also by america's test kitchen

A Very Chinese Cookbook

Kitchen Gear

Gatherings

The Healthy Back Kitchen

Everyday Bread

The Complete Modern Pantry

Boards

The Complete Plant-Based Cookbook

Cooking with Plant-Based Meat

The Outdoor Cook

Desserts Illustrated

Vegan Cooking for Two

Modern Bistro

Fresh Pasta at Home

More Mediterranean

The Complete Small Plates Cookbook

The Savory Baker

The New Cooking School Cookbook:
    Advanced Fundamentals

The New Cooking School Cookbook:
    Fundamentals

The Complete Autumn and Winter Cookbook

One-Hour Comfort

The Everyday Athlete Cookbook

Cook for Your Gut Health

Foolproof Fish

Five-Ingredient Dinners

The Ultimate Meal-Prep Cookbook

The Complete Salad Cookbook

The Chicken Bible

The Side Dish Bible

Meat Illustrated

Vegetables Illustrated

Bread Illustrated

Cooking for One

The Complete One Pot

How Can It Be Gluten-Free
    Cookbook Collection

The Complete Summer Cookbook

Bowls

100 Techniques

Easy Everyday Keto

Everything Chocolate

The Perfect Cookie

The Perfect Pie

The Perfect Cake

How to Cocktail

The Complete Guide to Healthy Drinks

Spiced

The Ultimate Burger

The New Essentials Cookbook

Dinner Illustrated

America's Test Kitchen Menu Cookbook

Cook's Illustrated Revolutionary Recipes

Tasting Italy: A Culinary Journey

Cooking at Home with Bridget and Julia

The Complete Mediterranean Cookbook

The Complete Vegetarian Cookbook

The Complete Cooking for Two Cookbook

The Complete Diabetes Cookbook

The Complete Slow Cooker

The Complete Make-Ahead Cookbook

Just Add Sauce

How to Braise Everything

How to Roast Everything

Nutritious Delicious

What Good Cooks Know

Cook's Science

The Science of Good Cooking

Master of the Grill

Kitchen Smarts

Kitchen Hacks

100 Recipes

The New Family Cookbook

The Cook's Illustrated Baking Book

The Cook's Illustrated Cookbook

The America's Test Kitchen Family
    Baking Book

America's Test Kitchen Twentieth Anniversary
    TV Show Cookbook

The Best of America's Test Kitchen
    (2007–2023 Editions)

The Complete America's Test Kitchen
    TV Show Cookbook 2001–2024

Ultimate Air Fryer Perfection

Healthy Air Fryer

Healthy and Delicious Instant Pot

Mediterranean Instant Pot

Cook It in Your Dutch Oven

Vegan for Everybody

Sous Vide for Everybody

Toaster Oven Perfection

Multicooker Perfection

Food Processor Perfection

Pressure Cooker Perfection

Instant Pot Ace Blender Cookbook

Naturally Sweet

Foolproof Preserving

Paleo Perfected

The Best Mexican Recipes

Slow Cooker Revolution Volume 2:
    The Easy-Prep Edition

Slow Cooker Revolution

The America's Test Kitchen D.I.Y. Cookbook

COOK'S COUNTRY TITLES

Big Flavors from Italian America

One-Pan Wonders

Cook It in Cast Iron

Cook's Country Eats Local

The Complete Cook's Country
TV Show Cookbook

FOR A FULL LISTING OF ALL OUR BOOKS:

CooksIllustrated.com

AmericasTestKitchen.com

praise for america's test kitchen titles

"This comprehensive guide is packed with delicious recipes and fun menu ideas but its unique draw is the personal narrative and knowledge-sharing of each ATK chef, which will make this a hit."

BOOKLIST ON GATHERINGS

"An exhaustive but approachable primer for those looking for a 'flexible' diet. Chock-full of tips, you can dive into the science of plant-based cooking or just sit back and enjoy the 500 recipes."

MINNEAPOLIS STAR TRIBUNE ON THE COMPLETE PLANT-BASED COOKBOOK

Best Overall Mediterranean Cookbook 2022

RUNNER'S WORLD ON THE COMPLETE MEDITERRANEAN COOKBOOK

"Here are the words just about any vegan would be happy to read: 'Why This Recipe Works.' Fans of America's Test Kitchen are used to seeing the phrase, and now it applies to the growing collection of plant-based creations in *Vegan for Everybody*."

THE WASHINGTON POST ON VEGAN FOR EVERYBODY

"True to its name, this smart and endlessly enlightening cookbook is about as definitive as it's possible to get in the modern vegetarian realm."

MEN'S JOURNAL ON THE COMPLETE VEGETARIAN COOKBOOK

"A mood board for one's food board is served up in this excellent guide . . . This has instant classic written all over it."

PUBLISHERS WEEKLY (STARRED REVIEW) ON BOARDS: STYLISH SPREADS FOR CASUAL GATHERINGS

"Reassuringly hefty and comprehensive, *The Complete Autumn and Winter Cookbook* by America's Test Kitchen has you covered with a seemingly endless array of seasonal fare . . . This overstuffed compendium is guaranteed to warm you from the inside out."

NPR ON THE COMPLETE AUTUMN AND WINTER COOKBOOK

"If you're one of the 30 million Americans with diabetes, *The Complete Diabetes Cookbook* by America's Test Kitchen belongs on your kitchen shelf."

PARADE.COM ON THE COMPLETE DIABETES COOKBOOK

"Another flawless entry in the America's Test Kitchen canon, *Bowls* guides readers of all culinary skill levels in composing one-bowl meals from a variety of cuisines."

BUZZFEED BOOKS ON BOWLS

Selected as the Cookbook Award Winner of 2021 in the Single Subject category

INTERNATIONAL ASSOCIATION OF CULINARY PROFESSIONALS (IACP) ON FOOLPROOF FISH

"The book's depth, breadth, and practicality makes it a must-have for seafood lovers."

PUBLISHERS WEEKLY (STARRED REVIEW) ON FOOLPROOF FISH

"*The Perfect Cookie* . . . is, in a word, perfect. This is an important and substantial cookbook . . . If you love cookies, but have been a tad shy to bake on your own, all your fears will be dissipated. This is one book you can use for years with magnificently happy results."

HUFFPOST ON THE PERFECT COOKIE

"The book offers an impressive education for curious cake makers, new and experienced alike. A summation of 25 years of cake making at ATK, there are cakes for every taste."

THE WALL STREET JOURNAL ON THE PERFECT CAKE

"In this latest offering from the fertile minds at America's Test Kitchen the recipes focus on savory baked goods. Pizzas, flatbreads, crackers, and stuffed breads all shine here . . . Introductory essays for each recipe give background information and tips for making things come out perfectly."

BOOKLIST (STARRED REVIEW) ON THE SAVORY BAKER

"The go-to gift book for newlyweds, small families, or empty nesters."

ORLANDO SENTINEL ON THE COMPLETE COOKING FOR TWO COOKBOOK

Selected as the Cookbook Award Winner of 2021 in the General category

INTERNATIONAL ASSOCIATION OF CULINARY PROFESSIONALS (IACP) ON MEAT ILLUSTRATED

"*Five-Ingredient Dinners* is as close to a sure thing to an easy meal as you'll find. . . . If you want to get cooking, cut down on take-out, and deliver a ton of flavor, you can't lose with these recipes."

PROVIDENCE JOURNAL ON FIVE-INGREDIENT DINNERS

THE COMPLETE
Beans & Grains
COOKBOOK

A Comprehensive Guide with
450+ Recipes

America's Test Kitchen

Kamut® is a registered trademark of Kamut International, Ltd.

Library of Congress Cataloging-in-Publication Data has been applied for.

ISBN 978-1-954210-67-7

AMERICA'S TEST KITCHEN
21 Drydock Avenue, Boston, MA 02210

Printed in Canada
10 9 8 7 6 5 4 3 2 1

Distributed by Penguin Random House Publisher Services
Tel: 800.733.3000

PICTURED ON FRONT COVER: Lupini Beans with Shallot, Urfa, and Cumin (page 40), Spiced Stuffed Peppers with Yogurt-Tahini Sauce (page 248), Antipasto Farro Salad with Arugula (page 169)

PICTURED ON BACK COVER: Basmati Rice Pilaf with Whole Spices (page 299) and Chana Masala (page 145), Braised Lamb Shoulder Chops with Fava Beans (page 198), Scarlet Runner Mole Burgers (page 70)

EDITORIAL DIRECTOR, BOOKS: Adam Kowit

EXECUTIVE FOOD EDITOR: Dan Zuccarello

DEPUTY FOOD EDITOR: Stephanie Pixley

EXECUTIVE MANAGING EDITOR: Debra Hudak

SENIOR EDITORS: Camila Chaparro, Kaumudi Marathé, and Sara Mayer

ASSOCIATE EDITOR: Sara Zatopek

TEST COOKS: Olivia Counter, Hannah Fenton, Laila Ibrahim, José Maldonado, and David Yu

EDITORIAL ASSISTANT: Julia Arwine

CONTRIBUTING EDITOR: Cheryl Redmond

ADDITIONAL EDITORIAL SUPPORT: Amelia Freidline, Katrina Ávila Munichiello, and April Poole

DESIGN DIRECTOR: Lindsey Timko Chandler

ASSOCIATE ART DIRECTOR: Kylie Alexander

PHOTOGRAPHY DIRECTOR: Julie Bozzo Cote

SENIOR PHOTOGRAPHY PRODUCER: Meredith Mulcahy

SENIOR STAFF PHOTOGRAPHERS: Steve Klise and Daniel J. van Ackere

STAFF PHOTOGRAPHER: Kevin White

ADDITIONAL PHOTOGRAPHY: Joseph Keller and Carl Tremblay

FOOD STYLING: Joy Howard, Sheila Jarnes, Catrine Kelty, Chantal Lambeth, Gina McCreadie, Kendra McNight, Ashley Moore, Christie Morrison, Marie Piraino, Elle Simone Scott, Kendra Smith, and Sally Staub

PROJECT MANAGER, PUBLISHING OPERATIONS: Katie Kimmerer

SENIOR PRINT PRODUCTION SPECIALIST: Lauren Robbins

PRODUCTION AND IMAGING COORDINATOR: Amanda Yong

PRODUCTION AND IMAGING SPECIALISTS: Tricia Neumyer and Dennis Noble

COPY EDITOR: Cheryl Redmond

PROOFREADER: Kelly Gauthier

INDEXER: Elizabeth Parson

CHIEF CREATIVE OFFICER: Jack Bishop

EXECUTIVE EDITORIAL DIRECTORS: Julia Collin Davison and Bridget Lancaster

Contents

welcome to america's test kitchen

This book has been tested, written, and edited by the folks at America's Test Kitchen, where curious cooks become confident cooks. Located in Boston's Seaport District in the historic Innovation and Design Building, it features 15,000 square feet of kitchen space including multiple photography and video studios. It is the home of *Cook's Illustrated* magazine and *Cook's Country* magazine and is the workday destination for more than 60 test cooks, editors, and cookware specialists. Our mission is to empower and inspire confidence, community, and creativity in the kitchen.

We start the process of testing a recipe with a complete lack of preconceptions, which means that we accept no claim, no technique, and no recipe at face value. We simply assemble as many variations as possible, test a half-dozen of the most promising, and taste the results blind. We then construct our own recipe and continue to test it, varying ingredients, techniques, and cooking times until we reach a consensus. As we like to say in the test kitchen, "We make the mistakes so you don't have to." The result, we hope, is the best version of a particular recipe, but we realize that only you can be the final judge of our success (or failure). We use the same rigorous approach when we test equipment and taste ingredients.

All of this would not be possible without a belief that good cooking, much like good music, is based on a foundation of objective technique. Some people like spicy foods and others don't, but there is a right way to sauté, there is a best way to cook a pot roast, and there are measurable scientific principles involved in producing perfectly beaten, stable egg whites. Our ultimate goal is to investigate the fundamental principles of cooking to give you the techniques, tools, and ingredients you need to become a better cook. It is as simple as that.

To see what goes on behind the scenes at America's Test Kitchen, check out our social media channels for kitchen snapshots, exclusive content, video tips, and much more. You can watch us work (in our actual test kitchen) by tuning in to *America's Test Kitchen* or *Cook's Country* on public television or on our websites. Listen to *Proof*, *Mystery Recipe*, and *The Walk-In* (AmericasTestKitchen.com/podcasts) to hear engaging, complex stories about people and food. Want to hone your cooking skills or finally learn how to bake—with an America's Test Kitchen test cook? Enroll in one of our online cooking classes.

However you choose to visit us, we welcome you into our kitchen, where you can stand by our side as we test our way to the best recipes in America.

- facebook.com/AmericasTestKitchen
- instagram.com/TestKitchen
- youtube.com/AmericasTestKitchen
- tiktok.com/@TestKitchen
- twitter.com/TestKitchen
- pinterest.com/TestKitchen

AmericasTestKitchen.com
CooksIllustrated.com
CooksCountry.com
OnlineCookingSchool.com

JOIN OUR COMMUNITY OF RECIPE TESTERS

Our recipe testers provide valuable feedback on recipes under development by ensuring that they are foolproof in home kitchens. Help the America's Test Kitchen book team investigate the how and why behind successful recipes from your home kitchen.

Introduction

Welcome to the World of Beans and Grains

Beans and grains have been sustaining the world for a very long time. They have also long been favorites in the test kitchen. *The Complete Beans and Grains Cookbook* is our deep dive into the vast, varied, and endlessly interesting topic of these two foods. We wanted to take beans and grains beyond the pantry and grocery store so we included heirloom beans and grains in our testing and recipe development. It was exciting to taste and create recipes for varieties of beans and grains we had not experienced before working on this book.

We love beans and grains for all of their proven health benefits. Carbs with benefits? We should all be eating more of them. This extensive collection of recipes makes it easy to eat more beans and grains, especially important if you want to follow the Mediterranean diet where they form a major source of daily protein. They are superstar foods that provide a vital source of nutrition in countries the world over: healthy, filling, flavorful, and inexpensive as well as shelf-stable.

We put beans and grains together in one cookbook because while each is commanding on its own, together they form a dynamic duo. They are partners in traditional recipes in many cuisines as well as in new favorite plant-based pairings. While they are also important nutritionally, what excites us most is the immense range of flavors and textures found in these two foods. Beans and grains are incredibly versatile in recipes for simple snacks to centerpiece dinners.

This comprehensive range of recipes gives you 450-plus ways to enjoy beans and grains that go far beyond plain rice and simple side dishes (although there are plenty of those included). You'll find easy dips, burgers and tacos, soups and stews, salads big and small, amazing side dishes, and months of dinners to make. There are endless takes on each of these categories along with everything in between. Beans and grains are beloved by vegetarians and vegans everywhere but we wanted to bring everyone to the table. While a lot of our recipes make beans and grains the starring ingredients, we also combine them with meat or fish where they play an important supporting role. Because beans can be so meaty and satisfying, some clever beanified dishes such as Bean Bourguignon will appeal to meat eaters even though they have no meat in the recipe. We have tagged all recipes that are meat- and dairy-free as Vegan.

Many recipes in the book use heirloom bean and grain varieties, which are great to cook and try. For those recipes we include a substitution line which gives a common grocery store alternative. We have also tagged recipes that can be prepared in 45 minutes or less as Fast, so it's easy to identify recipes that are especially weeknight-friendly. Cooking Fava Bean Pesto Pasta or Okinawan Taco Rice is sure to make mealtime more exciting.

Stuck in an inspiration rut? Find immediate and spectacular relief by just opening a can. You can roast some crunchy spiced chickpeas for a snack, blend an ultracreamy white bean soup, or mix up a dynamite chili. And you can't go wrong with quick-cooking red lentils for tacos or dal.

Even if you are an old hand at cooking beans and grains, there are hundreds of inventive recipes waiting for you. There are traditional recipes for Hoppin' John, Tacu Tacu, and Adasi. There are comfort classics including New England Baked Beans, Ribollita, and Arroz con Pollo. There are celebratory dinners such as Chickpea Bouillabaisse, Kibbeh bil Saineyeh, and Plov. And so much more.

Whether you're a novice or pro, vegan or carnivore, here's everything you need to know from our kitchen to yours. Let us guide you through the flavorful world of beans and grains to failproof and irresistible results.

About Beans

Simply put, beans are seeds. "Bean" is an umbrella term used to describe the seeds of thousands of flowering plants within the legume family, *Fabaceae*. There are several genera within the legume family, including *Vicia* (broad beans), *Pisum* (peas), *Lens* (lentils), and *Phaseolus*, which contains *Phaseolus vulgaris*, the common bean, which in turn includes black beans, pinto beans, navy beans, and even green beans. The "bean" category is a big one; the term is often applied to varieties that aren't really considered beans, such as lentils, peanuts, and certain types of peas. Still, when we think of beans, we're usually thinking of varieties of *Phaseolus vulgaris*.

The Bean Life Cycle

Beans are generally planted in the spring and then flower in the late spring and summer. The flowers themselves are edible, as are the fresh, tender seed pods that form. Many varieties of *Phaseolus vulgaris* are edible at several stages of the growing process. Green beans, sold and eaten fresh, are the young seed pods. Mature pods can also be harvested and eaten as so-called shelled beans. If left in the pods, the seeds develop their signature hues and markings as they dry. The dried beans are ready to be cooked and eaten or to be saved for replanting next season.

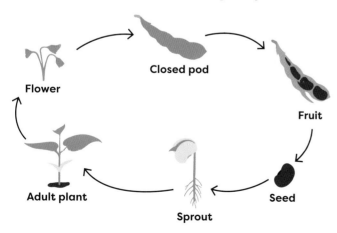

Bean Nomenclature

Common Beans

We refer to most of the beans on the market as common or supermarket beans. They are grown using commercial farming techniques on an industrial scale. In the past 200 years, bean breeders identified certain varieties of common beans that were easier to grow, transport, process, and sell than others. These beans make up most of what you can purchase at your local supermarket: bags and cans of dependable varieties that are both low-cost and consistently available. It is hard to know how long dried beans have been on the shelf (they could be a few years old) so consider them to be super-dried. Most of our recipes use common beans.

Heirloom Beans

Most common beans have an heirloom ancestor. When the commodity bean industry zeroed in on a handful of beans and ignored the rest, a few things happened. Many beans were lost to history, but the luckier ones were passed down and preserved by avid small-scale farmers and dogged seed collectors for their unique appearance or flavor. Heirloom bean farming has been kept strong by networks of family farms lovingly growing the same beans for generations on a small scale and selling them locally. These beans have adapted to the specific regions where they've been traditionally cultivated and are often vulnerable to diseases and pests when grown in other environments. Just like heirloom tomatoes show up at farmers' markets and specialty outlets during a small window of the year, so it is with heirloom beans.

In the past two decades, there has been a wider spotlight shone on heirloom beans in the United States, with the arrival of a few companies dedicated to preserving and cultivating these lesser-known varieties and selling them around the

country. One of the most famous is Rancho Gordo in Napa, California, which partners mostly with farmers on the West Coast and in Mexico. But it's not the only company in the game. Zürsun Idaho Heirloom Beans has been selling heirloom beans grown by family farms in Idaho's Snake River Valley since 1985. North Bay Trading Company provides beans and other heirloom foods from the Great Lakes region. Heirloom beans from these purveyors and more—including your own local farmers—can be purchased online, at specialty food stores, or at farmers' markets.

Color = Flavor

Many heirloom bean varieties are quite beautiful, with their vibrant colors and striking markings. The colorful flecks, speckles, or mottled undulations are due to genetic alterations in the seed coat, the thin membrane that covers the bean. There is a connection between their color and flavor. The genes don't just make the beans pretty; some of them direct the development of molecules called flavonoids, which color the bean and also make them taste delicious. Heirloom beans have a wider range of flavor variations than common beans do. They can taste slightly grassy (flageolets) or vegetal (orcas); have hints of nuts (royal coronas, scarlet runners) or mushrooms (Christmas lima beans); or even be reminiscent of candied bacon (canary beans). Many have a supercreamy, melt-in-your-mouth texture whereas common beans are more dense.

Some flavonoids leach into the cooking water, so most beans are at their most vivid and striking before they're cooked. Even brining causes some of the coloring to fade. Heirloom beans are usually shipped in the year they're harvested so they are fresher than commodity beans. Fresher beans means that they will cook faster and have more flavor.

Taste-Testing Beans

There is such a large array of common and heirloom beans available that we purchased a number of them to hold several tastings in the test kitchen. We were interested in the beans' different flavors and textures and wanted to figure out how best to use each variety. We brined and rinsed each sample of beans before simmering them (with garlic and bay leaf) until just tender and then tasted them plain. Almost every sample had its own distinct personality in terms of taste and texture. See our tasting notes in the descriptions that follow (pages 6–11).

FAQ

Are heirloom beans worth buying?

Yes, heirloom beans are definitely worth seeking out even though they are generally more expensive than supermarket beans. They open up a world of interesting new flavors and even textures. We tasted a variety of heirloom beans and lentils and liked every one that we tried.

Beanified Classics

We were so impressed with the meaty quality and texture of the beans we had tasted that when brainstorming recipe ideas for them we imagined subbing them into several classic recipes as the main ingredient. The end result was stellar recipes for Chickpea Bouillabaisse (page 144), Beans Marbella (page 140), and Bean Bourguignon (page 146) to name a few.

Dried Beans Used in Our Recipes

This compilation includes all of the beans that we tried and then figured out how best to cook. It was rewarding to think about and match up specific beans to specific recipes. There are multiple names for the same beans; we've listed the common names you might see at the grocery store.

Black Beans

Sometimes called "black turtle beans" because of their hard outer shell, black beans are most popular in Latin American and Caribbean countries. Because they hold their shape well, black beans are good for pot beans, soups, chilis, salads, and dishes mixed with rice. When cooked, these beans make a dark inky broth, which is sometimes used for other dishes or consumed alone. Black beans are commonly available at grocery stores both dried and canned; heirloom varieties are frequently available online.

Tasting notes: Small, dense, and creamy, with an earthy, sometimes "smoky" flavor, particularly heirloom varieties
Find them in: Coconut Black Bean Soup with Plantains (page 116), Avocado and Black Bean Toast (page 62), Black Bean and Cheese Arepas (page 84)

Black Chickpeas
(ceci neri, desi/kala chana)

Black chickpeas can refer to a dark, very wrinkly-skinned variety grown in southern parts of Italy (ceci neri), or a similarly small variety that is most commonly used in India and other parts of Asia (desi chana or kala chana). Because of their thick skin, black chickpeas need to soak and cook longer than white chickpeas, and they hold their shape well. Note that they lose a lot of color during cooking, turning more gray than black. Ceci neri are traditionally used in Italy for soups, stews, and pasta dishes. Desi/kala chana are creamier and commonly used in stews, curries, and stir-fries. Ceci neri and desi/kala chana are available online.

Tasting notes: More dense and thicker-skinned than regular chickpeas, with an "earthier, more herbaceous" flavor
Find them in: Roasted Vegetable and Black Chickpea Salad (page 163)

Black-Eyed Peas

Cowpeas, which are related to mung beans, are thought to have originated and been domesticated in Africa; they are commonly consumed there along with the Southern U.S. and Asia.

Black-eyed peas are one of the more well-known varieties of cowpeas identified by a dark black "eye" on a small pale cream-colored oval bean. Black-eyed peas hold their shape well, making them good for salads or rice dishes. They are also traditionally ground up to make fritters. Black-eyed peas, both dried and canned, are available at grocery stores.

Tasting notes: Firm, dense and creamy, with a distinctively earthy taste
Find them in: Texas Caviar (page 58), Black-Eyed Pea Fritters with Garlic and Herb Sauce (page 49), Pressure-Cooker Green Gumbo (page 335)

Canary Beans
(mayocoba beans, peruano beans)

Canary beans are a pale yellow, thin-skinned variety that is popular in Mexico (where it is known as mayocoba) and also Peru. These beans hold their shape well and so make a good option for pot beans, or soups and stews, but they're also well suited for dishes such as refried beans or tacu tacu that take advantage of their creamy texture. Canary beans, dried and canned, are available in well-stocked grocery stores; heirloom varieties are available online.

Tasting notes: Very creamy with a subtle sweetness; are soft but hold their shape well
Find them in: Tacu Tacu with Salsa Criolla (page 88)

Cannellini Beans

Related to red kidney beans, cannellini are most popular in Italy, where many heirloom varieties were bred and exist, though they originated in the Americas. They hold their shape well when cooked, making them good for salads, soups, stews, casseroles, blended into dips, or eaten simply dressed with oil. Cannellini beans are commonly available at grocery stores both dried and canned; heirloom varieties are frequently available online.

Tasting notes: Thin-skinned and tender with a creamy texture and nutty, "buttery" to "earthy" flavor
Find them in: Ribollita (page 114), White Beans with Caramelized Onions, Fennel, and Gruyère (page 209), Pasta e Fagioli (page 141)

Chickpeas
(garbanzo beans, kabuli chana)

Chickpeas are thought to be native to and domesticated in Turkey, and then spread throughout the Mediterranean and India. Chickpeas are now used throughout many cultures, and because they hold their shape well, are ideal for salads, soups, stews, curries, and casseroles, though one of their most well-known uses is blended into dips/spreads like hummus. Chickpea flour is also used in many cuisines for flatbreads, fritters, and crackers. Chickpeas are commonly available at grocery stores both dried and canned.

Tasting notes: Dense, firm, and "meaty"; hold their shape well but turn creamy when cooked, and make a smooth puree
Find them in: Chickpea Bouillabaisse (page 144), Chickpea Crackers (page 45), Buffalo Blue Cheese Chickpea Patties with Creamy Herb Sauce (page 69)

Christmas Lima Beans

Christmas lima beans are an heirloom bean. They are very large, flat, dark lima bean–shaped beans with maroon and white markings that fade slightly with cooking. These stunning beans are great for recipes where you want a striking bean that holds its shape when cooked—in salads, stews, or soups. Christmas limas are available online.

Tasting notes: Creamy "melt-in-your-mouth" yet meaty, with a vegetal flavor reminiscent of "mushrooms" and "chestnuts"
Find them in: Bean Bourguignon (page 146)

Cranberry Beans
(Roman beans, borlotti beans)

Plump, beige dried cranberry beans have maroon speckles that disappear upon cooking, leading to a uniform brown color. Cranberry beans are thought to have originated in Colombia (where they're known as the cargamanto bean) but are used in many Mediterranean cuisines, including Italy where they are called borlotti beans. They are a classic choice for pasta e fagioli or minestrone. Cranberry beans are available in well-stocked grocery stores both dried and canned (often labeled Roman beans); heirloom varieties are frequently available online.

Tasting notes: Thin-skinned, with a sweet and mild flavor that some liken to chestnuts; soft, velvety texture that makes a rich bean broth
Find them in: Burst Cherry Tomato Puttanesca with Roman Beans (page 210); Italian-Style Lamb Stew with Roman Beans, Green Beans, and Tomatoes (page 132)

Flageolets

Bred in France, long, skinny, medium-size flageolet beans are picked while still immature, which preserves their light green color when dried. These delicate beans cook to a light tan color, and tend to break down with extended cooking, but can be added to soups and stews towards the end of cooking. Classically they are added to cassoulet and paired with lamb. Flageolet beans are available online.

Tasting notes: Very creamy texture that dissolves on the tongue; mild with grassy "spring-like," "buttery" flavors
Find them in: Soupe au Pistou (page 111)

Gigante Beans

Gigante beans are extra-large, white flat runner beans similar in shape to lima beans (though they are not related). Commonly used in Greek cuisine, gigante beans originated in Mexico and Central America, like other runner beans. One of their traditional uses is in gigantes plaki, where they are baked with tomatoes, olive oil, onions, and herbs, but they are striking in any dish where a distinctive bean that holds its shape is desired, even lightly dressed on toast. Gigante beans are available online.

Tasting notes: Sweet mild taste, meaty and creamy texture
Find them in: Gigantes Plaki (page 212), Pressure-Cooker Gigante Bean Soup with Celery and Olives (page 331)

Great Northern Beans

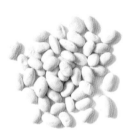

One of several beans that are oftentimes lumped interchangeably together as "white beans," great northern beans are larger than navy beans, and less kidney-shaped than cannellini. Great northern beans are thought to have their name because they are grown in colder northern climates, particularly the upper Midwest (Nebraska and Minnesota). They are commonly used in soups, stews, chiles, and casseroles. Great northern beans, both dried and canned, are available at grocery stores.

Tasting notes: Mild, nutty flavor and creamy texture
Find them in: Slow-Cooker Tuscan White Bean Soup (page 367), Slow-Cooker Garden Minestrone (page 371), Creamy White Bean Soup with Chorizo Oil and Garlicky Bread Crumbs (page 99)

Kidney Beans

Perhaps most well known in the U.S. as a bean for chili, kidney beans are also popular in certain regions of India, the Caribbean, Portugal, and Spain. Kidney beans come in a variety of shades of red, from dark to light, as well as white (usually called cannellini), and speckled and mottled varieties. Kidney beans, both dried and canned, are available at grocery stores.

Tasting notes: Faintly sweet, starchy texture
Find them in: Red Beans and Rice with Andouille (page 194), Habichuelas Guisadas con Calabaza (page 195)

Lima Beans
(butter beans)

Native to Peru (hence the name), lima beans are also known as butter beans, particularly smaller varieties and in the southern U.S. Lima beans are available dried, canned, and frozen. Lima beans are good for baked beans, salads, pot beans, succotash, or dips. While technically all the same variety, there are a range of size and colors of lima beans available—at the grocery store or through mail-order sources—including large white lima beans, baby limas, and green baby limas.

Tasting notes: Buttery and soft with a stronger vegetable flavor than most beans
Find them in: Cauliflower and Bean Paella (page 206), Succotash Salad with Butter Beans and Basil (page 283), Jamaican Oxtail (page 187)

Lupini Beans

Lupini (lupine) beans are a flat, round, beige bean most commonly consumed in the Mediterranean and the Middle East/North Africa, but also popular in parts of the Andean region of South America. Lupines are part of the pea genus and contain a potentially toxic alkaloid that has to be removed through a time-intensive soaking process of the dried beans, though newer varieties require less soaking. As a result, jarred lupini beans packed in brine or vacuum-packed cooked beans are often preferred to dried beans. Lupini beans are frequently prepared simply—with oil, salt, and a minimum of flavorings—and eaten as a snack, appetizer, or street food in Mediterranean countries. Jarred lupini beans are available in well-stocked grocery stores.

Tasting notes: Mild, nutty, with a very firm, "snappy" almost crunchy texture; thin edible skin that some slip off before consuming
Find them in: Lupini Beans with Garlic, Lemon, and Parsley (page 40)

Navy Beans

Navy beans are the smallest of the white bean category. Served as a staple in the U.S. Navy since the 1800s (hence the name), navy beans are a small white, slightly flat bean that originated in Peru. Navy beans are the traditional bean for Boston baked beans and Senate bean soup, but are also frequently used in cassoulet and other baked applications. Navy beans, both dried and canned, are commonly available at grocery stores.

Tasting notes: Creamy, mild flavor that makes them extremely versatile
Find them in: Slow-Cooker U.S. Senate Navy Bean Soup (page 367), New England Baked Beans (page 291), Hearty Vegetarian Chili (page 373)

Orca Beans

Named for the black and white orca whales, orca beans are a small heirloom bean with striking black and white mottling. These beans hold up well to extended cooking, retain their markings when cooked, and create dark and flavorful pot liquor. Good for chilis, soups, stews, pot beans, or mashed into dips. Orca beans are available online.

Tasting notes: Creamy and starchy with a potato-like flavor
Find them in: Lemon-Garlic Orca Bean Dip (page 53), Ultimate Beef Chili (page 150)

Pigeon Peas

First domesticated in India, and then transported throughout the world through the slave trade, pigeon peas get their English name from their historic use as feed for pigeons in Barbados. Pigeon peas are cultivated in tropical and semi-tropical areas (with the greatest production in India) and consumed in many regions of the world including Asia, Africa, and Latin America. In Latin America and the Caribbean, pigeon peas are commonly served stewed with toma-toes and onions or mixed with rice. In India split pigeon peas are commonly used for dal (toor dal), and in Kenya simmered in coco-nut milk and served with rice. Cooked peas can be added to soups, stews, curries, sauces, salads, and rice dishes. Pigeon peas—dried, canned, and frozen—are available in well-stocked grocery stores.

Tasting notes: Nutty flavor and "crisp" texture
Find them in: Glazed Caribbean Tofu with Rice and Pigeon Peas (page 224)

Pink Beans

Pink beans (commonly known by their name in Spanish, habichuelas rosadas) are popular in the Caribbean, particularly Puerto Rico. Pink beans are well suited for serving as pot beans with rice, in chiles, and as refried beans. Pink beans, dried and canned, are available in well-stocked grocery stores; heirloom varieties are available online.

Tasting notes: Rich, meaty flavor and smooth, creamy texture
Find them in: Pink Bean and Lima Bean Dip with Parsley (page 55)

Pinto Beans

Pinto beans get their name from their speckled or "painted" appearance. Popular in Mexico, particularly northern Mexico, and the western/Southwestern U.S., pinto beans hold their shape well so they are great for pot beans (charro beans), chilis, soups, and stews. Their creaminess makes them especially good for refried beans. Pinto beans, dried and canned, are available in most grocery stores; heirloom varieties are available online.

Tasting notes: Soft, creamy, with "mild nuttiness" but a neutral flavor that makes them versatile
Find them in: Tomatillo Chicken Huaraches (page 86); Pinto Bean, Ancho, and Beef Salad with Pickled Poblanos (page 164); Drunken Beans (page 291)

Royal Corona Beans

Huge royal corona beans are similar in appearance to large white lima beans or gigante beans (to which they are related) and are an heirloom variety grown in Europe, though with roots firmly in Mexico, like other runner bean varieties. These beans—which can be used in soups, stews, pot beans, salads, and casseroles—have a striking presence in any dish (and also when served alone) due to their immense size. Royal corona beans are available online.

Tasting notes: Thick-skinned, creamy, smooth, rich, and dense inside with faintly sweet, mild flavor
Find them in: Beans Marbella (page 140)

Scarlet Runner Beans

Beautiful, large, pink and black speckled beans, scarlet runner beans originated in Mexico. Scarlet runner beans hold their shape well and retain some of their markings after cooking, and also create a dark, thick pot liquor. These striking beans are well suited for applications that take advantage of their large size, meatiness and flavor: for example, braises or salads. Scarlet runner beans are available online.

Tasting notes: Thick-skinned, starchy, meaty, and faintly sweet, with smoky/roasted notes
Find them in: Scarlet Runner Mole Burgers (page 70)

Sea Island Red Peas

Sea Island red peas are an heirloom variety of cowpeas, domesticated in the Sea Islands (a chain of barrier islands off the Atlantic coast of South Carolina, Georgia, and Florida) and the low country region of South Carolina. Like other cowpeas, they are originally from West Africa. Sea Island red peas are the traditional pea used in Hoppin' John. Sea Island red peas are available online.

Tasting notes: Richly flavored, sweet and meaty
Find them in: Hoppin' John (page 190)

Small Red Beans

Small red beans are popular throughout the Caribbean and Central America, and also southern parts of the U.S. They are different in shape and size from red kidney beans, though the two are sometimes substituted for each other. They are also different from adzuki beans used to make red bean paste used in Chinese and other cuisines. Small red beans retain their shape during cooking, and are ideal for simmered dishes, soups, stews, chilis, and dishes mixed with rice (arroz con habichuelas in the Dominican Republic, or red beans and rice in Louisiana). Small red beans, dried and canned, are available in well-stocked grocery stores.

Tasting notes: Rich flavor and firm texture
Find them in: Slow-Cooker Red Beans and Rice with Okra and Tomatoes (page 387)

Split Peas

Split peas are "field peas," which are green or yellow peas that are allowed to mature in the pod, and specifically suited for drying. Like other split legumes (see red lentils), they are quick-cooking, and don't need to be pre-soaked like other dried beans.

Tasting notes: Starchy and sweet (particularly green peas), very creamy, puree-like texture when cooked
Find them in: Split Pea and Ham Soup (page 119)

Tepary Beans

Tepary beans are drought-resistant beans native to the Southwestern U.S. and Mexico, particularly in the northwest, but they have also been cultivated in Africa, Australia, and Asia. Both brown and white tepary beans are versatile and can be added to soups and stews, made into pot beans or refried beans, or pureed into dips. Tepary beans are available online.

Tasting notes: Small and dense with a slightly sweet to earthy flavor
Find them in: Tepary Bean Dip with Herb and Olive Salad (page 52), Tepary Bean Soup (page 106)

How to Cook Dried Beans

Cooking dried beans does take more time than opening a can but it isn't difficult to do and the results are unbeatable in terms of the heightened flavor and creamy texture of from-scratch beans. The cooking method is the same for all beans and the test kitchen's tried-and-true method could not be easier, as outlined in the five steps below. We prefer to cook beans on the stovetop because it is faster, you can adjust the heat, and you can easily monitor the beans' cooking and test them for doneness. Since it's impossible to know the age of your beans (which can have a large impact on how long it takes for the beans to cook), it's important to taste the beans for doneness rather than relying solely on recipe cook times.

ATK's Method for Cooking Dried Beans

1 Pick Over and Rinse

Before cooking, pick over 1 pound of dried beans to remove any small stones or debris and then rinse them.
How to: The easiest way to check the beans is to spread them on a large plate or rimmed baking sheet.

2 Brine and Then Rinse

To brine or not to brine? We definitely recommend brining dried beans prior to cooking. Overnight brining will give you the most tender beans with skins that stay in place. Brining (and soaking generally) speeds up cooking. Brining also helps beans maintain their shape throughout cooking, seasons them, and results in tender skins. Getting the skins to soften reduces the number of beans that explode during cooking, which is key for beans that cook up creamy rather than starchy.
How to: Dissolve 1½ tablespoons salt in 2 quarts cold water in a large container. Use a deep container (a bowl rather than a wide Dutch oven) to ensure that the beans remain submerged as they hydrate and swell. Add the pound of rinsed beans and soak at room temperature for at least 8 hours or up to 24 hours. Drain and rinse them well before using.

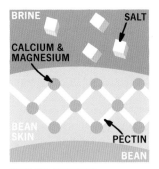

BEFORE BRINING
The strong pectin molecules in the bean's skin are tightly bound into a network by calcium and magnesium ions.

WHILE BRINING
Sodium replaces the calcium and magnesium ions, causing the pectin network to break down more readily, softening the skin and preventing exploding legumes.

3 Simmer Gently

Maintaining a gentle simmer prevents the beans from rupturing and prevents too much water from evaporating during cooking, ensuring that the beans stay submerged. Cooking them uncovered on the stovetop allows you to watch and taste them as they cook.
How to: Bring soaked beans and 7 cups water to simmer in large saucepan or Dutch oven. Simmer, uncovered, over medium-low heat until the beans are tender, about 40 minutes.

4 Test for Doneness

Taste the texture of the beans. After approximately 40 minutes of simmering, the beans should be just tender.

How to: To check for doneness, simply bite into a few beans. Be sure to taste more than one bean in the pot. It's a good idea to start checking your beans after 30 minutes.

5 Finish Off the Heat

Turning off the heat, covering the pot, and letting the beans steep after simmering allows them to gently finish cooking through without rupturing their skins.

How to: Remove the pan from the heat; stir in 1½ teaspoons salt, cover, and let sit for 15 minutes. Drain the beans.

Quick Brining

If you are pressed for time, a quick brine (water plus salt) for an hour is better than nothing but the test kitchen strongly recommends overnight brining. Longer brining results in superior texture and the creamiest beans. Quick-brined dried beans will be less creamy and may take longer to cook. Note that some recipes may call for simply soaking beans in water without any salt. To quick brine beans: Combine 1 pound dried beans with 1½ tablespoons salt in 2 quarts cold water in a large Dutch oven and bring to a boil. Remove from the heat, cover, and let sit for 1 hour. Drain and rinse well under cold water before continuing with the recipe.

Baking Soda and Acid

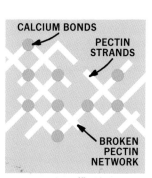

CALCIUM BONDS

PECTIN STRANDS

BROKEN PECTIN NETWORK

Some recipes call for adding baking soda when cooking beans. Baking soda works magic on beans (and grains) by raising the pH of their cooking liquid to make an alkaline environment. This weakens their cell walls and helps them to absorb water faster, which means the beans cook more quickly. In our Ultracreamy Hummus (page 50), adding ½ teaspoon of baking soda with the canned chickpeas breaks down the already-cooked skins and helps them slip off completely. Baking soda also helps to set the color of some beans, such as black beans and green beans, so their color stays bright instead of turning muddy.

Acid also affects how beans cook. The acid in tomatoes can prevent beans from becoming tender so we don't add them too early in the cooking process in recipes such as Hearty Tuscan Bean Stew with Sausage and Cabbage (page 137). The acid in wine slows down beans' cooking time so we add it about halfway through making Bean Bourguignon (page 146).

Pressure- or Slow-Cooking

An electric pressure cooker aka multicooker aka Instant Pot is a great way to cook dried beans: It cooks them in a fraction of their conventional cooking time. For more information about pressure-cooking beans and for pressure-cooker recipes, see pages 320–357. You can also use a slow cooker to cook dried beans (and lentils). Its cooking environment provides gentle, steady heat. For more information about slow-cooking beans and for slow-cooker recipes, see pages 358–391.

FAQ

Do all beans cook in the same amount of time?

The cooking time for dried beans can vary based on bean type, age, and whether the beans have been brined. The older the dried beans are, the longer they can take to cook; heirloom beans may cook faster. When we say beans take "about" 40 minutes to cook, we mean 10 minutes on either side of that, so start checking around 30 minutes. If your beans are really old (there's no way to tell), they may take longer than 50 minutes to cook.

10 Ways to Use a Pot of Beans

There's something comforting and satisfying about making a pot of beans to eat throughout the week. When cooked ahead and stored in the fridge or freezer, they are just as convenient as canned beans. Here are 10 ideas for what to do with those beans.

1 Eat some right away
Freshly cooked beans are delicious warm, at room temperature, or cold. They're so flavorful that all they need is a drizzle of olive oil, salt and pepper, and maybe a squeeze of lemon or lime juice.

2 Add beans to breakfast
Beans make a great toast topper: Add a crunchy element like pickled vegetables and a dollop of yogurt or cheese. Or try Breakfast Burritos (pages 77–78) or Breakfast Tacos (page 77) for a hearty start to the day.

3 Make a meze spread for guests
Get creative and flavor multiple batches of Simple Hummus (page 50) or let Lemon-Garlic Orca Bean Dip (page 53) be the centerpiece.

4 Have a taco party
Beans make a great addition to a taco spread; try Black Bean and Sweet Potato Tacos (page 76).

5 Build a bowl
Beans can be topped with just about anything for a simple "clean out the fridge" meal.

6 Pair with rice
Simply pair beans with rice and you've got a complete protein. Add some vegetables, herbs, and extra-virgin olive oil and vinegar, and you've made a great no-recipe meal.

7 Cook a flavorful burger
Make Black Bean Burgers (page 70) or Scarlet Runner Mole Burgers (page 70).

8 Stuff a vegetable for dinner
Try Loaded Sweet Potatoes (page 210) or Stuffed Peppers with Chickpeas, Goat Cheese, and Herbs (page 214).

9 Store some beans in the refrigerator (for up to 4 days)
Store a measured amount to speed up the making of any recipe.

10 Store some beans in the freezer (for up to 1 month)
The beans are ready when you are.

FAQ

What is the best way to store beans?
In the pantry: Dried beans degrade over time, so we recommend using them within six months of purchase. Uncooked beans should be stored in a cool, dry place in an airtight container.

In the refrigerator: Brined beans and fully cooked dried beans can be refrigerated for up to four days. They should be drained and stored outside of their brining or cooking liquid.

In the freezer: Drained brined or cooked beans can be frozen for up to one month. Pat them dry with paper towels and transfer them to a zipper-lock bag. Lay the bag flat to freeze to save space.

About Canned Beans

Canned beans are undeniably convenient, and in many recipes they work as well as dried beans. However, there are instances when dried beans are central to a recipe's success because their long cooking time adds thickness and body. Most recipes that call for dried beans require the beans to cook slowly with the other ingredients so that they release their starches and thicken the dish. When you replace them with canned beans and shorten the cooking time (canned beans are fully cooked and need only to warm through and soak up flavor), you can sacrifice both the flavor and the texture of the finished dish.

Canned Bean Equivalents
• 1 (15-ounce) can beans = 1½–1¾ cups drained beans plus ½ to ¾ cup liquid
• 3 cups canned beans = 1 cup uncooked dried beans

Rinsing Canned Beans
Canned beans are made by pressure-cooking dried beans directly in the can with water, salt, and sometimes preservatives. As the beans cook, starches and proteins leach into the liquid, thickening it. Whether canned bean liquid can be replaced with bean cooking water depends on the recipe. Our recipes indicate whether or not to rinse away the starchy liquid depending on the desired outcome.

A half-cup serving of canned beans can contain more than 400 milligrams of sodium. Given that we often drain and rinse beans before use, we were curious: Exactly how much sodium does that wash away? To find out, we sent cans of beans to a lab for analysis. The good news is that draining and rinsing beans lowers the sodium by 20.7 to 26.5 percent—or about 100 milligrams per ½ cup serving.

FAQ

Can cooked dried beans be substituted for canned in a recipe?
Yes, you can straight up replace canned beans with cooked dried beans in a recipe cup for cup. However, when beans and lentils are the star of a dish, we prefer the superior flavor and texture of dried. Dried beans soak up more liquid than canned so they soak up more flavor.

FAQ

What is the best way to get reluctant eaters to try more beans?
Start by preparing a crunchy or crisp snack or two that both kids and grownups will find hard to resist. Our Barbecue-Spiced Roasted Chickpeas (page 41) have all the appeal of BBQ potato chips but are a lighter, healthier option. Likewise, crispy Chickpea Fries (page 44) made from chickpea flour are hard to resist. For an easy family-friendly casserole for dinner, try Cheesy Bean and Tomato Bake (page 208), aka pizza beans, that's made with creamy cannellini beans.

About Lentils

Lentils, botanically named *Lens culinaris*, are a member of the legume family. Within the legume family lie the pulses, which are legumes harvested primarily for dried seeds, including lentils; kidney, pinto, and navy beans; peas; chickpeas; and a few others. There are 12 different types of lentils, varying in color from yellow to red-orange, green, brown, and black. The most commonly grown varieties are large brown lentils, small green lentilles du Puy, and petite red lentils. Lentils may be sold with or without their thin seed coat, and either whole or split in half. The differences in flavor and texture among the various types of lentils are surprisingly distinct; see page 17 to find out more about the three different types of lentils used in the recipes in this book.

Because of their small size and relatively high surface area-to-volume ratio, and their thin seed coat, lentils absorb water very rapidly and cook in much less time than other pulses. Like other dried beans, their skins can still blow out during cooking. To counter this, we like to brine lentils, so that the salt can help to weaken the pectin in the skins, allowing the lentils to stay intact, and not become mushy, during cooking.

Because lentils are smaller and cook faster, they are the perfect invitation to start cooking dried beans. Easy to find, inexpensive, and packed with nutrients, lentils are an ideal pantry staple; they are also one of the most versatile. We use them for soups and stews; in salads and rice pilaf; and in classic pairings with proteins such as salmon, chicken, and sausages. Although we like tiny, firm French lentilles du Puy and vibrant, tender red lentils, we most often reach for brown or green lentils, which are similar enough in flavor and texture to be used interchangeably in recipes.

Brining Lentils

As with dried beans, the test kitchen recommends brining lentils (again, some but not all) before cooking. Because lentils are smaller with a thinner coating, they don't need much time to brine. Lentils benefit from brining if we want them to keep their shape during cooking; the brine also seasons them throughout. The salt in the brine tenderizes the skin of the lentils, which helps to prevent blowouts as they cook. We don't brine split lentils since there's no seed coat. And in some recipes it is desirable for lentils to break down during cooking.

How to: Dissolve 1 teaspoon salt in 1 quart water in bowl. Add lentils and brine at room temperature for at least 1 hour or up to 24 hours. Drain and rinse well. (Drained lentils can be refrigerated for up to two days before cooking.)

Cooking Lentils

The variation in texture of lentils is considerable, ranging from earthy brown and green lentils that hold their shape when cooked to others, such as red lentils and split green lentils, that break down and get mushy by design. The firmer lentils should be perfectly intact without being crunchy and have tender, creamy interiors. They should be cooked gently in seasoned water or broth.

Ways to Cook Lentils

Although they are available canned, lentils are by far more commonly found dried. Dried lentils are fairly easy to cook and can be prepared in many ways for many different uses, from being eaten out of hand to becoming the base of a hearty dinner. They can be boiled, stewed, braised in the oven, or prepared in a pressure cooker (see page 322) or slow cooker (see page 360). We even shallow-fry them for Crispy Lentil and Herb Salad (page 160). Frying brined lentils in oil gives them a crisp-crunchy texture. Crispy fried lentils make an excellent snack (Cumin-Spiced Crispy Lentils page 42) or a crunchy topping for hummus and other dips, soup, or a grain bowl.

FAQ

What's the difference between split and whole lentils?
Split lentils don't have a seed coat and as a result cook much faster but they don't hold their shape. For that reason we like them in soups, stews, and dips. We reserve whole lentils with their seed coat for salads, braises, and sautés.

Lentils Used in Our Recipes

Brown or Green Lentils

Brown lentils are flat, large lentils that might be considered the "everyday" lentil found in every supermarket. They are sometimes also called "green lentils" because their color borders on green-brown, but are not the same as lentilles du Puy, or French green lentils (see below). These are all-purpose lentils, great in soups and salads or tossed with olive oil and herbs. Brown lentils hold their shape relatively well, but will break down with extended cooking. Both dried and canned brown lentils are available at grocery stores.

Tasting notes: Mild yet light and earthy flavor and creamy texture
Find them in: Adasi (page 148); Mujaddara (page 267); Lentil Salad with Oranges, Celery, and Feta (page 161)

Lentilles du Puy
(French green lentils)

Lentilles du Puy are a variety of green lentil that are smaller and rounder than the larger, flatter brown/green lentils and have dark speckles. Lentilles du Puy (or du Puy lentils) are only grown in the Puy region of France, whose volcanic soil is said to affect the flavor of the lentils grown in this region giving them more mineral-y and peppery notes. Interchangeable with French green lentils, lentilles du Puy have a thicker skin than regular green lentils, which means they hold their shape really well when cooked. They are great for salads, simmered with mirepoix and stock as a side dish, or in any dish where you want a firm yet tender lentil that can take center stage. Lentilles du Puy are available at well-stocked grocery stores or online.

Tasting notes: Mineral-y and peppery, with a firm texture
Find them in: Saumon aux Lentilles (page 203), Thai Red Curry with Lentils and Tofu (page 218), Lentilles du Puy with Spinach and Crème Fraîche (page 290), Cumin-Spiced Crispy Lentils (page 42)

Red Lentils
(masoor dal)

Red lentils are most commonly sold "split," meaning their seed coat has been removed and the inner part of the lentil has been split in half. In fact, most "red" lentils were originally brown/tan skinned lentils; removing their seed coat reveals their inner red-orange color. Red lentils cook more quickly than whole lentils and break down completely as well, making them ideal for soups, dals, purees, and mashes, or anywhere you want a thick puree.

Tasting notes: Delicate, earthy, nutty, slightly sweet flavor with floral notes
Find them in: Red Lentil Kibbeh (page 219), Palak Dal (page 147), Red Lentil Tacos (page 75)

About Other Legumes

The term "legume" refers to both the dried seeds, like lentils, and to the fresh pods. Fresh legumes, such as green beans and peas, have edible seeds inside. Green beans are grown and eaten for their pods, as are sugar snap peas and snow peas. Other fresh legumes such as English peas and fava beans have pods that are too tough to eat. Edamame are soybeans that are harvested while they are still green and young. They also come in an inedible pod that has to be split open to release the beans. Boiling and salting edamame's whole pods is an easy way to enjoy the delectable beans inside.

Peanuts are also legumes, edible seeds that grow in pods (their shells). Unlike tree nuts, peanuts grow below the surface of the soil. True fresh peanuts, called "green" peanuts, straight from the plant, are highly perishable and need to be eaten within a few days. For this reason, they are not usually found outside their growing regions.

Frozen Is OK

The test kitchen has always been a big fan of frozen peas. Shucked from the pod, quick-blanched, and individually frozen within hours of being harvested, they are often fresher-tasting than the "fresh" peas that you can buy that may have spent days in storage. We've also had great success using frozen green beans, fava beans, and edamame.

Fresh Beans Used in Our Recipes

English Peas
(garden peas, green peas, shell peas)

Originating in the Mediterranean basin, peas were originally grown for their dry seeds; in more modern times, it became more common to eat the seeds "green" when still immature. Today's peas were developed in England in the 16th century. The pod of English peas is discarded and only the seeds inside are consumed. Avoid overly large pods with visible bumps, which indicate more mature (and less sweet) peas. Shelled peas turn starchy faster, so shuck them just before cooking. If it's not spring, buy them frozen. Green peas are versatile; they can be added to soups, casseroles, pasta or rice dishes, and much more.

Tasting notes: Sweet and dense
Find them in: Roast Chicken with Bulgur, Peas, and Mint (page 230); Skillet Paella (page 259); Savory Oatmeal with Peas, Pecorino, and Pepper (page 272)

Fava Beans
(broad beans)

First cultivated in the Mediterranean, fava beans are flat, bright-green beans that grow in large, thick pods (which are discarded). Each bean has an outer skin or sheath around it which is typically removed before eating. Fava beans are available fresh, dried, canned, and frozen. Fresh beans—available seasonally—can be eaten raw, added to salads, made into pesto or pureed, or cooked like other spring vegetables. Dried favas are used in soups, stews, pastas, and falafel, and dishes like ful medames, a fava bean stew consumed for breakfast in Egypt and many countries of North and East Africa and the Middle East. Dried, canned, and frozen fava beans are available at well-stocked grocery stores.

Tasting notes: Delicate, buttery, nutty, and "spring-like" when fresh; dried favas are likened to chickpeas
Find them in: Green Fava Bean Toast (page 63), Braised Lamb Shoulder Chops with Fava Beans (page 198), Ful Medames (page 288)

Green Beans
(French beans, string beans, wax beans, snap beans, haricot verts)

What we call green beans (or also commonly string beans or snap beans due to the "snap" they make when their stem ends are removed) are the unripe fruit of the common bean. They come in different colors and sizes, and are harvested and consumed before the bean seeds inside have matured. Sold fresh, canned, and frozen, green beans can be consumed raw, pickled, or cooked in a variety of ways including blanching, stir-frying or sautéing, braising, or roasting.

Tasting notes: Slightly sweet, grassy flavor; can have a "snappy" texture if lightly cooked or raw
Find them in: Caesar Green Bean Salad (page 280), Cauliflower and Bean Paella (page 206), Classic Three Bean Salad (page 281)

Peanuts
(ground nuts)

Unlike most other legumes, peanuts grow underground, but like many other legumes, peanuts originated in South America. Peanuts are culinarily closer to a nut in both nutritional content (high in fat) and flavor, though botanically they are related to other legumes (pea and bean family). Peanuts are commonly made into pastes (peanut butter) or used whole, either roasted or raw.

Tasting notes: Quite mild, slightly bitter and earthy when raw; much more intensely nutty when toasted and/or ground
Find them in: West African Peanut Stew (page 131), Boiled Peanuts (page 40), Sichuan Snack Peanuts (page 41)

Snow Peas

Snow peas are edible-pod peas with a flattened shape and a pod with very thin, delicately crisp walls that is eaten whole. They were first cultivated in Holland in the 17th century, and can be eaten raw or cooked—blanched, sautéed, or stir-fried most commonly. Look for shiny pods with tiny immature peas visible through the pod walls; bigger peas mean greater maturity and more starchiness.

Tasting notes: Crunchy; vegetal and mildly sweet
Find them in: Chilled Soba Noodles with Spring Vegetables (page 165), Marinated Tofu and Vegetable Salad (page 158)

Soybean Products
(edamame, tofu, tempeh, miso)

Native to east Asia, soybeans are grown for multiple uses (both for human and animal consumption), including soymilk, tofu, tempeh, soybean oil, soy sauce, fermented soy beans and fermented soy-based pastes, including miso and doenjang. Edamame and soybean sprouts are forms of soybean eaten without additional processing, and can be added to stir-fries, salads, and other dishes. Tofu (which comes in many different varieties of firmness) and tempeh can be used in multiple ways including fried/sautéed/stir-fried/grilled, added to soups and stews, and simmered/braised.

Tasting notes: Very vegetal flavor, reminiscent of peas, but less sweet, and a crunchy firm texture.
Find them in: Edamame Salad with Pecorino and Mint (page 283), Edamame and Shrimp Salad (page 159), Tempeh Tacos (page 74), Bitter Melon with Tofu and Pork (page 193), Panko-Crusted Tofu with Cabbage Salad (page 223)

Sugar Snap Peas

Sugar snap peas are edible-pod peas with a rounded shape, similar to English peas, but with a less fibrous pod that is eaten whole. Snap peas are a cross between garden peas and snow peas. For the sweetest flavor, look for fat pods that are no longer than 2½ inches and uniform in color.

Tasting notes: Crisp; juicy and sweet
Find them in: Gochujang Meatballs with Edamame and Sugar Snap Peas (page 189); Pan-Seared Scallops with Sugar Snap Pea Slaw (page 201); Spicy Basil Noodles with Crispy Tofu, Snap Peas, and Bell Pepper (page 222)

About Grains

Like beans, grains are seeds. The edible seeds contain the embryos for future plants. The stored resources in seeds mean that grains can be a nutrient-dense food. Grains can be a major source of protein and fiber and are a vital food source for many parts of the world. Grains are the foundation of many cuisines and can be the starring ingredient in soups and stews, salads, and heartier dishes. They can also be milled into flours to create all kinds of breads, cakes, and more.

Grains are the edible seeds of specific grasses belonging to the *Poaceae* (also known as *Gramineae*) family. These plants are also called cereals. They produce many small, separate dry grains or kernels. Both quinoa and buckwheat are pseudo-cereal grains. Pseudo-cereals are non-grass, wild plants whose seeds are used in the same manner as cereals, but are underutilized due to the dominance of conventional cereal crops. A goal of modern agriculture was to increase the production of identical seed crops, making it more dependable and predictable, therefore raising only a handful of varieties year after year including wheat, oats, and rice.

Types of Grains

Common Grains

The cultivation of the major cereal plants—wheat, barley, oats, rice, corn— has played an integral role in sustaining human development and population growth. These grains were some of the first plants to be domesticated. Similar to commodity bean cultivation, specific grain varieties have been prioritized for their high yields, among other factors.

Heirloom Grains

Heirloom grains are grains that tend to be less processed and have remained largely unchanged for hundreds of years. They come from plants that have been carefully grown from the exact same seedline for hundreds of years. Some of those grains we use in our recipes include freekeh, Kamut, spelt, and teff. Like heirloom beans, heirloom grains are not mass produced. Dedicated farmers and scientists have attempted to create and store reserves of hereditary seeds in order to maintain and propagate the diversity of plant stocks.

Whole Grains

Whole grains have all parts of the kernel and so are the most nutritious choice. They are grains that have been minimally processed and had only their inedible husk removed while still containing their bran and germ. (The bran from any whole grain is a good source of fiber.) Whole grains lend a satisfying chew and earthy, nutty depth to dishes. Whole grains are both healthy and filling and they contain a number of key nutrients, such as antioxidants. We have recipes that use bulgur, farro, freekeh, and quinoa among others in this book. For more information, see pages 22–27.

FAQ

What is an ancient grain?
"Ancient grain" is largely a marketing term used to describe a category of grains and pseudo-cereals purported to have been minimally changed by selective breeding.

Anatomy of a Grain

Each grain, also called a kernel, has three parts:

Bran: the hard outer coating of a kernel. It contains most of the kernel's fiber. It also has vitamins and minerals.

Germ: the part that sprouts into a new plant. It has many vitamins, healthy fats, and other natural plant nutrients.

Endosperm: the energy supply for the seed. It mostly contains starches. It has small amounts of proteins and vitamins and very little fiber.

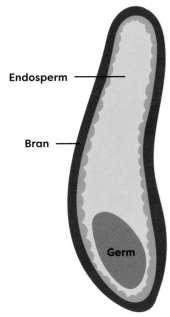

Refined Grains

Refined grains have had some or all of their germ and bran removed. These grains have a finer texture and a longer food storage life. The refining process takes out nearly all of the fiber and many other nutrients. White flour, white rice, and degermed cornmeal are examples of refined grains.

Enriched Grains

The nutrients removed from refined grains may be added back. These refined grains are called enriched grains. For example, when rice is refined, it loses vitamins, minerals, and fiber. Enriched white rice has these vitamins and minerals added back, but fiber usually isn't replaced.

Read the Package

The type of grain you are purchasing is not always written on the front of the package. To determine whether the grain has been processed and pearled, hulled, or presteamed, check the ingredient list. A pearled or semi-pearled grain has had some or all of the bran removed and will typically cook faster (pearl barley is an example), whereas a hulled grain has had just its outer husk removed. A presteamed grain means that some pre- or partial cooking has occurred. You can also take a look at the cooking time in the directions; if the grain requires more than 30 minutes to cook, it is most likely has not been pearled, hulled, or presteamed.

A Word About Whole-Grain Flours

Many whole grains are ground into flour, and many of those flours have the added benefit of being gluten-free. We experimented in the kitchen with various whole-grain flours and developed a variety of recipes such as crepes from buckwheat flour and spaetzle from sorghum flour.

Color matters and color is determined by the relative amount of bran and germ each contains: Darker flours deliver stronger flavor. Because the U.S. Food and Drug Administration doesn't regulate how much "whole grain" a product needs to contain to bear that label, any type of flour may bear this description.

Grains Used in Our Recipes

This listing is an introduction to all of the wonderful varieties of grains that we experimented with and ended up using in the book. The differences in their flavors and textures are quite distinct.

Buckwheat Flour

Earthy, nutty, mineral-y buckwheat flour is made from ground buckwheat groats and adds a nutty, slightly bitter flavor to dishes in which it is used, such as Japanese soba noodles and crepes from Brittany, France. It does not contain gluten, and as such cannot be used alone to make leavened breads, but it adds nutty flavor to quick breads and other baked goods.

Find it in: Galettes Complètes (page 93)

Buckwheat Groats
(kasha)

Buckwheat, despite its name, is not related to wheat but is in fact an herb that is related to sorrel and rhubarb. Native to Russia, buckwheat appears in cuisines all over the globe, particularly in Eastern Europe and Japan. Buckwheat has an assertive flavor and can be found in several forms. Grayish-green, hulled, crushed buckwheat seeds are known as buckwheat groats and have a mildly earthy flavor. They are often eaten as a staple like rice and are baked into puddings and porridges. Kasha is buckwheat groats that have been roasted. This process gives kasha a darker color and a noticeably earthier and roasty flavor. Kasha is often served pilaf-style and as a hot cereal, and it also is traditionally used in blintzes, combined with pasta to make a traditional Eastern European Jewish dish called kasha varnishkes, and included as part of a filling for pastries known as knishes. Kasha and buckwheat groats are not interchangeable.

Find it in: Buckwheat Tabbouleh (page 311)

Bulgur

Bulgur is made from parboiled or steamed wheat kernels/berries that are then dried, partially stripped of their outer bran layer, and coarsely ground. The result of this process is a highly nutritious grain that cooks relatively quickly—some types require only soaking. Perhaps best known as an element in tabbouleh, bulgur is actually quite versatile, and can be used in pilafs, stuffings, meat-based dishes (kibbeh) and salads. It is most commonly used in North Africa and the eastern Mediterranean. Coarse-grind bulgur, which requires simmering, is best suited for making pilaf. Note that medium-grind bulgur can work in multiple applications if you make adjustments to soaking or cooking times. Do not confuse bulgur with cracked wheat, which is not precooked and cannot be substituted for bulgur. When it's cooked, bulgur will be somewhat tender but still firm. Be sure to rinse bulgur, regardless of grain size, to remove excess starches that can turn the grain gluey.

Find it in: Kibbeh bil Saineyeh (page 250), Pan-Seared Chicken with Warm Bulgur Pilaf (page 229), Stuffed Eggplants with Bulgur (page 263)

Corn (dried)

Corn, one of the most important global food crops, was originally domesticated in Mexico from a wild grass called teosinte. While corn is featured prominently in the food of Mexico (where the most corn biodiversity still exists) and the Americas, corn is grown and consumed globally. There are many types of corn, which are classified based on kernel texture and composition, including sweet varieties for eating fresh, frozen, or canned (sweet corn); types for making cornmeal/flour (flour corn); and those used for hominy and ground products like polenta, grits, and masa harina (flint and dent corn). Popcorn is a particular type of flint corn whose starch makeup and kernel texture allow the kernels to explode when heated.

Find it in: Posole (page 136), Cheesy Baked Grits (page 313), Corn Pudding (page 315)

FAQ
Is corn a grain?

Fresh and frozen corn are considered to be vegetables not grains. Only once corn is dried is it considered to be a grain. Dried corn can be milled into flour and turned into foods such as tortillas and cornbread. Popcorn is considered to be a whole grain.

Cornmeal
(polenta, grits)

Cornmeal is ground from dried corn. Generally it is ground fairly fine and used to make cornbread and other baked goods. It has usually been degerminated, meaning that the hull and germ have been removed to lengthen its shelf life. Heirloom varieties of cornmeal contain the hull and (oil-rich) germ and therefore will go rancid more quickly. The final texture of the dish may vary if using an heirloom variety. Corn grits, like cornmeal, are ground from dried corn kernels, typically coarser than cornmeal. Polenta is also coarse-ground corn but is traditionally made from a different variety of corn: Where grits (and cornmeal) are made from dent corn (a low-sugar variety with pronounced corn flavor), polenta is made from flint corn, which has a harder starch kernel (so polenta retains a coarse texture when it's cooked). Note that many cornmeals are actually a blend of corn types and not a single kind.

The grind you choose depends on what you are making: Choose fine grind for baking recipes, coarse grind for polenta. We prefer degerminated coarse-ground cornmeal for both polenta and grits because it produces a soft-textured product with great corn flavor. Avoid instant or quick-cooking polenta for these recipes.

Find it in: Grilled Polenta Wedges with Grilled Scallions and Gorgonzola (page 46), Guanimes con Bacalao (page 143)

FAQ
Are polenta and grits the same thing?

Basically, yes. Both polenta and grits are made from coarse-ground corn. You can substitute grits for polenta and vice versa. Polenta is typically made from ground yellow corn, while grits can be made from ground yellow corn, white corn, or hominy.

Farro

Farro is hulled whole-wheat kernels with a sweet, nutty flavor and a chewy bite. Farro can be processed in four different ways: Whole-grain farro has the husk removed, but the bran and germ are intact; it requires soaking and has the longest cook time. Semi-pearled and pearled farro have part of the outer bran layer removed, reducing cook times from whole-grain farro, while quick-cooking farro has the entire bran layer removed, and the quickest cook times. We think farro is best cooked using an abundance of water (like pasta) to cook the grains more evenly. When cooked, the grains will be tender but have a slight chew, similar to al dente pasta. Farro is great as a pilaf, grain salad, in soups, or cooked like risotto (for farroto).

Find it in: Braised Short Ribs with Wild Mushroom Farrotto (page 244), Flank Steak with Farro and Mango Salsa (page 245), Wild Mushroom Ragout with Farro (page 270)

Fonio

Fonio is a tiny-grained relative of millet, cultivated in West Africa, including Senegal, Burkina Faso, Gambia, Mali, Nigeria, and Guinea. This fast-growing, drought-resistant grass is also fast-cooking, mild-tasting and highly versatile, usable in everything from pilafs to salads to veggie burgers or patties. Fonio has an earthy, grassy aroma and a texture most similar to couscous when cooked, readily absorbing flavors. Fonio is available online or in well-stocked grocery stores.

Find it in: Fonio, Sweet Potato, and Scallion Cakes (page 68); Curried Fonio with Roasted Vegetables and Hibiscus Vinaigrette (page 274)

Freekeh

Sometimes spelled frikeh or farik, freekeh is a nutrient-packed grain that's used in eastern Mediterranean and North African kitchens in pilafs, salads, and more. It has a nutty, slightly smoky flavor. Freekeh is made from durum wheat, which is harvested while immature and soft and then fire-roasted and rubbed to remove the chaff, or husk ("freekeh" means "to rub" in Arabic). It can then be left whole or cracked into smaller pieces. We found that simply boiling the grain like pasta is the most foolproof way to achieve a chewy, firm texture.

Find it in: Chorba Frik (page 121), Chicken and Spiced Freekeh with Cilantro and Preserved Lemon (page 240)

Hominy

Hominy is dried field (not sweet) corn kernels that have been nixtamalized or soaked in limewater, an alkaline solution of water and calcium hydroxide, which breaks down and gels some of the corn's carbohydrates and makes the corn nuttier and more complex-tasting, and also more nutritious. During the nixtamalization process, the hull and germ are removed, which allows the kernel to puff up, explaining hominy's giant size. Hominy can be either yellow or white, and can be used dried or canned. It's often used in stews, like Mexican posole, or ground into grits (hominy grits) or flour (see masa harina).

Find it in: Pressure-Cooker Pork Pozole Rojo (page 326), White Chicken Chili (page 152), Slow-Cooker Tomatillo Chili with Pork and Hominy (page 369)

Kamut
(khorasan wheat)

Kamut is also known as khorasan wheat, as that refers to the region of Afghanistan and Iran in which the ancient grain historically grew. Beyond being plumper than standard wheat, Kamut is extra delightful in any wheat berry application—soups, salads, pilafs, gratins—as it has a deep buttery flavor and a smooth texture that costars nicely with vibrant ingredients. Kamut can also be milled into flour.

Find it in: Popped Kamut (page 43), Warm Kamut with Carrots and Pomegranate (page 317)

Masa Harina

Masa harina (literally "dough flour" though often called "instant corn masa flour" in English) is nixtamalized corn that has been cooked, dried, and ground into flour and can be reconstituted to make "masa," the basis of tamales, tortillas, pupusas, and many other dishes. Nixtamalization is the process of soaking corn in limewater, an alkaline solution of water and calcium hydroxide, which breaks down and gels some of the corn's carbohydrates, allowing our bodies to absorb the nutrients present. It also makes the corn taste nuttier and more complex. Masa harina is generally a finely ground flour that mixed with water forms masa for making many corn-based products.

Find it in: Pupusas with Beans and Cheese (page 84), Tomatillo Chicken Huaraches (page 86)

Masarepa

Masarepa is also an instant corn flour made from precooked corn, but it is not nixtamalized. It can be made from yellow or white corn and is a finely milled flour. Masarepa is used for making arepas, corn cakes that are traditional in Colombia and Venezuela. Masarepa and masa harina cannot be substituted for each other.

Find it in: Black Bean and Cheese Arepas (page 84)

Millet

Millet is a small-seeded cereal grass that is super drought-resistant. It is a staple crop in many parts of the world, including Africa, India, and northern China. The mellow corn flavor and fine, fluffy texture of these tiny seeds when cooked make them extremely versatile in both savory and sweet applications, including pilafs, porridges, puddings, and pan-fried cakes. Millet can also be ground into a flour. Whole millet cooks relatively quickly, and when done cooking, all of the liquid will be absorbed and the grains will be fully tender.

Find it in: Millet Salad with Corn and Queso Fresco (page 169)

Oat Berries
(oat groats)

Labeled either oat berries or oat groats, this whole grain is simply whole oats that have been hulled and cleaned. They are the least processed oat product (other forms, such as rolled flat, cut, or ground oats, are processed further). Because they have hardly been processed, oat berries retain a high nutritional value. They have an appealing chewy texture and a mildly nutty flavor. Oats are usually thought of as a breakfast cereal, but oat berries make a great savory side dish cooked pilaf-style.

Find it in: Pressure-Cooker Southwestern Shrimp and Oat Berry Bowl (page 352), Beef and Oat Berry Soup (page 126)

Pearl Barley

A common ingredient in soups and composed grain dishes or salads, barley has a nutty, slightly sweet flavor that is similar to that of brown rice. Barley is available in multiple forms, but our favorite is pearl barley, which is hulled barley that has been polished to remove all or some of the bran, which decreases the cook time. Cooking times vary depending on the extent to which the barley is polished. Since there is often no way to tell how pearled the barley is by reading the label, we account for the differences by including a wide range in our cooking times. When cooked, barley is plump and tender but still somewhat firm in the center, with a bit of "bite."

Find it in: Barley with Celery and Miso Dressing (page 310), Chicken Barley Soup (page 124), Sheet-Pan Italian Chicken Sausages with Broccoli and Barley (page 239)

Quinoa

Quinoa originated in the Andes Mountains of South America, and while it is generally treated as a grain, it is actually the seed of the goosefoot plant. Quinoa is often referred to as a "supergrain" because it's high in nutritionally complete protein. The pin-head-size seeds can be white, red, black, or purple; they have a delicate crunch and mineral-y, nutty taste. When cooked, the seeds unfurl and expand to about three times their size. Cooked as a pilaf or for a salad, quinoa can be ready in about 20 minutes. Look for prewashed quinoa, which has been washed to remove its natural bitter protective coating, called saponin; if you buy unwashed quinoa (or if you are unsure whether it's washed), rinse it before cooking.

Find it in: Easy Baked Quinoa with Lemon, Garlic, and Parsley (page 318); Herbed Quinoa Cakes with Whipped Feta (page 66); Quinoa Lettuce Wraps with Feta and Olives (page 73)

Rye Berries

Rye is cultivated in the U.S., Asia, and Europe, particularly in areas that are unfavorable for other cereal crops due to cooler climates or poor soil quality. While rye may be most commonly known in its flour form, rye berries can be used similarly to other whole grains like wheat or oat berries: in salads, or grain bowls, or in stews, or added to breads. Rye berries have a nutty, earthy flavor with a slight tang, and a tender yet firm texture when cooked. Rye berries can be sprouted for use in salads or boiled as a side dish.

Find it in: Warm Rye Berries with Apple and Scallions (page 319), Sprouted Grain Salad (page 177)

Rye Flour

Rye flour, like wheat, contains gluten (though in lower amounts) and as such can be used in bread baking. Rye breads, such as pumpernickel, are traditional in the central, eastern, and northern European countries (the "rye belt") in which rye was an important staple crop. Rye flour adds a nutty, earthy, and slightly malty flavor to baked goods, similar to whole-wheat flour. Rye flour is classified as "light," "medium," or "dark," which indicates how much of the rye kernel is included in the flour; flours with more bran and germ are darker in color and more intense in rye flavor. Dark rye flour, also known as pumpernickel flour, is milled from the entire rye kernel giving the most pronounced rye flavor.

Find it in: Rye Crepes with Smoked Salmon, Crème Fraîche, and Pickled Shallots (page 94); Chicken and Rye Dumplings (page 130)

Spelt

Before modern wheat came spelt, a species that was domesticated around 5000 BCE. It was a staple crop and now is valued for its nutritional benefits. The heirloom grain is noted for being easier to digest than conventional wheat. It's not only an excellent source of fiber and protein, it's also rich in beneficial B vitamins as well as minerals like iron. Also called dinkel, hulled, or German wheat, spelt is sweet and nutty and here featured as nice chewy berries. Spelt flour has gained popularity as a substitute for all-purpose flour or other whole-wheat flours in baked goods.

Find it in: Spelt Salad with Pickled Fennel, Pea Greens, and Mint (page 171)

Steel-Cut Oats

Steel-cut oats are whole-grain oats that are partially cooked and then cut into pieces with steel blades. Dense and chewy with a strong buttery flavor, steel-cut oats take about 25 minutes longer to cook than rolled oats.

Find it in: Savory Oatmeal with Peas, Pecorino, and Pepper (page 272)

Wheat Berries

Wheat berries, often erroneously referred to as "whole wheat," are whole, unprocessed kernels of wheat. Since none of the grain has been removed, wheat berries are an excellent source of nutrition. Compared with more refined forms of wheat (cracked wheat, bulgur, and flour), wheat berries require a relatively long cooking time. In the test kitchen, we like to toast the dry wheat berries until they are fragrant, and then simmer them for about an hour until they are tender but still retain a good bite.

Find it in: Mushroom and Wheat Berry Soup (page 108); Wheat Berry Salad with Radicchio, Dried Cherries, and Pecans (page 172); Slow-Cooker Wheat Berries with Carrots and Orange (page 389)

Cooking Grains

Some grains, such as bulgur, cook in minutes, while others, such as barley, take much longer. We have perfected three basic methods for cooking grains. As for which method is preferred, that is really dependent on the grain. For instance, we love pilaf-style because it produces grains with a light and fluffy texture and a slightly toasted flavor but we don't recommend cooking most whole grains this way.

Grain Prep

Rinsing

We recommend rinsing and draining grains before cooking. The grains will roughly triple in volume once cooked.

How to: To remove excess surface starch, place the grains or rice in a fine-mesh strainer and rinse until cool water until the water runs clear, occasionally stirring lightly with your hand. Let drain briefly.

Sprouting

You can eat some whole grains raw by sprouting them. Sprouting grains is easy; you simply soak the seeds in successive batches of filtered water until they just begin to sprout. We like to eat them in Sprouted Grain Salad (page 177). For more information, see page 178.

Grain Cooking Methods

Grains can be simmered, boiled, and microwaved. The pasta method (boiling) is usually the best choice for longer-cooking grains like farro and wheat berries, while simmering using the pilaf method is a good choice for shorter-cooking grains such as quinoa and bulgur. In the test kitchen, we cooked a mountain of grains to determine the best way to cook each grain.

Boiling (the pasta method)

The pasta method involves boiling the grains in a large amount of water that is later drained off. Bring 2 or 4 quarts water to a boil in a large saucepan. Stir in the grains and ½ teaspoon salt. Return to a boil, then reduce to a simmer and cook until the grains are tender, following the times in the cooking chart (page 30). Drain.

Pilaf method

The pilaf method calls for simmering a measured amount of grains in a specific amount of water in a covered pot until the water is absorbed and the grains are tender. Rinse and dry the grains on a towel. Heat 1 tablespoon oil in a medium saucepan (preferably nonstick) over medium-high heat until shimmering. Stir in the grains and toast until lightly golden and fragrant, 2 to 3 minutes. Stir in the water and ¼ teaspoon salt. Bring the mixture to a simmer, then reduce the heat to low, cover, and continue to simmer until the grains are tender and have absorbed all of the water, following the times in the cooking chart (page 30). Off the heat, let the grains stand for 10 minutes, then fluff with a fork.

Microwaving

Rinse the grains. Combine the grain, 1 or 2 cups water, and ¼ teaspoon salt in a bowl. Cover and cook following the times and temperatures in the cooking chart (page 30) until the liquid is absorbed and the grains are tender. Carefully remove the bowl from the microwave and let sit covered for 5 minutes. Fluff the grains with a fork and serve.

Great Grains to Microwave
- Bulgur (fine-grind)
- Fonio
- Quinoa (any color)

Cooling

To cool cooked grains, spread them on a rimmed baking sheet and let cool for at least 15 minutes before using.

Reheating

To reheat cooked grains, microwave in a covered microwave-safe bowl until hot throughout, fluffing with a fork halfway through cooking (timing will vary depending on the quantity and type of grains used).

Storing Grains and Rice

In the pantry: To prevent open boxes and bags of grains and rice from spoiling, store them in an airtight container.

In the refrigerator: Cooked grains will last in the refrigerator for up to three days.

In the freezer: Store uncooked grains and rice in the freezer in an airtight container. Store cooked grains and rice in the freezer for up to three months. When grains are completely cooled, transfer them to a zipper-lock bag and lay it flat to freeze.

Grain Cooking Chart

The chart below contains all you need to know to cook our favorite grains. The recipes can be scaled up by increasing the amounts proportionally. The cooking times will remain the same.

TYPE OF GRAIN	COOKING METHOD	AMOUNT OF GRAIN	AMOUNT OF WATER	COOKING TIME
Pearl Barley	Boiled	1½ cups	4 quarts	20 to 40 minutes
	Pilaf-Style	X	X	X
	Microwave	X	X	X
Bulgur (medium- to coarse-grind)	Boiled	1 cup	4 quarts	15 to 20 minutes
	Pilaf-Style**	1 cup	1 cup	16 to 18 minutes
	Microwave	1 cup	1 cup	5 to 10 minutes
Bulgur (fine-grind)	Boiled	X	X	X
	Pilaf-Style	X	X	X
	Microwave	1 cup	2 cups	4 minutes
Buckwheat	Boiled	1 cup	2 quarts	10 to 12 minutes
	Pilaf-Style	1 cup	1½ cups	12 minutes
	Microwave	X	X	X
Farro	Boiled	1 cup	4 quarts	15 to 20 minutes
	Pilaf-Style	X	X	X
	Microwave	X	X	X
Fonio	Boiled	X	X	X
	Pilaf-Style	X	X	X
	Microwave	1 cup	2 cups	5 minutes
Freekeh	Boiled	1½ cups	4 quarts	30 to 45 minutes
	Pilaf-Style	X	X	X
	Microwave	X	X	X
Kamut	Boiled	1 cup	2 quarts	55 minutes to 1¼ hours
	Pilaf-Style	X	X	X
	Microwave	X	X	X
Millet	Boiled	X	X	X
	Pilaf-Style***	1 cup	2 cups	15 to 20 minutes
	Microwave	X	X	X
Oat Berries	Boiled	1 cup	4 quarts	30 to 40 minutes
	Pilaf-Style	1 cup	1½ cups	30 to 40 minutes
	Microwave	X	X	X
Quinoa (any color)	Boiled	X	X	X
	Pilaf-Style	1 cup	1 cup + 3 tablespoons	18 to 20 minutes
	Microwave	1 cup	2 cups	5 minutes on medium, then 5 minutes on high
Spelt	Boiled	1 cup	2 quarts	50 minutes to 1 hour 5 minutes
	Pilaf-Style	X	X	X
	Microwave	X	X	X
Wheat Berries	Boiled	1 cup	4 quarts	1 hour
	Pilaf-Style	X	X	X
	Microwave	X	X	X

** For pilaf, do not rinse, and skip the toasting step, adding the grain to the pot with the liquid.

*** For pilaf, increase the toasting time until the grains begin to pop, about 12 minutes.   X = Not recommended

Got Grains? Make a Grain Bowl

Grains make an ideal base to a bowl-style meal that you can fully customize. There are no hard and fast rules when it comes to building a great bowl, but there are a few elements that will take your bowls from boring to brilliant.

Base: Filling grains make a great bowl base. Tossing your grains with some sauce or dressing adds flavor to each and every bite.

Protein: The beauty of bowls is that they're flexible—you can add protein in the form of cooked chopped, ground, or shredded meat; eggs; beans; or tofu.

Vegetables: Vegetables boost a bowl's overall flavor, nutrition, visual appearance, and textural contrast. Try shredding, chopping, cutting matchsticks, or peeling ribbons. Try doing the same with fruit.

Sauce: Great bowls use sauces or dressings to amp up their flavor and moisture—both homemade and store-bought varieties are excellent options. Bright sauces can add a pop of color as well as a punch of extra flavor.

Crunch: Adding some crunch takes a bowl from good to great. Some of our favorite crunchy elements are as simple as raw radish slices or bean sprouts. Raid your pantry or fridge for other crunchy options.

About Rice

Anatomy of Rice

There's a wide world of rice beyond white. Colored rices—brown, black, and red—all have their bran intact, meaning that they are whole grains. It's the outer bran layer that gives rice its color. Try nutty red rice in a pot of Coconut Chicken Soup with Red Rice (page 122) or black rice in a stunning Black Rice and Sea Bean Salad (page 173) where the roasted flavor of the rice plays off the salty beans.

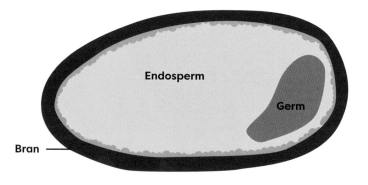

Rice Used in Our Recipes

Long-Grain White Rice

This broad category includes generic long-grain rice as well as aromatic varieties such as basmati, Texmati, and jasmine. The grains are slender and elongated and measure four to five times longer than they are wide. Long-grain white rice cooks up light and fluffy with firm, distinct grains, making it good for pilafs and salads. For this rice we often prefer the pilaf-style method of cooking, a sautéing method that adds toasted, nutty flavors to the rice. You can also use the simmering or absorption method by cooking the rice in water or broth.

Find it in: Congee with Stir-Fried Ground Pork (page 137), Jamaican Rice and Peas (page 305), Turmeric Rice and Chicken Salad with Herbs (page 175)

Medium-Grain White Rice

This category includes rices used to make risotto (Arborio) and paella (Valencia), as well as many Japanese and Chinese varieties. The grains are fat and cook up a bit sticky, resisting turning hard and crunchy as they cool (unlike long-grain rice). When simmered, the grains clump together, making this rice a good choice to accompany a stir-fry, but it also takes well to pilafs.

Find it in: Almost Hands-Free Risotto with Parmesan (page 303), Paella on the Grill (page 259), Cauliflower and Bean Paella (page 206)

Short-Grain White Rice 	The grains of short-grain rice are almost round, and the texture is quite sticky and soft when cooked. These qualities make it ideal for tossing with a light vinegar dressing and wrapping up in onigiri. It's often steamed or gently simmered.	Find it in: Onigiri (page 72), Garlicky Fried Rice with Bok Choy (page 265) **FAQ** **What is sushi rice?** Bags at the store labeled "sushi rice" contain Japanese-style short-grain rice. This rice has a higher starch content than other varieties, which gives it its sticky texture.
Brown Rice 	As with white rice, brown rice comes in a variety of grain sizes: short, medium, and long. Long-grain brown rice, the best choice for pilafs, cooks up fluffy with separate grains. Medium-grain brown rice is a bit more sticky, perfect for risotto, paella, and similar dishes. Short-grain brown rice is the starchiest and stickiest, ideal for sushi and puddings. The bran layer, valued for its fiber content, is also something of a nuisance: It slows absorption (brown rice takes nearly twice as long to cook as white) and causes uneven simmering on the stovetop, so we generally prefer boiling brown rice in an abundance of water or baking it.	Find it in: Brown Rice Pilaf with Dates and Pistachios (page 305), Miso Brown Rice Burgers (page 67), Gingery Chicken and Rice Soup with Shiitakes (page 123)
Black Rice 	Like brown rice, black rice is sold unpolished, with its bran layer still attached. But black rice contains anthocyanins, the same antioxidant compounds in blueberries and blackberries. These compounds are what turn the rice a deep purple as it cooks.	Find it in: Black Rice and Sea Bean Salad (page 173), Black Rice Bowls with Roasted Salmon and Miso Dressing (page 256)
Red Rice 	This category of whole-grain rice gets its color from its anthocyanin content, which colors its bran layer red, instead of the regular brown. Common varieties include West African red rice, Bhutanese (or Himalayan) red rice, and Thai red rice. Because it still contains the bran, red rice is considered a whole grain and contains more vitamins and minerals than white rice. Red rice tends to taste nuttier and subtly sweeter than other rices.	Find it in: Coconut Chicken Soup with Red Rice (page 122)
Wild Rice 	Wild rice isn't actually rice at all; it's an aquatic grass. Wild rice is North America's only native grain. It grows naturally in lakes and rivers and is also cultivated in man-made paddies in Minnesota, California, and Canada. Cultivated paddy rice is chewier and fairly neutral-tasting; natural wild rice is tender with a delicate fragrance and distinctive taste. We prefer brands that parboil the grains during processing, which leads to more even cooking later.	Find it in: Garlicky Wild Rice Soup with Artichokes (page 113), Harvest Salad (page 174), Wild Rice Stuffing (page 308)

Cooking Rice

Rinsing Rice

Rinsing white rice removes excess surface starch that would otherwise absorb water and swell, causing the grains to stick together. Brown rice has its bran layer intact, so there is little to no exterior starch to wash away.

DO rinse for pilaf, steamed rice, and rice salads, where you want separate, distinct grains. DON'T rinse for applications such as risotto; rinsing compromises the desirably creamy, sticky consistency.

How to: Rinse rice in fine-mesh strainer under cold running water until water runs clear.

> #### FAQ
>
> #### How can you tell when the water has become clear when rinsing raw rice?
> It can be hard to recognize when the water has become clear. This is because the water is aerated by its passage through the rice, which can give it a cloudy appearance; also, typically we're rinsing in the sink and the rinse water goes quickly down the drain. We recommend capturing some of the rinse water in a bowl to check whether it is starchy. Keep reserving and checking, a small amount at a time, until it is clear.

Rice Cooking Methods

Here are three simple methods for basic rice cooking: boiling, pilaf-style, and microwaving. Pilaf-style cooking is our favorite (though boiling rice in ample amounts of water is a great easy method when you want rice to round out a meal or fill a burrito). And after working on it for a while in the test kitchen, we can say that not only does the microwave work for rice, it works really well. Plus you can cook the rice right in the serving bowl. To make rice for a crowd, use the boiling method and double the amount of rice (don't add more water or salt).

Boiling

Bring the water to a boil in a large saucepan. Stir in the rice and 2½ teaspoons salt. Return to a boil, then reduce to a simmer and cook until the rice is tender, following the times in the cooking chart (page 35). Drain.

Pilaf

Rinse the rice. Heat 1 tablespoon oil in a medium saucepan (preferably nonstick) over medium-high heat until shimmering. Stir in the rice and cook until the edges of the grains begin to turn translucent, about 3 minutes. Stir in the water and ¼ teaspoon salt. Bring the mixture to a simmer, then reduce the heat to low, cover, and continue to simmer until the rice is tender and has absorbed all the water, following the cooking times below. Off the heat, place a clean folded dish towel under the lid and let the rice sit for 10 minutes. Fluff the rice with a fork.

Microwave

Rinse the rice. Combine the water, the rice, 1 tablespoon oil, and ¼ teaspoon salt in a bowl. Cover and microwave on high (full power) until the water begins to boil, 5 to 10 minutes. Reduce the microwave heat to medium (50 percent power) and continue to cook until the rice is just tender, following the cooking times below. Remove from the microwave and fluff with a fork. Cover the bowl with plastic wrap, poke several vent holes in the plastic with the tip of a knife, and let sit until completely tender, about 5 minutes.

Rice Cooking Chart

TYPE OF RICE	COOKING METHOD	AMOUNT OF RICE	AMOUNT OF WATER	COOKING TIME
Short- and Medium-Grain White Rice	Boiled	1 cup	4 quarts	10 to 15 minutes
	Pilaf-Style	1 cup	1¾ cups	10 to 15 minutes
	Microwave	X	X	X
Long-Grain White Rice	Boiled	1 cup	4 quarts	12 to 17 minutes
	Pilaf-Style	1 cup	1¾ cups	16 to 18 minutes
	Microwave	1 cup	2 cups	10 to 15 minutes
Short- and Medium-Grain Brown Rice	Boiled	1 cup	4 quarts	22 to 27 minutes
	Pilaf-Style	1 cup	1¾ cups	40 to 50 minutes
	Microwave	1 cup	2 cups	25 to 30 minutes
Long-Grain Brown Rice	Boiled	1 cup	4 quarts	25 to 30 minutes
	Pilaf-Style	1 cup	1¾ cups	40 to 50 minutes
	Microwave	1 cup	2 cups	25 to 30 minutes
Black Rice	Boiled	1½ cups	4 quarts	20 to 25 minutes
	Pilaf-Style	X	X	X
	Microwave	X	X	X
Red Rice	Boiled	1½ cups	4 quarts	27 to 31 minutes
	Pilaf-Style	X	X	X
	Microwave	X	X	X
Wild Rice	Boiled	1 cup	4 quarts	45 to 40 minutes
	Pilaf-Style	X	X	X
	Microwave	X	X	X
Basmati or Jasmine Rice	Boiled	1 cup	4 quarts	12 to 17 minutes
	Pilaf-Style	1 cup	1¾ cups	16 to 18 minutes
	Microwave	1 cup	2 cups	10 to 15 minutes

X = Not recommended

Useful Equipment

Cooking beans, grains, and rice requires very few pieces of kitchen equipment. A large saucepan, Dutch oven, fine-mesh strainer, and colander are used most often and items you likely have on hand. Here's a list of the pieces we reach for, along with the test kitchen's buying recommendations.

Fine-Mesh Strainer

A fine-mesh strainer is ideal for rinsing and draining rice and the smallest of grains. With a roomy, medium-depth basket of very fine, tight, stiff mesh, our favorite is the Rösle Fine Mesh Strainer, 7.9 inches. A long, wide hook allows it to sit securely on a variety of cookware, and its rounded steel handle was easy to hold. This strainer's sturdy construction makes it worth its high price: It looked as good as new even after serious abuse.

Colander

Whether beans or grains have been brined, soaked, or simply picked over for debris, before they go into a pot to cook, they should be rinsed of starch and dust. We like the RSVP International Precision Pierced 5 Qt. Colander for that purpose and for draining beans and grains after cooking. Its bowl is covered with tiny perforations, so liquids drain from it quickly. Its tall base lifts it high above water draining in a sink. This simple colander is the best we've ever tested. We also like that it's dishwasher-safe and didn't dent when we dropped it.

Large Saucepan

When we want to boil beans or grains or make a soup or stew with them, we turn to our long-time winner, the All-Clad Stainless 4-Qt. Sauce Pan. It has uniform, steady heating and good visibility inside the saucepan to monitor the progress of cooking and, if needed, browning. Its cup-shaped stay-cool handle is easy to grip, and a helper handle provides another grabbing point when the pan is full. Even after brutal whacking on concrete, this model still sat flat on the counter. Our Best Buy is the Tramontina Tri-Ply Clad 4 Qt. Sauce Pan.

Dutch Oven

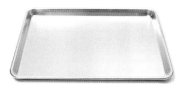

When we are making bean stews or cooking grains pilaf-style, we like to use our Le Creuset 7¼ Qt Round Dutch Oven. It is substantial enough to hold and distribute heat evenly without being unbearably heavy. The light-colored interior combined with low, straight sides gives us good visibility and makes it easy to monitor browning and thermometer position. The broad cooking surface saves us time since we can cook more food at once. This pot is expensive, but it is exceptionally resistant to damage. Our Best Buy is Cuisinart Chef's Enameled Cast Iron Casserole.

Rimmed Baking Sheet

Rimmed baking sheets, also called half-sheet pans, are true workhorses in the test kitchen. We use our Nordic Ware Bakers' Half Sheet to sort and clean beans and grains on and to spread out boiled rice and other grains so they can cool without clumping.

Baking Dish

When you are baking beans or grains, you want a dish that is easy to get in and out of the oven, like the Pyrex Easy Grab 3-Quart Oblong Baking Dish. With the largest handles in our testing, this relatively lightweight baking dish was by far the easiest model to grip and maneuver.

Nonstick Skillet

To cook ingredients to add to our bean dishes or to sauté the beans themselves, we use our OXO Good Grips Non-stick Pro 12" Open Frypan. The cooking surface is slick, both when new and after extensive use, and food never sticks. It's one of the lightest models we tested, so it is easy to lift and maneuver, but also sturdy and dent-resistant. We like its wide, comfortable handle. Its surface can get scratched, but it otherwise holds up well.

Potato Masher

For some bean and lentil recipes, cooked legumes need to be mashed to make a silky sauce or create uniform texture in a dish. That is where our Zyliss Stainless Steel Potato Masher comes in. This tall tool has a sturdy metal mashing plate supported by a long, curved handle made of slip-free plastic. The plethora of small holes on its mashing plate make an ultracreamy, smooth mash and its handle feels comfortable in hands of all sizes. Its round mashing plate eases effortlessly along the edges of every pan. And of course, it is also great for mashing all types of potatoes too.

Food Processor

A food processor like our winning Cuisinart Custom 14 Cup Food Processor makes an astonishing range of recipes faster, easier, and more approachable. Among other things, we use it for processing beans for dips, batters, and sauces. It has a compact, streamlined design that takes up less space than most food processors, despite having one of the largest capacities, all at a moderate price. Its blade and smooth, simple bowl are designed to be easy to handle, monitor during use, and clean. Its unusual feed tube placement allows for increased bowl visibility. It comes with three blades for chopping, shredding, and slicing that can all be stored inside the bowl, with no accessories box to deal with.

Electric Pressure Cooker

If you want to use an electric pressure cooker/multicooker to cook your beans and grains, our winning Instant Pot Pro 8Qt is your best bet. A great, easy-to-use appliance, its flat-bottomed interior pot allows for even searing. Stay-cool handles mean you

can easily move the pot, even when it's hot. The streamlined interface is easy to navigate. A "favorites" feature lets you save go-to recipes. It has a pressure-release switch that keeps your hand away from the hot steam when you vent the machine, and a diffuser on the vent makes the steam disperse slightly more gently. We like that we can disable the "keep warm" function so that the food doesn't keep cooking once it is done.

Stovetop Pressure Cooker

Cooking beans and grains in a pressure cooker greatly reduces their cooking time. Solidly constructed, with a low, wide profile that makes browning food easy, Fissler Vitaquick 8½ Quart Pressure Cooker is well engineered and has an automatic lock and an easy-to-monitor pressure valve. The only cooker to reach 250 degrees at high pressure, it cooks food to perfection in the time range suggested by the recipes.

Slow Cooker

If you like to use a slow cooker, we recommend the Cuisinart 6-Quart 3-in-1 Cook Central with searing capabilities. It has a lightweight, nonstick rectangular metal crock and stay-cool plastic handles. The crock sits directly over a built-in hotplate, so it tends to run a little hotter and cook foods faster than traditional ceramic slow cookers. It has a brown/sauté function that eliminates the need for a separate skillet. It cooks evenly and has built-in temperature sensors that prevent the contents from boiling. It is a solid performer that yields excellent cooking results for beans and grains.

Rice Cooker

A quality rice cooker guarantees perfectly cooked rice every time. Our favorite, the Zojirushi 5.5-Cup Neuro Fuzzy Rice Cooker & Warmer consistently produces excellent rice in both small and large batches. The water measurement markings on the cooking bowl, which are clearly labeled in white writing, are easy to read. The machine plays a song both when it starts cooking and when it switches to the "keep warm" setting. A timer counts down the final minutes of cooking. Plus, the handles on its cooking bowl protect our hands from heat. It keeps rice at a food-safe temperature for 12 hours, a helpful perk for people who like to enjoy rice at multiple times throughout the day. We also like the larger version of this model, the Zojirushi 10-Cup Neuro Fuzzy Rice Cooker & Warmer, which makes from 2 to 20 cups of cooked rice. Remember that leftover rice is perfect for turning into a stir-fry.

CHAPTER ONE

Snacks and Appetizers

● FAST (45 minutes or less)   ● VEGAN
Photo: Barbecue-Spiced Roasted Chickpeas

Lupini Beans with Shallot, Urfa, and Cumin

3 tablespoons extra-virgin olive oil
2 garlic cloves, sliced thin
1 (8-ounce) jar lupini beans in brine, rinsed
2 teaspoons grated lemon zest plus 1 tablespoon juice
1 tablespoon minced fresh parsley

Combine oil and garlic in medium saucepan and cook over medium heat until garlic begins to sizzle, about 3 minutes. Stir in beans and cook until warmed through, about 3 minutes, stirring occasionally. Off heat, stir in lemon zest and juice. Let sit until flavors meld, about 30 minutes. (Beans can be refrigerated for up to 2 days; bring to room temperature before serving.) Stir in parsley, transfer to bowl, and serve.

VARIATION

Lupini Beans with Shallot, Urfa, and Cumin
FAST VEGAN
Add 1 thinly sliced small shallot to oil with garlic. Add 1 teaspoon ground urfa pepper and ½ teaspoon cumin seeds to oil with beans.

Lupini Beans with Garlic, Lemon, and Parsley

Serves 4 (makes 1½ cups) | **Total Time** 10 minutes, plus 30 minutes resting FAST VEGAN

WHY THIS RECIPE WORKS Though less well-known in the United States, lupini beans are commonly eaten throughout the Mediterranean as a street snack or appetizer. Once you've tried them, you'll understand their inherent snackability. Salty from the brine they are soaked in, with a snappy texture, they meld well with simple flavors of the region: lemon, garlic, and parsley or shallots, urfa chile pepper, and cumin seeds. We strongly recommend seeking out cooked lupini; though you can buy dried lupini, they require a lengthy cooking and soaking process to remove the bitter alkaloid they contain. The outer skin is edible, though some people prefer to remove it before eating. Cooked lupini beans are sold packed in brine in jars; rinse them before using to remove excess salt.

Boiled Peanuts

Serves 16 (makes 16 cups) | **Total Time** 6¼ hours, plus 2 hours cooling VEGAN

WHY THIS RECIPE WORKS Boiled peanuts are a beloved snack in the southern United States, where they are sold in small paper bags from roadside stands. If you live outside the South, you may never have tasted this treat, but it's a delicious snack and nutritious alternative to shell-on roasted peanuts. For our recipe, we found that the typical method of boiling raw, shell-on (not roasted) peanuts in heavily seasoned water is the most common cooking method for good reason: It works best. Cooking the peanuts covered for 6 hours and letting them cool in the cooking water for another 2 hours ensures that they are perfectly tender. They should have the texture and consistency of a cooked dried bean. If you're using fresh green peanuts, which are available in late summer and early fall, reduce the cooking time to about 2 hours.

2 pounds raw, shell-on peanuts
Table salt for cooking peanuts

Combine peanuts, 2 gallons water, and 1 cup salt in 12-quart stockpot. Bring to boil over high heat. Reduce heat to low, cover, and simmer until peanuts are tender, about 6 hours, stirring occasionally. Remove from heat and let peanuts cool completely in water, about 2 hours. Strain and serve.

Sichuan Snack Peanuts

Serves 8 to 10 (makes 4 cups) | **Total Time** 20 minutes, plus 1 hour cooling VEGAN

WHY THIS RECIPE WORKS These spicy, pleasantly tongue-tingling peanuts are a popular drinking snack in Sichuan, China. They are easy to make and hard to resist. Though they're commonly made by slowly deep-frying raw, skinned peanuts, we found that we could achieve similar results (and skip the deep frying) by starting with unsalted dry-roasted peanuts, which are prepeeled. To amplify the peanuts' crunchiness, we toast them in 2 tablespoons of oil until they just begin to darken in color before tossing in a heady mix of salt, sugar, and spices, along with whole and ground Sichuan chiles and peppercorns. The ultra-aromatic chiles and peppercorns give these irresistible nuts their signature málà (numbing spicy) flavor. To seed the whole dried Sichuan chiles, snip off the stems with kitchen shears and scrape out the seeds with a toothpick. You can also use kitchen shears to slice the chiles. If you can't find Sichuan chili flakes, substitute gochugaru (Korean red pepper flakes). Alternatively, you can substitute red pepper flakes, but the nuts will be spicier and less aromatic.

3¼ cups (1 pound) unsalted dry-roasted peanuts
2 tablespoons peanut or vegetable oil
10 small dried Sichuan chiles, stemmed, seeded, and sliced ¼ inch thick on bias (optional)
1 tablespoon Sichuan peppercorns, plus 1 teaspoon ground Sichuan peppercorns
2 teaspoons Sichuan chili flakes
2 teaspoons sugar
1½ teaspoons table salt
½ teaspoon five-spice powder
½ teaspoon white pepper

1. Combine peanuts and oil in 14-inch flat-bottomed wok or 12-inch nonstick skillet over medium heat. Cook, stirring frequently, until peanuts begin to darken, 4 to 8 minutes.

2. Stir in sliced chiles, if using; whole and ground peppercorns; chili flakes; sugar; salt; five-spice powder; and white pepper. Cook, tossing slowly but constantly, until peanuts are evenly coated and spices are fragrant, about 1 minute. Transfer peanuts to bowl and let cool completely, about 1 hour. Stir to redistribute spices before serving. (Peanuts can be stored in airtight container for up to 1 week; shake before serving.)

Barbecue-Spiced Roasted Chickpeas

Serves 6 (makes 1⅔ cups) | **Total Time** 1¼ hours, plus 30 minutes cooling VEGAN

WHY THIS RECIPE WORKS You can turn a can of chickpeas into a crunchy, salty snack with a burst of heat. Roasted chickpeas have the crunch and saltiness of chips and pretzels, but they are packed with protein and lighter on oil. Our spiced roasted chickpeas have a crisp, airy texture that we achieve by first zapping the chickpeas in the microwave for about 10 minutes to burst them open at the seams so they release interior moisture. We then coat them with a small amount of olive oil and bake them in a 350-degree oven for about an hour. To keep them from burning, we crowd them toward the center of the pan. For a riff on barbecue potato chips, we dust the roasted chickpeas with a mix of smoked paprika, sugar, garlic powder, onion powder, salt, and cayenne. There is no need to rinse the chickpeas. This recipe calls for a metal baking pan; using a glass or ceramic baking dish will result in unevenly cooked chickpeas.

2 (15-ounce) cans chickpeas
3 tablespoons extra-virgin olive oil
1 tablespoon smoked paprika
1½ teaspoons sugar
1 teaspoon garlic powder
½ teaspoon onion powder
⅛ teaspoon table salt
⅛ teaspoon cayenne pepper

1. Adjust oven rack to middle position and heat oven to 350 degrees. Place chickpeas in colander and let drain for 10 minutes. Line large plate with double layer of paper towels. Spread chickpeas over plate in even layer. Microwave until exteriors of chickpeas are dry and many have split slightly at seams, 8 to 12 minutes.

2. Transfer chickpeas to 13 by 9-inch metal baking pan. Add oil and stir until evenly coated. Using spatula, spread chickpeas into single layer. Transfer to oven and roast for 30 minutes. While chickpeas are roasting, combine paprika, sugar, garlic powder, onion powder, salt, and cayenne in small bowl.

3. Stir chickpeas and crowd toward center of pan, avoiding edges of pan as much as possible. Continue to roast until chickpeas appear dry, slightly shriveled, and deep golden brown, 20 to 40 minutes longer. (To test for doneness, remove a few paler chickpeas and let cool briefly before tasting; if interiors are soft, return to oven for 5 minutes before testing again.)

Cumin-Spiced Crispy Lentils

4. Transfer chickpeas to large bowl. Toss with spice mixture to coat. Season with salt to taste. Let cool completely before serving, about 30 minutes. (Chickpeas can be stored in airtight container for up to 1 week.)

VARIATIONS

Smoked Paprika–Spiced Roasted Chickpeas VEGAN

Omit sugar and garlic powder. Substitute ground coriander for onion powder. Add ¼ teaspoon ground cumin to smoked paprika mixture in step 2.

Coriander-Turmeric Roasted Chickpeas VEGAN

Omit garlic powder and onion powder. Substitute 2 teaspoons paprika for smoked paprika and reduce sugar to ½ teaspoon. Add 1 teaspoon ground coriander, ½ teaspoon ground turmeric, ½ teaspoon ground allspice, and ½ teaspoon ground cumin to paprika mixture in step 2.

Cumin-Spiced Crispy Lentils

Serves 4 (makes 1 cup) | **Total Time** 35 minutes, plus 1 hour soaking VEGAN

WHY THIS RECIPE WORKS These spiced fried lentils are inspired by lentil preparations in the Middle East. The firm texture of small lentilles du Puy holds up well to quick frying in a saucepan. Brining the lentils before frying ensures that they turn tender and lightly crispy without burning. Crispy lentils are great to eat out of hand and they also make a crunchy topping for salads and hummus and other dips. Be sure to use a large saucepan to fry the lentils, as the oil mixture will bubble and steam.

Substitution: You can use dried brown lentils in place of the lentilles du Puy.

- 1 teaspoon table salt for brining
- ½ cup dried lentilles du Puy, picked over and rinsed
- ⅓ cup vegetable oil for frying
- ½ teaspoon ground cumin
- ¼ teaspoon table salt

1. Dissolve 1 teaspoon salt in 1 quart cold water in bowl. Add lentils and let sit at room temperature for at least 1 hour or up to 24 hours. Drain well and pat dry with paper towels.

2. Heat oil in large saucepan over medium heat until shimmering. Add lentils and cook, stirring constantly, until crisped and golden in spots, 8 to 12 minutes (oil should bubble

Buttered Popcorn

vigorously throughout; adjust heat as needed). Carefully drain lentils in fine-mesh strainer set over bowl; transfer lentils to paper towel–lined plate and discard oil. Sprinkle with cumin and ¼ teaspoon salt and toss to combine; let cool completely. Serve. (Cooled lentils can be stored in airtight container at room temperature for up to 24 hours.)

Buttered Popcorn

Serves 14 (makes 14 cups) | **Total Time** 20 minutes
FAST

WHY THIS RECIPE WORKS You'll be planning movie nights just to have this salty, buttery, no-kernel-left-unpopped popcorn. The key to perfectly popped stovetop popcorn is to heat three test kernels with vegetable oil in a saucepan until the kernels pop—that means the oil is hot enough. Adding the rest of the kernels off the burner and letting them sit for 30 seconds ensures all of the kernels heat up evenly. After that, it just takes a few minutes over medium-high heat with the lid slightly ajar for all the corn to pop. The kernels all pop at the same rate—no shaking required. We also created a bunch of choice seasonings.

   3 tablespoons vegetable oil
   ½ cup popcorn kernels
   2 tablespoons unsalted butter, melted
   ¼ teaspoon table salt

   1. Heat oil and 3 kernels in large saucepan over medium-high heat until kernels pop. Remove pan from heat, add remaining kernels, cover, and let sit for 30 seconds.

   2. Return saucepan to medium-high heat. Continue to cook with lid slightly ajar until popping slows to about 2 seconds between pops. Transfer popcorn to large bowl. Add melted butter and toss to coat popcorn. Add salt and toss to combine. Serve.

VARIATIONS
Parmesan-Pepper Popcorn **FAST**
Add ½ teaspoon pepper to butter before melting. Add ½ cup grated Parmesan to popcorn when tossing with butter.

Garlic and Herb Popcorn **FAST**
Add 2 minced garlic cloves and 1 tablespoon minced fresh or 1 teaspoon dried rosemary, thyme, or dill to butter before melting.

Hot and Sweet Popcorn **FAST**
Add 2 tablespoons sugar, 1 teaspoon ground cinnamon, and ½ teaspoon chili powder to butter before melting.

Cajun-Spiced Popcorn **FAST**
Add 1 teaspoon red pepper flakes, 1 teaspoon minced fresh thyme, ¾ teaspoon hot sauce, ½ teaspoon garlic powder, ½ teaspoon paprika, and ¼ teaspoon onion powder to butter before melting.

Popped Wheat Berries

Serves 6 (makes ¾ cup) | **Total Time** 1 hour **VEGAN**

WHY THIS RECIPE WORKS When it comes to popping, corn gets all the attention. But we experimented with different whole grain varieties and found that larger types—namely wheat berries, spelt, and Kamut—take on a hearty crunch and nutty flavor when they're popped, making them a terrific snack or wholesome topping for soups and salads. We also found that a brief simmer in salted water seasons the grains and softens their starch, so they aren't dense and tough when popped. (Note that the grains make a noise as they pop and will jump around the skillet, but they won't fully open like popcorn does.)

   ½ cup wheat berries
      Table salt for cooking grains
   1 teaspoon vegetable oil

   1. Bring 1 quart water to boil in medium saucepan. Add wheat berries and ½ teaspoon table salt and simmer for 15 minutes. Drain well, then spread over large plate lined with double layer of paper towels and let dry for 15 minutes.

   2. Combine dried wheat berries and oil in 10-inch skillet. Cook over medium heat, stirring constantly, until wheat berries are fragrant and deep golden brown, and popping slows, 6 to 8 minutes. (Wheat berries will jump around skillet and won't fully open.) Transfer wheat berries to bowl and season with salt to taste. Let cool completely before serving. (Wheat berries can be stored in airtight container for up to 1 week.)

VARIATIONS
Popped Spelt **VEGAN**
Substitute spelt for wheat berries.

Popped Kamut **VEGAN**
Substitute Kamut for wheat berries.

Chickpea Fries

Serves 6 to 8 | **Total Time** 1½ hours, plus 1 hour chilling
`VEGAN`

WHY THIS RECIPE WORKS Creamy, crispy chickpea fries—also known as panisse in France and panissa or panelle in Italy—are a popular European street snack perfect for batch-making at home and sharing with friends. These black pepper–forward snacks are nicely browned on the outside, with soft, custardy centers. To maintain the light flavors of our chickpea fries, we stick to the most foundational ingredients, staying away from distracting add-ins. We combine the ingredients and simmer them on the stovetop to remove the moisture, essential for hydrating the flour and keeping the fries intact. We let this batter solidify in the refrigerator before slicing it into batons and then frying the batons until they are crisp and golden.

- 1 cup (4½ ounces) chickpea flour
- ¾ teaspoon table salt
- ¼ teaspoon pepper
- 2¼ cups water
- 2 tablespoons extra-virgin olive oil
- 2 quarts vegetable oil for frying
  Lemon wedges
- 1 recipe dipping sauce (recipes follow)

1. Spray 8-inch square baking pan with vegetable oil spray. Combine chickpea flour, salt, and pepper in medium saucepan. Slowly whisk in water and olive oil until smooth. Bring to simmer over medium heat and cook, whisking constantly, until mixture is bubbling and slightly thickened, 3 to 4 minutes.

2. Stirring constantly with wooden spoon or rubber spatula, continue to cook over medium-low heat until batter is thickened to consistency of thick mashed potatoes and is no longer glossy, 6 to 8 minutes longer (spatula dragged through mixture should leave distinct trail).

3. Transfer batter to prepared pan and spread into even layer using greased rubber spatula. Let batter cool slightly, about 10 minutes. Cover with plastic wrap and refrigerate until batter is firm and fully set, at least 1 hour or up to 24 hours.

4. Turn mixture out onto cutting board. Cut into thirds to form 3 strips. Then cut each strip crosswise into 12 fries (you should have total of 36 fries).

5. Adjust oven rack to middle position and heat oven to 200 degrees. Set wire rack in rimmed baking sheet. Heat vegetable oil in large Dutch oven over medium-high heat to 375 degrees. Using spider skimmer or slotted spoon, carefully add half of fries to hot oil. Cook, without moving them, until fries begin to develop color, 30 seconds to 1 minute.

6. Continue to fry, stirring gently to prevent fries from sticking together or to bottom of pot, until fries are golden brown and crispy, 7 to 10 minutes longer. Adjust heat as needed to maintain oil temperature between 350 and 375 degrees.

7. Using spider skimmer or slotted spoon, transfer fries to prepared rack and season with salt and pepper to taste. Transfer to oven to keep warm. Return oil to 375 degrees and repeat frying with remaining fries. Serve with lemon wedges and dipping sauce.

Lemon and Herb Dipping Sauce
Makes 1 cup | **Total Time** 10 minutes `FAST`

- 1 cup mayonnaise
- 2 tablespoons capers, minced
- 1 tablespoon lemon zest plus 2 teaspoons juice
- 1 tablespoon minced fresh tarragon

Whisk all ingredients together in small bowl. Season with salt and pepper to taste. (Sauce can be refrigerated for up to 2 days.)

VARIATIONS

Calabrian Chile Dipping Sauce
Substitute 3 tablespoons minced fresh chives and 2 tablespoons jarred crushed Calabrian chiles for capers, lemon zest, and tarragon. Reduce lemon juice to 1 teaspoon.

Honey and Spice Dipping Sauce
Substitute 1 tablespoon honey, 2 teaspoons cider vinegar, and 2 teaspoons ras el hanout for capers, lemon zest and juice, and tarragon.

Chickpea Crackers

Serves 6 to 8 (makes about 35 crackers)
Total Time 45 minutes, plus 30 minutes cooling `VEGAN`

WHY THIS RECIPE WORKS These quick and easy crackers are made using chickpea flour, which is rich in protein, fiber, and flavor. Because it is a dense flour, we add some olive oil to help create a tender texture, while still keeping the crackers crisp and crunchy. Warm water is key in hydrating the chickpea flour and ensuring the dough is easy to roll out. The dough will feel dry after mixing in the bowl but should hold together when squeezed in the palm of your hand. It will come together fully after kneading on the counter. Don't be afraid to liberally flour the counter when rolling; it's necessary to roll the dough out to the proper thickness. We prefer 2-inch crackers but you can use any size round cutter with no change in the baking time. The earthy chickpea flavor lends itself well to additional flavors so we developed some variations based on herbes de Provence and turmeric and black pepper. The crackers pair well with cheese and dips, but are flavorful enough to be eaten on their own.

1 cup (4½ ounces) chickpea flour, plus extra for rolling
¼ teaspoon table salt
3 tablespoons plus 1 teaspoon warm water
1 tablespoon extra-virgin olive oil

1. Adjust oven rack to middle position and heat oven to 350 degrees. Line rimmed baking sheet with parchment paper. Whisk flour and salt together in large bowl. Stir in water and oil and mix until shaggy dough forms. Transfer to clean counter and knead dough until no dry flour remains. Shape into 4-inch round, wrap with plastic wrap and let rest for 10 minutes.

2. On well-floured counter, roll dough into 13-inch round (about ¹⁄₁₆ inch thick), flipping and flouring dough if it begins to stick to counter or resists rolling. Using 2-inch biscuit cutter, cut as many rounds from dough as possible and transfer to prepared sheet.

3. Combine scraps and knead briefly to form cohesive ball. Flatten and reroll dough into 8-inch round (about ¹⁄₁₆ inch thick). Repeat cutting rounds from dough and transferring to sheet. Arrange dough rounds so they are evenly spaced over sheet then poke each dough round in center with blunt end of toothpick or skewer.

4. Bake crackers until puffed and golden brown, 17 to 19 minutes, rotating sheet halfway through baking. Let crackers cool completely on sheet, about 30 minutes. Serve. (Crackers can be stored in airtight container at room temperature for up to 5 days.)

Chickpea Crackers

VARIATIONS

Turmeric–Black Pepper Chickpea Crackers `VEGAN`
Add 1 teaspoon ground turmeric and ½ teaspoon black pepper to flour mixture in step 1.

Herbes de Provence Chickpea Crackers `VEGAN`
Add 2 teaspoons herbes de Provence to flour mixture in step 1.

Farinata

Serves 6 to 8 (makes one 12-inch pancake)
Total Time 1 hour, plus 4 hours resting `VEGAN`

WHY THIS RECIPE WORKS On the Ligurian coast of Italy, the golden batter for this chickpea flour pancake is poured across a wide, shallow copper pan and slid into an extremely hot wood-burning pizza oven. The delectable result is a pancake that's crispy at the edges but plush and creamy inside. The simple batter consists of just chickpea flour, water, and salt, but letting it hydrate for an extended time after whisking the ingredients together causes the batter to thicken and turn smooth, making for a pancake that is dense and custardy. A well-seasoned 12-inch cast-iron skillet is the closest approximation to the traditional pan. Farinata is often served plain or with just one or two simple adornments. In this version, fresh rosemary added to the skillet before pouring in the batter and a sprinkling of sea salt and ground black pepper complement the savory cake.

- 1 cup (4½ ounces) chickpea flour
- 2 cups cold water
- ¾ teaspoon table salt
- 3 tablespoons extra-virgin olive oil
- 1 tablespoon chopped fresh rosemary
  Coarse sea salt

1. Whisk flour, cold water, and salt together in large bowl until smooth. Cover and let sit at room temperature for at least 4 hours or up to 24 hours.

2. Adjust oven rack to upper-middle position and heat oven to 400 degrees. Heat 12-inch cast-iron skillet over medium heat for 3 minutes. Add oil, swirl to coat evenly, and heat until shimmering. Add rosemary and cook until fragrant, about 30 seconds.

3. Whisk batter to recombine, then pour into skillet. Transfer skillet to oven and bake until top of pancake is dry and golden and edges begin to pull away from sides of skillet, 35 to 40 minutes. Remove skillet from oven and heat broiler.

4. Return skillet to oven and broil until pancake is spotty brown, 1 to 2 minutes. Let pancake cool slightly in skillet on wire rack for 5 minutes. Using thin spatula, loosen edges and underside of pancake from skillet, then carefully slide pancake onto cutting board. Season with sea salt and pepper to taste. Cut into wedges and serve warm.

NOTES FROM THE TEST KITCHEN

USING CHICKPEA FLOUR
Nutty-tasting chickpea flour, also sold as garbanzo flour, is high in protein and is gluten-free. Made by grinding whole dried chickpeas, this flour has a distinct bean flavor and dark color and is more often seen in dishes in the Middle East, France, and Italy. In addition to using chickpea flour to make crackers, fries, and pancakes, it is also used to make savory flatbreads (page 92). Bob's Red Mill is the brand we stock in the test kitchen but you can also use Italian chickpea flour (farina di ceci) or Indian chickpea flour (gram/besan). It is best stored in the refrigerator or freezer.

Farinata

Grilled Polenta Wedges with Grilled Scallions and Gorgonzola

Serves 6 to 8 (makes 16 wedges)
Total Time 55 minutes, plus 2½ hours cooling and chilling

WHY THIS RECIPE WORKS Grilled polenta triangles with a decadent sweet and smoky topping make a delicious alternative to crostini. Using a low liquid-to-cornmeal ratio when simmering the polenta ensures that the wedges will be sturdy enough to hold together during grilling. Fresh rosemary bolsters the outdoor flavors with its piney notes. After chilling in an 8-inch square baking pan, the cooked polenta is firm enough to slice into portions. Five minutes over a hot fire crisps and lightly chars the outside while the insides stay nice and soft. These versatile wedges lend themselves to plenty of other toppings, as well as to being served topping-free alongside grilled meat and vegetables. Be sure that the Gorgonzola is at room temperature so that it blends smoothly.

2 cups water

1 tablespoon chopped fresh rosemary

½ teaspoon table salt

1 cup coarse-ground cornmeal

3 tablespoons plus 1 teaspoon extra-virgin olive oil, divided

4 scallions, trimmed

4 ounces Gorgonzola cheese, softened

1 tablespoon heavy cream

1 tablespoon honey

1. Grease 8-inch square baking pan, line with parchment paper, and grease parchment. Bring water to boil in medium saucepan over medium-high heat. Stir in rosemary and salt. Slowly pour cornmeal into water in steady stream while whisking constantly and return to boil. Reduce heat to medium-low and continue cooking until grains of cornmeal are tender, about 30 minutes, stirring every few minutes. (Polenta should be very thick.) Off heat, stir in 3 tablespoons olive oil. Transfer polenta to prepared pan, smooth top using a rubber spatula, and let cool completely, about 30 minutes. Wrap tightly in plastic wrap and refrigerate until polenta is very firm, at least 2 hours or up to 3 days.

2. Remove polenta from pan and flip onto cutting board; discard parchment. Slice into 4 equal squares, then cut each square into 4 triangles; refrigerate until ready to grill. Toss scallions with remaining 1 teaspoon oil.

3A. FOR A CHARCOAL GRILL Open bottom vent completely. Light large chimney starter filled with charcoal briquettes (6 quarts). When top coals are partially covered with ash, pour evenly over half of grill. Set cooking grate in place, cover, and open lid vent completely. Heat grill until hot, about 5 minutes.

3B. FOR A GAS GRILL Turn all burners to high, cover, and heat grill until hot, about 15 minutes. Leave primary burner on high and turn off other burner(s).

4. Clean and oil cooking grate. Grill polenta triangles and scallions (covered if using gas) until polenta and scallions are lightly charred on both sides, 5 to 7 minutes, turning as needed. As polenta and scallions finish cooking, transfer polenta to serving platter and scallions to cutting board.

5. Chop scallions. Stir scallions, Gorgonzola, and cream in bowl until thoroughly combined. Season with salt and pepper to taste. Top polenta wedges with heaping teaspoon Gorgonzola mixture and drizzle with honey. Serve.

Grilled Polenta Wedges with Grilled Scallions and Gorgonzola

VARIATION

Grilled Polenta Wedges with Grilled Oranges and Ricotta

Omit scallions and Gorgonzola. Cut peel and pith from 1 orange. Slice orange crosswise into ¼-inch-thick rounds. Brush rounds with 1 teaspoon extra-virgin olive oil and grill until lightly charred on both sides, 5 to 7 minutes, flipping as needed. Halve orange slices to make half-moons. Stir 4 ounces (½ cup) whole-milk ricotta cheese, 1 tablespoon cream, and 1 teaspoon minced fresh thyme together in bowl. Season with salt and pepper to taste. Top polenta wedges with heaping teaspoon ricotta mixture and orange slices; drizzle with honey.

Bean and Beef Taquitos

Black-Eyed Pea Fritters with Garlic and Herb Sauce

Bean and Beef Taquitos

Serves 4 to 6 (makes 12 taquitos)
Total Time 1¼ hours, plus 20 minutes cooling

WHY THIS RECIPE WORKS Taquito means "little taco," but these filled and fried tortillas have outsize appeal. To develop a streamlined home method, we replaced long-braised chuck with spiced ground beef. To prevent the filling from falling out of the open ends of the taquitos, we thicken it with mashed pinto beans. Microwaving the corn tortillas makes them pliable enough to roll. A quick egg wash helps seal the taquitos, and switching from deep frying to shallow frying allows us to start cooking the taquitos seam side down, guaranteeing that they hold together. Serve with Mexican crema and hot sauce.

- 4 teaspoons vegetable oil, divided
- 8 ounces 90 percent lean ground beef
- 1 cup rinsed canned pinto beans
- 1 onion, halved and sliced thin
- 2 jalapeño chiles, stemmed, seeded, and minced
- 3 garlic cloves, minced
- 1 teaspoon ground cumin
- 1 teaspoon chili powder
- 1 (8-ounce) can tomato sauce
- ½ cup water
- 3 tablespoons minced fresh cilantro
- ½ teaspoon table salt
- ½ teaspoon pepper
- 12 (6-inch) corn tortillas
- 1 large egg, lightly beaten
- 1 cup vegetable oil for frying

1. Heat 1 teaspoon oil in 12-inch nonstick skillet over medium-high heat until just smoking. Add beef and cook, breaking up meat with wooden spoon, until no longer pink, about 5 minutes. Drain beef in colander. In separate bowl, mash beans to paste with potato masher.

2. Heat remaining 1 tablespoon oil in now-empty skillet over medium heat until shimmering. Add onion and cook until softened and lightly browned, 5 to 7 minutes. Stir in jalapeños, garlic, cumin, and chili powder and cook until fragrant, about 30 seconds. Stir in tomato sauce, water, cilantro, salt, pepper, drained beef, and mashed beans. Cook, stirring often, until mixture has thickened and begins to sizzle, about 10 minutes. Season with salt and pepper to taste, transfer to bowl, and let cool for 20 minutes.

3. Adjust oven rack to middle position and heat oven to 200 degrees. Line rimmed baking sheet with parchment paper. Set wire rack in second rimmed baking sheet. Stack 6 tortillas, wrap in damp dish towel, and place on plate; microwave until warm and pliable, about 1 minute.

4. Working with 1 tortilla at a time, brush edges of top half with beaten egg. Spread 3 tablespoons filling in tight row across lower half of tortilla, fold bottom of tortilla over filling, then pull back on tortilla to tighten around filling. Roll tightly, place seam side down on parchment-lined sheet, and cover with second damp towel. Microwave remaining 6 tortillas and repeat with remaining filling. (Taquitos can be covered with damp towel, wrapped tightly in plastic wrap, and refrigerated for up to 24 hours.)

5. Add remaining 1 cup oil to clean, dry 12-inch nonstick skillet and heat over medium-high heat to 350 degrees. Using tongs, place 6 taquitos seam side down in oil. Fry taquitos until golden on all sides, about 8 minutes, turning as needed and adjusting heat as needed to maintain oil temperature between 300 and 325 degrees. Transfer to prepared wire rack and place in oven to keep warm while repeating with remaining 6 taquitos. Serve.

Black-Eyed Pea Fritters with Garlic and Herb Sauce

Serves 8 to 10 (makes about 45 fritters)
Total Time 50 minutes, plus 8 hours soaking

WHY THIS RECIPE WORKS These simple and satisfying little fritters start with black-eyed peas that have been soaked overnight. We process the whole soaked black-eyed peas to a hummus-like texture, which makes for smooth fritters with a nice speckled appearance from the skins. Adding baking powder to the mix ensures a fluffier fritter. We use two spoons to safely guide the batter into the hot oil. Cooking the fritters at a relatively high temperature of 375 degrees guarantees that the interior stays moist while the exterior becomes perfectly crisp. The savory bean flavor pairs well with a garlic and herb sauce. (However, feel free to serve the fritters with your own favorite sauce.) Use a Dutch oven that holds 6 quarts or more for this recipe.

BLACK-EYED PEA FRITTERS
- 8 ounces (1¼ cups) dried black-eyed peas, picked over and rinsed
- 2 garlic cloves, minced
- 2 teaspoons baking powder
- 1 teaspoon table salt
- 3 quarts peanut oil or vegetable oil for frying

GARLIC AND HERB SAUCE
- 1 cup mayonnaise
- 2 tablespoons minced fresh parsley
- 1 tablespoon minced fresh chives
- 2 teaspoons Dijon mustard
- 2 garlic cloves, minced
- 2 teaspoons lemon juice
- ¼ teaspoon table salt

1. FOR THE FRITTERS Combine 2 quarts cold water and black-eyed peas in large container. Soak at room temperature for at least 8 hours or up to 24 hours. Drain and rinse well. (If you're pressed for time, see page 13 for information on quick brining your beans.)

2. FOR THE SAUCE Combine all ingredients in bowl; set aside until ready to serve. (Sauce can be refrigerated for up to 4 days.)

3. Transfer soaked black-eyed peas to food processor. Add 7 tablespoons water, garlic, baking powder, and salt and process until mixture is smooth and resembles hummus, about 2 minutes, scraping down sides of bowl as needed.

4. Adjust oven rack to middle position and heat oven to 200 degrees. Set wire rack in rimmed baking sheet and line with triple layer of paper towels. Add oil to large Dutch oven until it measures about 2 inches deep and heat over medium-high heat to 375 degrees. Carefully drop one-quarter of batter into oil, 1 tablespoon at a time (use spoon to carefully scrape batter from tablespoon measure into hot oil). Fry until deep golden brown, 4 to 8 minutes, stirring frequently with wire skimmer or slotted spoon. Adjust burner, if necessary, to maintain oil temperature between 350 and 400 degrees.

5. Using wire skimmer or slotted spoon, transfer fritters to prepared sheet. Transfer sheet to oven to keep fritters warm while frying remaining batter. Return oil to 375 degrees and repeat with remaining batter. Serve with reserved sauce.

Simple Hummus

Serves 8 (makes 2 cups) | **Total Time** 15 minutes, plus 30 minutes resting FAST VEGAN

WHY THIS RECIPE WORKS Hummus is composed of simple ingredients: chickpeas, tahini, olive oil, garlic, and lemon juice. This streamlined recipe produces a flavorful hummus with a light texture. We use convenient canned chickpeas and a food processor to quickly turn them into a smooth puree. To avoid a grainy hummus, rather than pureeing the chickpeas on their own, we create an emulsion. We grind the chickpeas and then slowly add a mixture of water and lemon juice. We whisk the olive oil and tahini together and drizzle the mixture into the chickpeas while processing; this creates a lush, light puree. Earthy cumin, garlic, and a pinch of cayenne keep the flavors balanced.

- ¼ cup water, plus extra as needed
- 3 tablespoons lemon juice
- 6 tablespoons tahini
- 2 tablespoons extra-virgin olive oil
- 1 (15-ounce) can chickpeas, rinsed
- 1 small garlic clove, minced
- ½ teaspoon table salt
- ¼ teaspoon ground cumin
  Pinch cayenne pepper

1. Combine water and lemon juice in small bowl. In separate bowl, whisk tahini and oil together.

2. Process chickpeas, garlic, salt, cumin, and cayenne in food processor until almost fully ground, 15 to 30 seconds. Scrape down sides of bowl with rubber spatula. With machine running, add lemon juice mixture in steady stream. Scrape down sides of bowl and continue to process for 1 minute. With machine running, add tahini mixture in steady stream and process until hummus is smooth and creamy, 15 to 30 seconds, scraping down sides of bowl as needed.

3. Transfer hummus to serving bowl, cover with plastic wrap, and let sit at room temperature until flavors meld, about 30 minutes. (Hummus can be refrigerated for up to 5 days; adjust consistency with up to 1 tablespoon warm water as needed.) Serve.

VARIATION

Big-Batch Simple Hummus FAST VEGAN
Makes 4 cups

Double all ingredients.

Ultracreamy Hummus

Ultracreamy Hummus

Serves 8 to 10 (makes 3 cups) | **Total Time** 45 minutes
FAST VEGAN

WHY THIS RECIPE WORKS This tahini-forward hummus is velvety-smooth and creamy, with a rich flavor. To achieve a perfectly smooth texture, we simmer canned chickpeas with water and baking soda for 20 minutes and then quickly remove their grainy skins by gently swishing them under a few changes of water. Tahini is a major source of richness and flavor in this hummus. To avoid the bitter flavors that can come from tahini made with heavily roasted sesame seeds, we choose a light-colored tahini, which indicates that the seeds were only gently toasted. For balanced garlic flavor, we steep the garlic in lemon juice and salt to extract its flavor and deactivate the enzyme that gives it a harsh bite. Finally, we add ample fresh lemon juice to give the hummus a bright flavor. The hummus will thicken slightly over time; add warm water, 1 tablespoon at a time, as needed to restore its creamy consistency.

- 2 (15-ounce) cans chickpeas, rinsed
- ½ teaspoon baking soda
- 4 garlic cloves, peeled
- ⅓ cup lemon juice (2 lemons), plus extra for seasoning
- 1 teaspoon table salt
- ¼ teaspoon ground cumin, plus extra for garnish
- ½ cup tahini, stirred well
- 2 tablespoons extra-virgin olive oil, plus extra for drizzling
- 1 tablespoon minced fresh parsley

1. Combine chickpeas, baking soda, and 6 cups water in medium saucepan and bring to boil over high heat. Reduce heat and simmer, stirring occasionally, until chickpea skins begin to float to surface and chickpeas are creamy and very soft, 20 to 25 minutes.

2. While chickpeas cook, mince garlic using garlic press or rasp-style grater. Measure out 1 tablespoon garlic and set aside; discard remaining garlic. Whisk lemon juice, salt, and reserved garlic together in small bowl and let sit for 10 minutes. Strain garlic-lemon mixture through fine-mesh strainer set over bowl, pressing on solids to extract as much liquid as possible; discard solids.

3. Drain chickpeas in colander and return to saucepan. Fill saucepan with cold water and gently swish chickpeas with your fingers to release skins. Pour off most of water into colander to collect skins, leaving chickpeas behind in saucepan. Repeat filling, swishing, and draining 3 or 4 times until most skins have been removed (this should yield about ¾ cup skins); discard skins. Transfer chickpeas to colander to drain.

4. Set aside 2 tablespoons whole chickpeas for garnish. Process garlic-lemon mixture, ¼ cup water, cumin, and remaining chickpeas in food processor until smooth, about 1 minute, scraping down sides of bowl as needed. Add tahini and oil and process until hummus is smooth, creamy, and light, about 1 minute, scraping down sides of bowl as needed. (Hummus should have pourable consistency similar to yogurt. If too thick, loosen with water, adding 1 teaspoon at a time.) Season with salt and extra lemon juice to taste.

5. Transfer to serving bowl and sprinkle with parsley, reserved chickpeas, and extra cumin. Drizzle with extra oil and serve. (Hummus can be refrigerated for up to 5 days; bring to room temperature before serving.)

VARIATION
Ultracreamy Hummus with Spiced Walnut Topping
FAST **VEGAN**

Do not overprocess; the topping should remain coarse-textured.

Omit parsley and cumin for garnish. Do not set aside 2 tablespoons whole chickpeas for garnish in step 4. Process ¾ cup extra-virgin olive oil, ⅓ cup walnuts, ¼ cup paprika, ¼ cup tomato paste, 2 garlic cloves, 1 teaspoon ground turmeric, ½ teaspoon ground cumin, ½ teaspoon ground allspice, ½ teaspoon table salt, and ¼ teaspoon cayenne pepper in clean food processor until uniform coarse puree forms, about 30 seconds, scraping down sides of bowl halfway through processing. Serve topping over hummus. (Topping can be refrigerated for up to 5 days.)

Sweet Potato Hummus

Serves 14 (makes 3½ cups) | **Total Time** 35 minutes, plus 30 minutes resting **VEGAN**

WHY THIS RECIPE WORKS This vibrant sweet potato hummus combines creamy chickpeas with earthy sweet potato. To bring out the sweet potato's subtle flavor, we tested mixing varying amounts with our classic hummus. We found that one large sweet potato (about 1 pound) provides just the right balance. Microwaving the sweet potato yields a flavor that is nearly as intense as roasting and a lot faster, which is important for such a simple dish. As for seasonings, we prefer less tahini than in traditional hummus, so we use just ¼ cup. To complement the sweet potato, we add warm spices: sweet paprika, coriander, cinnamon, and cumin. A dash of cayenne pepper and a clove of garlic cut the sweetness and accent the hummus well.

- 1 large sweet potato (about 1 pound), unpeeled
- ¾ cup water
- ¼ cup lemon juice (2 lemons)
- ¼ cup tahini
- 2 tablespoons extra-virgin olive oil, plus extra for drizzling
- 1 (15-ounce) can chickpeas, rinsed
- 1 small garlic clove, minced
- 1 teaspoon paprika
- 1 teaspoon table salt
- ½ teaspoon ground coriander
- ¼ teaspoon ground cumin
- ⅛ teaspoon ground cinnamon
- ⅛ teaspoon cayenne pepper

1. Prick sweet potato several times with fork, place on plate, and microwave until very soft, about 12 minutes, flipping halfway through microwaving. Slice potato in half lengthwise, let cool, then scrape sweet potato flesh from skin and transfer to food processor; discard skin.

2. Combine water and lemon juice in small bowl. In separate bowl, whisk tahini and oil together.

3. Process sweet potato, chickpeas, garlic, paprika, salt, coriander, cumin, cinnamon, and cayenne in food processor until almost fully ground, about 15 seconds. Scrape down bowl with rubber spatula. With machine running, add lemon juice mixture in steady stream. Scrape down bowl and continue to process for 1 minute. With machine running, add tahini mixture in steady stream and process until hummus is smooth and creamy, about 15 seconds, scraping down bowl as needed.

4. Transfer hummus to serving bowl, cover with plastic wrap and let sit at room temperature until flavors meld, about 30 minutes. (Hummus can be refrigerated for up to 5 days; bring to room temperature before serving and stir in 1 tablespoon warm water to loosen hummus texture if necessary.) Drizzle with extra oil before serving.

Tepary Bean Dip with Herb and Olive Salad

Serves 16 (makes 4 cups) | **Total Time** 1¾ hours, plus 8 hours soaking `VEGAN`

WHY THIS RECIPE WORKS Drought-resistant tepary beans are small but hearty. The two main types are brown and white. The earthy flavor and creamy texture of the white variety call out for a pureed treatment. This recipe is inspired by Michael Solomonov's "tehina" hummus, replacing chickpeas with tepary beans. It carries the familiar flavors of garlic, lemon, and tahini against the mild, almost sweet, white bean canvas. We soak and then cook the dried beans in a simple solution of baking soda and salt, which helps speed the deterioration of the tough pectin exterior and soften the beans. This results in a smooth puree with a uniform texture. We finish the hummus with a fresh herb salad that's simple to make but has complex flavors and textures with parsley and dill, briny kalamata olives, and a trio of nutty, crunchy seeds: pepitas, sunflower, and sesame. This hummus keeps surprisingly well in the fridge, but after one bite, you may find that storage won't be necessary.

Substitution: You can use dried cannellini beans in place of the tepary beans or use two 15-ounce cans cannellini beans. If using canned beans, skip steps 1 and 2.

½ teaspoon table salt for brining
¼ teaspoon baking soda for brining
8 ounces (1¼ cups) dried white tepary beans, picked over and rinsed
½ cup plus 2 teaspoons lemon juice (3 lemons), divided
4 garlic cloves, unpeeled
1 teaspoon table salt
⅔ cup tahini
¼ teaspoon ground cumin
¾ cup chopped fresh parsley
½ cup chopped fresh dill
½ cup pitted kalamata olives, sliced thin
2 tablespoons extra-virgin olive oil, plus extra for drizzling
2 tablespoons roasted pepitas
2 tablespoons roasted sunflower seeds
2 tablespoons white sesame seeds, toasted

1. Dissolve ½ teaspoon salt and baking soda in 8 cups cold water in large saucepan. Add beans, cover, and soak at room temperature for at least 8 hours or up to 24 hours. (If you're pressed for time, see page 13 for information on quick brining your beans.)

2. Bring beans (still in soaking liquid) to boil over high heat, skimming off any foam that rises to surface. Reduce heat to medium-low and simmer until beans are very tender (some beans will blow out), 1 hour to 1¼ hours. Drain and set aside.

3. Pulse ½ cup lemon juice, ⅓ cup water, garlic, and salt in food processor until coarse puree forms, about 20 pulses. Transfer to small bowl and let sit for at least 10 minutes or up to 30 minutes. Strain lemon juice mixture through fine-mesh strainer back into processor; discard solids. Add tahini to processor and process until smooth and well combined, 45 to 60 seconds. Scrape down sides of bowl and add cumin and beans. Process until mixture is very smooth, about 4 minutes. Season with salt to taste and adjust consistency with up to 2 tablespoons additional water as needed. (Dip can be refrigerated for up to 5 days; bring to room temperature before serving and adjust consistency with up to 1 tablespoon warm water as needed.)

4. Toss parsley, dill, olives, oil, and remaining 2 teaspoons lemon juice together in small bowl. Season with salt to taste. Transfer hummus to serving bowl and place herb salad in center. Sprinkle pepitas, sunflower seeds, and sesame seeds over top and drizzle with extra oil. Serve.

Lemon-Garlic Orca Bean Dip

DIP

1½ tablespoons table salt for brining
  8 ounces (1 cup) dried orca beans,
       picked over and rinsed
  1 teaspoon extra-virgin olive oil
  3 scallions
  2 teaspoons table salt for cooking beans
2½ tablespoons lemon juice
  2 garlic cloves, minced
  1 teaspoon ground cumin

TATBEELEH TOPPING

  2 jalapeño chiles, stemmed, seeded,
       and finely chopped
  ¼ cup finely chopped onion
  2 scallions, sliced thin
  1 tablespoon lemon juice
  ¼ cup minced fresh parsley
  ½ teaspoon table salt
  4 teaspoons extra-virgin olive oil,
       plus extra for drizzling
       Flake sea salt

1. FOR THE DIP Dissolve 1½ tablespoons salt in 2 quarts cold water in large container. Add beans and soak at room temperature for at least 8 hours or up to 24 hours. Drain and rinse well. (If you're pressed for time, see page 13 for information on quick brining your beans.)

2. Heat oil in Dutch oven over medium-high heat until shimmering. Reduce heat to medium, add scallions, and cook until spotty brown, 4 to 6 minutes, flipping halfway through cooking. Add soaked beans and 7 cups water to Dutch oven with scallions and bring to simmer. Simmer, partially covered, over medium-low heat until beans are very tender, about 40 minutes. Off heat, stir in 2 teaspoons salt, cover, and let sit for 15 minutes.

3. Drain beans, reserving 3 tablespoons cooking liquid and discarding charred scallions. Return beans to Dutch oven and stir in lemon juice, garlic, and cumin. Transfer 1½ cups bean mixture to food processor along with reserved cooking liquid and process until mostly smooth with some small pieces visible, about 10 seconds. Return processed beans to Dutch oven with remaining whole beans and stir to combine.

4. FOR THE TOPPING Combine all ingredients in bowl. Transfer warm dip to serving bowl and top with tatbeeleh topping. Drizzle with extra oil and sprinkle with sea salt. Serve.

Lemon-Garlic Orca Bean Dip

Serves 8 (makes 2 cups) | **Total Time** 1½ hours, plus 8 hours soaking `VEGAN`

WHY THIS RECIPE WORKS This bean dip is based on the flavors of ful medames, a popular Middle Eastern meze that's often served alongside hummus and falafel and eaten with pita. The flavors are fresh and simple, with garlic and lemon being the most prominent. We developed this recipe using orca beans, a striking heirloom variety that has flavor notes resemblant of potatoes. To preserve their beauty and add texture to the dip, we leave some beans whole. We top the dip with a version of tatbeeleh, a common topping for various meze that is made from green chiles, onion, lemon juice, and olive oil. We suggest serving this bright dip with warm pita or crackers. You can make the dip one day ahead; just be sure to gently warm it up before serving.

Substitution: You can use dried small white beans in place of the orca beans.

Navy Bean and Artichoke Dip

Pink Bean and Lima Bean Dip with Parsley

VARIATION
Quick Lemon-Garlic White Bean Dip
Total Time 35 minutes `FAST` `VEGAN`

You can make the dip one day ahead; just be sure to gently warm it up before serving.

DIP
- 1 teaspoon extra-virgin olive oil
- 3 scallions
- 2 (15-ounce) cans small white beans, 6 tablespoons liquid reserved, beans rinsed
- 2½ tablespoons lemon juice
- 2 garlic cloves, minced
- 1 teaspoon ground cumin
- ¼ teaspoon table salt

TATBEELEH TOPPING
- 2 jalapeño chiles, stemmed, seeded, and finely chopped
- ¼ cup finely chopped onion
- 2 scallions, sliced thin
- 1 tablespoon lemon juice
- ¼ cup minced fresh parsley
- ½ teaspoons table salt
- 4 teaspoons extra virgin olive oil, plus extra for drizzling
- Flake sea salt

1. FOR THE DIP Heat oil in Dutch oven over medium-high heat until shimmering. Reduce heat to medium, add scallions, and cook until spotty brown, 4 to 6 minutes, flipping halfway through cooking. Add beans, lemon juice, garlic, cumin, and salt and cook over medium-low heat until warmed through, about 10 minutes, stirring occasionally. Discard scallions.

2. Transfer 1½ cups bean mixture to food processor along with reserved bean liquid and process until mostly smooth with some small pieces visible, about 10 seconds. Return processed beans to Dutch oven with remaining whole beans and stir to combine.

3. FOR THE TOPPING Combine all ingredients in bowl. Transfer warm dip to serving bowl and top with tatbeelch topping. Drizzle with extra oil and sprinkle with sea salt. Serve.

Navy Bean and Artichoke Dip

Serves 8 (makes 2 cups) | **Total Time** 25 minutes, plus 30 minutes resting

WHY THIS RECIPE WORKS This light and fresh-tasting dip plays up the earthy flavor and velvety texture of navy beans. Vegetal artichokes partner well with the mild navy beans, adding some needed character. Using canned beans and jarred artichoke hearts keeps the recipe easy. To increase the creaminess of our dip, we incorporate Greek yogurt. A healthy dose of lemon juice, garlic, parsley, and scallion add fresh flavor and brightness.

- 1 teaspoon grated lemon zest plus 2 tablespoons juice
- 1 small garlic clove, minced
- 1 (15-ounce) can navy beans, 2 tablespoons liquid reserved, beans rinsed
- 1 cup jarred whole artichoke hearts packed in water, rinsed and patted dry, plus 2 tablespoons chopped
- ¼ cup fresh parsley leaves
- 1 scallion, white and light green parts cut into ½-inch pieces, dark green part sliced thin on bias
- ¾ teaspoon table salt
- ¼ teaspoon ground fennel
  Pinch cayenne pepper
- ¼ cup plain Greek yogurt
  Extra-virgin olive oil

1. Combine lemon zest and juice and garlic in bowl and let sit for 10 minutes.

2. Pulse garlic-lemon juice mixture, beans and reserved liquid, whole artichoke hearts, parsley, white and light green scallion pieces, salt, fennel, and cayenne in food processor until finely ground, 5 to 10 pulses, scraping down sides of bowl as needed. Process until uniform paste forms, about 1 minute, scraping down sides of bowl as needed.

3. Add yogurt and continue to process until smooth, about 15 seconds, scraping down sides of bowl as needed. Transfer to serving bowl, cover, and let sit at room temperature until flavors meld, about 30 minutes. (Dip can be refrigerated for up to 24 hours; bring to room temperature before serving.) Sprinkle with reserved chopped artichokes and dark green scallion parts, and drizzle with oil before serving.

Pink Bean and Lima Bean Dip with Parsley

Serves 8 (makes 2 cups) | **Total Time** 30 minutes, plus 30 minutes resting

WHY THIS RECIPE WORKS To create a bean dip that is creamy and complex-tasting we combine a starchy bean with a lighter legume. Pink beans, also called chili beans or habichuelas rosadas, are a relative of the kidney bean and have a rich, meaty flavor. They pair well with the lighter texture of lima beans. "Cooking" the raw garlic in lemon juice mellows it. Adding Greek yogurt to the dip gives it creamy body without robbing it of flavor. To further freshen the dip, we add lemon juice and a full ¼ cup of parsley. Letting the dip rest at room temperature allows the flavors to meld.

- 2 tablespoons lemon juice
- 1 small garlic clove, minced
- 1 cup frozen lima beans, thawed, divided
- 1 (15-ounce) can pink beans, 2 tablespoons liquid reserved, beans rinsed
- 1 scallion, white and light green parts cut into ½-inch pieces, green part sliced thin on bias
- ¼ cup fresh parsley leaves
- ¾ teaspoon table salt
- ¼ teaspoon garam masala
- ¼ teaspoon paprika
  Pinch cayenne pepper
- ⅓ cup plain Greek yogurt
  Extra-virgin olive oil

1. Combine lemon juice and garlic in bowl and let sit for 10 minutes. Measure out 2 tablespoons lima beans, chop coarse, and set aside for garnish.

2. Pulse garlic–lemon juice mixture, pink beans and reserved liquid, remaining whole lima beans, white and light green scallion pieces, parsley, salt, garam masala, paprika, and cayenne in food processor until finely ground, 5 to 10 pulses, scraping down sides of bowl as needed. Process until uniform paste forms, about 1 minute, scraping down sides of bowl as needed.

3. Add yogurt and continue to process until smooth, about 15 seconds, scraping down sides of bowl as needed. Transfer to serving bowl, cover, and let sit at room temperature until flavors meld, about 30 minutes. (Dip can be refrigerated for up to 24 hours; bring to room temperature before serving.) Sprinkle with reserved chopped lima beans and scallion greens, and drizzle with oil before serving.

Black Bean Dip

Greek Layer Dip

Black Bean Dip

Serves 8 (makes 2 cups) | **Total Time** 25 minutes, plus 30 minutes resting VEGAN

WHY THIS RECIPE WORKS Black beans are native to Mexico and are a staple ingredient in Mexican cooking. We wanted to highlight their rich flavor in a smooth and creamy dip. To keep this starter quick and easy, we use canned black beans. We pair the starchy beans with a lighter vegetable—in this case, onion—and infuse the mixture with aromatic spices. A combination of oregano, cumin, and chipotle in adobo provide earthy, spicy, and smoky notes. Since raw garlic tastes harsh, we first soak it in lime juice to mellow its flavor. We combine everything in a food processor, which gives the dip a smooth, luxurious texture. Letting the dip rest at room temperature for at least 30 minutes ensures that all the flavors meld nicely. A bit of cilantro stirred in just before serving adds a burst of freshness to the dip.

- 2 tablespoons lime juice
- 1 garlic clove, minced
- 1 teaspoon minced fresh oregano
- 2 (15-ounce) cans black beans, rinsed
- ½ onion, chopped
- 1 tablespoon extra-virgin olive oil
- 1 teaspoon minced canned chipotle chile in adobo sauce
- ½ teaspoon ground cumin
- ¼ teaspoon table salt
- 2 tablespoons minced fresh cilantro

1. Combine lime juice, garlic, and oregano in small bowl and let sit for 10 minutes.

2. Pulse lime juice mixture, beans, onion, oil, chipotle, cumin, and salt in food processor until fully ground, 5 to 10 pulses, scraping down sides of bowl as needed. Process until uniform paste forms, about 1 minute, scraping down sides of bowl as needed.

3. Transfer dip to serving bowl, cover, and let sit at room temperature until flavors meld, about 30 minutes. (Dip can be refrigerated for up to 24 hours; bring to room temperature before serving.) Stir in cilantro before serving.

Greek Layer Dip

Serves 8 to 10 | **Total Time** 15 minutes `FAST`

WHY THIS RECIPE WORKS Most layered dips are typically built in a deep bowl that showcases all the layers. For this recipe, we rethought the architecture a bit and chose to build our dip on a platter: A shallower dip means easier swiping to capture all of the layers on your chip. We start this party-worthy dip with a base of savory hummus and cover it with creamy, tangy Greek yogurt. Next comes a mixture of Greek salad vegetables, olives, and fresh mint. Finally we top it all with a good portion of crumbled feta cheese. You can substitute store-bought hummus here: Our favorite supermarket hummus, from Sabra, comes in a 17-ounce family size; two of these containers will equal 4¼ cups. For best results, be sure to assemble this dip shortly before serving, because it doesn't store well.

    1 recipe Big-Batch Simple Hummus (page 50)
 1½ cups plain Greek yogurt
    ½ English cucumber, cut into ¼-inch pieces
    ½ cup jarred roasted red peppers, rinsed,
        patted dry, and chopped
    ⅓ cup pitted kalamata olives, chopped
    4 scallions, sliced thin
    3 tablespoons extra-virgin olive oil, plus
        extra for drizzling
    2 tablespoons chopped fresh mint
    ¼ teaspoon table salt
    ¼ teaspoon pepper
    2 ounces feta cheese, crumbled (½ cup)

Spread hummus in single layer on large, shallow serving platter. Spread yogurt in even layer over hummus. Combine cucumber, red peppers, olives, scallions, oil, mint, salt, and pepper in bowl. Spoon vegetable mixture in even layer over yogurt. Sprinkle with feta and drizzle with extra oil. Serve.

Toasted Corn and Black Bean Salsa

Serves 8 (makes 2 cups) | **Total Time** 20 minutes, plus 1 hour chilling `VEGAN`

WHY THIS RECIPE WORKS When you're in the mood for a different kind of salsa, try this tomato-free one (which is still chock-full of vegetables). The black beans bring hearty texture and protein, while the combination of fresh toasted corn kernels and chopped red bell pepper gives the salsa bright color and contrasting vegetable flavor. Jalapeño, scallion, and garlic add pops of spicy intensity. In keeping with the Mexican theme, we round out this salsa with lime juice, cilantro, and cumin. In addition to serving it with tortilla chips, you can pile this satisfying salsa onto rice or even use it as a taco filling. To make the salsa spicier, add the chile seeds. Do not substitute frozen corn for the fresh corn here.

 1½ tablespoons extra-virgin olive oil, divided
    1 ear corn, kernels cut from cob
    1 red bell pepper, stemmed, seeded, and chopped fine
    ¾ cup rinsed canned black beans
    ½ jalapeño chile, stemmed, seeded, and minced
    1 scallion, sliced thin
    2 garlic cloves, minced
    2 tablespoons lime juice, plus extra for seasoning
    2 tablespoons minced fresh cilantro
    ½ teaspoon ground cumin
    ¼ teaspoon table salt
    ⅛ teaspoon pepper

1. Heat 1½ teaspoons oil in 10-inch nonstick skillet over medium-high heat until shimmering. Add corn and cook, stirring occasionally, until golden brown, about 4 minutes.

2. Transfer corn to medium serving bowl and stir in bell pepper, beans, jalapeño, scallion, garlic, lime juice, cilantro, cumin, salt, pepper, and remaining 1 tablespoon oil. Cover and refrigerate until flavors meld, about 1 hour. Season with extra lime juice to taste before serving. (Salsa can be refrigerated for up to 2 days; bring to room temperature before serving.)

CUTTING CORN FROM THE COB

After removing husk and silk, stand ear upright in large bowl. Use paring knife to slice kernels off cob.

Roasted Tomato Salsa with Black Beans

Serves 12 (makes 3 cups) | **Total Time** 45 minutes, plus 1 hour cooling   VEGAN

WHY THIS RECIPE WORKS For a hearty tomato salsa with black beans, we start by preparing a salsa asada, or "roasted salsa." We broil tomato and red jalapeño halves with sliced onion and whole garlic cloves until everything is well charred, ensuring deep smoky flavor. A bit of cumin provides an earthy undertone. Cooking the salsa a bit further on the stovetop intensifies the flavors and develops a saucier base, guaranteeing salsa that's thick enough to scoop up with chips. Fresh cilantro adds a citrusy, bright green pop. For a milder salsa, use one chile; for a spicy salsa, use all three chiles.

- 1½ pounds tomatoes, halved and cored
- 1 onion, sliced into ½-inch-thick rounds
- 1–3 red jalapeño or Fresno chiles, stemmed and halved lengthwise
- 3 garlic cloves, peeled
- 2 tablespoons lime juice, plus extra for seasoning
- 1 teaspoon table salt
- ½ teaspoon ground cumin
- 1 (15-ounce) can black beans, rinsed
- 2 teaspoons chopped fresh cilantro

1. Adjust oven rack 4 inches from broiler element and heat broiler. Line rimmed baking sheet with aluminum foil. Place tomatoes, cut side down, and onion on prepared sheet. Broil until tomatoes and onion are well charred, about 10 minutes; transfer to bowl. Place jalapeños, cut side down, and garlic on now-empty sheet and broil until chiles are well charred, 3 to 5 minutes.

2. Transfer chiles, garlic, half of tomatoes, and half of onions to food processor and process to thick puree, about 10 seconds; transfer to large saucepan. Pulse remaining broiled tomatoes and onions in now-empty food processor into ½-inch pieces, 2 to 3 pulses; transfer to saucepan.

3. Stir in lime juice, salt, and cumin and bring to boil over medium-high heat. Cook, stirring often, until salsa has thickened slightly and reduced to 2 cups, about 10 minutes.

4. Transfer tomato mixture to bowl and stir in black beans; let cool to room temperature. Cover loosely with plastic wrap and refrigerate until completely cooled, at least 1 hour. (Salsa can be refrigerated for up to 2 days; bring to room temperature before serving.) Stir in cilantro and season with salt and extra lime juice to taste. Serve.

Texas Caviar

Serves 10 to 12 (makes 7 cups)
Total Time 15 minutes, plus 1 hour resting   VEGAN

WHY THIS RECIPE WORKS Despite its name, there's no roe in this recipe. This black-eyed pea salad was created in 1940 by Helen Corbitt, the "mother of modern Texas cooking." Her original recipe marinated the peas in a simple tangy vinaigrette and tossed them with onion and garlic. We made a few tweaks to brighten the flavors. Canned black-eyed peas easily take the place of cooking dried. Green and red bell pepper, celery, scallions, and jalapeños provide plenty of crunch and heat, while a hearty amount of chopped herbs— both parsley and cilantro—freshens up the canned beans. We use a heavy hand with red wine vinegar and round out the characteristically punchy dressing with sugar and garlic. If you prefer a spicier salad, reserve and stir in some of the jalapeño seeds. The salad needs at least an hour for the flavors to meld, but the longer it sits, the better it tastes.

- ⅓ cup red wine vinegar
- 3 tablespoons vegetable oil
- 1 tablespoon sugar
- 2 garlic cloves, minced
- 1 teaspoon table salt
- ½ teaspoon pepper
- 2 (15-ounce) cans black-eyed peas, rinsed
- 6 scallions, sliced thin
- 1 red bell pepper, stemmed, seeded, and chopped
- 1 green bell pepper, stemmed, seeded, and chopped
- 2 jalapeño chiles, stemmed, seeded, and minced
- 1 celery rib, chopped fine
- ¼ cup chopped fresh cilantro
- ¼ cup chopped fresh parsley

Whisk vinegar, oil, sugar, garlic, salt, and pepper together in large bowl. Add black-eyed peas, scallions, bell peppers, jalapeños, celery, cilantro, and parsley and toss to combine. Season with salt and pepper to taste. Let sit for at least 1 hour before serving. (Salad can be refrigerated for up to 2 days; bring to room temperature before serving.)

Cheesy Nachos with Refried Beans

Serves 4 to 6 | **Total Time** 25 minutes `FAST`

WHY THIS RECIPE WORKS With the addition of refried beans, these crunchy, satisfying nachos are more than just cheese and chips and they will appeal to both meat eaters and vegetarians. A good nacho starts with good refried beans so we like to make our own. To guarantee no shortage of cheese, we shred a pound and a half combo of mild Jack and sharp cheddar to use. To ensure that our nachos are spicy, we add a hearty helping of sliced jalapeños. The chips come out hot and crisp and ready to be topped with sour cream, guacamole, salsa, or any of your favorite nacho toppings.

> **Substitution:** You can use one 14.5-ounce can of refried beans in place of the homemade.

- 12 ounces tortilla chips, divided
- 1¾ cups Refried Beans (page 295), divided
- 1 pound Monterey Jack cheese, shredded (4 cups), divided
- 8 ounces sharp cheddar cheese, shredded (2 cups), divided
- 2 large jalapeños, stemmed and sliced into thin rings, divided

1. Adjust oven rack to middle position and heat oven to 400 degrees. Spread half of tortilla chips in even layer in rimmed baking sheet. Dollop twelve 1 tablespoon-size spoonfuls of refried beans over chips. Sprinkle with 2 cups Monterey Jack, 1 cup cheddar, and half of jalapeños. Repeat with remaining tortilla chips, refried beans, 2 cups Monterey Jack, 1 cup cheddar, and jalapeños. Bake until cheese is melted, 7 to 10 minutes.

2. Remove nachos from oven and let cool for 2 minutes. Serve.

Roasted Tomato Salsa with Black Beans

Texas Caviar

Toasts, Patties, Tacos, and More

● FAST (45 minutes or less)   ● VEGAN
Photo: British-Style Beans on Toast

Avocado and Black Bean Toast

Serves 4 | **Total Time** 20 minutes | FAST | VEGAN

WHY THIS RECIPE WORKS Avocado toast is one of our favorite snacks, but we wanted a topped toast that is a bit more substantial and could stand alone as breakfast. We chose a bold southwestern flavor profile to liven up our morning: It's hard to argue with mashed black beans on toast elevated with a bit of spice, fresh tomato, and squeeze of lime. By simply mashing canned beans with hot water, oil, and lime zest and juice, we create a flavorsome, well-textured base. We really like the addition of spicy quick-pickled onions, which can be made up to a week ahead. (If you don't have them on hand, a pinch of red pepper flakes will provide heat.) For an accurate measure of boiling water, bring a full kettle of water to boil and then measure out the desired amount.

4 ounces cherry tomatoes, quartered
4 teaspoons extra-virgin olive oil, divided
Pinch plus ½ teaspoon table salt, divided
⅛ teaspoon pepper, divided
1 (15-ounce) can black beans, rinsed
¼ cup boiling water
½ teaspoon grated lime zest plus 1 tablespoon juice
4 (½-inch-thick) slices rustic bread
1 ripe avocado, halved, pitted, and sliced thin
¼ cup Quick Sweet-and-Spicy Pickled Red Onions (optional)
¼ cup fresh cilantro leaves

1. Combine tomatoes, 1 teaspoon oil, pinch salt, and pinch pepper in bowl; set aside. Mash beans, boiling water, lime zest and juice, remaining ½ teaspoon salt, remaining pinch pepper, and remaining 1 tablespoon oil with potato masher to coarse puree in second bowl, leaving some whole beans intact.

2. Adjust oven rack 4 inches from broiler element and heat broiler. Place bread on aluminum foil–lined rimmed baking sheet and broil until golden, 1 to 2 minutes per side.

3. Spread mashed bean mixture evenly on toasts, then top with avocado and season with salt to taste. Top with pickled onions, if using; tomatoes; and cilantro. Serve.

Avocado and Black Bean Toast

Quick Sweet-and-Spicy Pickled Red Onions

Makes 1 cup | **Total Time** 55 minutes | VEGAN

1 cup red wine vinegar
⅓ cup sugar
¼ teaspoon table salt
2 jalapeño chiles, stemmed, seeded, and cut into thin rings
1 red onion, halved and sliced thin

Microwave vinegar, sugar, and salt in bowl until steaming, 1 to 2 minutes. Stir in onion and jalapeño and let sit, stirring occasionally, for 45 minutes. Drain vegetables in colander. Serve. (Drained pickled onions can be refrigerated for up to 1 week.)

Green Fava Bean Toast

Serves 4 | **Total Time** 1¼ hours, plus 1¼ hours cooling
`VEGAN`

WHY THIS RECIPE WORKS Spring was our inspiration for this bean-topped toast, evident even in its beautiful color. We use earthy fresh fava beans two ways: cooked and mixed with avocado and pickled. We also double down on the dill, using a sprig in our pickles and heavily sprinkling chopped dill on the toast. Lemon and garlic perfectly accent the fava beans and pistachios give a nutty (and green) finishing touch. All in all, our hearty, meal-time toast is simple, yet delicious. We prefer the brighter flavor of fresh fava beans. Be sure to set up the ice water bath before cooking the fava beans, as plunging them immediately in the cold water after blanching retains their bright green color and ensures that they don't overcook.

Substitution: You can use 12 ounces (2½ cups) frozen shelled fava beans, thawed, in place of the fresh favas. Be sure to remove the sheath. Skip step 1 if using frozen favas.

2½ pounds fava beans, shelled (2½ cups)
 ½ cup red wine vinegar
 2 tablespoons sugar
 ⅛ teaspoon plus ¾ teaspoon table salt, divided
 1 sprig fresh dill plus ¼ cup torn fresh dill
 ¼ cup extra-virgin olive oil, plus extra for drizzling
 1 shallot, minced
 1 garlic clove, minced
 ½ teaspoon grated lemon zest plus 2 tablespoons juice
 1 avocado, halved, pitted, and cut into ½-inch pieces
 4 (½-inch-thick) slices rustic bread
 2 tablespoons chopped pistachios or pine nuts, toasted
    Flake sea salt

1. Bring 4 quarts water to boil in large pot. Fill large bowl halfway with ice and water. Add fava beans to boiling water and cook for 1 minute. Using slotted spoon, transfer fava beans to ice water and let cool, about 2 minutes. Transfer fava beans to triple layer of paper towels and dry well. Using paring knife, make small cut along edge of each bean through waxy sheath, then gently squeeze sheath to release bean; discard sheath. Set fava beans aside.

2. Bring vinegar, sugar, and ⅛ teaspoon salt to simmer in small saucepan over medium-high heat, stirring occasionally, until sugar has dissolved. Off heat, stir in ½ cup reserved fava beans and dill sprig; cover; and let cool to room temperature, about 1 hour. (Pickled favas can be refrigerated in airtight container for up to 1 week.)

3. Heat oil in medium saucepan over medium heat until shimmering. Add shallot and cook until softened, 1 to 3 minutes. Stir in garlic and lemon zest, and cook until fragrant, about 30 seconds. Stir in remaining reserved fava beans, 1 cup water, and remaining ¾ teaspoon salt and bring to simmer. Reduce heat to medium-low and cook until fava beans are softened and most of liquid has evaporated, 12 to 15 minutes. Let cool to room temperature, about 20 minutes.

4. Meanwhile, adjust oven rack 4 inches from broiler element and heat broiler. Place bread on aluminum foil–lined rimmed baking sheet and broil until golden, 1 to 2 minutes per side; set aside.

5. Mash avocado and lemon juice together until mostly smooth. Gently stir avocado into fava beans, trying not to break up fava beans too much. Spread fava bean mixture evenly over reserved toasts and top with pickled fava beans, pistachios, and sprinkle with dill. Drizzle with extra oil and sprinkle with sea salt. Serve.

PREPARING FRESH FAVA BEANS

1. To shell favas, use paring knife and your thumb to snip off tip of pod and pull apart sides to release beans. Blanch beans and dry well.

2. Use paring knife to make small cut along edge of bean through waxy sheath, then gently squeeze sheath to release bean.

British-Style Beans on Toast

Serves 4 | **Total Time** 45 minutes **FAST**

WHY THIS RECIPE WORKS Beans on toast is eaten every day in the U.K. for breakfast, lunch, and dinner. It is a quick meal that is often served at diners or made at home because it is comforting and hearty, as well as being easy on the wallet. The idea is that even after making or ordering this filling dish, you should have enough money left to afford a pint or two at the pub. Most of the time the topped toast is served with a fried egg, fried onions, or bacon on the side, but we decided to make it a little fancier and serve a fried egg on top. We make the sauce with a backbone of onion, carrot, and celery, and then add tomato paste, brown sugar, and Worcestershire sauce. We started out by draining our beans and then adding water to the sauce but soon realized we were throwing away that delicious bean liquid that makes a sauce so unctuous. Once we added that back in, our sauce was the perfect consistency. A dash of cider vinegar at the end brightens the dish and the fried egg on top elevates the beans on toast to perfection.

- 4 (½-inch-thick) slices rustic bread
- 2 (15-ounce) cans navy beans, undrained
- 2 tablespoons extra-virgin olive oil, divided
- ½ small onion, chopped fine
- 1 small carrot, peeled and chopped fine
- ⅓ cup minced celery
- 1 garlic clove, minced
- ¼ cup tomato paste
- 2 tablespoons packed brown sugar
- 1 tablespoon Worcestershire sauce
- ½ teaspoon plus pinch table salt, divided
- ½ teaspoon pepper, divided
- ½ teaspoon cider vinegar
- 4 large eggs

1. Adjust oven rack 4 inches from broiler element and heat broiler. Place bread on aluminum foil–lined baking sheet and broil until golden, 1 to 2 minutes per side; set aside.

2. Drain beans, reserving 1¼ cups liquid; set beans and their liquid aside. Heat 1 tablespoon oil in large saucepan over medium heat until shimmering. Add onion, carrot, and celery and cook until softened, 5 to 7 minutes. Add garlic and cook until fragrant, about 30 seconds. Stir in reserved bean liquid, tomato paste, sugar, Worcestershire sauce, ½ teaspoon salt, and ¼ teaspoon pepper and bring to boil. Reduce heat to low

and cook until flavors meld, about 5 minutes. Transfer sauce to blender and process until completely smooth, about 1 minute. Return sauce to now-empty saucepan.

3. Stir beans into sauce in saucepan, cover, and simmer over low heat until flavors meld and beans are warmed through, about 5 minutes. Stir in vinegar and season with salt and pepper to taste. Cover to keep warm while cooking eggs.

4. Heat remaining 1 tablespoon oil in 12-inch nonstick skillet over medium-high heat until shimmering. Add eggs to skillet and sprinkle with remaining pinch salt. Cover and cook for 1 minute. Remove skillet from heat and let sit, covered, for 15 to 45 seconds for runny yolks, 45 to 60 seconds for soft but set yolks, or about 2 minutes for medium-set yolks.

5. Spoon beans over reserved toasts, then top with eggs. Sprinkle eggs with remaining ¼ teaspoon pepper and serve.

Molletes

Serves 6 | **Total Time** 25 minutes, plus 30 minutes resting

WHY THIS RECIPE WORKS Somewhat akin to Italian bruschetta, Mexican molletes are a simple combination of toasted bread, refried beans, melted cheese, and fresh salsa. Individual bolillo rolls are most commonly used, but a standard loaf of French bread works well, and one long loaf is easier to handle than several small rolls. We remove some of the interior crumb so that the bread will cradle the beans and cheese, helping the molletes hold together. As for the cheese, Chihuahua—a good melting cheese that's similar to mild white cheddar—is commonly used in Mexico, but it can be hard to find in American stores. We opt for pepper Jack or mild cheddar instead. To build our molletes, we first butter and toast the hollowed-out bread and then spread it with refried beans and a generous handful of cheese. Once the cheese is just melted, we top the loaves with fresh homemade pico de gallo. To make sure the salsa doesn't make the bread soggy, we eliminate excess moisture by salting the chopped tomatoes. A minced jalapeño, lime juice, and some fresh cilantro round out our pico de gallo. The salsa provides the perfect contrast to the rich cheese and creamy beans. Avoid using rustic loaves with thick crusts in this recipe. We prefer our homemade Refried Beans (page 295), but you may use store-bought.

Molletes

2. Adjust oven rack to middle position and heat oven to 400 degrees. Line baking sheet with aluminum foil. Slice bread in half horizontally, then remove all but ¼ inch of interior crumb; discard removed crumb. Spread butter evenly inside hollowed bread and place cut side up on prepared sheet. Bake until lightly toasted and browned, about 8 minutes.

3. Let bread cool slightly. Spread refried beans evenly inside toasted bread and top with cheese. Bake until cheese is just melted, 5 to 7 minutes. Transfer bread to cutting board, top with salsa, and slice crosswise into 2-inch pieces. Serve warm.

Curried Chickpea Salad Sandwiches

Serves 6 | **Total Time** 15 minutes **FAST**

WHY THIS RECIPE WORKS This superfast and pantry-friendly bean-based sandwich filling offers all the satisfaction of a traditional deli-style option. Chickpeas' tender but not overly pasty texture combines with mayo to produce a creamy hummus-style puree. A hefty amount of curry powder flavors the chickpea mixture, bolstered by lemon juice and salt. Chopped celery provides crunch, and raisins a contrasting hint of sweetness that complements the curried flavor of the salad. Served on toasted hearty bread, these sandwiches make an inspired lunch choice.

- 3 tomatoes, cored and chopped
- ¼ teaspoon table salt, for salting tomatoes
- ½ cup finely chopped onion
- ½ cup fresh cilantro leaves
- 1 jalapeño chile, stemmed, seeded, and minced
- 2 tablespoons lime juice
- 1 garlic clove, minced
- 1 (16-inch) loaf French or Italian bread
- 4 tablespoons unsalted butter, softened
- 1 cup refried beans
- 8 ounces Chihuahua, pepper Jack cheese, or mild cheddar cheese shredded (2 cups)

1. Toss tomatoes with salt in colander and let drain for 30 minutes. Shake colander to drain and discard excess tomato juice. Transfer tomatoes to bowl and stir in onion, cilantro, jalapeño, lime juice and garlic. Season with salt and pepper to taste.

- 2 (15-ounce) cans chickpeas, rinsed, divided
- ½ cup mayonnaise
- ¼ cup water
- 1 tablespoon lemon juice
- 1 tablespoon curry powder
- ½ teaspoon table salt
- 2 celery ribs, chopped fine
- ½ cup raisins
- 12 slices hearty bread, toasted

1. Process ¾ cup chickpeas, mayonnaise, water, lemon juice, curry powder, and salt in food processor until smooth, about 30 seconds, scraping down sides of bowl as needed. Add remaining chickpeas to food processor and pulse until coarsely chopped with some larger pieces remaining, about 4 pulses.

2. Combine chickpea mixture, celery, and raisins in bowl and season with salt and pepper to taste. (Chickpea salad can be refrigerated for up to 3 days.) Spread chickpea salad evenly over 6 bread slices. Top with remaining bread slices and serve.

Herbed Quinoa Cakes
with Whipped Feta

Miso Brown Rice Burgers

Herbed Quinoa Cakes with Whipped Feta

Serves 4 | **Total Time** 1¾ hours, plus 1 hour cooling and chilling

WHY THIS RECIPE WORKS We wanted a light and flavorful quinoa cake that would hold together while searing. This recipe leans heavily on bright Mediterranean flavors. The perk in the flavor comes from the addition of apple cider vinegar and lemon juice, while a hint of sweetness comes from soaked raisins. We also add a generous amount of herbs to give the mixture a fresh note. The quinoa cakes are bound together with eggs and panko bread crumbs. We serve these satisfying cakes alongside a tangy whipped feta and recommend serving them with a green salad either for lunch or a light dinner. If you buy unwashed quinoa, rinse it and then spread it out on a clean dish towel to dry for 15 minutes. The patties hold together but tend to be delicate, so flip them carefully in step 6. If your whipped feta is very loose after whipping, you may need to refrigerate it for up to 90 minutes before serving.

WHIPPED FETA
- ¾ teaspoon lemon juice
- 1 small garlic clove, minced
- 4 ounces feta cheese, crumbled (1 cup)
- 1½ tablespoons milk
- 1 tablespoon extra-virgin olive oil
- 1½ teaspoons minced fresh oregano
- 1½ teaspoons minced fresh parsley

QUINOA CAKES
- ¼ cup golden raisins, chopped
- 3 tablespoons cider vinegar
- ⅛ teaspoon saffron (optional)
- 3 tablespoons extra-virgin olive oil, divided
- 1 small red onion, chopped fine
- 4 garlic cloves, minced
- 1 cup prewashed white quinoa
- 1 teaspoon table salt
- ½ cup panko bread crumbs
- 2 large eggs, lightly beaten
- ½ teaspoon grated lemon zest plus 2 teaspoons juice
- 2 ounces Parmesan cheese, grated (1 cup)
- ⅓ cup fresh chopped fresh parsley and/or dill
- 2 tablespoon chopped fresh oregano
- ¼ teaspoon pepper
- ¼ teaspoon ground allspice

1. FOR THE WHIPPED FETA Combine lemon juice and garlic in bowl and let sit for 10 minutes. Process feta, milk, and lemon juice mixture in food processor until feta mixture resembles ricotta cheese, about 15 seconds. Scrape down sides of bowl. With processor running, slowly drizzle in oil. Continue to process until mixture has Greek yogurt–like consistency (some small lumps will remain), 1½ to 2 minutes longer, stopping once to scrape down bottom and sides of bowl. Add oregano and parsley and pulse to combine. If whipped feta is very loose, refrigerate for up to 1½ hours. Set aside until ready to serve. (Dip can be refrigerated for up to 3 days. If refrigerated for longer than 1½ hours, let sit at room temperature for 30 minutes before serving.)

2. FOR THE QUINOA CAKES Microwave raisins; vinegar; saffron, if using; and 3 tablespoons water in small bowl until steaming, about 2 minutes. Let sit for 30 minutes until raisins are soft and plump. Drain raisins and set aside.

3. Heat 1 tablespoon oil in large saucepan over medium heat until shimmering. Add onion and cook until softened, 3 to 5 minutes. Stir in garlic and cook until fragrant, about 30 seconds. Stir in 2 cups water, quinoa, and salt and bring to simmer. Cover, reduce heat to medium-low, and cook until quinoa is tender, 10 to 15 minutes. Off heat, let quinoa sit, covered, until liquid is fully absorbed, about 10 minutes. Set aside and let cool uncovered for 30 minutes.

4. Line rimmed baking sheet with parchment paper. Process panko in clean, dry food processor until finely ground, around 30 seconds. Add eggs and lemon zest and pulse until mixture forms paste, about 5 pulses. Transfer panko mixture to large bowl and stir in cooled quinoa, reserved raisins, lemon juice, Parmesan, parsley, dill, oregano, pepper, and allspice.

5. Divide quinoa mixture into 8 equal portions. Using your lightly moistened hands, firmly pack each portion into tight ball, then flatten to 3-inch-wide patty; transfer to prepared sheet. Cover with plastic wrap and refrigerate until chilled and firm, at least 30 minutes or up to 24 hours.

6. Heat ½ tablespoon oil in 12-inch nonstick skillet over medium-low heat until shimmering. Carefully place 4 chilled quinoa patties in skillet and cook until crisp and golden brown on first side, 5 to 7 minutes. Gently flip patties using 2 spatulas, add ½ tablespoon oil to skillet, and cook until crisp and browned on second side, 4 to 6 minutes. Transfer to platter and tent with aluminum foil. Repeat with remaining 1 tablespoon oil and remaining chilled quinoa patties. Serve quinoa cakes with whipped feta.

Miso Brown Rice Burgers

Serves 4 | **Total Time** 2 hours, plus 30 minutes chilling

WHY THIS RECIPE WORKS Easy, inexpensive, and substantial, rice cakes should have a permanent place on any vegetarian table. Here we use hearty long-grain brown rice and give the dish a very flavorful twist. We pair the rice with red miso and shiitake mushrooms for depth of flavor and meatiness; ginger and garlic round out the flavors. Although we usually cook brown rice in the oven to ensure fluffy grains, that technique would work against us here. Instead, we turn to the stovetop method to aid in releasing starches that help hold the patties together when pan-fried. Once the rice is cool, we pulse it in a food processor to help break down the starches for even better binding. Then we mix the rice with egg, sesame oil, and the miso, plus scallions for some freshness, form the mixture into patties, and chill them briefly until firm. Just a few minutes in a hot skillet gives us crisp, browned rice patties. Although we prefer the flavor of red miso here, you can substitute white miso, but do not substitute "light" miso; its flavor is too mild.

- 3 tablespoons extra-virgin olive oil, divided
- 8 ounces shiitake mushrooms, stemmed and chopped
- 2 teaspoons grated fresh ginger
- 2 garlic cloves, minced
- 1½ cups long-grain brown rice, rinsed
- 3¾ cups water
- 1 teaspoon table salt, divided
- 4 scallions, chopped fine
- 1 large egg plus 1 large yolk, lightly beaten
- 3 tablespoons red miso
- 1½ teaspoons toasted sesame oil
- ¼ teaspoon pepper
- 8 hamburger buns, toasted if desired
- 1 recipe Sriracha Mayo (page 68)

1. Heat 1 tablespoon olive oil in large saucepan over medium heat until shimmering. Add mushrooms and cook until lightly browned, about 5 minutes. Stir in ginger and garlic and cook until fragrant, about 30 seconds. Add rice, water, and ½ teaspoon salt and bring to simmer. Reduce heat to low, cover, and cook until rice is tender, about 50 minutes, stirring occasionally. Spread rice mixture onto rimmed baking sheet and let cool for 15 minutes.

2. Pulse rice mixture in food processor until coarsely ground, about 10 pulses; transfer to large bowl. Stir in scallions, egg and yolk, miso, sesame oil, pepper, and remaining ½ teaspoon salt until well combined.

3. Line rimmed baking sheet with parchment paper. Divide rice mixture into 8 equal portions. Using your lightly moistened hands, firmly pack each portion into tight ball, then flatten to 3-inch-wide patty; transfer to prepared sheet. Cover with plastic wrap and refrigerate until chilled and firm, at least 30 minutes or up to 24 hours.

4. Heat 1 tablespoon olive oil in 12-inch nonstick skillet over medium-high heat until shimmering. Carefully place 4 chilled rice cakes in skillet and cook until crisp and browned on both sides, about 4 minutes per side, gently flipping using 2 spatulas halfway through cooking; transfer to platter and tent with aluminum foil. Repeat with remaining 1 tablespoon olive oil and remaining chilled rice cakes. Serve on buns with sriracha mayo.

Sriracha Mayo

Makes ¾ cup | **Total Time** 5 minutes **FAST**

½ cup mayonnaise
1 scallion, chopped fine
2 tablespoons sriracha
1 tablespoon lime juice

Combine all ingredients in bowl. (Mayo can be refrigerated for up to 2 days.)

Fonio, Sweet Potato, and Scallion Cakes

Serves 4 | **Total Time** 1¼ hours, plus 30 minutes chilling

WHY THIS RECIPE WORKS It's hard not to love fonio: This tiny-grained West African relative of millet is quick-cooking, mild-tasting, and highly versatile, usable in everything from pilafs to salads to veggie burgers or patties, as we've done here. This ancient grain just needs a quick simmer before we mix it with sweet potato, which we precook in the microwave. We add lots of scallions, ginger, a fresh green chile, garlic, and a generous amount of black pepper, flavors common in many parts of West Africa. While the sweet potato works well to keep the cakes together, an egg adds a bit more structure and gives the patties a crispy crust when cooked in a skillet. A final squeeze of lime adds the right amount of brightness for the cake's spicy flavors. To make this dish spicier, reserve and add the chile seeds to the fonio mixture as desired.

1 cup water
½ cup fonio
1 teaspoon table salt, divided
1 sweet potato (12 ounces), unpeeled, pricked all over with fork
3 tablespoons extra-virgin olive oil, divided
6 scallions, white and green parts separated and sliced thin
1 jalapeño chile, stemmed, seeded, and minced
2 garlic cloves, minced
1½ teaspoons grated fresh ginger
½ teaspoon pepper
1 large egg, lightly beaten
Lime wedges

1. Combine water, fonio, and ½ teaspoon salt in small saucepan and bring to simmer over medium heat. Reduce heat to low, cover, and simmer until liquid is absorbed, about 2 minutes. Off heat, let fonio sit, covered, for 10 minutes, then transfer to large bowl and gently fluff with fork, breaking up any large clumps. Set aside to cool.

2. While fonio cools, microwave sweet potato on plate until very soft, 6 to 9 minutes, flipping potato over halfway through microwaving. Immediately slice potato in half lengthwise to release steam and set aside to cool. Scoop out cooled flesh into bowl with fonio and mash with fork until smooth and well combined.

3. Heat 1 tablespoon oil in 12-inch nonstick skillet over medium heat until shimmering. Add scallion whites and jalapeño and cook until scallions are softened, about 2 minutes. Add garlic, ginger, and pepper and cook until fragrant, about 30 seconds. Transfer to bowl with fonio and let cool, about 5 minutes. Wipe out now-empty skillet with paper towels.

4. Line rimmed baking sheet with parchment paper. Add scallion greens, egg, and remaining ½ teaspoon salt to cooled fonio mixture and mix until well combined. Divide mixture into 8 equal portions. Using your lightly moistened hands, firmly pack each portion into tight ball, then flatten to 3-inch-wide patty; transfer to prepared sheet. Cover with plastic wrap and refrigerate until chilled and firm, at least 30 minutes or up to 24 hours.

5. Heat 1 tablespoon oil in now-empty skillet over medium heat until shimmering. Carefully place 4 chilled cakes in skillet and cook until crisp and deep golden brown on both sides, 4 to 5 minutes per side, gently flipping using 2 spatulas halfway through cooking; transfer to platter and tent with aluminum foil. Repeat with remaining 1 tablespoon oil and remaining cakes. Serve with lime wedges.

Buffalo Blue Cheese Chickpea Patties with Creamy Herb Sauce

Serves 6 | **Total Time** 1 hour, plus 1 hour chilling

WHY THIS RECIPE WORKS Chickpeas make great veggie burgers. Inspired by Buffalo chicken wings, we spice up these chickpea patties with hot sauce, carrots, celery, and blue cheese. The patties are simply made by pulsing the components in a food processor until there's a mix of finely chopped pieces and a few larger pieces. The variety of sizes is key in holding them together while still giving them a satisfying texture. We also make sure to remove excess liquid from the chickpeas to avoid overly wet patties that crack and fall apart. The addition of sour cream, eggs, and panko lightens the mixture and binds it together while the blue cheese and hot sauce give them their classic Buffalo flavor. A great protein-packed vegetarian alternative to beef burgers, these patties are hearty and sturdy enough to be enjoyed on a bun and are equally delicious crumbled over a wedge salad. Avoid overmixing the chickpea mixture in step 3 or the cakes will have a mealy texture. We used Frank's Red Hot Original Cayenne Pepper Sauce but other hot sauces can be used. If celery leaves are not available, substitute an equal amount of parsley leaves.

SAUCE

¼ cup mayonnaise
¼ cup sour cream
2 tablespoons milk
2 tablespoons chopped fresh cilantro
2 tablespoons minced fresh chives
1 tablespoon distilled white vinegar
2 teaspoons chopped fresh dill
1 teaspoon granulated garlic
1 teaspoon onion powder
¼ teaspoon pepper
⅛ teaspoon table salt

Fonio, Sweet Potato, and Scallion Cakes

PATTIES

2 (15-ounce) cans chickpeas, rinsed
2 celery ribs, chopped, plus ¼ cup celery leaves
1 carrot, chopped
1 shallot, chopped
2 large eggs
⅓ cup sour cream
6 tablespoons extra-virgin olive oil, divided
3 tablespoons hot sauce, plus extra for serving
½ teaspoon table salt
1 cup panko bread crumbs
1 ounce blue cheese, finely crumbled (¼ cup)
6 hamburger buns, toasted if desired

1. FOR THE SAUCE Stir all ingredients until smooth. Set aside until ready to serve. (Sauce can be refrigerated in airtight container for up to 4 days.)

2. FOR THE PATTIES Line rimmed baking sheet with triple layer paper towels and spread chickpeas over towels; pat dry. Let sit for 15 minutes.

3. Pulse celery and celery leaves, carrot, and shallot in food processor until finely chopped, about 15 pulses, scraping down sides of bowl as needed. Add dried chickpeas and pulse until chickpeas are evenly broken down and pieces are no larger than ¼ inch, about 6 pulses. Whisk eggs, sour cream, 2 tablespoons oil, hot sauce, and salt together in large bowl. Add chickpea mixture, panko, and blue cheese and mix until just combined. Cover and refrigerate for at least 1 hour or up to 24 hours.

4. Divide chickpea mixture into 6 equal portions. Using your lightly moistened hands, firmly pack each portion into tight ball, then flatten to 3 ½-inch-wide patty.

5. Heat 1 tablespoon oil in 12-inch nonstick skillet over medium heat until shimmering. Carefully place 3 patties in skillet and cook until crisp and well browned on first side, about 5 minutes. Gently flip patties using 2 spatulas, add 1 tablespoon oil, and cook until crisp and well browned on second side, 3 to 5 minutes. Transfer to platter and tent with aluminum foil. Repeat with remaining 2 tablespoons oil and remaining 3 patties. Transfer patties to buns and serve with reserved herb sauce and additional hot sauce.

Black Bean Burgers

Serves 6 | Total Time 1 hour, plus 1 hour chilling

WHY THIS RECIPE WORKS Earthy black beans make a really satisfying nonmeat burger. We were after burgers that featured bean flavor at their heart with just enough seasoning and mix-ins to give them a little zest and intrigue. To start we spread the beans on paper towels to rid them of moisture. For great-tasting, cohesive burgers, we grind tortilla chips in the food processor to use as a flavorful starchy binder. We then pulse the beans with the chips so the beans maintain some texture. Eggs and flour, which contains sticky amylopectin, help to hold the burger mix together. To keep the preparation simple, we add no-cook seasonings that bolster the flavor of the burgers. Letting the mixture sit in the refrigerator for an hour gives the starches time to soak up moisture from the eggs, so the patties are easier to shape.

2 (15-ounce) cans black beans, rinsed
2 large eggs, lightly beaten
2 tablespoons all-purpose flour
4 scallions, minced
3 tablespoons minced fresh cilantro
2 garlic cloves, minced

1 teaspoon ground cumin
1 teaspoon hot sauce
½ teaspoon ground coriander
¼ teaspoon table salt
¼ teaspoon pepper
1 ounce tortilla chips, crushed coarse (½ cup)
¼ cup vegetable oil, divided
6 hamburger buns, toasted if desired

1. Line rimmed baking sheet with triple layer paper towels and spread beans over towels, pat dry. Let sit for 15 minutes.

2. Whisk eggs and flour in large bowl until uniform paste forms. Stir in scallions; cilantro; garlic; cumin; hot sauce, if using; coriander; salt; and pepper until well combined.

3. Process tortilla chips in food processor until finely ground, about 30 seconds. Add black beans and pulse until beans are roughly broken down, about 5 pulses. Transfer black bean mixture to bowl with egg mixture and mix until well combined. Cover and refrigerate for at least 1 hour or up to 24 hours.

4. Divide bean mixture into 6 equal portions. Using your lightly moistened hands, firmly pack each portion into tight ball, then flatten to 3 ½-inch-wide patty.

5. Heat 1 tablespoon oil in 12-inch nonstick skillet over medium heat until shimmering. Carefully place 3 patties in skillet and cook until crisp and well browned on first side, about 5 minutes. Gently flip patties using 2 spatulas, add 1 tablespoon oil, and cook until crisp and well browned on second side, 3 to 5 minutes. Transfer to platter and tent with aluminum foil. Repeat with remaining 2 tablespoons oil and remaining 3 patties. Transfer burgers to buns and serve.

Scarlet Runner Mole Burgers

Serves 6 | Total Time 1¾ hours, plus 8½ hours brining and chilling

WHY THIS RECIPE WORKS Native to Mexico, scarlet runner beans are distinctive in flavor with notes of chocolate and roasted coffee beans. It felt especially appropriate to use these meaty beans for a vegetarian burger. Staying true to the bean's roots, this burger is inspired by Oaxacan flavors. It contains several bold seasonings with a particular emphasis on smoky chili spices. To balance all that out, we add lime and crema to give the burger some brightness. The addition of bread crumbs, pepitas, and eggs help keep the burger together. The final result is a flavorful burger that's crispy on the outside and soft on the inside, but without being mushy. We recommend serving it with Avocado Crema and Quick Sweet-and-Spicy Pickled Red Onions (page 62) on a burger roll. If you can't find Mexican crema, you can substitute sour cream.

> **Substitution:** You can use dried black beans or two (15-ounce) cans rinsed black beans in place of the dried scarlet runner beans; skip steps 1 and 2 if using canned.

1½ tablespoons table salt for brining
  8 ounces (1⅓ cups) dried scarlet runner beans, picked over and rinsed
    Table salt for cooking beans, plus ¾ teaspoon salt
  1 cup panko bread crumbs
  ¼ cup raw, unsalted pepitas
  ½ onion, chopped fine
  2 large eggs, lightly beaten
  ⅓ cup chopped fresh cilantro
  2 tablespoons Mexican crema
  2 garlic cloves, minced
1½ teaspoons ground cumin
1½ teaspoons ancho chile powder
1½ teaspoons minced canned chipotle chile in adobo sauce, plus 1 teaspoon adobo sauce
  1 teaspoon smoked paprika
  ½ teaspoon grated lime zest plus 1 tablespoon juice
  2 tablespoons extra-virgin olive oil, divided
  6 hamburger buns, toasted if desired
    Avocado Crema (page 76; optional)

1. Dissolve 1½ tablespoons salt in 2 quarts cold water in large container. Add beans and soak at room temperature for at least 8 hours or up to 24 hours. Drain and rinse well. (If you're pressed for time, see page 13 for information on quick brining your beans.)

2. Bring soaked beans and 7 cups water to simmer in large saucepan. Simmer, partially covered, over medium-low heat until beans are tender, 30 to 40 minutes. Remove from heat, stir in 1½ teaspoons salt, cover, and let beans sit until completely tender, about 15 minutes. Drain beans.

3. Line rimmed baking sheet with parchment paper. Process panko in food processor until finely ground, about 30 seconds. Add pepitas and process until finely chopped, about 15 seconds; transfer to large bowl. Working in 2 batches, process half of cooked beans, onion, eggs, cilantro, crema, garlic, cumin, ancho, chipotle plus adobo sauce, paprika, lime zest and juice, and salt in now-empty processor until coarsely ground, 15 to 20 seconds, scraping down sides of bowl as needed; add to bowl with panko mixture.

Scarlet Runner Mole Burgers

4. Stir remaining cooked beans into processed bean-panko mixture until well combined. Divide bean mixture into 6 equal portions. Using your lightly moistened hands, firmly pack each portion into tight ball, then flatten to 3½-inch-wide patty; transfer to prepared sheet. Cover with plastic wrap and refrigerate until chilled and firm, at least 30 minutes or up to 24 hours.

5. Heat ½ tablespoon oil in 12-inch nonstick skillet over medium-low heat until shimmering. Carefully place 3 patties in skillet and cook until crisp and golden brown on first side, about 5 minutes. Gently flip patties using 2 spatulas, add ½ tablespoon oil to skillet, and cook until crisp and golden brown on second side, about 5 minutes. Transfer to platter and tent with aluminum foil. Repeat with remaining 1 tablespoon oil and remaining 3 patties. Transfer burgers to buns and serve with avocado crema, if using.

Onigiri

Makes 6 onigiri | **Total Time** 1¼ hours

WHY THIS RECIPE WORKS Onigiri, also called omusubi, are a popular snack in Japan. They're made from sticky rice that's molded into shapes and wrapped with pieces of nori, a seaweed (see page 98) which provides a convenient spot to hold the onigiri. Triangles are the most common shape, but you'll also see onigiri circles, cylinders, or even adorable animal shapes. These savory, chewy snacks can be served plain, filled or mixed with flavorful ingredients, or brushed with a salty-sweet glaze and charcoal-grilled or pan-fried, a style called "yaki." Filling and easy to eat (no utensils needed), onigiri make a satisfying on-the-go snack for busy days. If you have an onigiri rice mold, you can use it to shape the rice balls into triangles in step 6 instead of shaping them by hand.

1¼ cups short-grain white rice
1½ cups water
¼ teaspoon table salt
1 (8-by-7½-inch) sheet nori
¼ cup drained canned tuna
1 tablespoon mayonnaise
½ teaspoon soy sauce
White or black sesame seeds, raw or toasted (optional)

1. Set fine-mesh strainer over large bowl and set in sink. Place rice in strainer and rinse under cold running water, emptying bowl a few times as it fills, until water in bowl is clear, 1½ to 2 minutes. Shake strainer to drain rice well and transfer to medium saucepan.

2. Stir water and salt into rice in saucepan and bring to boil. Reduce heat to low, cover saucepan, and cook for 20 minutes. Remove rice from heat and let sit, covered, for 10 minutes.

3. Meanwhile, use kitchen shears to cut three 1-inch-wide strips from nori sheet. Cut strips in half crosswise (you should have 6 pieces). Set aside. Stir together tuna, mayonnaise, and soy sauce.

4. Rinse and dry now-empty large bowl. Use rubber spatula to transfer cooked rice to bowl. Let cool until easy to handle but still very warm, about 5 minutes.

5. Line ½-cup dry measuring cup with plastic wrap. Using rubber spatula and your damp hands, fill plastic-lined measuring cup with warm rice. Use back of 1-teaspoon measuring spoon to make indentation in center of rice. Add 1 teaspoon tuna mixture to indentation. Place 1 teaspoon rice on top of filling. Gather edges of plastic together; lift out of measuring cup and twist and gently squeeze to form rice into ball, enclosing filling inside.

6. Using your hands, gently flatten ball on counter into disk about 1 inch thick. Turn disk onto edge and press to flatten. Rotate and flatten edges a few times to shape into 3-inch long by 1-inch thick triangle. Unwrap rice triangle and place 1 end of 1 nori strip in center of triangle. Wrap nori around 1 edge to other side, pressing lightly to adhere. Place onigiri on serving plate and return plastic to measuring cup. Top onigiri with ¼ teaspoon filling. Repeat with remaining filling and remaining rice.

7. Sprinkle outsides of onigiri with sesame seeds, if using. Serve. (Onigiri can be wrapped individually in plastic wrap and refrigerated in airtight container for up to 24 hours.)

FILLING AND SHAPING ONIGIRI

1. Use back of 1-teaspoon measuring spoon to make indentation in center of rice. Add 1 teaspoon filling to indentation. Place 1 teaspoon rice on top of filling.

2. Using plastic, lift rice out of cup. Twist and squeeze rice into ball. Gently flatten ball into disk.

3. Rotate and flatten edges a few times to shape into a triangle 3 inches long on each side and about 1 inch thick.

4. Unwrap rice triangle and place 1 end of 1 nori strip in center of triangle. Wrap nori around 1 edge to other side, pressing lightly to adhere.

Quinoa Lettuce Wraps with Feta and Olives

Serves 4 | **Total Time** 45 minutes, plus 20 minutes cooling

WHY THIS RECIPE WORKS Whatever the filling, lettuce wraps make a perfect light lunch. We fill these with an easy and flavorful vegetarian quinoa salad. To complement the quinoa's nuttiness, we pair it with salty feta, briny olives, and fresh mint and oregano. Rather than crumbling the feta into the salad, we blend it with some yogurt and vinegar to make a flavorful vinaigrette. Once the quinoa cools, we toss it with cucumber, tomatoes, olives, shallot, and some of the vinaigrette, reserving the rest for drizzling once we portion our salad into the lettuce leaves. The large, crisp leaves of Boston or Bibb lettuce make perfectly sized cups. If you buy unwashed quinoa, rinse it and then spread it out on a clean dish towel to dry for 15 minutes.

VINAIGRETTE

- 4 ounces feta cheese, crumbled (1 cup)
- ½ cup plain yogurt
- ¼ cup minced fresh mint
- 3 tablespoons red wine vinegar
- 2 tablespoons minced fresh oregano or 1½ teaspoons dried
- ½ teaspoon table salt
- ¼ teaspoon pepper
- ½ cup extra-virgin olive oil

SALAD

- 1½ cups prewashed white quinoa
- 2¼ cups water
- ½ teaspoon table salt
- 2 tomatoes, cored, seeded, and cut into ¼-inch pieces
- 1 cucumber, halved lengthwise, seeded, and cut into ¼-inch pieces
- 1 shallot, minced
- ¼ cup pitted kalamata olives, chopped
- 2 heads Boston or Bibb lettuce (1 pound), leaves separated

1. FOR THE VINAIGRETTE Process feta, yogurt, mint, vinegar, oregano, salt, and pepper in blender until smooth, about 15 seconds. With blender running, slowly add oil until emulsified, about 30 seconds. (Vinaigrette can be refrigerated for up to 24 hours.)

Onigiri

Quinoa Lettuce Wraps with Feta and Olives

2. FOR THE SALAD Toast quinoa in large saucepan over medium-high heat, stirring often, until very fragrant and quinoa makes continuous popping sound, 5 to 7 minutes. Stir in water and salt and bring to simmer. Cover, reduce heat to low, and simmer gently until most of water has been absorbed and quinoa is nearly tender, about 15 minutes. Spread quinoa onto rimmed baking sheet and let cool for 20 minutes; transfer to large bowl.

3. Add tomatoes, cucumber, shallot, olives, and ⅔ cup vinaigrette to quinoa and toss to combine. Season with salt and pepper to taste. Serve with lettuce leaves, spooning ⅓ cup quinoa mixture into each leaf and drizzling with remaining vinaigrette.

Tomato and Corn Tostadas with Baked Eggs

Serves 4 | **Total Time** 55 minutes

WHY THIS RECIPE WORKS We liked the idea of pairing crunchy, crisp corn tostadas with creamy beans; soft, rich eggs; and flavorful roasted vegetables. We start by roasting cherry tomatoes, corn, and onion with smoky chipotle and aromatic spices. To keep it easy, we bake the eggs in divots made in the vegetable mixture. A slather of warm refried beans and a sprinkle of queso fresco and cilantro finish off our tostadas perfectly. We prefer our homemade Refried Beans (page 295), but you may use store-bought.

1½ pounds cherry tomatoes, halved
1½ cups fresh or thawed frozen corn
1 onion, halved and sliced thin
2 tablespoons vegetable oil
3 garlic cloves, minced
2 teaspoons minced canned chipotle chile in adobo sauce
2 teaspoons minced fresh oregano or ½ teaspoon dried
1 teaspoon ground cumin
½ teaspoon ground coriander
½ teaspoon table salt
¼ teaspoon pepper
8 (6-inch) corn tortillas
¾ cup vegetable oil for frying
8 large eggs
1 cup refried beans, warmed
2 ounces queso fresco, crumbled (½ cup)
3 tablespoons chopped fresh cilantro

1. Adjust oven rack to middle position and heat oven to 500 degrees. Line rimmed baking sheet with aluminum foil. Toss tomatoes, corn, onion, 2 tablespoons oil, garlic, chipotle, oregano, cumin, coriander, salt, and pepper together, then spread onto prepared sheet. Roast tomato mixture, stirring occasionally, until tomatoes are softened and skins begin to shrivel, 10 to 15 minutes. Remove sheet from oven.

2. Meanwhile, using fork, poke center of each tortilla 3 or 4 times (to prevent puffing and allow for even cooking). Heat ¾ cup oil in 8-inch skillet over medium heat to 350 degrees. Line second rimmed baking sheet with several layers of paper towels.

3. Working with 1 tortilla at a time, add to hot oil and place metal potato masher on top to keep tortilla flat and submerged in oil. Fry until crisp and lightly browned, 45 to 60 seconds (no flipping is necessary). Transfer fried tortilla to paper towel–lined sheet. Repeat with remaining tortillas.

4. Using spoon, make 8 indentations, 2 to 3 inches wide, in tomato mixture in sheet. Crack 1 egg into each indentation. Bake until egg whites are just set and yolks are still runny, 5 to 7 minutes, rotating sheet halfway through baking.

5. Spread 2 tablespoons warm refried beans over each tostada, then top with tomato mixture and eggs. Sprinkle with queso fresco and cilantro and serve immediately.

Tempeh Tacos

Serves 4 to 6 | **Total Time** 30 minutes   FAST   VEGAN

WHY THIS RECIPE WORKS Much more than just a stand-in for more traditional beef or chicken versions, these tempeh tacos have their own nutty flavor and tender but firm texture. Rather than rely on questionable supermarket seasoning packets, we created our own taco mix to complement the tempeh. Chili powder and dried oregano add the right depth without overpowering the tempeh. To make their flavor fuller and rounder, we bloom the spices briefly in hot oil. This simple step gives the filling a rich, deep flavor that is markedly better than stirring the spices in raw. For a light sauce to carry the flavors of the spices and keep the filling cohesive, we use a combination of tomato sauce and vegetable broth. To give the sauce sweet-and-sour balance, we add brown sugar and lime juice.

Tempeh Tacos

1 tablespoon vegetable oil
1 onion, chopped fine
3 tablespoons chili powder
4 garlic cloves, minced
1 teaspoon dried oregano
1 pound tempeh, crumbled into ¼-inch pieces
1 (8-ounce) can tomato sauce
1 cup vegetable broth
1 teaspoon packed brown sugar
2 tablespoons minced fresh cilantro
1 tablespoon lime juice
12 taco shells, warmed

1. Heat oil in 12-inch skillet over medium heat until shimmering. Add onion and cook until softened, about 5 minutes. Stir in chili powder, garlic, and oregano and cook until fragrant, about 30 seconds. Stir in tempeh and cook until lightly browned, about 5 minutes.

2. Stir in tomato sauce, broth, and sugar and simmer until thickened, about 2 minutes. Off heat, stir in cilantro and lime juice and season with salt and pepper to taste. Serve with taco shells.

Red Lentil Tacos

Serves 4 to 6 | **Total Time** 50 minutes, plus 30 minutes resting VEGAN

WHY THIS RECIPE WORKS Convenient, vibrant, and nutritious, red lentils are perfect for a quick weeknight dinner. Here, we use them to emulate a traditional ground beef taco filling. They cook and break down quickly; the resulting meaty texture, combined with warm spices and peppers, makes a great vegetarian alternative to fill a taco. We love the refreshing crunch of pickled radishes on these tacos but you can use your favorite taco toppings.

SPICY PICKLED RADISHES
10 radishes, trimmed and sliced thin
½ cup lime juice (4 limes)
1 jalapeño chile, stemmed and sliced thin
1 teaspoon sugar
¼ teaspoon table salt

TACO FILLING
2 tablespoons vegetable oil
1 small onion, chopped fine
1 green bell pepper, stemmed, seeded, and chopped fine
2 tablespoons chili powder
3 garlic cloves, minced
2 teaspoons ground cumin
2 teaspoons ground coriander
1 teaspoon dried oregano
½ teaspoon table salt
¼ teaspoon cayenne pepper
1 cup red lentils, picked over and rinsed
3 cups vegetable broth
12 (6-inch) corn tortillas, warmed

1. FOR THE SPICY PICKLED RADISHES Combine all ingredients in bowl. Cover and let sit at room temperature for 30 minutes. Drain vegetables in colander. Serve. (Drained pickles can be refrigerated for up to 24 hours.)

2. FOR THE TACO FILLING Heat oil in 12-inch nonstick skillet over medium heat until shimmering. Add onion and bell pepper and cook until softened, about 5 minutes. Stir in chili powder, garlic, cumin, coriander, oregano, salt, and cayenne and cook until fragrant, about 30 seconds.

3. Stir in lentils and broth and bring to boil. Reduce heat to medium-low, partially cover, and simmer vigorously until lentils have broken down and all liquid has evaporated, 15 to 20 minutes. Serve with tortillas and reserved pickled radishes.

Black Bean and Sweet Potato Tacos

Serves 4 | **Total Time** 55 minutes | **VEGAN**

WHY THIS RECIPE WORKS Tacos are often focused on rich meats. One great thing about the proliferation of taco restaurants is that many feature plant-based fillings, from cauliflower to mushrooms and more. It inspired us to create this delicious pantry-friendly combination of black beans, sweet potatoes, and onion, which we season with fragrant garlic, cumin, coriander, and oregano. Roasting the vegetables produces caramelized exteriors and tender interiors. The black beans ramp up the protein for a satiating meal. For a tangy, spicy finish, sprinkle the tacos with Quick Sweet-and-Spicy Pickled Red Onions (page 62).

- 3 tablespoons extra-virgin olive oil
- 3 garlic cloves, minced
- 1½ teaspoons ground cumin
- 1½ teaspoons ground coriander
- 1 teaspoon minced fresh oregano or ¼ teaspoon dried
- 1 teaspoon table salt
- ½ teaspoon pepper
- 12 ounces sweet potatoes, peeled and cut into ½-inch pieces
- 1 onion, halved and sliced ½ inch thick
- 1 (15-ounce) can black beans, rinsed
- ¼ cup chopped fresh cilantro
- 12 (6-inch) corn or flour tortillas, warmed
- 1 recipe Avocado Crema; optional

1. Adjust oven racks to upper-middle and lower-middle positions and heat oven to 450 degrees. Whisk oil, garlic, cumin, coriander, oregano, salt, and pepper together in large bowl. Add potatoes and onion and toss to coat.

2. Spread vegetable mixture in even layer over 2 aluminum foil–lined rimmed baking sheets. Roast vegetables until tender and golden brown, about 30 minutes, stirring vegetables and switching and rotating sheets halfway through baking.

3. Return vegetables to now-empty bowl, add beans and cilantro, and gently toss to combine. Serve with tortillas and crema, if using.

VARIATION

Black Bean, Sweet Potato, and Poblano Tacos **VEGAN**
Roast 4 poblano chiles, stemmed, seeded, and cut into ½-inch-wide strips with potatoes and onions.

Black Bean and Sweet Potato Tacos

Avocado Crema

Makes ½ cup | **Total Time** 10 minutes | **FAST**

- ½ avocado, chopped coarse
- ¼ cup chopped fresh cilantro
- 3 tablespoons water
- 1 tablespoon lime juice
- 1 tablespoon plain yogurt or Mexican crema

Process all ingredients in food processor until completely smooth, about 1 minute, scraping down sides of bowl as needed. Season with salt and pepper to taste. Serve. (Crema can be refrigerated with plastic wrap pressed flush to surface for up to 2 days.)

Breakfast Tacos with Pinto Beans and Cotija Cheese

Serves 4 | **Total Time** 20 minutes **FAST**

WHY THIS RECIPE WORKS Beans are often served alongside Mexican egg dishes such as huevos rancheros or migas, so we thought, why not put them directly into the eggs? To tenderize and lend richness to the eggs without adding moisture, we skip dairy and other watery liquids in favor of olive oil. We cook the eggs quickly in more olive oil over medium-high heat, stirring constantly to create large curds. We then fold in the beans and cilantro once the curds are well established but still a little wet so that the eggs can set up around the beans and pull the dish together. A bit of cotija—a dry, crumbly, salty Mexican cheese—is a worthy addition. Served with a stack of warm tortillas and a bottle of hot sauce, these eggs make a quick, fresh breakfast. This recipe can be easily halved, if desired; use a 10-inch skillet.

3 tablespoons extra-virgin olive oil, divided
¼ cup jarred sliced jalapeños, chopped coarse
2 garlic cloves, minced
1 (15-ounce) can pinto beans, rinsed
¼ cup chopped fresh cilantro, divided
8 large eggs
¼ teaspoon table salt
¼ teaspoon pepper
1 ounce cotija or feta cheese, crumbled (¼ cup)
12 (6-inch) corn or flour tortillas, warmed

1. Cook 1 teaspoon oil, jalapeños, and garlic in 12-inch nonstick skillet over medium heat until fragrant, about 1 minute. Stir in beans and 3 tablespoons cilantro and cook until moisture has evaporated, about 1 minute. Transfer bean mixture to bowl and set aside. Wipe skillet clean with paper towels.

2. Beat eggs, 2 tablespoons oil, salt, and pepper with fork in bowl until eggs are thoroughly combined and color is pure yellow. Heat remaining 2 teaspoons oil in now-empty skillet over medium-high heat until shimmering. Add egg mixture and, using rubber spatula, constantly and firmly scrape along bottom and sides of skillet until eggs begin to clump and spatula just leaves trail on bottom of skillet, 1 to 2 minutes. Reduce heat to low and gently but constantly fold eggs until clumped and just slightly wet, 30 to 60 seconds. Fold in reserved bean mixture. Transfer to serving dish, sprinkle with cotija and remaining 1 tablespoon cilantro. Serve with tortillas.

Kale and Black Bean Breakfast Burritos

Kale and Black Bean Breakfast Burritos

Serves 6 | **Total Time** 45 minutes **FAST**

WHY THIS RECIPE WORKS Breakfast burritos often rely on greasy meat for bulk and flavor. To fill our burritos with healthier options, we swap in black beans and kale along with fluffy scrambled eggs. To build a flavorful base, we sauté aromatic onion, garlic, a poblano, and cumin and then add our beans, mashing half of them to create a cohesive mixture. Next, we quickly braise kale until tender, then use the same skillet to scramble eggs before folding in the kale. We spread the bean mixture onto tortillas, add the kale-egg scramble, and finish with tomato and a drizzle of olive oil. Softening the tortillas in the microwave makes them easy to roll. Serve with hot sauce, if desired.

2 tablespoons extra-virgin olive oil, divided, plus extra for drizzling
1 small onion, chopped fine
1 poblano chile, stemmed, seeded, and chopped fine
¾ teaspoon table salt, divided
2 garlic cloves, minced
½ teaspoon ground cumin
1 (15-ounce) can black beans, rinsed
¾ cup water, divided
12 ounces kale, stemmed and chopped
8 large eggs
2 tablespoons milk
¼ teaspoon pepper
6 (10-inch) flour tortillas
1 tomato, cored and chopped fine

1. Heat 1 tablespoon oil in 12-inch nonstick skillet over medium-high heat until shimmering. Add onion, poblano, and ¼ teaspoon salt and cook until softened, about 5 minutes. Stir in garlic and cumin and cook until fragrant, about 30 seconds. Stir in beans and ½ cup water and cook until beans are warmed through, about 4 minutes. Off heat, mash half of beans to chunky paste; transfer to bowl and cover to keep warm; set aside. Wipe out skillet.

2. In now-empty skillet, heat 2 teaspoons oil over medium-high heat until shimmering. Add kale and ¼ teaspoon salt, cover, and cook until kale begins to wilt, about 2 minutes. Stir in remaining ¼ cup water, cover, and cook until kale is tender, 2 to 4 minutes; transfer to second bowl. Wipe out skillet.

3. Beat eggs, milk, pepper, and remaining ¼ teaspoon salt with fork in bowl until eggs are thoroughly combined and color is pure yellow. Heat remaining 1 teaspoon oil in now-empty skillet over medium-high heat until shimmering. Add egg mixture and, using rubber spatula, constantly and firmly scrape along bottom and sides of skillet until eggs begin to clump and spatula leaves trail on bottom of skillet, 1 to 2 minutes. Off heat, gently stir in kale and constantly fold eggs and kale until clumped and just slightly wet, 30 to 60 seconds. Cover to keep warm.

4. Wrap tortillas in damp dish towel and microwave until warm and pliable, about 1 minute. Arrange tortillas on counter. Spread reserved bean mixture evenly across center of each tortilla. Top with kale-egg mixture, then sprinkle with tomato and drizzle with extra oil to taste. Working with 1 burrito at a time, fold sides of tortilla over filling, then fold up bottom of tortilla and roll tightly around filling. Serve immediately.

Breakfast Burritos with Poblano, Beans, Corn, and Crispy Potatoes

Serves 4 | Total Time 50 minutes

WHY THIS RECIPE WORKS Breakfast burritos first appeared on a menu in 1975 at Tia Sophia's in Santa Fe, New Mexico, but now they're beloved around the country as a handheld, hearty, and customizable morning meal. For this potatoey burrito version, we wanted potatoes that stayed extra-crispy. Frozen tater tots, thawed and then smashed flat in the skillet, did the trick. Along with the tots, we add fluffy scrambled eggs, pinto beans, sharp cheddar cheese, and sautéed vegetables for a vegetarian filling. A potent chipotle sour cream sauce provides tang and heat without adding excess moisture, keeping the burritos neat and portable. Browning the rolled burritos in a hot skillet right before serving produces a crispy golden exterior and helps them stay sealed. If you are spice averse, omit the cayenne pepper and reduce the chipotle chile to 1 tablespoon. To thaw frozen tater tots, either let them sit in the refrigerator for 24 hours or arrange them on a paper towel–lined plate and microwave them for 1½ minutes.

CHIPOTLE SOUR CREAM
¼ cup sour cream
2 tablespoons minced canned chipotle chile in adobo sauce
2 teaspoons lime juice
1 garlic clove, minced
¼ teaspoon cayenne pepper
¼ teaspoon table salt

BURRITOS
6 tablespoons vegetable oil, divided
2 cups frozen tater tots, thawed and patted dry
1 poblano chile, stemmed, seeded, and chopped
½ cup canned pinto beans, rinsed
½ cup frozen corn
¼ cup chopped onion
1 teaspoon chili powder
½ teaspoon table salt
8 large eggs, lightly beaten
3 ounces sharp cheddar cheese, shredded (¾ cup)
4 (10-inch) flour tortillas

Breakfast Burritos with Poblano, Beans, Corn, and Crispy Potatoes

4. Wrap tortillas in damp dish towel and microwave until warm and pliable, about 1 minute. Arrange tortillas on counter. Spread about 1½ tablespoons reserved chipotle sour cream across bottom third of each tortilla, leaving 1-inch border. Top chipotle sour cream with tater tots and eggs. Working with 1 burrito at a time, fold sides of tortilla over filling, then fold up bottom of tortilla and roll tightly around filling.

5. Wipe skillet clean with paper towels. Heat remaining 1 tablespoon oil in again-empty skillet over medium heat until shimmering. Arrange burritos in skillet seam side down and cook until crisp and golden, about 1 minute per side. Serve.

FILLING, ROLLING, AND CRISPING A BURRITO

1. Divide filling among tortillas, then fold sides of tortillas over filling.

2. Fold up bottom and roll tightly.

3. Arrange burritos seam side down in skillet and cook until crisp and golden.

1. FOR THE CHIPOTLE SOUR CREAM Combine all ingredients in bowl; set aside.

2. FOR THE BURRITOS Heat 3 tablespoons oil in 12-inch nonstick skillet over medium-high heat until shimmering. Add tater tots to skillet and press with spatula or underside of dry measuring cup to flatten slightly. Cook until crispy and deep golden brown, about 4 minutes per side. Transfer tater tots to paper towel–lined plate and set aside. Wipe skillet clean with paper towels.

3. Heat 2 tablespoons oil in now-empty skillet over medium heat until shimmering. Add poblano, beans, corn, onion, chili powder, and salt and cook until softened, 6 to 8 minutes. Add eggs and, using rubber spatula, constantly and firmly scrape along bottom and sides of skillet until eggs begin to clump and spatula leaves trail on bottom of skillet, 1 to 2 minutes. Off heat, gently stir in cheddar and constantly fold eggs and cheddar until clumped and just slightly wet, 30 to 60 seconds. Cover to keep warm.

Falafel

Serves 6 (makes 24 falafel) | **Total Time** 55 minutes, plus 8 hours soaking

WHY THIS RECIPE WORKS For moist, tender falafel packed with flavorful seasonings, we start by soaking dried chickpeas overnight to soften them slightly before grinding them into coarse bits along with onion, herbs, garlic, and spices. Instead of binding the dough with uncooked flour, which yields bready fritters, we mix in a cooked flour paste that adds moisture without making the dough too fragile to form and fry. Cooking the fritters at a relatively low 325 degrees allows their particularly moist interiors to fully cook by the time their exteriors are brown and crisp. Use a Dutch oven that holds 6 quarts or more. An equal amount of chickpea flour can be substituted for the all-purpose flour; if using, increase the water in step 3 to ½ cup. Do not substitute canned or quick-soaked chickpeas; they will make leaden falafel.

- 8 ounces (1¼ cups) dried chickpeas, picked over and rinsed
- ¾ cup fresh cilantro leaves and stems
- ¾ cup fresh parsley leaves
- ½ onion, chopped fine
- 2 garlic cloves, minced
- 1½ teaspoons ground coriander
- 1 teaspoon ground cumin
- 1 teaspoon table salt
- ¼ teaspoon cayenne pepper
- ¼ cup all-purpose flour
- 2 teaspoons baking powder
- 2 quarts vegetable oil for frying
- 4 to 6 (8-inch) pitas, halved
- 1 recipe Tahini-Yogurt Sauce (page 81)

1. Place chickpeas in large container and cover with water by 2 to 3 inches. Soak at room temperature for at least 8 hours or up to 24 hours. Drain and rinse well.

2. Process cilantro, parsley, onion, garlic, coriander, cumin, salt, and cayenne in food processor for 5 seconds. Scrape down sides of bowl. Continue to process until mixture resembles pesto, about 5 seconds. Add chickpeas and pulse 6 times. Scrape down sides of bowl. Continue to pulse until chickpeas are coarsely chopped and resemble sesame seeds, about 6 more pulses. Transfer mixture to large bowl and set aside.

3. Whisk flour and ⅓ cup water in bowl until no lumps remain. Microwave, whisking every 10 seconds, until mixture thickens to stiff, smooth, pudding-like consistency that forms mound when dropped from end of whisk into bowl, 40 to 80 seconds. Stir baking powder into flour paste.

4. Add flour paste to chickpea mixture and, using rubber spatula, mix until fully incorporated. Divide mixture into 24 portions and gently roll into golf ball–size spheres, transferring spheres to parchment paper–lined rimmed baking sheet once formed. (Formed falafel can be refrigerated for up to 2 hours.)

5. Set wire rack in second rimmed baking sheet and line with triple layer of paper towels. Heat oil in large Dutch oven over medium-high heat to 325 degrees. Add half of falafel and fry, stirring occasionally, until deep brown, about 5 minutes. Adjust burner, if necessary, to maintain oil temperature of 325 degrees. Using slotted spoon or wire skimmer, transfer falafel to prepared rack to drain. Return oil to 325 degrees and repeat with remaining falafel. Stuff each pita half with falafel balls and serve immediately with tahini-yogurt sauce.

Ta'ameya with Tahini-Yogurt Sauce

Serves 4 (makes 16 ta'ameya) | **Total Time** 1 hour

WHY THIS RECIPE WORKS Falafel (balls or patties) nestled into pita bread and adorned with vegetables and tahini sauce is a delectable street cart food across the Mediterranean. While a lot of falafel is made from ground chickpeas, falafel in Egypt, known as ta'ameya there, uses sweet, nutty fava beans. The fried patties have a gorgeous green hue amplified by plentiful fresh herbs and scallions. They're flavored with warm spices and often coated with sesame seeds, which increase the crispness that encases luscious, creamy interiors. Ground pita and an egg are key (and resourceful) binders, and baking powder gives the mash a soft fluffiness. No falafel is complete without toppings, and creamy tahini-yogurt sauce plus juicy tomatoes, crisp cucumbers, and onions, add richness and freshness. Be sure to set up the ice water bath before cooking the fava beans, as plunging them immediately in the cold water after blanching retains their bright green color and ensures that they don't overcook. You can use a quarter of an English cucumber in place of the Persian cucumbers. When taking the temperature of the frying oil, tilt the skillet so the oil pools on one side.

Substitution: You can use 1 pound 5 ounces (4⅓ cups) frozen shelled fava beans, thawed, in place of the fresh favas. Be sure to remove the sheath. Skip step 1 if using frozen favas.

4⅓ pounds fava beans, shelled (4⅓ cups)
¾ cup torn pita, plus 2 (8-inch) pitas, halved
½ teaspoon fennel seeds, toasted and cracked
¼ cup chopped fresh cilantro and/or parsley
1 large egg, lightly beaten
2 scallions, sliced thin
2 garlic cloves, minced
½ teaspoon baking powder
½ teaspoon ground coriander
½ teaspoon ground cumin
½ teaspoon table salt
¼ teaspoon pepper
2 teaspoons sesame seeds
½ cup extra-virgin olive oil for frying
1 tomato, cored and chopped
2 Persian cucumbers, halved lengthwise and sliced thin
½ red onion, sliced thin
½ cup Tahini-Yogurt Sauce
1 recipe Pink Pickled Turnips (optional; page 82)
1 teaspoon nigella seeds (optional)

Ta'ameya with Tahini-Yogurt Sauce

1. Bring 4 quarts water to boil in large pot. Fill large bowl halfway with ice and water. Add fava beans to boiling water and cook for 1 minute. Using slotted spoon, transfer fava beans to ice water and let cool, about 2 minutes. Transfer fava beans to triple layer of paper towels and dry well. Using paring knife, make small cut along edge of each bean through waxy sheath, then gently squeeze sheath to release bean; discard sheath. Set fava beans aside.

2. Process torn pita pieces and fennel seeds in food processor until finely ground, about 15 seconds. Add fava beans, cilantro, egg, scallions, garlic, baking powder, coriander, cumin, salt, and pepper and pulse until fava beans are coarsely chopped and mixture is cohesive, about 15 pulses, scraping down sides of bowl as needed. Working with 2 tablespoons mixture at a time, shape into 2-inch-wide patties and transfer to large plate (you should have 16 patties). Sprinkle sesame seeds evenly over falafel patties and press lightly to adhere.

3. Set wire rack in rimmed baking sheet and line with triple layer of paper towels. Heat oil in 12-inch nonstick skillet over medium heat to 350 degrees. Add half of ta'ameya and fry until deep golden brown, 2 to 3 minutes per side, using 2 spatulas to carefully flip patties. Transfer to prepared rack to drain and repeat with remaining ta'ameya, adjusting heat as needed if ta'ameya begins to brown too quickly. Stuff each pita half with ta'ameya, tomato, cucumbers, and onion, and top with tahini-yogurt sauce; pickled turnips if using; and nigella seeds, if using. Serve.

Tahini-Yogurt Sauce
Makes 1 cup | **Total Time** 40 minutes `FAST`

⅓ cup tahini
⅓ cup plain Greek yogurt
¼ cup water
3 tablespoons lemon juice
1 garlic clove, minced
¾ teaspoon table salt

Whisk all ingredients in bowl until combined. Season with salt and pepper to taste. Let sit until flavors meld, about 30 minutes. (Sauce can be refrigerated for up to 4 days.)

Pink Pickled Turnips

Makes Two 1-pint jars (4 cups) | **Total Time** ¾ hour, plus 2 days chilling VEGAN

1¼ cups white wine vinegar
1¼ cups water
2½ tablespoons sugar
1½ tablespoons kosher salt
3 garlic cloves, smashed and peeled
¾ teaspoon whole allspice berries
¾ teaspoon black peppercorns
1 pound turnips, peeled and cut into 2 by ½-inch sticks
1 small beet, trimmed, peeled, and cut into 1-inch pieces

1. Bring vinegar, water, sugar, salt, garlic, allspice, and peppercorns to boil in medium saucepan over medium-high heat. Cover, remove from heat, and let steep for 10 minutes. Strain brine through fine-mesh strainer, then return to saucepan.
2. Place two 1-pint jars in bowl and place under hot running water until heated through, 1 to 2 minutes; shake dry. Pack turnips vertically into hot jars with beet pieces evenly distributed throughout.
3. Return brine to brief boil. Using funnel and ladle, pour hot brine over vegetables to cover. Let jars cool to room temperature, cover with lids, and refrigerate for at least 2 days before serving. (Pickled turnips can be refrigerated for up to 1 month; turnips will soften over time.)

Sumac Onions

Makes 2 cups | **Total Time** 1¼ hours VEGAN

1 red onion, halved and ¼-inch thick
2 tablespoons lemon juice
2 tablespoons red wine vinegar
1 tablespoon extra-virgin olive oil
1 tablespoon ground sumac
½ teaspoon sugar
¼ teaspoon table salt

Combine all ingredients in bowl. Let sit, stirring occasionally for 1 hour. (Onions can be refrigerated for up to 1 week).

Spiced Chickpea Gyros with Tahini Yogurt

Serves 4 | **Total Time** 30 minutes FAST

WHY THIS RECIPE WORKS Looking for a vegetarian meal in a hurry? Try this fresh take on pita sandwiches. It reimagines protein-rich canned chickpeas by making them the star filling. Mashing the chickpeas lightly breaks their skins and allows them to soak up the flavors of the seasonings. Red onion, pepperoncini, and cucumber add three different kinds of crunch.

1 cup plain Greek yogurt
¼ cup tahini
1 teaspoon table salt, divided
2 (15-ounce) cans chickpeas, rinsed
2 tablespoons chili-garlic sauce
2 teaspoons ground cumin
4 (8-inch) pitas, lightly toasted
½ English cucumber, halved lengthwise and sliced thin on 3-inch bias
½ cup pepperoncini, stemmed and sliced into thin rings
¼ cup thinly sliced red onion

1. Combine yogurt, tahini, and ½ teaspoon salt in bowl; set aside. Using potato masher, very coarsely mash chickpeas in medium bowl. Stir in chili-garlic sauce, cumin, and remaining ½ teaspoon salt; set aside.
2. Spread reserved yogurt sauce evenly over 1 side of each pita (use all of it). Divide reserved chickpea mixture, cucumber, pepperoncini, and onion evenly among pitas. Fold pitas in half, wrap tightly in parchment paper, and serve.

Shawarma-Spiced Tofu Wraps

Serves 4 to 6 | **Total Time** 1 hour, plus 1 hour chilling

WHY THIS RECIPE WORKS Crispy charred tofu fingers burst with bold spices and garlic in this satisfying and texturally varied vegetarian sandwich. The flavors of street cart Middle Eastern shawarma are the inspiration, a marinade to deeply season the tofu relying on classic shawarma spices of sumac, fenugreek, paprika, cumin, and garlic. Lemon juice and honey provide well-rounded, complex flavor, the latter also delivering impeccable caramelization. The intense heat of the broiler ably blooms the flavors, burnishing them on the crispy tofu. Tossing the finished tofu in some reserved marinade amplifies the smoky flavor. We wrap the tofu in warm, fluffy pitas and then pile on some shawarma topping treats: tomatoes, sumac onions, pickles, and fresh herbs, plus a finishing drizzle of cooling, creamy tahini-yogurt sauce. The tofu fingers are delicate and may break while turning; this will not affect the final wraps.

28	ounces firm or extra-firm tofu
½	cup extra-virgin olive oil
6	garlic cloves, minced
1½	tablespoons ground sumac
1	tablespoon ground fenugreek
2	teaspoons smoked paprika
1½	teaspoons ground cumin
1	teaspoon table salt
¼	cup lemon juice (2 lemons)
3	tablespoons honey
4–6	(8-inch) pitas, warmed
1	tomato, cored and chopped
½	cup chopped fresh parsley and/or mint
½	cup dill pickle slices
½	cup Sumac Onions (optional; page 82)
½	cup Tahini-Yogurt Sauce (page 81)

1. Cut tofu crosswise into ½-inch-thick slabs, then slice slabs lengthwise into ½-inch-thick fingers. Spread tofu over paper towel–lined rimmed baking sheet, let drain for 20 minutes, then gently press dry with paper towels.

2. Microwave oil, garlic, sumac, fenugreek, paprika, cumin, and salt in medium bowl, stirring occasionally, until fragrant, 30 to 60 seconds. Whisk in lemon juice and honey until honey has dissolved. Measure out and reserve ¼ cup marinade. (Reserved marinade can be refrigerated for up to 24 hours; bring to room temperature and whisk to recombine before using.)

3. Arrange tofu in single layer on second rimmed baking sheet and spoon marinade evenly over top. Using your hands, gently turn tofu to coat with marinade. Cover and refrigerate for at least 1 hour or up to 24 hours.

4. Adjust oven rack 6 inches from broiler element and heat broiler. Line rimmed baking sheet with aluminum foil. Transfer tofu to prepared sheet and arrange in single layer, spaced evenly apart. Broil tofu until well browned on first side, 10 to 15 minutes, rotating sheet halfway through broiling. Gently flip tofu and continue to broil until well browned on second side, 10 to 15 minutes, rotating sheet halfway through broiling. Transfer tofu and reserved marinade to large bowl and gently toss to coat. Divide tofu evenly among pitas and top with tomato; parsley; pickles; sumac onions, if using; and tahini-yogurt sauce. Serve.

Spiced Chickpea Gyros with Tahini Yogurt

Shawarma-Spiced Tofu Wraps

Black Bean and Cheese Arepas

Serves 4 (makes 8 arepas) | **Total Time** 1 hour

WHY THIS RECIPE WORKS Arepas are a type of corn cake popular in Latin countries. The Venezuelan variety is served as sandwiches that are split open and stuffed with anything from meat and cheese to beans, corn, even fish. The arepas are made simply using masarepa (an instant flour made from precooked corn) along with water and salt, but getting the consistency right can be a challenge. We found that using just a half-cup more water than masarepa produces a dough that is easy to shape, and a small amount of baking powder lightens its texture. We shape the dough into rounds, brown them in a skillet, and finish them in the oven. Our filling mixes canned black beans with Monterey Jack cheese. Cilantro adds freshness, lime juice a bit of acidity, and chili powder a hint of heat.

AREPAS
- 2 cups (10 ounces) masarepa blanca
- 1 teaspoon table salt
- 1 teaspoon baking powder
- 2½ cups warm water
- ¼ cup vegetable oil, divided

BLACK BEAN FILLING
- 1 (15-ounce) can black beans, rinsed
- 4 ounces Monterey Jack cheese, shredded (1 cup)
- 2 tablespoons minced fresh cilantro
- 2 scallions, sliced thin
- 1 tablespoon lime juice
- ¼ teaspoon chili powder

1. FOR THE AREPAS Adjust oven rack to middle position and heat oven to 400 degrees. Whisk masarepa, salt, and baking powder together in large bowl. Gradually add water, stirring until combined. Using generous ⅓ cup dough for each round, form into eight 3-inch rounds, each about ½ inch thick.

2. Heat 2 tablespoons oil in 12-inch nonstick skillet over medium-high heat until shimmering. Add 4 arepas and cook until golden on both sides, about 4 minutes per side. Transfer arepas to wire rack set in rimmed baking sheet. Wipe out skillet with paper towels and repeat with remaining 2 tablespoons oil and remaining 4 arepas. (Fried arepas can be refrigerated for up to 3 days or frozen for up to 1 month. Increase baking time as needed; if frozen, do not thaw before baking.) Bake arepas on wire rack until they sound hollow when tapped on bottom, about 10 minutes.

3. FOR THE FILLING Meanwhile, using potato masher or fork, mash beans in bowl until most are broken. Stir in Monterey Jack, cilantro, scallions, lime juice, and chili powder and season with salt and pepper to taste.

4. Using fork, gently split hot, baked arepas open. Stuff each with generous 3 tablespoons filling. Serve.

Pupusas with Beans and Cheese

Serves 4 (makes 8 pupusas) | **Total Time** 50 minutes, plus 20 minutes resting

WHY THIS RECIPE WORKS Pupusas are savory stuffed corn cakes with a long history in El Salvador and Honduras. There, these enticing packages are made by stuffing beans, cheese, braised meats, or some combination thereof into a ball of corn flour dough called masa. Masa harina, also known as "dough flour," is masa that has been dried and ground again into flour. Hydrating the masa harina with boiling rather than room-temperature water allows the starches in the flour to absorb it more quickly and completely, resulting in a well-hydrated dough that is easy to work with and doesn't dry out when cooked. The proper ratio of masa dough to filling ensures that each bite of pupusa includes plenty of melted cheese filling. Pressing the stuffed pupusas into 4-inch disks between sheets of plastic ensures uniform thickness and allows us to cook four pupusas at once in a 12-inch skillet. The crunch and acidic brightness of curtido (a spicy slaw) and fresh salsa perfectly complement the tender, savory patties. For an accurate measurement of boiling water, bring a kettle of water to a boil and then measure out the desired amount. Properly hydrated masa dough should be tacky, requiring damp hands to keep it from sticking to your palms. If the dough feels the slightest bit dry at any time, knead in warm tap water, 1 teaspoon at a time, until the dough is tacky. An occasional leak while frying the pupusas is to be expected, and the browned cheese is delicious.

- 2 cups (8 ounces) masa harina
- 1 teaspoon table salt, divided
- 2 cups boiling water, plus warm tap water as needed
- 2 teaspoons vegetable oil, divided
- 1 (15-ounce) can kidney beans, rinsed
- 5 ounces Monterey Jack cheese, shredded (1¼ cups)
- ½ teaspoon ground cumin
- ½ teaspoon dried oregano
- ⅛ teaspoon cayenne pepper
- 1 recipe Quick Salsa
- 1 recipe Curtido (page 86)

1. Using marker, draw 4-inch circle in center of 1 side of 1-quart or 1-gallon zipper-lock bag. Cut open seams along both sides of bag but leave bottom seam intact so bag opens completely.

2. Mix masa harina and ½ teaspoon salt together in medium bowl. Add boiling water and 1 teaspoon oil and mix with rubber spatula until soft dough forms. Cover dough and let rest for 20 minutes.

3. While dough rests, line rimmed baking sheet with parchment paper. Place beans in medium bowl and mash with potato masher or fork until chunky paste forms. Add Monterey Jack, cumin, oregano, cayenne, and remaining ½ teaspoon salt and stir until well combined. Form mixture into 8 balls, weighing about 1½ ounces each, and place balls on 1 half of prepared sheet.

4. Knead dough in bowl for 15 to 20 seconds. Test dough's hydration by flattening golf ball–size piece. If cracks larger than ¼ inch form around edges, add warm tap water, 2 teaspoons at a time, until dough is soft and slightly tacky. Transfer dough to counter, shape into large ball, and divide into 8 equal pieces. Using your damp hands, roll 1 dough piece into ball and place on empty half of prepared sheet. Cover with damp dish towel. Repeat with remaining dough pieces.

5. Place open cut bag marked side down on counter. Place 1 dough ball in center of circle. Fold other side of bag over ball. Gently press dough to 4-inch diameter, using flat-bottomed pot or pie plate and using circle drawn on bag as guide. Turn out disk into your palm and place 1 ball filling in center. Bring sides of dough up around filling and pinch top to seal. Remoisten your hands and roll ball until smooth, smoothing any cracks with your damp fingertip. Return ball to bag and slowly press to 4-inch diameter. Pinch closed any small cracks that form at edges. Return pupusa to sheet and cover with damp dish towel. Repeat with remaining dough and filling.

6. Heat remaining 1 teaspoon oil in 12-inch nonstick skillet over medium-high heat until shimmering. Wipe skillet clean with paper towels. Carefully lay 4 pupusas in skillet and cook until spotty brown on both sides, 2 to 4 minutes per side. Transfer to platter and repeat with remaining 4 pupusas. Serve warm with salsa and curtido.

Pupusas with Beans and Cheese

Quick Salsa

Makes 2 cups | **Total Time** 1¼ hours

FAST **VEGAN**

- ¼ small red onion
- 2 tablespoons minced fresh cilantro
- ½ small jalapeño chile, seeded and minced
- 1 (14.5-ounce) can diced tomatoes, drained
- 2 teaspoons lime juice, plus extra for seasoning
- 1 small garlic clove, minced
- ¼ teaspoon table salt
- Pinch pepper

Pulse onion, cilantro, and jalapeño in food processor until finely chopped, 5 pulses, scraping down sides of bowl as needed. Add tomatoes, lime juice, garlic, salt, and pepper and process until smooth, 20 to 30 seconds. Season with salt and extra lime juice to taste.

Tomatillo Chicken Huaraches

Serves 4 (makes 4 huaraches) | **Total Time** 1½ hours, plus 30 minutes resting

WHY THIS RECIPE WORKS Generously sized huaraches are named for the iconic huarache woven leather sandal. The hearty huaraches of Mexico City consist of masa dough filled and topped with varying proteins, vegetables, cheeses, and sauces. This version features a stuffing of rich refried beans with a topping of shredded chicken mixed with tomatillo salsa; it's all garnished with radishes and queso fresco. Well-hydrated dough is important because you need to shape and flatten the dough twice: once before adding the stuffing and once after you fold the dough around it. For an accurate measurement of boiling water, bring a kettle of water to a boil and then measure out the desired amount. Properly hydrated masa dough should be tacky, requiring damp hands to keep it from sticking. If the dough feels the slightest bit dry at any time, knead in warm tap water, 1 teaspoon at a time, until the dough is tacky. We like using Perfect Poached Chicken (page 176) here, but any cooked chicken would work.

3 cups (12 ounces) masa harina
1¾ teaspoons table salt, divided
4 cups boiling water, plus warm tap water as needed
1 (15-ounce) can pinto beans, rinsed
¼ cup chicken broth
5 tablespoons lard, divided
½ onion, chopped fine
½ jalapeño chile, stemmed, seeded, and minced
2 garlic cloves, minced
1 teaspoon ground cumin
1 tablespoon chopped fresh cilantro plus ¼ cup fresh cilantro leaves
1 teaspoon lime juice
3 cups cooked chicken, shredded into bite-size pieces
3 cups jarred tomatillo salsa
4 radishes, sliced thin
4 ounces queso fresco, crumbled (1 cup)

1. Whisk masa harina and 1¼ teaspoons salt together in large bowl. Add boiling water and mix with rubber spatula until soft dough forms. Cover with damp dish towel and let rest for 30 minutes.

Curtido

Serves 4 | **Total Time** 1¼ hours VEGAN

1 cup cider vinegar
½ cup water
1 tablespoon sugar
1½ teaspoons table salt
½ head green cabbage, cored and sliced thin (6 cups)
1 onion, sliced thin
1 large carrot, peeled and shredded
1 jalapeño chile, stemmed, seeded, and minced
1 teaspoon dried oregano
1 cup chopped fresh cilantro

Whisk vinegar, water, sugar, and salt in large bowl until sugar is dissolved. Add cabbage, onion, carrot, jalapeño, and oregano and toss to combine. Cover and refrigerate for at least 1 hour or up to 24 hours. Toss slaw, then drain. Return slaw to bowl and stir in cilantro.

2. Meanwhile, process beans and broth in food processor until smooth, about 30 seconds, scraping down sides of bowl as needed; set aside. Heat 1 tablespoon lard in 12-inch nonstick skillet over medium heat until shimmering. Add onion, jalapeño, and remaining ½ teaspoon salt and cook over medium heat until vegetables are softened and beginning to brown, 5 to 7 minutes.

3. Stir in garlic and cumin and cook until fragrant, about 30 seconds. Stir in reserved beans and cook, stirring often, until well combined and thickened slightly, about 5 minutes. Off heat, stir in chopped cilantro and lime juice and season with salt and pepper to taste; set aside to cool slightly. Once cool enough to handle, divide beans into 4 equal portions using greased ⅓-cup dry measuring cup. Transfer to large plate and set aside. Wipe out skillet.

4. Adjust oven rack to middle position and heat oven to 200 degrees. Set wire rack in rimmed baking sheet. Once dough has rested for 30 minutes, test dough's hydration by flattening golf ball–size piece. If cracks larger than ¼ inch form around edges, knead in warm tap water by hand, 2 teaspoons at a time, until dough is soft and slightly tacky. Transfer dough to counter, shape into large ball, divide into 4 equal pieces, and place on parchment-lined second rimmed baking sheet. Cover dough with damp dish towel. Cut open seams along both sides of 1-gallon zipper-lock bag, leaving bottom seam intact.

5. Working with 1 piece of dough at a time, repeat testing hydration and add extra water as needed. Shape dough into rough oval, about 4 inches long, then enclose in split bag (oval should be perpendicular to counter edge and seam of bag should be on your right). Press dough flat into ½-inch-thick, 6-inch-long oval using flat-bottomed pot or pie plate. Peel away plastic, smooth any cracks around edges of round, and place 1 reserved refried bean portion in center of dough oval. (If at any time dough feels dry, moisten your hands to smooth out any cracks and make dough pliable.)

6. Grasping side edges of zipper-lock bag, lift to bring sides of dough up around filling and press edges of dough to seal. Remoisten your hands, unfold bag, and smooth any cracks with your damp fingers. Flip dough seam side down, enclose in split bag, and slowly press dough flat into a 9-inch oval about ¼ inch thick between split bag. Return shaped dough to sheet, and cover with damp dish towel while shaping remaining dough.

7. Heat 1 tablespoon lard in clean, dry skillet over medium-high heat until shimmering. Gently place 1 dough oval in skillet and cook until dark spotty brown on first side, 4 to 6 minutes. Using 2 spatulas, gently flip huarache and continue to cook until second side is crispy and dark spotty brown, 4 to 6 minutes; transfer to prepared rack and hold in warm oven. Repeat with remaining lard and remaining dough ovals.

8. Meanwhile, microwave chicken and salsa in large bowl until warmed through, 1 to 3 minutes. Top huaraches with chicken-salsa mixture and sprinkle with radishes, queso fresco, and cilantro leaves. Serve.

SHAPING HUARACHES

1. Shape dough piece into 4-inch oval and enclose in split plastic bag. Using flat-bottomed pot or pie plate, press dough into 6-inch oval about ½ inch thick.

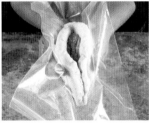

2. Smooth any cracks around edges of round and place bean mixture in center of masa. Grasping side edges of bag, lift to bring sides of dough up around filling; pinch top of dough to seal.

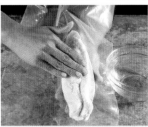

3. Remoisten your hands, unfold bag, and smooth any cracks with your damp fingers.

4. Flip dough seam side down, enclose in split bag, and press dough flat into 9-inch oval about ¼ inch thick between split bag using flat-bottomed pot or pie plate.

Tacu Tacu with Salsa Criolla

Serves 4 | **Total Time** 2¾ hours, plus 8½ hours brining and resting

WHY THIS RECIPE WORKS Tacu tacu is a Peruvian rice and bean cake commonly served at breakfast or lunch. For breakfast, it is topped with eggs and for lunch, it's often served with a side of steak. Regardless of time of day, tacu tacu is normally accompanied by salsa criolla, a Peruvian onion salsa. The lime in the salsa really perks up this dish while the onions add a nice crunch. The bean of choice is the canary bean; a creamy mild-flavored variety. Following traditional preparation, we blend a portion of the beans to help bind the mixture together. Tacu tacu has a mild kick due to the addition of aji amarillo paste, a yellow chili pepper paste that is a staple in Peruvian cuisine. We ultimately decided to serve it with eggs and salsa criolla for a delicious filling breakfast. This is a great way to use up leftover rice; substitute 2 cups day-old cooked rice for the cup of dried rice.

Substitution: You can use dried cannellini beans or two (15-ounce) cans rinsed cannellini beans in place of the dried canary beans; skip steps 1 and 3 if using canned beans.

TACU TACU

- 1½ tablespoons table salt for brining
- 8 ounces (1 cup) dried canary beans, picked over and rinsed
  Table salt for cooking beans plus ¾ teaspoon plus ⅛ teaspoon salt, divided
- 1 cup long-grain white rice, rinsed
- 5 tablespoons extra-virgin olive oil, divided
- ½ red onion, chopped fine
- 2 tablespoons aji amarillo paste
- 3 garlic cloves, minced to paste
- 1 teaspoon ground cumin
- ¾ teaspoon dried oregano
- ¼ teaspoon pepper, divided
- 1 cup vegetable broth
- 3 tablespoon chopped fresh cilantro
- 4 large eggs
  Lime wedges

SALSA CRIOLLA

- ½ red onion, sliced thin
- 1 tablespoon lime juice
- ¼ teaspoon table salt
  Pinch pepper
- 2 tablespoon chopped fresh cilantro

Tacu Tacu with
Salsa Criolla

1. FOR THE TACU TACU Dissolve 1½ tablespoons salt in 2 quarts cold water in large container. Add beans and soak at room temperature for at least 8 hours or up to 24 hours. Drain and rinse well. (If you're pressed for time, see page 13 for information on quick brining your beans.)

2. FOR THE SALSA CRIOLLA Soak onion in ice water for 10 minutes. Drain well and pat dry with paper towels. Combine onion, lime juice, salt, and pepper in bowl. Cover with plastic wrap and refrigerate for at least 30 minutes or up to 2 days. Stir in cilantro just before serving.

3. Bring soaked beans and 7 cups water to simmer in large saucepan. Simmer, partially covered, over medium-low heat until beans are tender, 30 to 40 minutes. Remove from heat, stir in 1½ teaspoons salt, cover, and let sit until completely tender, about 15 minutes.

4. Drain beans and transfer to large bowl. Process 1 cup cooked beans in food processor until smooth, about 30 seconds, scraping sides of processor as needed. Transfer to bowl with remaining cooked beans, stirring and mashing as needed to combine; set aside.

5. Meanwhile, bring rice, 1½ cups water, and ¼ teaspoon salt to simmer in medium saucepan over medium-high heat. Reduce heat to medium-low, cover and simmer gently until rice is tender and all liquid has been absorbed, 11 to 13 minutes. Remove from heat and let sit, covered, for 10 minutes. Fluff rice with fork and set aside.

6. Adjust oven racks to upper-middle and lower-middle positions and heat oven to 200 degrees. Heat 1 tablespoon oil in 12-inch nonstick skillet over medium heat until shimmering. Add onion and cook, stirring occasionally, until softened and just beginning to brown, 5 to 7 minutes. Stir in aji amarillo paste, garlic, cumin, oregano, ⅛ teaspoon pepper, and ½ teaspoon salt and cook until fragrant, about 1 minute. Off heat, add reserved bean mixture and reserved rice and stir to combine. Return skillet to medium heat, stir in broth, and bring to simmer. Cook liquid is absorbed and rice mixture thickens, 3 to 5 minutes, stirring frequently; mixture should be sticky. Transfer to bowl, stir in cilantro, and let sit for 10 minutes.

7. In clean, dry skillet, heat ½ tablespoon oil over medium heat until shimmering. Add one-quarter rice and bean mixture and, using rubber spatula, press mixture against 1 side of skillet while tilting skillet towards tacu tacu (tilting makes it easier to pack rice and bean mixture firmly). Firmly press mixture until it is a rough oval and measures about 8 inches in length. Cook until golden brown along edges, 2 to 4 minutes.

8. Place skillet flat on stovetop and, using 2 spatulas, carefully flip tacu tacu. (If it breaks, firmly press into side of skillet matching shape of tacu tacu to bring back together.) Add ½ tablespoon oil to skillet and nestle tacu tacu into side of skillet that matches its shape. Repeat firmly pressing tacu tacu into side of skillet while tilting skillet slightly. Cook until golden brown along edges, 2 to 4 minutes. Carefully slide tacu tacu onto serving plate and transfer to oven to keep warm. Repeat with remaining rice and bean mixture and 3 tablespoons oil.

9. Heat remaining 1 tablespoon oil in clean, dry skillet over medium heat until shimmering. Add eggs to skillet and sprinkle with remaining ⅛ teaspoon salt and remaining ⅛ teaspoon pepper. Cover and cook for 1 minute. Remove skillet from heat and let sit, covered, for 15 to 45 seconds for runny yolks, 45 to 60 seconds for soft but set yolks, or about 2 minutes for medium-set yolks. Top each tacu tacu with 1 egg and serve with salsa criolla and lime wedges.

MAKING TACU TACU

1. Cook rice and grains with aromatics, then add broth, cooking until mixture is sticky.

2. Tilt skillet slightly and press rice and bean mixture firmly into side of skillet to create cohesive cake.

3. After browning 1 side, flip tacu tacu using 2 spatulas, and continue to cook until golden brown on second side.

Poblano and Corn Hand Pies

Serves 8 (makes 16 hand pies) | **Total Time** 1¾ hours, plus 1¼ hours chilling and cooling

WHY THIS RECIPE WORKS Stuffed with pinto beans, corn, poblano chiles, scallions, and pepper Jack cheese, these satisfying hand pies pack a belly-warming heat. They're also great to make ahead and keep on hand for portable meals or snacks. Vegetable shortening creates a dough that's easy to work with and sturdy enough to stuff with the filling mixture while baking up tender and flaky. Using vegetable broth instead of water enhances the dough's savory quality. For the filling, mashing a portion of the pinto beans with some of their canning liquid creates a moist binder so that it won't fall out messily when you take a bite. We oil and preheat the baking sheets to make a searing-hot cooking surface for the hand pies, which helps give them crisp, golden-brown crusts without the need for deep frying. Poking each hand pie with the tines of a fork before baking provides a vent for the steam to escape. The tangy crema is wonderful for dolloping or dipping.

CREMA

½ cup mayonnaise

½ cup sour cream

2 tablespoons lime juice

2 tablespoons whole milk

FILLING

1 (15-ounce) can pinto beans, rinsed with 3 tablespoons liquid reserved, divided

1½ cups frozen corn, thawed

6 ounces pepper Jack cheese, shredded (1½ cups)

3 scallions, white parts minced, green parts sliced thin

2 tablespoons vegetable oil

3 poblano chiles, stemmed, seeded, and cut into ¼-inch pieces

2 garlic cloves, minced

2 teaspoons minced fresh oregano or ½ teaspoon dried

1½ teaspoons ground cumin

1½ teaspoons ground coriander

½ teaspoon table salt

¼ teaspoon pepper

DOUGH

4 cups (20 ounces) all-purpose flour

2 teaspoons table salt

1 teaspoon baking powder

8 tablespoons vegetable shortening, cut into ½-inch pieces

1 cup vegetable broth

2 large eggs, lightly beaten

5 tablespoons vegetable oil, divided

1. FOR THE CREMA Whisk all ingredients together in bowl. Refrigerate until ready to serve.

2. FOR THE FILLING Place one-quarter of beans in large bowl; add reserved bean liquid; and, using potato masher or fork, mash coarse. Stir in corn, pepper Jack, scallion greens, and remaining beans.

3. Heat oil in 12-inch nonstick skillet over medium-high heat until shimmering. Add poblanos and scallion whites and cook, stirring occasionally, until softened, 3 to 5 minutes. Stir in garlic, oregano, cumin, coriander, salt, and pepper and cook until fragrant, about 30 seconds. Transfer poblano mixture to bowl with bean mixture and stir well to combine. Season with salt and pepper to taste and let cool slightly. Refrigerate until completely cool, 45 minutes to 1 hour.

4. FOR THE DOUGH Meanwhile, process flour, salt, and baking powder in food processor until combined, about 3 seconds. Add shortening and pulse until mixture resembles coarse cornmeal, 6 to 8 pulses. Add broth and eggs and pulse until dough just comes together, about 5 pulses. Transfer dough to lightly floured counter and knead until dough forms smooth ball, about 20 seconds. Divide dough into 16 equal pieces. With your cupped hand, form each piece into smooth, tight ball.

5. Adjust oven racks to upper-middle and lower-middle positions, place 1 rimmed baking sheet on each rack, and heat oven to 425 degrees. Working with 1 dough ball at a time, roll each dough ball on lightly floured counter into 6-inch circle, covering dough rounds with plastic while rolling remaining dough. Place heaping ¼ cup filling in center of dough round. Brush edges of dough with water and fold dough over filling. Press to seal, trim any ragged edges, and crimp edges with tines of fork. Pierce top of each hand pie once with fork.

6. Drizzle 2 tablespoons oil over surface of each hot baking sheet, then return sheets to oven for 2 minutes. Brush tops of hand pies with remaining 1 tablespoon oil. Carefully place 8 hand pies on each prepared sheet and bake until golden brown, 20 to 25 minutes, switching and rotating sheets halfway through baking. Transfer hand pies to wire rack and let cool completely, about 30 minutes. Serve with crema.

New Mexican Bean-and-Cheese Turnovers with Green Chile

Serves 8 (makes 8 turnovers) | **Total Time** 2¼ hours, plus 30 minutes cooling

WHY THIS RECIPE WORKS The golden, stuffed bean-and-cheese sopaipillas we ate at Mary & Tito's Cafe in Albuquerque, New Mexico, came smothered in a lightly spicy green chile sauce that beautifully coated every bite. To re-create them, we use refried beans enhanced with porky lard and onion. We stuff the beans and some cheddar cheese in a homemade flour tortilla dough. Sealing the dough with water and twisting the sealed edge keeps the filling from oozing out while frying. Without access to New Mexican chiles, we approximate their flavor using Anaheim chiles and a jalapeño. Broiling the chiles adds smokiness while intensifying their sweetness for a punchy chile sauce. Use a Dutch oven that holds 6 quarts or more for this recipe. We prefer our homemade Refried Beans (page 295), but you may use store-bought. You can substitute vegetable shortening for the lard, if desired.

New Mexican Bean-and-Cheese Turnovers with Green Chile

DOUGH

2¾ cups (13¾ ounces) all-purpose flour
1½ teaspoons table salt
½ teaspoon baking powder
6 tablespoons lard, cut into ½-inch pieces
¾ cup plus 2 tablespoons water

GREEN CHILE SAUCE

2 pounds Anaheim chiles
1 jalapeño chile
2 tablespoons lard
1 cup finely chopped onion
3 garlic cloves, minced
1 tablespoon all-purpose flour
1 cup chicken broth
1 teaspoon table salt
8 ounces mild cheddar cheese, shredded (2 cups), divided
2 cups refried beans, divided
2 quarts peanut or vegetable oil, for frying

1. FOR THE DOUGH Whisk flour, salt, and baking powder together in large bowl. Rub lard into flour mixture with your fingers until mixture resembles coarse meal. Stir in water until combined. Turn out dough onto clean counter and knead briefly to form cohesive ball, 6 to 8 turns. Divide dough into 8 equal portions, about 2¾ ounces each (scant ⅓ cup), then roll into balls. Transfer dough balls to plate, cover with plastic wrap, and refrigerate until firm, at least 30 minutes or up to 2 days.

2. FOR THE GREEN CHILE SAUCE Adjust oven rack 6 inches from broiler element and heat broiler. Line rimmed baking sheet with aluminum foil. Arrange Anaheims and jalapeño in single layer on prepared sheet. Broil until chiles are soft and mostly blackened, about 5 minutes per side, rotating sheet halfway through broiling. Transfer chiles to bowl and cover with plastic; let cool for 10 minutes.

3. Remove skins from chiles with spoon. Stem and seed Anaheims, then chop into ¼-inch pieces. Stem (but do not seed) jalapeño; chop into ¼-inch pieces.

4. Heat lard in large saucepan over medium heat until shimmering. Add onion and cook until softened, about 3 minutes. Stir in garlic and cook until fragrant, about 30 seconds. Stir in flour and cook for 1 minute. Stir in broth, salt, Anaheims, and jalapeño and bring to simmer. Simmer until slightly thickened, about 6 minutes. Season with salt to taste; cover and set aside.

5. Keeping other dough balls covered with damp dish towel, roll 1 dough ball into 7-inch circle on lightly floured counter. Lightly squeeze ¼ cup cheddar cheese in your palm to form ball. Place cheese in center of dough round, followed by ¼ cup refried beans. Moisten edges of dough round with water. Fold dough round in half, creating half-moon shape to enclose filling, and press to seal.

6. Moisten top of sealed edge with water. Starting at 1 end, fold, slightly twist, and pinch dough diagonally across sealed edge between your thumb and index finger. Continue pinching and twisting dough around seam to create decorative rope edge. Transfer to parchment paper–lined baking sheet. Repeat with remaining dough balls, cheese, and refried beans. Using paring knife, poke ½-inch hole in center of each sopaipilla. (Filled sopaipillas can be covered and refrigerated for up to 24 hours.)

7. Line baking sheet with triple layer of paper towels. Add oil to large Dutch oven until it measures about 1½ inches deep and heat over medium-high heat to 375 degrees. Add 4 sopaipillas to oil and fry until golden brown, about 3 minutes per side. Adjust burner as needed to maintain oil temperature between 350 and 375 degrees. Transfer fried sopaipillas to prepared sheet. Return oil to 375 degrees and repeat with remaining 4 sopaipillas.

8. Reheat green chile sauce over medium-high heat until hot. Serve sopaipillas topped with chile sauce.

Cauliflower Chickpea Flatbread with Romesco

Serves 4 to 6 (makes two 12-inch flatbreads)
Total Time 2 hours

WHY THIS RECIPE WORKS Cauliflower pizza crusts have firmly secured their place on supermarket shelves, thanks to the undeniable appeal of a vegetable-based crust. But it can be tricky to create a cauliflower crust or flatbread that doesn't either crumble or stick to the pan (or both) when you try to serve it. This cauliflower-based flatbread takes a cue from Farinata (page 45) to create a strong, durable structure by incorporating chickpea flour. To add irresistible crispness, we stir in a generous amount of grated Parmesan cheese, which essentially fries in the oven to create a gloriously crisp crust. If you don't have a baking peel, use a rimless or overturned baking sheet to slide the flatbreads onto the baking stone. If you don't have a baking stone, you can use a preheated rimless or overturned baking sheet; however, the breads will be less crisp. Don't top the second flatbread until right before you bake it.

- 1 head cauliflower (2 pounds), cored and cut into ¾-inch florets (about 7 cups), divided
- 1 cup chickpea flour
- 2 large eggs
- ½ cup extra-virgin olive oil, divided, plus extra for drizzling
- 3 garlic cloves, minced, divided
- 2 teaspoons chopped fresh oregano or ¾ teaspoon dried
- 1 teaspoon table salt, divided
- 6 ounces Parmesan cheese, grated (3 cups)
- 1¼ cups fresh parsley leaves, divided
- ⅔ cup jarred roasted red peppers, rinsed, patted dry, and chopped
- ¼ cup walnuts, toasted
- 1 tablespoon sherry vinegar
- 6 anchovy fillets, rinsed, patted dry, and chopped fine (optional), divided
- ¼ cup ricotta cheese, divided

1. One hour before baking, adjust oven rack to upper-middle position, set baking stone on rack, and heat oven to 475 degrees. Process 4 cups cauliflower florets, chickpea flour, eggs, ¼ cup oil, two-thirds garlic, oregano, and ¼ teaspoon salt in food processor until thick, smooth batter forms, about 3 minutes, scraping down sides of bowl as needed. Transfer batter to large bowl and stir in Parmesan.

2. Line baking peel with 16 by 12-inch piece of parchment paper with long edge perpendicular to handle and spray parchment well with vegetable oil spray. Transfer half of batter (about 2 cups) to center of prepared parchment and top with second greased sheet parchment. Gently press batter into 12-inch round (about ¼ inch thick), then discard top piece parchment. Carefully slide round, still on parchment, onto stone and bake until edges are browned and crisp and top is golden, about 12 minutes, rotating halfway through baking (parchment will darken). Transfer crust to wire rack set in rimmed baking sheet and discard bottom parchment. Repeat with remaining batter to make second crust.

3. In clean, dry processor work bowl, process ¼ cup parsley, red peppers, walnuts, vinegar, remaining garlic, and ¼ teaspoon salt until smooth, about 30 seconds, scraping down sides of bowl as needed. With processor running, slowly add 3 tablespoons oil until incorporated. (Romesco sauce can be refrigerated for up to 3 days.)

4. Heat remaining 1 tablespoon oil in 12-inch nonstick skillet over medium-high heat until shimmering. Add remaining 3 cups cauliflower florets and remaining ½ teaspoon salt and cook, stirring frequently, until florets are spotty brown and crisp-tender, 12 to 15 minutes.

5. Working with 1 crust at a time, spread half of sauce (about ⅓ cup) in thin layer over crust, leaving ¼-inch border. Scatter half of cauliflower and half of anchovies, if using, evenly over top. Place flatbread (still on wire rack in sheet) on stone and bake until warmed through, about 5 minutes.

6. Transfer flatbread to cutting board. Sprinkle evenly with ½ cup parsley, dollop half of ricotta in small spoonfuls evenly over flatbread, and drizzle with oil to taste. Slice into 8 slices and serve immediately. Repeat topping and baking for second flatbread.

Greek Pita Pizzas with Hummus

Serves 4 | **Total Time** 30 minutes **FAST**

WHY THIS RECIPE WORKS These simple personal pizzas, which rely on toasted pita rounds for the crusts, make a quick, easy-to-assemble family-friendly meal or snack. Topping the pizzas with prepared hummus in lieu of tomato sauce, along with feta, onion, and kalamata olives, gives them a Greek-inspired flavor in little time, while lightly dressed arugula, added just before serving, makes them appealingly fresh. If you cannot fit all four pitas on a single baking sheet, use two baking sheets and bake on the upper-middle and lower-middle racks, switching and rotating the baking sheets halfway through baking. We prefer our homemade Simple Hummus (page 50), but you may use store-bought.

- ¼ cup extra-virgin olive oil, divided
- 4 (8-inch) pitas
- 2 tablespoons red wine vinegar
- ¼ teaspoon pepper
- ⅛ teaspoon table salt
- 1 small red onion, halved and sliced thin
- ½ cup pitted kalamata olives, chopped
- ½ cup hummus
- 4 ounces whole-milk block mozzarella cheese, shredded (1 cup)
- 4 ounces feta cheese, crumbled (1 cup)
- 2 ounces (2 cups) baby arugula

1. Adjust oven rack to middle position and heat oven to 475 degrees. Brush 2 tablespoons oil over both sides of pitas and lay on rimmed baking sheet. Bake pitas until golden brown, about 5 minutes, flipping halfway through baking.

2. Meanwhile, whisk remaining 2 tablespoons oil, vinegar, pepper, and salt together in bowl. Measure out 2 tablespoons vinaigrette and toss with onion and olives.

3. Spread 2 tablespoons hummus evenly over each pita. Sprinkle with mozzarella and feta, then top with onion mixture. Bake pitas until cheese is melted and spotty brown, 6 to 8 minutes, rotating baking sheet halfway through baking.

4. Whisk remaining vinaigrette to recombine, then add arugula and toss gently to coat. Top pizzas with arugula and serve.

Galettes Complètes

Serves 4 (makes 4 crepes) | **Total Time** 1¼ hours

WHY THIS RECIPE WORKS In Brittany, France, crepes are made from earthy, mineral-y buckwheat flour. This classic preparation has them partially folded around nutty Gruyère cheese and salty-sweet ham, with an egg cracked into the well. They're cooked until the eggs are set and then sprinkled with fresh herbs, making for a lovely presentation. Since buckwheat is naturally gluten-free, you can't use just buckwheat flour in the batter, or you'll end up with brittle crepes that tear. Blending in some all-purpose flour gives them more resilience. Though these galettes are traditionally made one by one in a skillet, arranging four on a baking sheet and sliding them into the oven lets you serve more people at once. The crepes will

Cauliflower Chickpea Flatbread with Romesco

Galettes Complètes

give off steam as they cook, but if at any point the skillet begins to smoke, remove it from the burner and turn down the heat. Stacking the crepes on a wire rack lets excess steam escape so that they won't stick together. The batter yields 10 crepes, but only four are needed. You can double the filling amount to make eight filled crepes; prep the second batch on a second baking sheet while the first batch is in the oven. Extra crepes also freeze well, or you can stash them in the fridge for a couple days.

CREPES

- ½ teaspoon vegetable oil
- ¾ cup (3⅜ ounces) buckwheat flour
- ¼ cup (1¼ ounces) all-purpose flour
- ¾ teaspoon table salt
- 2 cups milk
- 3 large eggs
- 4 tablespoons unsalted butter, melted and cooled

FILLING

- 4 thin slices deli ham (2 ounces)
- 5½ ounces Gruyère cheese, shredded (1⅓ cups)
- 4 large eggs
- 1 tablespoon unsalted butter, melted
- 4 teaspoons chopped fresh chives

1. FOR THE CREPES Adjust oven rack to middle position and heat oven to 450 degrees. Heat oil in 12-inch nonstick skillet over low heat for at least 5 minutes. While skillet heats, whisk buckwheat flour, all-purpose flour, and salt together in medium bowl. In second bowl, whisk together milk and eggs. Add half of milk mixture to flour mixture and whisk until smooth. Add melted butter and whisk until incorporated. Whisk in remaining milk mixture until smooth.

2. Using paper towel, wipe out skillet, leaving thin film of oil on bottom and sides. Increase heat to medium and let skillet heat for 1 minute. Test heat of skillet by placing 1 teaspoon batter in center and cooking for 20 seconds. If mini crepe is golden brown on bottom, skillet is properly heated; if it is too light or too dark, adjust heat accordingly and retest.

3. Lift skillet off heat and pour ⅓ cup batter into far side of skillet; swirl gently in clockwise direction until batter evenly covers bottom of skillet. Return skillet to heat and cook crepe, without moving it, until surface is dry and crepe starts to brown at edges, loosening crepe from sides of skillet with rubber spatula, about 35 seconds. Gently slide spatula underneath edge of crepe, grasp edge with your fingertips, and flip crepe. Cook until second side is lightly spotted, about 20 seconds. Transfer crepe to wire rack. Return skillet to heat for 10 seconds before repeating with remaining batter. As crepes are done, stack on rack. (Crepes can be wrapped tightly in plastic wrap and refrigerated for up to 3 days or stacked between sheets of parchment paper and frozen for up to 1 month. Allow frozen crepes to thaw completely in refrigerator before using.)

4. FOR THE FILLING Line rimmed baking sheet with parchment paper and spray with vegetable oil spray. Arrange 4 crepes spotty side down on prepared sheet (they will hang over edge). (Reserve remaining crepes for another use.) Working with 1 crepe at a time, place 1 slice of ham in center of crepe, followed by ⅓ cup Gruyère, covering ham evenly. Make small well in center of cheese. Crack 1 egg into well. Fold in 4 sides, pressing to adhere.

5. Brush crepe edges with melted butter and transfer sheet to oven. Bake until egg whites are uniformly set and yolks have filmed over but are still runny, 8 to 10 minutes. Using thin metal spatula, transfer each crepe to plate and sprinkle with chives. Serve immediately.

Rye Crepes with Smoked Salmon, Creme Fraîche, and Pickled Shallots

Serves 4 (makes 8 crepes) | **Total Time** 1¼ hours, plus 30 minutes cooling

WHY THIS RECIPE WORKS For big-personality crepes with a subtle spiciness, try rye flour. Although it contains less gluten than whole-wheat flour, it still contains enough to form sturdy crepes. Rye flour also absorbs moisture at a different rate than whole-wheat flour, so we use 2½ cups milk to make the batter fluid enough for easy portioning and cooking. Pairing these earthy rye crepes with a smoked salmon filling takes its inspiration from classic blini toppings. Mixing crème fraîche with lemon, chives, and chopped capers makes for a briny, bright mixture to pair with the rich smoked salmon. Sliced shallots quickly pickled with vinegar and sugar offer a tangy contrasting crunch. The batter makes 11 crepes, but only eight are needed. Extra crepes also freeze well, or you can stash them in the fridge for a couple days.

Rye Crepes with Smoked Salmon, Creme Fraîche, and Pickled Shallots

RYE CREPES

½ teaspoon vegetable oil
1 cup (5½ ounces) rye flour
½ teaspoon table salt
2½ cups milk
3 large eggs
4 tablespoons unsalted butter, melted and cooled

FILLING

⅓ cup distilled white vinegar
2 tablespoons sugar
2 shallots, sliced thin
¾ cup crème fraîche
3 tablespoons capers, rinsed and chopped
3 tablespoons finely chopped chives
1½ teaspoons grated lemon zest plus
    1½ tablespoons juice
¼ teaspoon table salt
¼ teaspoon pepper
8 ounces smoked salmon

1. FOR THE CREPES Heat oil in 12-inch nonstick skillet over low heat for at least 5 minutes. While skillet heats, whisk flour and salt together in medium bowl. In second bowl, whisk together milk and eggs. Add half of milk mixture to flour mixture and whisk until smooth. Add melted butter and whisk until incorporated. Whisk in remaining milk mixture until smooth.

2. Using paper towel, wipe out skillet, leaving thin film of oil on bottom and sides. Increase heat to medium and let skillet heat for 1 minute. Test heat of skillet by placing 1 teaspoon batter in center and cooking for 20 seconds. If mini crepe is golden brown on bottom, skillet is properly heated; if it is too light or too dark, adjust heat accordingly and retest.

3. Lift skillet off heat and pour ⅓ cup batter into far side of skillet; swirl gently in clockwise direction until batter evenly covers bottom of skillet. Return skillet to heat and cook crepe, without moving it, until surface is dry and crepe starts to brown at edges, loosening crepe from sides of skillet with rubber spatula, about 35 seconds. Gently slide spatula underneath edge of crepe, grasp edge with your fingertips, and flip crepe. Cook until second side is lightly spotted, about 20 seconds. Transfer crepe to wire rack. Return skillet to heat for 10 seconds before repeating with remaining batter. As crepes are done, stack on rack. (Crepes can be wrapped tightly in plastic wrap and refrigerated for up to 3 days or stacked between sheets of parchment paper and frozen for up to 1 month. Allow frozen crepes to thaw completely in refrigerator before using.)

4. FOR THE FILLING Combine vinegar and sugar in small bowl and microwave until sugar is dissolved and vinegar is steaming, about 30 seconds. Add shallots and stir to combine. Cover and let cool completely, about 30 minutes. Drain shallots and discard liquid.

5. Combine crème fraîche, capers, chives, lemon zest and juice, salt, and pepper in medium bowl.

6. Place crepes on large plate and invert second plate over crepes. Microwave until crepes are warm, 30 to 45 seconds (45 to 60 seconds if crepes have cooled completely). Working with 1 crepe at a time, spread 2 tablespoons crème fraîche mixture across bottom half of crepe, followed by 1 ounce smoked salmon and one-quarter of shallots. Fold crepes in half and then into quarters. Transfer to plate and serve.

● FAST (45 minutes or less)   ● VEGAN

Photo: Acquacotta

Miso Soup with Wakame and Tofu

Serves 4 | **Total Time** 45 minutes `FAST`

WHY THIS RECIPE WORKS Miso soup is a classic Japanese warmer made with its namesake fermented soybean paste mixed into a stock called dashi (a combination of water, kombu, and dried bonito flakes cooked together). This stock makes an umami-rich backbone for the sweet and savory miso. The soup can include a variety of additions, most traditionally tofu (soy bean curd) and wakame but also seafood and vegetables. Here we keep it simple, focusing on the flavor of the dashi and using silken tofu as protein. The tofu doesn't even require cooking. It is simply placed in individual bowls with the wakame to warm, once the soup has been heated and flavored with miso. Do not wash or wipe off the chalky, white powder on the exterior of the kombu; it is a source of flavor. To create a vegan dashi, omit the bonito flakes. Drizzle with sesame oil or Chili Oil (page 119), or sprinkle with sesame seeds, crumbled nori, or furikake.

DASHI
8 cups water
½ ounce kombu
2 cups bonito flakes

SOUP
1 tablespoon wakame
¼ cup white or red miso
7 ounces silken tofu, cut into ½-inch pieces
3 scallions, sliced thin

1. FOR THE DASHI Bring water and kombu to boil in large saucepan over medium heat. When water reaches boil, immediately remove from heat and discard kombu or save for another use. Stir in bonito flakes and let sit for 5 minutes. Strain dashi through fine-mesh strainer into large container; discard solids. (Dashi can be refrigerated for up to 5 days.)

2. FOR THE SOUP Soak wakame in cold water until softened, about 15 minutes; drain and set aside. Whisk miso and 1 cup dashi in small bowl until combined. Bring remaining dashi to simmer in now-empty saucepan over medium-high heat. Off heat, stir in miso mixture.

3. Divide tofu and wakame among individual serving bowls. Ladle soup into bowls, sprinkle with scallions, and serve immediately.

NOTES FROM THE TEST KITCHEN

GETTING TO KNOW JAPANESE SEAWEED
Seaweed has long played a role in Japanese cuisine. It is used to flavor stocks and soups, as a garnish for rice and noodle dishes, and as a key ingredient for maki, commonly referred to as rolled sushi. Three types of seaweed are the most common: kombu, nori, and wakame.

KOMBU Kombu is a dried kelp rich in flavor-enhancing glutamic acid. It is used extensively in Japanese cooking, one of its most popular applications being in dashi, Japan's multipurpose base for soups, stews, and sauces. When purchasing kombu, which is primarily sold in dried, thick sheets, take note of the chalky, white powder on the exterior. This is an indication of the glutamic acid content and translates to increased flavor.

NORI Nori (Japanese for seaweed), in addition to being used to wrap sushi, is crumbled and used as a garnish for soup, rice, and noodles. Nori is available plain or seasoned with a mixture of soy sauce, sugar, and spices. It is often toasted before being added to a dish to release its flavor and make it more pliable for rolling sushi. A popular Japanese condiment, furikake, is also made with nori.

WAKAME Wakame is a traditional garnish in miso soup and many Japanese salads. It is available dried in thin sheets, shreds (or flakes), or fresh-salted. Both dried and fresh varieties are used in soups and salads. Dried wakame must be rehydrated in water for at least 3 to 15 minutes before using, while fresh-salted wakame should be rinsed briefly to remove the excess salt, then soaked in water for 1 to 2 minutes.

5-Ingredient Black Bean Soup

Serves 4 | **Total Time** 25 minutes `FAST`

WHY THIS RECIPE WORKS For a flavorful soup that's quick and pantry-friendly, we turn to a can of beans, which gives us two ingredients in one. The bean liquid provides body, silky texture, and flavor—enough so that we don't need many herbs or aromatics to make the dish sing. Smoky, fruity chipotle chiles in adobo give the soup character and deep flavor. Blending half the beans after cooking thickens it the soup. Greek yogurt adds

**5-Ingredient
Black Bean Soup**

VARIATIONS

Chickpea and Garlic Soup `FAST`

Toast 6 garlic cloves in large saucepan over medium heat until skins are just beginning to brown, about 5 minutes. Let cool slightly, then discard skins. Substitute canned chickpeas for black beans, garlic for chipotle, and lemon wedges for lime wedges. Add 1 teaspoon grated lemon zest to blender with soup.

White Bean and Sun-Dried Tomato Soup `FAST`

Substitute canned white beans for black beans, ⅓ cup chopped oil-packed sun-dried tomatoes for chipotle, and lemon wedges for lime wedges. Add ¼ cup grated Parmesan cheese to blender with soup.

Lentil and Chorizo Soup `FAST`

Omit yogurt and chipotle. Cook 8 ounces chopped Spanish-style chorizo sausage in large saucepan over medium heat until fat is rendered, 5 to 7 minutes. Transfer sausage to bowl; do not clean saucepan. Substitute canned brown lentils for black beans. Add 1 teaspoon red wine vinegar to blender with soup. Sprinkle with sausage before serving.

Creamy White Bean Soup with Chorizo Oil and Garlicky Bread Crumbs

Serves 4 to 6 | **Total Time** 45 minutes `FAST`

WHY THIS RECIPE WORKS A humble can of white beans can become a luxuriously silky soup without any special equipment and with ingredients you probably already have in your pantry. We start by briefly simmering great northern beans and their seasoned canning liquid with softened aromatic vegetables and herbs. Heating the beans causes their starches to hydrate, which makes the soup especially creamy, and blending the beans with a small amount of liquid helps their skins break down so the puree is completely smooth. Chicken broth plus a little Parmesan cheese and butter boost the soup's flavor and richness. Chorizo oil and garlicky bread crumbs are quick-to-make but impressive garnishes that complement the neutral soup base with vibrant color, flavor, and texture. Use a conventional blender here; an immersion blender will not produce as smooth a soup.

creaminess and tartness. Change the beans for a whole new soup. For more spice, use the larger amount of chipotle. Serve with fresh cilantro, diced avocado, crumbled cheese (try cotija), hot sauce, crema, and/or crumbled tortilla chips or croutons.

> **Substitution:** You can use canned lentils in place of the black beans.

- 2 (15-ounce) cans black beans, undrained
- 2½ cups vegetable broth, plus extra as needed
- 1–3 teaspoons minced canned chipotle chile in adobo sauce
- ¼ cup plain Greek yogurt or sour cream
  Lime wedges

1. Bring beans and their liquid, broth, and chipotle to simmer in large saucepan over medium-low heat, and cook, stirring occasionally, until beans begin to break down, 5 to 7 minutes.

2. Process half of soup in blender until smooth, about 1 minute. Return processed soup to saucepan and bring to brief simmer. Off heat, stir in yogurt and adjust consistency with extra hot broth as needed. Season with salt and pepper to taste. Serve with lime wedges.

CHORIZO OIL AND GARLICKY BREAD CRUMBS

- 5 tablespoons extra-virgin olive oil, divided
- ¼ cup panko bread crumbs
- 1 garlic clove, minced
  Pinch table salt
- 2½ ounces Spanish-style chorizo sausage, chopped fine

SOUP

- 2 tablespoons extra-virgin olive oil
- ½ cup chopped onion
- ⅓ cup minced celery
- 3 sprigs fresh thyme
- 2 garlic cloves, sliced thin
  Pinch cayenne pepper
- 2 (15-ounce) cans great northern beans, undrained
- 2 tablespoons grated Parmesan cheese
- 2 cups chicken broth, divided
- 2 tablespoons unsalted butter
- ½ teaspoon lemon juice, plus extra for seasoning

1. FOR THE CHORIZO OIL AND GARLICKY BREAD CRUMBS Cook 1 tablespoon oil and panko in 8-inch skillet over medium heat until golden brown, 3 to 5 minutes, stirring frequently. Add garlic and cook until fragrant, about 30 seconds. Transfer to bowl and stir in salt. Heat remaining ¼ cup oil and chorizo in now-empty skillet over medium heat until chorizo is crispy, about 2 minutes, stirring frequently. Using slotted spoon, transfer chorizo to paper towel–lined plate and cover skillet to keep oil warm.

2. FOR THE SOUP Heat oil in large saucepan over medium heat until shimmering. Add onion and celery and cook, stirring frequently, until softened but not browned, 6 to 8 minutes. Add thyme sprigs, garlic, and cayenne and cook, stirring constantly, until fragrant, about 1 minute. Add beans and their liquid and stir to combine. Reduce heat to medium-low, cover, and cook, stirring occasionally, until beans are warmed through and just starting to break down, 6 to 8 minutes. Remove saucepan from heat and discard thyme sprigs.

3. Process bean mixture and Parmesan in blender on low speed until thick, smooth puree forms, about 2 minutes. With blender running, add 1 cup broth and butter. Increase speed to high and continue to process until butter is incorporated and mixture is pourable, about 1 minute.

4. Return soup to clean saucepan and whisk in remaining 1 cup broth. Cover and bring to simmer over medium heat, adjusting consistency with up to 1 cup hot water as needed. Off heat, stir in lemon juice. Season with salt and extra lemon juice to taste. Drizzle each portion of soup with chorizo oil and sprinkle with chorizo and bread crumbs. Serve.

OTHER GARNISHES FOR CREAMY WHITE BEAN SOUP

Consider our simple soup a blank slate on which you can build visual, textural, and flavor appeal with different garnishes. Substitute any of these quick-to-make combinations for the chorizo oil and garlicky bread crumbs to complement the white beans' subtle savory flavor.

Herb Oil and Crispy Capers `FAST` `VEGAN`

Omit chorizo oil and crispy bread crumb topping. Combine ⅓ cup extra-virgin olive oil and ¼ cup rinsed and dried capers in medium bowl (capers should be mostly submerged). Microwave until capers are darkened in color and have shrunk, about 5 minutes, stirring halfway through microwaving. Using slotted spoon, transfer capers to paper towel–lined plate (they will continue to crisp as they cool); set aside. Stir 2 tablespoons minced fresh parsley and 1 tablespoon chopped fresh basil into reserved caper oil. Drizzle each portion of soup with herb oil, sprinkle with capers, and serve.

Extra-Virgin Olive Oil and Quick Pickled Celery `VEGAN`

Omit chorizo oil and crispy bread crumb topping. Microwave ½ cup unseasoned rice vinegar, 1 tablespoon sugar, and ½ teaspoon table salt in medium bowl until simmering, 1 to 2 minutes. Stir in 1 finely chopped celery rib and let sit for 15 minutes. Drain celery, discarding liquid. Drizzle each portion of soup with 1 teaspoon extra-virgin olive oil and sprinkle with celery.

Lemony Yogurt and Crispy Leeks

Omit chorizo oil and crispy bread crumb topping. Halve white and light green part of 1 leek lengthwise, then slice into very thin 2-inch-long strips. Wash and dry thoroughly. Toss with 2 tablespoons all-purpose flour in medium bowl. Stir in ½ cup vegetable oil. Microwave for 5 minutes. Stir and microwave for 2 minutes. Repeat stirring and microwaving in 2-minute increments until leeks begin to brown (4 to 6 minutes total), then repeat stirring and microwaving in 30-second increments until leeks are deep golden (30 seconds to 2 minutes total). Using slotted spoon, transfer leeks to paper towel–lined plate; discard oil. Let leeks drain and turn crispy, about 5 minutes, then season with salt to taste. Meanwhile, whisk ½ cup plain Greek yogurt, 3 tablespoons water, and 1 teaspoon lemon zest and 2 teaspoons juice in bowl until smooth. Season with salt to taste. Drizzle each portion of soup with yogurt and sprinkle with leeks.

TWO REASONS WHY OUR CREAMY WHITE BEAN SOUP IS SUPERSMOOTH

This soup is so lush and silky you'd think it was pureed in a professional-quality blender, passed through a restaurant-grade sieve, and enriched with cream. But it's nothing but beans, broth, butter, seasonings—and two effective techniques.

COOK CANNED BEANS

Heating canned beans loosens their starch granules (which we perceive as gritty on the tongue) and allows water to dilute the starch so that it's imperceptible.

PUREE WITH MINIMAL LIQUID

Blending the beans with a little liquid (more liquid is added later) allows for lots of friction that helps grind their skins into a smooth puree. The liquid creates just enough of a vortex to keep the blender running.

Creamy Chickpea, Broccoli Rabe, and Garlic Soup

Creamy Chickpea, Broccoli Rabe, and Garlic Soup

Serves 4 to 6 | **Total Time** 45 minutes `FAST` `VEGAN`

WHY THIS RECIPE WORKS In this silky soup, canned chickpeas provide protein, the bean liquid helps create body and creamy texture, and broccoli rabe adds fiber and color. But the standout flavor comes from 17 cloves of garlic. Because the garlic is treated in different ways (broiled with broccoli rabe, dry-toasted still in its skin, and turned into garlic chips to toss with lemon zest and chives for garnish), it practically transforms into three entirely different ingredients. Then lemon juice and chives become a vibrant stir-in to the silky soup served with the crunchy garlic-lemon zest chips.

6 tablespoons extra-virgin olive oil, divided
1 pound broccoli rabe, trimmed and cut into 1-inch lengths
17 garlic cloves (1 minced, 8 sliced thin, 8 unpeeled)
1 teaspoon table salt, divided
1 teaspoon grated lemon zest plus 2 tablespoons juice
3 tablespoons minced fresh chives, divided
2 (15-ounce) cans chickpeas, undrained
2½ cups water

1. Adjust oven rack 4 inches from broiler element and heat broiler. Brush rimmed baking sheet with 1 tablespoon oil. Toss broccoli rabe with 2 tablespoons oil, minced garlic, and ½ teaspoon salt, then spread in even layer over prepared sheet. Broil until exposed leaves are well browned, about 2 minutes. Toss to expose unbrowned leaves, then return sheet to oven and broil until most leaves are well browned and stalks are crisp-tender, about 2 minutes; set aside.

2. Cook remaining 3 tablespoons oil and sliced garlic in large saucepan over medium heat, stirring constantly once garlic starts to sizzle, until garlic is light golden, 3 to 5 minutes. Using slotted spoon, transfer garlic to bowl and toss with lemon zest and 1 teaspoon chives. Set aside.

3. Carefully wipe out saucepan. Toast unpeeled garlic in now-empty saucepan over medium heat until skins are beginning to brown, about 5 minutes. Remove from saucepan and let cool. Peel garlic, then return to now-empty saucepan along with chickpeas and their liquid, water, and remaining ½ teaspoon salt. Bring to simmer and cook over medium-low heat until chickpeas begin to break down, 5 to 7 minutes.

4. Working in batches, process soup in blender until smooth, about 2 minutes. Return soup to again-empty saucepan, stir in broccoli rabe, and adjust consistency with extra hot water as needed. Cook over medium heat until warmed through, about 2 minutes. Stir in lemon juice and remaining chives. Serve with garlic chips.

REMOVING GARLIC PEELS IN BULK

Put garlic cloves in zipper-lock bag. Shut tight. Beat bag gently with rolling pin to release peels. Separate garlic from peels to use as needed.

Gingery Coconut Carrot Soup with Tofu Croutons

Serves 4 | **Total Time** 1 hour VEGAN

WHY THIS RECIPE WORKS The sweet flavors of carrots, ginger, and coconut milk meet savory crispy tofu in this sumptuous but pantry-friendly vegan soup. We add more oomph to a weeknight soup that requires no stock by using tofu in two unusual ways, making croutons out of some tofu by crisping it in the skillet and using the rest to thicken our puree. First, carrots are cooked with aromatic ginger, water, and coconut milk until tender and blendable. Then they are processed with firm tofu, which helps create a creamy, silky, filling meal. Our croutons and dry-roasted peanuts contrast with the silkiness of the orange soup and make a crunchy garnish too. Although time-intensive, draining and pressing the tofu will guarantee crispy tofu, so don't skimp on this step.

14 ounces extra-firm tofu, cut lengthwise into 3 equal slabs, divided
¾ teaspoon table salt, divided
⅛ teaspoon pepper
2 tablespoons extra-virgin olive oil
1 pound carrots, peeled and cut into ½-inch pieces
1 tablespoon grated fresh ginger
1½ cups water
1 (14-ounce) can coconut milk
½ cup unsalted dry-roasted peanuts, chopped

1. Place tofu on paper towel–lined plate and let drain for 20 minutes, then gently press dry with paper towels. Sprinkle with ¼ teaspoon salt and pepper. Heat oil in large saucepan over medium-high heat until shimmering. Add 2 tofu slabs and cook, flipping as needed, until lightly browned on both sides, 6 to 8 minutes. Transfer tofu to cutting board and cut into ½-inch pieces; set aside.

2. Add carrots and remaining ½ teaspoon salt to oil left in saucepan and cook, stirring occasionally, until lightly browned, 6 to 8 minutes. Stir in ginger and cook until fragrant, about 1 minute. Stir in water and coconut milk, scraping up any browned bits, and bring to simmer. Cook, covered, over medium-low heat until carrots are tender, 10 to 15 minutes.

3. Transfer 1 cup soup and remaining tofu slab to blender and process until smooth, about 2 minutes. Stir pureed soup and reserved browned tofu into remaining soup in saucepan and adjust consistency with extra hot water as needed. Season with salt and pepper to taste. Serve with peanuts.

Tanabour

Serves 6 | **Total Time** 1¾ hours

WHY THIS RECIPE WORKS Tanabour, or spas, is a nourishing, filling Armenian grain-and-yogurt soup. Its name comes from "tan" (a yogurt drink in Armenian) and "abour" (soup); "spas," which means "to serve," refers to the fact that the dish requires a spoon. Though tanabour can be made using a wide variety of grains, ours uses pearl barley, since— lacking hulls—it cooks to a tender, plump consistency without breaking down entirely. We choose Greek yogurt, which gives the soup milky tang, the requisite thickness and richness, and an exceptional satiny texture. We also add an egg yolk for more richness and extra body. Finally, we garnish the soup with cilantro and Aleppo pepper–infused melted butter. Make sure to prevent the soup from curdling by only warming it to between 180 and 185 degrees—still plenty hot for serving. Dried mint is widely used in Middle Eastern cooking; its flavor is quite different from that of fresh mint, so if you can't find it, it's better to omit it than to substitute fresh.

    4 tablespoons unsalted butter, divided
    1 onion, chopped fine
    1 teaspoon dried mint
    1 teaspoon table salt
    ½ teaspoon pepper
       Pinch baking soda
    ¾ cup pearl barley
    4 cups vegetable broth
    2 cups water
 1½ cups plain Greek yogurt
    1 large egg yolk
    ¼ cup chopped fresh cilantro, divided
    1 teaspoon ground dried Aleppo pepper

1. Melt 2 tablespoons butter in large saucepan over medium heat. Add onion, mint, salt, pepper, and baking soda and cook, stirring occasionally, until onion has broken down into soft paste and is just starting to stick to saucepan, 6 to 8 minutes.

2. Stir in barley and cook, stirring frequently, until grains are translucent around edges, about 3 minutes. Add broth and water and bring to boil. Reduce heat to low and simmer gently, partially covered, until barley is very tender, 50 minutes to 1 hour, stirring occasionally. Meanwhile, whisk yogurt and egg yolk together in large bowl.

3. Remove saucepan from heat. Whisking vigorously, gradually add 2 cups barley mixture to yogurt mixture. Stirring constantly, add yogurt-barley mixture back to saucepan. Cover and let sit for 10 minutes to thicken.

4. Heat soup over medium heat, stirring occasionally, until temperature registers between 180 and 185 degrees (do not allow soup to boil or yogurt will curdle). Remove from heat, stir in 2 tablespoons cilantro, and season with salt to taste. (Soup should have consistency of buttermilk; if thicker, adjust by adding hot water, 2 tablespoons at a time.)

5. Melt remaining 2 tablespoons butter in 8-inch skillet over medium-high heat. Off heat, stir in Aleppo pepper. Ladle soup into bowls, drizzle each portion with 1 teaspoon spiced butter, sprinkle with remaining 2 tablespoons cilantro, and serve.

Gingery Coconut Carrot Soup with Tofu Croutons

Tanabour

Avgolemono

Serves 4 to 6 | **Total Time** 1 hour 10 minutes

WHY THIS RECIPE WORKS Avgolemono, or Greek chicken and rice soup, gets its name from the egg-lemon mixture that thickens and flavors this rich-tasting dish. Our version contains tender shreds of chicken that are poached to perfection by sitting off the heat in the hot broth used to cook our long-grain rice. We flavor the broth with citrusy coriander and lemon zest that gives it savory depth and enhances the soup's characteristic lemon flavor. To use amylose, a starch molecule in rice, we puree some of the rice in the blender along with the eggs, yolks, and lemon juice. That gives us a starchy egg-lemon-rice puree to stir into the broth so the avgolemono has the perfect consistency. Use a vegetable peeler to remove strips of zest from the lemons.

- 1½ pounds boneless, skinless chicken breasts, trimmed
- 1¾ teaspoons table salt
- 12 (3-inch) strips lemon zest plus 6 tablespoons juice, plus extra juice for seasoning (3 lemons)
- 2 sprigs fresh dill, plus 2 teaspoons chopped
- 2 teaspoons coriander seeds
- 1 teaspoon black peppercorns
- 1 garlic clove, smashed and peeled
- 8 cups chicken broth
- 1 cup long-grain white rice, rinsed
- 2 large eggs plus 2 large yolks

1. Cut each chicken breast in half lengthwise and pat dry with paper towels. Toss with salt and let sit at room temperature for at least 15 minutes or up to 30 minutes. Cut 8-inch square of triple-thickness cheesecloth. Place lemon zest, dill sprigs, coriander seeds, peppercorns, and garlic in center of cheesecloth and tie into bundle with kitchen twine.

2. Bring broth, rice, and spice bundle to boil in large saucepan over high heat. Reduce heat to low, cover, and cook for 5 minutes. Turn off heat, add chicken, cover, and let sit for 15 minutes.

3. Transfer chicken to large plate and discard spice bundle. Using 2 forks, shred chicken into bite-size pieces. Using ladle, transfer 1 cup cooked rice to blender (leave any liquid in pot). Add lemon juice and eggs and yolks to blender and process until smooth, about 1 minute.

4. Return chicken and any accumulated juices to pot. Return soup to simmer over high heat. Remove pot from heat and stir in egg mixture until fully incorporated. Stir in chopped dill and season with salt, pepper, and extra lemon juice to taste. Serve.

Kimchi and Tofu Soup

Serves 4 to 6 | **Total Time** 40 minutes **FAST** **VEGAN**

WHY THIS RECIPE WORKS This spicy Korean soup is typically served sizzling hot tableside in an earthenware bowl. To make it at home, without the traditional earthenware serving vessel, we build the soup in a large saucepan. It gets its protein from tofu and its tang and heat from cabbage kimchi and gochujang, a Korean chile-soybean paste. For supple, tender bites, we use silken tofu and keep the pieces large to start. As the soup cooks and is stirred, the tofu breaks up into bite-size pieces. If enoki mushrooms (see page 106) are unavailable, substitute thinly sliced white mushrooms. To make this vegan be sure to use a vegan kimchi. Serve with steamed rice.

- 1 tablespoon vegetable oil
- 6 scallions, white parts sliced thin and green parts cut into 1-inch pieces
- 4 garlic cloves, minced
- 2 teaspoons grated fresh ginger
- 1–3 tablespoons gochujang
- 6 cups vegetable broth
- 28 ounces silken tofu, cut into rough 2-inch pieces
- 1 cup cabbage kimchi, drained and chopped coarse
- 8 ounces daikon radish, trimmed and cut into ½-inch pieces
- 2 tablespoons soy sauce
- 2 ounces enoki mushrooms, trimmed

Cook oil, scallion whites, garlic, ginger, and gochujang in large saucepan over medium-high heat until fragrant, about 2 minutes. Stir in broth, tofu, kimchi, radish, and soy sauce. Bring to simmer and cook, stirring occasionally, until flavors meld, about 15 minutes. Stir in scallion greens and season with salt and pepper to taste. Top individual portions with mushrooms before serving.

Spring Vegetable Soup with Charred Croutons

Serves 4 | **Total Time** 1¼ hours **VEGAN**

WHY THIS RECIPE WORKS The arrival of spring means green vegetables are back. That calls for a soup that shows them off. Here we showcase vibrantly colored in-season snap peas, which are rich in both protein and fiber and need no more than 60 seconds of cooking. First, we cook the green part of a leek, fennel fronds, and parsley briefly; puree them; and set them aside. For the soup base, we cook the white part of the leek, carrots, and garlic, and then add vegetable broth. Just before serving, we add the pureed vegetables to the liquid, along with sliced snap peas and asparagus so they stay perfectly crisp-tender and maintain their bright green hue. We add a touch of vinegar for welcome tartness. The incredible color of this showstopper is punctuated by crunchy, generously sized charred croutons, which help soak up the brothy goodness.

- 5 ounces rustic sourdough bread, cut into 1½-inch pieces
- ½ teaspoon table salt, plus salt for blanching vegetables
- ¼ teaspoon baking soda for blanching vegetables
- 2 cups fresh parsley leaves, chopped coarse
- 1 small leek, white and light green parts sliced into thin rounds and washed thoroughly; dark green part sliced thin and washed thoroughly
- 1 fennel bulb, fronds chopped coarse, stalks discarded, bulb cored and cut into ¼-inch pieces
- ¼ cup plus 3 tablespoons extra-virgin olive oil, divided
- 1½ teaspoons pepper
- 3 garlic cloves, sliced thin
- 2 carrots, peeled and cut into ¼-inch-thick rounds
- 4 cups vegetable broth
- 4 ounces thick asparagus spears, trimmed and sliced into ⅛-inch-thick rounds
- 4 ounces snap peas, strings removed, cut into ½-inch pieces
- 2 tablespoons white wine vinegar

1. Adjust oven rack 8 inches from broiler element and heat broiler. Arrange bread in even layer on rimmed baking sheet. Broil until bread is charred on top, 1 to 2 minutes. Flip bread pieces and continue to broil until second side is charred, 1 to 2 minutes. Set aside.

2. Bring 10 cups water to boil in large saucepan over high heat. Meanwhile, set up ice bath by filling large bowl halfway with ice and water. Add 1½ teaspoons salt, baking soda, parsley leaves, dark green leek, and fennel fronds to boiling water and cook for 1 minute. Drain in fine-mesh strainer or colander and immediately transfer, still in strainer, to ice bath. (Keeping the mixture in the strainer or colander makes retrieving them from the ice bath much easier.)

3. Transfer 1 cup ice and 1 cup water from ice bath to blender. Remove blanched mixture from ice bath, squeeze out excess water, and transfer to blender. Process until mostly smooth, about 1 minute. Stop blender and scrape down sides of blender jar with rubber spatula. With blender running, slowly drizzle in ¼ cup oil. Continue to process until mixture is smooth, 30 to 45 seconds. Stir in salt and set aside.

Kimchi and Tofu Soup

Spring Vegetable Soup with Charred Croutons

GETTING TO KNOW MUSHROOMS

Mushrooms add complex meatiness to food and there are many varieties available today. If possible, buy fresh mushrooms loose so you can inspect their quality; pick ones with large caps and minimal stems. For dried mushrooms, choose large, smooth ones free of holes, dust, grit, and wormholes.

WHITE These mild, meaty mushrooms are the most affordable and easily available. Their firm texture makes them suitable for grilling, sautéing, roasting, even marinating, whole or sliced.

CREMINI Brown cremini have the same shape as white mushrooms, but are more intensely flavored than their pale cousins; they have a rich, sweet taste, like a caramelized white mushroom. Look for whole, intact caps; avoid discoloration or dry, shriveled patches. Though we think cremini are firmer and more flavorful than less expensive white mushrooms, the two are interchangeable.

ENOKI These long-stemmed, small-capped mushrooms are usually sold clustered. Very mild and faintly nutty, with a delicately crisp texture, they need no cooking. Simply stir them into soup before serving.

OYSTER Oyster mushrooms are beige, cream, or gray in color, with a clean, savory, subtly briny taste. Since they are delicate, they are best cooked only briefly.

PORCINI Often sold dried, porcini are shelf-stable, with concentrated meaty flavor and an earthy aroma. Because porcini are foraged, they vary in cleanliness. Always remove grit before using; we swish them in a bowl of water to loosen dirt, and then rinse them. We use them in various dishes, such as Italian Wedding Soup with Kale and Farro (page 125) and Almost Hands-Free Risotto with Porcini (page 303).

SHIITAKE Esteemed in Japan and China, shiitakes range from tan to dark brown in color and have a woody, earthy, savory, and meaty flavor. We use them in Teriyaki Stir-Fried Beef with Green Beans and Shiitakes (page 187) and Hot and Sour Soup (page 118), as they make a great substitute for wood ear mushrooms, which are popular in Chinese cuisine.

4. Heat remaining 3 tablespoons oil and pepper in Dutch oven over medium-low heat until pepper begins to sizzle, about 1 minute. Add leek and garlic and cook, stirring occasionally, until softened, about 3 minutes. Add carrots and fennel and continue to cook, stirring occasionally, until slightly softened at edges, about 3 minutes.

5. Add broth, increase heat to medium-high, and bring to simmer, about 5 minutes. Reduce heat to medium-low and gently simmer until carrots and fennel are slightly tender but still firm, about 3 minutes.

6. Stir asparagus, snap peas, vinegar, and pureed mixture into soup. Season with salt and pepper to taste. Divide soup and charred croutons among warmed shallow bowls. Serve immediately.

TRIMMING SNAP PEAS AND SNOW PEAS

Snap off the stem end and remove the string before cutting or cooking snap peas or snow peas.

Tepary Bean Soup

Serves 4 to 6 | **Total Time** 2¼ hours, plus 8 hours brining VEGAN

WHY THIS RECIPE WORKS Drought-resistant white and brown tepary beans are native to the American southwest and northern Mexico. We use white tepary beans in Tepary Bean Dip with Herb and Olive Salad (page 52). Brown tepary beans, when dried, are small and flat and look a bit more like lentils than common beans. So we substitute them for lentils in a take on the traditional Greek faki soupa (lentil soup). We soak the beans overnight with salt and baking soda, which helps to reduce cooking time and yields tender, creamy beans. However, baking soda also weakens the cell-wall structure of the other vegetables in the soup. In order to maintain the texture of our vegetables, we sauté the vegetables separately, adding them to the pot partway through cooking. In keeping with the dish's Greek inspiration, we finish the soup with a splash of red wine vinegar and fresh parsley.

Substitution: You can use dried kidney beans in place of the tepary beans.

½ teaspoon table salt for brining

¼ teaspoon baking soda for brining

8 cups water

1¼ cups dried brown tepary beans, picked over and rinsed

¼ cup plus 2 tablespoons extra-virgin olive oil, divided

1 onion, chopped

2 carrots, peeled and chopped

1 celery rib, chopped

2 garlic cloves, minced

¼ teaspoon table salt

2 cups vegetable broth

1 tablespoon tomato paste

2 bay leaves

3 tablespoons red wine vinegar

2 tablespoons minced fresh parsley

1. Dissolve ½ teaspoon salt and baking soda in water in Dutch oven. Add beans, cover, and soak at room temperature for at least 8 hours or up to 24 hours. Bring beans (still in soaking liquid) to boil over high heat, skimming off any foam that rises to surface. Reduce heat to medium-low and simmer, uncovered, until beans are tender, about 45 minutes. Do not drain beans.

2. Meanwhile heat ¼ cup oil in 10-inch skillet over medium heat until shimmering. Stir in onion, carrots, celery, garlic, and salt and cook until onion is translucent, 5 to 7 minutes. Remove from heat.

3. Add softened vegetables, broth, tomato paste, and bay leaves to pot and stir to combine. Bring to boil over high heat, then reduce heat to medium-low and simmer, uncovered, until soup has thickened and flavors have melded, about 30 minutes. Off heat, stir in vinegar and season with salt to taste. Divide soup among warmed bowls, sprinkle with parsley, and drizzle with remaining 2 tablespoons oil. Serve.

Wild Rice and Mushroom Soup

Serves 6 to 8 | **Total Time** 2 hours 20 minutes

WHY THIS RECIPE WORKS This creamy soup bursts with umami. Tomato paste, soy sauce, dry sherry, and garlic amplify the mushrooms' taste. Cooking the cremini and onion with tomato paste over high heat develops a flavorful fond, and dried shiitakes deliver more flavor. We cook the wild rice separately in the oven, adding baking soda to help tenderize it faster, and reserve the cooking liquid to add more flavor. We like cremini mushrooms here but you can substitute white mushrooms, if desired.

Wild Rice and Mushroom Soup

1 sprig fresh thyme

4¼ cups water, divided, plus extra as needed

1 bay leaf

5 garlic cloves, peeled (1 whole, 4 minced)

1½ teaspoons table salt, divided

¼ teaspoon baking soda

1 cup wild rice, rinsed

4 tablespoons unsalted butter

1 pound cremini mushrooms, trimmed and sliced ¼ inch thick

1 onion, chopped fine

1 teaspoon tomato paste

1 teaspoon pepper

⅔ cup dry sherry

4 cups vegetable broth

1 tablespoon soy sauce

¼ ounce dried shiitake mushrooms, finely ground using spice grinder

¼ cup cornstarch

½ cup heavy cream

¼ cup minced fresh chives

¼ teaspoon grated lemon zest

MAKING WILD RICE ACT LIKE STEAK

We brown meat as a matter of course, since the deeper color is an indication of the Maillard reaction, the process triggered by heat that causes a food's proteins and sugars to recombine into new flavor compounds that boost complexity. To achieve richer flavor in ordinary rice, we often toast the raw grains in the pan. But toasting doesn't work with wild rice, since it is technically a grass seed with a hard pectin-rich coating that must break down before the proteins and sugars on the inside can brown. We stumbled upon another way to achieve browning: adding baking soda to the cooking water. Baking soda not only breaks down the pectin seed coat to speed up cooking, it also lowers the temperature necessary for browning to occur—from at least 300 degrees to below water's boiling point of 212. Another factor in our favor: Wild rice is high in the amino acids lysine and glycine, proteins that are particularly sensitive to browning. We end up with a deep-brown stock that enriches the taste of soup.

1. Adjust oven rack to middle position and heat oven to 375 degrees. Bring 4 cups water, thyme sprig, bay leaf, whole garlic clove, ¾ teaspoon salt, and baking soda to boil in medium saucepan over high heat. Add rice and return to boil. Cover saucepan; transfer to oven; and bake until rice is tender, 35 to 50 minutes. Drain rice in fine-mesh strainer set in 4-cup liquid measuring cup, discarding thyme sprig, bay leaf, and garlic. Add enough water to reserved cooking liquid to measure 3 cups.

2. Melt butter in Dutch oven over high heat. Add cremini mushrooms, onion, tomato paste, pepper, minced garlic, and remaining ¾ teaspoon salt and cook, stirring occasionally, until vegetables are browned and dark fond develops on bottom of pot, about 15 minutes.

3. Stir in sherry, scraping up any browned bits, and cook until nearly evaporated, about 2 minutes. Stir in broth, soy sauce, shiitake mushrooms, and reserved rice cooking liquid and bring to boil. Reduce heat to low; cover; and simmer until onion and mushrooms are tender, about 20 minutes.

4. Whisk cornstarch and remaining ¼ cup water together in bowl. Stir cornstarch slurry into soup and simmer until thickened, about 2 minutes. Off heat, stir in rice, cream, chives, and lemon zest. Cover and let sit for 20 minutes. Season with salt and pepper to taste. Serve.

Mushroom and Wheat Berry Soup

Serves 8 | **Total Time** 2 hours `VEGAN`

WHY THIS RECIPE WORKS For this rich, substantial, and savory soup, we pair mushrooms with wheat berries, which are whole, unprocessed kernels of wheat. To bring out their nutty taste, we toast them in a dry Dutch oven, while we slowly cook our cremini mushrooms in a covered pot to concentrate flavors and extract their juices. To amplify the earthiness of the wheat berries and cremini, we build a flavorful base from ground dried shiitake mushrooms, as we do for our Wild Rice and Mushroom Soup (page 107), adding tomato paste, soy sauce, dry sherry, and plenty of garlic. Grinding the shiitakes ensures their flavor permeates the broth. After simmering our wheat berries, we finish the soup with sturdy mustard greens and lemon zest for freshness. We use a spice grinder to process the dried shiitake mushrooms, but a blender works too.

- 1 cup wheat berries, rinsed
- 3 tablespoons extra-virgin olive oil, divided
- 1½ pounds cremini mushrooms, trimmed and sliced thin
- ¼ teaspoon table salt
- 1 onion, chopped fine
- 6 garlic cloves, minced
- 2 teaspoons tomato paste
- 1 cup dry sherry
- 8 cups vegetable broth
- 1 tablespoon soy sauce
- 1 sprig fresh thyme
- 1 bay leaf
- ½ ounce dried shiitake mushrooms, finely ground using spice grinder
- 4 ounces mustard greens, stemmed and chopped
- ¼ teaspoon grated lemon zest

1. Toast wheat berries in Dutch oven over medium heat, stirring often, until fragrant and beginning to darken, about 5 minutes; transfer to bowl.

2. Heat 2 tablespoons oil in now-empty pot over medium heat until shimmering. Add cremini mushrooms and salt, cover, and cook until mushrooms have released their liquid, about 3 minutes. Uncover, increase heat to medium-high, and cook until mushrooms begin to brown, 5 to 7 minutes; transfer to plate.

3. Heat remaining 1 tablespoon oil in now-empty pot over medium heat until shimmering. Add onion and cook until softened, about 5 minutes. Stir in garlic and tomato paste and cook until slightly darkened, about 2 minutes.

Mushroom and Wheat Berry Soup

4. Stir in sherry, scraping up any browned bits, and cook until nearly evaporated, about 2 minutes. Stir in toasted wheat berries, broth, soy sauce, thyme, bay leaf, and ground shiitakes and bring to boil over medium-high heat. Cover, reduce heat to low, and simmer until wheat berries are tender but still chewy, 45 minutes to 1 hour. Discard bay leaf and thyme sprig.

5. Off heat, stir in reserved cremini and any accumulated juices, mustard greens, and lemon zest, cover, and let sit until greens are wilted, about 5 minutes. Season with salt and pepper to taste, and serve.

GRINDING DRIED MUSHROOMS

When mushrooms are dried, their flavor is concentrated and they become shelf-stable. Grind dried mushrooms into a fine powder with a spice grinder, blender, or mortar and pestle. Sprinkle the powder on anything you like for a meaty boost.

Minestra di Farro

Serves 6 to 8 | **Total Time** 35 minutes **FAST**

WHY THIS RECIPE WORKS Farro is a staple grain in Italy's Umbria region where it predates common wheat. The Umbrians employ the good-for-you grain both whole, in soups and stews, and as flour, which they use to make gnocchi, pasta, and even crepes. In this classic vegetable and farro soup, they use the grain coarsely ground and it thickens and flavors the hearty dish with its nuttiness. While ground farro isn't readily available in most American grocery stores, it's easy to create your own; six pulses in a blender are enough to break up the grain into smaller pieces. While a prosciutto bone may be a traditional flavor booster for this soup, we use readily accessible pancetta to deliver a similarly rich, salty note, while leeks, celery, and carrots contribute sweetness. A sprinkling of fresh parsley and some freshly grated Pecorino Romano finish this humble but tasty soup. Use the entire leek (dark and light green parts) in this recipe. We prefer the flavor and texture of whole farro in this recipe. Do not use pearl, quick-cooking, or presteamed farro (check the ingredient list on the package to determine this) for the whole farro.

1 cup whole farro, rinsed and dried
3 ounces pancetta, chopped fine
1 pound whole leeks, trimmed, chopped, and washed thoroughly
2 carrots, peeled and chopped
1 celery rib, chopped
8 cups chicken broth
2 tablespoons minced fresh parsley
   Grated Pecorino Romano cheese

1. Pulse farro in blender until about half of grains are broken into smaller pieces, about 6 pulses; set aside.

2. Cook pancetta in Dutch oven over medium-low heat until browned and fat is rendered, about 5 minutes. Stir in leeks, carrots, and celery and cook until softened and lightly browned, 5 to 7 minutes.

3. Stir in broth and farro, bring to simmer, and cook until farro is tender with slight chew, 15 to 30 minutes. Stir in parsley and season with salt and pepper to taste. Serve with Pecorino.

Butternut Squash and White Bean Soup with Sage Pesto

Soupe au Pistou

Butternut Squash and White Bean Soup with Sage Pesto

Serves 6 to 8 | **Total Time** 1 hour 40 minutes

WHY THIS RECIPE WORKS This hearty soup can stand on its own as a meal. Instead of pureeing all the squash, we pair chunks of it with creamy cannellini beans and their liquid, which goes in toward the end of cooking to warm through and break down slightly, adding starch and silkiness. We cut the squash bulb into wedges, cook them in vegetable broth until soft, and mash them to make a "squash stock" that gives our soup base body and flavor. We then cook the neck portion of the squash, cut into chunks, in this stock, for more butternut flavor. Adding butter to the stock at the start of its simmering time allows it to fully emulsify, giving the soup base richness and a more velvety texture. A swirl of sage pesto, quickly made in the food processor, lends just the right bright, fresh finish.

PESTO
- ½ cup walnuts, toasted
- 2 garlic cloves, minced
- 1 cup fresh parsley leaves
- ½ cup fresh sage leaves
- ¾ cup extra-virgin olive oil
- 1 ounce Parmesan cheese, grated (½ cup), plus extra for serving

SOUP
- 1 (2- to 2½-pound) butternut squash, peeled
- 4 cups vegetable broth
- 3 cups water
- 4 tablespoons unsalted butter
- 1 tablespoon soy sauce
- 1 tablespoon vegetable oil
- 1 pound leeks, white and light green parts only, halved lengthwise, sliced thin, and washed thoroughly
- 1 tablespoon tomato paste
- 2 garlic cloves, minced
- ¾ teaspoon table salt
- ¼ teaspoon pepper
- 3 (15-ounce) cans cannellini beans, undrained
- 1 teaspoon white wine vinegar

1. FOR THE PESTO Pulse walnuts and garlic in food processor until coarsely chopped, about 5 pulses. Add parsley and sage. With processor running, slowly add oil until incorporated. Transfer to bowl, stir in Parmesan, and season with salt and pepper to taste; set aside.

2. FOR THE SOUP Cut round bulb section off squash and cut in half lengthwise. Discard seeds, then cut each half into 4 wedges.

3. Bring squash wedges, broth, water, butter, and soy sauce to boil in medium saucepan over high heat. Reduce heat to medium, partially cover, and simmer vigorously until squash is very tender and starting to fall apart, about 20 minutes. Remove pot from heat and use potato masher to mash squash, still in broth, until completely broken down. Cover to keep warm; set aside.

4. While broth cooks, cut neck of squash into ½-inch pieces. Heat oil in Dutch oven over medium heat until shimmering. Add leeks and tomato paste and cook, stirring occasionally, until leeks are softened and tomato paste is darkened, about 5 minutes. Add garlic and cook until fragrant, about 30 seconds. Add squash pieces, salt, and pepper and cook, stirring occasionally, for 5 minutes. Add squash broth and bring to simmer. Partially cover and cook for 10 minutes.

5. Add beans and their liquid, partially cover, and cook, stirring occasionally, until squash is just tender, 15 to 20 minutes. Stir in vinegar and season with salt and pepper to taste. Serve, passing pesto and extra Parmesan separately.

PREPPING BUTTERNUT SQUASH

Peel away tough outer skin using vegetable peeler, then trim off top and bottom of squash before cutting it.

1. Slice squash in half width-wise, separating solid, narrow neck piece from hollow, rounded bottom.

2. Slice solid neck piece lengthwise into evenly sized planks, then cut into pieces as directed.

3. Slice bottom piece in half, remove seeds with spoon, then cut into pieces as directed.

Soupe au Pistou

Serves 6 to 8 | **Total Time** 1¾ hours, plus 8 hours brining

WHY THIS RECIPE WORKS Provence's version of minestrone, soupe au pistou, is light and bright, using fresh, seasonal produce, pasta, and beans. White beans are traditionally used but we like French flageolet beans; these delicate, light green and white beans with subtle vegetal notes add to the bounty already present in this soup. We add the viscous, seasoned liquid left over from cooking the dried beans, too. This makes for a soup that is still brothy but also has some body and starch. The soup is finished with a dollop of fragrant pistou, France's version of pesto.

Substitution: You can use two undrained 15-ounce cans of cannellini beans for the dried flageolet beans; skip steps 2 and 3.

PISTOU
- 1 cup fresh basil leaves
- 1 ounce Parmesan cheese, grated (½ cup)
- ⅓ cup extra-virgin olive oil
- 1 garlic clove, minced

SOUP
- 1½ tablespoons table salt for brining
- 8 ounces (1¼ cups) dried flageolet beans, picked over and rinsed
- 1 tablespoon extra-virgin olive oil
- 1 leek, white and light green parts only, halved lengthwise, sliced ½ inch thick, and washed thoroughly
- 1 celery rib, cut into ½-inch pieces
- 1 carrot, peeled and sliced ¼ inch thick
- 1½ teaspoons table salt
- 2 garlic cloves, minced
- ½ cup tubetti or ditalini
- 8 ounces green beans, trimmed and cut into ½-inch lengths
- 1 small zucchini, halved lengthwise, seeded, and cut into ¼-inch pieces
- 1 large tomato, cored, seeded, and cut into ¼-inch pieces

1. FOR THE PISTOU Process all ingredients in food processor until smooth, scraping down sides of bowl as needed, about 15 seconds, set aside until ready to serve. (Pistou can be refrigerated for up to 4 hours.)

2. FOR THE SOUP Dissolve 1 ½ tablespoons salt in 2 quarts cold water in large container. Add beans and soak at room temperature for at least 8 hours or up to 24 hours. Drain and rinse well. (If you're pressed for time, see page 13 for information on quick brining your beans.)

3. Bring soaked beans and 7 cups water to simmer in Dutch oven. Simmer, partially covered, over medium-low heat until beans are tender, 30 to 40 minutes. Remove from heat, stir in salt, cover, and let sit until completely tender, about 15 minutes. Strain beans, reserving 3 cups cooking liquid, adding water if necessary to reach volume. Reserve beans and measured cooking liquid.

4. Heat oil in now-empty Dutch oven over medium heat until shimmering. Add leek, celery, carrot, and salt and cook until vegetables are softened, 8 to 10 minutes. Stir in garlic and cook until fragrant, about 30 seconds. Stir in reserved bean cooking liquid and 4 cups water and bring to simmer.

5. Stir in pasta and simmer until slightly softened, about 5 minutes. Stir in green beans and simmer until bright green but still crunchy, 3 to 5 minutes. Stir in reserved beans, zucchini, and tomato and simmer until pasta and vegetables are tender, about 3 minutes. Season with salt and pepper to taste. Serve, topping individual portions with reserved pistou.

Hearty 15-Bean and Vegetable Soup

Hearty 15-Bean and Vegetable Soup

Serves 10 | **Total Time** 2 hours 40 minutes, plus 8 hours brining `VEGAN`

WHY THIS RECIPE WORKS For the ultimate bean soup, with an array of textures and colors and supercharged with hearty vegetables, a 15-bean soup mix is a convenient starting point. But we discard the seasoning packet, knowing we can add flavor in a fresher way. Bean soup mixes can disappoint because different beans cook at different rates, leaving some beans blown out and disintegrating while others stay hard. To prevent blowouts, we brine the beans to soften their skins. Then we bring the soup to a simmer before transferring it to the oven to cook gently in the low, constant heat. To build flavor, we sauté aromatics and add thyme, bay leaves, and savory dried porcini. Swiss chard, mushrooms, and a tomato balance the beans with hearty vegetable flavor. You can find 15-bean soup mix with other bagged dried beans in the supermarket; any 1-pound bag of multiple bean varieties will work. Be sure to taste several beans to ensure they are all tender before serving.

1½ tablespoons table salt for brining
1 pound 15-bean soup mix, flavoring pack discarded, dried beans picked over and rinsed
2 tablespoons extra-virgin olive oil
1 small onion, chopped
1 carrot, peeled and chopped fine
1 pound Swiss chard, stems chopped, leaves sliced into ½-inch-wide strips
½ ounce dried porcini mushrooms, rinsed and minced
12 ounces white mushrooms, trimmed and quartered
6 garlic cloves, minced
2 teaspoons minced fresh thyme or ½ teaspoon dried
8 cups vegetable broth
2 bay leaves
1 large tomato, cored and chopped

1. Dissolve 1 ½ tablespoons salt in 2 quarts cold water in large container. Add beans and soak at room temperature for at least 8 hours or up to 24 hours. Drain and rinse well. (If you're pressed for time, see page 13 for information on quick brining your beans.)

2. Adjust oven rack to lower-middle position and heat oven to 250 degrees. Heat oil in Dutch oven over medium heat until shimmering. Add onion, carrot, chard stems, and porcini mushrooms and cook until vegetables are softened, 7 to 10 minutes.

3. Stir in white mushrooms, cover, and cook until mushrooms have released their liquid, about 5 minutes. Uncover and continue to cook until mushrooms are browned, 5 to 10 minutes.

4. Stir in garlic and thyme and cook until fragrant, about 30 seconds. Stir in soaked beans, broth, and bay leaves and bring to boil. Cover pot, transfer to oven, and cook until beans are almost tender, 1 to 1¼ hours.

5. Stir in chard leaves and tomato and continue to cook in oven, covered, until beans and vegetables are fully tender, 30 to 40 minutes. Discard bay leaves and season with salt and pepper to taste. Serve.

Garlicky Wild Rice Soup with Artichokes

Serves 4 | **Total Time** 1½ hours

WHY THIS RECIPE WORKS Wild rice, with its distinct chew and shape, shines in soups and holds up to long cooking, the substantial grains adding hearty texture and filling fiber without stodginess. Though wild rice is a North American ingredient, this soup's profile takes inspiration from spring flavors in the south of France. An abundance of aromatics gets it off to a flavorful start; leek, garlic, anchovies, wine, and thyme all contribute to a pleasantly potent backbone. We cook the rice until it's almost done, and then stir in asparagus and artichokes (which we've sautéed to achieve browning), so everything—from hearty rice to light asparagus—finishes cooking at the same time. Stirring in a combination of fresh tarragon, lemon, and additional garlic off the heat ensures that their flavors have presence.

    3 tablespoons extra-virgin olive oil, divided
    3 cups jarred whole baby artichoke hearts packed in
       water, quartered, rinsed, and patted dry
    1 leek, white and light green parts only, halved length-
       wise, sliced ¼ inch thick, and washed thoroughly
    8 garlic cloves, minced, divided
    4 anchovy fillets, rinsed, patted dry, and minced
    1 teaspoon minced fresh thyme or ¼ teaspoon dried
    ¼ cup dry white wine
    6 cups vegetable broth

Garlicky Wild Rice Soup with Artichokes

    1 cup wild rice, rinsed
    2 bay leaves
    1 pound asparagus, trimmed and cut into 1-inch pieces
    2 tablespoons minced fresh tarragon
    1 teaspoon grated lemon zest plus 1 tablespoon juice

1. Heat 2 tablespoons oil in Dutch oven over medium heat until shimmering. Add artichokes and cook until browned, 8 to 10 minutes. Transfer to bowl and set aside.

2. Heat remaining 1 tablespoon oil in now-empty pot over medium heat until shimmering. Stir in leek and cook until softened and beginning to brown, 5 to 7 minutes. Stir in half of garlic, anchovies, and thyme and cook until fragrant, about 30 seconds. Stir in wine, scraping up any browned bits, and cook until nearly evaporated, about 1 minute.

3. Stir in broth, rice, and bay leaves and bring to simmer. Cover, reduce heat to medium-low, and simmer gently for 35 minutes. Stir in reserved artichokes and asparagus and cook, covered, until rice and vegetables are tender, about 10 minutes.

4. Remove pot from heat and discard bay leaves. Stir in tarragon, lemon zest and juice, and remaining garlic and season with salt and pepper to taste. Serve.

Acquacotta

Serves 8 to 10 | **Total Time** 1½ hours

WHY THIS RECIPE WORKS Don't let the Italian name acquacotta ("cooked water") deceive you. In this Tuscan cousin of the better-known minestrone and ribollita, water, vegetables, beans, and herbs are transformed into a satisfying meal when whole eggs or yolks are whisked into the broth before it's ladled over stale bread. Creamy cannellini beans, tender fennel, and faintly bitter escarole provide bulk and chicken broth amps up the flavor of soffritto, a mix of sautéed onion, celery, and garlic. We use a food processor to finely chop these ingredients and the canned tomatoes that flavor the broth. If your cheese has a rind, slice it off the wedge and add it to the broth in step 3 (remove it before serving).

SOUP

- 1 large onion, chopped coarse
- 2 celery ribs, chopped coarse
- 4 garlic cloves, peeled
- 1 (28-ounce) can whole peeled tomatoes
- ½ cup extra-virgin olive oil
- ¾ teaspoon table salt
- ⅛ teaspoon red pepper flakes
- 8 cups chicken broth
- 1 fennel bulb, 2 tablespoons fronds minced, stalks discarded, bulb halved, cored, and cut into ½-inch pieces
- 2 (15-ounce) cans cannellini beans, drained with liquid reserved, beans rinsed
- 1 small head escarole (10 ounces), trimmed and cut into ½-inch pieces (8 cups)
- 2 large egg yolks
- ½ cup chopped fresh parsley
- 1 tablespoon minced fresh oregano
  Grated Pecorino Romano cheese
  Lemon wedges

TOAST

- 10 (½-inch-thick) slices thick-crusted country bread
- ¼ cup extra-virgin olive oil

1. FOR THE SOUP Pulse onion, celery, and garlic in food processor until very finely chopped, 15 to 20 pulses, scraping down sides of bowl as needed. Transfer to Dutch oven. Add tomatoes and their juice to now-empty processor and pulse until tomatoes are finely chopped, 10 to 12 pulses; set aside.

2. Stir oil, salt, and pepper flakes into onion mixture in pot. Cook over medium-high heat, stirring occasionally, until light brown fond begins to form on bottom of pot, 12 to 15 minutes. Stir in reserved tomatoes, increase heat to high, and cook, stirring frequently, until mixture is very thick and rubber spatula leaves distinct trail when dragged across bottom of pot, 9 to 12 minutes.

3. Add broth and fennel bulb to pot and bring to simmer. Reduce heat to medium-low and simmer until fennel begins to soften, 5 to 7 minutes. Stir in beans and escarole and cook until fennel is fully tender, about 10 minutes.

4. Whisk egg yolks and reserved bean liquid together in bowl, then stir into soup. Stir in parsley, oregano, and fennel fronds. Season with salt and pepper to taste.

5. FOR THE TOAST Adjust oven rack about 5 inches from broiler element and heat broiler. Place bread on aluminum foil–lined rimmed baking sheet and drizzle with oil. Broil until bread is deep golden brown.

6. Place 1 slice bread in bottom of each individual bowl. Ladle soup over toasted bread. Serve, passing Pecorino and lemon wedges separately.

Ribollita

Serves 8 to 10 | **Total Time** 2¼ hours, plus 8 hours brining

WHY THIS RECIPE WORKS Despite its humble origins, ribollita is arguably the best known Tuscan soup: Meaning "reboiled" in Italian, this hearty soup was traditionally made by peasants using leftover vegetable soup reheated with leftover bread (sometimes multiple times), creating a mixture that many recipes say should be thick enough to eat with a fork. Here we use Marcella beans, named after Italian chef Marcella Hazan, which are grown in California from Italian seed. These thin-skinned heirloom cannellini have an incredibly creamy texture. While the beans cook on the stovetop, we toast fresh (or stale, if you have it) bread so it will not completely break down when added to the hot soup. Lacinato kale and the classic trio of onions, celery, and carrots, boosted with a bit of pancetta for depth, give deep flavor. A restrained amount of canned tomatoes add acidity and color, and fresh herbs and a finishing splash of lemon juice bring a bright herbaceous note to balance the earthy flavors. Lacinato kale (also known as Tuscan kale or cavolo nero) is traditional in this recipe but you can substitute curly kale.

Substitution: You can use dried cannellini beans in place of the Marcella beans.

Ribollita

1. Dissolve 1½ tablespoons table salt in 2 quarts cold water in large container. Add beans and soak at room temperature for at least 8 hours or up to 24 hours. Drain and rinse well. (If you're pressed for time, see page 13 for information on quick brining your beans.)

2. Adjust oven rack to middle position and heat oven to 250 degrees. Add pancetta to large Dutch oven and cook over medium heat until pancetta is browned and fat is rendered, about 10 minutes, stirring frequently. Add oil, onion, carrots, and celery and cook until onions are browned, 10 to 12 minutes, stirring frequently. Stir in garlic and cook until fragrant, about 30 seconds.

3. Stir in soaked beans, broth, 4 cups water, and bay leaves and bring to simmer. Reduce heat to low, and simmer, covered, until beans are tender, 25 to 35 minutes.

4. While beans cook, arrange bread in single layer on rimmed baking sheet, and bake until bread is dry and crisp, about 30 minutes. Set aside.

5. Stir kale, tomatoes and reserved juice, salt, rosemary, thyme, and pepper into soup. Increase heat to high and return soup to simmer, then reduce heat to low, cover pot and cook until kale is tender, about 15 minutes.

6. Off heat, discard bay leaves and stir in bread and lemon juice. Cover and let sit for 15 minutes. Whisk soup vigorously until bread is broken down, about 2 minutes. Serve, drizzling individual servings with extra oil and seasoning with pepper to taste.

1½	tablespoons table salt for brining
1	pound (2½ cups) dried Marcella beans, picked over and rinsed
4	ounces pancetta, chopped fine
2	tablespoons extra-virgin olive oil, plus extra for drizzling
1	large onion, chopped fine
2	carrots, peeled and chopped
2	celery ribs, chopped
4	garlic cloves, minced
4	cups chicken broth
2	bay leaves
8	ounces rustic Italian bread, cut into 1-inch pieces
1	pound lacinato kale, stemmed and chopped into 1-inch pieces
1	(14.5-ounce) can whole peeled tomatoes, drained with juice reserved, chopped
1½	teaspoons table salt
1	teaspoon minced fresh rosemary or ¼ teaspoon dried
1	teaspoon minced fresh thyme or ¼ teaspoon dried
1	teaspoon pepper
4	teaspoons lemon juice

Lablabi

Serves 4 to 6 | **Total Time** 1¼ hours, plus 8 hours brining

VEGAN

WHY THIS RECIPE WORKS Dinner—or lunch, or breakfast—is served with this simple but superlatively satisfying Tunisian chickpea soup. And it's really all about the chickpeas: They're simmered in only water until they're just tender and their flavor becomes omnipresent, giving the soup meatiness, rather than broth doing that job. Traditional aromatics (garlic, cumin, and harissa paste) are added in the final minutes of simmering to make an invigorating broth. This soup is traditionally enhanced with extras for a meal; crusty bread, one of the most common, is highly recommended to help soak up all the delectable broth. A squeeze of lemon and a dollop of additional harissa are also traditional and add freshness. Then myriad other toppings can make the dish as filling as you wish, from hard-cooked eggs to canned tuna. Don't be afraid to try several different combinations.

Lablabi

1. **FOR THE SOUP** Dissolve 1½ tablespoons salt in 2 quarts cold water in large container. Add chickpeas and soak at room temperature for at least 8 hours or up to 24 hours. Drain and rinse well. (If you're pressed for time, see page 13 for information on quick brining your chickpeas.)

2. Bring chickpeas and 10 cups water to boil in Dutch oven. Reduce heat and simmer, stirring occasionally until chickpeas are just tender, 30 to 45 minutes.

3. Stir in onion, ¼ cup harissa, garlic, cumin, and salt and cook until onion is softened and chickpeas are tender, 10 to 15 minutes. Off heat, stir in lemon juice and season with salt to taste. Divide soup among individual bowls and top with cilantro and remaining ¼ cup harissa.

4. **FOR THE TOPPINGS** Serve with your preferred toppings.

Harissa

Makes 1 cup | **Total Time** 10 minutes

`FAST` `VEGAN`

¾ cup extra-virgin olive oil
12 garlic cloves, minced
¼ cup paprika
2 tablespoons ground coriander
2 tablespoons ground dried Aleppo pepper
2 teaspoons ground cumin
1½ teaspoons caraway seeds
1 teaspoon table salt

Combine all ingredients in bowl and microwave until bubbling and very fragrant, about 1 minute, stirring halfway through microwaving. Let cool completely before serving. (Harissa can be refrigerated for up to 4 days. Bring to room temperature before serving.)

SOUP

1½ tablespoons table salt for brining
1 pound (2¾ cups) dried chickpeas, picked over and rinsed
1 onion, chopped fine
½ cup Harissa, divided
4 garlic cloves, minced
2 teaspoons ground cumin
1 teaspoon table salt
2 tablespoons lemon juice
¼ cup chopped fresh cilantro

TOPPINGS

Crusty bread
Extra-virgin olive oil
Canned tuna
Capers, rinsed
Pitted green olives
Lemon wedges
Hard-cooked eggs
Greek yogurt

Coconut Black Bean Soup with Plantains

Serves 6 | **Total Time** 1 hour 25 minutes, plus 8 hours brining `VEGAN`

WHY THIS RECIPE WORKS Earthy black beans and fried sweet plantains are a frequent pairing across many countries and cuisines. To transform this duo into a soup, we create a savory base of bell peppers, serrano chile, garlic, cumin, and oregano, and add soaked dried black beans. Instead of simmering the beans in water or broth, we use coconut milk for richness and a hint of sweetness. While the soup simmers, we fry diced ripe plantains and make sweet-tart pickled red onions. Pureeing some of the cooked beans creates plenty of body for the soup while we keep the rest whole for texture. A final squeeze of lime juice and chopped cilantro rounds out the dish, before we top it with chunks of sweet plantain and crunchy pickled onions. Look for very ripe plantains that yield to firm pressure and are dark yellow and heavily blackened, indicating that they are sweet.

1½ tablespoons table salt for brining
1 pound (2½ cups) dried black beans, picked over and rinsed
¼ cup plus 1 teaspoon vegetable oil, divided
2 green bell peppers, stemmed, seeded, and chopped fine
1 serrano chile, stemmed, seeded, and minced
1¼ teaspoons plus ¼ teaspoon table salt, divided
1 large red onion, chopped fine, divided
5 garlic cloves, minced
1 tablespoon ground cumin
1 teaspoon dried oregano
5 cups vegetable broth
1 (14-ounce) can coconut milk
¼ cup red wine vinegar
2 very ripe plantains, peeled, quartered lengthwise and sliced ½ inch thick
½ cup chopped fresh cilantro, divided
1 teaspoon grated lime zest plus 1 tablespoon juice

1. Dissolve 1½ tablespoons salt in 2 quarts cold water in large container. Add beans and soak at room temperature for at least 8 hours or up to 24 hours. Drain and rinse well. (If you're pressed for time, see page 13 for information on quick brining your beans.)

2. Heat 2 tablespoons oil in large Dutch oven over medium heat until shimmering. Add bell peppers, serrano, ½ teaspoon salt, and three-quarters of onion and cook until vegetables are softened and onions are lightly browned, 12 to 15 minutes. Stir in garlic, cumin, and oregano and cook until fragrant, about 30 seconds. Stir in soaked beans, broth, and coconut milk and bring to simmer. Reduce heat to low and simmer, covered, until beans are tender, 25 to 30 minutes, stirring occasionally.

Coconut Black
Bean Soup
with Plantains

PEELING PLANTAINS

1. To peel, cut off both ends of plantain, then make 1 cut lengthwise through skin, but not into fruit.

2. Pull away skin from side of plantain.

3. While beans cook, heat 1 teaspoon oil in 12-inch nonstick skillet over medium heat until shimmering. Add remaining one-quarter of onion and ⅛ teaspoon salt and cook until softened, 3 to 5 minutes. Stir in vinegar and cook until evaporated, about 1 minute. Transfer onion to small bowl; set aside. Wipe skillet clean with paper towels.

4. Heat remaining 2 tablespoons oil in now-empty skillet over medium heat until shimmering; add plantains and cook until tender and dark brown on all sides, 5 to 7 minutes, turning as needed. Transfer to paper towel–lined plate and sprinkle with ⅛ teaspoon salt; set aside.

5. Process 1½ cups cooked beans and 2 cups soup liquid in blender until smooth, about 30 seconds, then return to pot. Off heat, stir in ¼ cup cilantro, lime zest and juice, and remaining ¾ teaspoon salt. Serve, topping individual servings with plantains, red onions and remaining ¼ cup cilantro.

Hot and Sour Soup

Serves 4 to 6 | **Total Time** 1 hour 10 minutes

WHY THIS RECIPE WORKS "This soup is a warm hello," says Jeffrey Pang, one of the authors of our *A Very Chinese Cookbook*. Jeffrey adds, "Many small family-run restaurants I frequented would greet customers with a complimentary bowl of hot and sour soup. It's like the Chinese equivalent of bread and butter at a French bistro." He explains that because he always associated this soup with restaurant dining, his family rarely made it at home. "Turns out, it's easier to make a batch than you'd think," he says, explaining that it is tempting to substitute ingredients but because this soup has "such a specific taste, I really suggest you don't." He recommends extra-firm tofu, "otherwise it'll disintegrate in the soup." He also suggests using Chinese black vinegar. "It's fairly inexpensive and its malty sweet flavor is integral to this soup. And the floral headiness of white pepper just can't be replicated with black pepper. Don't compromise on those ingredients, and you'll make a superb hot and sour soup I'll want to come over for sometime." Serve with vinegar or white pepper. For a more authentic hot and sour soup experience, use wood ear mushrooms instead of shiitakes.

Hot and Sour Soup

7 ounces extra-firm tofu, cut into ½-inch pieces

1 (6-ounce) boneless pork chop, trimmed

6 cups chicken broth

3 tablespoons soy sauce, plus extra for seasoning

1 (5-ounce) can bamboo shoots, sliced thin lengthwise

4 ounces shiitake mushrooms, stemmed and sliced ¼ inch thick

3 tablespoons plus 1 teaspoon water, divided

3 tablespoons plus ½ teaspoon cornstarch, divided

5 tablespoons Chinese black vinegar, plus extra for seasoning

1 teaspoon white pepper

1 teaspoon toasted sesame oil

1–3 teaspoons Chili Oil (page 119)

1 large egg

3 scallions, sliced thin on bias

1. Spread tofu on paper towel–lined plate and let drain for 20 minutes. Place pork chop on large plate and freeze until firm, about 15 minutes. Holding knife parallel to cutting board, slice pork chop into 2 thin cutlets. Slice each cutlet crosswise into thin strips.

2. Bring broth and soy sauce to simmer in large saucepan over medium heat. Add bamboo shoots and mushrooms and cook until mushrooms are just tender, about 2 minutes. Stir in tofu and pork and cook until pork is no longer pink, about 2 minutes.

3. Whisk 3 tablespoons water, 3 tablespoons cornstarch, vinegar, and white pepper together in bowl, then stir mixture into soup. Increase heat to medium-high and cook, stirring occasionally, until soup thickens and turns translucent, about 1 minute. Remove soup from heat, stir in sesame oil and chili oil, and season with extra soy sauce to taste.

4. Whisk remaining 1 teaspoon water and remaining ½ teaspoon cornstarch together in small bowl, then whisk in egg until combined. Using large soup spoon, add egg mixture to hot soup by slowly drizzling very thin streams into soup in circular motion. Without stirring soup, let soup sit off heat for 1 minute. Return soup to simmer over medium-high heat. Sprinkle individual portions with scallions before serving with extra soy sauce and vinegar.

Chili Oil

Makes 1½ cups | **Total Time** 40 minutes, plus 12 hours resting `VEGAN`

- ½ cup Sichuan chili flakes
- 2 tablespoons sesame seeds
- 2 tablespoons Sichuan peppercorns, coarsely ground, divided
- ½ teaspoon table salt
- 1 cup vegetable oil
- 1 (1-inch) piece ginger, unpeeled, sliced into ¼-inch-thick rounds and smashed
- 3 star anise pods
- 5 cardamom pods, crushed
- 2 bay leaves

1. Combine chili flakes, sesame seeds, half of peppercorns, and salt in heatproof bowl. Cook oil, ginger, star anise, cardamom, bay leaves, and remaining peppercorns in small saucepan over low heat, stirring occasionally, until spices have darkened and mixture is very fragrant, 25 to 30 minutes.

2. Strain mixture through fine-mesh strainer into bowl with chili flake mixture (mixture may bubble slightly); discard solids in strainer. Stir well to combine. Let sit at room temperature until flavors meld, about 12 hours, before using. (Oil can be stored in airtight container for up to 3 months; flavor will mature over time.)

Split Pea and Ham Soup

Serves 6 to 8 | **Total Time** 1 hour 50 minutes

WHY THIS RECIPE WORKS In this soup, split peas are the main feature, traditionally accompanied by a leftover meaty ham shank. But what if you don't have a leftover ham bone? We set out to create a richly flavorful broth with tender shreds of meat to accompany the split peas. It turns out that ham steak is also very meaty and provides the soup with a fuller pork flavor without making the soup too greasy. A few strips of raw bacon add the richness and smokiness that the bone would provide. Four ounces of regular sliced bacon can be used, but the thinner slices are harder to remove from the soup. Unsoaked split peas break down just as well as soaked and are better at absorbing the flavor of the soup. If the soup is too thin at the end of step 2, increase the heat and simmer, uncovered, until the desired consistency is reached. If it is too thick, thin it with a little water. We like to garnish the soup with croutons, fresh peas, chopped mint, and a drizzle of aged balsamic vinegar.

- 2 tablespoons unsalted butter
- 1 large onion, chopped fine
- ½ teaspoon table salt
- 2 garlic cloves, minced
- 7 cups water
- 1 pound ham steak, skin removed, cut into quarters
- 3 slices thick-cut bacon
- 1 pound (2 cups) split peas, picked over and rinsed
- 2 sprigs fresh thyme
- 2 bay leaves
- 2 carrots, peeled and cut into ½-inch pieces
- 1 celery rib, cut into ½-inch pieces

1. Melt butter in Dutch oven over medium-high heat. Add onion and salt and cook, stirring often, until onion is softened, about 5 minutes. Stir in garlic and cook until fragrant, about 30 seconds. Stir in water, ham steak, bacon, peas, thyme, and bay leaves. Increase heat to high and bring to simmer, stirring frequently to keep peas from sticking to bottom. Reduce heat to low, cover, and simmer until peas are tender but not falling apart, about 45 minutes.

2. Remove ham steak and cover with plastic wrap to prevent it from drying out; set aside. Stir in carrots and celery and simmer, covered, until vegetables are tender and peas have almost completely broken down, about 30 minutes.

3. Shred ham into small bite-size pieces. Discard thyme, bay leaves, and bacon slices. Return ham to soup and season with salt and pepper to taste. Serve.

Hearty Spanish-Style Lentil and Chorizo Soup with Kale

Chorba Frik

Hearty Spanish-Style Lentil and Chorizo Soup with Kale

Serves 6 to 8 | **Total Time** 2¾ hours, plus 30 minutes brining

WHY THIS RECIPE WORKS Our version of Spain's thick and smoky lentil soup pairs dried lentils suspended in a rich broth with flavor-packed sausage and hearty greens. We use lentilles du Puy (French green lentils) because if you plan to make this soup ahead and store it in the fridge or freezer, the lentils won't get overly soft. Brining them briefly before cooking prevents blowouts and ensures that they are well seasoned. Browning links of Spanish chorizo and then simmering them in the soup gives a juicy texture, and we sweat finely chopped aromatics in the chorizo's fat for added depth of flavor. We finish the soup with tadka, an Indian technique in which a mixture of spices are bloomed in oil (see page 148). Sherry vinegar brightens the soup. If Spanish-style chorizo is not available, kielbasa sausage can be substituted. Red wine vinegar can be used instead of sherry vinegar. We prefer sweet smoked paprika for this recipe.

> **Substitution:** We like lentilles du Puy for this recipe; however you can use dried brown, black, or regular green lentils. Note that cooking times will vary depending on the type used. Do not use red or yellow lentils, or canned lentils.

- 1 pound (2¼ cups) dried lentilles du Puy, picked over and rinsed
- 2 teaspoons table salt for brining
- 1 large onion
- 5 tablespoons extra-virgin olive oil, divided
- 1½ pounds Spanish-style chorizo sausage, pricked with fork several times
- 3 carrots, peeled and cut into ¼-inch pieces
- 3 tablespoons minced fresh parsley, divided
- 1 teaspoon table salt
- 3 tablespoons sherry vinegar, plus extra for seasoning
- 2 bay leaves
- ⅛ teaspoon ground cloves
- 12 ounces kale, stemmed and cut into ½-inch pieces
- 2 tablespoons sweet smoked paprika
- 3 garlic cloves, minced
- ½ teaspoon pepper
- 1 tablespoon all-purpose flour

1. Place lentils and 2 teaspoons salt in large container, cover with 4 cups boiling water, and let soak for 30 minutes. Drain well.

2. Meanwhile, finely chop three-quarters of onion (you should have about 1 cup) and grate remaining quarter (you should have about 3 tablespoons). Heat 2 tablespoons oil in Dutch oven over medium heat until shimmering. Add chorizo and cook until browned on all sides, 6 to 8 minutes. Transfer chorizo to large plate and set aside. Reduce heat to low and add chopped onion, carrots, 1 tablespoon parsley, and salt. Cover and cook, stirring occasionally, until vegetables are very soft but not brown, 25 to 30 minutes. If vegetables begin to brown, add 1 tablespoon water to pot.

3. Add lentils and vinegar to vegetables in pot, increase heat to medium-high, and cook, stirring frequently, until vinegar starts to evaporate, 3 to 4 minutes. Add 7 cups water, reserved chorizo, bay leaves, and cloves; bring to simmer. Reduce heat to low, cover, and cook for 15 minutes. Stir in kale and cook until lentils and kale are tender, about 15 minutes. Off heat, remove chorizo from lentils and discard bay leaves. When chorizo is cool enough to handle, cut in half lengthwise, then cut each half into ¼-inch-thick slices.

4. Heat remaining 3 tablespoons oil in small saucepan over medium heat until shimmering. Add paprika, grated onion, garlic, and pepper and cook, stirring constantly, until fragrant, 2 minutes. Add flour and cook, stirring constantly, for 1 minute. Stir paprika mixture into lentils and continue to cook until flavors meld and soup has thickened, 10 to 15 minutes. Return chorizo to soup.

5. Stir in remaining 2 tablespoons parsley and season with salt, pepper, and up to 2 teaspoons vinegar to taste. Serve.

Chorba Frik

Serves 4 to 6 | **Total Time** 1½ hours

WHY THIS RECIPE WORKS Stews and soups are a universal starter on Ramadan iftar dinner tables worldwide, as they hydrate the body and prepare it for digestion after a day of fasting. Chorba, meaning soup, with its many variations, is widely consumed in Algeria, Tunisia, Morocco, and Libya. Chorba frik, a soup packed with freekeh, is a favorite culinary tradition. The focal ingredient is the freekeh. Consumed throughout the Mediterranean for thousands of years, freekeh is made from roasted durum wheat harvested while the grains are still young and green. Through simmering, the grain retains its pleasantly chewy texture and imparts a signature smoky, nutty flavor to the dish. Though the stewy dish varies from household to household, its foundation is consistent: A nourishing bowl of aromatic, well-spiced tomato-based broth simmered with plentiful freekeh, chorba also contains lots of fresh cilantro, morsels

of meat, and sometimes chickpeas. Our recipe uses a can of chickpeas as well as two bone-in chicken thighs, making the soup even more filling without detracting from the grain. Do not use whole freekeh in this recipe.

1 (14.5-ounce) can whole peeled tomatoes
2 (5- to 7-ounce) bone-in chicken thighs, trimmed
1¼ teaspoons table salt, divided
2 tablespoons extra-virgin olive oil
1 onion, chopped fine
1 celery rib, minced
1 cup minced fresh cilantro, plus ¼ cup leaves for serving
2 tablespoons tomato paste
3 garlic cloves, minced
1 tablespoon ground coriander
1 tablespoon paprika
2 teaspoons ground cumin
½ teaspoon pepper
¼ teaspoon ground cinnamon
¼ teaspoon cayenne pepper
6 cups water
1 (15-ounce) can chickpeas, undrained
½ cup cracked freekeh, rinsed
1 teaspoon dried mint
Lemon wedges

1. Pulse tomatoes and their juice in food processor until pureed, about 30 seconds. Pat chicken dry with paper towels and sprinkle with ¼ teaspoon salt. Heat oil in Dutch oven over medium-high heat until just smoking. Cook chicken skin side down until well browned, about 5 minutes; transfer chicken to plate. Pour off all but 2 tablespoons fat from pot.

2. Add onion, celery, and remaining 1 teaspoon salt to fat in pot and cook over medium heat until softened, about 5 minutes. Stir in minced cilantro, tomato paste, garlic, coriander, paprika, cumin, pepper, cinnamon, and cayenne and cook until fragrant, about 1 minute. Stir in pureed tomatoes, water, chickpeas and their liquid, and freekeh, scraping up any browned bits. Nestle chicken and any accumulated juices into pot and bring to simmer. Adjust heat as needed to maintain simmer and cook until freekeh is tender and chicken registers 195 degrees and easily shreds with fork, 35 to 45 minutes.

3. Transfer chicken to cutting board and let cool slightly. Once cool enough to handle, shred chicken into bite-size pieces using 2 forks, and discard skin and bones. Stir shredded chicken and any accumulated juices back into pot and season with salt and pepper to taste. Sprinkle with cilantro leaves and dried mint. Serve with lemon wedges.

Coconut Chicken Soup with Red Rice

Gingery Chicken and Rice Soup with Shiitakes

Coconut Chicken Soup with Red Rice

Serves 6 to 8 | **Total Time** 2 hours 10 minutes

WHY THIS RECIPE WORKS A rice variety with a red husk and nutty flavor, red rice is minimally processed; it is hearty and nutritious. We like its pretty grains and full-bodied flavor in this soup. We first brown bone-in chicken breasts and thighs, and then cook onion in the reserved fat. Then we add aromatics, water, and salt to build a flavorful broth, in which we cook both rice and mushrooms. Rich coconut milk and earthy rehydrated shiitake mushrooms with their liquid deepen flavor. Bone-in chicken parts hold up to a longer cook time and guarantee tender chicken pieces. Herbs round out the comforting warmth and add freshness.

2 (12-ounce) bone-in split chicken breasts, trimmed
2 (5- to 7-ounce) bone-in chicken thighs, trimmed
2 tablespoons vegetable oil, divided
1 onion, chopped
8 cups water
2 lemongrass stalks, trimmed to bottom 6 inches and sliced thin
1 (1-inch) piece ginger, peeled and sliced into ¼-inch-thick rounds
3 garlic cloves, smashed and peeled
1½ teaspoons table salt
½ ounce dried shiitake mushrooms, rinsed and minced
4 ounces white mushrooms, trimmed and sliced thin
⅔ cup red rice, rinsed
1 tablespoon fish sauce
1 (14-ounce) can coconut milk
¼ cup minced fresh cilantro
2 scallions, chopped fine
Lime wedges

1. Pat chicken dry with paper towels. Heat 1 tablespoon oil in Dutch oven over medium-high heat until just smoking. Place chicken breasts and thighs skin side down in pot and cook until well browned, about 5 minutes. Transfer chicken to plate and discard skin.

2. Pour off all but 1 tablespoon fat left in pot. Add onion and cook over medium heat until softened, about 5 minutes. Stir in water, browned chicken and any accumulated juices, lemongrass, ginger, garlic, and salt, scraping up any browned bits, and bring to simmer. Reduce heat to low and cook until chicken thighs register at least 175 degrees, and chicken breasts register 160 degrees, about 30 minutes.

3. Transfer chicken to large plate and set aside to cool slightly. Strain cooking liquid through fine-mesh strainer, reserving broth and discarding solids. Once cool enough to handle, using 2 forks, shred chicken into bite-size pieces. Discard bones. Combine 1 cup reserved broth and shiitake mushrooms in bowl, cover, and let sit until softened, about 5 minutes. Drain mushrooms in fine-mesh strainer, reserving liquid, and set aside.

4. Heat remaining 1 tablespoon oil in now-empty Dutch oven over medium heat until shimmering. Add white mushrooms and cook until softened, about 3 minutes. Add rice, fish sauce, reserved broth, reserved mushroom soaking liquid, and soaked shiitakes. Bring to simmer and cook over medium-low heat until rice is tender, 30 to 35 minutes. Stir in shredded chicken and coconut milk and cook until warmed through, about 5 minutes. Season with salt and pepper to taste. Off heat, stir in cilantro and scallions. Serve with lime wedges.

Gingery Chicken and Rice Soup with Shiitakes

Serves 6 to 8 | **Total Time** 1 hour 20 minutes

WHY THIS RECIPE WORKS In search of a new spin on age-old chicken and rice soup, we turned to another classic pairing of miso, ginger, and scallion that plays well with rich and nutty brown rice. Miso and shiitakes create an umami-rich broth with the help of seared, bone-in chicken thighs. Ginger adds warmth and vibrancy that helps to lighten the soup. While ginger is commonly added at the beginning of cooking along with other aromatics, we find that adding the ginger near the end of cooking helps it retain volatile compounds that might otherwise get lost during simmering. The scallions and cilantro round out the soup, along with rice wine vinegar for an added pop of acidity. We use brown rice in this soup not only for its nutty flavor and chewy texture, but also for the added health benefits.

2 pounds bone-in chicken thighs, trimmed
1½ teaspoons table salt, divided
¾ teaspoon pepper, divided
1 tablespoon vegetable oil
1 onion, chopped fine
6 ounces shiitake mushrooms, stemmed and sliced thin
2 garlic cloves, minced
6 cups water
4 cups chicken broth
⅔ cup long-grain brown rice, rinsed
2 tablespoons miso
1 tablespoon grated fresh ginger
1 tablespoon unseasoned rice wine vinegar
2 scallions, white parts sliced thin, green parts cut into 1-inch pieces
½ cup chopped fresh cilantro
Toasted sesame oil

1. Pat chicken dry with paper towels and sprinkle with ¼ teaspoon salt and ¼ teaspoon pepper. Heat vegetable oil in Dutch oven over medium-high heat until shimmering. Add chicken and cook until well browned on both sides, 8 to 10 minutes. Transfer to large plate; remove and discard skin. Set aside.

2. Pour off all but 1 tablespoon fat from pot. Add onion, mushrooms, 1 teaspoon salt, and remaining ½ teaspoon pepper and cook over medium heat until just beginning to brown, 5 to 7 minutes. Add garlic and cook until fragrant, about 30 seconds.

3. Stir in water, broth, rice, and reserved chicken thighs and any accumulated juices, scraping up any browned bits, and bring to boil. Reduce heat to medium-low and simmer until chicken registers at least 175 degrees, about 10 minutes. Transfer chicken to large plate to cool slightly and continue to cook soup, simmering gently, until rice is tender, 15 to 20 minutes.

4. Using wide, shallow spoon, skim excess fat from surface of soup. Using 2 forks, shred chicken into bite-size pieces; discard bones. Stir miso, ginger, vinegar, scallions, and shredded chicken into soup and cook until warmed through, about 3 minutes. Season with salt and pepper to taste. Serve, passing cilantro and sesame oil separately.

Chicken Orzo Soup with Kale and Chickpeas

Serves 6 | **Total Time** 55 minutes

WHY THIS RECIPE WORKS For an aromatic, nourishing weeknight dinner that is on the table in under an hour, try this chicken and pasta soup. We add extra protein in the form of chickpeas, include kale for color and nutrition, and flavor the soup with smoky cumin and fragrant coriander seed. We like to use our Perfect Poached Chicken (page 176) but you can use store-bought rotisserie chicken here. Blooming the aromatics and spices in rendered chicken fat at the start builds flavor before we add broth and water and simmer our other ingredients. A little lemon juice goes a long way in adding brightness to the finished soup.

2 tablespoons extra-virgin olive oil
1 onion, chopped fine
  Pinch red pepper flakes
3 garlic cloves, minced
¼ teaspoon ground cumin
¼ teaspoon ground coriander
4 cups chicken broth
4 cups water
3 ounces curly kale, stemmed and cut into ½-inch pieces (6 cups)
1 (15-ounce) can chickpeas, rinsed
½ cup orzo
2 cups cooked chicken, shredded into bite-size pieces
2 tablespoons lemon juice

1. Heat oil in Dutch oven over medium heat until shimmering. Add onion and pepper flakes and cook, stirring occasionally, until onion is softened, about 5 minutes. Add garlic, cumin, and coriander and cook until fragrant, about 1 minute. Add broth and water; increase heat to high and bring to simmer. Stir in kale, chickpeas, and orzo, reduce heat to medium-low, and simmer, partially covered, for 10 minutes.

2. Add chicken and cook until orzo and kale are tender, about 2 minutes. Off heat, stir in lemon juice and season with salt and pepper to taste. Serve.

Chicken Barley Soup

Serves 6 | **Total Time** 1½ hours

WHY THIS RECIPE WORKS Pearl barley cooks faster than regular barley because both its hull and bran have been removed and it releases starch into cooking liquid, two reasons we like using it for soups. For this dish, we cook pearl barley until tender, with carrots and celery, in a broth made aromatic with onion, garlic, and herbs such as bay leaf and thyme. We like to shred our Perfect Poached Chicken (page 176) and warm it through in the soup, but you can use store-bought rotisserie chicken here. With a splash of lemon juice before serving to add a welcome burst of freshness, this hearty meal is ready.

2 tablespoons unsalted butter
1 onion, chopped fine
½ teaspoon dried thyme
  Pinch red pepper flakes
2 garlic cloves, minced
4 cups chicken broth
4 cups water
¾ cup pearl barley
1 bay leaf
2 celery ribs, cut into ¼-inch pieces
2 carrots, peeled and cut into ¼-inch pieces
2 cups cooked chicken, shredded into bite-size pieces
1 tablespoon lemon juice

1. Melt butter in Dutch oven over medium heat. Add onion, thyme, and pepper flakes and cook, stirring occasionally, until onion is softened, about 5 minutes. Add garlic and cook until fragrant, about 1 minute. Add broth, water, barley, and bay leaf, increase heat to high and bring to simmer. Reduce heat to medium-low and simmer, partially covered, for 15 minutes.

2. Add celery and carrots and simmer, partially covered, until vegetables start to soften, about 15 minutes.

3. Add chicken and cook until barley and vegetables are tender, about 10 minutes. Off heat, stir in lemon juice and season with salt and pepper to taste. Serve.

Italian Wedding Soup with Kale and Farro

Serves 6 | **Total Time** 1¾ hours

WHY THIS RECIPE WORKS Traditional Italian wedding soup is so named because of the harmonious marriage of meatballs, greens, and pasta in a savory, fortified broth. We love the idea of a hearty, meal-in-a-bowl soup but wanted to take the soup in a grain-forward direction. We replace ditalini with hearty farro; the nutty whole grain rounds out the soup perfectly. For a fast path to a complex broth, we simmer chicken broth with aromatic fennel, onion, garlic, and dried porcini mushrooms, adding white wine for sharpness and Worcestershire sauce for meaty depth. Instead of traditional beef and pork, we prepare turkey meatballs, flavored with parsley, Parmesan, and minced fennel fronds. We poach them gently in the broth so they are delicate and tender. Chopped kale brings its characteristic assertive texture. Be sure to use 93 percent lean ground turkey, not ground turkey breast (also labeled 99 percent fat-free), in this recipe.

Italian Wedding Soup with Kale and Farro

- 1 tablespoon extra-virgin olive oil
- 1 fennel bulb, ¼ cup fronds minced, stalks discarded, bulb halved, cored, and sliced thin
- 1 onion, sliced thin
- 5 garlic cloves (4 peeled and smashed, 1 minced to paste)
- ¼ ounce dried porcini mushrooms, rinsed and minced
- ½ cup dry white wine
- 1 tablespoon Worcestershire sauce
- 4 cups chicken broth
- 4 cups water
- 1 slice hearty white sandwich bread, torn into 1-inch pieces
- 5 tablespoons milk
- 12 ounces ground turkey
- ¼ cup grated Parmesan cheese
- ¼ cup minced fresh parsley
- 1 teaspoon table salt, divided
- ⅛ teaspoon pepper
- 1 cup whole farro, rinsed
- 8 ounces kale, stemmed and cut into ½-inch pieces

1. Heat oil in Dutch oven over medium-high heat until shimmering. Stir in fennel, onion, smashed garlic, and mushrooms and cook, stirring frequently, until just softened and lightly browned, 5 to 7 minutes. Stir in wine and Worcestershire and cook for 1 minute. Stir in broth and water and bring to simmer. Reduce heat to low, cover, and simmer for 30 minutes.

2. Meanwhile, combine bread and milk in large bowl and, using fork, mash mixture to uniform paste. Add turkey, Parmesan, parsley, ½ teaspoon salt, pepper, fennel fronds, and minced garlic and knead gently with your hands until evenly combined. Using your wet hands, roll heaping teaspoon-sized balls of meat mixture into meatballs and transfer to rimmed baking sheet. (You should have 35 to 40 meatballs.) Cover with greased plastic wrap and refrigerate for 30 minutes.

3. Strain broth through fine-mesh strainer set over large bowl, pressing on solids to extract as much broth as possible; discard solids. Wipe pot clean with paper towels and return strained broth to pot.

4. Bring broth to boil over medium-high heat. Add farro and remaining ½ teaspoon salt, reduce heat to medium-low, cover, and simmer until farro is just tender, about 15 minutes. Uncover, stir in meatballs and kale and cook, stirring occasionally, until meatballs are cooked through and farro is tender, 5 to 7 minutes. Season with salt and pepper to taste, and serve.

Madzoon ov Kofte

Serves 6 | **Total Time** 1¼ hours

WHY THIS RECIPE WORKS Bulgur is a grain popular across the Middle East and it adds heft to a number of dishes like this soup, madzoon ov kofte, a version of the Armenian yogurt soup Tanabour (page 102). Adding meatballs to the soup makes it a nourishing, hearty meal but instead of using the time-consuming stuffed, spiced meatballs that are more traditional, we use easy-to-make meatballs from ground beef and quick-cooking bulgur, with baking soda to make them light and airy. Pasta and chickpeas make the dish even more hearty. We use Greek yogurt for the base, since it is rich and thick, with just the right amount of tartness. As with our tanabour, we garnish the soup with cilantro and Aleppo pepper–infused melted butter. Dried mint is widely used in Middle Eastern cooking; its flavor is quite different from that of fresh mint, so if you can't find it, it's better to omit it than to substitute fresh. You can use small elbow macaroni instead of the pasta shells.

8	ounces 85 percent lean ground beef
3	tablespoons water
1¾	teaspoons table salt, divided
¼	teaspoon baking soda, divided
½	cup medium-grind bulgur, rinsed
¼	cup chopped fresh cilantro, divided
2	teaspoons ground dried Aleppo pepper, divided
1	teaspoon ground coriander
½	teaspoon pepper, divided
4	tablespoons unsalted butter, divided
1	onion, chopped fine
1	teaspoon dried mint
4	cups chicken broth
1	(15-ounce) can chickpeas, undrained
4	ounces (1 cup) small pasta shells
1½	cups plain Greek yogurt
1	large egg yolk

1. Toss beef with water, 1 teaspoon salt, and ⅛ teaspoon baking soda in bowl until thoroughly combined. Add bulgur, 1 tablespoon cilantro, 1 teaspoon Aleppo pepper, coriander, and ¼ teaspoon pepper and mix by hand until uniform. Transfer meat mixture to cutting board and press into 6-inch square. Using bench scraper or sharp knife, divide mixture into 36 squares (6 rows by 6 rows). Using your lightly moistened hands, roll each square into smooth ball and leave on cutting board.

2. Melt 2 tablespoons butter in large saucepan over medium heat. Add onion, mint, remaining ¾ teaspoon salt, remaining ¾ teaspoon baking soda, and remaining ¼ teaspoon pepper and cook, stirring occasionally, until onion has broken down into soft paste and is just starting to stick to saucepan, 6 to 8 minutes.

3. Stir in broth, chickpeas and their liquid, and meatballs and bring to boil. Simmer over medium-low heat for 5 minutes, stirring occasionally. Add pasta and continue to cook until pasta is tender. While pasta cooks, whisk yogurt and egg yolk together in large bowl.

4. Remove saucepan from heat. Using ladle, transfer 1½ cups broth to liquid measuring cup (try to avoid meatballs, pasta, and chickpeas). Whisking vigorously, gradually add broth to yogurt mixture. Add half of yogurt-broth mixture back to saucepan and stir to combine. Stir in remaining yogurt-broth mixture. Cover and let sit for 10 minutes to thicken.

5. Heat soup over medium heat, stirring occasionally, until temperature registers between 180 and 185 degrees (do not allow soup to boil or yogurt will curdle). Remove from heat, stir in 1 tablespoon cilantro, and season with salt to taste. (Broth should have consistency of buttermilk; if thicker, adjust by adding hot water, 2 tablespoons at a time.)

6. Melt remaining 2 tablespoons butter in small skillet over medium-high heat. Off heat, stir in remaining 1 teaspoon Aleppo pepper. Ladle soup into bowls, drizzle each portion with 1 teaspoon spiced butter, sprinkle with remaining 2 tablespoons cilantro, and serve.

Beef and Oat Berry Soup

Serves 6 to 8 | **Total Time** 1½ hours

WHY THIS RECIPE WORKS Oat berries—the husked kernels of wholesome oat groats—paired with tender meat and rich flavorful broth make for a soup that looks and tastes like it simmered all day though it didn't. We turn to blade steaks here, a flavorful and relatively inexpensive cut of meat from the shoulder. Trimmed and cut into half-inch pieces, this cut becomes tender and rich in the same time it takes for the oat berries to soften. Beef broth, bolstered with tomato paste and dried porcini mushrooms, creates the rich, long-simmered flavor we want. Stirring in chopped baby kale at the end saves us prep and cook time, and finishing with just a little red wine vinegar brings brightness to this hearty grain and beef stew. Before using the blade steaks, trim and discard their interior line of gristle.

3 tablespoons extra virgin olive oil, divided

1½ pounds beef blade steaks, trimmed and cut into ½-inch pieces

1¾ teaspoons table salt, divided

¾ teaspoon pepper, divided

4 carrots, peeled and chopped

2 celery ribs, chopped

1 onion, chopped fine

1 tablespoon minced fresh thyme or 1 teaspoon dried

3 garlic cloves, minced

1 tablespoon tomato paste

¼ ounce dried porcini mushrooms, rinsed and minced

4 cups beef broth

4 cups water

1 cup oat berries (groats), rinsed

5 ounces baby kale, chopped coarse

2 teaspoons red wine vinegar

1. Heat 1 tablespoon oil in Dutch oven over medium-high heat until just smoking. Pat beef dry with paper towels and season with ½ teaspoon salt and ½ teaspoon pepper. Brown half of beef on all sides, 5 to 7 minutes, turning as needed; transfer to bowl. Repeat with remaining beef.

2. Add carrots, celery, onion, remaining 1¼ teaspoons salt, remaining ¼ teaspoon pepper, and remaining 2 tablespoons oil to fat left in pot and cook over medium heat until vegetables are softened and lightly browned, 5 to 7 minutes. Stir in thyme, garlic, tomato paste, and mushrooms and cook until fragrant, about 30 seconds.

3. Stir in browned beef and any accumulated juices, broth, water, and oat berries, scraping up any browned bits. Bring to simmer, then reduce heat to low and cook, covered, until oat berries and beef are tender, about 40 minutes.

4. Stir in kale and vinegar and let sit until kale is wilted, about 1 minute. Season with salt and pepper to taste. Serve.

TRIMMING BLADE STEAKS

1. Cut each steak lengthwise, leaving center line of gristle attached to one half.

2. Slice away gristle from half to which it is attached. Cut both halves into ½-inch pieces.

Madzoon ov Kofte

Beef and Oat Berry Soup

Stews

● FAST (45 minutes or less) ● VEGAN

Photo: Chana Masala

Chicken and
Rye Dumplings

West African
Peanut Stew

Chicken and Rye Dumplings

Serves 6 to 8 | **Total Time** 2 hours

WHY THIS RECIPE WORKS Tender chicken and vegetables in a creamy gravy are traditionally topped by light dumplings. To feature nutty rye flour, we adapt ingredients to match the earthier grain while keeping the original's coziness. Cremini, porcini, and leeks give savory depth. White wine, fresh thyme, and lemon juice add brightness. Using a proportion of half rye flour and half all-purpose flour in the dough allows rye's nutty flavor to shine without turning the texture gummy. Wait to start the dumpling dough until you've cooked through step 3.

STEW

- 3 pounds bone-in chicken thighs, trimmed
- 1¼ teaspoons table salt, divided
- ¾ teaspoon pepper, divided
- 2 teaspoons extra-virgin olive oil, plus extra as needed
- 1½ pounds cremini mushrooms, trimmed and quartered
- 2 leeks, white and light green parts only, halved lengthwise, sliced ½ inch thick, and washed thoroughly
- 2 carrots, peeled, halved lengthwise and sliced ¼ inch thick on bias
- ¼ ounce dried porcini mushrooms, rinsed and minced
- 3 garlic cloves, minced
- 2 teaspoons minced fresh thyme or ¾ teaspoon dried
- 3 tablespoons all-purpose flour
- ¼ cup dry white wine
- 5 cups chicken broth
- 2 bay leaves
- 1 tablespoon lemon juice
- 3 tablespoons minced fresh chives

DUMPLINGS

- ⅔ cup (3⅓ ounces) all-purpose flour
- ⅔ cup (3⅔ ounces) medium or light rye flour
- 2 teaspoons baking powder
- ½ teaspoon table salt
- ⅔ cup milk, warmed to 110 degrees
- 3 tablespoons unsalted butter, melted

1. FOR THE STEW Pat chicken dry with paper towels, then sprinkle with ½ teaspoon salt and ½ teaspoon pepper. Heat oil in Dutch oven over medium-high heat until just smoking. Add half of chicken and cook until well browned on both sides, about 5 minutes per side; transfer to plate.

Repeat with remaining chicken. Pour off all but 3 tablespoons fat from pot (or add extra oil as needed to equal 3 tablespoons). Remove and discard skin from chicken.

2. Add cremini mushrooms and ¼ teaspoon salt to fat in pot and cook over medium heat until fond forms, about 7 minutes. Add leeks and carrots and cook until leeks soften, about 5 minutes. Stir in porcini mushrooms, garlic, and thyme and cook until fragrant, about 30 seconds. Stir in flour and cook for 30 seconds. Stir in wine, scraping up any browned bits. Whisk in chicken broth, then add bay leaves and chicken and any accumulated juices. Bring to simmer, then reduce heat to low, and cook, covered, until chicken registers at least 175 degrees, 20 to 25 minutes.

3. Transfer chicken to cutting board and let cool slightly. Once cool enough to handle, shred chicken into bite-size pieces using 2 forks, and discard bones. Discard bay leaves, then return shredded chicken to stew.

4. FOR THE DUMPLINGS Whisk all-purpose flour, rye flour, baking powder, and salt together in medium bowl. Combine milk and melted butter in 2-cup liquid measuring cup, then stir milk mixture into flour mixture until incorporated and no dry flour remains.

5. Add remaining ½ teaspoon salt, remaining ¼ teaspoon pepper, and lemon juice to stew, then bring to vigorous simmer. Using greased tablespoon measure, drop rounded portions of dumpling batter evenly over top of stew; you should have about 16 dumplings. Cover, reduce heat to low, and cook until dumplings have doubled in size, and toothpick inserted into center of dumpling comes out clean, about 10 minutes. Off heat, remove lid and let sit for 10 minutes. Sprinkle with chives and serve.

West African Peanut Stew

Serves 6 to 8 | **Total Time** 1¼ hours

WHY THIS RECIPE WORKS Peanuts are fresh legumes, edible seeds that grow in pods (their shells). We wanted to make use of them as more than just a snack. Peanut stew, originally called groundnut stew, is common across West Africa. Peanut stews vary greatly there; what connects each unique take is the building of a flavorful broth in which to cook the proteins. As Adwoa Difie Antwi, a Ghanaian friend of one of our test cooks, says, "We often rely on the broth we create [to cook] the meat. This broth brings out the flavor of the meat into the soup." Instead of processing whole peanuts, we turn to peanut butter. Rather than relying on spices, we build up flavor by cooking vegetables, peppers, garlic, and

ginger in the rendered fat from chicken thighs along with peanut oil. Blending the vegetable base with chicken stock ensures the peanut butter incorporates evenly as it thickens the stew. To balance the heartiness, we use mustard greens for freshness and brightness. Many variations of this stew use large quantities of palm oil so that pockets of oil form along the surface of the stew, creating a luxurious and velvety texture. We find that using the combination of peanut oil and the fat from the chicken also creates a rich velvety texture. You can use vegetable oil in place of the peanut oil. We prefer to use natural, unsweetened peanut butter in this recipe. If you can't find Scotch bonnet chiles, you can substitute habanero chiles. Serve with rice (see pages 298–299), if desired.

2   pounds bone-in chicken thighs, trimmed
1   tablespoon peanut oil
2   onions, chopped
6   garlic cloves, minced
1–2 Scotch bonnet chiles, minced
1   tablespoon tomato paste
1   (28-ounce) can whole peeled tomatoes
3   cups chicken broth
1   cup creamy natural peanut butter
8   ounces mustard greens, stemmed and
    cut into 1-inch pieces
2   tablespoons grated fresh ginger
1   teaspoon table salt
½   cup dry-roasted peanuts, chopped

1. Pat chicken dry with paper towels. Heat oil in Dutch oven over medium-high heat until just smoking. Cook chicken skin side down until well browned, about 5 minutes. Transfer to plate and discard skin.

2. Add onions to fat in pot and cook over medium heat until softened, about 5 minutes. Stir in garlic, Scotch bonnet, and tomato paste and cook until fragrant, about 1 minute. Transfer to food processor along with tomatoes and their juice and process until smooth, 1 to 2 minutes, scraping down sides of processor bowl as needed.

3. Return tomato mixture to now-empty pot and stir in broth and peanut butter until incorporated. Stir in chicken and bring to simmer. Cook over medium heat until stew has thickened and chicken registers 175 degrees, about 25 minutes.

4. Transfer chicken to cutting board. Once cool enough to handle, cut chicken into 1-inch pieces, discarding bones. Stir chicken, mustard greens, ginger, and salt into sauce in pot and cook until mustard greens are wilted, about 2 minutes. Season with salt and pepper to taste. Sprinkle with peanuts and serve.

Italian-Style Lamb Stew with Roman Beans, Green Beans, and Tomatoes

Serves 6 to 8 | **Total Time** 3 hours

WHY THIS RECIPE WORKS In this deeply flavorful lamb stew, tender pieces of lamb are paired with two kinds of beans—meaty, creamy, mildly sweet Roman beans (also called cranberry beans) and green beans, for fresh contrast. Boneless lamb shoulder is perfect for braising, turning meltingly tender as it cooks, and gives us the same bold flavor as lamb leg for less money. We brown the meat before building our stewing liquid with onions, garlic, tomatoes, and rosemary. A little flour ensures a stew with the spoon-clinging consistency we desire. For the liquid, we use a combination of water and white wine to keep the clean lamb flavor in the foreground. To prevent the beans from breaking down completely, we add them halfway through cooking. A final sprinkling of basil just before serving adds pleasant freshness.

- 1 (3-pound) boneless lamb shoulder, pulled apart at seams, trimmed, and cut into 1½-inch pieces
- 1¾ teaspoons table salt, divided
- ½ teaspoon pepper
- 3 tablespoons vegetable oil, divided
- 3 onions, chopped
- 3 garlic cloves, minced
- ¼ cup all-purpose flour
- 1¾ cups water, divided
- ½ cup dry white wine
- 1 (14.5-ounce) can diced tomatoes
- 1 tablespoon minced fresh rosemary or 1 teaspoon dried
- 2 (15-ounce) cans Roman beans, rinsed
- 12 ounces green beans, trimmed and halved
- ¼ cup chopped fresh basil

1. Adjust oven rack to lower-middle position and heat oven to 300 degrees. Pat lamb dry with paper towels and sprinkle with 1 teaspoon salt and pepper. Heat 1 tablespoon oil in Dutch oven over medium-high heat until just smoking. Add half of lamb and brown on all sides, 6 to 8 minutes; transfer to large bowl. Repeat with 1 tablespoon oil and remaining lamb.

2. Add remaining 1 tablespoon oil, onions, and ¼ teaspoon salt to now-empty pot and cook over medium heat, stirring often, until onions are softened, about 5 minutes. Stir in garlic and cook until fragrant, about 30 seconds. Stir in flour and cook for 30 seconds.

3. Whisk in 1 cup water and wine, scraping up any browned bits and smoothing out any lumps. Slowly whisk in remaining ¾ cup water. Add tomatoes and their juice, rosemary, remaining ½ teaspoon salt, and browned lamb and any accumulated juices, and bring to simmer. Cover, transfer pot to oven, and cook for 1 hour.

4. Remove pot from oven. Stir in beans and sprinkle green beans over top. Return covered pot to oven and cook until meat and vegetables are tender, 50 minutes to 1 hour. Stir in basil and season with salt and pepper to taste. Serve.

Mapo Tofu

Serves 4 to 6 | **Total Time** 1 hour

WHY THIS RECIPE WORKS The most famous culinary export of Sichuan is named for an old widow whose face was scarred by smallpox. The legend goes that she ran a restaurant near Chengdu and was famous for this dish. People traveled far and wide to sample it, and in time it garnered the name mapo tofu or "pockmarked old woman tofu." A thrilling introduction to Sichuan cuisine, mapo tofu is an unapologetically fiery show-case for tofu and the spices that made the region famous. Ground pork is a flavoring, not a primary component of the dish. We start with cubed soft tofu, poaching it gently in chicken broth to help the cubes stay intact in the braise. For the sauce base, we use ginger, garlic, and four Sichuan pantry powerhouses: doubanjiang (toban djan), douchi, Sichuan chili flakes, and Sichuan peppercorns. We finish the dish with cornstarch to create velvety thickness. Serve with steamed rice (see page 298).

- 28 ounces soft tofu, cut into ½-inch cubes
- 1 cup chicken broth
- 6 scallions, sliced thin
- 8 ounces ground pork
- 1 teaspoon vegetable oil, plus extra as needed
- 9 garlic cloves, minced
- ⅓ cup doubanjiang (broad bean chile paste)
- 1 tablespoon grated fresh ginger
- 1 tablespoon douchi (fermented black beans)
- 1 tablespoon Sichuan chili flakes
- 1 tablespoon Sichuan peppercorns, toasted and ground coarse
- 2 tablespoons hoisin sauce
- 2 teaspoons toasted sesame oil
- 2 tablespoons water
- 1 tablespoon cornstarch

Mapo Tofu

1. Place tofu, broth, and scallions in large bowl and microwave, covered, until steaming, 5 to 7 minutes. Let stand while preparing remaining ingredients.

2. Cook pork and vegetable oil in 14-inch flat-bottomed wok over medium heat, breaking up meat with wooden spoon, until meat just begins to brown, 5 to 7 minutes. Using slotted spoon, transfer pork to separate bowl. Pour off all but ¼ cup fat from wok. (If necessary, add vegetable oil to equal ¼ cup.)

3. Add garlic, doubanjiang, ginger, douchi, chili flakes, and peppercorns to fat left in wok and cook over medium heat until spices darken and oil begins to separate from paste, 2 to 3 minutes.

4. Gently pour tofu with broth into wok, followed by hoisin, sesame oil, and cooked pork. Cook, stirring gently and frequently, until simmering, 2 to 3 minutes. Whisk water and cornstarch together in small bowl. Add cornstarch mixture to wok and continue to cook, stirring frequently, until sauce has thickened, about 3 minutes. Serve.

SICHUAN PANTRY INGREDIENTS

The boldly flavored seasonings featured in Mapo Tofu also appear in many Sichuan and other Chinese dishes. They keep indefinitely and are worth seeking out to produce authentic flavors.

SICHUAN PEPPERCORNS A key seasoning, these small reddish-brown husks (and more assertive green husks) aren't true peppercorns but the dried fruit rinds of the prickly ash. They don't contribute heat per se but offer a unique tingling or buzzing sensation known as ma. The peppercorns are often ground before using—you can do this in a spice grinder or mortar and pestle.

DRIED CHILES AND SICHUAN CHILI FLAKES

Dried Sichuan chiles come in many varieties. What you want are bright red chiles with moderate heat, 1 to 2 inches long and ½ inch wide at the stem. We find that tien tsin chiles are readily available at the market and online. Dried arbols chiles can also be used. Sichuan chili flakes are made by crushing dried chiles and are a convenient option when a lot is needed, such as with Chili Oil (page 119). Sichuan chiles are also sold as a powder; however, we prefer the coarse texture of the flakes. Gochugaru (Korean red pepper flakes) are a suitable alternative.

DOUBANJIANG An essential flavoring in Sichuan cuisine, this deep reddish-brown paste is made from red chiles, broad (fava) beans, salt, and wheat flour. It adds spicy, meaty depth to dishes. It's worth seeking out doubanjiang from the town of Pixian (look for Pixian on the label); bright red and chunkier than standard doubanjiang, it has a more assertive, richer flavor.

DOUCHI Salty, savory, and with a hint of funk to finish, fermented black soybeans add incredible depth of flavor to many dishes. They are packed with a hefty amount of salt so be sure to rinse before using.

YACAI Sometimes called suimiyacai, yacai is made by sun-drying mustard stalks, rubbing them with salt, applying spices and sugar, and allowing the stalks to ferment for months. Its unique spice, tang, and complexity make it perfect for our Gan Bian Si Ji Dou (page 284).

Brazilian Black Bean and Pork Stew

Serves 6 to 8 | **Total Time** 3 hours

WHY THIS RECIPE WORKS Feiojada, a black bean–pork stew, is traditionally loaded with pork cuts and pig parts such as feet, ears, tail, and snout. Considered one of Brazil's national dishes, it's as much an event as a meal. For a version with fewer cuts of meat that still feels celebratory, we use three pork cuts that pack a punch and require minimal prep: boneless pork butt, bacon, and smoky linguiça sausage. Adding baking soda to the black beans helps the beans keep their dark hue, giving the stew a striking color. Molho apimentado, a fresh, salsa-like hot sauce traditionally served alongside, brings pleasing heat and cuts through the braise's richness.

STEW

- 1 (3½- to 4-pound) boneless pork butt roast, pulled apart at seams, trimmed, and cut into 1½-inch pieces
- 1½ teaspoons table salt, divided
- ½ teaspoon pepper
- 3 tablespoons vegetable oil, divided
- 4 slices bacon, chopped fine
- 1 onion, chopped fine
- 4 garlic cloves, minced
- 1 tablespoon chili powder
- 1 teaspoon ground cumin
- 1 teaspoon ground coriander
- 7 cups water
- 1 pound (2½ cups) dried black beans, picked over and rinsed
- 2 bay leaves
- ⅛ teaspoon baking soda
- 1 pound linguiça sausage, cut into ½-inch pieces

HOT SAUCE

- 2 tomatoes, cored, seeded, and chopped fine
- 1 onion, chopped fine
- 1 small green bell pepper, stemmed, seeded, and chopped fine
- 1 jalapeño chile, stemmed, seeded, and minced
- ⅓ cup white wine vinegar
- 3 tablespoons extra-virgin olive oil
- 1 tablespoon minced fresh cilantro
- ½ teaspoon table salt

1. FOR THE STEW Adjust oven rack to lower-middle position and heat oven to 325 degrees. Pat pork dry with paper towels and season with 1 teaspoon salt and pepper. Heat 1 tablespoon oil in Dutch oven over medium-high heat until just smoking. Add half of pork and brown well on all sides, 7 to 10 minutes; transfer to large bowl. Repeat with 1 tablespoon oil and remaining pork.

2. Add bacon to fat left in pot and cook over medium heat until crisp, 5 to 7 minutes. Stir in remaining 1 tablespoon oil, onion, and ¼ teaspoon salt and cook until onion is softened, about 5 minutes. Stir in garlic, chili powder, cumin, and coriander and cook until fragrant, about 30 seconds.

3. Stir in water, beans, bay leaves, baking soda, remaining ¼ teaspoon salt, and browned pork and any accumulated juices, and bring to simmer. Cover, transfer pot to oven, and cook for 1½ hours.

4. Remove pot from oven and stir in linguiça. Return covered pot to oven and cook until meat and beans are fully tender, about 30 minutes.

5. FOR THE HOT SAUCE While stew cooks, combine all ingredients in bowl and let sit at room temperature until flavors meld, at least 30 minutes.

6. Remove stew from oven and discard bay leaves. Season with salt and pepper to taste, and serve with hot sauce.

French Pork and White Bean Stew

Serves 8 to 10 | **Total Time** 5 hours, plus 8¼ hours brining and resting

WHY THIS RECIPE WORKS Inspired by cassoulet, this simpler braise combines many elements of the classic: tender white beans, succulent pork, and juicy garlic sausages. Baking the dish in the oven keeps the cooking mostly hands-off. We replace the common addition of duck confit with salt pork for richness. A crispy bread crumb crust covers the braise. We use half of our crumbs to absorb the excess liquid in the casserole. Then we uncover the pot, add the remaining crumbs, and let the dish cook until they are crisp. If you can't find fresh French garlic sausages, substitute Irish bangers or bratwurst.

- 1½ tablespoons table salt for brining
- 1 pound (2½ cups) dried cannellini beans, picked over and rinsed
- 2 celery ribs
- 4 sprigs fresh thyme

1 bay leaf

1½ pounds fresh French garlic sausage

4 ounces salt pork, rinsed

¼ cup vegetable oil, divided

1½ pounds boneless pork butt roast, cut into 1-inch pieces

1 large onion, chopped fine

2 carrots, peeled and cut into ¼-inch pieces

4 garlic cloves, minced

1 tablespoon tomato paste

½ cup dry white wine

1 (14.5-ounce) can diced tomatoes

4 cups chicken broth

4 slices hearty white sandwich bread, torn into rough pieces

½ cup chopped fresh parsley

1. Dissolve salt in 2 quarts cold water in large container. Add beans and soak at room temperature for at least 8 hours or up to 24 hours. Drain and rinse well. (If you're pressed for time, see page 13 for information on quick brining your beans.)

2. Adjust oven rack to lower-middle position and heat oven to 300 degrees. Using kitchen twine, tie together celery, thyme sprigs, and bay leaf; set aside. Place sausage and salt pork in medium saucepan and add cold water to cover by 1 inch. Bring to boil over high heat, then reduce heat to maintain simmer and cook for 5 minutes. Transfer sausage to cutting board to cool slightly, then cut into 1-inch pieces. Remove salt pork from water; set aside.

3. Heat 2 tablespoons oil in Dutch oven over medium-high heat until just smoking. Add sausage and brown on all sides, 8 to 12 minutes; transfer to bowl. Add pork butt roast and brown on all sides, 8 to 12 minutes. Add onion and carrots and cook, stirring constantly, until onion is translucent, about 2 minutes. Add garlic and tomato paste and cook, stirring constantly, until fragrant, about 30 seconds. Return sausage to pot; add wine, scraping up any browned bits; and cook until reduced slightly, about 30 seconds. Stir in tomatoes, reserved celery bundle, and reserved salt pork.

4. Stir in broth and beans, pressing beans into even layer. If any beans are completely exposed, add up to 1 cup water to submerge (beans may still break surface of liquid). Increase heat to high, bring to simmer, and cover; transfer pot to oven. Cook until beans are tender, about 1½ hours. Discard celery bundle and salt pork. Using wide spoon, skim fat from surface and discard. Season with salt and pepper to taste. Increase oven temperature to 350 degrees and bake, uncovered, for 20 minutes.

5. Meanwhile, pulse bread and remaining 2 tablespoons oil in food processor until crumbs are no larger than ⅛ inch, 8 to 10 pulses. Transfer to bowl and stir in parsley.

Brazilian Black Bean and Pork Stew

French Pork and White Bean Stew

6. Sprinkle ½ cup bread crumb mixture evenly over top of beans, cover tightly, and bake for 15 minutes. Uncover and bake for 15 minutes. Sprinkle remaining bread crumb mixture evenly over top and bake until golden brown, about 30 minutes. Let rest for 15 minutes before serving.

Posole

Serves 6 to 8 | **Total time** 3 hours

WHY THIS RECIPE WORKS Posole is a beloved Mexican stew that is also a favorite in New Mexico. Our recipe is a version of the New Mexican style, using hominy—dried corn that's been soaked in lye to remove its skin—which is a key ingredient in traditional posole. Sautéing the hominy in rendered pork fat makes it sweet, toasty, and chewy; we add it to the stew at the end to preserve these qualities. Toasting dried ancho chiles deepens their flavor, and steeping them in hot broth gives the stew ample depth. Browning the pork enhances the flavor of both meat and broth. Serve with sliced radishes, green cabbage, chopped avocado, hot sauce, and cilantro.

    ¾ ounce dried ancho chiles
    8 cups chicken broth, divided
    2 pounds boneless country-style pork ribs, trimmed
    1 teaspoon table salt, divided
    ¾ teaspoon pepper, divided
    3 tablespoons vegetable oil, divided
    3 (15-ounce) cans white hominy, rinsed
    2 onions, chopped
    5 garlic cloves, minced
    1 tablespoon minced fresh oregano
    1 tablespoon lime juice

1. Adjust oven rack to middle position and heat oven to 350 degrees. Place chiles on rimmed baking sheet and bake until puffed and fragrant, about 6 minutes. When chiles are cool enough to handle, remove stems and seeds. Combine chiles and 1 cup broth in bowl. Cover with plastic wrap and microwave until bubbling, about 2 minutes. Let sit until softened, 10 to 15 minutes.

2. Pat pork dry with paper towels and sprinkle with ½ teaspoon salt and ¼ teaspoon pepper. Heat 2 tablespoons oil in Dutch oven over medium-high heat until just smoking. Cook pork until well browned all over, about 10 minutes. Transfer pork to plate. Add hominy to now-empty pot and cook, stirring frequently, until fragrant and hominy begins to darken, 2 to 3 minutes. Transfer hominy to clean bowl.

3. Heat remaining 1 tablespoon oil in again-empty pot over medium heat until shimmering. Add onions and cook until softened, about 5 minutes. Stir in garlic and cook until fragrant, about 30 seconds. Process onion mixture and softened chile mixture in blender until smooth, about 1 minute. Combine remaining 7 cups broth, pureed onion-chile mixture, pork, oregano, remaining ½ teaspoon salt, and remaining ½ teaspoon pepper in now-empty pot and bring to boil. Reduce heat to low and simmer, covered, until meat is tender, 1 to 1½ hours.

4. Transfer pork to cutting board. Add hominy to pot and simmer, covered, until tender, about 30 minutes. Using large spoon, skim fat from broth. When meat is cool enough to handle shred into bite-size pieces using 2 forks, discarding fat. Return pork to pot and cook until warmed through, about 1 minute. Off heat, stir in lime juice and season with salt and pepper to taste. Serve.

NOTES FROM THE TEST KITCHEN

FREEZING AND REHEATING SOUPS, STEWS, AND CHILIS

Since soups, stews, and chilis make a generous number of servings, it is convenient to stock your freezer with leftovers to reheat easily. To freeze them correctly, first you'll need to cool the pot. As tempting as it might seem, don't transfer the hot contents straight to the freezer or refrigerator. This can increase the fridge's internal temperature to unsafe levels for all other food. Letting the pot cool on the countertop for an hour helps the temperature drop to about 75 degrees, at which point you can transfer it safely to the freezer. For faster cooling, you can divide the pot's contents into a number of storage containers to allow the heat to dissipate more quickly or cool it rapidly by using a frozen bottle of water to stir the contents of the pot. To reheat soups, stews, and chilis, first thaw them, then simmer them gently on the stovetop in a sturdy, heavy-bottomed pot.

While most soups, stews, and chilis store just fine, those that contain pasta or dairy (plant-based or traditional) do not. The pasta turns bloated and mushy and the dairy curdles as it freezes. Instead, make and freeze the dish without the pasta or dairy component. When you have thawed and heated the dish through, you can stir in uncooked pasta and simmer until just tender or stir in the dairy and continue to heat gently until hot (do not boil).

Hearty Tuscan Bean Stew with Sausage and Cabbage

Serves 8 | **Total time** 2¼ hours, plus 8 hours brining

WHY THIS RECIPE WORKS In Tuscany, creamy beans elevate rustic stews. To avoid tough, exploded beans, we brine them overnight, which softens the skins. Gently cooking the beans in a 250-degree oven produces perfectly cooked ones that stay intact. Sausage, cabbage, and carrots add heft; garlic, onion, and oregano lend aromatic nuance. Usually, we recommend not adding tomatoes too early, as the acid prevents the beans from becoming tender; here, we use that knowledge to our advantage, adding the tomatoes early so the beans don't become too soft.

- 1½ tablespoons table salt for brining
- 1 pound (2½ cups) dried cannellini beans, picked over and rinsed
- 1 tablespoon extra-virgin olive oil, plus extra for drizzling
- 1½ pounds sweet Italian sausage, casings removed
- 1 large onion, chopped
- 2 carrots, peeled and cut into ½-inch pieces
- 2 celery ribs, cut into ½-inch pieces
- 8 garlic cloves, peeled and crushed
- 4 cups chicken broth
- 3 cups water
- 2 bay leaves
- ½ head savoy cabbage, cut into 1-inch pieces
- 1 (14.5-ounce) can diced tomatoes, drained
- 1 sprig fresh oregano

1. Dissolve 1½ tablespoons salt in 2 quarts cold water in large container. Add beans and soak at room temperature for at least 8 hours or up to 24 hours. Drain and rinse well. (If you're pressed for time, see page 13 for more information on quick brining your beans.)

2. Adjust oven rack to lower-middle position and heat oven to 250 degrees. Cook oil and sausage in Dutch oven over medium heat, stirring often and breaking meat into small pieces with wooden spoon, until sausage is no longer pink, about 5 minutes; transfer sausage to paper towel–lined plate. Stir onion, carrots, and celery into fat left in pot and cook until softened and lightly browned, 10 to 16 minutes.

3. Stir in garlic and cook until fragrant, about 1 minute. Stir in broth, water, bay leaves, and beans. Increase heat to high and bring to simmer. Cover, transfer to oven, and cook until beans are almost tender (very center of beans will still be firm), 45 minutes to 1 hour.

4. Stir browned sausage, cabbage, and tomatoes into pot. Return pot to oven and cook, covered, until beans and greens are fully tender, 30 to 40 minutes.

5. Remove pot from oven and stir in oregano; cover and let sit off heat for 15 minutes. Discard bay leaves and oregano and season with salt and pepper to taste. If desired, use back of spoon to press some beans against side of pot to thicken stew. Drizzle portions with extra oil before serving.

Congee with Stir-Fried Ground Pork

Serves 4 to 6 | **Total Time** 1½ hours

WHY THIS RECIPE WORKS Great congee (savory Chinese rice porridge) features soft, barely intact grains gently bound by their silky, viscous cooking liquid; the result should be fluid but thick and creamy enough to suspend toppings. Our formula starts with a 13:1 ratio of liquid to long-grain white rice, which produces an appropriately loose porridge (we cut the water with a little chicken broth for a savory backbone). Then we simmer the rice vigorously to encourage the grains to break

Posole

Congee with Stir-Fried
Ground Pork

Jamaican Stew Peas
with Spinners

down in about 45 minutes, partially covering the pot to help the contents cook quickly while minimizing evaporation. To prevent the congee from boiling over, we rinse excess starch from the raw rice and wedge a wooden spoon between the lid and the side of the pot, giving steam a chance to escape. Meanwhile, we make a quick, savory stir-fried pork topping. Serve with Microwave-Fried Shallots (page 139), if desired.

Substitution: You can use jasmine rice in place of conventional long-grain white rice.

CONGEE

- ¾ cup long-grain white rice
- 1 cup chicken broth
- ¾ teaspoon table salt

STIR-FRIED PORK

- 8 ounces ground pork
- ¼ teaspoon table salt
- ⅛ teaspoon baking soda
- 1 garlic clove, minced
- 1 teaspoon minced fresh ginger
- 1 teaspoon soy sauce
- 1 teaspoon Shaoxing wine
- 1 teaspoon cornstarch
- ½ teaspoon sugar
- ¼ teaspoon white pepper
- 1 teaspoon vegetable oil

    Scallions, sliced thin on bias
    Fresh cilantro leaves
    Dry-roasted peanuts, chopped coarse
    Chili oil
    Soy sauce
    Chinese black vinegar

1. FOR THE CONGEE Place rice in fine-mesh strainer and rinse under cold running water until water runs clear. Drain well and transfer to Dutch oven. Add broth, salt, and 9 cups water and bring to boil over high heat. Reduce heat to maintain vigorous simmer. Cover pot, tucking wooden spoon horizontally between pot and lid to hold lid ajar. Cook, stirring occasionally, until mixture is thickened, glossy, and reduced by half, 45 to 50 minutes.

2. FOR THE STIR-FRIED PORK While rice cooks, toss pork, 1 tablespoon water, salt, and baking soda in bowl until thoroughly combined. Add garlic, ginger, soy sauce, Shaoxing wine, cornstarch, sugar, and white pepper and toss until thoroughly combined.

3. Heat oil in 12-inch nonstick skillet over medium-high heat until just smoking. Add pork mixture and cook, breaking up meat into ¼-inch pieces with wooden spoon, until pork is no longer pink and just beginning to brown. Serve congee in bowls, spooning pork over congee and passing scallions, cilantro, peanuts, chili oil, soy sauce, and vinegar separately.

Microwave-Fried Shallots

Makes ½ cup | **Total Time** 25 minutes **FAST**

3 shallots, sliced thin
½ cup vegetable oil, for frying

Combine shallots and oil in medium bowl. Microwave for 5 minutes. Stir and continue to microwave 2 minutes longer. Repeat stirring and microwaving in 2-minute increments until beginning to brown (4 to 6 minutes). Repeat stirring and microwaving in 30-second increments until deep golden brown (30 seconds to 2 minutes). Using slotted spoon, transfer shallots to paper towel–lined plate; season with salt to taste. Let drain and crisp, about 5 minutes. (Shallots can be stored in an airtight container for up to 1 month.)

Jamaican Stew Peas with Spinners

Serves 6 to 8 | **Total Time** 3 hours, plus 8 hours soaking

WHY THIS RECIPE WORKS In a *Cook's Country* story, Dionne Reid recalls returning home to Montego Bay and being welcomed by her grandmother with a pot of stew peas redolent of coconut and bold herbs, and brimming with red peas, salted pig tails, and dumplings known as spinners. In her version, Dionne swaps in small red beans for Jamaican dried red peas, soaking them overnight and saving the ruddy soaking liquid to add to the stew. Instead of salted pigs' tails or salted beef, she uses more readily available smoked ham hocks (a nod to cooks who make stew peas using the leftover bone from a Christmas ham). Fine-tuning spices and aromatics—garlic, allspice berries, celery, thyme, and a Scotch bonnet chile—gives the stew rich, nuanced flavor. Chicken broth and coconut milk add creamy, savory flavor. The final addition is spinners: rustic flour-and-water dumplings you "spin" between your palms before dropping into the stew. If you can't find a Scotch bonnet, use a habanero. Serve with white rice (see pages 298–299).

Substitution: You can use dried kidney beans in place of the small red beans.

1 pound (2 cups) dried small red beans, picked over and rinsed
6 cups plus 3 tablespoons water, divided
4 sprigs fresh thyme, plus 1 tablespoon chopped
1 Scotch bonnet chile, pierced once with tip of paring knife
1 bay leaf
1 teaspoon whole allspice berries
1 tablespoon unrefined coconut oil
1 onion, chopped
1 green bell pepper, stemmed, seeded, and chopped
1 large celery rib, chopped (¾ cup)
3 tablespoons minced garlic (9 cloves)
2 teaspoons garlic powder
1¼ teaspoons table salt, divided
½ teaspoon pepper
2 (12-ounce) smoked ham hocks
2 cups chicken broth
1 (14-ounce) can coconut milk
½ cup all-purpose flour
6 scallions, chopped

1. Combine beans and 6 cups cold water in large container; soak at room temperature for at least 8 hours or up to 24 hours.

2. Bundle thyme sprigs, Scotch bonnet, bay leaf, and allspice in cheesecloth; secure with kitchen twine; and set aside. Heat oil in Dutch oven over medium heat until shimmering. Add onion, bell pepper, celery, garlic, garlic powder, ½ teaspoon salt, and pepper and cook, stirring occasionally, until onion is translucent, 6 to 8 minutes.

3. Add beans and their soaking liquid, ham hocks, broth, cheesecloth bundle, and ½ teaspoon salt. Increase heat to high and bring to boil. Reduce heat to low and cook, uncovered, stirring occasionally, until beans start to soften and liquid is slightly reduced, about 1½ hours, adjusting heat as needed to maintain vigorous simmer. Stir in coconut milk and continue to cook until beans are completely soft (it's OK if some skins crack) and sauce thickens, about 30 minutes.

4. While stew simmers, whisk flour and remaining ¼ teaspoon salt together in bowl. Make well in center. Gradually add remaining 3 tablespoons water to flour mixture, stirring until shaggy mass forms. Knead in bowl until dough clears sides of bowl and forms tight ball (if dough seems too dry to shape, add up to 2 teaspoons water, ½ teaspoon at a time). Pinch off about 1 teaspoon dough and roll between your palms to form 3-inch-long dumpling with tapered ends. Transfer to plate and repeat with remaining dough (you should have 14 to 16 dumplings).

5. Taste stew; adjust spiciness, if desired, by pressing cheesecloth bundle against side of pot with back of spoon to release juice of Scotch bonnet. Discard bundle and transfer ham hocks to plate to cool slightly. Gently drop dumplings into stew. Simmer, without stirring, until dumplings are set, about 5 minutes. While dumplings cook, debone ham hocks and cut meat into ½-inch pieces (you'll have ½ to ⅔ cup meat); discard bones, skin, and fat. Stir meat, scallions, and chopped thyme into stew. Season with salt and pepper to taste. Simmer until flavors have melded and scallions have softened slightly, 10 to 15 minutes. Serve.

MAKING SPINNERS

These dumplings are an essential component of stew peas. As they poach, some of the flour sloughs off, giving the broth body. To make one, pinch off about 1 teaspoon of dough and roll it between your palms to form a 3-inch-long dumpling with tapered ends.

Beans Marbella

Serves 4 to 6 | **Total Time** 4 hours, plus 8 hours brining

WHY THIS RECIPE WORKS This enticing stew is a beanified version of a timeless classic: Chicken Marbella from *The Silver Palate Cookbook*. The combination of sweet prunes, briny olives, and tangy red wine vinegar marries nicely with Royal Corona beans—strikingly large runner beans that have a hearty, meat-like character while cooking up tender and creamy. Royal Corona beans lean towards the sweeter end of the bean spectrum so we add a small amount of pancetta and anchovies for savory depth and umami. We also pare down the amount of brown sugar to 3 tablespoons (the original recipe has 1 cup!) to account for the natural sweetness in the beans. Due to their size, Royal Corona beans have a longer than average cook time, so instead of cooking the beans separately, we take advantage of this time and cook the beans and sauce together to allow them to integrate. We also removed wine from the sauce, as it tends to impede bean cook time. Instead we add red wine vinegar at the end for a bright hit of acidity. Serve with crusty bread.

Substitution: You can use large lima beans in place of the Royal Coronas. If using large lima beans, start checking for doneness at 2 hours in step 2. Royal Corona beans will take closer to 3 hours to cook.

1½ tablespoons table salt for brining
1 pound (2½ cups) dried Royal Corona beans, picked over and rinsed
1 tablespoon extra-virgin olive oil
4 ounces pancetta, cut into 1-inch long by ¼-inch wide lardons
4 garlic cloves, minced
4 anchovy fillets, rinsed, patted dry and minced
¼ teaspoon red pepper flakes
2 tablespoons all-purpose flour
3 tablespoons packed brown sugar
1 cup pitted prunes, halved, divided
¾ cup pitted green olives, halved, divided
¼ cup capers, divided
2 bay leaves
½ teaspoon dried oregano
1½ teaspoons table salt
½ teaspoon pepper
2 tablespoons red wine vinegar
¼ cup chopped fresh parsley

1. Dissolve 1½ tablespoons table salt in 2 quarts cold water in large container. Add beans and soak at room temperature for at least 8 hours or up to 24 hours. Drain and rinse well. (If you're pressed for time, see page 13 for information on quick brining your beans.)

2. Adjust oven rack to middle position and preheat oven to 325 degrees. Heat oil in Dutch oven over medium heat until shimmering. Add pancetta and cook until browned, 5 to 7 minutes. Add garlic, anchovies, and pepper flakes and cook until fragrant, about 30 seconds. Stir in flour and cook for 30 seconds. Slowly whisk in 7 cups water and brown sugar, scraping up any browned bits and smoothing out any lumps. Stir in beans, half of prunes, half of olives, half of capers, bay leaves, oregano, salt, and pepper. Bring to simmer, then cover pot and transfer to oven. Cook until beans are tender, 2 to 3 hours, stirring every 30 minutes.

3. Stir remaining prunes, remaining olives, remaining capers, and vinegar into pot. Cover pot and let rest off heat until prunes have softened, about 10 minutes. Discard bay leaves. Stir in parsley and season with salt and pepper to taste. Serve.

Pasta e Fagioli

Serves 6 to 8 | **Total Time** 1¾ hours,
plus 8 hours brining

WHY THIS RECIPE WORKS This pasta-and-bean stew makes for a hearty meal, combining creamy Marcella beans with ditalini, finely chopped vegetables, and pancetta in a savory tomato broth. It seems apropos that the delicate, thin-skinned heirloom cannellini beans used for this Italian American dish are named for Italian cooking authority Marcella Hazan, who was partial to their creamy texture and bright, buttery flavor. For a shortcut, rather than boiling the pasta in a separate pot, we add it directly into the soup towards the end. We recommend serving the soup with grated Parmesan cheese on top for more savory richness. To make this soup vegetarian, omit the pancetta and substitute vegetable broth for the chicken broth. When reheating leftovers, add more broth or water as necessary.

> **Substitution:** You can use dried cannellini beans in place of the Marcella beans.

- 1½ tablespoons table salt for brining
- 1 pound (2½ cups) dried Marcella beans, picked over and rinsed
- 2 tablespoons extra-virgin olive oil
- 2 onions, chopped fine
- 2 carrots, chopped fine
- 2 celery ribs, chopped fine
- 4 ounces pancetta, chopped fine
- ½ teaspoon table salt
- ½ teaspoon pepper
- 2 tablespoons tomato paste
- 4 garlic cloves, minced
- 2 teaspoons minced fresh rosemary or ¾ teaspoon dried
- 1 teaspoon minced fresh thyme or ¼ teaspoon dried
- ¼ teaspoon red pepper flakes
- ⅛ teaspoon sugar
- 1 (14.5-ounce) can diced tomatoes
- 4 cups chicken broth
- 8 ounces ditalini
- 2 teaspoons lemon juice
- 3 tablespoons chopped fresh parsley
- 2 ounces Parmesan cheese, grated (1 cup)

Beans Marbella

Pasta e Fagioli

1. Dissolve 1½ tablespoons salt in 2 quarts cold water in large container. Add beans and soak at room temperature for at least 8 hours or up to 24 hours. Drain and rinse well. (If you're pressed for time, see page 13 for information on quick brining your beans.)

2. Heat oil in large saucepan over medium heat until shimmering. Add onions, carrots, celery, pancetta, salt, and pepper and cook until vegetables are softened, about 10 minutes.

3. Stir in tomato paste, garlic, rosemary, thyme, pepper flakes, and sugar and cook until fragrant, about 2 minutes. Stir in diced tomatoes and their liquid, broth, 4 cups water, and beans. Bring to boil, reduce heat to medium-low, and simmer until beans are tender, about 40 minutes, stirring occasionally.

4. Increase heat to medium-high and bring to boil. Add pasta and cook, stirring occasionally, until pasta is al dente, about 10 minutes. Off heat, stir in lemon juice and parsley. Serve with Parmesan.

Garlicky Shrimp, Tomato, and White Bean Stew

Serves 4 to 6 | **Total Time** 1¼ hours, plus 15 minutes brining

WHY THIS RECIPE WORKS This riff on white bean stew pairs cannellini beans with shrimp, garlic, and fresh basil, giving it a summery feel (though it's satisfying to eat any time of the year). Canned beans and canned tomatoes make the dish fast and doable; plus, the liquid from one of the cans of beans lends good body to the stew. For more seafood flavor, we make a quick concentrated stock with the shrimp shells and use it to simmer the beans. We also cook the shrimp with the beans rather than separately, and we sauté minced anchovies with the aromatics. To season the shrimp and keep them plump and juicy, we brine them briefly, add them late in the cooking process so they don't overcook, and reduce the heat so they cook gently. The basil and lemon juice and zest provide freshness and nice acidity. We prefer untreated shrimp, but if your shrimp are treated with added salt or preservatives like sodium tripolyphosphate, skip brining in step 1 and increase the salt to ½ teaspoon in step 3.

2 tablespoons sugar for brining
1 tablespoon table salt for brining
1 pound large shell-on shrimp (26 to 30 per pound), peeled, deveined, tails removed, and shells reserved
¼ cup extra-virgin olive oil, divided
1 onion, chopped fine
4 garlic cloves, peeled, halved lengthwise, and sliced thin
2 anchovy fillets, rinsed, patted dry, and minced
¼ teaspoon red pepper flakes
¼ teaspoon table salt
⅛ teaspoon pepper
2 (15-ounce) cans cannellini beans (1 can drained and rinsed, 1 can undrained)
1 (14.5-ounce) can diced tomatoes, drained
¼ cup shredded fresh basil
½ teaspoon grated lemon zest plus 1 tablespoon juice

1. Dissolve sugar and 1 tablespoon salt in 1 quart cold water in large container. Submerge shrimp in brine, cover, and refrigerate for 15 minutes. Remove shrimp from brine and pat dry with paper towels.

2. Heat 1 tablespoon oil in 12-inch skillet over medium heat until shimmering. Add shrimp shells and cook, stirring frequently, until they begin to turn spotty brown and skillet starts to brown, 5 to 6 minutes. Remove skillet from heat and carefully add 1 cup water. When bubbling subsides, return skillet to medium heat and simmer gently, stirring occasionally, for 5 minutes. Strain mixture through colander set over large bowl. Discard shells and reserve liquid (you should have about ¼ cup). Wipe skillet clean with paper towels.

3. Heat 2 tablespoons oil, onion, garlic, anchovies, pepper flakes, salt, and pepper in now-empty skillet over medium-low heat. Cook, stirring occasionally, until onion is softened, about 5 minutes. Add 1 can drained beans, 1 can beans and their liquid, tomatoes, and shrimp stock and bring to simmer. Simmer, stirring occasionally, for 15 minutes.

4. Reduce heat to low, stir in shrimp, cover, and cook, stirring once during cooking, until shrimp are just opaque, 5 to 7 minutes. Remove skillet from heat and stir in basil and lemon zest and juice. Season with salt and pepper to taste. Transfer to serving dish, drizzle with remaining 1 tablespoon oil, and serve.

Guanimes con Bacalao

Guanimes con Bacalao

Serves 4 | **Total Time** 1¾ hours, plus 24 hours soaking

WHY THIS RECIPE WORKS Guanimes con bacalao is a stew eaten throughout Puerto Rico. It combines briny salt cod (bacalao) with fruity peppers in a rich sauce, offset by simple cornmeal dumplings (guanimes). We make the dumplings with cornmeal, salt, and water and cook them in boiling water. The salt cod soaks in water for 24 hours; we then boil it for 10 minutes to soften it and remove much, but not all, of its salinity, because some is essential for seasoning the stew. Onions, garlic, Cubanelle pepper, and ajíes dulces (sweet chiles native to Latin America) are cooked in annatto oil until they soften before the salt cod is added to the pot to simmer with the vegetables. If possible, use pieces of salt cod that vary in thickness. The thicker pieces will remain saltier after soaking and boiling, and the thinner pieces will be less salty. It's ideal to have this variety. If you can find only thinner tail pieces of salt cod (about ½ inch or less), then soak it for only 18 hours (still changing the water once). We strongly recommend weighing the cornmeal here. If you can't find ajíes dulces, you can substitute ½ cup of chopped red bell pepper.

BACALAO

- 1 pound salt cod
- ½ cup vegetable oil
- 1½ teaspoons annatto seeds
- 2¼ cups chopped onion
- 1 large Cubanelle pepper (5 ounces), stemmed, seeded, halved crosswise, and cut into thin strips (1 cup)
- 4 ounces ajíes dulces, stemmed, seeded, and chopped (½ cup)
- 5 garlic cloves, minced
- ¾ teaspoon table salt
- ½ teaspoon dried oregano
- 2 tablespoons tomato paste
- ⅓ cup coarsely chopped fresh cilantro leaves and stems
- ¼ cup thinly sliced pimento-stuffed Manzanilla olives

GUANIMES

- ¾ teaspoon table salt
- 1¼ cups (6¼ ounces) cornmeal

1. FOR THE BACALAO Rinse salt cod of excess surface salt. Place cod in medium bowl and cover with about 2 quarts water. Transfer to refrigerator and let cod soak for 24 hours, changing water halfway through soaking.

2. Heat oil and annatto seeds in small saucepan over low heat, swirling occasionally, until bubbles begin to form around seeds and oil takes on deep orange color, about 5 minutes. Remove from heat and let sit for 10 minutes. Strain oil through fine-mesh strainer into liquid measuring cup and set aside; discard seeds. (Annatto oil can be stored in airtight container for up to 1 week.)

3. Drain cod. Place cod in large saucepan, cover with 2 quarts water, and bring to boil over high heat. Reduce heat to medium and simmer for 10 minutes. Reserve 1 cup cooking water. Drain cod; transfer to bowl; and let sit until cool enough to handle, 5 to 10 minutes. Using your fingers or potato masher, flake or mash cod until finely shredded. (Shredded cod can be refrigerated for up to 2 days.)

4. Heat ¼ cup annatto oil in 12-inch nonstick skillet over medium heat until shimmering. Add onion, Cubanelle, ajíes dulces, garlic, salt, and oregano and cook, stirring occasionally, until vegetables are softened, about 7 minutes.

5. Stir in tomato paste and cook for 1 minute. Stir in cod and reserved cooking water and bring to simmer. Reduce heat to low; cover; and cook, stirring occasionally, until mixture deepens in color and flavors meld, about 15 minutes. Off heat, stir in cilantro and olives. Season with salt to taste and cover to keep warm.

6. FOR THE GUANIMES Bring 1½ cups water and salt to boil in medium saucepan over high heat. Once boiling, immediately remove from heat. Using wooden spoon, quickly stir in cornmeal until mixture thickens and no lumps remain. Let mixture cool for 3 to 5 minutes. Divide guanimes mixture into 20 equal portions, about 1 tablespoon each. Roll guanimes between your lightly moistened hands to form smooth balls and transfer to plate. (Shaped guanimes can be refrigerated in zipper-lock bag for up to 24 hours.)

7. Bring 3 quarts water to boil in large saucepan over high heat. (Simultaneously begin reheating bacalao mixture if necessary.) Drop guanimes into boiling water and cook until beginning to float, about 5 minutes. Using spider skimmer or slotted spoon, transfer 5 guanimes to each of 4 serving bowls. Top with bacalao mixture and drizzle with remaining annatto oil to taste. Serve.

Chickpea Bouillabaisse

Serves 4 to 6 | **Total Time** 1½ hours

WHY THIS RECIPE WORKS Versatile chickpeas are at home in many cuisines. Here they pair well with the potent flavors of classic bouillabaisse. We use leeks, fennel, garlic, tomato paste, and saffron to ensure a flavorful broth. In lieu of fish stock, we use chicken broth and canned chickpea liquid to create the dish's traditional body. Chickpeas add heft and an ultrasavory presence while potatoes, white wine, pastis, and orange zest stay true to the Provençal flavors. The vibrant rouille-topped croutons complete the dish, adding acidity and brightness. We prefer the robust flavor of extra-virgin olive oil in the rouille; you can use a combination of vegetable oil and extra-virgin olive oil if you prefer a more neutral flavor.

BOUILLABAISSE

- 2 tablespoons extra-virgin olive oil
- 1 large leek, white and light green parts only, halved lengthwise, sliced thin, and washed thoroughly
- 1 fennel bulb, stalks discarded, bulb halved, cored, and sliced thin
- ¼ teaspoon table salt
- 4 garlic cloves, minced
- 1 tablespoon tomato paste
- 1 tablespoon unbleached all-purpose flour
- ¼ teaspoon saffron threads, crumbled
- ¼ teaspoon ground cayenne pepper
- 2 (15-ounce) cans chickpeas, undrained
- 3 cups chicken broth
- 1 (14.5-ounce) can diced tomatoes, drained

- 12 ounces Yukon Gold potatoes, cut into ¾-inch pieces
- ½ cup dry white wine
- ¼ cup pastis or Pernod
- 1 (3-inch) strip orange zest
- 1 tablespoon chopped fresh tarragon or parsley

ROUILLE AND CROUTONS

- 3 tablespoons water
- ¼ teaspoon saffron threads, crumbled
- 1 baguette
- 4 teaspoons lemon juice
- 2 teaspoons Dijon mustard
- 1 large egg yolk
- 2 small garlic cloves, minced
- ¼ teaspoon ground cayenne pepper
  Pinch table salt
- ½ cup plus 2 tablespoons extra-virgin olive oil, divided

1. FOR THE BOUILLABAISSE Adjust oven rack to lower-middle position and heat oven to 375 degrees. Heat oil in Dutch oven over medium-high heat until shimmering. Add leek, fennel, and salt and cook, stirring often, until vegetables begin to soften, about 5 minutes. Stir in garlic, tomato paste, flour, saffron, and cayenne and cook until fragrant, about 30 seconds. Stir in chickpeas and their liquid, broth, tomatoes, potatoes, wine, pastis, and orange zest. Bring to simmer and cook over medium-low heat, partially covered, until potatoes are tender, about 20 minutes.

2. FOR THE ROUILLE AND CROUTONS While bouillabaisse cooks, microwave water and saffron in medium bowl until water is steaming, 15 to 30 seconds; set aside for 5 minutes. Cut 4-inch piece of baguette; remove and discard crust. Tear crustless bread into 1-inch pieces (you should have about 1 cup). Stir bread pieces and lemon juice into saffron-infused water and let sit for 5 minutes. Using whisk, mash soaked bread mixture until uniform paste forms, 1 to 2 minutes. Whisk in mustard, egg yolk, garlic, cayenne, and salt. Whisking constantly, slowly drizzle in ¼ cup oil in steady stream until smooth mayonnaise-like consistency is reached, about 4 minutes, scraping down bowl as necessary. Slowly whisk in ¼ cup oil until smooth; set aside until ready to serve.

3. Cut remaining baguette into ¾-inch-thick slices. Toss slices with remaining 2 tablespoons oil until coated, then arrange in single layer on rimmed baking sheet. Bake until light golden brown, 10 to 15 minutes.

4. Discard orange peel from bouillabaisse. Stir in tarragon and season with salt and pepper to taste. Serve, dolloping individual serving bowls with rouille and spreading rouille over croutons.

Chana Masala

Serves 4 to 6 | **Total Time** 50 minutes   `VEGAN`

WHY THIS RECIPE WORKS Chana masala (spiced chickpeas) is arguably one of North India's best-known vegetarian dishes, and can be quick and easy to prepare, with most ingredients coming from the pantry. We use canned chickpeas because their flavor and texture are nearly indistinguishable from those cooked from dried, and we don't drain them because the canning liquid adds body and savory depth to the dish. An aromatic onion, garlic, ginger, and chile paste forms the base of our recipe along with canned tomatoes. Since canned chickpeas still retain a bit of snap, we simmer them in the tomato sauce until they turn soft. Adding spices like cumin, turmeric, and fennel seeds at the start of cooking ensures that they permeate the dish. Sweet, delicate garam masala goes in toward the end to preserve its aroma. Chopped onion, chile, and cilantro make a vibrant, textured, fresh garnish. This dish is often paired with bhature, deep-fried breads that puff up as they cook. It can also be served with rice or naan.

- 1 small red onion, quartered, divided
- 10 sprigs fresh cilantro, stems and leaves separated
- 1 (1½-inch) piece ginger, peeled and chopped coarse
- 2 garlic cloves, chopped coarse
- 2 serrano chiles, stemmed, halved, seeded, and sliced thin crosswise, divided
- 3 tablespoons vegetable oil
- 1 (14.5-ounce) can whole peeled tomatoes
- 1 teaspoon paprika
- 1 teaspoon ground cumin
- ½ teaspoon ground turmeric
- ½ teaspoon fennel seeds
- 2 (15-ounce) cans chickpeas, undrained
- 1½ teaspoons garam masala
- ½ teaspoon table salt
  Lime wedges

1. Chop three-quarters of onion coarse; reserve remaining quarter for garnish. Cut cilantro stems into 1-inch lengths. Process chopped onion, cilantro stems, ginger, garlic, and half of serranos in food processor until finely chopped, scraping down sides of bowl as necessary, about 20 seconds. Cook onion mixture and oil in large saucepan over medium-high heat, stirring frequently, until onion is fully softened and beginning to stick to saucepan, 5 to 7 minutes.

Chickpea Bouillabaisse

Chana Masala

Bean Bourguignon

2. While onion mixture cooks, process tomatoes and their juice in now-empty food processor until smooth, about 30 seconds. Add paprika, cumin, turmeric, and fennel seeds to onion mixture and cook, stirring constantly, until fragrant, about 1 minute. Stir in chickpeas and their liquid and processed tomatoes and bring to boil. Adjust heat to maintain simmer, then cover and simmer for 15 minutes. While mixture cooks, chop reserved onion fine.

3. Stir garam masala and salt into chickpea mixture and continue to cook, uncovered and stirring occasionally, until chickpeas are softened and sauce is thickened, 8 to 12 minutes. Season with salt to taste. Transfer to wide, shallow serving bowl. Sprinkle with chopped onion, remaining serranos, and cilantro leaves and serve, passing lime wedges separately.

Bean Bourguignon

Serves 4 to 6 | **Total Time** 2 hours, plus 8 hours brining VEGAN

WHY THIS RECIPE WORKS Creamy, chestnut-like Christmas lima beans meet tender, earthy portobello mushrooms in a rich, velvety sauce for a vegan version of the French classic, as luxurious and satisfying as the original. The ability of mushrooms to create fond, plus umami-boosting miso, soy sauce, and tomato paste, create a supremely savory sauce. Simmering beans in this acidic sauce slows down their cook time, leading to uneven results, so we cook them separately and add them to the sauce for the last 15 minutes to infuse them with the stew's flavors. You can substitute dried shiitake mushrooms for the porcini and yellow or red miso for white. Leave the mushroom gills intact; they enhance the stew's color and flavor. Serve over Creamy Parmesan Polenta (page 313).

> **Substitution:** You can use dried large lima beans in place of the Christmas lima beans.

Palak Dal

- 1½ tablespoons table salt for brining
- 8 ounces (1⅓ cups) dried Christmas lima beans, picked over and rinsed
- ½ teaspoon table salt, plus salt for cooking beans
- ¼ cup extra-virgin olive oil, divided
- 1½ pounds portobello mushroom caps, cut into 1-inch pieces
- ¼ teaspoon pepper

2 carrots, peeled, and chopped fine
1 large shallot, minced
½ ounce dried porcini mushrooms, rinsed and minced
4 garlic cloves, minced
2 teaspoons minced fresh thyme or ¾ teaspoon dried
3 tablespoons all-purpose flour
1 cup plus 2 tablespoons dry red wine, divided
2 tablespoons white miso
2 tablespoons soy sauce
1 tablespoon tomato paste
2 bay leaves
1 cup frozen pearl onions, thawed
¼ cup minced fresh parsley

1. Dissolve 1½ tablespoons table salt in 2 quarts cold water in large container. Add beans and soak at room temperature for at least 8 hours or up to 24 hours. Drain and rinse well. (If you're pressed for time, see page 13 for information on quick brining your beans.)

2. Bring soaked beans and 7 cups water to simmer in large saucepan. Simmer, partially covered, over medium-low heat until beans are tender, 20 to 30 minutes. Remove from heat, stir in 1½ teaspoons salt, cover, and let sit for 15 minutes. Drain beans and set aside.

3. While beans cook, add ¼ cup water and 2 tablespoons oil to Dutch oven and bring to simmer over medium-high heat. Add portobello mushrooms, salt, and pepper. Cover and cook for 5 minutes, stirring occasionally (mushrooms will release liquid).

4. Uncover and continue to cook, stirring occasionally, until pot is dry and dark fond forms, 6 to 8 minutes longer. Add carrots, shallot, and remaining 2 tablespoons oil to pot and cook, stirring frequently, until vegetables start to brown, 3 to 4 minutes. Add porcini mushrooms, garlic, and thyme and cook until fragrant, about 30 seconds. Stir in flour and cook for 30 seconds. Whisk in 1 cup wine, scraping up any browned bits.

5. Whisk in miso, soy sauce, and tomato paste, then stir in 5 cups water and bay leaves. Bring to boil over high heat. Reduce heat to maintain vigorous simmer and cook, stirring occasionally and scraping bottom of pot to loosen any browned bits, until sauce is reduced and has consistency of heavy cream, 20 to 25 minutes.

6. Stir in cooked beans, pearl onions, and remaining 2 tablespoons wine. Cover and cook over low heat, stirring occasionally, until pearl onions are tender, about 15 minutes. Discard bay leaves and stir in parsley. Serve.

Palak Dal

Serves 4 to 6 | **Total Time** 1¼ hours

WHY THIS RECIPE WORKS In India, both raw lentils and the stews made with them are called "dal." It is a staple of the vegetarian Indian meal: quick, affordable, flavorful, and packed with protein. We use quick-cooking red lentils for this weeknight dish. Spinach is the vegetable component. Once the lentils soften, a vigorous whisk transforms them into a porridge-like stew, no blender or food processor needed. Seasoning the lentils with tadka (see page 148) just before serving gives the dish complexity, a gorgeous appearance, and an enticing aroma. Yellow mustard seeds can be substituted for brown. Monitor the spices and aromatics carefully during frying and reduce the heat if needed to prevent scorching. Serve with naan and/or Basmati Rice Pilaf (page 299).

4½ cups water
1½ cups (10½ ounces) dried red lentils, picked over and rinsed
1 tablespoon grated fresh ginger
¾ teaspoon ground turmeric
6 ounces (6 cups) baby spinach
1½ teaspoons table salt
3 tablespoons ghee
1½ teaspoons brown mustard seeds
1½ teaspoons cumin seeds
1 large onion, chopped
15 curry leaves, roughly torn (optional)
6 garlic cloves, sliced
4 whole dried arbol chiles
1 serrano chile, halved lengthwise
1½ teaspoons lemon juice, plus extra for seasoning
⅓ cup chopped fresh cilantro

1. Bring water, lentils, ginger, and turmeric to boil in large saucepan over medium-high heat. Reduce heat to maintain vigorous simmer. Cook, uncovered, stirring occasionally, until lentils are soft and starting to break down, 18 to 20 minutes.

2. Whisk lentils vigorously until coarsely pureed, about 30 seconds. Continue to cook until lentils have consistency of loose polenta or oatmeal, up to 5 minutes. Stir in spinach and salt and continue to cook until spinach is fully wilted, 30 to 60 seconds. Cover and set aside off heat.

3. Melt ghee in 10-inch skillet over medium-high heat. Add mustard seeds and cumin seeds and cook, stirring constantly, until seeds sizzle and pop, about 30 seconds.

Add onion and cook, stirring frequently, until onion is just starting to brown, about 5 minutes. Add curry leaves, if using; garlic, arbols; and serrano and cook, stirring frequently, until onion and garlic are golden brown, 3 to 4 minutes.

4. Add lemon juice to lentils and stir to incorporate. (Dal should have consistency of loose polenta. If too thick, loosen with hot water, adding 1 tablespoon at a time.) Season with salt and extra lemon juice to taste. Transfer dal to serving bowl and spoon onion mixture on top. Sprinkle with cilantro and serve.

NOTES FROM THE TEST KITCHEN

TADKA

A tadka (other names: Baghaar, phodni, or chownk) is a classic Indian seasoning technique. Whole spices like brown (also called black) mustard seeds and/or cumin seeds are bloomed in hot ghee or oil along with powdered turmeric or asafetida and chiles to bring out their flavor and aroma. A tadka can be used at the beginning of cooking or drizzled on at the end as a potent garnish. Since Indian cooks often use a tadka for lentils, we use it traditionally for Palak Dal (page 147) and adapt the technique for Hearty Spanish-Style Lentil and Chorizo Soup (page 120).

Adasi

Serves 4 to 6 | **Total Time** 2 hours

WHY THIS RECIPE WORKS Often enjoyed for breakfast, this humble lentil stew is a staple for Iranians. "Adasi" translates to "lentils" and can be prepared in infinite ways. At its most simple, it is lentils cooked in water with salt. However, spices, potatoes, chiles, tomato paste, herbs, and toppings such as caramelized onions, hard boiled eggs, and yogurt are all customary and welcomed. The texture of adasi can range from thick to brothy. We like it loose and porridge-like, with tender lentils that melt into an aromatic sauce. We complement the lentils' creamy texture with caramelized onions and a crispy garlic-mint crumble. While dried mint is more commonly used as a topping, we like the sweet, delicate texture of fried fresh mint leaves. Finally, a dash of golpar, a spice made from the seedpods of the Persian hogweed plant, adds bitter notes and a woodsy aroma, so use it sparingly.

Substitution: You can use dried brown lentils in place of the green lentils.

ADASI
- 4 tablespoons unsalted butter, divided
- 1 onion, chopped fine
- 1¼ teaspoons table salt, divided
- 1½ teaspoons ground cumin
- 1 teaspoon pepper
- ¾ teaspoon ground turmeric
- 10 cups water
- 1 pound (2¼ cups) dried green lentils, picked over and rinsed
  Golpar (optional)
  Lime wedges

TOPPINGS
- 1 tablespoon unsalted butter
- 1 onion, halved and sliced thin
- 1 teaspoon plus pinch sugar, divided
- ⅛ teaspoon plus pinch table salt, divided
- ¼ cup chopped garlic (10 cloves)
- ¼ cup vegetable oil for frying
- ¼ cup chopped fresh mint

1. FOR THE ADASI Melt 2 tablespoons butter in large saucepan over medium heat. Add onion and ¼ teaspoon salt and cook until softened, about 5 minutes. Stir in cumin, pepper, and turmeric and cook until fragrant, about 1 minute. Stir in water, lentils, and remaining 1 teaspoon salt and bring to simmer. Reduce heat to medium-low and cook until thickened to consistency of loose oatmeal, about 1¼ hours, stirring often so lentils don't stick to bottom of saucepan.

2. FOR THE TOPPINGS While lentils simmer, melt butter in 10-inch nonstick skillet over medium-low heat. Add onion, 1 teaspoon sugar, and ⅛ teaspoon salt, cover, and cook, stirring occasionally, until onion is softened, 8 to 10 minutes. Uncover and continue to cook, stirring occasionally, until onion is deep golden brown, about 10 minutes. Remove from heat and cover with lid to keep warm until ready to serve.

3. Combine garlic and oil in medium bowl. Microwave for 3 to 4 minutes, stirring every minute, until garlic is light golden. Stir in mint and microwave until garlic is golden brown and mint is translucent, about 1 minute longer. Strain garlic-mint mixture through fine-mesh strainer set over bowl. Transfer garlic-mixture to paper towel–lined plate, sprinkle with remaining pinch sugar and remaining pinch salt and let sit for at least 5 minutes until crisp. Set aside until ready to serve.

4. Stir remaining 2 tablespoons butter into lentils. Serve, passing caramelized onions; garlic-mint topping; lime wedges; and golpar, if using, separately.

Classic Ground Beef Chili

Serves 4 to 6 | **Total Time** 1½ hours

WHY THIS RECIPE WORKS Good ground beef chili should come together easily and relatively quickly, but it shouldn't taste as if it did. The flavors should be rich and balanced, the texture thick and hearty. To create deeply satisfying chili, we start by browning the beef to develop fond in a Dutch oven. After building this flavor base, we bloom dried spices in hot oil to bring out their lively personalities. We puree half the kidney beans with canned tomatoes to thicken the chili without having to simmer it all day, adding the remaining beans later on to give our chili heft and texture. For a spicier chili, use the greater amount of chipotle. Serve with your favorite chili garnishes.

Adasi

Classic Ground Beef Chili

- 1 (28-ounce) can whole peeled tomatoes
- 2 (15-ounce) cans kidney beans, rinsed, divided
- 1 tablespoon vegetable oil
- 1½ pounds 85 percent lean ground beef
- 1 onion, chopped fine
- 1½ teaspoons table salt
- 1 teaspoon pepper
- 3 tablespoons chili powder
- 1–2 tablespoons minced canned chipotle chile in adobo sauce
- 1 tablespoon ground coriander
- 1 tablespoon garlic powder
- 2 teaspoons ground cumin
- 2 teaspoons dried oregano
- 2 cups water, plus extra as needed

1. Process tomatoes and their juice and half of beans in food processor until smooth, about 30 seconds; set aside.

2. Heat oil in Dutch oven over medium-high heat until just smoking. Add beef, onion, salt, and pepper and cook, breaking up meat with wooden spoon, until any liquid has evaporated and fond begins to form on bottom of pot, 12 to 14 minutes. Add chili powder, chipotle, coriander, garlic powder, cumin, and oregano and cook, stirring frequently, until fragrant, about 2 minutes.

3. Stir in water, scraping up any browned bits. Stir in tomato mixture and remaining beans and bring to simmer. Reduce heat to medium-low, cover partially, and cook until thickened and flavors meld, about 45 minutes. (If chili begins to stick to bottom of pot or looks too thick, stir in extra water as needed.) Season with salt and pepper to taste. Serve.

Five-Alarm Chili

Serves 6 to 8 | **Total Time** 2 hours

WHY THIS RECIPE WORKS As the name implies, five-alarm chili should be spicy enough to make you break a sweat—but it has to have rich, complex chile flavor too. Mellowed with a bit of sugar and enriched with creamy pinto beans, our chili is well balanced and spicy without being harsh. We use a combination of fruity dried anchos, smoky chipotle chiles in adobo sauce, fresh jalapeños, and chili powder to create layers of spicy flavor. Ground beef adds meaty bulk, and pureeing the chiles along with canned tomatoes and corn tortilla chips creates extra body and another layer of flavor. Serve with your favorite chili garnishes.

- 2 ounces (4 to 6) dried ancho chiles, stemmed, seeded, and cut into 1-inch pieces
- 1 (28-ounce) can whole peeled tomatoes
- ¾ cup crushed corn tortilla chips
- ¼ cup canned chipotle chile in adobo sauce plus 2 teaspoons adobo sauce
- 2 tablespoons vegetable oil, divided
- 2 pounds 85 percent lean ground beef
- 1 teaspoon table salt
- ½ teaspoon pepper
- 2 pounds onions, chopped fine
- 2 jalapeño chiles, stemmed, seeds reserved, and minced
- 6 garlic cloves, minced
- 2 tablespoons ground cumin
- 2 tablespoons chili powder
- 1 tablespoon dried oregano
- 2 teaspoons ground coriander
- 2 teaspoons sugar
- 1 teaspoon cayenne pepper
- 1½ cups beer
- 3 (15-ounce) cans pinto beans, rinsed

1. Combine anchos and 1½ cups water in bowl and microwave until softened, about 3 minutes. Drain anchos and discard liquid. Process anchos, tomatoes and their juice, 2 cups water, tortilla chips, chipotle, and adobo sauce in blender until smooth, about 1 minute.

2. Heat 2 teaspoons oil in Dutch oven over medium-high heat until just smoking. Add beef, salt, and pepper and cook, breaking up meat with wooden spoon, until all liquid has evaporated and meat begins to sizzle, 10 to 15 minutes. Drain in colander and set aside.

3. Heat remaining 4 teaspoons oil in now-empty Dutch oven over medium-high heat until shimmering. Add onions and jalapeños with their seeds and cook until onions are beginning to brown, 5 to 7 minutes. Stir in garlic, cumin, chili powder, oregano, coriander, sugar, and cayenne and cook until fragrant, about 30 seconds. Pour in beer and bring to simmer.

4. Stir in beans, reserved chile-tomato mixture, and reserved cooked beef and return to simmer. Cover, reduce heat to low, and cook, stirring occasionally, until thickened, 50 minutes to 1 hour. (If chili begins to stick to bottom of pot or looks too thick, stir in extra water as needed.) Season with salt to taste, and serve.

Ultimate Beef Chili

Serves 6 to 8 | **Total Time** 3 hours, plus 8 hours brining

WHY THIS RECIPE WORKS Our ultimate chili starts with tender, full-flavored chunks of meaty blade steak, and we pair them with orca beans, black-and-white heirloom beans with a potato-like flavor that are well suited for long, slow cooking. For complexity, we use ground dried ancho and arbol chiles; for grassy heat, we add fresh jalapeños. Light molasses brings welcome sweetness, and cocoa powder adds depth. A small amount of cornmeal thickens the dish. Because much of the chili flavor is held in the fat, we stir in the fat that rises to the top rather than discarding it. You can substitute dried New Mexican or guajillo chiles for the anchos; each dried arbol may be replaced with ⅛ teaspoon cayenne pepper. Serve with your favorite chili garnishes.

Substitution: You can use dried pinto beans in place of the orca beans.

- 1½ tablespoons table salt for brining
- 8 ounces (1¼ cups) dried orca beans, picked over and rinsed
- 2½ ounces (6) dried ancho chiles, stemmed, seeded, and torn into 1-inch pieces
- 2–4 dried arbol chiles, stemmed, seeded, and halved
- 3 tablespoons cornmeal
- 2 teaspoons dried oregano
- 2 teaspoons ground cumin
- 2 teaspoons unsweetened cocoa powder
- 1½ teaspoons table salt, divided
- 2½ cups chicken broth, divided
- 2 onions, cut into ¾-inch pieces
- 3 small jalapeño chiles, stemmed, seeded, and cut into ½-inch pieces

       3 tablespoons vegetable oil, divided
       4 garlic cloves, minced
       1 (14.5-ounce) can diced tomatoes
       2 teaspoons molasses
    3½ pounds blade steak, ¾ inch thick,
          trimmed and cut into ¾-inch pieces
    1½ cups mild lager, divided

1. Dissolve 1½ tablespoons salt in 2 quarts cold water in large container. Add beans and soak at room temperature for at least 8 hours or up to 24 hours. Drain and rinse well. (If you're pressed for time, see page 13 for information on quick brining your beans.)

2. Adjust oven rack to lower-middle position and heat oven to 300 degrees. Toast anchos in 12-inch skillet over medium-high heat, stirring frequently, until fragrant, 4 to 6 minutes, reducing heat if chiles begin to smoke. Transfer to food processor and let cool (do not clean skillet).

3. Add arbols, cornmeal, oregano, cumin, cocoa, and ½ teaspoon salt to processor with toasted anchos and process until finely ground, about 2 minutes. With processor running, slowly add ½ cup broth and process until smooth paste forms, about 45 seconds, scraping down sides of bowl as needed. Transfer paste to bowl. Pulse onions in now-empty processor until coarsely chopped, about 4 pulses. Add jalapeños and pulse until consistency of chunky salsa, about 4 pulses, scraping down sides of bowl as needed.

4. Heat 1 tablespoon oil in Dutch oven over medium-high heat. Add onion mixture and cook, stirring occasionally, until moisture has evaporated and vegetables are softened, 7 to 9 minutes. Add garlic and cook until fragrant, about 1 minute. Stir in tomatoes and their juice, molasses, and chile paste, then add beans and remaining 2 cups broth. Bring to boil, then reduce heat to low and simmer.

5. Meanwhile, heat 1 tablespoon oil in now-empty skillet over medium-high heat until shimmering. Pat beef dry with paper towels and sprinkle with remaining 1 teaspoon salt. Brown half of beef on all sides, about 10 minutes; transfer to pot with bean mixture. Add ¾ cup beer to skillet, scraping up any browned bits, and bring to simmer. Transfer beer to pot with bean mixture. Repeat with remaining 1 tablespoon oil, remaining beef, and remaining ¾ cup beer. Stir to combine and return mixture in pot to simmer.

6. Cover pot and transfer to oven. Cook until meat and beans are fully tender, 1½ to 2 hours. Let chili sit, uncovered, for 10 minutes. (If chili begins to stick to bottom of pot or looks too thick, stir in extra water as needed.) Stir well, season with salt to taste, and serve.

Five-Alarm Chili

Ultimate Beef Chili

White Chicken Chili

White Chicken Chili

Serves 4 to 6 | **Total Time** 45 minutes FAST

WHY THIS RECIPE WORKS A big steaming pot of chili gets everybody crowding around for a bowl on cold weekends and game days. Usually chili needs to simmer for hours, making it an all-day affair, but this mildly spiced, tomato-free chicken version is ready in less than an hour. Canned hominy and store-bought broth, blended until smooth, create a thick base for the chicken, which we brown before poaching in the broth and then shred before adding to the finished chili. We leave some of the hominy kernels whole to stir into the chili to add warm corn flavor and a pleasingly chewy texture. Tomatillo salsa and cilantro give freshness without veering into green chili territory. Serve with your favorite chili garnishes.

2 (15-ounce) cans white or yellow hominy, rinsed, divided
4 cups chicken broth, divided
1½ pounds boneless, skinless chicken breasts, trimmed
½ teaspoon table salt
½ teaspoon pepper
2 tablespoons vegetable oil, divided

3 poblano chiles, stemmed, seeded, and chopped
1 onion, chopped fine
2 tablespoons all-purpose flour
3 garlic cloves, minced
1 teaspoon ground cumin
1 teaspoon ground coriander
⅛ teaspoon cayenne pepper
½ cup jarred tomatillo salsa or salsa verde
2 tablespoons minced fresh cilantro

1. Process 1½ cups hominy and 1 cup broth in blender until smooth, about 10 seconds; set aside.

2. Pat chicken dry with paper towels and sprinkle with salt and pepper. Heat 1 tablespoon oil in Dutch oven over medium-high heat until just smoking. Add chicken and cook until lightly browned on both sides, about 5 minutes; transfer to plate.

3. Add remaining 1 tablespoon oil, poblanos, and onion to fat left in pot and cook over medium heat until vegetables are softened, about 5 minutes. Stir in flour, garlic, cumin, coriander, and cayenne and cook until fragrant, about 1 minute. Slowly whisk in remaining 3 cups broth, scraping up any browned bits and smoothing out any lumps.

4. Stir in pureed hominy mixture and remaining hominy. Add browned chicken, along with any accumulated juices, cover, and simmer gently until chicken registers 160 degrees, about 10 minutes. Transfer chicken to cutting board; using 2 forks, shred into bite-size pieces.

5. Return chili to simmer. Stir in shredded chicken and tomatillo salsa and cook until heated through, about 1 minute. Stir in cilantro and season with salt and pepper to taste. Serve.

Classic Turkey Chili

Serves 6 to 8 | **Total Time** 1½ hours

WHY THIS RECIPE WORKS Turkey chili is a great alternative to classic ground beef chili, providing a leaner but no less flavorful meal, with kidney beans adding texture and heartiness. Ground turkey is full of moisture—more so than ground beef—but it's virtually impossible to keep the juices in the meat unless you give it some help to stay moist and tender while simmering. Treating the turkey with salt and baking soda helps the meat retain moisture, so it doesn't shed liquid during cooking. To buttress the mild turkey flavor we aren't shy with seasonings, incorporating ¼ cup of chili powder, six cloves of garlic, and plenty of other spices. Be sure to use ground turkey, not ground turkey breast (also labeled 99 percent fat-free), in this recipe. Serve with your favorite chili garnishes.

2 pounds ground turkey
1 tablespoon water, plus extra as needed
1 teaspoon table salt, divided
¼ teaspoon baking soda
¼ cup chili powder
6 garlic cloves, minced
1 tablespoon ground cumin
2 teaspoons ground coriander
1 teaspoon red pepper flakes
1 teaspoon dried oregano
½ teaspoon cayenne pepper
2 tablespoons vegetable oil
2 onions, chopped fine
2 red bell peppers, stemmed, seeded,
    and cut into ½-inch pieces
1 (28-ounce) can diced tomatoes
1 (28-ounce) can tomato puree
2 (15-ounce) cans kidney beans, drained and rinsed

1. Toss turkey, 1 tablespoon water, ½ teaspoon salt, and baking soda in bowl until thoroughly combined; set aside for 20 minutes. Combine chili powder, garlic, cumin, coriander, pepper flakes, oregano, and cayenne in bowl.

2. Heat oil in Dutch oven over medium heat until shimmering. Add onions, bell peppers, and remaining ½ teaspoon salt and cook until softened, 8 to 10 minutes. Increase heat to medium-high, add turkey, and cook, breaking up meat with wooden spoon, until no longer pink, 4 to 6 minutes. Stir in chili powder mixture and cook until fragrant, about 30 seconds. Stir in tomatoes and their juice and tomato puree and bring to simmer. Reduce heat to low, cover, and simmer gently, stirring occasionally, for 1 hour.

3. Stir in beans, cover, and continue to cook until slightly thickened, about 45 minutes. (If chili begins to stick to bottom of pot or looks too thick, stir in extra water as needed.) Season with salt and pepper to taste. Serve.

Pumpkin Turkey Chili

Serves 4 to 6 | **Total Time** 3 hours

WHY THIS RECIPE WORKS Pumpkin puree gives turkey chili a silky texture and subtle squash flavor that complements the chili's smokier notes. Black beans offer both color contrast and texture. To safeguard against rubbery turkey, we use the technique from our Classic Turkey Chili (page 152), treating the ground poultry with salt and baking soda. To give our dish a smoky, aromatic backbone, we make our own spice blend by

grinding toasted ancho chiles, cumin, coriander, paprika, and oregano. The result is a chili with deep, rich flavor. Be sure to use ground turkey, not ground turkey breast (also labeled 99 percent fat-free), in this recipe. Serve with your favorite chili garnishes.

1 pound ground turkey
1 tablespoon plus 2 cups water, divided
¾ teaspoon table salt, divided
¼ teaspoon baking soda
4 dried ancho chiles, stemmed, seeded,
    and torn into 1-inch pieces
1½ tablespoons ground cumin
1½ teaspoons ground coriander
1½ teaspoons dried oregano
1½ teaspoons paprika
1 teaspoon pepper
1 (28-ounce) can whole peeled tomatoes
2 tablespoons extra-virgin olive oil
2 onions, chopped fine
2 red bell peppers, stemmed, seeded,
    and cut into ½-inch pieces
6 garlic cloves, minced
1 cup canned unsweetened pumpkin puree
2 (15-ounce) cans black beans, rinsed

1. Toss turkey, 1 tablespoon water, ¼ teaspoon salt, and baking soda in bowl until thoroughly combined; set aside for 20 minutes.

2. Meanwhile, toast anchos in Dutch oven over medium-high heat, stirring frequently, until fragrant, 4 to 6 minutes, reducing heat if anchos begin to smoke. Transfer to food processor and let cool for 5 minutes.

3. Add cumin, coriander, oregano, paprika, and pepper to food processor with anchos and process until finely ground, about 2 minutes; transfer mixture to bowl. Process tomatoes and their juice in now-empty food processor until smooth, about 30 seconds.

4. Heat oil in now-empty pot over medium heat until shimmering. Add onions, bell peppers, and remaining ½ teaspoon salt and cook until softened, 8 to 10 minutes. Increase heat to medium-high, add turkey, and cook, breaking up meat with wooden spoon, until no pink remains, 4 to 6 minutes. Stir in spice mixture and garlic and cook until fragrant, about 30 seconds. Stir in pureed tomatoes, pumpkin, and remaining 2 cups water, and bring to simmer. Reduce heat to low, cover, and simmer gently, stirring occasionally, for 1 hour.

5. Stir in beans, cover, and continue to cook until slightly thickened, about 45 minutes. (If chili begins to stick to bottom of pot or looks too thick, stir in extra water as needed.) Season with salt to taste. Serve.

Ultimate Vegetarian Chili

Serves 6 to 8 | **Total Time** 4 hours, plus 8 hours brining and 20 minutes resting VEGAN

WHY THIS RECIPE WORKS This vegetarian chili is something to get excited about. Our goal was to build a chili as savory and deeply satisfying as any meat chili—one that even meat lovers would want to eat. We start our recipe with dried beans. As the beans cook, they shed flavor and starch that help to build a better chili. Two kinds of beans plus bulgur give our chili a substantial, hearty texture. For the chiles, we chose a combination of dried ancho and New Mexican chiles, toast them in the oven until fragrant, and then grind them. A combination of umami-rich ingredients—tomatoes, mushrooms, and (surprisingly) soy sauce—adds deep, savory flavor. Ground walnuts contribute even more savoriness, plus richness and body. We recommend a mix of at least two types of beans, one creamy (such as cannellini or navy) and one earthy (such as pinto, black, or red kidney). For a spicier chili, use both jalapeños. Serve with your favorite chili garnishes.

- 3 tablespoons table salt for brining
- 1 pound (2½ cups) assorted dried beans, picked over and rinsed
- 1 ounce (about 2) ancho chiles
- ½ ounce (about 2) New Mexican chiles
- ½ ounce dried shiitake mushrooms, chopped coarse
- 4 teaspoons dried oregano
- ½ cup walnuts, toasted
- 1 (28-ounce) can diced tomatoes, drained with juice reserved
- 3 tablespoons tomato paste
- 3 tablespoons soy sauce
- 1–2 jalapeño chiles, stemmed and chopped coarse
- 6 garlic cloves, minced
- ¼ cup vegetable oil
- 2 pounds onions, chopped fine
- 1¼ teaspoons table salt
- 1 tablespoon ground cumin
- ⅔ cup medium-grind bulgur
- ¼ cup minced fresh cilantro

1. Dissolve 3 tablespoons salt in 4 quarts cold water in large container. Add beans and soak at room temperature for at least 8 hours or up to 24 hours. Drain and rinse well. (If you're pressed for time, see page 13 for information on quick brining your beans.)

2. Adjust oven rack to middle position and heat oven to 300 degrees. Arrange ancho and New Mexican chiles on rimmed baking sheet and toast until fragrant and puffed, about 8 minutes. Transfer to plate, let cool for 5 minutes, then remove stems and seeds. Working in batches, grind toasted chiles, mushrooms, and oregano in spice grinder until finely ground.

3. Process walnuts in food processor until finely ground, about 30 seconds; transfer to bowl. Process drained tomatoes, tomato paste, soy sauce, jalapeño(s), and garlic in food processor until tomatoes are finely chopped, about 45 seconds.

4. Heat oil in Dutch oven over medium-high heat until shimmering. Add onions and salt and cook, stirring occasionally, until onions begin to brown, 8 to 10 minutes. Reduce heat to medium, add ground chile mixture and cumin, and cook, stirring constantly, until fragrant, about 1 minute. Stir in beans and 7 cups water and bring to boil. Cover pot, transfer to oven, and cook for 45 minutes.

5. Stir in bulgur, ground walnuts, tomato mixture, and reserved tomato juice and continue to cook in oven, covered, until beans are fully tender, about 2 hours. Remove pot from oven, stir well, and let stand, uncovered, for 20 minutes. Stir in cilantro and season with salt to taste before serving. (Chili can be refrigerated for up to 3 days.)

Four-Chile Vegetarian Chili

Serves 6 | **Total Time** 1¾ hours VEGAN

WHY THIS RECIPE WORKS This robust and flavorful plant-based chili can compete with the best meaty chilis out there. We sauté a base of onion and fresh poblano chile in plenty of olive oil until lightly browned; the oil's fat unlocks the flavors of the chiles and seasonings. Then we add tomato paste and minced garlic, along with dried oregano and a heap of warm, earthy ground cumin. We let it all sizzle until the tomato paste begins to darken and the sugars caramelize. Many recipes call for store-bought chili powder, but we toast torn dried ancho and guajillo chiles, reconstitute them in water, and then blitz them in a blender with tomatoes and canned chipotle chile to create a significantly more complex chili. To account for the lack of meat, we incorporate soy sauce and dried porcini mushrooms in addition to the tomato paste to contribute umami, or savory flavor. The soy sauce and tomato paste combine to provide a concentrated salty-sweet tang while the reconstituted mushrooms add depth and a slightly smoky element. We use a medley of canned beans—black, pinto, and kidney—to create an appealing mosaic of colors, flavors, and textures, along with mild barley, which contributes a pleasant, chewy bite. We like using a mix of beans here, but you can use all of one type or any combination of the three. Do not use hulled, hull-less, quick-cooking, or presteamed barley (check the ingredient list on the package to determine this) in this recipe. Use more or fewer chipotle chiles depending on your desired level of spiciness. Serve with your favorite chili garnishes.

- 1 ounce (2 or 3) dried ancho chiles, stemmed, seeded, and torn into 1-inch pieces
- ½ ounce (3 or 4) dried guajillo chiles, stemmed, seeded, and torn into 1-inch pieces
- 1 (28-ounce) can whole peeled tomatoes
- 1–3 canned chipotle chiles in adobo sauce
- 3 tablespoons soy sauce
- 2¼ teaspoons table salt, divided
- ¼ cup extra-virgin olive oil
- 1 onion, chopped
- 1 poblano chile, stemmed, seeded, and chopped
- 3 tablespoons tomato paste
- 6 garlic cloves, minced
- 2 tablespoons ground cumin
- 1 tablespoon dried oregano
- 1 (15-ounce) can pinto beans, rinsed
- 1 (15-ounce) can black beans, rinsed
- 1 (15-ounce) can red kidney beans, rinsed
- ¾ cup pearl barley
- ½ ounce dried porcini mushrooms, rinsed and chopped fine
- ½ cup chopped fresh cilantro

1. Place anchos and guajillos in Dutch oven and cook over medium heat, stirring often, until fragrant and darkened slightly but not smoking, 3 to 5 minutes. Immediately transfer anchos and guajillos to bowl and cover with hot water. Let sit until chiles are soft and pliable, about 5 minutes.

2. Drain anchos and guajillos and combine with tomatoes and their juice, 1 cup water, chipotle(s), soy sauce, and 1½ teaspoons salt in blender. Process until smooth, 1 to 2 minutes; set aside.

3. Heat oil in now-empty Dutch oven over medium-high heat until shimmering. Add onion, poblano, and remaining ¾ teaspoon salt. Cook, stirring occasionally, until onion begins to brown, 3 to 5 minutes. Stir in tomato paste, garlic, cumin, and oregano and cook until tomato paste darkens, 1 to 2 minutes.

4. Stir in pinto, black, and kidney beans; barley; mushrooms; chile puree; and 2½ cups water. Bring to boil. Reduce heat to medium-low and simmer, stirring occasionally, until barley is tender, 35 to 45 minutes. Let sit off heat for 10 minutes (chili will continue to thicken as it sits). Season with salt to taste. Stir in cilantro and serve.

Ultimate Vegetarian Chili

Four-Chile Vegetarian Chili

Meal Salads

● FAST (45 minutes or less)   ● VEGAN
Photo: Sprouted Grain Salad

Marinated Tofu and Vegetable Salad

Serves 4 | **Total Time** 40 minutes FAST

WHY THIS RECIPE WORKS Tofu takes particularly well to marinating, which is a great way to imbue flavor in recipes where the tofu is served raw. In this dinner salad, we marinate tofu with a bright dressing and combine it with crunchy snow peas, sliced tender napa cabbage, and a bright bell pepper. A sriracha-based salad dressing does double duty as the marinade, bringing in a touch of heat and tons of flavor. Firm tofu is tender and supple when eaten raw, but still pleasantly sturdy. Note that this recipe uses unseasoned rice vinegar; we don't recommend using seasoned rice vinegar in its place. Do not use silken tofu.

28 ounces firm tofu, cut into ¾-inch pieces
¼ cup unseasoned rice vinegar
2 tablespoons sriracha
2 teaspoons honey
¼ teaspoon table salt
3 tablespoons toasted sesame oil
½ small head napa cabbage, cored and sliced thin (4 cups)
6 ounces snow peas, strings removed, cut in half crosswise
1 red bell pepper, stemmed, seeded, and cut into ½-inch pieces
2 scallions, sliced thin on bias
2 tablespoons toasted sesame seeds

1. Pat tofu dry with paper towels. Whisk vinegar, sriracha, honey, and salt together in large bowl. Whisking constantly, slowly drizzle in sesame oil until emulsified. Gently toss tofu in dressing, then cover and refrigerate for 20 minutes.

2. Add cabbage, snow peas, and bell pepper to bowl with tofu and toss gently to combine. Season with salt and pepper to taste and sprinkle with scallions and sesame seeds. Serve.

Kale Salad with Crispy Tofu and Miso-Ginger Dressing

Serves 4 | **Total Time** 30 minutes FAST VEGAN

WHY THIS RECIPE WORKS This plant-based salad uses kale as a hearty base with a satisfying, crispy fried tofu topping powered by the delicate but distinct flavors of white miso, ginger, and toasted sesame oil. Dressing the kale first gives the tough greens time to soften while we pan-fry cubes of tofu. To tie the salad together, avocado and roasted cashews offer both heft and textural contrast to the tofu and greens while fresh cilantro leaves sprinkled on before serving add delightful freshness. Split the tofu horizontally into thirds and make ½-inch-thick planks before making the remaining cuts to cube it.

¼ cup seasoned rice vinegar
3 tablespoons toasted sesame oil
3 tablespoons white miso
1 tablespoon grated fresh ginger
1 pound curly kale, stemmed and chopped coarse
2 carrots, peeled and shredded
14 ounces firm tofu, cut into ½-inch pieces
½ teaspoon table salt
⅓ cup cornstarch
¼ cup vegetable oil for frying
2 avocados, halved, pitted, and cut into ½-inch pieces
½ cup roasted cashews, chopped coarse

1. Whisk vinegar, sesame oil, miso, and ginger together in large bowl. Add kale and carrots and toss to combine. Season with salt and pepper to taste.

2. Pat tofu dry with paper towels. Sprinkle with salt, then toss tofu with cornstarch in bowl.

3. Heat vegetable oil in 12-inch nonstick skillet over medium-high heat until shimmering. Add tofu and cook, turning as needed, until crispy and browned on all sides, 10 to 15 minutes, breaking up any pieces that stick together. Transfer to paper towel–lined plate. Divide kale among 4 individual serving bowls, then top with avocados, cashews, and tofu. Serve.

Edamame and Shrimp Salad

Serves 4 | **Total Time** 25 minutes **FAST**

WHY THIS RECIPE WORKS Immature soy beans—
edamame—are great in salads because their bright, fresh
flavor and satisfying texture pair perfectly with leafy greens.
Tart vinaigrettes and bold-flavored vegetables can easily over-
power the beans' mildness, though. So we choose rice vinegar
for its mild acidity, incorporating honey for some sweetness
and to help emulsify the dressing. The subtle pepperiness and
delicate, tender leaves of baby arugula work well as a flavor
and texture complement, and sweet sautéed shrimp turns this
bright salad into dinner. Mint and basil bring a light, summery
flavor; thinly sliced shallot gives mild allium notes; and radishes
provide crunch and color. Garlic contributes aroma and flavor
without taking over the dish, and a sprinkling of roasted sunflower seeds adds nuttiness and depth.

- 12 ounces extra-large shrimp (21 to 25 per pound),
  peeled, deveined, and tails removed
- 1¼ teaspoons table salt, divided
- ¼ teaspoon pepper
- ¼ cup extra-virgin olive oil, divided
- 2 tablespoons unseasoned rice vinegar
- 1 tablespoon honey
- 1 small garlic clove, minced
- 3 cups frozen shelled edamame beans,
  thawed and patted dry
- 2 ounces (2 cups) baby arugula
- ½ cup shredded fresh basil
- ½ cup chopped fresh mint
- 2 radishes, trimmed, halved, and sliced thin
- 1 shallot, halved and sliced thin
- ¼ cup roasted sunflower seeds

1. Pat shrimp dry with paper towels and sprinkle with
¼ teaspoon salt and pepper. Heat 1 tablespoon oil in 12-inch
nonstick skillet over medium-high heat until just smoking. Add
shrimp in single layer and cook, without stirring, until spotty
brown and edges turn pink on bottom, about 1 minute. Flip
shrimp and continue to cook until all but very center is opaque,
about 30 seconds; transfer shrimp to plate and let cool slightly.

2. Whisk vinegar, honey, garlic, and remaining 1 teaspoon
salt together in large bowl. Whisking constantly, slowly drizzle
in remaining 3 tablespoons oil until emulsified. Add shrimp,
edamame, arugula, basil, mint, radishes, and shallot and toss
to combine. Season with salt and pepper to taste. Sprinkle
with sunflower seeds and serve.

Edamame and Shrimp Salad

Kale Salad with Crispy Tofu
and Miso-Ginger Dressing

Crispy Lentil
and Herb Salad

Lentil Salad with Oranges,
Celery, and Feta

Crispy Lentil and Herb Salad

Serves 4 | **Total Time** 35 minutes, plus 1 hour brining

WHY THIS RECIPE WORKS Many lentil salads are made with boiled lentils, but we decided to fry ours in this salad inspired by lentil preparations in countries such as India, Lebanon, Syria, and Turkey. Brining the lentils before frying is crucial to ensure that they cook, turn tender and lightly crispy, but don't burn. We tested various lentils and found that the firm texture of lentilles du Puy holds up especially well to quickly frying in a saucepan. Instead of tossing the components together with a dressing, we use yogurt as an anchor, spreading it on a platter and topping it with a lightly dressed blend of fresh herbs tossed with the crunchy lentils and sweet bits of dried cherries. Pita is a must for scooping everything up in one perfect bite. Be sure to use a large saucepan to fry the lentils, as the oil mixture will bubble and steam.

Substitution: You can use brown lentils in place of the lentilles du Puy.

- 1 teaspoon table salt for brining
- ½ cup dried lentilles du Puy, picked over and rinsed
- ⅓ cup vegetable oil for frying
- ½ teaspoon ground cumin
- ¼ teaspoon plus pinch table salt, divided
- 1 cup plain Greek yogurt
- 3 tablespoons extra-virgin olive oil, divided
- 1 teaspoon grated lemon zest plus 1 teaspoon juice
- 1 garlic clove, minced
- ½ cup fresh parsley leaves
- ½ cup torn fresh dill
- ½ cup fresh cilantro leaves
- ¼ cup dried cherries, chopped
  Pomegranate molasses
  Pitas, warmed

1. Dissolve 1 teaspoon salt in 1 quart water in bowl. Add lentils and brine at room temperature for at least 1 hour or up to 24 hours. Drain and rinse well; pat dry with paper towels.

2. Heat vegetable oil in large saucepan over medium heat until shimmering. Add lentils and cook, stirring constantly, until crispy and golden in spots, 8 to 12 minutes (oil should bubble vigorously throughout; adjust heat as needed). Carefully drain lentils in fine-mesh strainer set over bowl, then transfer lentils to paper towel–lined plate. Discard oil. Sprinkle with cumin and ¼ teaspoon salt and toss to combine; set aside. (Cooled lentils can be stored in airtight container at room temperature for up to 24 hours.)

3. Whisk yogurt, 2 tablespoons olive oil, lemon zest and juice, and garlic together in bowl and season with salt and pepper to taste. Spread yogurt mixture over serving platter. Toss parsley, dill, cilantro, remaining pinch salt, and remaining 1 tablespoon olive oil together in bowl, then gently stir in lentils and cherries. Season with salt and pepper to taste and arrange on top of yogurt mixture, leaving 1-inch border. Drizzle with pomegranate molasses. Serve with warm pitas.

Lentil Salad with Oranges, Celery, and Feta

Serves 4 to 6 | **Total Time** 1¼ hours, plus 1 hour brining

WHY THIS RECIPE WORKS The most important part of making a lentil salad is perfecting the cooking of the lentils so they maintain their shape and firm-tender bite. This requires two key steps. The first is to brine the lentils in salt water. With brining, the lentils' skins soften, which leads to fewer blowouts. The second step is to cook the lentils in the oven, which heats them gently and uniformly. Once the lentils are perfectly cooked, all we have left to do is to pair the earthy legumes with a tart vinaigrette and boldly flavored and textured mix-ins: soft feta, crunchy pecans, crisp celery, and tangy orange slices.

> **Substitution:** You can use brown lentils in place of the green lentils.

- 1 teaspoon table salt for brining
- 1 cup dried green lentils, picked over and rinsed
- ¼ teaspoon table salt, plus salt for cooking lentils
- 2 tablespoons cider vinegar
- 1 shallot, minced
- 1 tablespoon honey
- ½ teaspoon dried mint
- ¼ cup extra-virgin olive oil
- 1 orange
- 2 celery ribs, sliced thin on bias, plus ¼ cup celery leaves
- ¼ cup pecans, toasted and chopped coarse, divided
- 1 ounce feta cheese, crumbled (¼ cup)

1. Dissolve 1 teaspoon salt in 1 quart water in bowl. Add lentils and brine at room temperature for at least 1 hour or up to 24 hours. Drain and rinse well.

2. Adjust oven rack to middle position and heat oven to 325 degrees. Combine drained lentils, 4 cups water, and ½ teaspoon salt in medium saucepan. Cover, transfer to oven, and bake until lentils are tender, 40 minutes to 1 hour. Drain lentils well.

3. Whisk vinegar, shallot, honey, mint, and salt together in large bowl. While whisking constantly, slowly drizzle in oil until combined. Cut away peel and pith from orange. Cut orange into 8 wedges then slice crosswise into ¼-inch-thick slices. Add drained lentils, orange slices, celery and leaves, and 2 tablespoons pecans and toss to combine. Season with salt and pepper to taste. Sprinkle with feta and remaining 2 tablespoons pecans. Serve warm or at room temperature.

Fattoush with Chickpeas

Serves 4 to 6 | **Total Time** 45 minutes **FAST** **VEGAN**

WHY THIS RECIPE WORKS This Levantine salad combines fresh, flavorful produce, crisp pita chips, and bright herbs with chickpeas, an ingredient favored in the region. Many recipes call for eliminating excess moisture from the salad by seeding and salting the cucumbers and tomatoes. We skip this step in order to preserve the crisp texture of the cucumber and the flavorful seeds and jelly of the tomatoes. Instead, we make the pita moisture-repellent by brushing its craggy sides with plenty of olive oil before baking. The oil prevents the pita chips from absorbing so much liquid from the salad that they became soggy while still allowing the chips to pick up flavor from the lemony dressing. However, serve this salad as soon as you've made it so that the pita doesn't sit too long. Despite the oil, it will get soggy over time. The success of fattoush depends on ripe, in-season tomatoes.

- 2 (8-inch) pitas
- ½ cup extra-virgin olive oil, divided
- 1 garlic clove, minced
- ½ teaspoon grated lemon zest plus ¼ cup juice (2 lemons)
- ¼ teaspoon table salt
- 1 (15-ounce) can chickpeas, rinsed
- 1 pound tomatoes, cored and cut into ¾-inch pieces
- 1 English cucumber, peeled and sliced ⅛ inch thick
- 1 cup baby arugula, chopped coarse
- ½ cup chopped fresh mint
- 4 scallions, sliced thin

1. Adjust oven rack to middle position and heat oven to 375 degrees. Using kitchen shears, cut around perimeter of each pita and separate into 2 thin rounds. Cut each round in half. Place pitas, smooth side down, on wire rack set in rimmed baking sheet. Brush ¼ cup oil over surface of pitas. (Pitas do not need to be uniformly coated. Oil will spread during baking.) Bake until pitas are crisp and pale golden brown, 10 to 14 minutes. Set aside to cool. (Cooled pitas can be stored in zipper-lock bag for up to 24 hours.)

2. Meanwhile, whisk garlic, lemon zest and juice, salt, and remaining ¼ cup oil together in large bowl. Add chickpeas and let sit until flavors meld, about 10 minutes.

3. Add tomatoes, cucumber, arugula, mint, and scallions, then break pitas into ½-inch pieces over top. Toss to combine. Season with salt and pepper to taste. Serve immediately.

Hearty Green Salad with Chickpeas, Pickled Cauliflower, and Seared Halloumi

Serves 4 | **Total Time** 35 minutes FAST

WHY THIS RECIPE WORKS A textured salad thoughtfully composed with greens, beans, juicy, crisp vegetables and/or tangy fruit, and a bright, creamy dressing is a welcome low-effort meal. Canned chickpeas are a powerhouse ingredient, a supereasy way to add protein to salad. First we quick-pickle cauliflower florets and use the brine as the acid base for the dressing. Some of the brine then goes into a vinaigrette to dress green leaf lettuce and radicchio, and we combine the rest into a thick, creamy dressing with Greek yogurt and tahini to coat the other components. In addition to the chickpeas and pickled cauliflower, we top the greens with pan-seared slabs of briny halloumi and juicy grapes.

½ cup cider vinegar
4 teaspoons honey
2 teaspoons table salt, divided
½ head cauliflower (1 pound), cored and cut into 1-inch florets (3 cups)
1 teaspoon plus ¼ cup extra-virgin olive oil, divided
8 ounces halloumi cheese, cut into 8 slices
1 small head green leaf lettuce (8 ounces), torn into bite-size pieces

1 small head radicchio (6 ounces), cored and sliced thin
1 (15-ounce) can chickpeas, rinsed
6 tablespoons plain Greek yogurt
¼ cup tahini
1 garlic clove, minced
1 teaspoon ground dried Aleppo pepper
12 ounces seedless red grapes, halved (2 cups)

1. Whisk vinegar, honey, and 1½ teaspoons salt together in medium bowl. Add cauliflower and stir to coat. Microwave until simmering, 1½ to 2 minutes. Stir, then cover and let sit, stirring occasionally, until cauliflower is crisp-tender, about 5 minutes. Using slotted spoon, transfer cauliflower to small plate, leaving liquid in bowl.

2. Heat 1 teaspoon oil in 12-inch nonstick skillet over medium-high heat until shimmering. Add halloumi and cook until brown on both sides, 60 to 90 seconds per side. Remove from heat and cover to keep warm.

3. Transfer ¼ cup pickling liquid to large bowl. Add remaining ¼ cup oil and whisk to combine. Add lettuce and radicchio, season with salt and pepper to taste, and toss to combine. Distribute greens evenly between 4 shallow serving bowls. Place chickpeas in now-empty bowl.

4. Add yogurt, tahini, garlic, Aleppo pepper, and remaining ½ teaspoon salt to remaining pickling liquid and whisk until combined. Add ½ cup yogurt mixture to chickpeas and toss to combine. Top greens with cauliflower, halloumi, and grapes and drizzle remaining yogurt mixture over top. Divide chickpea mixture evenly among bowls and serve.

Warm Broccoli, Chickpea, and Avocado Salad

Serves 4 | **Total Time** 45 minutes FAST VEGAN

WHY THIS RECIPE WORKS Canned chickpeas and broccoli florets get nice and crispy in a skillet, delivering roasted flavor to this salad without requiring the oven. For a creamy dressing without any mayo, we mash together avocado, olive oil, and pickled jalapeño brine to coat every inch of the chickpeas and broccoli. We set some avocado chunks aside to add to the salad later, with shallots and pickled jalapeños. They add crunch, softness, and more heat, and cut through the creamy dressing.

Warm Broccoli, Chickpea, and Avocado Salad

3. Add shallot, pickled jalapeños, and remaining avocado to bowl and toss gently to combine. Season with salt and pepper to taste. Serve.

Roasted Vegetable and Black Chickpea Salad

Serves 4 to 6 | Total Time 2 hours, plus 8 hours brining

WHY THIS RECIPE WORKS Think of black chickpeas as the sophisticated grown-up version of the humble common chickpea. An heirloom variety, they are commonly used in India and Italy. Black chickpeas boast a firm texture and an earthy, nutty, almost smoky flavor and can be used in place of chickpeas in just about any application. To highlight their stunning color and unique flavor, instead of making just a dip or a puree, we created a main course, special occasion–worthy salad. We pair the chickpeas with roasted vegetables that stand up to their meaty texture and flavor. Roasted delicata squash and golden beets make for a nice visual contrast while their natural sweetness tempers the earthiness of the chickpeas. A bed of herbed yogurt anchors the components of this dish and makes the salad feel cohesive and composed. A drizzle of fiery harissa ensures that the flavors don't lean too sweet. We prefer golden beets because they don't discolor the rest of the salad, but you can use red beets.

Substitution: You can use dried common chickpeas in place of black chickpeas.

2 avocados, halved, pitted, and cut into ½-inch pieces, divided

½ cup pickled jalapeños, chopped, plus ¼ cup brine

7 tablespoons extra-virgin olive oil, divided

1½ pounds broccoli florets, cut into 2-inch pieces

1 teaspoon table salt, divided

¾ teaspoon pepper, divided

2 (15-ounce) cans chickpeas, rinsed

1 large shallot, sliced thin

1. Mash ½ cup avocado, jalapeño brine, and 2 tablespoons oil in serving bowl with fork until combined; set dressing aside. Heat 3 tablespoons oil in 12-inch nonstick skillet over medium heat until shimmering. Add broccoli, ¾ teaspoon salt, and ½ teaspoon pepper and cook, stirring occasionally, until broccoli is dark brown and crispy in spots, about 20 minutes. Add to bowl with reserved dressing.

2. Heat remaining 2 tablespoons oil in now-empty skillet over medium-high heat until shimmering. Add chickpeas, remaining ¼ teaspoon salt, and remaining ¼ teaspoon pepper and cook until lightly browned, 6 to 10 minutes. Add to bowl with broccoli and dressing.

1½ tablespoons table salt for brining

8 ounces dried black chickpeas, picked over and rinsed

½ teaspoon table salt, divided, plus salt for cooking beans

1 pound golden beets, trimmed

1 delicata squash (12 to 16 ounces), ends trimmed, halved lengthwise, seeded, and sliced crosswise ½ inch thick

3 tablespoons extra-virgin olive oil, divided, plus extra for drizzling

1 cup plain Greek yogurt

¼ cup chopped fresh cilantro, divided

¾ teaspoon grated lemon zest, divided, plus 1½ tablespoons juice

¼ cup Harissa (page 116)

½ cup pomegranate seeds

¼ cup shelled pistachios, toasted and chopped

1. Dissolve 1½ tablespoons salt in 2 quarts cold water in large container. Add beans and brine at room temperature for at least 8 hours or up to 24 hours. Drain and rinse well. (If you're pressed for time, see page 13 for information on quick brining your beans.)

2. Adjust oven rack to middle position and heat oven to 425 degrees. Bring soaked beans and 7 cups water to simmer in large saucepan. Simmer, partially covered, over medium-low heat until beans are tender, 30 to 40 minutes. Remove from heat, stir in 1½ teaspoons salt, cover, and let sit for 15 minutes. Drain well and set aside.

3. Meanwhile, wrap beets individually in aluminum foil and place on aluminum foil-lined rimmed baking sheet. Roast for 30 minutes.

4. Toss squash with 1 tablespoon oil and ¼ teaspoon salt in bowl. Remove sheet with beets from oven and arrange beets on 1 half of sheet. Spread squash in even layer on other side of sheet, then return to oven and roast until beets and squash are tender (you will need to unwrap beets to test them), about 15 minutes.

5. Remove beets and squash from oven and carefully open beet foil packets. Once beets are cool enough to handle, carefully rub off skins using paper towels. Slice beets into ½-inch-thick wedges, and, if large, cut in half crosswise.

6. Whisk yogurt, 1 tablespoon oil, 1 tablespoon cilantro, ¼ teaspoon lemon zest, and ⅛ teaspoon salt together in bowl; set aside. Whisk remaining 1 tablespoon oil, remaining ½ teaspoon lemon zest, lemon juice, and remaining ⅛ teaspoon salt together in large bowl. Add reserved drained beans, beets, and squash and toss to combine. Season with salt and pepper to taste.

7. Spread yogurt mixture over wide serving platter. Arrange bean-vegetable mixture over top, then drizzle with harissa and sprinkle with pomegranate seeds, pistachios, and remaining 3 tablespoons cilantro. Drizzle with extra oil and serve.

White Bean and Tuna Salad

Serves 4 to 6 | **Total Time** 10 minutes **FAST**

WHY THIS RECIPE WORKS For this pantry-friendly salad, using stellar ingredients is key. Canned cannellini beans make it quick and bulk up the protein-rich fish. Olive oil–packed tuna is more moist and rich than tuna packed in water; the oil contributes fresh, fruity flavor. There's no need for a dressing; all ingredients are simply stirred together, with sherry vinegar adding a pop of brightness.

1 (6-ounce) container olive oil–packed tuna
2 (15-ounce) cans cannellini beans, rinsed
¼ cup extra-virgin olive oil
¼ cup coarsely chopped fresh parsley
1 shallot, sliced thin
4 teaspoons sherry vinegar
¼ teaspoon table salt
¼ teaspoon red pepper flakes

Remove tuna from container and discard packing oil. Coarsely flake tuna into medium bowl. Add beans, oil, parsley, shallot, vinegar, salt, and pepper flakes and stir to combine. Season with salt and pepper to taste. Serve.

Pinto Bean, Ancho, and Beef Salad with Pickled Poblanos

Serves 4 | **Total Time** 40 minutes, plus 30 minutes cooling

WHY THIS RECIPE WORKS This bean salad pays homage to some beloved Mexican ingredients. Ancho chiles, frequently used in Mexican cuisine, are dried poblanos; we use ancho chile powder as a rub for our steak, and we quick-pickle poblanos

Roasted Vegetable and Black Chickpea Salad

for sweet-sour spiciness. Grated jicama brings crunch to canned pinto beans, red onion, cilantro, and lime juice. The dressed salad is a refreshing counterpoint to the rich, chile spice–rubbed skirt steak, which we sear in a skillet. Crumbled cotija adds a salty bite. We top the salad with finely chopped unsweetened chocolate to round out the dish with complex bitterness. It is important to chop the chocolate fine; bigger pieces of chocolate will be overpoweringly bitter.

1 cup red wine vinegar
⅓ cup sugar
1¼ teaspoons table salt, divided
4 ounces poblano chiles, stemmed, seeded, and sliced ⅛ inch thick
1 (1-pound) skirt steak, trimmed and cut into thirds
2 teaspoons ancho chile powder
¾ teaspoon pepper, divided
2 tablespoons vegetable oil, divided
2 (15-ounce) cans pinto beans, rinsed
12 ounces jicama, peeled and grated (1½ cups)
½ cup finely chopped red onion
¼ cup chopped fresh cilantro leaves and stems, plus extra for sprinkling
3 tablespoons lime juice (2 limes)
1½ ounces cotija cheese, crumbled (⅓ cup)
½ ounce unsweetened chocolate, chopped fine (optional)

1. Microwave vinegar, sugar, and ¼ teaspoon salt in medium bowl until simmering, 3 to 4 minutes. Whisk to dissolve any residual sugar and salt, then stir in poblanos. Let sit, stirring occasionally, for 30 minutes. Drain and set aside.

2. Meanwhile, pat steak dry with paper towels, then sprinkle with chile powder, ¼ teaspoon pepper, and ½ teaspoon salt. Heat 1 tablespoon oil in 12-inch skillet over medium-high heat until just smoking. Add steak and cook until well browned and meat registers 120 to 125 degrees (for medium-rare), about 2 minutes per side. Transfer steak to cutting board, tent with aluminum foil, and let rest for 5 minutes.

3. Combine beans, jicama, onion, cilantro, lime juice, remaining ½ teaspoon salt, remaining ½ teaspoon pepper, and remaining 1 tablespoon oil in bowl and toss to combine. Season with salt and pepper to taste then transfer to serving platter. Slice steak thin against grain and arrange over top of salad. Sprinkle with cotija; chocolate, if using; reserved poblanos; and extra cilantro. Serve.

Chilled Soba Noodles with Spring Vegetables

Serves 4 to 6 | **Total Time** 30 minutes `FAST` `VEGAN`

WHY THIS RECIPE WORKS Earthy Japanese soba noodles are made with buckwheat flour, which contains no gluten. The deeper the color, the more buckwheat the noodles contain (and the richer they taste). Soba are as enjoyable chilled as they are hot. Here an umami-packed miso dressing coats them to make a refreshing cold noodle salad. We cook soba noodles in unsalted boiling water until they are tender but still resilient and rinse them under cold running water to remove excess sticky starch. We then toss the noodles with the dressing, which clings to and flavors them without overpowering their unique taste. A mix of raw vegetables cut in varying sizes provide crunch and color. Strips of toasted nori add more texture and a subtle briny flavor. If dried arbol chiles are unavailable, you can substitute ¼ to ½ teaspoon red pepper flakes. You can use yellow, red, or brown miso instead of the white.

3 tablespoons white miso
3 tablespoons mirin
2 tablespoons toasted sesame oil
1 tablespoon sesame seeds
1 teaspoon grated fresh ginger
1–2 dried arbol chiles (each about 2 inches long), stemmed, seeded, and chopped fine
8 ounces dried soba noodles
⅓ English cucumber, quartered lengthwise, seeded, and sliced thin on bias
4 ounces snow peas, strings removed, cut lengthwise into matchsticks
4 radishes, trimmed, halved, and sliced thin
3 scallions, sliced thin on bias
1 (8-inch square) sheet nori, toasted and cut into 2-inch-long matchsticks (optional)

1. Whisk miso, mirin, oil, 1 tablespoon water, sesame seeds, ginger, and arbols in large bowl until combined.

2. Meanwhile, bring 4 quarts water to boil in large pot. Add noodles and cook, stirring occasionally, until noodles are cooked through but still retain some chew. Drain noodles and rinse under cold running water until chilled. Drain well and transfer to bowl with dressing. Add cucumber; snow peas; radishes; scallions; and nori, if using, and toss to combine. Season with salt to taste. Serve.

Barley Salad with Celery and Miso Dressing

Serves 6 to 8 | **Total Time** 1¼ hours `VEGAN`

WHY THIS RECIPE WORKS Barley is a nutty but neutral grain, so it pairs well with most seasonings and can deliver satisfying chew and heartiness. In this simple salad, we pair barley with soy sauce, miso, toasted sesame oil, and seasoned rice vinegar. For grains that are distinct and boast a tender chew, we cook barley like pasta—boiled in a large volume of salted water and then drained—to rid the grains of much of their sticky starch, which would otherwise cause them to clump. Once the barley is cooked, we let it cool briefly on a rimmed baking sheet to help it dry thoroughly and then toss it with an acid-heavy dressing, crunchy celery and carrots, and aromatics and herbs to create a colorful, textured, and refreshing salad. The cooking time for pearl barley will vary from product to product, so start checking the barley for doneness after about 25 minutes.

1½ cups pearl barley
     Table salt for cooking barley
  3 tablespoons seasoned rice vinegar
  1 tablespoon white miso
  1 tablespoon soy sauce
  1 tablespoon toasted sesame oil
  1 tablespoon vegetable oil
  2 teaspoons grated fresh ginger
  1 garlic clove, minced
  1 teaspoon packed brown sugar
  ¼ teaspoon red pepper flakes
  2 celery ribs, sliced thin on bias
  2 carrots, peeled and shredded
  ½ cup minced fresh cilantro

1. Bring 4 quarts water to boil in large pot. Add barley and 1 tablespoon salt and boil gently until grains are tender with slight chew, 25 to 45 minutes. Drain barley, spread onto rimmed baking sheet, and let cool until no longer steaming, 5 to 7 minutes.

2. Whisk vinegar, miso, soy sauce, sesame oil, vegetable oil, ginger, garlic, sugar, and pepper flakes together in large bowl. Add barley and toss to coat. Add celery, carrots, and cilantro and toss to combine. Season with salt and pepper to taste. Serve.

Bulgur Salad with Curry Roasted Sweet Potatoes and Chickpeas

Serves 4 to 6 | **Total Time** 1¼ hours

WHY THIS RECIPE WORKS Bulgur is made from wheat berries that have been steamed or boiled and ground into fine, medium, coarse, or very coarse grains. Because the wheat berries are parcooked, bulgur is often just soaked in some liquid to make it edible. When it is cooked again, as in this recipe, it takes very little time and becomes somewhat tender but is still firm. Tabbouleh may be the most iconic bulgur dish; however, bulgur's appearance in salads shouldn't end there. For a satisfying, many-flavored dinner salad, we combine bulgur with kale and top it with protein-rich chickpeas and sweet potatoes spiced with curry powder. Tossing the chopped kale with the warm bulgur softens the sturdy leaves. Look for small sweet potatoes that weigh about 8 ounces each. Don't confuse bulgur with cracked wheat, which has a much longer cooking time and will not work in this recipe.

  1 pound sweet potatoes, unpeeled, cut
     lengthwise into 1-inch-thick wedges
  1 (15-ounce) can chickpeas, rinsed
  ½ cup extra-virgin olive oil, divided, plus
     extra for drizzling
  1 tablespoon curry powder
1½ teaspoons table salt, divided, plus
     salt for cooking bulgur
1¼ cups medium-grind bulgur
  5 tablespoons cider vinegar
  6 ounces kale, stemmed and chopped
  4 ounces goat cheese, crumbled (1 cup)
  ½ cup walnuts, toasted and chopped
  ⅓ cup dried cranberries

1. Adjust oven rack to middle position and heat oven to 450 degrees. Line rimmed baking sheet with parchment paper. Toss sweet potatoes, chickpeas, 1 tablespoon oil, curry powder, and ½ teaspoon salt together in large bowl. Arrange in single layer on prepared sheet. Roast until sweet potatoes are lightly browned and tender, about 20 minutes.

2. Meanwhile, bring 2 quarts water to boil in large saucepan. Add bulgur and 1 teaspoon salt, reduce heat to medium-low, and simmer until grains are tender, 5 to 8 minutes. Drain bulgur.

3. Whisk vinegar, remaining 7 tablespoons oil, and remaining 1 teaspoon salt together in now-empty bowl. Add drained bulgur and kale and toss to combine, then season with salt and pepper to taste. Divide bulgur mixture, sweet potatoes, and chickpeas evenly among 4 individual bowls. Top with goat cheese, walnuts, and cranberries. Drizzle with extra oil and serve.

Bulgur Salad with Spinach, Chickpeas, and Apples

Serves 4 to 6 | **Total Time** 45 minutes **FAST**

WHY THIS RECIPE WORKS You'll love the colorful combination of ingredients in this simple, inspired salad. Spinach and chickpeas, a pairing that's always a winner, add plant-powered heft to the bulgur, and plenty of chopped apples interrupt the earthiness with sweet crunch. All the components are dressed in a lemony, smoked paprika–spiced, honey-sweetened vinaigrette; the honey rounds out the smokiness of the peppery paprika. We briefly microwave the mix to bloom the smoked paprika. Once the salad is composed, toasted walnuts add a final layer of crunch.

1½ cups medium-grind bulgur
½ teaspoon table salt, plus salt for cooking bulgur
5 tablespoons extra-virgin olive oil
1 shallot, minced
1 teaspoon smoked paprika
½ teaspoon grated lemon zest plus ¼ cup juice (2 lemons)
1 tablespoon honey
1 (15-ounce) can chickpeas, rinsed
10 ounces frozen chopped spinach, thawed and squeezed dry
2 apples, cored and cut into ½-inch pieces
½ cup walnuts, toasted and chopped

1. Bring 2 quarts water to boil in large saucepan. Add bulgur and 1 teaspoon salt, reduce heat to medium-low, and simmer until tender, 5 to 8 minutes. Drain bulgur, spread onto rimmed baking sheet, and let cool for 15 minutes.

2. Meanwhile, whisk oil, shallot, paprika, and lemon zest together in large bowl. Microwave until bubbling and fragrant, about 30 seconds. Whisk in lemon juice, honey, and salt.

3. Add cooled bulgur, chickpeas, spinach, and apples to vinaigrette and toss to combine. Season with salt and pepper to taste, and sprinkle with walnuts. Serve.

Bulgur Salad with Curry Roasted Sweet Potatoes and Chickpeas

Bulgur Salad with Spinach, Chickpeas, and Apples

**Farro Salad with
Roasted Eggplant**

Farro Salad with Roasted Eggplant

Serves 4 to 6 | **Total Time** 1¼ hours `VEGAN`

WHY THIS RECIPE WORKS Nutty, earthy farro is one of the fastest-cooking whole grains around and it works to make the perfect good-for-you grain salad. While the farro cooks, we broil cubed eggplant until it's nice and brown, which brings essential meatiness and savory, caramelized flavor to the salad. A hefty amount of jarred roasted red peppers add sweetness and extra veggie goodness. Once the farro is cooled, we toss everything together with thinly sliced scallions and a lemony dressing that permeates the whole dish. Do not use pearl, quick-cooking, or presteamed farro (check the ingredient list on the package to determine this) in place of the whole farro.

1½ cups whole farro
 ½ teaspoon table salt, plus salt for cooking farro
1½ pounds eggplant, cut into ½-inch pieces
 6 tablespoons extra-virgin olive oil, divided
 1 teaspoon grated lemon zest plus 1 tablespoon juice
1½ cups jarred roasted red peppers, rinsed, patted dry, and cut into ½-inch pieces
 3 scallions, sliced thin
 ¼ teaspoon pepper

1. Adjust oven rack 4 inches from broiler element and heat broiler. Bring 4 quarts water to boil in large pot. Add farro and 1 tablespoon salt and cook until grains are tender with slight chew, 15 to 30 minutes. Drain farro, spread onto rimmed baking sheet, and let cool for 15 minutes.

2. Meanwhile, toss eggplant with 3 tablespoons oil, then transfer to aluminum foil–lined rimmed baking sheet and spread into even layer. Broil eggplant until well browned, 15 to 17 minutes, stirring halfway through.

3. Whisk remaining 3 tablespoons oil and lemon zest and juice together in large bowl. Add cooled farro, eggplant, red peppers, scallions, pepper, and salt and toss to combine. Season with salt and pepper to taste. Serve.

Millet Salad with Corn and Queso Fresco

Antipasto Farro Salad with Arugula

Serves 6 to 8 | **Total Time** 1¼ hours

WHY THIS RECIPE WORKS Farro makes a great salad base. Since the grain is from Italy, we think it's fitting to use it to make an antipasto salad. Once the farro is cooked and completely cool, we toss it with diced salami and provolone cheese; halved cherry tomatoes; chopped olives; marinated artichokes; and a bold dressing of red wine vinegar, olive oil, and dried oregano. We also fold in peppery arugula and a big handful of basil for a substantial yet summery dish. We prefer a small, individually packaged, dry Italian-style salami such as Genoa or soppressata, but unsliced deli salami can be used. Buy a piece of mild provolone from the deli counter rather than presliced provolone. We prefer the flavor and texture of whole farro in this recipe. Do not use pearl, quick-cooking, or presteamed farro (check the ingredient list on the package to determine this) for the whole farro.

1½ cups whole farro
½ teaspoon table salt, plus salt for cooking farro
⅓ cup extra-virgin olive oil
2 tablespoons red wine vinegar
1 teaspoon Dijon mustard
½ teaspoon dried oregano
½ teaspoon pepper
12 ounces cherry tomatoes, halved
4 ounces link salami, cut into ¼-inch pieces (1 cup)
4 ounces mild provolone cheese, cut into ¼-inch pieces (1 cup)
1 cup marinated artichoke hearts, chopped
½ cup chopped pitted green olives
3 ounces (3 cups) baby arugula
1 cup chopped fresh basil

1. Bring 4 quarts water to boil in large pot. Add farro and 1 tablespoon salt and cook until grains are tender with slight chew, 15 to 30 minutes. Drain farro, spread onto rimmed baking sheet, and let cool for 15 minutes.

2. Whisk oil, vinegar, mustard, oregano, pepper, and salt together in large bowl. Add farro, tomatoes, salami, provolone, artichokes, and olives and toss to combine. Fold in arugula and basil. Season with salt and pepper to taste. Serve.

Millet Salad with Corn and Queso Fresco

Serves 4 to 6 | **Total Time** 1 hour

WHY THIS RECIPE WORKS The mellow corn flavor and fine texture of tiny millet seeds make them versatile in savory dishes. We feature the small seeds in a salad that enhances the grain's sweet flavor, and we add corn to complement the millet's natural flavor and create texture. Millet seeds release starch as they cook, which can create large clumps. We found that boiling the millet like pasta results in distinct, individual cooked seeds because the seeds can't clump together. This makes them perfect for tossing with dressing. Spreading out the millet on a baking sheet first allows it to cool and further prevents clumping. Then we proceed to build the flavors of our salad; cherry tomatoes, queso fresco, and a minced jalapeño give the dish some southwestern flavor. For our dressing, we whip up a quick, bright vinaigrette using lime zest and juice. A small amount of mayonnaise helps emulsify the dressing so that it coats the millet evenly. Chopped cilantro adds freshness and color.

1 cup millet
¼ teaspoon table salt, plus salt for cooking millet
1 teaspoon grated lime zest plus 2½ tablespoons juice (2 limes), divided
2 teaspoons honey
½ teaspoon mayonnaise
3 tablespoons extra-virgin olive oil
8 ounces cherry tomatoes, quartered
½ cup frozen corn, thawed
1½ ounces queso fresco, crumbled (⅓ cup)
¼ cup chopped fresh cilantro
1 jalapeño chile, stemmed, seeded, and minced

1. Bring 3 quarts water to boil in large pot. Add millet and 1 teaspoon salt and cook until grains are tender, about 20 minutes. Drain millet, spread onto rimmed baking sheet, and drizzle with 1½ teaspoons lime juice. Let cool for 15 minutes.

2. Whisk honey, mayonnaise, salt, and lime zest and remaining 2 tablespoons lime juice together in large bowl. Whisking constantly, slowly drizzle in oil until emulsified. Add millet and toss to combine. Fold in tomatoes, corn, queso fresco, cilantro, and jalapeño. Season with salt and pepper to taste. Serve.

Quinoa, Black Bean, and Mango Salad with Lime Dressing

Serves 4 to 6 | **Total Time** 1 hour `VEGAN`

WHY THIS RECIPE WORKS The quinoa seed is often called a "supergrain" because it's a nutritionally complete protein. Quinoa originated in South America, is widely used there, and has become popular here too. To feature its delicate texture and nuttiness in a salad that makes a great main course, we toast the quinoa to bring out its flavor before adding liquid to the pan and simmering the grains until they are nearly tender. Then, as we do with other grains, we spread the quinoa on a rimmed baking sheet to cool without clumping. The residual heat finishes cooking it, giving us fluffy grains. Black beans, mango, and bell pepper add heartiness, flavor, and color to the salad and the blended dressing is a refreshing mix of jalapeño, cilantro, and lime juice. Scallions bring bite, and avocado provides creaminess. If you buy unwashed quinoa, rinse it and then spread it out on a clean dish towel to dry for 15 minutes.

1½ cups prewashed white quinoa
2¼ cups water
1½ teaspoons table salt, divided
 5 tablespoons lime juice (3 limes)
½ jalapeño chile, seeded and chopped
¾ teaspoon ground cumin
½ cup extra-virgin olive oil
⅓ cup fresh cilantro leaves
 1 red bell pepper, stemmed, seeded, and chopped
 1 mango, peeled, pitted, and cut into ¼-inch pieces
 1 (15-ounce) can black beans, rinsed
 2 scallions, sliced thin
 1 avocado, halved, pitted, and sliced thin

1. Toast quinoa in large saucepan over medium-high heat, stirring often, until very fragrant and quinoa makes continuous popping sound, 5 to 7 minutes. Stir in water and ½ teaspoon salt and bring to simmer. Cover, reduce heat to low, and simmer gently until most of water has been absorbed and quinoa is nearly tender, about 15 minutes. Let sit off heat, covered, for 10 minutes. Spread quinoa onto rimmed baking sheet and let cool for 15 minutes.

Quinoa, Black Bean, and Mango Salad with Lime Dressing

2. Meanwhile, process lime juice, jalapeño, cumin, and remaining 1 teaspoon salt in blender until jalapeño is finely chopped, about 15 seconds. With blender running, add oil and cilantro and process until smooth and emulsified, about 20 seconds.

3. Combine cooled quinoa, bell pepper, mango, beans, scallions, and dressing in large bowl and toss to combine. Season with salt and pepper to taste. Serve, topping individual portions with avocado.

Quinoa Taco Salad

Serves 4 | **Total Time** 1½ hours

WHY THIS RECIPE WORKS We reworked taco salad with quinoa, making it hearty, tasty, and nutritious. When properly seasoned, quinoa is a surprisingly good replacement for ground beef: Toasted and simmered in broth with chipotles in adobo, tomato paste, anchovy paste, and cumin, it acquires a rich, spiced, meaty flavor. We substitute escarole for lettuce to add a welcome hint of bitter crunch and cut back on cheese, opting for queso fresco; and we add lots of fragrant cilantro. Black beans, avocado, cherry tomatoes, and scallions complete the picture. This salad is so hearty that it doesn't even need tortilla chips, but you can certainly serve it with tortilla chips or multigrain chips. If you buy unwashed quinoa, rinse it and then spread it out on a clean dish towel to dry for 15 minutes.

¾ cup prewashed white quinoa
3 tablespoons extra-virgin olive oil, divided
1 small onion, chopped fine
½ teaspoon table salt, divided
2 teaspoons minced canned chipotle chile in adobo sauce
2 teaspoons tomato paste
1 teaspoon anchovy paste (optional)
½ teaspoon ground cumin
1 cup vegetable broth
2 tablespoons lime juice
¼ teaspoon pepper
1 head escarole (1 pound), trimmed and sliced thin
2 scallions, sliced thin
½ cup chopped fresh cilantro, divided
1 (15-ounce) can black beans, rinsed
8 ounces cherry tomatoes, quartered
1 ripe avocado, halved, pitted, and chopped
2 ounces queso fresco, crumbled (½ cup)

1. Toast quinoa in large saucepan over medium-high heat, stirring often, until very fragrant and quinoa makes continuous popping sound, 5 to 7 minutes; transfer to bowl.

2. Heat 1 tablespoon oil in now-empty saucepan over medium heat until shimmering. Add onion and ¼ teaspoon salt and cook until onion is softened and lightly browned, 5 to 7 minutes.

3. Stir in chipotle; tomato paste; anchovy paste, if using; and cumin and cook until fragrant, about 30 seconds. Stir in broth and quinoa, increase heat to medium-high, and bring to simmer. Cover, reduce heat to low, and simmer until quinoa is tender and liquid has been absorbed, 18 to 22 minutes, stirring halfway through cooking. Let sit off heat, covered, for 10 minutes. Spread quinoa onto rimmed baking sheet and let cool for 15 minutes.

4. Whisk lime juice, pepper, remaining 2 tablespoons oil, and remaining ¼ teaspoon salt together in large bowl. Add escarole, scallions, and ¼ cup cilantro and toss to combine. Gently fold in beans, tomatoes, and avocado. Season with salt and pepper to taste, then transfer to serving platter. Top with quinoa, queso fresco, and remaining ¼ cup cilantro. Serve.

Spelt Salad with Pickled Fennel, Pea Greens, and Mint

Serves 4 to 6 | **Total Time** 1½ hours, plus 30 minutes cooling

WHY THIS RECIPE WORKS Whole grains (minimally processed and still containing their bran and germ) are a livelier, more nutritious alternative to rice or pasta, lending a satisfying bite and earthy, nutty depth to salads. That makes spelt an ideal choice here. We find it easiest (and quickest) to cook the grain like pasta, simply simmering the kernels in a pot of water until they are tender but still chewy. We combine the spelt with tart and crunchy pickled fennel, pea tendrils, and mint and toss them with a bright dressing for a salad that is delicious as a light main. Pea tendrils are also called pea greens or pea shoots. Watercress can be used in place of the pea tendrils. If using refrigerated grains, let them come to room temperature before making the salad.

Substitution: You can use any whole grain in place of the spelt; note that cooking times may change (see chart on page 30).

1 cup spelt, rinsed
½ teaspoon table salt, divided, plus salt for cooking spelt
⅓ cup cider vinegar
2 tablespoons sugar
1 small fennel bulb, 1 tablespoon fronds minced, stalks discarded, bulb halved, cored, and sliced thin
3 tablespoons extra-virgin olive oil
2 tablespoons lemon juice
1 small shallot, minced
¼ teaspoon pepper
2 ounces pea tendrils, torn into bite-size pieces (2 cups)
¼ cup torn fresh mint
1 ounce feta cheese, crumbled (¼ cup)

1. Bring 2 quarts water to boil in large saucepan. Add spelt and 2 teaspoons salt and boil gently until grains are tender, 50 minutes to 1 hour 5 minutes. Drain spelt, spread onto rimmed baking sheet, and let cool for 15 minutes.

2. Bring vinegar, sugar, and ¼ teaspoon salt to simmer in small saucepan over medium-high heat, stirring occasionally, until sugar dissolves. Off heat, stir in fennel. Cover and let cool completely, about 30 minutes. (Pickled fennel can be refrigerated for up to 3 days.) Drain and discard liquid.

3. Whisk oil, lemon juice, shallot, pepper, and remaining ¼ teaspoon salt together in large bowl. Add cooled spelt, pea tendrils, mint, fennel fronds, and ½ cup pickled fennel (reserve remaining picked fennel for another use) to dressing and toss to combine. Season with salt and pepper to taste. Sprinkle with feta. Serve.

Oat Berry, Chickpea, and Arugula Salad

Serves 4 to 6 | **Total Time** 1¼ hours

WHY THIS RECIPE WORKS Oats are not just for breakfast anymore. Chewy, nutty oat berries (whole oats that have been hulled) make a wonderful base for a substantial grain salad. To ensure that the oat berries retain the perfect chewy, tender texture when served cold, we cook them in a large amount of water, pasta-style, and then drain and rinse them under cold water to stop the cooking so that the grains don't end up mushy. Assertive, peppery arugula pairs well with the oat berries, and we add chickpeas for more heft, a complementary buttery flavor, and creamy texture. Roasted red peppers bring sweetness while feta gives creaminess and salty bite. A simple lemon and cilantro dressing spiked with cumin, paprika, and cayenne provides the perfect amount of spice and brightness.

- 1 cup oat berries (groats), rinsed
- ¼ teaspoon table salt, plus salt for cooking oat berries
- 2 tablespoons lemon juice
- 2 tablespoons minced fresh cilantro
- 1 teaspoon honey
- 1 garlic clove, minced
- ¼ teaspoon ground cumin
- ⅛ teaspoon paprika
  Pinch cayenne pepper
- 3 tablespoons extra-virgin olive oil
- 1 (15-ounce) can chickpeas, rinsed
- 6 ounces (6 cups) baby arugula
- ½ cup jarred roasted red peppers, patted dry and chopped
- 2 ounces feta cheese, crumbled (½ cup)

1. Bring 2 quarts water to boil in large saucepan. Add oat berries and ½ teaspoon salt and cook, partially covered, until grains are tender but still chewy, 45 to 50 minutes. Drain oat berries and rinse under cold running water until cool. Drain well.

2. Whisk lemon juice, cilantro, honey, garlic, cumin, paprika, cayenne, and salt together in large bowl. Whisking constantly, slowly drizzle in oil until emulsified, then stir in drained oat berries, chickpeas, arugula, red peppers, and feta. Season with salt and pepper to taste. Serve.

Wheat Berry Salad with Radicchio, Dried Cherries, and Pecans

Serves 4 to 6 | **Total Time** 1¾ hours

WHY THIS RECIPE WORKS The earthy, nutty flavor and firm chew of wheat berries make them an ideal base for a colorful, textured, and vibrant salad when paired with blue cheese, dried cherries, and pecans; delicious as a light main. We find it easiest (and quickest) to cook the wheat berries like pasta, simply simmering them in a pot of water until they are tender but still chewy. We combine the cooked wheat berries with radicchio and parsley and toss them with a bright red wine–shallot vinaigrette before adding the flavorful toppings.

Substitution: You can use any whole grain in place of the wheat berries; note that cooking times may change (see chart on page 30).

- 1 cup wheat berries, rinsed
- ½ teaspoon table salt, plus salt for cooking wheat berries
- 3 tablespoons extra-virgin olive oil
- 2 tablespoons red wine vinegar
- 1 small shallot, minced
- ½ teaspoon pepper
- 1 cup chopped radicchio
- 1 cup fresh parsley leaves
- ½ cup pecans, toasted and chopped coarse, divided
- ¼ cup dried cherries
- 1 ounce blue cheese, crumbled (¼ cup)

1. Bring 2 quarts water to boil in large saucepan. Add wheat berries and 2 teaspoons salt and boil gently until grains are tender, 1 hour to 1 hour 20 minutes. Drain wheat berries, spread onto rimmed baking sheet, and let cool for 15 minutes.

2. Whisk oil, vinegar, shallot, pepper, and salt together in large bowl. Add wheat berries, radicchio, parsley, half of pecans, and cherries and toss to combine. Season with salt and pepper to taste. Sprinkle with blue cheese and remaining pecans. Serve.

Black Rice and Sea Bean Salad

Serves 4 to 6 | **Total Time** 1½ hours

WHY THIS RECIPE WORKS Black rice, also known as purple rice or forbidden rice, is an ancient grain that was once reserved for Chinese emperors. It is easy to overcook, so the best approach is to use the pasta method, giving it space to move around in lots of boiling water. After draining the rice, we let it cool completely on a baking sheet. This ensures perfectly cooked grains with chew but no mushiness. The deliciously roasted, nutty flavor of black rice plays off salty, crunchy sea beans; sweet-tart grapefruit; fresh, floral mint; and honey in the dressing to create a salad that contrasts tastes, colors, and textures in a superflavorful way. Sea beans (see page 174) develop their strong, briny flavor from the salty water and air in the marshes where they typically grow upright. One hurdle is tempering their saltiness. Blanching them first helps; it also gives them a vibrant green color, which looks stunning when tossed with the black rice.

- 5 ounces sea beans, trimmed and cut into 2-inch lengths
- 1½ cups black rice
- 1 grapefruit
- ¼ cup white wine vinegar
- 1 shallot, minced
- 1 garlic clove, minced
- 1 teaspoon honey
- 6 tablespoons extra-virgin olive oil
- 2 tablespoons chopped fresh mint

1. Bring 4 quarts water to boil in large pot. Fill large bowl halfway with ice and water. Add sea beans to boiling water and cook until crisp-tender, about 1 minute. Using slotted spoon, transfer sea beans to ice bath and let sit until cool, about 5 minutes.

2. Transfer sea beans to triple layer of paper towels and dry well. Return water in pot to boil. Add rice and cook until rice is tender, 20 to 25 minutes. Drain rice, spread onto rimmed baking sheet, and let cool for 15 minutes.

3. Cut away peel and pith from grapefruit. Quarter grapefruit, then slice crosswise into ¼-inch-thick pieces. Whisk vinegar, shallot, garlic, and honey together in large serving bowl. Whisking constantly, slowly drizzle in oil until emulsified. Add sea beans, rice, grapefruit, and mint and toss to coat. Season with salt and pepper to taste. Serve.

Black Rice and Sea Bean Salad

Oat Berry, Chickpea, and Arugula Salad

USING SEA BEANS

Sea beans are members of the genus *Salicornia* and can be found on the beach or in salt marshes and other saline environments. If you live in a coastal area, you can forage for them, and you can even grow sea beans in your garden, though they will lose much of their salinity if grown in soil away from the ocean. Also commonly known as glasswort, pickle weed, sea asparagus, or saltwort, this plant's crunchy stems and salty flavor quickly bring to mind raw green beans or cucumbers, and like both vegetables, sea beans work well in salads and pickled applications. The leaves and shoots of this succulent plant can be eaten raw but are also sturdy enough to stand up to stir-frying or steaming. Sea beans can be found in the late spring and summer months. They should be small sprigs that are firm and bright green; avoid any sprigs that are limp or slimy. As the weather turns colder, sea beans will turn red, a sign that they have developed woody stems and have become too salty to enjoy eating. Store sea beans wrapped in a damp paper towel inside a plastic produce bag for up to a week.

Harvest Salad

Harvest Salad

Serves 4 to 6 | **Total Time** 1¾ hours

WHY THIS RECIPE WORKS When autumn is in the air, fall food is on our minds. Hearty wild rice; caramelized roasted sweet potatoes; and crunchy, tart apples make for a perfect seasonal salad meal that fills you up but also stores well. To continue the harvest theme, we whisk up a cider and caraway vinaigrette, toasting and cracking the seeds but leaving them whole for appealing texture. For toppings, feta cheese adds briny contrast and dried cranberries contribute color and more tartness, helping turn mealtime into an autumn harvest affair. To crack the caraway seeds, rock the bottom edge of a skillet over the toasted seeds on a cutting board until they crack. For extra crunch, serve this salad topped with Savory Seed Brittle (page 175).

- ½ cup wild rice
- ½ teaspoon table salt, divided, plus salt for cooking rice
- 1 pound sweet potatoes, unpeeled, halved lengthwise and sliced crosswise ¼ inch thick
- 5 tablespoons extra-virgin olive oil, divided
- 2 tablespoons plus 2 teaspoons cider vinegar
- 4 teaspoons Dijon mustard
- 2 teaspoons caraway seeds, toasted and cracked
- ¼ teaspoon pepper
- 8 ounces (8 cups) baby kale
- 1 Granny Smith apple, cored and cut into ½-inch pieces
- 4 ounces feta cheese, crumbled (1 cup)
- ¼ cup dried cranberries

1. Bring 2 quarts water to boil in large saucepan. Add rice and ½ teaspoon salt and cook until rice is tender, 35 to 40 minutes. Drain rice, spread onto rimmed baking sheet, and let cool for 15 minutes.

2. Meanwhile, adjust oven rack to middle position and heat oven to 400 degrees. Toss potatoes, 1 tablespoon oil, and ¼ teaspoon salt together in bowl, then spread in even layer on aluminum foil–lined rimmed baking sheet. Roast until potatoes are beginning to brown, 15 to 20 minutes, flipping slices halfway through roasting. Let potatoes cool for 5 minutes.

3. Whisk vinegar, 2 tablespoons water, mustard, caraway seeds, pepper, and remaining ¼ teaspoon salt together in bowl. Whisking constantly, slowly drizzle in remaining ¼ cup oil until emulsified. Toss kale with half of vinaigrette in large bowl to coat, then season with salt and pepper to taste. Transfer to serving platter and top with cooled rice, cooled sweet potatoes, apple, feta, and cranberries. Drizzle with remaining vinaigrette and serve.

Savory Seed Brittle

Makes 2 cups | **Total Time** 1¼ hours, plus
1 hour cooling

This topping adds crunch and salty-sweetness to
any salad. Do not use quick or instant oats in
this recipe.

- 2 tablespoons maple syrup
- 1 large egg white
- 1 tablespoon extra-virgin olive oil
- 1 tablespoon soy sauce
- 1 tablespoon caraway seeds, crushed
- ½ teaspoon table salt
- ¼ teaspoon pepper
- ½ cup old-fashioned rolled oats
- ⅓ cup raw, unsalted sunflower seeds
- ⅓ cup raw, unsalted pepitas
- 2 tablespoons sesame seeds
- 2 tablespoons nigella seeds

1. Adjust oven rack to upper-middle position and heat
oven to 300 degrees. Line 8-inch square baking pan
with parchment paper and spray parchment with vegetable oil spray. Whisk maple syrup, egg white, oil,
soy sauce, caraway seeds, salt, and pepper together
in large bowl. Stir in oats, sunflower seeds, pepitas,
sesame seeds, and nigella seeds until well combined.
2. Transfer oat mixture to prepared pan and spread
into even layer. Using stiff metal spatula, press oat
mixture until very compact. Bake until golden brown
and fragrant, 45 to 55 minutes, rotating pan halfway
through baking.
3. Transfer pan to wire rack and let brittle cool completely, about 1 hour. Break cooled brittle into pieces
of desired size, discarding parchment. (Brittle can be
stored in airtight container for up to 1 month.)

Turmeric Rice and Chicken Salad with Herbs

Serves 4 | **Total Time** 1 hour

WHY THIS RECIPE WORKS Shawarma, a street-food
favorite throughout the Middle East, inspired this rice and
chicken salad. Traditional seasonings—garlic, turmeric,
paprika, cumin, and cinnamon—lend their aromatic flavors.
For fluffy, well-seasoned rice that doesn't clump or get hard
as it cools, we boil the grains in an abundance of salted water,
then spread them on a baking sheet to prevent clumping. We
add crunchy sliced cucumbers, radishes, juicy tomatoes, and
cilantro, the torn leaves bringing intense bursts of freshness
and flavor to every bite. A lemony herbed yogurt is drizzled
over the salad to complete it. We like to use our Perfect
Poached Chicken (page 176) but you can use store-bought
rotisserie chicken here. You can use 6 ounces of English
cucumber if Persian cucumbers are not available.

- 1 cup long-grain white rice
- ½ teaspoon table salt, plus salt for cooking rice
- 3 tablespoons extra-virgin olive oil
- 2 garlic cloves, minced
- 1 teaspoon ground cumin
- 1 teaspoon paprika
- 1 teaspoon ground turmeric
- ⅛ teaspoon cayenne pepper
  Pinch ground cinnamon
- 3 tablespoons lemon juice
- 2 cups cooked chicken, chopped
- 6 ounces cherry tomatoes, halved
- 2 Persian cucumbers, quartered lengthwise and sliced
  crosswise ¼ inch thick
- 3 radishes, trimmed, quartered, and sliced thin
- 1 cup torn fresh cilantro
- ½ cup Herb-Yogurt Sauce (page 176)

1. Bring 4 quarts water to boil in large pot. Add rice and
1½ teaspoons salt and cook, stirring occasionally, until rice is
tender but not soft, about 15 minutes. Drain rice, spread onto
rimmed baking sheet, and let cool for 15 minutes.
2. Microwave oil, garlic, cumin, paprika, turmeric, cayenne,
and cinnamon in medium bowl until simmering and fragrant,
30 to 60 seconds. Let cool slightly, then whisk in lemon juice
and salt.
3. Combine rice, dressing, chicken, tomatoes, cucumbers,
radishes, and cilantro in large bowl and toss to combine. Season
with salt and pepper to taste. Serve with herb-yogurt sauce.

Perfect Poached Chicken

Makes 4 cups | **Total Time** 50 minutes

This chicken is great to have on hand for use in salad.

> 4 (6- to 8-ounce) boneless, skinless chicken breasts, trimmed
> Table salt for cooking chicken

1. Cover chicken breasts with plastic wrap and pound thick ends gently until 3/4 inch thick. Whisk 4 quarts cool water with 2 tablespoons salt in Dutch oven.
2. Arrange chicken in steamer basket without overlapping. Submerge basket in pot. Heat over medium heat, stirring occasionally, until water registers 175 degrees, 15 to 20 minutes.
3. Turn off heat, cover pot, remove from burner, and let sit until chicken registers 160 degrees, 17 to 22 minutes. Transfer chicken to cutting board and let cool for 10 to 15 minutes. Slice, chop, or shred as desired. Serve. (Chicken can be refrigerated for up to 2 days. Let come to room temperature before using in salads.)

Herb-Yogurt Sauce

Makes 1 cup | **Total Time** 5 minutes, plus 30 minutes chilling **FAST**

This topping can instantly take any salad to the next level.

> 1 cup plain whole-milk yogurt
> 1 teaspoon grated lemon zest plus 2 tablespoons juice
> 2 tablespoons minced fresh cilantro
> 2 tablespoons minced fresh mint
> 1 garlic clove, minced

Whisk all ingredients together in bowl. Cover and refrigerate until flavors meld, at least 30 minutes. Season with salt and pepper to taste. (Sauce can be refrigerated for up to 4 days.)

Nam Khao

Serves 4 to 6 | **Total Time** 2 hours

WHY THIS RECIPE WORKS Nam khao, a rice salad found at restaurants and street stalls throughout Laos, is said to come from Tha Deua, a Laotian port village. A blend of crunchy, soft, tangy, salty, sweet, and nutty flavors, nam khao traditionally features tightly packed deep-fried rice balls with a crunchy crust and chewy interior. The balls are broken into bite-size pieces and tossed with fermented pork sausage, herbs, and a citrus dressing. For our version, rather than form balls, we fry half the cooked rice in loose clusters and toss it with plain cooked rice for a blend of crunchy and chewy. We substitute sweet and salty Chinese sausage for the traditional fermented pork sausage (ham steaks are a great substitution too). Cilantro, mint, scallions, and peanuts make a crunchy, fragrant finish. Do not use basmati rice here. Use a Dutch oven that holds 6 quarts or more for this recipe.

> 2¼ cups water
> 1½ cups jasmine rice, rinsed
> 3 tablespoons lime juice (2 limes)
> 2 tablespoons fish sauce
> 1½ tablespoons palm sugar or packed brown sugar
> 1 tablespoon Thai red curry paste
> 1 teaspoon grated fresh ginger
> 2 shallots, sliced thin
> 1 teaspoon vegetable oil
> 2 ounces Chinese sausage, cut into ½-inch pieces
> 1½ quarts peanut or vegetable oil for frying
> ½ cup fresh cilantro leaves
> ½ cup fresh mint leaves, torn
> 4 scallions, sliced thin on bias
> ¼ cup dry-roasted peanuts, chopped coarse

1. Bring water and rice to simmer in large saucepan over high heat. Reduce heat to low, cover, and simmer gently until rice is tender and water has been fully absorbed, about 10 minutes. Off heat, lay clean dish towel underneath lid and let sit for 10 minutes. Spread rice onto greased large plate and let cool for 10 minutes.
2. Meanwhile, whisk lime juice, fish sauce, sugar, curry paste, and ginger in large bowl until sugar has dissolved. Stir in shallots and set aside.
3. Heat vegetable oil in large Dutch oven over medium heat until shimmering. Add sausage and cook until spotty brown, about 3 minutes; transfer to separate bowl. Wipe pot clean with paper towels.

4. Line rimmed baking sheet with triple layer of paper towels. Add peanut oil to now-empty pot until it measures about 1 inch deep and heat over medium-high heat to 400 degrees. Shape half of rice into rough 2-inch clusters. Carefully add half of rice clusters to hot oil and cook, without stirring them, until light golden brown, about 5 minutes. Adjust burner, if necessary, to maintain oil temperature between 375 and 400 degrees. Using slotted spoon or spider skimmer, transfer fried rice to prepared sheet. Return oil to 400 degrees and repeat with remaining rice clusters; transfer to sheet and let drain for 10 minutes.

5. Using your fingers, break up fried rice into bite-size pieces. Add fried rice, sausage, cilantro, mint, scallions, and remaining cooked rice to dressing and toss gently to combine. Season with salt and pepper to taste. Transfer salad to serving platter and sprinkle with peanuts. Serve.

Sprouted Grain Salad

Serves 4 to 6 | **Total Time** 45 minutes, plus 32¾ hours sprouting and cooling

WHY THIS RECIPE WORKS It's about time that sprouted grains get the attention they deserve. Not only are they brimming with health benefits, but their delicately chewy texture and sweet, nutty flavor are also a welcome change from cooked grains. This salad is inspired by California cuisine, which focuses on fresh produce and bright tastes. Sprouting the grains, rather than cooking them, preserves the nutrients we worked so hard to achieve as well as minimizes prep. We keep the ingredient list simple, combining the sprouted grains with cucumber, avocado, and blackberries and tossing them in a pomegranate molasses vinaigrette. Once coated, the grains cling to the avocado and cucumbers, ensuring that they are enjoyed in every bite. Thinly sliced pickled shallot adds pops of acidity while the blackberries bring refreshing bursts of sweetness. We top the salad with microgreens and crispy lentils. We prefer Persian cucumbers here but one English cucumber, coarsely chopped into ¾-inch pieces, can be used instead. Do not use farro, barley, or buckwheat in this recipe as they tend to become mucilaginous while sprouting. If microgreens are unavailable, you can use watercress or chopped arugula. For efficiency, let the shallot pickle while you prepare the rest of the salad.

SPROUTED GRAIN

1 cup rye, wheat, or spelt berries, rinsed

Nam Khao

SALAD

⅓ cup red wine vinegar
2 tablespoons sugar
   Pinch plus ½ teaspoon table salt, divided
1 large shallot, sliced thin
4 Persian cucumbers
2 avocados, halved, pitted, and chopped coarse
¾ cup blackberries, halved
⅓ cup Pomegranate Molasses Vinaigrette (page 178)
¼ cup Cumin-Spiced Crispy Lentils (page 42)
½ cup microgreens (optional)

1. FOR THE SPROUTED GRAIN Combine rye berries and 2 cups filtered water in bowl, cover tightly with plastic wrap, and let sit at room temperature until rye berries are softened, at least 8 hours or up to 16 hours. Drain rye berries in fine-mesh strainer, rinse with filtered water, return to now-empty bowl and cover with plastic. Puncture plastic with paring knife 8 to 10 times and let grains sit at room temperature, draining and rinsing grains with filtered water every 6 to 8 hours, until grains begin to sprout, 24 to 36 hours.

Sprouted Grain Salad

Pomegranate Molasses Vinaigrette
Makes ⅔ cup | **Total Time** 10 minutes **FAST**

    2 tablespoons water
 1½ tablespoons pomegranate molasses
    1 small shallot, minced
    1 tablespoon honey
    1 tablespoon cider vinegar
    ¼ teaspoon table salt
    ¼ teaspoon pepper
    ¼ cup extra-virgin olive oil

Whisk water, pomegranate molasses, shallot, honey, vinegar, salt, and pepper together in medium bowl. While whisking constantly, slowly drizzle in oil until combined. (Vinaigrette can be refrigerated for up to 24 hours, whisk to recombine before serving.)

MAKING A ROLL CUT
A roll cut is used on long vegetables to make pieces with 2 angled sides, creating more surface area and visual appeal.

Starting at 1 end, hold knife at 45-degree angle (relative to cucumber) and make diagonal cut. Roll cucumber 90 degrees (quarter turn) and cut again at same angle. Continue rolling and cutting along length of cucumber.

2. FOR THE SALAD Bring vinegar, sugar, and pinch salt to simmer in small saucepan over medium-high heat, stirring occasionally, until sugar dissolves. Off heat, stir in shallot. Cover and set aside to cool completely, about 30 minutes. Drain shallot, discarding liquid, and set aside until ready to serve.

3. Trim ends of Persian cucumbers. Starting at 1 end, hold knife at 45-degree angle (relative to cucumber) and make diagonal cut. Roll cucumber 90 degrees (quarter turn) and cut again at same angle. Continue rolling and cutting along length of cucumber. Repeat trimming and cutting remaining cucumbers. Toss cucumbers and ¼ teaspoon salt in large bowl and let sit for 15 minutes.

4. Add avocados, blackberries, reserved pickled shallot, sprouted grains, pomegranate molasses vinaigrette, and remaining ¼ teaspoon salt to bowl with salted cucumbers and toss gently to combine. Season with salt and pepper to taste, then transfer to serving platter and top with crispy lentils and microgreens, if using. Serve.

NOTES FROM THE TEST KITCHEN

SPROUTING GRAINS
Grains that have been sprouted are said to have an improved texture and flavor, and their vitamins, minerals, and protein become easier to absorb. Sprouting activates enzymes that are dormant in dried seeds and grains. These enzymes increase digestibility and taste sweeter because enzymes break starches down into simple sugars. Since sprouted grains are consumed raw, the treatment of them during sprouting is crucial: Use only filtered water for soaking and rinsing and be sure to use the grains within four days of starting the sprouting process.

Hearty Green Salad with Spicy Peanut Chicken

Serves 4 | **Total Time** 35 minutes, plus 20 minutes cooling

WHY THIS RECIPE WORKS This peanutty, vegetable-packed spicy chicken salad is an easy meal to toss together. We start by quick-pickling shallots and serrano chiles. Some of the brine goes into a vinaigrette to dress the napa cabbage and watercress, and we turn the rest into a thick, creamy dressing with peanut butter and chili-garlic sauce to coat the other components, similar to our technique for Warm Broccoli, Chickpea, and Avocado Salad (page 162). We top the greens with microwave-steamed broccolini, juicy mango, and shredded carrot, along with pickled shallots and chiles. The chicken adds heft while peanuts give crunch and reflect the peanut butter in the dressing. A garnish of Thai basil and mint gives herby freshness. We like to use our Perfect Poached Chicken (page 176) but you can use store-bought rotisserie chicken here. The shallot and serrano can be refrigerated in the pickling liquid for up to a week.

- ½ cup unseasoned rice vinegar
- 2 tablespoons sugar
- 1½ teaspoons table salt
- 2 shallots, sliced thin and separated into rings
- 2 serrano chiles, stemmed, halved, seeded, and sliced thin crosswise
- 12 ounces broccolini, trimmed and cut into 1-inch lengths
- ½ cup creamy peanut butter
- 2–3 tablespoons Asian chili-garlic sauce
- 4 teaspoons fish sauce
- 1 garlic clove, minced
- 1 small head napa cabbage, halved, cored, and sliced thin (9 cups)
- 2 cups watercress, torn into bite-size pieces
- ½ cup fresh Thai basil leaves
- ½ cup fresh mint leaves
- 2 mangos, peeled, pitted, and cut into ½-inch pieces
- 2 carrots, peeled and shredded
- 2 cups cooked chicken, shredded into bite-size pieces
- ½ cup dry-roasted peanuts, chopped fine

1. Microwave vinegar, sugar, and salt in small bowl until simmering, about 1 minute. Stir in shallots and serranos and let sit, stirring occasionally, until shallots are pink and slightly softened, about 20 minutes. Using slotted spoon, transfer shallots and serranos to large plate, leaving liquid in bowl.

2. Combine broccolini and ¼ cup water in medium bowl. Cover and microwave until crisp-tender, 1½ to 2 minutes. Using slotted spoon, transfer broccolini to plate with shallot and serrano. Discard water. In now-empty bowl, whisk ¼ cup pickling liquid, peanut butter, chili-garlic sauce, and ½ cup water until smooth. Set aside.

3. Whisk together fish sauce, garlic, and remaining pickling liquid in large bowl. Add cabbage, watercress, Thai basil, and mint and toss to combine. Season with salt and pepper to taste, then distribute evenly among 4 shallow serving bowls. Sprinkle each salad with pickled shallot and serrano. Arrange broccolini, mango, and carrot in piles over top of greens. Drizzle ¼ cup reserved peanut dressing over vegetables and mango in each bowl. Add chicken to remaining reserved peanut dressing and stir to coat evenly. Divide chicken among salads, then sprinkle with peanuts. Serve.

Hearty Green Salad with Spicy Peanut Chicken

Bean Dinners

● FAST (45 minutes or less)   ● VEGAN

Photo: Fregula with Chickpeas, Tomatoes, and Fennel

Apricot-Glazed Chicken with Chickpeas, Chorizo, and Spinach

Serves 4 | **Total Time** 45 minutes   `FAST`

WHY THIS RECIPE WORKS A few potent ingredients give this simple dinner a sophisticated balance of flavors: chew and protein from chickpeas and chicken, sweetness from apricot preserves, smoky spice from chorizo sausage and smoked paprika. We first brown the chicken to start crisping the skin. We then add our other ingredients to the skillet, placing the chicken on top and brushing it with a seasoned apricot glaze before letting everything cook together in a hot oven. Tender fresh baby spinach, stirred in at the end, offsets the earthy, smoky flavors.

- ¼ cup apricot preserves
- 2 teaspoons grated lemon zest, plus lemon wedges for serving
- ¾ teaspoon table salt, divided
- ½ teaspoon pepper, divided
- 4 (10- to 12-ounce) bone-in split chicken breasts, trimmed and halved crosswise
- 1 tablespoon vegetable oil
- 1 (15-ounce) can chickpeas, rinsed
- 6 ounces Spanish-style chorizo sausage, cut into ½-inch pieces
- 1 onion, chopped
- 1½ teaspoons smoked paprika
- 8 ounces (8 cups) baby spinach

1. Adjust oven rack to middle position and heat oven to 450 degrees. Combine preserves, lemon zest, ⅛ teaspoon salt, and ⅛ teaspoon pepper in bowl; set aside. Pat chicken dry with paper towels and sprinkle with ½ teaspoon salt and ¼ teaspoon pepper.

2. Heat oil in 12-inch ovensafe skillet over medium-high heat until just smoking. Place chicken skin side down in skillet and cook until well browned on first side, 5 to 7 minutes. Flip chicken and continue to cook until lightly browned on second side, about 3 minutes; transfer to plate.

3. Off heat, combine chickpeas, chorizo, onion, paprika, remaining ⅛ teaspoon salt, and remaining ⅛ teaspoon pepper in now-empty skillet. Place chicken skin side up on top of chickpea mixture and brush with reserved apricot mixture. Transfer skillet to oven and roast until chicken registers 160 degrees, 20 to 25 minutes.

4. Transfer chicken to serving platter, tent with aluminum foil, and let rest while finishing chickpea mixture. Return skillet to medium-high heat (skillet handle will be hot), add spinach, 1 handful at a time, and cook until wilted, about 2 minutes. Season with salt and pepper to taste. Transfer chickpea mixture to platter with chicken. Serve with lemon wedges.

Skillet-Roasted Chicken with Garlicky Spinach and Beans

Serves 4 | **Total Time** 45 minutes   `FAST`

WHY THIS RECIPE WORKS This pairing of chicken and white beans is the perfect way to use a cut-up whole chicken. The variety of parts cook at similar rates. While the chicken rests, we cook creamy cannellini beans with wine and spinach, which pick up the flavorful juices left from the chicken. You can start with a 4-pound chicken or use 3 pounds of mixed bone-in chicken pieces. The skillet may appear crowded at first; the chicken will shrink as it cooks. You will need a 12-inch nonstick skillet with a tight-fitting lid for this recipe.

- 3 pounds bone-in chicken pieces (split breasts cut in half, drumsticks, thighs, and wings), trimmed
- 1½ teaspoons table salt, divided
- ½ teaspoon pepper
- 1 tablespoon extra-virgin olive oil, plus extra for serving
- 1 shallot, finely chopped
- 6 garlic cloves, sliced thin
- ⅛ teaspoon pepper flakes
- 1 (15-ounce) can cannellini beans, rinsed
- ½ cup dry white wine
- 1 pound (16 cups) baby spinach, divided
- 1 teaspoon grated lemon zest

1. Pat chicken dry with paper towels and sprinkle with 1 teaspoon salt and pepper. Swirl oil evenly over surface of cold 12-inch nonstick skillet. Place chicken, skin side down, in even layer in skillet and cook over medium heat until skin is crisp and well browned, 15 to 17 minutes.

2. Flip chicken and continue to cook until second side is well browned, breasts and wings register 160 degrees, and leg pieces register at least 175 degrees, 12 to 16 minutes, turning pieces as needed during last few minutes of cooking to ensure even cooking. Transfer each piece of chicken to plate once it reaches its target temperature and tent with aluminum foil.

Skillet-Roasted Chicken with Garlicky Spinach and Beans

African stews is also traditionally used in Tunisia to prepare a "tajine," an egg dish that's chock-full of proteins, herbs, and spices. Many Tunisians today cook tajine in a baking dish; we use a skillet. We include white beans, which become highly flavorful when cooked with spices and tomato paste, and tender pieces of sautéed chicken thighs. Bread crumbs absorb extra moisture and set the tajine's texture while nuggets of cheese melt into satisfying pools along its surface.

- 12 large eggs
- ½ cup panko bread crumbs, toasted, divided
- ½ cup minced fresh parsley
- 1 ounce Parmesan cheese, grated (½ cup)
- 3 tablespoons water
- ½ teaspoon table salt, divided
- ½ teaspoon pepper, divided
- 3 tablespoons extra-virgin olive oil
- 1½ pounds boneless, skinless chicken thighs, trimmed and cut into ½-inch pieces
- 1 tablespoon tomato paste
- 6 garlic cloves, minced
- 1 tablespoon ras el hanout
- ¼ teaspoon cayenne pepper
- 1 cup canned cannellini beans, rinsed
- 4 ounces Monterey Jack cheese, cut into ½-inch pieces (1 cup)

3. Add shallot, garlic, pepper flakes, and ¼ teaspoon salt to fat remaining in skillet and cook over medium heat until fragrant, about 1 minute. Stir in beans and wine; bring to simmer; and cook, stirring occasionally, until beans are just beginning to break down, about 5 minutes.

4. Mound half of spinach over beans and cook, covered, until spinach is mostly wilted, 1 to 2 minutes. Using tongs, stir in remaining spinach and remaining ¼ teaspoon salt. Cook, covered, until spinach is fully wilted, 1 to 2 minutes longer. Off heat, stir in lemon zest. Transfer bean mixture to bowls and drizzle with extra oil. Top with chicken and serve.

Tunisian Tajine with White Beans

Serves 4 to 6 | **Total Time** 55 minutes

WHY THIS RECIPE WORKS The word "tagine"—or "tajine" as in Tunisia—tells a story of history and custom. The classic earthenware vessel used to cook eponymous North

1. Adjust oven rack to upper-middle position and heat oven to 350 degrees. Whisk eggs, ¼ cup panko, parsley, Parmesan, water, ¼ teaspoon salt, and ¼ teaspoon pepper together in bowl; set aside.

2. Heat oil in 12-inch ovensafe nonstick skillet over medium-high heat until shimmering. Add chicken, tomato paste, remaining ¼ teaspoon salt, and remaining ¼ teaspoon pepper and cook, stirring occasionally, until chicken is well browned, 6 to 8 minutes. Stir in garlic, ras el hanout, and cayenne and cook until fragrant, about 1 minute. Stir in beans and cook until heated through, about 5 minutes.

3. Reduce heat to medium-low and stir in egg mixture. Cook, using spatula to scrape bottom of skillet, until large curds form but eggs are still very wet, about 2 minutes. Smooth egg mixture into even layer. Nestle Monterey Jack into egg curds and sprinkle top with remaining ¼ cup panko. Transfer skillet to oven and bake until tajine is slightly puffy and surface bounces back when lightly pressed, 10 to 12 minutes. Using oven mitt, remove skillet from oven. Being careful of hot skillet handle, use rubber spatula to loosen tajine from skillet and transfer to cutting board. Let sit for 5 minutes before slicing and serving.

Mustard-Roasted Chicken with Warm Green Bean and Potato Salad

Mustard-Roasted Chicken with Warm Green Bean and Potato Salad

Serves 4 | **Total Time** 1¼ hours

WHY THIS RECIPE WORKS Green beans and red potatoes team up as substantial and flavorful supporting players to bone-in chicken parts in this meal. A simple coating of mustard elevates the chicken to flavorful bistro fare. You can prepare the potatoes and green beans while the chicken roasts and supercharge the vinaigrette with the meaty, mustardy fond and juices from the chicken. Dressing the vegetables while warm helps them absorb maximum flavor. Use small red potatoes measuring 1 to 2 inches in diameter. If your potatoes are larger than 2 inches, cut them into 1-inch pieces.

 3 tablespoons plus 1 teaspoon Dijon mustard, divided
 ¼ cup extra-virgin olive oil, divided
 2 teaspoons soy sauce
 1 garlic clove, minced
 1 teaspoon minced fresh rosemary
 ¼ teaspoon pepper, divided
 3 pounds bone-in chicken pieces (split breasts halved crosswise, drumsticks, and/or thighs), trimmed
 ½ teaspoon table salt, plus salt for cooking vegetables
1½ pounds small red potatoes, halved
 8 ounces green beans, trimmed and halved
 2 tablespoons white wine vinegar
 1 tablespoon capers, rinsed and minced
 2 tablespoons chopped fresh parsley

1. Adjust oven rack to upper-middle position and heat oven to 475 degrees. Combine 3 tablespoons mustard, 1 tablespoon oil, soy sauce, garlic, rosemary, and ⅛ teaspoon pepper in small bowl; set aside.

2. Pat chicken dry with paper towels and sprinkle with salt and remaining ⅛ teaspoon pepper. Place chicken skin side up on rimmed baking sheet, arranging breast pieces in center and leg and/or thigh pieces around perimeter. Brush chicken with mustard mixture. Roast until breasts register 160 degrees and drumsticks/thighs register 175 degrees, 25 to 30 minutes, rotating sheet halfway through roasting. Transfer sheet to wire rack and tent with aluminum foil. Let chicken rest for 5 minutes.

Braised Chicken and Lentils

3. Meanwhile, bring 2 quarts water to boil in large saucepan over medium-high heat. Add potatoes and 1½ tablespoons salt, return to boil, and cook for 10 minutes. Add green beans and cook until both vegetables are tender, about 5 minutes. Drain well, return to pot, and cover to keep warm.

4. Whisk vinegar, capers, and remaining 1 teaspoon mustard together in large bowl. Whisking constantly, slowly drizzle in remaining 3 tablespoons oil until incorporated. Transfer chicken to serving platter. Scrape up any browned bits and pour any accumulated juices from sheet into bowl with dressing; whisk to combine. Add warm vegetables, toss gently to combine, and season with salt and pepper to taste. Sprinkle chicken and salad with parsley and serve.

Braised Chicken and Lentils

Serves 4 | **Total Time** 1½ hours

WHY THIS RECIPE WORKS Hearty, earthy lentils lend a rustic touch to any meal, and they take particularly well to bold flavors with a bit of spice and smoke. In this braise, we flavor meaty bone-in chicken thighs with smoked paprika, which blooms as the thighs brown in a Dutch oven. We build on that savory foundation by sautéing aromatic vegetables in the flavored chicken fat to create a fond. Red pepper flakes add spice, while fresh tomatoes and tomato paste contribute layers of savory flavor. We nestle the browned chicken thighs into the lentils, fortifying them with chicken stock and some extra smoked paprika. Braising the mixture uncovered in the oven thickens the lentils to just the right consistency. A splash of sherry vinegar at the end brightens the dish and helps break down some of the lentils further to add body and creaminess.

- 2½ teaspoons table salt, divided
- 2 teaspoons smoked paprika, divided
- ¾ teaspoon pepper, divided
- 8 (5- to 7-ounce) bone-in chicken thighs, trimmed
- 2 teaspoons extra-virgin olive oil
- 2 large plum tomatoes, cored and chopped
- 1 onion, chopped fine
- 1 carrot, peeled and chopped fine
- 6 garlic cloves, minced
- 2 tablespoons tomato paste
- 1 teaspoon chopped fresh thyme
- ½ teaspoon red pepper flakes

- 4 cups chicken broth
- 1 cup dried green or brown lentils, picked over and rinsed
- 1 tablespoon sherry vinegar
- ½ cup chopped fresh cilantro

1. Adjust oven rack to middle position and heat oven to 375 degrees. Combine 2 teaspoons salt, 1 teaspoon paprika, and ½ teaspoon pepper in small bowl. Pat chicken dry with paper towels and sprinkle with salt mixture.

2. Heat oil in Dutch oven over medium-high heat until just smoking. Add chicken, skin side down, and cook until well browned, 12 to 16 minutes; transfer chicken to plate.

3. Add tomatoes, onion, carrot, remaining ½ teaspoon salt, and remaining ¼ teaspoon pepper to fat left in pot and reduce heat to medium. Cook, stirring often, until tomatoes begin to break down, 3 to 5 minutes. Stir in garlic, tomato paste, thyme, and pepper flakes and cook, stirring constantly, until fond begins to form on bottom of pot, 3 to 4 minutes.

4. Stir in broth, scraping up browned bits. Stir in lentils and remaining 1 teaspoon paprika. Nestle chicken into lentil mixture, skin side up, and bring to simmer over high heat. Transfer pot to oven and cook, uncovered, until chicken registers at least 185 degrees, 35 to 40 minutes.

5. Transfer chicken to clean plate. Return pot (handles will be hot) to stovetop and continue to cook lentil mixture over medium heat, stirring often, until liquid is thickened and lentils are fully tender, 5 to 7 minutes. Add vinegar and whisk vigorously until liquid is creamy, about 30 seconds (lentil mixture will thicken as it cools). Season with salt and pepper to taste. Transfer lentils to shallow serving bowls and top with chicken. Sprinkle with cilantro and serve.

NOTES FROM THE TEST KITCHEN

GREEN LENTILS VERSUS LENTILLES DU PUY
For our Braised Chicken and Lentils we chose regular green lentils, which tend to break down a bit as they cook, making for a creamier final dish. Lentilles du Puy hold their shape better than regular green lentils, making them ideal in dishes where they need to stay more intact, such as lentil salads. As for flavor, green lentils are more mild and earthy, while lentilles du Puy are more peppery and complex. We like both types of lentils equally but use them in different types of dishes.

Sirloin Steak Tips with Charro Beans

Serves 4 | Total Time 35 minutes **FAST**

WHY THIS RECIPE WORKS Charro beans—pinto beans named after charros, or Mexican cowboys—are a traditional Tex-Mex recipe, commonly served alongside carne asada, thin steaks that are marinated and grilled until well charred. For a quick skillet dinner, we pair the beans with spice-rubbed steak tips, which are easy to cook and deliver big meaty flavor. Cooking the beans in the skillet used for searing the steak tips infuses them with flavor, making for a unified dish. Quick-pickled red onion and jalapeño add brightness and spice to the mild beans and rich, savory steak. We garnish the dish with fresh cilantro. Sirloin steak tips are often sold as flap meat.

- ½ small red onion, sliced thin
- ¼ cup distilled white vinegar
- 1 small jalapeño chile, stemmed, seeded, and sliced thin
- 2 pounds sirloin steak tips, trimmed and cut into 2-inch pieces
- 2½ teaspoons ground cumin, divided
- 1¾ teaspoons table salt, divided
- 1½ teaspoons pepper, divided
- 2 tablespoons vegetable oil
- 3 garlic cloves, minced
- 3 (15-ounce) cans pinto beans, rinsed
- 1½ cups chicken broth
- ¼ cup fresh cilantro leaves

1. Combine onion, vinegar, and jalapeño in small bowl. Cover and microwave until hot, about 2 minutes; set aside.

2. Pat beef dry with paper towels and sprinkle with ½ teaspoon cumin, 1 teaspoon salt, and 1 teaspoon pepper. Heat oil in 12-inch nonstick skillet over medium-high heat until just smoking. Add beef and cook until browned on all sides and meat registers 120 to 125 degrees (for medium-rare), about 7 minutes. Transfer beef to large plate and tent with aluminum foil.

3. Reduce heat to medium, add garlic and remaining 2 teaspoons cumin to fat left in now-empty skillet, and cook until fragrant, about 30 seconds. Stir in beans, broth, remaining ¾ teaspoon salt, and remaining ½ teaspoon pepper. Using potato masher, lightly mash beans until about one-quarter of beans are broken down. Bring to simmer and cook until thickened and liquid is fully incorporated into bean mixture, about 4 minutes. Serve steak with beans, reserved pickled onion mixture, and cilantro.

Sirloin Steak Tips with Charro Beans

CUTTING FLAP MEAT INTO STEAK TIPS

Flap meat, often called steak tips, can be purchased as a whole steak or precut into strips or cubes. Cubes of meat labeled "steak tips" can be cut from random parts of the cow. To ensure authenticity (and sirloin flavor), we like to buy larger pieces of flap meat and cut it ourselves.

1. Trim meat.

2. Cut meat into 2-inch pieces.

Teriyaki Stir-Fried Beef with Green Beans and Shiitakes

Serves 4 | **Total Time** 45 minutes **FAST**

WHY THIS RECIPE WORKS A stir-fry makes a quick weeknight meal. Here, crunchy green beans and meaty shiitakes, browned first and steamed to finish, provide a flavorful contrast to flank steak. Quick-cooking and ultrabeefy flank steak works well in stir-fries; slicing the meat against the grain and treating it with baking soda ensure the meats turns out tender with a pleasant, not overwhelming, chewiness. Tossing the meat with soy sauce and cornstarch heightens its savory flavor, and searing it in batches ensures optimal browning. We mash fresh ginger and garlic in the center of the pan to unlock their flavor before we toss all the ingredients with a teriyaki sauce. You can substitute 1 tablespoon of white wine or sake mixed with 1 teaspoon of sugar for the mirin. You will need a 14-inch flat-bottomed wok or 12-inch nonstick skillet, each with a tight-fitting lid, for this recipe. Serve with rice (pages 298–299).

 1 (1½-pound) flank steak, trimmed
 3 tablespoons water, divided
 ¼ teaspoon baking soda
 3 garlic cloves, minced
 1 tablespoon grated fresh ginger
 3 tablespoons vegetable oil, divided
 ½ cup chicken broth
 3 tablespoons soy sauce, divided
 2 tablespoons sugar
 1 tablespoon mirin
 1¾ teaspoons cornstarch, divided
 ¼ teaspoon red pepper flakes
 8 ounces shiitake mushrooms, stemmed and cut
   into 1-inch pieces
 12 ounces green beans, trimmed and halved
 4 scallions, white parts quartered lengthwise, green
   parts cut into 1½-inch lengths

1. Cut steak with grain into 2½- to 3-inch-wide strips and place on large plate; freeze until firm, about 15 minutes. Cut strips crosswise against grain into ⅛-inch-thick slices. Combine 1 tablespoon water and baking soda in medium bowl. Add beef and toss to coat; let sit for 5 minutes.

2. Combine garlic, ginger, and 1 tablespoon oil in small bowl; set aside. Whisk broth, 2 tablespoons soy sauce, sugar, mirin, 1 teaspoon cornstarch, and pepper flakes in second small bowl until sugar has dissolved; set aside. Add remaining 1 tablespoon soy sauce and remaining ¾ teaspoon cornstarch to beef and toss until well combined.

3. Heat 2 teaspoons oil in 14-inch flat-bottomed wok or 12-inch nonstick skillet over medium-high heat until just smoking. Add half of beef and increase heat to high. Cook, tossing beef slowly but constantly, until no longer pink, 2 to 6 minutes; transfer to clean medium bowl. Repeat with 2 teaspoons oil and remaining beef; transfer to bowl with first batch of beef.

4. Heat remaining 2 teaspoons oil in now-empty wok over medium-high heat until just smoking. Add mushrooms and green beans and cook, tossing slowly but constantly, until spotty brown, 2 to 6 minutes. Add remaining 2 tablespoons water (water will sputter), cover, and cook until green beans are crisp-tender, 2 to 3 minutes.

5. Push vegetables to 1 side of wok and reduce heat to medium. Add garlic mixture to clearing and cook, mashing mixture into pan, until fragrant, about 30 seconds. Stir garlic mixture into vegetables.

6. Whisk broth mixture to recombine, then add to pan along with beef and any accumulated juices and scallions. Increase heat to high and cook, tossing constantly, until sauce has thickened, about 30 seconds. Serve.

Jamaican Oxtail

Serves 6 to 8 | **Total Time** 5 hours, plus 4 hours marinating

WHY THIS RECIPE WORKS A staple of Jamaican cuisine, oxtails are a cut from the tail of the cow that features a round bone surrounded by a small amount of meat. This recipe from photographer and food writer Jillian Atkinson is based on a dish her grandmother prepared. The oxtail is first cooked in caramelized sugar, known as browning, which forms the foundation of the dish. From there, writes Atkinson, "a long cooking time tenderizes the meat, extracts gelatin from the bone, and delivers a treasured stickiness that requires you to lick your lips while you eat." Some dark soy sauce helps to strike a balance between salty and sweet while vinegar adds acidity. Tender butter beans, also called baby lima beans, are added toward the end of cooking. This dish is traditionally served with Jamaican Rice and Peas (page 305). You can substitute a habanero for the Scotch bonnet. In step 6, make sure you have the hot water ready to add as soon as the sugar has properly browned.

| **Substitution:** You can use 1½ cups (about 8 ounces) frozen beans in place of the canned.

OXTAIL

- 5 pounds oxtails, 2 to 2½ inches thick, trimmed
- 2 onions, halved and sliced thin
- 10 sprigs fresh thyme
- 2 scallions, crushed with side of knife, then chopped
- 2 tablespoons distilled white vinegar
- 1 tablespoon table salt
- 1 tablespoon pepper
- 1 tablespoon Worcestershire sauce
- 1 tablespoon dark soy sauce
- 3 garlic cloves, chopped
- 1 teaspoon onion powder
- 1 teaspoon granulated garlic
- 8 whole allspice berries
- 6 cups hot water
- 1 Scotch bonnet chile
- 1 (15-ounce) can butter beans, rinsed
- ¼ cup ketchup

BROWNING

- ¼ cup sugar
- ¼ cup hot water

1. FOR THE OXTAIL Place oxtails in large bowl and fill with cold water. Agitate to remove any loose bone and fat fragments. Drain and repeat, then drain again.

2. Add onions, thyme sprigs, scallions, vinegar, salt, pepper, Worcestershire, soy sauce, garlic, onion powder, granulated garlic, and allspice berries to bowl with oxtails and toss to thoroughly combine. Cover and refrigerate for at least 4 hours or up to 24 hours.

3. Brush marinade off oxtails and transfer oxtails to plate; reserve marinade to use in step 9.

4. FOR THE BROWNING Add sugar to center of large Dutch oven. Place pot over medium-low heat and cook, without stirring, until edges of sugar begin to liquefy and turn golden, about 4 minutes. Using long-handled wooden spoon or heat-resistant rubber spatula, pull edges of melted sugar inward to help melt remaining sugar.

5. Continue to cook until sugar turns dark chocolate brown, 4 to 6 minutes, stirring often for even cooking. (Browning will smoke; we recommend turning on your hood vent.)

6. Carefully add ¼ cup hot water to browning (mixture will sputter and let off steam) and stir to incorporate. Simmer until reduced by half and large bubbles break surface, 1½ to 2 minutes.

7. Add oxtails to browning and increase heat to medium-high (pot will be crowded). Cook, turning oxtails frequently, until oxtails have picked up significant color from sugar-based browning, some fond has begun to form on bottom of pot, and most moisture has cooked off to point where sizzling can be heard, 10 to 12 minutes.

8. Add 6 cups hot water to pot and bring to boil. Cover; reduce heat to medium-low; and cook at strong simmer for 2½ hours, stirring and turning oxtails occasionally.

9. Stir reserved marinade into pot. Poke small hole in Scotch bonnet with tip of paring knife and add to pot. Cover and continue to simmer until largest oxtails are fork-tender and meat begins to fall easily off bone, about 1 hour, stirring occasionally and being mindful to not burst Scotch bonnet as you stir.

10. Stir in butter beans and continue to simmer, covered, until meat falls easily off bone, about 30 minutes. Stir in ketchup and cook, uncovered, until liquid has thickened and reduced to just below surface of oxtails, 5 to 15 minutes. Serve.

BUYING OXTAILS

Depending on which part of the tail they come from, oxtail pieces can vary in diameter from ¾ inch to 4 inches. (Thicker pieces are cut close to the body; thinner pieces come from the end of the tail.) Try to buy oxtail packages with pieces approximately 2 inches thick and between 2 and 4 inches in diameter; they will yield more meat for your dish. Because of their varying diameters, keep in mind that you'll want to judge the doneness of the dish by the largest oxtails.

Tamale Pie

Serves 6 to 8 | **Total Time** 1½ hours

WHY THIS RECIPE WORKS Tamale pie—lightly seasoned, tomatoey ground beef with cornbread topping—borrows the flavor of traditional Mexican tamales for an easy-to-make pie. The addition of canned black beans makes our pie heartier, while corn and canned diced tomatoes contribute additional flavor and texture. Ninety percent lean ground beef gives us a good balance of richness and flavor. We bloom chili powder, oregano, and garlic with some sautéed onion and jalapeño to intensify their flavors and stir Monterey Jack cheese into the mixture to enrich the filling and help thicken it. To finish our pie, we make a simple cornmeal batter, which we spread over the filling before baking. After 30 minutes in the oven, our rich, hearty pie has a crunchy, flavorful topping that's reminiscent of real tamale dough and perfectly complements the spicy filling.

- 3 tablespoons vegetable oil, divided
- 1 pound 90 percent lean ground beef
- 1 onion, chopped fine
- 1 jalapeño chile, stemmed, seeded, and minced
- ½ teaspoon table salt, divided
- 2 tablespoons chili powder
- 1 tablespoon minced fresh oregano or 1 teaspoon dried
- 2 garlic cloves, minced
- 1 (15-ounce) can black beans, rinsed
- 1 (14.5-ounce) can diced tomatoes
- 1 cup fresh or frozen corn
- 2½ cups water
- ¾ cup coarse cornmeal
- 4 ounces Monterey Jack cheese, shredded (1 cup)

1. Adjust oven rack to lower-middle position and heat oven to 375 degrees. Heat 1 tablespoon oil in 12-inch skillet over medium-high heat until just smoking. Add beef and cook, breaking up meat with wooden spoon, until just beginning to brown, about 5 minutes.

2. Stir in onion, jalapeño, and ¼ teaspoon salt and cook until softened, about 5 minutes. Stir in chili powder, oregano, and garlic and cook until fragrant, about 30 seconds. Stir in beans, tomatoes and their juice, and corn and simmer until most of liquid has evaporated, about 3 minutes. Off heat, season with salt and pepper to taste.

3. Bring water to boil in large saucepan. Add remaining ¼ teaspoon salt and then slowly pour in cornmeal while whisking vigorously to prevent clumping. Reduce heat to medium and cook, whisking constantly, until cornmeal thickens, about 3 minutes. Stir in remaining 2 tablespoons oil.

4. Stir Monterey Jack into beef mixture, then scrape into deep-dish pie plate (or other 3-quart baking dish). Spread cornmeal mixture over top and seal against edge of dish. Cover with aluminum foil and bake until crust has set and filling is hot throughout, about 30 minutes. Let casserole cool for 10 minutes. Serve.

Gochujang Meatballs with Edamame and Sugar Snap Peas

Gochujang Meatballs with Edamame and Sugar Snap Peas

Serves 4 to 6 | **Total Time** 55 minutes

WHY THIS RECIPE WORKS We love frozen edamame—protein-packed soybeans harvested while still green—for their quick cooking time, bright color, and "meaty" but fresh texture. Combined with fresh sugar snap peas, they serve as a bed for gingery-garlicky meatballs, all tossed in a slightly spicy, sweet, and savory sauce to create an easy and satisfying meal. Intensely flavored gochujang forms the backbone of our sauce, complemented by savory soy sauce and nutty sesame oil with a bit of honey and rice vinegar to balance out all the flavors. Roasting the meatballs in the oven is quick and keeps the stovetop spatter-free. Just a few minutes in a hot skillet thaws the edamame and keeps the snap peas snappy before we add the roasted meatballs and sauce. Toasted sesame seeds and scallion greens makes a fresh finish. Even after thorough cooking, the meatballs may retain some pink color; use a meat thermometer to ensure that they're cooked to temperature before serving. Do not thaw the edamame before adding them to the skillet in step 4.

¼ cup water

3 tablespoons gochujang

3 tablespoons soy sauce

2 tablespoons toasted sesame oil

2 tablespoons honey

1 tablespoon unseasoned rice vinegar

3 garlic cloves, minced, divided

1¼ teaspoons grated fresh ginger, divided

1 pound 85 percent lean ground beef

½ cup panko bread crumbs

2 large eggs, lightly beaten

3 scallions, white parts minced, green parts sliced thin on bias, divided

¾ teaspoon table salt

¼ teaspoon pepper

1 teaspoon vegetable oil

8 ounces frozen shelled edamame (1 ½ cups)

8 ounces sugar snap peas, strings removed, halved crosswise on bias

2 tablespoons sesame seeds, toasted

1. Adjust oven rack to upper middle position and heat oven to 400 degrees. Whisk water, gochujang, soy sauce, sesame oil, honey, rice vinegar, one-third of garlic, and ¼ teaspoon ginger together in bowl; set aside.

2. Spray rimmed baking sheet with vegetable oil spray. Combine beef, panko, eggs, scallion whites, salt, pepper, remaining garlic, and remaining 1 teaspoon ginger and mix with your hands until thoroughly combined. Divide mixture into 16 portions. Roll portions between your wet hands to form meat-balls and arrange on prepared sheet. Transfer to oven and roast until meatballs register 160 degrees, 16 to 20 minutes.

3. Heat vegetable oil in 12-inch nonstick skillet over medium-high heat until just smoking. Add edamame and snap peas and cook until snap peas are bright green, about 2 minutes. Reduce heat to medium-low; add meatballs and reserved gochujang mixture; and cook until sauce thickens, about 2 minutes, gently turning meatballs to coat. Sprinkle with scallion greens and sesame seeds and serve.

Hoppin' John

Serves 4 to 6 | **Total Time** 2½ hours

WHY THIS RECIPE WORKS *Cook's Country*'s Toni Tipton-Martin and Bryan Roof went on the road to visit Ms. Emily Meggett, a matriarch of the Gullah Geechee community on Edisto Island, South Carolina. During that visit,

they cooked hoppin' John, based on the recipe from her cookbook *Gullah Geechee Home Cooking: Recipes from the Matriarch of Edisto Island*. This recipe is inspired by that cook-through. Hoppin' John is a blend of earthy peas, rich pork, and sweet onion nestled among tender, fluffy grains of rice. We use Sea Island red peas, small heirloom legumes which are a variety of cowpea/black-eyed pea originally from West Africa and popular in South Carolina's Lowcountry and Sea Islands (hence their name). They are the traditional choice for Hoppin' John and their small size belies their rich flavor. We combine well-rinsed peas with water and a halved ham hock. As we drain the cooked peas, we reserve their cooking liquid and the pieces of ham hock to use in the finished dish. We brown salt pork and use it to infuse long-grain rice with meaty flavor and then cook everything together to blend the flavors effectively. If you prefer your rice and peas with less meat, you can leave out the pieces of ham hock. If you can't find Sea Island red peas locally, you can order them online.

PEAS

1 cup Sea Island red peas

1 smoked ham hock, split in half vertically along bone Table salt for cooking beans

HOPPIN' JOHN

6 ounces salt pork, rinsed, patted dry, and cut into ¾-inch pieces

¼ cup vegetable oil or lard

1 cup chopped onion

3 scallions, sliced ½ inch thick

1½ cups long-grain or Carolina Gold rice, unrinsed

1 teaspoon table salt

¾ teaspoon pepper

¾ teaspoon granulated garlic

½ teaspoon onion powder

1. FOR THE PEAS Place peas in medium bowl and cover with water. Slosh peas around with your hand to knock off loose dirt. Let peas settle, then pour off excess water along with any floating peas; repeat rinsing and pouring off excess water until no peas float.

2. Combine rinsed peas, 4 quarts water, ham hock, and 1 tablespoon salt in Dutch oven. Bring to boil over high heat. Reduce to medium-low; cover; and simmer until peas are tender, 50 minutes to 1 hour.

3. Reserve 2¼ cups pea cooking liquid and transfer ham hock pieces to plate to cool. Drain peas in colander in sink. (Cooked peas can be refrigerated for up to 24 hours or frozen for up to 1 month. Defrost before proceeding with recipe.)

When cool enough to handle, chop ham hock into ½-inch pieces and reserve ¾ cup for hoppin' John, if desired (reserve remaining ham for another use or discard).

4. FOR THE HOPPIN' JOHN Combine salt pork and oil in large saucepan. Cover and cook over medium heat until pork is evenly browned, 10 to 12 minutes, stirring occasionally and being mindful of splatter. (Pork will initially stick to bottom of pot but will eventually release as it browns.)

5. Add onion and scallions to salt pork and cook until softened, about 3 minutes. Stir in rice until grains are evenly coated with oil and cook, stirring often, until edges of rice are translucent, about 2 minutes. Stir in salt; pepper; granulated garlic; onion powder; cooked peas; reserved pea cooking liquid; and chopped ham hock, if using, and bring to simmer. Once simmering, cover pot with sheet of aluminum foil, then cover with lid. Reduce heat to low and cook for 20 minutes without removing lid.

6. Off heat, let hoppin' John sit, covered, for 10 minutes. Fluff rice with carving fork. Transfer to shallow serving dish. Serve.

HALVING A HAM HOCK

Cut ham hock along bone before cooking so that meat and peas finish cooking at same time.

Hoppin' John

'Nduja with Beans and Greens

Serves 4 | **Total Time** 25 minutes **FAST**

WHY THIS RECIPE WORKS Humble canned beans come to the rescue when you need to pull together a quick, wholesome weeknight dinner. Here we pair creamy cannellini beans and just-tender kale with rich 'nduja sausage—a slightly spicy specialty of the southern Italian province of Calabria that packs a punch of umami. A crispy-edged fried egg perched on top offers the perfect contrast to the heartier ingredients. If you can't find 'nduja, use Italian sausage and cook it in a bit of oil.

'Nduja with Beans and Greens

**Pork Chops with Garlicky
Beans and Greens**

6 ounces 'nduja, casings removed
2 (15-ounce) cans cannellini beans (1 can rinsed,
   1 can undrained)
1 pound kale, stemmed and chopped
½ teaspoon pepper, divided
1 ounce Parmesan cheese, grated (½ cup), divided
1 tablespoon extra-virgin olive oil, plus extra for drizzling
¼ teaspoon table salt
4 large eggs

1. Cook 'nduja in Dutch oven over medium-high heat, breaking up meat with wooden spoon, until meat darkens in color and fat is rendered, 3 to 5 minutes. Stir in beans and their liquid, kale, and ¼ teaspoon pepper and bring to simmer. Reduce heat to medium-low, cover, and cook, stirring occasionally, until kale is tender and sauce has thickened slightly, 5 to 7 minutes. Off heat, stir in ¼ cup Parmesan.

2. Meanwhile, heat oil in 12-inch nonstick skillet over medium-high heat until shimmering. Add eggs to skillet and sprinkle with salt and remaining ¼ teaspoon pepper. Cover and cook for 1 minute. Remove from heat and let sit for 15 to 45 seconds for runny yolks, 45 to 60 seconds for soft but set yolks, or about 2 minutes for medium-set yolks.

3. Serve beans and kale with fried eggs, sprinkling with remaining ¼ cup Parmesan and drizzling with extra oil to taste.

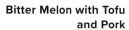

**Bitter Melon with Tofu
and Pork**

Pork Chops with Garlicky Beans and Greens

Serves 4 | **Total Time** 55 minutes

WHY THIS RECIPE WORKS A can of rinsed and drained cannellini beans adds heft and helps make a complete skillet meal when paired with lightly sweet pork chops and pleasantly bitter lacinato kale. Meaty 1-inch-thick rib chops are tender and flavorful and don't cook too quickly, giving the hearty greens time to soften. We sprinkle the raw chops with plenty of salt, freshly ground black pepper, and ground fennel; fennel's sweet, licorice-like flavor is a great partner for pork. Then we sear the chops (on one side only) in a bit of olive oil in a non-stick skillet before transferring them to a plate. Undercooking them during this step allows us to finish cooking them on top of our beans and greens in the oven, letting the pork juices flavor both the beans and vegetables underneath. The finishing touch? Parmesan cheese stirred in before serving, plus extra to pass at the table.

4 (10-ounce) bone-in pork rib chops, about 1 inch thick, trimmed

1 tablespoon grated lemon zest plus 2 teaspoons juice

1½ teaspoons ground fennel

1½ teaspoons table salt, divided

¾ teaspoon pepper

¼ cup extra-virgin olive oil, divided

1 onion, halved and sliced thin

4 garlic cloves, sliced thin

½ teaspoon red pepper flakes

2 cups chicken broth

1 pound kale, stemmed and cut into 2-inch pieces

1 (15-ounce) can cannellini beans, rinsed

1 ounce Parmesan cheese, grated (½ cup), plus extra for serving

1. Adjust oven rack to middle position and heat oven to 350 degrees. Using kitchen shears, snip through fat surrounding loin muscle of each chop in 2 places, about 2 inches apart. Pat chops dry with paper towels and sprinkle all over with lemon zest, fennel, 1¼ teaspoons salt, and pepper.

2. Heat 2 tablespoons oil in ovensafe 12-inch nonstick skillet over medium-high heat until just smoking. Add chops and cook until well browned on 1 side, about 5 minutes. Transfer chops, browned side up, to plate.

3. Add onion and garlic to fat left in skillet and cook over medium-high heat until garlic begins to brown, about 2 minutes. Add pepper flakes and cook until fragrant, about 30 seconds. Stir in broth and remaining ¼ teaspoon salt. Add kale, 1 handful at a time, and cover (lid will not sit snugly on skillet at first; this is OK). Cook until kale is fully wilted, about 10 minutes, stirring occasionally.

4. Off heat, stir in beans. Place chops, browned side up, on top of kale mixture. Transfer skillet to oven and roast, uncovered, until chops register 140 degrees, 14 to 17 minutes. Transfer chops to serving platter. Stir Parmesan, lemon juice, and remaining 2 tablespoons oil into kale mixture. Serve with chops, passing extra Parmesan separately.

Bitter Melon with Tofu and Pork

Serves 4 | **Total Time** 1¼ hours, plus 50 minutes resting

WHY THIS RECIPE WORKS Goya champuru is a popular Okinawan stir-fry dish containing tofu, pork belly, bitter melon, and egg. When cooked, bitter melon has the texture and crunch of young zucchini. To tame its bitterness, we first soak the melon in water. We toss slices of pork belly with baking soda to help tenderize the meat; we then render some fat from the pork belly, cook onions in it, add the bitter melon and pieces of firm tofu, and lightly stir-fry them. Katsuobushi (bonito flakes) boosts the dish's umami; toasted sesame oil adds a sweet, nutty element. We prefer our homemade Shichimi Togarashi (page 194), but you may use store-bought.

8 ounces center-cut fresh pork belly, about 1½ inches thick, skin removed

¼ teaspoon baking soda

4 teaspoons soy sauce, divided, plus extra for serving

1 bitter melon (10 ounces), halved lengthwise, seeded, and sliced thin on bias

½ teaspoon table salt

14 ounces firm tofu, cut into 1-inch pieces

2 teaspoons vegetable oil, plus extra as needed

1 small onion, halved and sliced thin

2 tablespoons sake

½ cup katsuobushi, divided

2 teaspoons toasted sesame oil

1 teaspoon shichimi togarashi

1. Cut pork into 2-inch-wide strips and place on large plate; freeze until firm, about 30 minutes. Slice strips crosswise ⅛ inch thick. Combine 1 tablespoon water and baking soda in medium bowl. Add pork and toss to coat; let sit for 5 minutes. Add 1 teaspoon soy sauce and toss to coat.

2. Meanwhile, combine bitter melon and 4 cups water in large bowl and let sit, swishing melon occasionally, until water turns cloudy, about 5 minutes. Drain melon, toss with salt in now-empty bowl, and let sit for 30 minutes. Rinse, drain, and pat dry. Spread tofu on paper towel–lined rimmed baking sheet and let drain for 20 minutes.

3. Heat vegetable oil in 12-inch nonstick skillet over medium-high heat until just smoking. Add pork and increase heat to high. Cook, tossing pork slowly but constantly, until no longer pink, 2 to 6 minutes. Using slotted spoon, transfer pork to clean bowl. Pour off all but 2 teaspoons fat from pan. (If necessary, add extra vegetable oil to equal 2 teaspoons.) Add onion to fat left in pan and cook, tossing slowly but constantly, until softened and lightly browned, 4 to 6 minutes.

4. Add melon and sake and cook, tossing slowly but constantly, until melon just begins to soften, about 1 minute. Add pork and any accumulated juices, tofu, 2 tablespoons water, and remaining 1 tablespoon soy sauce and cook, tossing slowly but constantly, until tofu is warmed through, about 2 minutes. Off heat, carefully stir in ¼ cup katsuobushi and sesame oil. Sprinkle with remaining ¼ cup katsuobushi and shichimi togarashi. Serve, passing extra soy sauce separately.

Shichimi Togarashi

Makes ¼ cup
Total Time 10 minutes **FAST** **VEGAN**

- 1½ teaspoons grated orange zest
- 4 teaspoons sesame seeds, toasted
- 1 tablespoon paprika
- 2 teaspoons pepper
- ½ teaspoon garlic powder
- ½ teaspoon ground ginger
- ¼ teaspoon cayenne pepper

Microwave orange zest in small bowl, stirring occasionally, until dry and no longer clumping together, about 2 minutes. Stir in sesame seeds, paprika, pepper, garlic powder, ginger, and cayenne. (Shichimi togarashi can be stored in airtight container for up to 1 week.)

Italian Sausage with Lentils and Kale

Serves 4 | **Total Time** 45 minutes **FAST**

WHY THIS RECIPE WORKS This quick weeknight meal pairs canned lentils and fresh greens with Italian sausage for hearty satisfaction. Cooking the sausages on top of the lentil mixture infuses this one-skillet dish with rich, meaty flavor. We combine yogurt and whole-grain mustard to make a simple, tangy sauce to drizzle on the dish. For a spicier kick, use hot Italian sausage. We prefer curly kale for this recipe, but other varieties will work.

- 2 teaspoons extra-virgin olive oil
- 1½ pounds sweet Italian sausage
- 2 shallots, peeled, halved, and sliced thin
- 3 garlic cloves, minced
- 10 ounces kale, stemmed and chopped
- ¾ cup chicken broth
- ¼ teaspoon table salt
- ¼ teaspoon pepper
- 1 (15-ounce) can lentils, rinsed
- 3 tablespoons plain yogurt
- 2 tablespoons whole-grain mustard
- 1 tablespoon water

1. Adjust oven rack to middle position and heat oven to 375 degrees. Heat oil in 12-inch skillet over medium-high heat until just smoking. Add sausage and cook until browned all over, about 5 minutes; transfer to plate.

2. Reduce heat to medium, add shallots and garlic to now-empty skillet, and cook until vegetables start to brown, about 3 minutes. Stir in kale, broth, salt, and pepper; cover and cook until wilted, about 5 minutes.

3. Stir in lentils. Arrange browned sausage on top of lentil mixture and transfer skillet to oven. Cook, uncovered, until sausage registers 160 degrees, about 12 minutes. Whisk yogurt, mustard, and water together in bowl; drizzle over top. Serve.

Red Beans and Rice with Andouille

Serves 4 | **Total Time** 1 hour

WHY THIS RECIPE WORKS For red beans and rice with weeknight ease, canned kidney beans bring convenience and a bonus: The bean liquid, mixed with chicken broth, offers meatiness and body without need for long simmering with a traditional hambone. Smoky, spicy andouille sausage balances the sweetness of the beans, while celery, bell pepper, and oregano create a strong vegetable base. Toasting the rice in oil until the edges turn translucent helps the grains to hold their shape. We cook the rice and beans together with the broth, bean liquid, and sautéed onion for 20 minutes and let them sit for 10 minutes before fluffing with a fork. Rinse the rice in a fine-mesh strainer until the water runs almost clear, about 2 minutes, stirring the rice a few times with your hand.

Substitution: You can use canned small red beans in place of the kidney beans.

- 2¼ cups chicken broth, plus extra as needed
- 1 (15-ounce) can kidney beans, drained with liquid reserved
- 2 tablespoons vegetable oil
- 8 ounces andouille sausage, sliced ¼ inch thick
- ½ onion, chopped fine
- ¼ cup finely chopped green bell pepper
- ¼ cup minced celery
- ½ teaspoon table salt
- ½ teaspoon pepper
- 1½ cups long-grain white rice, rinsed
- 3 garlic cloves, minced

Red Beans and Rice with Andouille

Habichuelas Guisadas con Calabaza

Serves 4 to 6 | **Total Time** 1¾ hours, plus 8 hours soaking

WHY THIS RECIPE WORKS Stewed red kidney beans served atop salt pork–studded rice tell a rich history of one of Puerto Rico's most comforting dishes. This version was developed for us by Von Diaz, a writer, documentary producer, and author of *Coconuts and Collards: Recipes and Stories from Puerto Rico to the Deep South.* If you can't find jamón de cocinar, you can substitute an equal volume of chopped ham steak. Kabocha or butternut squash are good substitutes for calabaza (no need to peel the kabocha; butternut should be peeled). We prefer our homemade Sofrito (page 196) and Sazón (page 196), but you may use store-bought. Serve with Arroz con Tocino (page 300) and lime wedges, if desired.

- 8 ounces (1¼ cups) dried red kidney beans, picked over and rinsed
- 2 tablespoons extra-virgin olive oil
- ½ cup finely chopped jamón de cocinar (4 ounces)
- ½ cup Sofrito (page 196)
- 1 tablespoon Sazón (page 196)
- 1 tablespoon tomato paste
- 1 (8-ounce) can tomato sauce
- 2 cups chicken broth
- 1 bay leaf
- 1 tablespoon kosher salt
- 1 pound seeded calabaza squash, cut into 1-inch pieces (2½ cups)
- ½ cup pimento-stuffed green olives
- 2 teaspoons red wine vinegar, plus extra for seasoning
- ¼ teaspoon pepper
- ½ cup fresh cilantro leaves

1. Cover beans with at least 2 inches water in large bowl and soak at room temperature for at least 8 hours or up to 24 hours. Drain well. (If you're pressed for time, see page 13 for information on quick brining your beans.)

2. Heat oil in Dutch oven over medium heat until shimmering. Add jamón and cook until lightly browned, 3 to 5 minutes. Stir in sofrito and cook, stirring often, until liquid is evaporated, 3 to 5 minutes.

- 2 teaspoons paprika
- ½ teaspoon dried thyme
- 1 bay leaf
- 2 teaspoons red wine vinegar
- 2 scallions, thinly sliced
  Hot sauce

1. Add enough broth to reserved bean liquid to equal 2½ cups and stir to combine; set aside. Heat oil in 12-inch nonstick skillet over medium-high heat until shimmering. Add andouille, onion, bell pepper, celery, salt, and pepper and cook until vegetables are softened and beginning to brown, about 8 minutes.

2. Add rice and cook, stirring frequently, until edges begin to turn translucent and rice is fragrant, about 2 minutes. Stir in garlic, paprika, and thyme and cook until fragrant, about 30 seconds. Stir in bay leaf, beans, and reserved broth mixture and bring to boil. Cover, reduce heat to medium-low, and cook, without stirring, for 20 minutes.

3. Off heat, let sit, covered, for 10 minutes. Discard bay leaf. Gently fluff rice with fork and stir in vinegar. Season with salt and pepper to taste, and sprinkle with scallions. Serve with hot sauce.

3. Stir in sazón and tomato paste and cook until mixture begins to darken in color, about 30 seconds. Stir in tomato sauce, scraping up any browned bits. Add broth, 2 cups water, bay leaf, salt, and drained beans. Bring to boil over high heat. Cover; reduce heat to medium-low; and simmer until beans are completely tender but not falling apart, 40 to 50 minutes.

4. Stir in calabaza and olives. Add extra water (up to 1 cup) if liquid has reduced below level of beans. Bring to simmer over medium-high heat. Cover, reduce heat to low, and cook until calabaza is fork-tender but not falling apart, 10 to 15 minutes. Stir in vinegar and pepper. Season with salt and vinegar to taste, and sprinkle with cilantro. Serve.

Habichuelas Guisadas con Calabaza

Sofrito

Makes 2¼ cups
Total Time 10 minutes `FAST` `VEGAN`

This recipe is adapted from *Coconuts and Collards: Recipes and Stories from Puerto Rico to the Deep South* by Von Diaz. Sofrito, a loose paste made from a mix of onion, garlic, sweet peppers, culantro (which is called chadon beni in the Caribbean and sawtooth coriander elsewhere), and cilantro, is pillar of Puerto Rican cuisine. Diaz writes of how sofrito, which is European in origin, is traditionally pounded or ground into a paste in Puerto Rico, reflecting indigenous and African influence. If you can't find ajies dulces or ajies amarillos, you can substitute half of a red, orange, or yellow bell pepper. If you can't find culantro, substitute cilantro.

- 1 red bell pepper, stemmed, seeded, and quartered
- 3 ajies dulces or ajies amarillos, stemmed, seeded, and chopped coarse
- 6 large garlic cloves, peeled
- 1 large onion, chopped coarse
- 6 fresh culantro leaves and tender stems, chopped coarse
- 6 fresh cilantro sprigs, chopped coarse

Process bell pepper, ajies dulces, and garlic in large (14-cup) food processor until mixture is smooth, about 1 minute, scraping down sides of bowl as needed. Add onion and process until smooth, about 30 seconds. Add culantro and cilantro and process until herbs are finely minced, about 30 seconds. (Sofrito can be refrigerated for up to 1 week or frozen for up to 3 months.)

Sazón

Makes ½ cup
Total Time 10 minutes `FAST` `VEGAN`

Sazón is one of the most commonly used seasonings in Puerto Rican cuisine and throughout Latin America. It adds flavor to everything, and thanks to annatto and turmeric it adds a pleasing warm color too. If you can't find annatto, you can substitute paprika. This recipe is adapted from *Coconuts and Collards: Recipes and Stories from Puerto Rico to the Deep South* by Von Diaz.

- 2 tablespoons table salt
- 2 tablespoons ground annatto
- 1 tablespoon garlic powder
- 1 tablespoon onion powder
- 1 tablespoon ground cumin
- 1 tablespoon ground turmeric
- ½ teaspoon pepper

Combine all ingredients in bowl. (Sazón can be stored in airtight container for up to 3 months.)

PUERTO RICAN RICE AND BEANS

Rice and beans are ubiquitous across Latin America and the Caribbean, with seemingly limitless variations. In Cuban congrí and Jamaican rice and peas, beans and rice are cooked together with aromatics in the same pot. But more often, beans are stewed separately and served atop white rice. According to Von Diaz, "Puerto Rican arroz con habichuelas (rice and beans) is an extension of indigenous Taíno and African foodways, with ingredients introduced by colonization that were creatively adapted. Beans and legumes thrive on the island and were an essential component of the Taíno diet. The iconic legumes for arroz con habichuelas are dark red kidney beans, which are known locally as colorá (or habichuelas coloradas). They are larger than other common varieties and have a creamy texture and rich flavor." Rice tells a story here too. "It was brought to the island during Spanish colonization and ultimately cultivated by enslaved African workers who brought knowledge of rice cultivation from their native countries," Diaz says. "Among the most traditional preparations is Arroz con Tocino (page 300), where white rice is cooked with rendered salt pork and a bit of fresh garlic, adding richness and dimension that enhances the flavor of what it's served with."

Whole-Wheat Spaghetti with Greens, Beans, and Pancetta

Serves 6 | **Total Time** 1½ hours

WHY THIS RECIPE WORKS Wheaty pasta, hearty greens, and savory beans are humble ingredients that can combine to make a rustic, full-flavored dish. For a meal that's not only complex-tasting and satisfying but also quick and easy, we start with kale or collard greens, which require just a quick braise. This means we can easily infuse them with aromatic flavors of onion, garlic, spicy red pepper flakes, and chicken broth. The canned beans, greens, and sauce only need to cook with the pasta for a few minutes to create magic. We prefer whole-wheat pasta to regular, as the wheat stands up to the bold flavors of the sauce and complements the earthiness of the greens. To round out the dish, we add crisp, savory pancetta and silky fontina. A sprinkling of Parmesan bread crumbs gives the creamy pasta a bit of textural contrast.

⅓ cup panko bread crumbs

2 tablespoons extra-virgin olive oil, divided

¾ plus ⅛ teaspoon table salt, divided, plus salt for cooking pasta

⅛ teaspoon pepper

2 tablespoons grated Parmesan cheese

3 ounces pancetta, cut into ½-inch pieces

1 onion, chopped fine

3 garlic cloves, minced

¼–½ teaspoon red pepper flakes

1½ pounds kale or collard greens, stemmed and cut into 1-inch pieces, divided

1½ cups chicken broth

1 (15-ounce) can cannellini beans, rinsed

1 pound whole-wheat spaghetti

4 ounces fontina cheese, shredded (1 cup)

1. Combine panko, 1 tablespoon oil, ⅛ teaspoon salt, and pepper in 8-inch nonstick skillet. Cook over medium heat, stirring frequently, until evenly browned, 3 to 4 minutes. Transfer to bowl and stir in Parmesan; set aside until ready to serve.

2. Heat remaining 1 tablespoon oil in 12-inch skillet over medium heat until shimmering. Add pancetta and cook, stirring occasionally, until crisp, 5 to 7 minutes. Using slotted spoon, transfer pancetta to paper towel–lined plate.

3. Add onion to fat left in pan and cook over medium heat until softened and lightly browned, 5 to 7 minutes. Stir in garlic and pepper flakes and cook until fragrant, about 30 seconds. Add half of greens and cook, stirring occasionally, until starting to wilt, about 2 minutes. Add remaining greens, broth, and remaining ¾ teaspoon salt and bring to simmer. Reduce heat to medium, cover (pan will be very full), and cook, stirring occasionally, until greens are tender, about 15 minutes (mixture will be somewhat soupy). Off heat, stir in beans and pancetta.

4. Meanwhile, bring 4 quarts water to boil in large pot. Add pasta and 1 tablespoon salt and cook, stirring often, until just shy of al dente. Reserve ½ cup cooking water, then drain pasta and return to pot. Add greens mixture and cook over medium heat, tossing to combine, until pasta absorbs most of liquid, about 2 minutes.

5. Off heat, stir in fontina. Season with salt and pepper to taste, and adjust consistency with reserved cooking water as needed. Serve, sprinkling individual portions with reserved Parmesan panko.

Braised Lamb Shoulder Chops with Fava Beans

Serves 4 | **Total Time** 1½ hours

WHY THIS RECIPE WORKS Fava beans and lamb are both quintessential springtime items, so it's no wonder they're often paired together. This weeknight braise uses the flavors of Italian lamb and fava bean ragus. We chose lamb shoulder chops for their natural tenderness and fatty marbling, which gives deep, rich flavor to our sauce. We build a sauce base by sautéing mirepoix with garlic, anchovy, tomato paste, and red pepper flakes; then we add red wine, broth, and the browned chops. Simmering for just 15 to 20 minutes creates a luxurious sauce for the fava beans to soak up. The fava beans along with lemon juice and mint provide a bright counterpoint to the rich lamb chops. Be sure to set up the ice water bath before cooking the fava beans, as plunging them immediately in the cold water after blanching retains their bright green color and ensures that they don't overcook. You will need a 12-inch skillet with a tight-fitting lid for this recipe. Serve with crusty bread or Creamy Parmesan Polenta (page 313).

Substitution: You can use 1 pound (3¼ cups) frozen shelled fava beans, thawed, in place of fresh. Be sure to remove the sheath. Skip step 1 if using frozen favas.

- 3 pounds fava beans, shelled (3 cups)
- 4 (6- to 10-ounce) lamb shoulder chops, ¾ inch thick, trimmed
- 1 teaspoon table salt, divided
- ¼ teaspoon pepper
- 1 tablespoon extra-virgin olive oil
- 1 small onion, chopped fine
- 1 carrot, peeled and chopped fine
- 1 celery rib, chopped fine
- 2 garlic cloves, minced
- 2 anchovy fillets, rinsed, patted dry, and minced
- 1 tablespoon tomato paste
- ⅛ teaspoon red pepper flakes
- ⅓ cup dry red wine
- 1¼ cups chicken broth
- 2 teaspoons lemon juice
- 2 tablespoons shredded fresh mint

1. Bring 4 quarts water to boil in large pot over high heat. Fill large bowl halfway with ice and water. Add fava beans to boiling water and cook for 1 minute. Drain fava beans, transfer to ice water, and let sit until chilled, about 2 minutes. Transfer fava beans to triple layer of paper towels and dry well. Using paring knife, make small cut along edge of each bean through waxy sheath, then gently squeeze sheath to release bean; discard sheath. Set fava beans aside.

2. Cut 2 slits, about 2 inches apart, through outer layer of fat and silverskin on each lamb chop. Pat lamb chops dry with paper towels and sprinkle with ½ teaspoon salt and pepper. Heat oil in 12-inch skillet over medium-high heat until just smoking. Add lamb chops and cook until browned on both sides, 8 to 10 minutes. Transfer to large plate and set aside.

3. Pour off all but 1 tablespoon fat from skillet. Add onion, carrot, celery, and remaining ½ teaspoon salt and cook over medium heat until softened, about 5 minutes. Add garlic, anchovies, and pepper flakes and cook until fragrant, about 30 seconds. Add tomato paste and cook for 1 minute. Add wine and simmer, scraping up any browned bits, until reduced to glaze, about 1 minute. Add broth and return chops and any accumulated juice to skillet. Bring to simmer then reduce heat to low, cover, and simmer until chops are cooked through but tender, 15 to 20 minutes.

4. Transfer chops to clean plate and tent with aluminum foil. Add reserved fava beans to liquid in skillet and simmer over medium heat until favas are warmed through and sauce has thickened slightly, about 4 minutes. Stir in lemon juice and season with salt and pepper to taste. Return chops and any accumulated juices to skillet, sprinkle with mint, and serve.

One-Pot Lamb Meatballs with Eggplant and Chickpeas

Serves 4 to 6 | **Total Time** 1 hour

WHY THIS RECIPE WORKS For this boldly flavored dish, we drew inspiration from the flavors commonly used in Moroccan tagines, stewed dishes cooked in earthenware pots of the same name. Our Dutch oven version features lemony lamb meatballs in a tomato-based sauce, spiced with harissa and studded with eggplant and chickpeas for more substance and nutty flavor. The spice blend ras el hanout connects the meatballs and the sauce while golden raisins and green olives bring sweetness and brininess. Fresh herbs add visual pop and bright flavor. We prefer our homemade Harissa (page 116), but you may use store-bought.

Spicy Lamb with Lentils and Yogurt

¼ cup harissa

2 teaspoons grated lemon zest

½ cup coarsely chopped fresh cilantro, divided

½ cup coarsely chopped fresh mint, divided

1. FOR THE MEATBALLS Combine lamb, panko, egg, ras el hanout, lemon zest, garlic, and salt in large bowl and mix with your hands until thoroughly combined. Divide mixture into 16 even portions. Roll portions between your wet hands to form meatballs.

2. Heat oil in Dutch oven over medium-high heat until just smoking. Add meatballs and cook until well browned all over, about 5 minutes. Transfer meatballs to large plate, leaving fat in pot.

3. FOR THE EGGPLANT AND SAUCE Heat fat left in pot over medium-high heat until just smoking. Add eggplant, onion, garlic, ras el hanout, and salt and cook until vegetables are beginning to soften, 8 to 10 minutes, stirring frequently.

4. Stir in tomatoes, chickpeas, raisins, water, olives, harissa, and lemon zest. Nestle meatballs into sauce. Reduce heat to medium-low; cover; and cook until eggplant is very tender and meatballs register 160 degrees, about 10 minutes.

5. Off heat, stir in ¼ cup cilantro and ¼ cup mint. Sprinkle remaining ¼ cup cilantro and remaining ¼ cup mint over top and serve.

Spicy Lamb with Lentils and Yogurt

Serves 4 | **Total Time** 1¼ hours, plus 20 minutes resting

WHY THIS RECIPE WORKS This skillet recipe combines earthy lentils with warm-spiced ground lamb for a hearty but not fussy meal. Cilantro and tomatoes add freshness, while Greek yogurt stirred in at the end brings the dish together. Sautéing the aromatics creates a fond and then deglazing the pan dissolves all that complex flavor into the dish. Garam masala and red pepper flakes add a punch of warm-spiced flavor. Adding a tiny amount of baking soda tenderizes the ground lamb by raising its pH. Note that you will need ¾ cup of cilantro, so shop accordingly. We prefer how small green lentilles du Puy hold their shape in this recipe. We prefer our homemade Garam Masala (page 216), but you may use store-bought.

MEATBALLS

1 pound ground lamb

½ cup panko bread crumbs

1 large egg, lightly beaten

1 tablespoon ras el hanout

2 teaspoons grated lemon zest

2 garlic cloves, minced

1 teaspoon table salt

2 tablespoons extra-virgin olive oil

EGGPLANT AND SAUCE

1 pound eggplant, cut into ½-inch pieces

1 onion, chopped fine

4 garlic cloves, minced

1 tablespoon ras el hanout

1 teaspoon table salt

1 (28-ounce) can crushed tomatoes

1 (15-ounce) can chickpeas, rinsed

¾ cup golden raisins

½ cup water

½ cup pitted green olives, halved

1 pound ground lamb

¾ teaspoon table salt, divided, plus salt for cooking lentils

¼ teaspoon baking soda

1 cup dried lentilles du Puy, picked over and rinsed

3 garlic cloves, minced

1 tablespoon tomato paste

2 teaspoons garam masala

1 teaspoon red pepper flakes

1 teaspoon grated fresh ginger

1 tablespoon vegetable oil

1 onion, chopped

2 naan breads

2 tomatoes, cored and cut into ½-inch pieces

¾ cup chopped fresh cilantro, divided

¾ cup plain Greek yogurt, divided

1. Toss lamb with 2 tablespoons water, ½ teaspoon salt, and baking soda in bowl until thoroughly combined; set aside for 20 minutes.

2. While lamb sits, bring lentils, 4 cups water, and 1 teaspoon salt to boil in medium saucepan over high heat. Reduce heat to low and simmer until lentils are just tender, 18 to 22 minutes. Drain well.

3. Adjust oven rack to middle position and heat oven to 400 degrees. Combine garlic, tomato paste, garam masala, pepper flakes, and ginger in small bowl. Heat oil in 12-inch skillet over medium heat until shimmering. Add onion and remaining ¼ teaspoon salt and cook until softened and lightly browned, 5 to 7 minutes. Stir in garlic mixture and cook, stirring constantly, until bottom of skillet is dark brown, 1 to 2 minutes.

4. Add 1 cup water and bring to boil, scraping up any browned bits. Reduce heat to medium-low, add lamb in 2-inch chunks to skillet, and bring to gentle simmer. Cover and cook until lamb is cooked through, 10 to 12 minutes, stirring and breaking up lamb chunks with 2 forks halfway through cooking. Uncover skillet, increase heat to medium, stir in drained lentils, and cook until liquid is mostly absorbed, 3 to 5 minutes.

5. While lamb cooks, place naan on rimmed baking sheet and bake until warmed through, about 5 minutes.

6. Off heat, stir tomatoes, ½ cup cilantro, and 2 tablespoons yogurt into lentils and season with salt and pepper to taste. Sprinkle with remaining ¼ cup cilantro. Serve with naan and remaining yogurt.

Shrimp with Long Beans and Garlic Sauce

Shrimp with Long Beans and Garlic Sauce

Serves 4 | **Total Time** 45 minutes, plus 30 minutes resting

WHY THIS RECIPE WORKS Chinese long beans, also called asparagus beans, have a flavor and a chew that is distinct from sweet green beans. They make a dramatic presentation alongside tender pink shrimp in this stir-fry. Many traditional recipes for these serpentine beans employ a double-cooking technique of deep frying followed by stir-frying, which renders them tender and juicy. To skip the deep frying, we microwave the beans before stir-frying them, making this an easy weeknight dish. We finish cooking the beans with the shrimp in a flavorful mix of soy sauce, Shaoxing wine, doubanjiang, garlic, scallions, and ginger. If doubanjiang is unavailable, substitute 1 teaspoon sambal. We prefer untreated shrimp, but if your shrimp are treated with added salt or preservatives like sodium tripolyphosphate, skip step 1. You will need a 14-inch flat-bottomed wok or 12-inch nonstick skillet, each with a tight-fitting lid, for this recipe.

Substitution: You can use haricots verts or thin green beans in place of long beans. Trim but do not halve them.

1 pound extra-large shrimp (21 to 25 per pound), peeled, deveined, and tails removed

1 teaspoon sugar

½ teaspoon table salt

⅓ cup plus 2 tablespoons Shaoxing wine, divided

2 tablespoons soy sauce

1 tablespoon doubanjiang (broad bean chile paste)

1 teaspoon Chinese black vinegar

2 teaspoons cornstarch

1½ pounds long beans, trimmed and halved crosswise

¼ cup vegetable oil, divided

6 garlic cloves, sliced thin

3 large scallions, white parts chopped fine, green parts cut into 1-inch pieces

2 tablespoons grated fresh ginger

1. Combine shrimp, sugar, and salt in medium bowl; let sit for 30 minutes.

2. Whisk ⅓ cup Shaoxing wine, soy sauce, doubanjiang, and vinegar together in small bowl. Whisk remaining 2 tablespoons Shaoxing wine and cornstarch together in second small bowl; set aside.

3. Rinse long beans but do not dry. Place in large bowl; cover; and microwave until tender, 6 to 12 minutes, tossing every 3 minutes. Using tongs, transfer beans to paper towel–lined plate and let drain. Do not clean bowl.

4. Heat 1 tablespoon oil in 14-inch flat-bottomed wok or 12-inch nonstick skillet over medium-high heat until just smoking. Add half of long beans and increase heat to high. Cook, tossing beans slowly but constantly, until softened and well charred, 5 to 10 minutes; transfer to now-empty bowl. Repeat with 1 tablespoon oil and remaining beans; transfer to bowl with first batch of beans.

5. Cook remaining 2 tablespoons oil, garlic, scallion whites, and ginger in now-empty pan over medium-high heat until garlic is just beginning to brown, about 1 minute. Add Shaoxing wine–soy sauce mixture and shrimp and bring to simmer. Reduce heat to medium-low; cover; and cook, tossing occasionally, until shrimp are just cooked through, 3 to 5 minutes.

Pan-Seared Scallops with Sugar Snap Pea Slaw

Pan-Seared Scallops with Sugar Snap Pea Slaw

Serves 4 | **Total Time** 40 minutes | FAST

WHY THIS RECIPE WORKS Tender scallops and crisp sugar snap peas form a playful juxtaposition in this easy dinner. The sugar snaps form an integral part of a mixed vegetable slaw that makes a refreshing and simple counterpoint to the rich, buttery scallops. For golden-brown and juicy scallops that rival those made on the most powerful restaurant range, we sear them in a smoking-hot skillet, and then finish them with a butter baste. The snap peas, cucumber, and radishes are simply sliced thin and tossed with mayo, chives, and lemon juice for a salad that can rest and develop flavor as the scallops quickly cook. Purchase large sea scallops rather than smaller bay scallops, which are far too easy to overcook. We recommend buying "dry" scallops, which don't have STPP added. These will brown better and have a creamier texture.

SLAW

- 8 ounces sugar snap peas, strings removed, sliced thin on bias
- 1 English cucumber, halved lengthwise, seeded, and sliced thin crosswise
- 6 radishes, trimmed, halved lengthwise, and sliced thin
- ¼ cup mayonnaise
- 2 tablespoons chopped fresh chives
- ¼ teaspoon grated lemon zest plus 2 tablespoons juice
- ¼ teaspoon table salt

SCALLOPS

- 1½ pounds large sea scallops, tendons removed
- ¾ teaspoon table salt
- ½ teaspoon pepper
- 2 tablespoons vegetable oil, divided
- 2 tablespoons unsalted butter, divided

1. FOR THE SLAW Toss all ingredients in bowl until thoroughly combined.

2. FOR THE SCALLOPS Place scallops on rimmed baking sheet lined with clean dish towel. Place second clean dish towel on top of scallops and press gently to blot liquid. Let scallops sit at room temperature for 10 minutes while towels absorb moisture.

3. Pat scallops thoroughly dry with paper towels. Sprinkle scallops on both sides with salt and pepper. Heat 1 tablespoon oil in 12-inch nonstick skillet over high heat until just smoking. Add half of scallops in single layer, flat side down, and cook, without moving them, until well browned, 1½ to 2 minutes.

4. Add 1 tablespoon butter to skillet. Using tongs, flip scallops. Continue to cook, using large spoon to continually baste scallops with melted butter (tilt skillet so butter pools to 1 side), until sides of scallops are firm and centers are opaque, 30 to 90 seconds (remove smaller scallops as they finish cooking). Transfer scallops to large plate and tent with aluminum foil. Wipe skillet clean with paper towels and repeat cooking with remaining 1 tablespoon oil, scallops, and 1 tablespoon butter. Serve immediately with slaw.

Roasted Trout with White Bean and Tomato Salad

Serves 4 | Total Time 30 minutes `FAST`

WHY THIS RECIPE WORKS Creamy cannellini beans and bright tomatoes tossed with the appealing Mediterranean flavors of shallots, parsley, lemon juice, capers, rosemary, and

Roasted Trout with White Bean and Tomato Salad

garlic make for a fresh and vivid salad that accompanies whole trout. Since whole trout have already been boned and butterflied, you can easily roast this rich, flavorful fish (just throw it on the baking sheet) and make the complementary side in the meantime. Adding the trout to a preheated baking sheet in the oven ensures that it develops a nice, crisp skin with no effort. Spooned over the butterflied fillets, the salad makes a beautiful presentation and a complete and colorful dinner.

- ½ cup extra-virgin olive oil, divided, plus extra for drizzling
- 2 shallots, minced
- ¼ cup lemon juice, plus lemon wedges for serving
- 2 tablespoons capers, rinsed and chopped
- 2 garlic cloves, minced
- 4 teaspoons minced fresh rosemary
- 4 (8- to 10-ounce) boneless, butterflied whole trout
- ½ teaspoon table salt
- ¼ teaspoon pepper
- 2 (15-ounce) cans cannellini beans, rinsed
- 12 ounces cherry tomatoes, halved
- ¼ cup chopped fresh parsley

1. Adjust oven rack to middle position, place rimmed baking sheet on rack, and heat oven to 450 degrees. Whisk ¼ cup oil, shallots, lemon juice, capers, garlic, and rosemary together in large bowl; set aside.

2. Pat trout dry with paper towels and sprinkle with salt and pepper. Add remaining ¼ cup oil to preheated sheet, tilting to coat evenly, and return to oven for 4 minutes.

3. Carefully place trout skin side down on hot sheet; return to oven and cook until trout flakes apart when gently prodded with paring knife, 7 to 9 minutes.

4. Add beans, tomatoes, and parsley to reserved dressing in bowl and toss to coat. Season with salt and pepper to taste, and drizzle with extra oil to taste. Serve with trout and lemon wedges.

Saumon aux Lentilles

Serves 4 | **Total Time** 1¼ hours

WHY THIS RECIPE WORKS This French-inspired dinner is a classic coupling of earthy pulses and rich fish. We first build a flavorful base for the lentils, gently cooking onion, carrots, and celery in olive oil until soft and adding fruity tomato paste and plenty of garlic before the lentils and water go in. When the lentils are fully softened and most of the moisture in the pot has evaporated or been absorbed, we focus on the salmon, briefly brining it in a saltwater solution to season the fish and ensure that it retains plenty of moisture as it cooks. Unconventionally, we place the salmon skin side down in a cold nonstick skillet that has been strewn with salt and pepper. As the pan heats up, the salmon begins to release some of the fat that lies just beneath the skin, crisping it and enabling us to cook the fish without any additional fat. Mustard and sherry vinegar stirred into the lentils brighten them and contrast with the rich fish. A drizzle of extra-virgin olive oil adds grassy top notes. To ensure uniform cooking, buy a 1½-pound center-cut salmon fillet and cut it into four pieces. If using wild salmon, check for doneness earlier and cook it until it registers 120 degrees.

LENTILS

- 2 tablespoons extra-virgin olive oil, divided
- 1 large onion, chopped fine
- 1 celery rib, chopped fine
- 1 carrot, peeled and chopped fine
- ¾ teaspoon table salt
- 1 tablespoon minced garlic (3–4 cloves)
- 1 tablespoon tomato paste

- ½ teaspoon dried thyme
- ½ teaspoon pepper
- 2½ cups water
- 1 cup dried lentilles du Puy, picked over and rinsed
- 1 tablespoon sherry vinegar
- 2 teaspoons Dijon mustard
- 1 tablespoon chopped fresh parsley

SALMON

- ¼ cup table salt for brining
- 4 (6-ounce) skin-on salmon fillets
- ¾ teaspoon table salt, divided
- ¾ teaspoon pepper, divided

1. FOR THE LENTILS Heat 1 tablespoon oil in medium saucepan over medium heat until shimmering. Add onion, celery, carrot, and salt and stir to coat vegetables. Cover and cook, stirring occasionally, until vegetables are softened but not browned, 8 to 10 minutes. Add garlic, tomato paste, thyme, and pepper and cook, stirring constantly, until fragrant, about 2 minutes. Stir in water and lentils. Increase heat and bring to boil. Adjust heat to simmer. Cover and cook, stirring occasionally, until lentils are soft but not mushy and have consistency of thick risotto, 40 to 50 minutes. Remove from heat and keep covered.

2. FOR THE SALMON While lentils are cooking, dissolve ¼ cup salt in 1 quart water in narrow container. Submerge salmon in brine and let stand for 15 minutes. Remove salmon from brine and pat dry with paper towels. Allow to stand while lentils finish cooking.

3. Sprinkle bottom of 12-inch nonstick skillet evenly with ½ teaspoon salt and ½ teaspoon pepper. Place fillets, skin side down, in skillet and sprinkle tops of fillets with remaining ¼ teaspoon salt and remaining ¼ teaspoon pepper. Heat skillet over medium-high heat and cook fillets, without moving them, until fat begins to render, skin begins to brown, and bottom ¼ inch of fillets turns opaque, 6 to 8 minutes.

4. Using tongs and thin spatula, flip fillets and continue to cook without moving them until centers are still translucent when checked with tip of paring knife and register 125 degrees (for medium-rare), 5 to 8 minutes. Transfer fillets, skin side up, to clean plate.

5. Warm lentils briefly if necessary. Stir in vinegar, mustard, and remaining 1 tablespoon oil. Season with salt, pepper, and vinegar to taste. Transfer lentils to wide, shallow serving bowl. Arrange salmon skin side up on lentils. Sprinkle with parsley and serve.

Grilled Swordfish with Eggplant, Tomato, and Chickpea Salad

Serves 4 | **Total Time** 1¼ hours

WHY THIS RECIPE WORKS Since meaty swordfish stands up so well to grilling, we decided to cook swordfish steaks simultaneously with some eggplant for an easy and elegant grilled dinner. We give a flavor boost to the fish by coating it with a paste of cilantro, onion, garlic, and warm spices, which bloom over the hot fire, reserving part of the paste to dress the eggplant salad. We remove the fish when the interior is just opaque; it continues to cook a little more from residual heat as it rests while we prepare the accompanying vegetables. After grilling the eggplant until soft and charred, we chop it into chunks and mix it with juicy cherry tomatoes and canned chickpeas, and then dress it with the remaining cilantro mixture for a vibrant salad. If swordfish isn't available, you can substitute halibut.

1 cup fresh cilantro leaves
½ red onion, chopped coarse
6 tablespoons extra-virgin olive oil, divided
3 tablespoons lemon juice
4 garlic cloves, chopped
1 teaspoon ground cumin
1 teaspoon paprika
¾ teaspoon table salt, divided
¼ teaspoon cayenne pepper
⅛ teaspoon ground cinnamon
4 (6- to 8-ounce) skin-on swordfish steaks, 1 to 1½ inches thick
1 large eggplant, sliced into ½-inch-thick rounds
⅛ teaspoon pepper
6 ounces cherry tomatoes, halved
1 (15-ounce) can chickpeas, rinsed

1. Process cilantro, onion, 3 tablespoons oil, lemon juice, garlic, cumin, paprika, ½ teaspoon salt, cayenne, and cinnamon in food processor until smooth, about 2 minutes, scraping down sides of bowl as needed. Measure out and reserve ½ cup cilantro mixture. Transfer remaining cilantro mixture to large bowl and set aside.

2. Brush swordfish with reserved ½ cup cilantro mixture. Brush eggplant with remaining 3 tablespoons oil and sprinkle with pepper and remaining ¼ teaspoon salt.

3A. FOR A CHARCOAL GRILL Open bottom vent completely. Light large chimney starter filled with charcoal briquettes (6 quarts). When top coals are partially covered with ash, pour two-thirds evenly over half of grill, then pour remaining coals over other half of grill. Set cooking grate in place, cover, and open lid vent completely. Heat grill until hot, about 5 minutes.

3B. FOR A GAS GRILL Turn all burners to high, cover, and heat grill until hot, about 15 minutes. Leave primary burner on high and turn other burner(s) to medium-high.

4. Clean cooking grate, then repeatedly brush grate with well-oiled paper towels until black and glossy, 5 to 10 times. Place swordfish and eggplant on hotter part of grill. Cook swordfish, uncovered, until streaked with dark grill marks, 6 to 9 minutes, gently flipping steaks using 2 spatulas halfway through cooking. Cook eggplant, flipping as needed, until softened and lightly charred, about 8 minutes; transfer to serving platter and tent with aluminum foil.

5. Gently move swordfish to cooler part of grill and continue to cook, uncovered, until fish flakes apart when gently prodded with paring knife and registers 140 degrees, 1 to 3 minutes per side; transfer to platter and tent with foil. Let swordfish rest while finishing salad.

Grilled Swordfish with Eggplant, Tomato, and Chickpea Salad

6. Chop eggplant coarse and add to bowl with reserved cilantro mixture along with tomatoes and chickpeas. Gently toss to combine and season with salt and pepper to taste. Serve.

Fava Bean Pesto Pasta

Serves 4 to 6 | **Total Time** 40 minutes `FAST`

WHY THIS RECIPE WORKS Creamy fava beans make an ideal base for pesto, which taps into their rich body. Buzz most of the blanched beans in a food processor with some almonds, olive oil, Pecorino Romano, dill, and lemon, and you've got a velvety, protein-rich pasta sauce. Then toss in a handful of whole ones for bursts of grass-green color and supple smoothness. Blanching and shocking the beans makes it easy to remove their waxy sheath without compromising their texture or fresh, nutty flavor. The cooking process softens pectin in the coating, making it flexible enough to be squeezed or peeled away. Look for fresh fava beans at farmers' markets or in the produce section of supermarkets; choose bright green, unblemished pods.

> **Substitution:** You can use an equal amount of frozen shelled fava beans in place of fresh. Do not thaw before using. Be sure to remove the sheath. Skip step 1 if using frozen favas.

1½ pounds fava beans, shelled (1¼ cups), divided
½ cup plus 1½ teaspoons fresh dill, divided
½ cup slivered almonds
6 tablespoons extra-virgin olive oil
¼ cup grated Pecorino Romano cheese
½ teaspoon table salt, plus salt for cooking pasta
1 pound spaghetti
1 tablespoon grated lemon zest

1. Bring 4 quarts water to boil in large pot. Fill large bowl halfway with ice and water. Add fava beans to boiling water and cook for 1 minute. Using slotted spoon, transfer fava beans to ice water and let cool, about 2 minutes. (Set aside cooking water.) Transfer fava beans to triple layer of paper towels and dry well. Using paring knife, make small cut along edge of each bean through waxy sheath, then gently squeeze sheath to release beans; discard sheath.

2. Transfer one-third of beans to small bowl. Add remaining beans to food processor along with ½ cup dill, almonds, oil, Pecorino, and salt. Process until combined, about 1 minute, scraping down sides of bowl halfway through processing (pesto will be quite thick and not completely smooth). Transfer pesto to large bowl.

3. Return cooking water to boil. Add pasta and 1 tablespoon salt and cook, stirring often, until al dente. Reserve 2 cups cooking water, then drain pasta.

4. Add lemon zest and 1½ cups cooking water to pesto and whisk until combined. Add pasta and reserved beans and toss until pasta is coated in creamy, lightly thickened sauce, 1 to 2 minutes, adjusting consistency with remaining cooking water as needed. Sprinkle with remaining 1½ teaspoons dill and season with salt to taste. Serve immediately.

NOTES FROM THE TEST KITCHEN

WHAT MAKES FAVAS SO CREAMY?
Water-soluble proteins within the bean makes them luxuriously creamy, even when cooked briefly. In fact, fava protein is sometimes used to add richness to vegan cheese and other dairy-free products.

Fava Bean Pesto Pasta

Cauliflower and Bean Paella

Serves 4 | **Total Time** 1¼ hours VEGAN

WHY THIS RECIPE WORKS Paella de verduras—a common, versatile approach to the beloved rice dish that's prepared throughout Spain—showcases vegetables rather than merely using them to flavor the rice. Here we feature green beans and butter beans, plus chunky cauliflower florets. In lieu of a meaty fond, we add savory backbone with a retooled Spanish sofrito, using browned bell pepper, umami-rich tomato paste, and lots of garlic to make a complex flavor base. Smoked paprika, saffron, and nutty-tasting dry sherry add brightness and depth. We parcook the beans and cauliflower on their own and then place the vegetables on top of the rice so they can finish cooking with the rest of the dish. Continuing to cook the rice after the liquid in the pan has evaporated creates a caramelized, crisp-chewy layer called a socarrat that adds even more complexity. Letting the paella rest for a few minutes before serving helps the socarrat layer firm up so it is even crispier and releases easily from the pan.

Substitution: You can use Bomba or Arborio rice in place of the Calasparra.

- 3 tablespoons extra-virgin olive oil, divided
- 2½ cups 2- to 2½-inch cauliflower florets
- ¾ teaspoon table salt, divided
- 6 ounces green beans, trimmed and cut into 2- to 2½-inch pieces
- 1 red bell pepper, stemmed, seeded, and chopped fine
- 1 tablespoon tomato paste
- 3 garlic cloves, minced
- 1 teaspoon smoked paprika
- ¼ teaspoon saffron threads, crumbled
- ¼ cup dry sherry
- 1 cup Calasparra rice
- 1 (15-ounce) can butter beans, rinsed
- 3½ cups vegetable broth
  Lemon wedges

1. Heat 1½ tablespoons oil in 12-inch skillet over medium heat until shimmering. Add cauliflower and ¼ teaspoon salt and cook, stirring frequently, until cauliflower is spotty brown, 3 to 5 minutes. Add green beans and ¼ teaspoon salt. Continue to cook, stirring frequently, until green beans are dark green, 2 to 4 minutes. Transfer vegetables to bowl.

2. Heat remaining 1½ tablespoons oil in now-empty skillet over medium heat until shimmering. Add bell pepper and remaining ¼ teaspoon salt and cook, stirring occasionally,

Cauliflower and Bean Paella

until bell pepper starts to brown, 7 to 10 minutes. Add tomato paste and cook, stirring constantly, until bell pepper pieces are coated in tomato paste, about 1 minute. Add garlic, paprika, and saffron and cook, stirring constantly, until fragrant, about 30 seconds. Stir in sherry and cook, stirring frequently, until excess moisture has evaporated and bell pepper mixture forms large clumps, 1 to 2 minutes.

3. Add rice and stir until very well combined. Off heat, smooth into even layer. Scatter butter beans evenly over rice. Scatter cauliflower and green beans evenly over butter beans. Gently pour broth all over, making sure rice is fully submerged (it's OK if parts of vegetables aren't submerged).

4. Bring to boil over high heat. Adjust heat to maintain gentle simmer and cook until broth is just below top of rice, 12 to 17 minutes. Cover and cook until rice is cooked through, about 5 minutes. Uncover and cook until rice pops and sizzles and all excess moisture has evaporated (to test, use butter knife to gently push aside some rice and vegetables), 3 to 7 minutes. (If socarrat is desired, continue to cook, rotating skillet quarter turn every 20 seconds, until rice on bottom of skillet is well browned and slightly crusty [use butter knife to test], 2 to 5 minutes.) Let rest off heat for 5 minutes. Serve, passing lemon wedges separately.

FOR THE BEST PAELLA, USE ONE OF THESE SPANISH RICES

These renowned rices, beloved by Spanish cooks, cook up plump, soft, and creamy. Rice has been an important agricultural product in Spain since the Moors arrived from North Africa nearly 1,300 years ago and built the infrastructure necessary to cultivate it. This grain is now part of the fabric of Spanish cuisine—most famously, in its paellas.

The most renowned paella rices come from one of Spain's three regulated denominaciones de origen protegida (DOP): Calasparra, Valencia, and Delta del Ebro. Some of these rices are sold under the name of their DOP (such as arroz de Calasparra), and others are labeled by cultivar—Bomba, which is grown in all three regions, is one such rice. In addition to cooking up plump, soft, and creamy, short-grain rices such as Bomba and arroz de Calasparra boast several qualities that make them a more desirable choice than long-grain rices in paella. First, these rices' starch structure allows them to absorb more of the rich flavors of the stock and aromatics of a paella without turning to mush and to endure the roughhousing of boiling without breaking. Paella rice also has a high degree of pearling, meaning it has concentrated starch at its center that gives the rice a bright-white color and extra creaminess when cooked. When purchasing Bomba rice or arroz de Calasparra for recipes such as our Cauliflower and Bean Paella (page 206), look for DOP on the label for the highest quality.

White Bean and Mushroom Gratin

Serves 4 to 6 | **Total Time** 1½ hours, plus 20 minutes resting VEGAN

WHY THIS RECIPE WORKS Our vegetarian gratin features creamy white beans; meaty cremini mushrooms; tender carrots; and a crisp, toasty layer of bread. The gravy's flavor is created from the fond developed by carefully sautéing mushrooms and aromatics and deglazing with nutty dry sherry. The combination of flour and starchy canned bean liquid thickens the gravy. We bake the gratin in a low oven after topping it with lightly seasoned and oiled bread cubes. As it bakes, the lower portion of the bread merges with the gratin, creating a lovely soft texture, while the upper portion dries out. Then, by flipping on the broiler for just a few minutes, we toast the bread until it is golden brown and crisp. The final product is complex in flavor and features a variety of textures. We prefer a round rustic loaf (also known as a boule) with a chewy, open crumb and a sturdy crust for this recipe.

½ cup extra-virgin olive oil, divided
10 ounces cremini mushrooms, trimmed and sliced ½ inch thick
¾ teaspoon table salt
½ teaspoon pepper, divided
4–5 slices country-style bread, cut into ½-inch pieces (5 cups)
¼ cup minced fresh parsley, divided
1 cup water
1 tablespoon all-purpose flour
1 small onion, chopped fine
5 garlic cloves, minced
1 tablespoon tomato paste
1½ teaspoons minced fresh thyme
⅓ cup dry sherry
2 (15-ounce) cans great northern beans, undrained
3 carrots, peeled, halved lengthwise, and cut into ¾-inch pieces

1. Adjust oven rack to middle position and heat oven to 300 degrees. Heat ¼ cup oil in 12-inch skillet over medium-high heat until shimmering. Add mushrooms, salt, and ¼ teaspoon pepper and cook, stirring occasionally, until mushrooms are well browned, 8 to 12 minutes.

2. While mushrooms cook, toss bread, 3 tablespoons parsley, remaining ¼ cup oil, and remaining ¼ teaspoon pepper together in bowl; set aside. Stir water and flour in second bowl until no lumps of flour remain; set aside.

3. Reduce heat to medium; add onion to skillet; and continue to cook, stirring frequently, until onion is translucent, 4 to 6 minutes. Reduce heat to medium-low; add garlic, tomato paste, and thyme; and cook, stirring constantly, until bottom of skillet is dark brown, 2 to 3 minutes. Add sherry and cook, scraping up any browned bits.

4. Add beans and their liquid, carrots, and flour mixture. Bring to boil over high heat. Off heat, arrange bread mixture over surface in even layer. Transfer skillet to oven and bake for 40 minutes. (Liquid should have consistency of thin gravy.)

5. Leave skillet in oven and turn on broiler. Broil until croutons are golden brown, 4 to 7 minutes. Remove gratin from oven and let sit for 20 minutes. Sprinkle with remaining 1 tablespoon parsley and serve.

White Bean Gratin with Rosemary and Parmesan

Serves 4 | **Total Time** 20 minutes **FAST**

WHY THIS RECIPE WORKS A creamy, bubbly gratin is a comforting and supremely satisfying way to take advantage of convenient canned beans. Mashing some of the beans before adding them to the dish gives the finished product the saucy texture of long-simmered beans in just 10 minutes. Broiling the beans in chicken broth allows them to absorb the rich flavor. For a straightforward and savory casserole, we limit the supporting ingredients to the classics: onion, garlic, rosemary. You will need an 8-inch broiler-safe baking dish or pan for this recipe. This recipe can be easily doubled using a 13 by 9-inch broiler-safe baking pan.

    1 onion, chopped fine
    2 tablespoons extra-virgin olive oil
    3 garlic cloves, minced
    1 teaspoon minced fresh rosemary or ¼ teaspoon dried
    2 (15-ounce) can cannellini beans, rinsed, divided
    ½ cup vegetable broth
    2 ounces Parmesan cheese, grated (1 cup)

1. Microwave onion, oil, garlic, and rosemary in medium bowl, stirring occasionally, until onion is softened, about 5 minutes.

2. Adjust oven rack to middle position and heat broiler. Add ⅔ cup beans to bowl with onion mixture and mash with potato masher until smooth. Stir in broth and remaining whole beans until combined. Transfer mixture to 8-inch square broiler-safe baking dish or pan and sprinkle evenly with Parmesan. Broil until mixture is bubbling around edges and cheese is golden brown, 5 to 7 minutes. Transfer dish to wire rack and let cool slightly before serving.

Cheesy Bean and Tomato Bake

Serves 4 to 6 | **Total Time** 55 minutes

WHY THIS RECIPE WORKS This quick bake is family-friendly and supereasy, perfect to cook with your kids. It's a dinner they will devour and all it takes is some creamy canned cannellini beans, cheese, tomatoes, and onions. Oregano, garlic, and panko lend a helping hand, adding more flavor and some crunch.

White Bean Gratin with Rosemary and Parmesan

Cheesy Bean and Tomato Bake

- 3 tablespoons extra-virgin olive oil, divided
- 1 small onion, chopped fine
- ¾ teaspoon table salt
- 3 garlic cloves, minced
- 1 teaspoon dried oregano
  Pinch red pepper flakes (optional)
- 1 (28-ounce) can crushed tomatoes
- ⅓ cup water
  Pinch sugar
- 2 (15-ounce) cans cannellini beans, rinsed
- 4 ounces mozzarella cheese, shredded (1 cup), divided
- ½ ounce Parmesan cheese, grated (¼ cup)
- ½ cup panko bread crumbs

1. Adjust oven rack to middle position and heat oven to 475 degrees. Heat 1 tablespoon oil in 12-inch skillet over medium heat until shimmering. Add onion and salt and cook until softened, about 5 minutes. Stir in garlic; oregano; and pepper flakes, if using, and cook until fragrant, about 30 seconds.

2. Stir in tomatoes, water, and sugar and bring to boil. Reduce heat to medium-low and simmer, stirring occasionally, until slightly thickened, about 10 minutes.

3. Stir in beans and cook until warmed through, about 5 minutes. Remove skillet from heat. Stir in half of mozzarella and Parmesan, then spread beans into even layer. Sprinkle remaining mozzarella evenly over top. Combine panko and remaining 2 tablespoons oil in bowl, then sprinkle evenly over top of cheese in skillet.

4. Bake until cheese is melted and panko is well browned, 5 to 8 minutes. Remove skillet from oven and let cool for 5 minutes. Serve.

White Beans with Caramelized Onions, Fennel, and Gruyère

Serves 6 | **Total Time** 2 hours

WHY THIS RECIPE WORKS Combining canned white beans with the elements of French onion soup—cheesy croutons and all—makes a comforting favorite even more cozy. We start by caramelizing onion and fennel (for faintly sweet, licorice background notes) in the rendered fat of crisped pancetta. Sherry, beef broth, and canned cannellini beans and their canning liquid give the mixture sauciness, but also body.

After a short simmer to allow the flavors to meld, we top our skillet dinner with a layer of crisp croutons and handfuls of Gruyère and Parmesan cheese before placing it in a hot oven. A final sprinkle of fennel fronds and crispy pancetta makes this dish as pretty as it is satisfying. Use the large holes of a box grater to shred the Gruyère and Parmesan. We like using a baguette for this recipe for its crust, but you will have some left over; you can use another crusty bread instead.

Substitution: We like cannellini's creaminess, size, and thin skins but any canned white bean will work.

- 8 ounces baguette, cut into 1-inch pieces
- 4 ounces pancetta, cut into ¼-inch pieces
- 1 large onion, halved and sliced ¼ inch thick through root end
- 1 fennel bulb, 2 tablespoons fronds minced, stalks discarded, bulbs halved, cored, and sliced thin
- ½ cup water
- ½ teaspoon table salt
- 3 garlic cloves, minced
- 2 teaspoons minced fresh thyme or ¾ teaspoon dried
- ½ teaspoon pepper
- ½ cup dry sherry
- 2 (15-ounce) cans cannellini beans, undrained
- 1 cup beef broth
- 1 bay leaf
- 4 ounces Gruyère cheese, shredded (1 cup)
- 2 ounces Parmesan cheese, shredded (⅔ cup)

1. Adjust oven rack to middle position and heat oven to 250 degrees. Arrange bread in single layer on rimmed baking sheet and bake until bread is dry and crisp, about 30 minutes. Set aside. Increase oven temperature to 500 degrees.

2. Add pancetta to 12-inch skillet and cook over medium-low heat until fat is rendered and pancetta is crisp, about 10 minutes. Using slotted spoon, transfer pancetta to paper-towel lined plate; set aside.

3. Pour off all but 2 tablespoons fat left in skillet (add extra oil as needed to equal 2 tablespoons), then add onion, fennel, water, and salt and bring to boil over medium-high heat. Cover and cook until water has evaporated and onion starts to sizzle, 8 to 10 minutes.

4. Uncover; reduce heat to medium-low; and cook until onion is softened and well browned, adjusting heat as needed to prevent scorching, about 20 minutes, stirring frequently.

5. Increase heat to medium; add garlic, thyme, and pepper; and cook until fragrant, about 30 seconds. Stir in sherry, scraping up browned bits, and cook until evaporated, 3 to 5 minutes. Stir in beans and their liquid, broth, and bay leaf and bring to simmer. Cover; reduce heat to low; and cook until thickened slightly, about 15 minutes.

6. Discard bay leaf, then arrange reserved bread evenly over bean mixture. Sprinkle with Gruyère, Parmesan, and reserved pancetta. Transfer to oven and bake until cheese is melted and bubbly, 5 to 7 minutes. Let cool for 5 minutes, then sprinkle with fennel fronds and serve.

Burst Cherry Tomato Puttanesca with Roman Beans

Serves 4 | **Total Time** 40 minutes **FAST**

WHY THIS RECIPE WORKS Creamy canned Roman beans (also known as cranberry beans) turn punchy, bold puttanesca sauce into a quick and easy one-pan meal. For a fast, fresh tomato sauce, we use sweet, readily available cherry tomatoes and cook them with a two-step process: First we let them blister, undisturbed, in a hot skillet. Then we add the beans along with the classic puttanesca ingredients—anchovies, capers, olives, and pepper flakes—and cook a few more minutes until the tomatoes turn juicy and are partially broken down. Crispy panko bread crumbs flavored with lemon and basil finish our dish with bright flavor and contrasting texture. Make sure the cherry tomatoes are no larger than 1 inch in diameter or they won't burst in the given time range.

- 3 tablespoon extra-virgin olive oil, divided, plus extra for drizzling
- ½ cup panko bread crumbs
- ¼ cup minced fresh basil
- 1 teaspoon grated lemon zest
- ⅛ teaspoon pepper
- 1 pound cherry tomatoes
- 2 (15-ounce) cans Roman beans, rinsed
- ½ cup pitted kalamata olives, chopped coarse
- 3 tablespoons capers, rinsed and minced
- 3 anchovy fillets, rinsed, patted dry, and minced
- 3 garlic cloves, minced
- ½ teaspoon table salt
- ¼ teaspoon red pepper flakes
- ¼ teaspoon sugar

1. Heat 1 tablespoon oil and panko in 12-inch skillet over medium heat, stirring occasionally until panko is golden brown, 4 to 5 minutes. Transfer panko to medium bowl and let cool to room temperature, about 10 minutes. Stir in basil, lemon zest, and pepper. Wipe skillet clean.

2. Heat remaining 2 tablespoons oil in now-empty skillet over medium heat until shimmering. Add tomatoes and stir to coat evenly in oil. Cook, partially covered, without stirring until tomatoes have blistered on bottom, about 3 minutes.

3. Stir in beans, olives, capers, anchovies, garlic, salt, pepper flakes, and sugar and continue to cook until beans are warmed through and tomato juices have formed a light sauce, about 3 minutes. Serve, topping individual portions with panko mixture and drizzling with extra oil.

Loaded Sweet Potatoes

Serves 4 to 6 | **Total Time** 1 hour

WHY THIS RECIPE WORKS For a quick dinner that kids and grownups alike will love, we start with sweet potatoes, which are a little heartier than your standard starchy russets, and load them up with black beans and cheese to make a hearty meal, with a little zing coming from chipotle chiles. First we microwave the sweet potatoes, scoop out the tasty insides, and pop the shells in the oven. The sweet potato flesh gets mashed up with cheddar and chipotle chiles in adobo sauce (use more or less depending on how spicy you like things). Once the shells are a little crispy, we layer on the black beans and scallions and dollop the cheesy mashed sweet potatoes on top. A final sprinkle of more gooey cheese adds richness and keeps the filling from drying out.

- 4 small sweet potatoes (8 ounces each), unpeeled, lightly pricked all over with fork
- 6 ounces cheddar cheese, shredded (1½ cups), divided
- 1–2 tablespoons minced canned chipotle chile in adobo sauce
- ¼ teaspoon table salt
- 1 (15-ounce) can black beans, rinsed
- 1 tablespoon extra-virgin olive oil
- 3 scallions, white parts minced, green parts sliced thin

1. Adjust oven rack to middle position and heat oven to 425 degrees. Microwave potatoes on large plate, flipping every 3 minutes, until paring knife glides easily through flesh, 9 to 12 minutes. Let potatoes cool for 5 minutes.

2. Halve each potato lengthwise. Using spoon, scoop flesh from each potato half into medium bowl, leaving ⅛- to ¼-inch thickness of flesh; set aside. Place shells cut side up on wire rack set in rimmed baking sheet and bake until dry and slightly crispy, about 10 minutes.

3. Meanwhile, mash reserved potato flesh with potato masher until smooth. Stir in ¾ cup cheddar, chipotle, and salt until well combined. Season with salt and pepper to taste.

4. Toss beans with oil and scallion whites, then divide evenly among parbaked shells. Top with mashed potato mixture and sprinkle with remaining ¾ cup cheddar. Return filled potatoes to rack in baking sheet and bake until spotty brown and warmed through, about 20 minutes. Sprinkle with scallion greens. Serve.

Cuban-Style Black Beans and Rice

Serves 6 to 8 as a main dish or 8 to 10 as a side dish | **Total Time** 2¼ hours, plus 8 hours soaking VEGAN

WHY THIS RECIPE WORKS Beans and rice is a familiar combination the world over, but the Cuban dish is unique in that the rice is cooked in the inky concentrated liquid left over from cooking the beans, thus rendering the grains flavorful too. We simmer a portion of the sofrito (the traditional combination of garlic, bell pepper, and onion) with our beans to infuse them with flavor and then use the liquid to cook our rice and beans together. Lightly browning the remaining sofrito vegetables and spices with rendered salt pork adds complex meatiness, and finishing the dish in the oven eliminates the crusty bottom that can form when the dish is cooked on the stove. It is important to use lean—not fatty—salt pork. If you can't find it, substitute six slices of bacon. If using bacon, decrease the cooking time in step 4 to 8 minutes. You will need a Dutch oven with a tight-fitting lid for this recipe. For a vegan version, use water instead of chicken broth, omit the salt pork, add 1 tablespoon tomato paste with the vegetables in step 4, and increase the amount of salt in step 5 to 1½ teaspoons.

Burst Cherry Tomato Puttanesca with Roman Beans

Loaded Sweet Potatoes

Cuban-Style Black Beans and Rice

1. Dissolve 1½ tablespoons salt in 2 quarts cold water in large container. Add beans and soak at room temperature for at least 8 hours or up to 24 hours. Drain and rinse well. (If you're pressed for time, see page 13 for information on quick brining your beans.)

2. Combine soaked beans, broth, 2 cups water, 1 bell pepper half, 1 onion half (with root end), halved garlic head, bay leaves, and 1 teaspoon salt in Dutch oven. Bring to simmer over medium-high heat, cover, and reduce heat to low. Cook until beans are just soft, 30 to 40 minutes. Discard bell pepper, onion, garlic, and bay leaves, then drain beans in colander set over large bowl, reserving 2½ cups bean cooking liquid. (If you don't have enough bean cooking liquid, add water to equal 2½ cups.) Do not wash out Dutch oven.

3. Adjust oven rack to middle position and heat oven to 350 degrees. Cut remaining bell peppers and onion into 2-inch pieces and process in food processor until broken into rough ¼-inch pieces, about 8 pulses, scraping down sides of bowl as necessary; set vegetables aside.

4. In now-empty Dutch oven, cook 1 tablespoon oil and salt pork over medium-low heat, stirring frequently, until lightly browned and rendered, 15 to 20 minutes. Add remaining 1 tablespoon oil, reserved processed vegetables, cumin, and oregano. Increase heat to medium and cook, stirring frequently, until vegetables are softened and beginning to brown, 10 to 15 minutes. Add minced garlic and cook, stirring constantly, until fragrant, about 1 minute. Add rice and stir to coat, about 30 seconds.

5. Stir in beans, reserved bean cooking liquid, vinegar, and remaining ½ teaspoon salt. Increase heat to medium-high and bring to simmer. Cover and transfer to oven. Bake until liquid is absorbed and rice is tender, about 30 minutes. Fluff with fork and let rest, uncovered, for 5 minutes. Serve, passing scallions and lime wedges separately.

1½ tablespoons table salt for brining
1 cup dried black beans, picked over and rinsed
2 cups chicken broth
2 large green bell peppers, halved and seeded, divided
1 large onion, halved at equator and peeled, root end left intact, divided
1 head garlic, 5 cloves removed and minced, remaining head halved at equator with skin left intact
2 bay leaves
1½ teaspoons table salt, divided
2 tablespoons extra-virgin olive oil, divided
6 ounces salt pork, cut into ¼-inch pieces
4 teaspoons ground cumin
1 tablespoon minced fresh oregano
1½ cups long grain white rice, rinsed
2 tablespoons red wine vinegar
2 scallions, sliced thin
Lime wedges

Gigantes Plaki

Serves 4 to 6 | **Total Time** 2¼ hours, plus 8 hours soaking

WHY THIS RECIPE WORKS Gigantes plaki is a popular bean dish that can be found throughout Greece both as meze at tavernas and on family dining tables, most often during Lent. The name simply refers to the type of beans (gigantes) and the style of cooking them in a baking dish in the oven (plaki). The beans absorb the juices and flavors of generous amounts of olive oil, tomatoes, and aromatics, becoming creamy, luxurious, and meaty-textured within a scrumptious casserole with caramelized edges and an intriguing aroma.

Gigantes Plaki

1. Dissolve 1½ tablespoons salt in 2 quarts cold water in large container. Add beans and soak at room temperature for at least 8 hours or up to 24 hours. Drain and rinse well. (If you're pressed for time, see page 13 for more information on quick brining your beans.)

2. Bring soaked beans and 3 quarts water to boil in Dutch oven. Reduce heat and simmer, stirring occasionally, until beans are tender, 1 to 1½ hours. (Skim any loose bean skins or foam from surface of liquid as beans cook.) Drain beans and set aside. Wipe out pot with paper towels.

3. Adjust oven rack to middle position and heat oven to 400 degrees. Heat oil in now-empty pot over medium heat until shimmering. Add onion, carrots, celery, and salt and cook until softened and beginning to brown, 7 to 10 minutes. Stir in tomato paste, garlic, oregano, and cinnamon and cook until fragrant, about 30 seconds. Add tomatoes and their juices and 1¼ cups water, scraping up any browned bits. Stir in reserved beans, honey, and bay leaves, and bring to simmer. Season with salt and pepper to taste.

4. Transfer bean mixture to 13 by 9-inch baking dish, smoothing top with rubber spatula. Transfer dish to oven and bake until beans are cooked through and edges are golden brown and bubbling, 30 to 45 minutes. Let cool for 15 minutes, then sprinkle with dill and drizzle with extra oil. Serve.

Onion, celery, carrots, and garlic form the base of the aromatics along with beloved Greek oregano; hints of warmth from cinnamon and sweetness from a touch of honey balance the acidity of the tomato-heavy sauce.

1½ tablespoons table salt for brining
1 pound (2½ cups) dried gigante beans or dried large lima beans, picked over and rinsed
¼ cup extra-virgin olive oil, plus extra for drizzling
1 onion, chopped
2 carrots, peeled and chopped
2 celery ribs, chopped
1 teaspoon table salt
2 tablespoons tomato paste
4 garlic cloves, minced
1 tablespoon chopped fresh oregano or 1 teaspoon dried
¼ teaspoon ground cinnamon
1 (14.5-ounce) can whole peeled tomatoes, drained with juice reserved, chopped
1 tablespoon honey
2 bay leaves
2 tablespoons chopped fresh dill

Espinacas con Garbanzos

Serves 4 | **Total Time** 50 minutes VEGAN

WHY THIS RECIPE WORKS Espinacas con garbanzos is a regional spinach and chickpea dish native to Seville. In Spain, spinach loves chickpeas, as this dish shows. The dish, which has a strong Arab influence, is substantial and full of flavor. Briefly simmering canned chickpeas (uniformly tender, well seasoned, and convenient) in a combination of chicken broth and chickpea canning liquid tenderizes them and ensures that the flavor of this main ingredient is extra savory. A picada (a paste of garlic and bread cooked in plenty of olive oil) thickens and seasons the sauce like magic. Smoked paprika and spices such as cumin, cinnamon, and saffron imbue this extra-special picada with heady aromas, and tomatoes and vinegar boost its tang. Red wine vinegar can be substituted for the sherry vinegar.

1 loaf crusty bread, divided

2 (15-ounce) cans chickpeas (1 can drained and rinsed, 1 can undrained)

1½ cups vegetable broth

6 tablespoons extra-virgin olive oil, divided

6 garlic cloves, minced

1 tablespoon smoked paprika

1 teaspoon ground cumin

¼ teaspoon table salt

⅛ teaspoon ground cinnamon

⅛ teaspoon cayenne pepper

1 small pinch saffron

2 small plum tomatoes, halved lengthwise, flesh shredded on large holes of box grater and skins discarded

4 teaspoons sherry vinegar, plus extra for seasoning

10 ounces frozen chopped spinach, thawed and squeezed dry

1. Cut 1½-ounce piece from loaf of bread (thickness will vary depending on size of loaf) and tear into 1-inch pieces. Process in food processor until finely ground (you should have ¾ cup crumbs). Combine chickpeas and broth in large saucepan and bring to boil over high heat. Adjust heat to maintain simmer and cook until level of liquid is just below top layer of chickpeas, about 10 minutes.

2. While chickpeas cook, heat ¼ cup oil in 10-inch nonstick skillet over medium heat until just shimmering. Add bread crumbs and cook, stirring frequently, until deep golden brown, 3 to 4 minutes. Add garlic, paprika, cumin, salt, cinnamon, cayenne, and saffron and cook until fragrant, 30 seconds. Stir in tomatoes and vinegar and remove from heat.

3. Stir bread mixture and spinach into chickpeas in saucepan. Continue to simmer, stirring occasionally, until mixture is thick and stew-like, 5 to 10 minutes. Off heat, stir in remaining 2 tablespoons oil. Cover and let sit for 5 minutes. Season with salt and extra vinegar to taste. Serve with remaining bread.

Stuffed Peppers with Chickpeas, Goat Cheese, and Herbs

Serves 6 | **Total Time** 1½ hours

WHY THIS RECIPE WORKS For a light and summery take on stuffed peppers, we nixed the typical meat-and-rice filling. Instead, we roast bell peppers until they are slightly blistered and soft and make a hearty stuffing for them with coarsely mashed chickpeas and chunks of crispy toasted bread, flavored with garlic, scallion, parsley, and capers. Lemon zest adds brightness, and 6 ounces of goat cheese is just enough to bind the filling without overpowering the other flavors.

½ cup extra-virgin olive oil, divided, plus extra for drizzling

6 (7- to 8-ounce) bell peppers

1½ teaspoons table salt, divided

1¼ teaspoons pepper, divided

1 (15-ounce) can chickpeas, rinsed

7 ounces baguette, cut into ½-inch pieces (4 cups)

8 garlic cloves, minced

¼ teaspoon red pepper flakes

8 scallions, sliced

¼ cup minced fresh parsley

¼ cup minced fresh basil

3 tablespoons capers, chopped

1 tablespoon grated lemon zest plus 1 tablespoon juice

6 ounces goat cheese, crumbled (1½ cups)

Espinacas con Garbanzos

1. Adjust oven rack to upper-middle position and heat oven to 475 degrees. Grease 13 by 9-inch baking pan with 1 tablespoon oil. Cut off top ½ inch of bell peppers and reserve; discard stems and seeds. Arrange bell peppers and their tops cut side down in prepared pan. Brush bell peppers and tops with 1 tablespoon oil, then sprinkle with ½ teaspoon salt and ¼ teaspoon pepper.

2. Roast until bell peppers are softened and beginning to blister, about 20 minutes. Flip bell peppers cut side up and let sit until cool enough to handle, about 5 minutes. Adjust oven temperature to 350 degrees.

3. Using potato masher, mash chickpeas coarse in large bowl. Chop bell pepper tops into ¼-inch pieces and add to bowl with chickpeas.

4. Heat ¼ cup oil in 12-inch nonstick skillet over medium heat until shimmering. Add bread and cook, stirring occasionally, until light golden brown and crispy, 5 to 7 minutes. Push bread to 1 side of skillet and add remaining 2 tablespoons oil to skillet. Add garlic and pepper flakes and cook until fragrant, about 30 seconds. Stir garlic mixture and ½ teaspoon salt into bread in skillet then transfer to bowl with chickpea mixture to cool completely, about 10 minutes.

5. Stir scallions, parsley, basil, capers, lemon zest and juice, remaining ½ teaspoon salt, and remaining 1 teaspoon pepper into chickpea mixture. Gently fold in goat cheese until combined.

6. Divide filling evenly among bell peppers, mounding slightly. Bake until filling registers between 100 and 120 degrees and begins to brown on top, 15 to 20 minutes. Transfer to platter and drizzle with extra oil. Serve.

Vegetable Tagine with Chickpeas and Olives

Serves 4 | **Total Time** 45 minutes FAST VEGAN

WHY THIS RECIPE WORKS Traditional North African tagines—fragrant stews of vegetables, beans, dried fruits, and slowly braised meats—are long-simmered affairs. But emphasizing the chickpeas and vegetables and skipping the meat makes this tagine fast enough for any weeknight without sacrificing flavor. We use canned chickpeas for speed, and we microwave the potatoes and carrots before adding them to the pot to streamline the process even further. Using a combination of garam masala and paprika shortens the spice list. Green olives, golden raisins, and lemon emphasize Moroccan flavors. We prefer our homemade Garam Masala (page 216), but you may use store-bought.

Vegetable Tagine with Chickpeas and Olives

1 pound red potatoes, cut into ½-inch pieces
1 pound carrots, peeled and cut into ½-inch pieces
¼ cup extra-virgin olive oil, divided
1 teaspoon table salt
½ teaspoon pepper
1 onion, halved and sliced thin
4 (3-inch) strips lemon zest, sliced into matchsticks, plus 2 tablespoons juice
5 garlic cloves, minced
4 teaspoons paprika
2 teaspoons Garam Masala (page 216)
3 cups vegetable broth
2 (15-ounce) cans chickpeas, rinsed
½ cup pitted green olives, halved
½ cup golden raisins
¼ cup minced fresh cilantro

1. Microwave potatoes, carrots, 2 tablespoons oil, salt, and pepper in covered bowl until vegetables begin to soften, about 10 minutes.

2. Meanwhile, heat remaining 2 tablespoons oil in Dutch oven over medium-high heat until shimmering. Add onion and lemon zest and cook until onion begins to brown, about 8 minutes. Stir in garlic, paprika, and garam masala and cook until fragrant, about 30 seconds.

3. Add microwaved potatoes and carrots to Dutch oven and stir to coat with spices. Stir in broth, chickpeas, olives, and raisins. Cover and simmer gently until flavors blend, about 10 minutes. Uncover and simmer until vegetables are tender and sauce is slightly thickened, about 7 minutes. Stir in lemon juice and cilantro and season with salt and pepper to taste. Serve.

Garam Masala

Makes ½ cup
Total Time 5 minutes FAST VEGAN

   3 tablespoons black peppercorns
   8 teaspoons coriander seeds
   4 teaspoons cardamom pods
2½ teaspoons cumin seeds
1½ (3-inch) cinnamon sticks, broken into pieces

Process all ingredients in spice grinder until finely ground, about 30 seconds. (Garam masala can be stored in airtight container for up to 1 month.)

Fregula with Chickpeas, Tomatoes, and Fennel

Serves 4 to 6 | **Total Time** 1 hour

WHY THIS RECIPE WORKS As befits an Italian island situated in the Mediterranean, the food of Sardinia is at once unique to its isolated, rugged environment and reflective of the influence of the many invaders who reached the island's shores. Fregola sarda, or fregula, is one such example: a sun-dried and toasted spherical pasta, it is hand-rolled from semolina, similar to North African couscous. Chickpeas provide our fregula recipe with heartiness, and grape tomatoes give it bursts of sweet acidity along with enough liquid to create a risotto-like texture. We use licorice-scented fennel (a fresh bulb for sweetness, and seeds for more intense flavor) and piney rosemary—typical Sardinian aromatics—to give the dish its savory underpinnings. A final sprinkling of Pecorino Romano (try

Pecorino Sardo, made from the typical sheep's milk of Sardinia, if you can find it) adds just the right amount of richness and salt to complement the dish.

   3 tablespoons extra-virgin olive oil, plus extra for drizzling
   1 fennel bulb, ¼ cup fronds minced, stalks discarded, bulb halved, cored, and sliced thin
   1 onion, chopped fine
   3 garlic cloves, minced
   2 teaspoons minced fresh rosemary or ¾ teaspoon dried
   1 teaspoon fennel seeds
   ½ teaspoon table salt
   ½ teaspoon pepper
   ¼ teaspoon red pepper flakes
   4 cups water
   2 (15-ounce) cans chickpeas, undrained
  10 ounces grape tomatoes
   8 ounces (1⅓ cups) fregula
   1 tablespoon lemon juice
     Grated Pecorino Romano cheese

1. Heat oil in Dutch oven over medium heat until shimmering. Add fennel and onion and cook until vegetables are softened, 5 to 7 minutes. Stir in garlic, rosemary, fennel seeds, salt, pepper, and pepper flakes and cook until fragrant, about 30 seconds.

2. Stir in water, chickpeas and their liquid, tomatoes, and fregula and bring to boil. Reduce heat to medium-low and simmer until fregula is tender, about 25 minutes, stirring occasionally. Stir in lemon juice and fennel fronds and season with salt and pepper to taste. Serve, drizzling individual portions with extra oil and passing Pecorino separately.

Maftoul with Carrots and Chickpeas

Serves 4 | **Total Time** 35 minutes FAST VEGAN

WHY THIS RECIPE WORKS Maftoul, also known as Palestinian couscous, is traditionally made by hand-rolling bulgur in moistened wheat flour (generally a mix of whole-wheat and white flours) to create small balls of pasta. Its beige color and extra-nutty flavor make maftoul a unique addition to the hand-rolled pastas of the Mediterranean, like North African couscous (from which maftoul was likely derived) and Sardinian fregula, both made from semolina. While maftoul is traditionally served with a brothy stew of chicken, onions, and chickpeas ("maftoul" refers to both the pasta and the finished dish), we

Maftoul with Carrots and Chickpeas

1. Bring 2 quarts water to boil in medium saucepan. Add maftoul and 1½ teaspoons salt and cook, stirring occasionally, until just tender, 10 to 25 minutes. Drain and set aside.

2. While maftoul cooks, heat oil in large saucepan over medium-high heat until shimmering. Add onion and cook until softened and beginning to brown, 5 to 7 minutes. Reduce heat to medium, stir in garlic and baharat and cook until fragrant, about 30 seconds. Add carrots, broth, chickpeas, and salt and bring to boil. Reduce heat to maintain simmer and cook, stirring occasionally, until carrots are tender, 8 to 10 minutes.

3. Remove saucepan from heat; stir in reserved maftoul; and let sit, covered, until most of broth has been absorbed but dish is still saucy, 3 to 5 minutes. Stir in parsley and lemon juice and season with salt and pepper to taste. Serve.

Big-Batch Meatless Meat Sauce with Chickpeas and Mushrooms

Makes 6 cups; enough for 2 pounds pasta | **Total Time** 1 hour VEGAN

WHY THIS RECIPE WORKS Having a big batch of red sauce portioned out in the freezer can be a lifesaver on busy nights. We add protein and heft with chopped chickpeas. For this crowd-pleasing meatless version of a classic tomato-meat sauce, we start with cremini mushrooms and tomato paste—both rich sources of savory umami. Extra-virgin olive oil does double duty, both enriching the sauce and helping to toast the aromatics: garlic, dried oregano, and red pepper flakes. To thin the sauce without diluting its flavor, we add vegetable broth. Make sure to rinse the chickpeas after pulsing them in the food processor or the sauce will be too thick.

lean on the heartiness of this nutty, wholesome ingredient, and create a legume- and vegetable-forward dish, fragrant with warm spices. We prefer our homemade Baharat (page 243), but you may use store-bought. Because the size of maftoul can vary considerably, we provide a wide range of cook times. You can use an equal amount (by weight) of fregula or moghrabieh in place of the maftoul.

- 8 ounces (1⅓ cups) maftoul
- ½ teaspoon table salt, plus salt for cooking maftoul
- 2 tablespoons extra-virgin olive oil
- 1 red onion, sliced ½ inch thick
- 2 garlic cloves, minced
- 1 tablespoon baharat
- 1 pound carrots, peeled, cut crosswise into 1½- to 2-inch lengths, and halved lengthwise or quartered if thick
- 2 cups vegetable broth
- 1 (15-ounce) can chickpeas, rinsed
- ½ cup minced fresh parsley
- 1 tablespoon lemon juice

- 10 ounces cremini mushrooms, trimmed
- 1 onion, chopped
- 1 (15-ounce) can chickpeas, rinsed
- 6 tablespoons extra-virgin olive oil, divided
- 1 teaspoon table salt
- ¼ cup tomato paste
- 5 garlic cloves, minced
- 1¼ teaspoons dried oregano
- ¼ teaspoon red pepper flakes
- 1 (28-ounce) can crushed tomatoes
- 2 cups vegetable broth
- 2 tablespoons chopped fresh basil

1. Working in batches, pulse mushrooms in food processor until pieces are no larger than ⅛ to ¼ inch, 7 to 10 pulses, scraping down sides of bowl as needed; transfer to bowl. Pulse onion in now-empty food processor until finely chopped, 7 to 10 pulses, scraping down sides of bowl as needed; set aside separately. Pulse chickpeas in again-empty food processor until chopped into ¼-inch pieces, 7 to 10 pulses. Transfer chickpeas to fine-mesh strainer and rinse under cold running water until water runs clear; drain well.

2. Heat 5 tablespoons oil in Dutch oven over medium-high heat until shimmering. Add mushrooms and salt and cook, stirring occasionally, until mushrooms are browned and fond has formed on bottom of pot, about 8 minutes.

3. Stir in onion and cook until softened, about 5 minutes. Add tomato paste and cook, stirring constantly, until mixture is rust-colored, 1 to 2 minutes. Reduce heat to medium and push vegetables to sides of pot. Add remaining 1 tablespoon oil, garlic, oregano, and pepper flakes to center and cook, stirring constantly, until fragrant, about 30 seconds. Stir in tomatoes and broth and bring to simmer over high heat. Reduce heat to low and simmer sauce for 5 minutes, stirring occasionally.

4. Stir drained chickpeas into sauce in pot and simmer until sauce is slightly thickened, about 15 minutes. Stir in basil and season with salt and pepper to taste. (Sauce can be refrigerated for up to 2 days or frozen for up to 1 month.)

Thai Red Curry with Lentils and Tofu

Serves 4 | **Total Time** 1 hour, plus 20 minutes resting

WHY THIS RECIPE WORKS Thai curries embrace a delicate balance of flavors, textures, temperatures, and colors to produce lively, satisfying meals. This fresh-tasting curry features hearty lentils and tofu instead of meat, and uses just enough coconut milk to create a rich, fragrant sauce. We start by cooking the lentils in an aromatic red curry broth until they're tender but still slightly al dente and have absorbed most of the liquid. Then we stir in the coconut milk and add vibrant red bell pepper slices, snow peas, and cubes of tofu at the very end, simply warming them through to maintain the vegetables' color and crisp-fresh texture. A generous handful of fresh basil and a sprinkle of scallions gives the dish a brisk, heady finish. Do not use light coconut milk. You will need a 12-inch skillet with a tight-fitting lid.

Substitution: You can use brown, black, or regular green lentils in place of the lentilles de Puy but cooking times will vary (see page 16). Do not use red or yellow lentils in this recipe.

14 ounces extra-firm tofu, cut into ½-inch pieces
¼ teaspoon table salt
⅛ teaspoon pepper
1 tablespoon vegetable oil
1 tablespoon Thai red curry paste
2½ cups water
2 tablespoons fish sauce
1 cup dried lentilles du Puy, picked over and rinsed
½ cup canned coconut milk
1 red bell pepper, stemmed, seeded, and cut into ¼-inch-wide strips
4 ounces snow peas, strings removed, halved crosswise
½ cup coarsely chopped fresh basil
1 tablespoon lime juice
2 scallions, sliced thin

1. Spread tofu on paper towel–lined baking sheet and let drain for 20 minutes. Gently press dry with paper towels and sprinkle with salt and pepper.

2. Heat oil in 12-inch skillet over medium heat until shimmering. Add curry paste and cook, stirring constantly, until fragrant, about 1 minute. Stir in water, fish sauce, and lentils and bring to simmer. Cover, reduce heat to low, and simmer gently, stirring occasionally, until lentils are tender and about two-thirds of liquid has been absorbed, 30 to 35 minutes.

3. Stir in coconut milk until well combined. Add tofu, bell pepper, and snow peas, and increase heat to medium-high. Cover and cook, stirring occasionally, until tofu is warmed through and vegetables are crisp-tender, about 2 minutes.

4. Off heat, stir in basil and lime juice. Season with salt to taste, and sprinkle with scallions. Serve.

Herb Vegetable and Lentil Bake with Feta

Serves 4 | **Total Time** 55 minutes

WHY THIS RECIPE WORKS Dinner doesn't get much fresher than this. Lentils provide filling protein and a complementary earthy flavor to a garden's worth of roasted vegetables in this summery meal. In-season fennel, potatoes, zucchini, and tomatoes have a fresh sweetness that benefits from the savor of a cumin rub, and using canned lentils makes stirring them into the bake easy. Leaving the core in the fennel (it softens nicely) ensures that the pretty wedges stay intact and are easy to flip. Near the end of roasting, we sprinkle the vegetables with feta for a salty, briny flavor; it softens and browns appealingly over the dish. The finishing touch is a drizzle of an herbaceous oil made with handfuls of parsley, dill, and mint. Use small potatoes measuring 1 to 2 inches in diameter.

HERB OIL

- ½ cup fresh parsley leaves
- ¼ cup fresh dill
- ¼ cup fresh mint leaves
- ¼ cup extra-virgin olive oil
- 2 tablespoons lemon juice
- 1 garlic clove, minced

ROASTED VEGETABLES

- 8 ounces small Yukon gold or red potatoes, quartered
- 1 large fennel bulb, stalks discarded, bulb halved, core left intact, and cut through core into ½-inch-thick wedges
- 2 tablespoons extra-virgin olive oil, divided
- ¾ teaspoon ground cumin
- ¾ teaspoon table salt, divided
- ½ teaspoon pepper, divided
- 2 zucchini, cut ½ inch thick on bias
- 8 ounces cherry tomatoes
- 2 shallots, sliced thin
- 1 (15-ounce) can lentils, rinsed
- 4 ounces feta cheese, crumbled (1 cup)

1. FOR THE HERB OIL Pulse all ingredients in food processor until coarsely chopped, about 10 pulses, scraping down sides of bowl as needed. Transfer to bowl and season with salt to taste; set aside until ready to serve.

2. FOR THE ROASTED VEGETABLES Adjust oven rack to upper-middle position and heat oven to 475 degrees. Toss potatoes, fennel, 1 tablespoon oil, cumin, ½ teaspoon salt, and ¼ teaspoon pepper together in bowl. Arrange vegetables cut side down on rimmed baking sheet and cover tightly with aluminum foil. Roast until vegetables are beginning to brown and are nearly tender, 15 to 20 minutes.

3. Remove foil and flip fennel wedges. Toss zucchini, tomatoes, shallots, lentils, remaining 1 tablespoon oil, remaining ¼ teaspoon salt, and remaining ¼ teaspoon pepper together in bowl. Scatter evenly over top of vegetables on

sheet, then sprinkle with feta. Roast until tomatoes blister, feta starts to soften and brown slightly, and vegetables are tender, about 15 minutes. Drizzle with reserved herb oil and serve.

Red Lentil Kibbeh

Serves 4 | **Total Time** 1 hour

WHY THIS RECIPE WORKS Kibbeh is a popular Middle Eastern dish made from bulgur, minced onions, varying spices, and (traditionally) ground meat. During Lent, those who observe often prepare this common meal with lentils in lieu of meat, as the texture of the two is similar. Here, both the color and flavor of the red lentils are enhanced by two red pastes: Tomato paste brings sweetness and an umami quality, and harissa adds complexity. We give the bulgur a head start before adding the quicker-cooking lentils to the same pan, which allows both components to finish cooking at the same time. Lemon juice and parsley brighten the kibbeh. The spoonable mixture can be served on its own with some Bibb lettuce and yogurt, and it makes a showstopping addition to a larger spread, alongside dips or with nuts, pickled radishes, and pita. We prefer our homemade Harissa (page 116), but you may use store-bought.

Red Lentil Kibbeh

- 3 tablespoons extra-virgin olive oil, divided
- 1 onion, chopped fine
- 1 red bell pepper, stemmed, seeded, and chopped fine
- 1 teaspoon table salt
- 2 tablespoons harissa
- 2 tablespoons tomato paste
- ½ teaspoon cayenne pepper (optional)
- 4 cups water
- 1 cup medium-grind bulgur, rinsed
- ¾ cup dried red lentils, picked over and rinsed
- ½ cup chopped fresh parsley
- 2 tablespoons lemon juice, plus lemon wedges for serving
- 1 head Bibb lettuce (8 ounces), leaves separated
- ½ cup plain yogurt

1. Heat 1 tablespoon oil in large saucepan over medium heat until shimmering. Add onion, bell pepper, and salt and cook until softened, about 5 minutes. Stir in harissa; tomato paste; and cayenne, if using, and cook, stirring frequently, until fragrant, about 1 minute.

2. Stir in water and bulgur and bring to simmer. Reduce heat to low; cover; and simmer gently until bulgur is barely tender, about 8 minutes. Stir in lentils; cover; and continue to cook, stirring occasionally, until lentils and bulgur are tender, 8 to 10 minutes.

3. Off heat, lay clean dish towel underneath lid and let mixture sit for 10 minutes. Stir in 1 tablespoon oil, parsley, and lemon juice and stir vigorously until mixture is cohesive. Season with salt and pepper to taste. Transfer to platter and drizzle with remaining 1 tablespoon oil. Spoon kibbeh into lettuce leaves and drizzle with yogurt. Serve with lemon wedges.

Enfrijoladas

Serves 4 to 6 | **Total Time** 55 minutes

WHY THIS RECIPE WORKS Enfrijoladas are straightforward Tex-Mex comfort food: Corn tortillas, which retain their structure and chew through cooking, are coated with refried beans, folded into quarters, placed in a baking dish, topped with cheese, and baked. For the best flavor, we make quick homemade "refried" black beans, making sure that a portion of our bean mixture is thick enough to cling to the tortillas. We then thin the rest of the mixture with broth and pour it over the tortillas for extra bean flavor, before adding a generous coating of shredded Monterey Jack cheese. After just 10 minutes in the oven, the enfrijoladas are melty-hot and ready to enjoy.

Enfrijoladas

- 2 (15-ounce) cans black beans, rinsed, divided
- 2 cups vegetable broth, divided
- 1 tablespoon vegetable oil
- 1 onion, chopped fine
- 1 jalapeño chile, stemmed, seeded, and minced
- ½ teaspoon table salt
- 3 garlic cloves, minced
- 2 teaspoons chili powder
- 2 teaspoons minced fresh oregano or ½ teaspoon dried
- 1 teaspoon ground cumin
- 2 tablespoons tomato paste
- 12 (6-inch) corn tortillas
  Vegetable oil spray
- 4 ounces Monterey Jack cheese, shredded (1 cup)
- 2 scallions, sliced thin
- 2 tablespoons minced fresh cilantro

1. Adjust oven rack to middle position and heat oven to 400 degrees. Process 2 cups beans and 1 cup broth in food processor until smooth, about 30 seconds, scraping down sides of bowl as needed. Add remaining beans and pulse until coarsely ground, about 5 pulses.

2. Heat oil in 12-inch nonstick skillet over medium heat until shimmering. Add onion, jalapeño, and salt and cook until onion is softened, about 5 minutes. Stir in garlic, chili powder, oregano, and cumin and cook until fragrant, about 30 seconds. Stir in tomato paste and cook for 1 minute. Stir in processed beans and cook, stirring often, until well combined and thickened slightly, about 3 minutes. Let bean mixture cool slightly.

3. Spray both sides of tortillas with oil spray. Stack tortillas, wrap in damp dish towel, and place on plate; microwave until warm and pliable, about 1 minute.

4. Working with 1 tortilla at a time, dip into bean mixture to coat both sides and fold into quarters; shingle folded tortillas in 3 columns widthwise in 13 by 9-inch baking dish.

5. Whisk remaining 1 cup broth into remaining bean mixture and pour over tortillas. Sprinkle with Monterey Jack and bake until tortillas are heated through and cheese is melted, about 10 minutes. Sprinkle with scallions and cilantro and serve.

MAKING ENFRIJOLADAS

1. Dip tortilla into bean mixture to coat both sides, then fold into quarters.

2. Shingle folded tortillas in 3 columns across length of 13 by 9-inch baking dish.

Pinto Bean, Swiss Chard, and Monterey Jack Enchiladas

Serves 4 to 6 | **Total Time** 1 hour 40 minutes

WHY THIS RECIPE WORKS Cheesy, meaty fillings are pretty typical for enchiladas; this satisfying pinto bean version uses no meat but still delivers tons of flavor. We keep things green by wilting flavorsome Swiss chard and crisp, slightly bitter green peppers with garlic and onions. To add creamy cohesiveness and protein, we mash half a can of pinto beans and mix in our greens; we then stir in the rest of the beans whole for contrasting texture. A quick simmer of convenient canned tomato sauce with aromatics and spices provides a robust sauce to round out the flavors of the filling. Traditional recipes call for frying the tortillas one at a time, but we found that brushing them with oil and microwaving works just as well—and without the mess of frying. A topping of a cilantro sauce or crema and chopped avocado is ideal—tangy, creamy, fresh-tasting, and rich.

CILANTRO SAUCE

- ¼ cup mayonnaise
- ¼ cup sour cream
- 3 tablespoons water
- 3 tablespoons minced fresh cilantro
- ¼ teaspoon table salt

ENCHILADAS

- ¼ cup vegetable oil, divided
- 2 onions, chopped fine, divided
- ¾ teaspoon table salt, divided
- 3 tablespoons chili powder
- 2 teaspoons ground cumin
- 2 teaspoons sugar
- 6 garlic cloves, minced, divided
- 2 (8-ounce) cans tomato sauce
- ½ cup water
- 1 pound Swiss chard, stemmed and sliced into ½-inch-wide strips
- 2 green bell peppers, stemmed, seeded, and cut into ½-inch pieces
- 1 (15-ounce) can pinto beans, rinsed, divided
- 12 (6-inch) corn tortillas
- 4 ounces Monterey Jack cheese, shredded (1 cup)
- 1 avocado, halved, pitted, and cut into ½-inch pieces
- ¼ cup fresh cilantro leaves
  Lime wedges

1. FOR THE CILANTRO SAUCE Whisk all ingredients together in bowl. Cover and refrigerate until ready to serve.

2. FOR THE ENCHILADAS Adjust oven rack to middle position and heat oven to 450 degrees. Heat 1 tablespoon oil in large saucepan over medium heat until shimmering. Add half of onions and ½ teaspoon salt and cook until softened, about 5 minutes. Stir in chili powder, cumin, sugar, and half of garlic and cook until fragrant, about 30 seconds. Stir in tomato sauce and water, bring to simmer, and cook until slightly thickened, about 7 minutes. Season with salt and pepper to taste; set aside.

3. Heat 1 tablespoon oil in Dutch oven over medium heat until shimmering. Add remaining onions and remaining ¼ teaspoon salt and cook until softened and lightly browned, 5 to 7 minutes. Add remaining garlic and cook until fragrant, about 30 seconds. Add chard and bell peppers, cover, and cook until chard is tender, 6 to 8 minutes. Using potato masher, mash half of beans coarse in large bowl. Stir in chard-pepper mixture, ¼ cup reserved sauce, and remaining whole beans.

4. Grease 13 by 9-inch baking dish. Spread ½ cup sauce over bottom of prepared dish. Brush both sides of tortillas with remaining 2 tablespoons oil. Stack tortillas, wrap in damp dish towel, and place on plate; microwave until warm and pliable, about 1 minute. Working with 1 warm tortilla at a time, spread ¼ cup chard filling across center. Roll tortilla tightly around filling and place seam side down in dish, arranging enchiladas in 2 columns across width of dish. Cover completely with remaining sauce and sprinkle Monterey jack over top.

5. Cover dish tightly with greased aluminum foil and bake until enchiladas are heated through, 15 to 20 minutes. Let enchiladas cool for 10 minutes. Drizzle with cilantro sauce and sprinkle with avocado and cilantro. Serve with lime wedges.

Spicy Basil Noodles with Crispy Tofu, Snap Peas, and Bell Pepper

Serves 4 | **Total Time** 50 minutes

WHY THIS RECIPE WORKS Spicy basil noodles are like a wake-up call for the sleepy palate. This brightly flavored Thai-inspired dish combines tender rice noodles with fragrant fresh basil and a spicy, aromatic sauce. Pan-fried tofu offers both creamy and crispy textures that pair well with the tender rice noodles, and stir-fried snap peas and red bell pepper strips add some crunch. We infuse our dish with subtle heat by creating a paste of hot chiles, garlic, and shallots in the food processor. Cooking the mixture briefly deepens its flavor and mellows the harshness of the raw aromatics. Fish sauce, brown sugar, lime juice, and chicken broth add sweet and savory flavors and give our sauce a bit of body. At the very end we stir in a generous 2 cups of basil, keeping its trademark fresh flavor and color intact.

12 ounces (⅜-inch-wide) rice noodles
14 ounces extra-firm tofu, cut into 1-inch pieces
8 Thai, serrano, or jalapeño chiles, stemmed and seeded
6 garlic cloves, peeled
4 shallots, peeled
2 cups vegetable or chicken broth
¼ cup fish sauce
¼ cup packed brown sugar
3 tablespoons lime juice (2 limes)
¼ teaspoon table salt
⅛ teaspoon pepper
½ cup cornstarch
7 tablespoons vegetable oil, divided
6 ounces snap peas, strings removed
1 red bell pepper, stemmed, seeded, sliced into ¼-inch-wide strips, halved crosswise
2 cups fresh Thai basil leaves or sweet basil leaves

1. Cover noodles with very hot tap water in large bowl and stir to separate. Let noodles soak until softened, pliable, and limp but not fully tender, 35 to 40 minutes; drain. Spread tofu out over paper towel–lined baking sheet and let drain for 20 minutes.

2. Meanwhile, pulse chiles, garlic, and shallots in food processor into smooth paste, about 30 pulses, scraping down bowl as needed; set aside. Whisk broth, fish sauce, sugar, and lime juice together in bowl.

3. Adjust oven rack to upper-middle position and heat oven to 200 degrees. Gently pat tofu dry with paper towels, sprinkle with salt and pepper, then toss with cornstarch in bowl. Transfer coated tofu to strainer and shake gently over bowl to remove excess cornstarch. Heat 3 tablespoons oil in 12-inch nonstick skillet over medium-high heat until just smoking. Add tofu and cook, turning as needed, until all sides are crisp and browned, about 8 minutes; transfer to paper towel–lined plate and keep warm in oven.

4. Wipe out skillet with paper towels, add 1 tablespoon oil, and heat over high heat until just smoking. Add snap peas and bell pepper and cook, stirring often, until vegetables are crisp-tender and beginning to brown, 3 to 5 minutes; transfer to separate bowl.

5. Add remaining 3 tablespoons oil to now-empty skillet and heat over medium-high heat until shimmering. Add processed chile mixture and cook until moisture evaporates and color deepens, 3 to 5 minutes. Add drained noodles and broth mixture and cook, tossing gently, until sauce has thickened and noodles are well coated and tender, 5 to 10 minutes.

6. Stir in cooked vegetables and basil and cook until basil wilts slightly, about 1 minute. Top individual portions with crispy tofu and serve.

Stir-Fried Tofu and Bok Choy

Serves 4 | **Total Time** 45 minutes **FAST** **VEGAN**

WHY THIS RECIPE WORKS Tofu stir-fries make a quick and tasty vegetarian meal, but many recipes result in lackluster tofu and vegetables in a gummy sauce. Several key techniques help produce creamy tofu with a browned crust and crisp-tender vegetables, all lightly coated in a flavorful sauce. Removing as much of the tofu's moisture as possible by letting it drain on a paper towel–lined baking sheet helps it brown in its relatively short cooking time. Coating the pieces in cornstarch further promotes a crispy crust while keeping the interior creamy, and also makes a craggy surface that holds the sauce nicely. We stir-fry the tofu in a skillet over high heat before adding the slower-cooking vegetables, which ensures that the bok choy and carrots don't get soggy. We then sauté the aromatics, add back the tofu with bok choy greens, and pour in a sauce lightly thickened with cornstarch that clings beautifully to the tofu and vegetables.

SAUCE

- ½ cup vegetable broth
- ¼ cup soy sauce
- 2 tablespoons Shaoxing wine
- 1 tablespoon sugar
- 2 teaspoons cornstarch
- 1 teaspoon toasted sesame oil

STIR-FRY

- 14 ounces extra-firm tofu, cut into 1-inch pieces
- ⅓ cup cornstarch
- 3 scallions, minced
- 3 garlic cloves, minced
- 1 tablespoon grated fresh ginger
- 3 tablespoons vegetable oil, divided
- 1 small head bok choy (1 pound), stalks and greens separated, stalks sliced thin, and greens cut into 1-inch pieces
- 2 carrots, peeled and cut into matchsticks

1. FOR THE SAUCE Whisk all ingredients together in bowl.

2. FOR THE STIR-FRY Spread tofu out over paper towel–lined baking sheet and let drain for 20 minutes. Gently pat tofu dry with paper towels, then toss with cornstarch in bowl. Transfer coated tofu to strainer and shake gently over bowl to remove excess cornstarch.

Stir-Fried Tofu and Bok Choy

3. Combine scallions, garlic, ginger, and 1 teaspoon oil in bowl; set aside. Heat 2 tablespoons oil in 12-inch nonstick skillet over high heat until just smoking. Add tofu and cook until crisp and well browned on all sides, 10 to 15 minutes; transfer to bowl.

4. Add remaining 2 teaspoons oil to skillet and return to high heat until shimmering. Add bok choy stalks and carrots and cook until vegetables are crisp-tender, about 4 minutes. Clear center of skillet; add garlic mixture; and cook, mashing mixture into skillet, until fragrant, about 30 seconds. Stir garlic mixture into vegetables.

5. Return tofu to skillet. Stir in bok choy greens. Whisk sauce to recombine, then add to skillet. Cook, stirring constantly, until sauce is thickened, 1 to 2 minutes. Serve.

Panko-Crusted Tofu with Cabbage Salad

Serves 4 | **Total Time** 35 minutes `FAST`

WHY THIS RECIPE WORKS Japanese katsu involves frying up a thin panko-breaded chicken or pork cutlet and serving it with a sweet and savory tonkatsu sauce. We use tofu "cutlets" instead of meat. To help the panko crust adhere, we dredge slices of tofu in a mixture of flour and egg, creating a glue-like paste that locks the panko in place. Ketchup, Worcestershire, soy sauce, garlic powder, and a pinch of sugar make up the tonkatsu sauce. Last but not least is the crunchy cabbage, which needs nothing more than a quick toss with some rice vinegar, toasty sesame oil, and a pinch of sugar for seasoning. To take things a step further, you can layer the cutlets, sauce, and shredded cabbage between slices of white sandwich bread or fluffy Japanese milk bread.

¼ cup ketchup
4 teaspoons Worcestershire sauce
2 teaspoons soy sauce
1 teaspoon garlic powder
1 teaspoon sugar, divided
2 large eggs
2 tablespoon all-purpose flour
1⅓ cups panko bread crumbs
14 ounces extra-firm tofu
½ teaspoon table salt
1 cup vegetable oil, for frying
2½ teaspoons unseasoned rice vinegar
1½ teaspoons toasted sesame oil
3 cups shredded red or green cabbage

1. Whisk ketchup, Worcestershire, soy sauce, garlic powder, and ½ teaspoon sugar together in small bowl; set aside.

2. Whisk eggs and flour together in shallow dish. Place panko in large zipper-lock bag and lightly crush with rolling pin; transfer crumbs to second shallow dish. Slice tofu lengthwise into four ½-inch-thick slabs, pat dry with paper towels, and sprinkle with salt. Working with 1 slab at a time, dip tofu in egg mixture, allowing excess to drip off, then coat all sides with panko, pressing gently to adhere; transfer to large plate.

3. Place wire rack in rimmed baking sheet and line rack with triple layer of paper towels. Heat vegetable oil in 12-inch nonstick skillet over medium-high heat until shimmering. Add tofu and cook until deep golden brown, 2 to 3 minutes per side. Transfer tofu to prepared rack and let drain.

Glazed Caribbean Tofu with Rice and Pigeon Peas

4. Combine vinegar, sesame oil, and remaining ½ teaspoon sugar in small bowl. Add cabbage, toss to coat, and season with salt and pepper to taste. Drizzle tofu with reserved sauce. Serve.

Glazed Caribbean Tofu with Rice and Pigeon Peas

Serves 4 | **Total Time** 1 hour, plus 20 minutes resting
`VEGAN`

WHY THIS RECIPE WORKS This simple dish is a study in flavor and texture contrasts: crisp, spicy-sweet tofu accompanied by creamy, savory rice and hearty pigeon peas. Incorporating the earthy, nutty flavor of pigeon peas into this comforting dish is as easy as opening a can. We start our rice and peas side dish while the tofu drains, boosting savoriness with jalapenos and onion, and adding coconut milk to the cooking liquid for creaminess. We cook the tofu until golden and crisp and then coat it with a glaze of pineapple preserves, lime juice, and pepper flakes. Served alongside our rich rice, the tofu is anything but mild-mannered.

28 ounces firm tofu

1 tablespoon curry powder

1½ teaspoons table salt, divided

¼ teaspoon pepper

1 onion, chopped fine

2 jalapeño chiles, stemmed, seeded, and minced

¼ cup vegetable oil, divided

1½ cups long-grain white rice

1 (15-ounce) can pigeon peas, rinsed

1 (14-ounce) can coconut milk

1 cup plus 3 tablespoons water, divided

½ cup pineapple preserves

2 tablespoons lime juice

¼ teaspoon red pepper flakes

2 scallions, sliced thin

1. Cut tofu in half lengthwise, then cut each half crosswise into 6 slices. Spread tofu out over paper towel–lined baking sheet and let drain for 20 minutes. Gently pat tofu dry with paper towels, sprinkle with curry powder, ½ teaspoon salt, and pepper.

2. Meanwhile, cook onion, jalapeño, and 2 tablespoons oil in large saucepan over medium-high heat until softened, about 3 minutes. Stir in rice and cook until opaque, about 1 minute. Stir in peas, coconut milk, 1 cup water, and remaining 1 teaspoon salt. Bring to boil, then reduce heat to low, cover, and cook until rice is tender, about 20 minutes. Season with salt and pepper to taste.

3. Microwave pineapple preserves until bubbling, about 1 minute, then whisk in lime juice, pepper flakes, and remaining 3 tablespoons water.

4. Heat remaining 2 tablespoons oil in 12-inch nonstick skillet over medium-high heat until just smoking. Add half of tofu and cook until golden and crisp on all sides, about 5 minutes; transfer to paper towel–lined plate. Repeat with remaining tofu, then return first batch of tofu to skillet. Add pineapple mixture and simmer, turning tofu to coat, until glaze thickens, about 1 minute. Sprinkle with scallions and serve with rice.

Braised Tofu with Winter Squash and Coconut Milk

Serves 4 | **Total Time** 1 hour, plus 20 minutes resting

VEGAN

WHY THIS RECIPE WORKS Nothing is better in the colder months than a hearty braised dish with layers of flavor, but most braising recipes are centered around meat. For a satisfying, rich vegetarian braise, we turn to tofu and a combination of butternut squash and eggplant, which we brown first in a skillet. To build a flavorful base, we sauté onion, garlic, ginger, and lemongrass until softened and fragrant. For the braising liquid, we combine vegetable broth with coconut milk, which adds richness and a creamy texture. The vegetables need only 20 minutes to cook through and lend their flavors to the sauce, which we finish with some cilantro, lime juice, and soy sauce.

14 ounces extra-firm tofu, cut into ¾-inch pieces

¼ teaspoon table salt

⅛ teaspoon pepper

3 tablespoons vegetable oil, divided

1½ pounds butternut squash, peeled, seeded, and cut into ½-inch pieces (4½ cups)

1 pound eggplant, cut into ½-inch pieces

1 onion, chopped fine

8 garlic cloves, minced

2 tablespoons grated fresh ginger

1 lemongrass stalk, trimmed to bottom 6 inches and bruised with back of chef's knife

1 (14-ounce) can coconut milk

½ cup vegetable broth

½ cup minced fresh cilantro

4 teaspoons lime juice

Soy sauce

2 scallions, sliced thin

1. Spread tofu over paper towel–lined baking sheet, let drain for 20 minutes, then gently press dry with paper towels. Sprinkle with salt and pepper.

2. Meanwhile, heat 1 tablespoon oil in 12-inch nonstick skillet over medium-high heat until shimmering. Add squash and cook until golden brown, 8 to 10 minutes; transfer to large bowl.

3. Add 1 tablespoon oil to now-empty skillet and heat over medium-high heat until shimmering. Add eggplant and cook until golden brown, 5 to 7 minutes; transfer to bowl with squash.

4. Add remaining 1 tablespoon oil to skillet and heat over medium heat until shimmering. Add onion and cook until softened and lightly browned, 5 to 7 minutes. Stir in garlic, ginger, and lemongrass and cook until fragrant, about 30 seconds. Stir in coconut milk, broth, browned squash-eggplant mixture, and drained tofu. Bring to simmer, reduce heat to medium-low, and cook until vegetables are softened and sauce is slightly thickened, 15 to 20 minutes.

5. Off heat, discard lemongrass. Stir in cilantro and lime juice. Season with soy sauce and pepper to taste. Sprinkle with scallions and serve.

Grain Dinners

Chicken

Beef

Lamb

Pork

Seafood

Vegetarian

● FAST (45 minutes or less)   ● VEGAN
Photo: Chicken and Spiced Freekeh with Cilantro and Preserved Lemon

Lemon-Oregano Chicken with Farro

Serves 4 | **Total Time** 45 minutes `FAST`

WHY THIS RECIPE WORKS Nutty farro makes a hearty side dish. Here an easy lemony incarnation adds heft to this boldly flavored chicken dinner. Traditionally, farro is soaked overnight and then cooked gradually for more than an hour. After testing out a few cooking techniques, we found that boiling the farro in a lot of water and then draining it (we call this the pasta method) yields nicely firm but tender farro—no soaking necessary. Mixing the cooked and cooled farro with chopped cucumber, tomato, pepperoncini, and feta makes for a vibrant side. We prefer the flavor and texture of whole farro for this recipe. Do not use pearl, quick-cooking, or presteamed farro (check the ingredient list on the package to determine this) for the whole farro.

1½ cups whole farro

1¾ teaspoons table salt, plus salt for cooking farro

6 tablespoons extra-virgin olive oil, divided

1 tablespoon minced fresh oregano

1½ teaspoons grated lemon zest plus 2 tablespoons juice

¾ teaspoon pepper

4 (6- to 8-ounce) boneless, skinless chicken breasts, trimmed

¼ cup thinly sliced pepperoncini, plus 1 tablespoon brine

½ English cucumber, cut into ½-inch pieces

1 tomato, cored and cut into ½-inch pieces

2 ounces feta cheese, crumbled (½ cup)

1. Bring 2 quarts water to boil in large saucepan. Add farro and 1 tablespoon salt. Return to boil; reduce heat to medium-low; and simmer until farro is tender with slight chew, 15 to 30 minutes. Drain in colander and rinse under cold water until chilled. Drain well and set aside.

2. Meanwhile, combine 1 tablespoon oil, oregano, lemon zest, pepper, and salt in small bowl. Rub each chicken breast all over with 1 teaspoon oregano mixture. Heat 1 tablespoon oil in 12-inch nonstick skillet over medium-high heat until just smoking. Cook until chicken is golden brown and registers 160 degrees, about 6 minutes per side. Transfer chicken to carving board.

Lemon-Oregano Chicken with Farro

3. Whisk pepperoncini brine, lemon juice, remaining ¼ cup oil, and remaining 2 teaspoons oregano mixture together in large bowl. Measure out and reserve 2 tablespoons dressing. Add cucumber, tomato, feta, farro, and pepperoncini to remaining dressing and toss to combine. Slice chicken ½ inch thick and serve with farro salad, drizzling chicken with reserved dressing.

Pomegranate-Glazed Chicken with Farro Salad

Serves 4 | **Total Time** 1 hour

WHY THIS RECIPE WORKS A Mediterranean-inspired salad of farro and chopped cucumbers, tomatoes, and mint dressed with a lemon-yogurt vinaigrette perfectly complements pomegranate-glazed chicken. Pomegranate molasses, seasoned with a bit of cinnamon and salt, acts as an intensely flavorful glaze for simple roasted chicken breasts. Brushing on the glaze in two applications during roasting produces richly burnished skin.

Substitution: We prefer the flavor and texture of whole farro for this recipe. Pearl farro can be used in place of whole farro but the texture may be softer. Do not use quick-cooking or presteamed farro (read the ingredient list on the package to determine this) in this recipe.

1½ cups whole farro
¾ teaspoon table salt, divided, plus salt for cooking farro
4 (12-ounce) bone-in split chicken breasts, trimmed and halved crosswise
¼ teaspoon pepper, divided
¼ cup extra-virgin olive oil, divided
6 tablespoons pomegranate molasses
1 teaspoon ground cinnamon
2 tablespoons plain Greek yogurt
1 shallot, minced
2 tablespoons lemon juice
1 English cucumber, halved lengthwise and cut into ¼-inch pieces
8 ounces cherry tomatoes, halved
¼ cup chopped fresh mint

1. Adjust oven rack to middle position and heat oven to 450 degrees. Set wire rack in aluminum foil–lined rimmed baking sheet. Bring 2 quarts water to boil in large saucepan. Add farro and 1 tablespoon salt. Return to boil; reduce heat to medium-low; and simmer until farro is tender with slight chew, 15 to 30 minutes. Drain in colander and rinse under cold water until chilled. Drain well and set aside.

2. Meanwhile, pat chicken dry with paper towels and sprinkle with ½ teaspoon salt and ⅛ teaspoon pepper. Heat 1 tablespoon oil in 12-inch skillet over medium-high heat until just smoking. Cook chicken skin side down until well browned, 5 to 7 minutes. Flip chicken and brown lightly on second side, about 3 minutes; transfer skin side up to prepared rack.

3. Combine pomegranate molasses, cinnamon, and ⅛ teaspoon salt in bowl. Brush top of chicken with half of pomegranate glaze. Transfer to oven and roast for 10 minutes. Brush chicken with remaining pomegranate glaze and continue to roast until chicken registers 160 degrees, 5 to 10 minutes. Cover with aluminum foil and let rest.

4. Whisk yogurt, shallot, lemon juice, remaining 3 tablespoons oil, remaining ⅛ teaspoon salt, and remaining ⅛ teaspoon pepper together in large bowl; set aside.

5. Add cooled farro, cucumber, tomatoes, and mint to bowl with vinaigrette and toss gently to combine. Season with salt and pepper to taste. Serve with chicken.

Pan-Seared Chicken with Warm Bulgur Pilaf

Serves 4 | **Total Time** 25 minutes **FAST**

WHY THIS RECIPE WORKS This speedy weeknight dinner builds lots of flavor starting with the fond, those yummy browned bits left on the bottom of the pan after we pan-sear quick-cooking boneless chicken breasts. While the chicken rests, we sauté cherry tomatoes in the same skillet before deglazing the pan with water to create a flavorful cooking liquid. Then it's the grain's turn. Bulgur soaks up all of the chickeny, tomatoey flavors in a mere 5 minutes. We toss salty kalamata olives and crumbled feta into the pilaf to finish our delicious one-pan dinner.

4 (6- to 8-ounce) boneless, skinless chicken breasts, trimmed and pounded to ½-inch thickness
1 teaspoon table salt, divided
¼ teaspoon pepper
3 tablespoons extra-virgin olive oil, divided plus extra for drizzling
10 ounces cherry tomatoes, halved
1½ cups water
1 cup fine-grind bulgur
4 ounces feta cheese, crumbled (1 cup)
½ cup pitted kalamata olives, halved

1. Pat chicken dry with paper towels and sprinkle with ½ teaspoon salt and pepper. Heat 1 tablespoon oil in 12-inch nonstick skillet over medium-high heat until just smoking. Add chicken and cook until golden brown and registers 160 degrees, 6 to 8 minutes per side. Transfer to cutting board, tent with aluminum foil, and let rest while cooking bulgur.

2. Meanwhile, add tomatoes to skillet and cook until skins blister and begin to release their juices, 1 to 2 minutes. Stir in water and bring to boil, scraping up any browned bits. Stir in bulgur and remaining ½ teaspoon salt. Cover, remove from heat, and let sit for 5 minutes.

3. Fluff bulgur with fork and stir in feta, olives, and remaining 2 tablespoons oil. Season with salt and pepper to taste. Slice chicken and serve with bulgur pilaf, drizzling with extra oil to taste.

Roast Chicken with Bulgur, Peas, and Mint

Serves 4 | **Total Time** 1¾ hours

WHY THIS RECIPE WORKS Bulgur's small shape and absorptive qualities are tailor-made for soaking up the savory juices from a roast chicken. This one-pan recipe goes the extra mile by cutting slits in the chicken skin, allowing more juices to drain onto the skillet, where they brown and concentrate into a rich liquid for the bulgur. Roasting the chicken breast side up in a preheated skillet set in a 400-degree oven helps the legs finish cooking at the same time as the breast, and the temperature is just low enough to prevent the juices from smoking. While the roast chicken rests, we cook our bulgur side dish in the drippings, brightened with lemon juice. We match the nutty bulgur with sweet peas and fresh mint. Layered on top of the bulgur, the frozen peas heat through off heat while the bulgur turns tender.

- 1½ teaspoons table salt, divided
- ½ teaspoon pepper
- 1 (4-pound) whole chicken, giblets discarded
- 1 tablespoon unsalted butter, melted
- ½ teaspoon vegetable oil
- 1 shallot, minced
- ¾ cup medium-grind bulgur, rinsed
- ½ cup water
- 5 teaspoons lemon juice
- 1 cup frozen peas
- 1 tablespoon chopped fresh mint

1. Adjust oven rack to middle position and heat oven to 400 degrees. Stir 1¼ teaspoons salt and pepper together in small bowl. Place chicken breast side up on cutting board. Using kitchen shears, thoroughly trim excess fat and skin from cavity. Lift 1 drumstick and use paring knife to cut ½-inch slit in skin where drumstick and thigh meet. Turn chicken on side so breast faces edge of counter. Cut ½-inch slit in skin where top of thigh meets breast. Repeat both cuts on opposite side of chicken. Tuck wingtips behind back. Sprinkle about one-third of salt mixture into cavity. Brush top and sides of chicken with melted butter. Sprinkle remaining salt mixture evenly over all sides of chicken.

2. Heat oil in 12-inch skillet over medium-high heat until shimmering. Place chicken breast side up in skillet; transfer to oven; and roast until thickest part of breast registers 150 to 155 degrees, 1 hour to 1 hour 10 minutes, rotating skillet halfway through roasting. Transfer chicken to carving board and let rest for 15 minutes (chicken temperature will continue to rise as it rests).

3. Meanwhile, pour pan juices into fat separator. Add 2 teaspoons fat to now-empty skillet. Add shallot and cook over medium-high heat, stirring occasionally, until softened, about 3 minutes. Add bulgur and stir until well combined. Stir in ¼ cup defatted pan juices, water, lemon juice, and remaining ¼ teaspoon salt and bring to gentle simmer. Spread peas in even layer over bulgur; turn off heat; cover; and let sit until bulgur is just tender and all liquid is absorbed, about 10 minutes.

4. Carve chicken and transfer to platter. Fluff bulgur, stir in mint, season with salt to taste, and transfer to bowl. Serve chicken with bulgur.

Chicken and Rice with Coconut-Ginger Sauce

Serves 4 | **Total Time** 1¼ hours

WHY THIS RECIPE WORKS This one-pot recipe features chicken and rice seasoned with a pungent stir-together coconut-ginger sauce inspired by Malaysian flavors. Cooking chicken thighs skin side down browns the skin and builds a foundation of flavor. We use thighs here because they don't dry out as much as breasts do when baked with the rice. Cooking the vegetables in some of the rendered chicken fat helps jump-start their cooking and carries the chicken flavor into the rice. To prevent mushy rice, we use a ratio of rice to cooking liquid that takes into account the juices that are released from the chicken as it cooks. We add ¾ cup of a coconut-ginger sauce to the rice to cook those flavors into it. Resting the parcooked thighs on a platter before combining them with the rice prevents the juices they exude during resting from soaking into the rice and making it mushy. Fluffing the cilantro and scallions into the rice (versus just scattering them over the finished dish) allows their flavors to penetrate the dish. Adding fresh lime juice to the sauce at the end brightens it up nicely.

COCONUT-GINGER SAUCE
- ⅓ cup canned coconut milk
- ¼ cup packed brown sugar
- 3 tablespoons fish sauce
- 1 tablespoon grated fresh ginger
- 3 garlic cloves, minced
- 1 tablespoon sriracha
- 1 tablespoon lime juice

CHICKEN, VEGETABLES, AND RICE

- 8 (5- to 7-ounce) bone-in chicken thighs, trimmed
- 2 teaspoons table salt, divided
- 1 teaspoon vegetable oil
- 1 red bell pepper, stemmed, seeded, and cut into 1½-inch pieces
- 1 red onion, cut into 1½-inch pieces
- 1½ cups long-grain white rice, rinsed
- ¾ cup water
- ½ cup chopped fresh cilantro
- 4 scallions, sliced thin

1. FOR THE COCONUT-GINGER SAUCE Combine coconut milk, sugar, fish sauce, ginger, garlic, and sriracha in bowl. Set aside.

2. FOR THE CHICKEN, VEGETABLES, AND RICE Adjust oven rack to middle position and heat oven to 350 degrees. Pat chicken dry with paper towels and sprinkle all over with 1 teaspoon salt. Heat oil in Dutch oven over medium-high heat until just smoking. Add half of chicken, skin side down, and cook until skin is well browned, 6 to 8 minutes. Transfer to plate skin side up. Repeat with remaining chicken.

3. Pour off all but 1 tablespoon fat from pot and heat over medium heat until shimmering. Add bell pepper and onion and cook until vegetables are spotty brown, about 3 minutes. Stir in rice, water, ¾ cup coconut-ginger sauce, and remaining 1 teaspoon salt, scraping up any browned bits, and bring to boil. Nestle chicken into rice mixture skin side up. Cover; transfer to oven; and bake until chicken registers at least 185 degrees, about 25 minutes.

4. Transfer pot to wire rack and let sit, covered, for 15 minutes. Transfer chicken to serving platter. Fluff rice with fork, stir in cilantro and scallions, and season with salt and pepper to taste. Stir lime juice into remaining coconut-ginger sauce and serve with chicken and rice.

One-Pot Chicken and Spinach Rice

Serves 4 to 6 | **Total Time** 1½ hours

WHY THIS RECIPE WORKS This satisfying version of chicken and rice was inspired by Greek spanakorizo, a vegetarian spinach rice pilaf commonly garnished with feta, lemon, and olive oil. Adding chicken and chicken broth to the mix makes for a hearty, ultracomforting one-pot square meal. We start by rendering the fat out of bone-in, skin-on chicken

Roast Chicken with Bulgur, Peas, and Mint

Chicken and Rice with Coconut-Ginger Sauce

thighs. A 12-inch cast-iron skillet works great here because there is room to brown eight thighs in one batch, and the relatively deep skillet holds all that rice and spinach. Briefly sautéing the rinsed rice helps ensure a fluffy pilaf. To the schmaltzy rice, onion, and garlic, we add chicken broth, fresh lemon juice, a handful of briny kalamata olives, and thawed frozen spinach. After nestling the thighs back into the skillet, we pop it covered into the oven to cook the chicken and rice through evenly. Finally, we plate up the tender pieces of chicken; sprinkle some fresh scallions and mint onto the rice; and finish it with crumbles of potent, salty feta cheese. We developed this recipe using Cavender's All Purpose Greek Seasoning but you can also make your own.

- 1 tablespoon Greek seasoning
- 1½ teaspoons kosher salt
- ¾ teaspoon pepper
- 8 (5- to 7-ounce) bone-in chicken thighs, trimmed
- 2 tablespoons extra-virgin olive oil, plus extra for drizzling
- 1 onion, chopped fine
- 4 garlic cloves, minced
- 1½ cups long-grain white rice, rinsed
- 2 cups chicken broth
- 10 ounces frozen spinach, thawed, squeezed dry, and chopped coarse
- ¼ cup pitted kalamata olives, chopped
- 1½ tablespoons lemon juice, plus lemon wedges for serving
- 2 ounces feta cheese, crumbled (½ cup)
- ¼ cup chopped fresh mint
- 2 scallions, sliced thin

1. Adjust oven rack to middle position and heat oven to 350 degrees. Combine Greek seasoning, salt, and pepper in bowl. Pat chicken dry with paper towels and sprinkle with 4 teaspoons Greek seasoning mixture.

2. Heat oil in 12-inch cast-iron skillet over medium-high heat until just smoking. Add chicken skin side down and cook, without moving it, until skin is crispy and golden, 7 to 9 minutes. Flip chicken and continue to cook until golden on second side, about 5 minutes. Transfer chicken to plate.

3. Pour off all but about 2 tablespoons fat from skillet and heat over medium-high heat until shimmering. Add onion and cook until softened, 3 to 5 minutes. Add garlic and cook until fragrant, about 30 seconds. Stir in rice and remaining 1¼ teaspoons Greek seasoning mixture and cook until edges of grains begin to turn translucent, about 2 minutes.

4. Stir in broth, spinach, olives, and lemon juice and bring to simmer. Nestle chicken into skillet along with any accumulated juices. Place large sheet of aluminum foil over skillet, then cover with lid. Transfer to oven and bake for 20 minutes.

5. Remove skillet from oven and let sit, covered, for 15 minutes. Transfer chicken to platter. Fluff rice with fork and sprinkle with feta, mint, and scallions. Drizzle with extra oil and serve with chicken and lemon wedges.

Homemade Greek Seasoning

Makes about ¼ cup | **Total Time** 10 minutes

`FAST` `VEGAN`

You can also sprinkle this seasoning over eggs and baked potatoes and add it to salad dressings. One lemon yields 1 tablespoon of zest.

- 1 tablespoon grated lemon zest
- 2 tablespoons dried oregano
- 1 teaspoon table salt
- 1 teaspoon pepper
- 1 teaspoon garlic powder

1. Spread lemon zest evenly on plate and microwave until dry and zest separates easily when crumbled between your fingers, about 2 minutes, stirring halfway through microwaving.

2. Combine oregano, salt, pepper, garlic powder, and lemon zest in small bowl. (Seasoning can be stored at room temperature for up to 1 week.)

Khao Man Gai

Serves 4 to 6 | **Total Time** 2¼ hours

WHY THIS RECIPE WORKS After *Cook's Country* Editorial Director Bryan Roof feasted on the deservedly famous chicken and rice at Nong's Khao Man Gai in Portland, Oregon, we were inspired to create a version. Following the lead of the cooks at Nong's we begin by gently poaching a whole chicken with garlic and ginger. While the chicken rests, we cook jasmine rice in the poaching liquid to make a rich, poultry-infused rice to serve alongside the sliced and shredded chicken. A bright, savory, spicy sauce wakes things up, and we serve it all with a small bowl of broth for sipping and cilantro and cucumber for a fresh, beautiful finish. Use a Dutch oven with at least a 7-quart capacity to comfortably fit the chicken.

One tablespoon of chili-garlic sauce can be substituted for the Thai chiles. Thai soybean paste is sometimes labeled yellow bean sauce or soybean sauce. If it's unavailable, you can substitute red miso.

CHICKEN AND BROTH

- 12 cups water
- 1 (2-inch) piece ginger, peeled and sliced into ¼-inch-thick rounds
- 2 tablespoons table salt
- 6 garlic cloves, smashed and peeled
- 1 (3½- to 4-pound) whole chicken, giblets discarded

RICE

- 1 tablespoon vegetable oil
- 1 shallot, chopped fine
- 1 (2-inch) piece ginger, peeled and cut in half lengthwise
- 2 garlic cloves, minced
- ¼ teaspoon table salt
- 2 cups jasmine rice, rinsed
- 1 cup fresh cilantro leaves and stems
- ½ English cucumber, sliced into thin rounds

SAUCE

- ¼ cup Thai soybean paste
- ¼ cup soy sauce
- ¼ cup distilled white vinegar
- 2 tablespoons sugar
- 3 garlic cloves, minced
- 2 Thai chiles, stemmed and minced
- 1 teaspoon grated fresh ginger
- 2 scallions, sliced thin

1. FOR THE CHICKEN AND BROTH Combine water, ginger, salt, and garlic in large Dutch oven. Add chicken to pot, breast side up, and bring to simmer over high heat. Place large sheet of aluminum foil over pot, then cover with lid. Reduce heat to low and simmer until breast registers 160 degrees and thighs register at least 175 degrees, 25 to 35 minutes.

2. Transfer chicken to bowl, tent with foil, and let rest while making rice. Using slotted spoon, skim foamy residue from surface of chicken broth. Set aside 3 cups broth for cooking rice. Cover remaining broth.

3. FOR THE RICE Heat oil in large saucepan over medium heat until shimmering. Add shallot, ginger, garlic, and salt and cook until shallot is softened, about 2 minutes. Add rice and cook, stirring frequently, until edges begin to turn translucent, about 2 minutes.

Khao Man Gai

4. Stir in reserved 3 cups broth and bring to boil over medium-high heat. Stir once more, then cover and reduce heat to low. Cook for 20 minutes. Without removing lid, remove saucepan from heat and let sit, covered, for 10 minutes.

5. FOR THE SAUCE Whisk all ingredients in bowl until sugar is dissolved, about 1 minute. (Sauce can be refrigerated for up to 2 days.)

6. Rewarm remaining broth over medium heat. Using boning knife, remove breast meat from chicken carcass; discard skin. Remove chicken leg quarters by dislocating thigh joint from carcass. Using 2 forks, shred leg quarter meat into bite-size pieces; discard skin and bones. Slice breasts crosswise ½ inch thick.

7. Transfer rice to large serving platter. Arrange shredded chicken on top of rice. Arrange sliced breast meat on top of shredded chicken. Place cilantro in pile in 1 corner of platter and shingle cucumber along side of platter.

8. Portion four to six 1-cup servings of remaining hot broth into individual soup bowls and sprinkle with scallions (you will have more than 6 cups broth; reserve extra broth for another use). Serve chicken and rice with sauce and portions of broth.

Chicken Biryani

Chicken Biryani

Serves 4 | Total Time 1¾ hours

WHY THIS RECIPE WORKS In a classic chicken biryani, spiced basmati rice is lavished with butter, studded with dried fruit and nuts, and layered with sauced bone-in chicken. It's all baked together before being topped with deep-fried onions and fresh herbs. We realized we could skip the step of marinating the chicken, prepare the entire dish on the stovetop (rather than transferring it to the oven), and cook the onions and chicken in the same pan. Rich, meaty chicken thighs give our dish a lot of flavor without much work, and wrapping the spices in a bundle of cheesecloth allows us to easily infuse the rice cooking water with the bold flavors of spices without having to fish them out of the finished dish. Garlic, jalapeño, currants, cilantro, and mint finish our biryani with a blend of heat, sweetness, and fresh herb flavor. You will need a 3½- to 4-quart saucepan about 8 inches in diameter for this recipe. Do not use a wide Dutch oven, as it will adversely affect both the layering of the dish and the final cooking times.

YOGURT SAUCE

- 1 cup plain yogurt
- 2 tablespoons minced fresh cilantro
- 2 tablespoons minced fresh mint
- 1 garlic clove, minced

CHICKEN AND RICE

- 10 cardamom pods, preferably green, smashed
- 1 cinnamon stick
- 1 (2-inch) piece ginger, peeled, sliced into ½-inch-thick rounds, and smashed
- ½ teaspoon cumin seeds
- 12 cups water
- 2 teaspoons table salt, divided
- 4 (5- to 7-ounce) bone-in chicken thighs, trimmed
- ¼ teaspoon pepper
- 3 tablespoons unsalted butter
- 2 onions, halved and sliced thin
- 2 jalapeño chiles, stemmed, seeded, and minced
- 4 garlic cloves, minced
- 1¼ cups basmati rice, rinsed
- ½ teaspoon saffron threads, crumbled
- ¼ cup dried currants or raisins
- 2 tablespoons chopped fresh cilantro
- 2 tablespoons chopped fresh mint

1. FOR THE YOGURT SAUCE Combine all ingredients in bowl; season with salt and pepper to taste and set aside. (Sauce can be covered and refrigerated for up to 2 days.)

2. FOR THE CHICKEN AND RICE Wrap cardamom pods, cinnamon stick, ginger, and cumin seeds in small piece of cheesecloth and secure with kitchen twine. Bring water, spice bundle, and 1½ teaspoons salt to boil in medium saucepan. Reduce heat to medium, partially cover, and simmer until spices have infused water, at least 15 minutes (but no longer than 30 minutes).

3. Meanwhile, pat chicken dry with paper towels and sprinkle with pepper and remaining ½ teaspoon salt. Melt butter in 12-inch nonstick skillet over medium-high heat. Add onions and cook, stirring often, until soft and dark brown around edges, 10 to 12 minutes. Stir in jalapeños and garlic and cook, stirring often, until fragrant, about 2 minutes. Transfer onion mixture to bowl, season with salt to taste, and set aside. Wipe out skillet with paper towels.

4. Cook chicken thighs, skin side down, in now-empty skillet over medium-high heat until well browned, 6 to 8 minutes, reducing heat if pan begins to scorch. Flip chicken skin side up and continue to cook until lightly browned on second side, about 3 minutes. Transfer chicken to plate; discard skin. Tent with aluminum foil.

5. If necessary, return spice-infused water to boil; add rice and cook for 5 minutes, stirring occasionally. Drain rice through fine-mesh strainer, reserving ¾ cup cooking liquid; discard spice bundle. Transfer rice to medium bowl and stir in saffron and currants (rice will turn splotchy yellow).

6. Spread half of rice evenly in bottom of now-empty saucepan using rubber spatula. Scatter half of onion mixture over rice, then place chicken thighs, skinned side up, on top of onions, along with any accumulated juices. Sprinkle evenly with cilantro and mint, scatter remaining onion mixture over herbs, then cover with remaining rice. Pour reserved cooking liquid evenly over rice.

7. Cover saucepan and cook over medium-low heat until rice is tender and chicken is cooked through, about 30 minutes (if large amount of steam is escaping from pot, reduce heat to low).

8. Run heatproof rubber spatula around inside rim of saucepan to loosen any affixed rice. Spoon biryani into individual bowls, scooping from bottom of pot. Serve, passing yogurt sauce separately.

Chicken Fried Rice with Sausage and Dried Shrimp

Serves 4 to 6 | **Total Time** 1½ hours, plus 20 minutes cooling

WHY THIS RECIPE WORKS Juicy chicken thighs pair with salty-sweet Chinese sausage and umami-packed dried shrimp in this supersavory fried rice. Fried rice typically starts with day-old rice; the overnight chill firms up the grains so they remain distinct and don't become mushy during stir-frying. This recipe offers a workaround by making a faux leftover rice, which achieves the firmness of leftover rice in under an hour. Cooking components separately avoids overcrowding the pan and maintains a heat level that is key for good stir-frying, resulting in fluffy eggs, tender chicken, and tender-firm grains of rice. Bean sprouts bring a welcome crunch and scallions add freshness. It is worth seeking out dried shrimp but they can be omitted if they're unavailable. You will need a 14-inch flat-bottomed wok or 12-inch nonstick skillet for this recipe. If using a wok, make sure that it is well seasoned so that the rice does not stick.

Substitution: You can use 6 cups day-old cooked rice in place of making the rice in this recipe; skip steps 1 and 2 and bring the leftover rice to room temperature before using.

- 6 tablespoons vegetable oil, divided
- 2 cups jasmine rice, rinsed
- 2⅔ cups plus 1 tablespoon water, divided
- ¼ teaspoon baking soda
- 8 ounces boneless, skinless chicken thighs, trimmed and cut into ½-inch pieces
- ¼ teaspoon cornstarch
- 6 scallions, white and green parts separated and sliced thin
- ¼ cup dried shrimp, chopped
- 2 garlic cloves, minced
- 2 tablespoons fish sauce
- 2 tablespoons Shaoxing wine
- 4 teaspoons soy sauce
- 1 teaspoon toasted sesame oil
- 1 teaspoon table salt
- ¼ teaspoon pepper
- 4 ounces Chinese sausage or ham steak, cut into ½-inch pieces
- 2 large eggs
- 2 ounces (1 cup) bean sprouts

1. Heat 2 tablespoons vegetable oil in large saucepan over medium heat until shimmering. Add rice and stir to coat grains with oil, about 30 seconds. Add 2⅔ cups water, increase heat to high, and bring to boil. Reduce heat to low, cover, and simmer until all liquid is absorbed, about 18 minutes.

2. Off heat, remove lid and place dish towel folded in half over saucepan; replace lid. Let sit until rice is just tender, about 8 minutes. Spread cooked rice onto rimmed baking sheet and let cool on wire rack for 10 minutes. Transfer sheet to refrigerator and let rice chill for 20 minutes.

3. Meanwhile, combine remaining 1 tablespoon water and baking soda in medium bowl. Add chicken and toss to coat; let sit for 5 minutes. Add cornstarch to chicken and toss until well combined.

4. Combine scallion whites, dried shrimp, garlic, and 2 tablespoons vegetable oil in small bowl; set aside. Whisk fish sauce, Shaoxing wine, soy sauce, sesame oil, salt, and pepper together in second small bowl; set aside.

5. Heat 1 tablespoon vegetable oil in 14-inch flat-bottomed wok or 12-inch nonstick skillet over medium heat until shimmering. Add sausage and cook, tossing sausage slowly but constantly, until spotty brown, 2 to 4 minutes. Add chicken and increase heat to high. Cook, tossing slowly but constantly, until chicken is no longer pink, 2 to 6 minutes; transfer to clean medium bowl.

6. Heat remaining 1 tablespoon vegetable oil in now-empty pan over high heat until shimmering. Add eggs and scramble quickly using rubber spatula. Continue to cook, scraping slowly but constantly along bottom and sides of pan, until eggs just form cohesive mass, 15 to 30 seconds (eggs will not be completely dry). Transfer to bowl with sausage and chicken and break up any large egg curds.

7. Break up any large clumps of rice with your fingers. Add reserved scallion whites mixture to now-empty pan and cook over medium heat, mashing mixture into pan, until fragrant, about 30 seconds. Add rice, bean sprouts, reserved fish sauce mixture, sausage-egg mixture, and scallion greens and cook, tossing constantly, until mixture is evenly coated, about 3 minutes. Increase heat to medium-high and cook, tossing occasionally, until mixture is heated through, about 4 minutes. Serve.

Arroz con Pollo

Serves 6 | **Total Time** 1½ hours

WHY THIS RECIPE WORKS For a full-flavored arroz con pollo, we briefly marinate bone-in chicken thighs in a mixture of vinegar, salt, pepper, and oregano. We start the chicken skin-on to maximize the flavorful renderings but then remove the skin after cooking. Next we stew the meat with tomato sauce, olives, capers, and rice until it becomes fall-off-the-bone tender. About half an hour before the chicken finishes cooking, we add medium-grain rice (which we prefer for its creamy texture), stirring it a few times to ensure even cooking. Using spoons rather than forks to pull the cooked meat apart produces appealing chunks instead of shreds.

> **Substitution:** You can use long-grain white rice in place of medium-grain. Increase the amount of water to ¾ cup.

6 garlic cloves, minced
5 teaspoons distilled white vinegar, divided
1½ teaspoons minced fresh oregano or ½ teaspoon dried
1¾ teaspoons table salt, divided
½ teaspoon pepper
4 pounds bone-in chicken thighs, trimmed
2 tablespoons extra-virgin olive oil, divided
1 onion, chopped fine
1 small green bell pepper, stemmed, seeded, and chopped fine
¼ teaspoon red pepper flakes
¼ cup minced fresh cilantro, divided
1¾ cups chicken broth
1 (8-ounce) can tomato sauce
¼ cup water, plus extra as needed
3 cups medium-grain white rice
½ cup pitted green Manzanilla olives, halved
1 tablespoon capers, rinsed
½ cup jarred whole pimentos, cut into 2 by ¼-inch strips
Lemon wedges

1. Adjust oven rack to middle position and heat oven to 350 degrees. Combine garlic, 1 tablespoon vinegar, oregano, 1 teaspoon salt, and pepper in large bowl. Add chicken, toss to coat, and cover; let sit at room temperature for 15 minutes.

2. While chicken marinates, heat 1 tablespoon oil in Dutch oven over medium heat until shimmering. Add onion and bell pepper and cook until softened, 5 to 7 minutes. Stir in pepper flakes and cook until fragrant, about 30 seconds. Stir in 2 tablespoons cilantro.

3. Push vegetables to side of pot and increase heat to medium-high. Add chicken, skin side down, to cleared area of pot and brown lightly, 2 to 4 minutes per side, reducing heat if chicken begins to burn. Stir in broth, tomato sauce, and water and bring to simmer. Cover, reduce heat to medium-low, and simmer for 20 minutes.

4. Stir in rice, olives, capers, and remaining ¾ teaspoon salt and bring to simmer. Cover, transfer pot to oven, and cook, stirring often, until chicken registers 175 degrees, rice is tender, and liquid has been absorbed, about 30 minutes. (If pot appears dry and begins to scorch after 20 minutes, stir in additional ¼ cup water.)

5. Remove pot from oven and transfer chicken to cutting board; cover pot and set aside. Let chicken cool slightly, then shred into bite-size pieces using 2 soupspoons; discard skin and bones. Toss chicken chunks, pimentos, remaining 2 teaspoons vinegar, remaining 1 tablespoon oil, and remaining 2 tablespoons cilantro in clean bowl and season with salt and pepper to taste.

6. Place chicken on top of rice, cover, and let sit until warmed through, about 5 minutes. Serve with lemon wedges.

Chicken Katsu with Tonkatsu Sauce, Cabbage Salad, and Rice

Serves 4 to 6 | **Total Time** 1 hour, plus 15 minutes resting

WHY THIS RECIPE WORKS Japanese panko-breaded chicken cutlets (chicken katsu) served with a tangy barbecue sauce over rice and a crunchy cabbage salad makes for an outstanding weeknight meal. We start the rice first and work on the rest of the meal while the rice cooks. Using tongs to dredge and coat the chicken keeps our hands batter-free. We keep the first batch of cutlets warm in a 200-degree oven while cooking the second batch.

> **Substitution:** You can use medium-grain white rice such as Calrose in place of the short-grain.

1¾ cups plus 2 tablespoons water
1½ cups short-grain white rice, rinsed
 1 tablespoon soy sauce, divided
 2 teaspoons lemon juice
 1 teaspoon toasted sesame oil
 ¼ small head green cabbage (5 ounces), cored and sliced thin
 4 scallions, sliced thin on bias
 ¼ cup ketchup
 2 tablespoons Worcestershire sauce
 1 teaspoon Dijon mustard
 2 cups panko bread crumbs
 2 large eggs
 ½ teaspoon table salt
 8 (4-ounce) chicken cutlets, ½ inch thick, trimmed
 ½ cup vegetable oil, divided

1. Bring water and rice to boil in large saucepan over high heat. Cover, reduce heat to low, and cook until liquid is absorbed, about 10 minutes. Remove pot from heat and let sit, covered, until tender, about 15 minutes. Fluff rice with fork and cover to keep warm.

2. Meanwhile, whisk 1 teaspoon soy sauce, lemon juice, and sesame oil together in medium bowl. Add cabbage and scallions and toss to combine. Season with salt and pepper to taste and refrigerate until ready to serve.

Arroz con Pollo

Chicken Katsu with Tonkatsu Sauce, Cabbage Salad, and Rice

3. Whisk ketchup, Worcestershire, mustard, and remaining 2 teaspoons soy sauce together in small bowl; set aside. Place panko in large zipper-lock bag and lightly crush with rolling pin. Transfer crumbs to shallow dish. Beat eggs with salt in second shallow dish.

4. Working with 1 cutlet at a time, dredge in egg mixture, allowing excess to drip off, then coat all sides with panko, pressing gently to adhere. Transfer to large plate. Place wire rack in rimmed baking sheet and line rack with paper towels.

5. Heat ¼ cup vegetable oil in 12-inch skillet over medium-high heat until shimmering. Add 4 cutlets and cook until deep golden brown, 2 to 3 minutes per side. Transfer cutlets to prepared rack, season with salt to taste, and tent with aluminum foil. Wipe skillet clean with paper towels. Repeat with remaining ¼ cup vegetable oil and remaining 4 cutlets.

6. Slice fried cutlets into ½-inch-wide strips. Drizzle chicken with sauce and serve over rice with cabbage salad.

Roast Chicken with Quinoa, Swiss Chard, and Lime

Serves 4 | **Total Time** 1¾ hours, plus 20 minutes resting

Roast Chicken with Quinoa, Swiss Chard, and Lime

WHY THIS RECIPE WORKS The quinoa accompanying this roast chicken gets depth of flavor from the rich roasting juices, earthy Swiss chard, and lime juice and zest. For a golden-brown, juicy, tender roast chicken, we trim off excess skin and fat from the cavity and cut small slits in the skin above and below the thigh. Then we brush the skin with melted butter instead of oil to facilitate browning. Roasting the chicken breast side up in a preheated skillet set in a 400-degree oven helps the legs finish cooking at the same time as the breast. While the bird rests, we cook an ultraflavorful side dish of quinoa with Swiss chard. We like the convenience of prewashed quinoa; rinsing removes the quinoa's bitter protective coating (called saponin). If you buy unwashed quinoa, rinse it and then spread it out on a clean dish towel to dry for 15 minutes.

1½ teaspoons table salt, divided
½ teaspoon pepper
1 (4-pound) whole chicken, giblets discarded
1 tablespoon unsalted butter, melted
½ teaspoon vegetable oil

8 ounces Swiss chard, stems cut into ¼-inch pieces, leaves sliced into ½-inch-wide strips
½ small onion, chopped fine
1 garlic clove, minced
½ teaspoon ground cumin
¾ cup prewashed quinoa
¾ cup water
¼ teaspoon grated lime zest plus 5 teaspoons juice

1. Adjust oven rack to middle position and heat oven to 400 degrees. Stir 1¼ teaspoons salt and pepper together in small bowl. Place chicken breast side up on cutting board. Using kitchen shears, thoroughly trim excess fat and skin from cavity. Lift 1 drumstick and use paring knife to cut ½-inch slit in skin where drumstick and thigh meet. Turn chicken on side so breast faces edge of counter. Cut ½-inch slit in skin where top of thigh meets breast. Repeat both cuts on opposite side of chicken. Tuck wingtips behind back. Sprinkle about one-third of salt mixture into cavity. Brush top and sides of chicken with melted butter. Sprinkle remaining salt mixture evenly over all sides of chicken.

2. Heat oil in 12-inch skillet over medium-high heat until shimmering. Place chicken breast side up in skillet; transfer to oven; and roast until thickest part of breast registers 150 to 155 degrees, 1 hour to 1 hour 10 minutes, rotating skillet halfway through roasting. Transfer chicken to carving board and let rest for 15 minutes (chicken temperature will continue to rise as it rests).

3. Meanwhile, pour pan juices into fat separator. Add 2 teaspoons fat to now-empty skillet. Add chard stems and onion and cook over medium-high heat, stirring occasionally, until onion is translucent, about 5 minutes. Add garlic and cumin and cook, stirring constantly, until fragrant, about 30 seconds. Add quinoa and stir until well combined. Stir in ¼ cup defatted pan juices, water, lime juice, and remaining ¼ teaspoon salt and bring to simmer. Spread chard leaves in even layer over quinoa; reduce heat to low; cover; and cook until quinoa is just tender and all liquid is absorbed, about 15 minutes.

4. Carve chicken and transfer to platter. Fluff quinoa, stir in lime zest, season with salt to taste, and transfer to bowl. Serve chicken with quinoa.

Sheet-Pan Italian Chicken Sausages with Broccoli and Barley

Serves 4 | **Total Time** 45 minutes FAST

WHY THIS RECIPE WORKS It's hard to get more hands-off than this weeknight sheet-pan dinner. While chicken sausage and broccoli roast, quick-cooking barley cooks on the stove and is ready in just 10 minutes. You start by preheating the oven with the sheet pan inside—that way, the fennel-studded Italian chicken sausage and broccoli sizzle when they hit the pan, jump-starting the browning process. Once everything is cooked, just mix the barley into the roasted broccoli, add some garlic and Parmesan, and you're in business.

 5 tablespoons extra-virgin olive oil, divided
 12 ounces broccoli florets, cut into 1½-inch pieces
 ¾ teaspoon table salt, divided
 ¼ teaspoon pepper
 1½ pounds fully cooked Italian chicken sausage
 1½ cups water
 1 cup quick-cooking barley
 1 ounce Parmesan cheese, grated (½ cup)
 1 garlic clove, minced

Sheet-Pan Italian Chicken Sausages with Broccoli and Barley

1. Adjust oven rack to lowest position and heat oven to 425 degrees. Brush rimmed baking sheet with 1 tablespoon oil. Transfer sheet to oven and heat until oil is just smoking, 3 to 5 minutes.

2. Toss broccoli with 2 tablespoons oil, ½ teaspoon salt, and pepper. Arrange sausage and broccoli in single layer on preheated sheet. Roast until sausage is browned on bottom, about 12 minutes. Flip sausage, stir broccoli, and continue to roast until sausage is browned on second side and broccoli is tender, about 12 minutes. Transfer sausage to platter and tent with aluminum foil; transfer broccoli to serving bowl.

3. Meanwhile, bring water and remaining ¼ teaspoon salt to boil in medium saucepan. Add barley, cover, reduce heat to low, and cook until tender and most of water is absorbed, about 10 minutes.

4. Add barley, Parmesan, garlic, and remaining 2 tablespoons oil to roasted broccoli in serving bowl, toss gently to combine, and season with salt and pepper to taste. Serve with sausage.

Chicken and Spiced Freekeh with Cilantro and Preserved Lemon

Serves 4 to 6 | **Total Time** 1½ hours

WHY THIS RECIPE WORKS Freekeh appears often with moist chicken in the Middle East, especially in Lebanon. Freekeh's distinctly toasty flavors play well with both rich spices, like smoked paprika and intensely floral cardamom, and bright preserved lemon. Here, the high-fiber grain combines with shredded chicken thigh meat, making for a satiating one-pot meal. Freshly chopped cilantro and toasted pistachios offer grassy notes along with a satisfying crunch. If you can't find preserved lemons, you can substitute 1 tablespoon lemon zest or make our Quick Preserved Lemon. Freekeh is sometimes spelled frikeh or farik. Use cracked freekeh that is roughly the size of steel-cut oats. Do not use whole freekeh in this recipe; it will not cook through in time.

- 4 (5- to 7-ounce) bone-in chicken thighs, trimmed
- ½ teaspoon table salt
- ¼ teaspoon pepper
- 1 tablespoon extra-virgin olive oil, plus extra for drizzling
- 1 onion, chopped fine
- 4 garlic cloves, minced
- 1½ teaspoons smoked paprika
- ¼ teaspoon ground cardamom
- ¼ teaspoon red pepper flakes
- 2¼ cups chicken broth
- 1½ cups cracked freekeh, rinsed
- ¼ cup plus 2 tablespoons chopped fresh cilantro, divided
- ½ cup shelled unsalted pistachios, toasted and chopped
- 2 tablespoons rinsed and minced preserved lemons

1. Adjust oven rack to lower-middle position and heat oven to 350 degrees. Pat chicken thighs dry with paper towels and sprinkle with salt and pepper. Heat oil in Dutch oven over medium-high heat until just smoking. Add chicken and cook until well browned, 8 to 10 minutes.

2. Transfer chicken to plate and discard skin. Add onion to fat left in pot and cook over medium heat until softened, about 5 minutes. Stir in garlic, paprika, cardamom, and pepper flakes and cook until fragrant, about 30 seconds. Stir in broth, scraping up any browned bits, then stir in freekeh.

3. Nestle chicken into freekeh mixture and add any accumulated juices. Cover, transfer pot to oven, and cook until freekeh is tender and chicken registers 195 degrees, 35 to 40 minutes.

4. Remove pot from oven. Transfer chicken to cutting board, let cool slightly, then shred into bite-size pieces using 2 forks; discard bones.

5. Meanwhile, gently fluff freekeh with fork. Lay clean dish towel over pot, replace lid, and let sit for 5 minutes. Stir in chicken, ¼ cup cilantro, pistachios, and preserved lemon. Season with salt and pepper to taste. Sprinkle with remaining 2 tablespoons cilantro and drizzle with extra oil. Serve.

Quick Preserved Lemon

Makes about 2 tablespoons | **Total Time** 10 minutes
FAST **VEGAN**

A floral, pungent, and elegant Moroccan staple.

- 8 (2-inch) strips lemon zest, minced, plus 2 teaspoons juice
- 1 teaspoon water
- ½ teaspoon sugar
- ½ teaspoon table salt

Combine all ingredients in bowl and microwave at 50 percent power until liquid evaporates, about 2 minutes, stirring and mashing lemon with back of spoon every 30 seconds; let cool to room temperature. (Lemon mixture can be refrigerated for up to 1 week.)

Lemony Chicken Meatballs with Quinoa and Carrots

Serves 4 | **Total Time** 1¼ hours

WHY THIS RECIPE WORKS Almost every ingredient pulls double duty in this pantry dinner. Fluffy white quinoa (other types are too crunchy) provides the base—along with carrots—and helps keep the meatballs tender. Hummus and lemon zest add moisture to the meatballs, and additional hummus is thinned with lemon juice to make a creamy, drizzle-able sauce. Even the carrot tops are used. Be sure to use ground chicken, not ground chicken breast (also labeled 99 percent fat free) here. If you buy unwashed quinoa, rinse it and then spread it out on a clean dish towel to dry for 15 minutes.

**Lemony Chicken
Meatballs with
Quinoa and Carrots**

1½ cups prewashed white quinoa

1¾ cups water

1¼ teaspoons table salt, divided

¾ cup garlic hummus, divided

1 teaspoon grated lemon zest plus 2½ tablespoons juice

4 teaspoons plus ¼ cup extra-virgin olive oil, divided

1 pound ground chicken

¼ teaspoon pepper

1 pound carrots with their greens, carrots peeled and sliced thin on bias, ⅓ cup greens chopped

1. Cook quinoa in medium saucepan over medium-high heat, stirring frequently, until very fragrant and making continuous popping sounds, 5 to 7 minutes. Stir in water and ½ teaspoon salt and bring to simmer. Reduce heat to low, cover, and simmer until quinoa is tender and water is absorbed, 18 to 22 minutes, stirring once halfway through cooking. Remove pot from heat and let sit, covered, for 5 minutes, then gently fluff with fork and set aside to cool slightly. Meanwhile, whisk ½ cup hummus, lemon juice, and 4 teaspoons oil together in bowl. Season with salt and pepper to taste; set hummus sauce aside until ready to serve.

2. Combine chicken, 1 cup cooled quinoa, lemon zest, ½ teaspoon salt, pepper, and remaining ¼ cup hummus in large bowl. Using your wet hands, gently knead until combined. Pinch off and roll mixture into 20 tightly packed 1½-inch-wide meatballs.

3. Heat 3 tablespoons oil in 12-inch nonstick skillet over medium-high heat until shimmering. Add meatballs and cook until well browned and cooked through, 9 to 11 minutes, turning gently as needed. Transfer meatballs to plate and tent with aluminum foil to keep warm.

4. Add carrots, 3 tablespoons water, and remaining ¼ teaspoon salt to now-empty skillet. Cover and cook over medium-high heat for 2 minutes. Uncover and cook until carrots are tender and spotty brown, 3 to 4 minutes. Stir in remaining 3 cups cooled quinoa, reduce heat to medium, and cook until quinoa is warmed through, about 2 minutes. Stir in remaining 1 tablespoon oil and season with salt and pepper to taste. Sprinkle quinoa with carrot greens, drizzle with olive oil to taste, and serve with meatballs and hummus sauce.

One-Pan Turkey Meatballs with Coconut Rice

Serves 4 | **Total Time** 1¼ hours, plus 15 minutes chilling

WHY THIS RECIPE WORKS Boldly flavored turkey meatballs cook up perfectly juicy and tender nestled in a skillet of creamy coconut rice in this easy one-pan meal. We pack the meatballs with cilantro, scallions, and ginger for fresh brightness and add chili-garlic sauce and fish sauce for heat and savory depth. After browning the meatballs, we sauté red bell pepper strips, and then add rice and cook it until the grains are translucent around the edges (a step that adds nutty flavor and prevents clumping). To cook the rice, we swap out one-third of the water for coconut milk—just enough for a noticeable delicacy and coconut sweetness but not so much that the finished dish is stodgy. The meatballs and rice finish cooking together in the covered skillet, and then we round out the meal by stirring in thawed frozen peas. We finish the dish with more fresh cilantro and scallions, a squeeze of lime juice, and some chopped peanuts for a welcome crunch. Be sure to use 93 percent lean ground turkey, not ground turkey breast (also labeled 99 percent fat-free), in this recipe. Turn the meatballs gently in step 2 so that they won't break.

1 pound ground turkey
½ cup panko bread crumbs
6 scallions, sliced thin, divided
½ cup chopped fresh cilantro, divided
1 large egg, lightly beaten
2 tablespoons Asian chili-garlic sauce, plus extra for serving
2 tablespoons fish sauce, divided
1 tablespoon grated fresh ginger
1 teaspoon table salt, divided
2 tablespoons vegetable oil
2 red bell peppers, stemmed, seeded, and sliced into ¼-inch-thick strips (2 cups)
1 cup long-grain white rice, rinsed
1½ cups water
⅔ cup canned coconut milk
½ cup frozen peas, thawed
¼ cup dry-roasted peanuts, chopped coarse
Lime wedges

1. Combine turkey, panko, two-thirds of scallions, ¼ cup cilantro, egg, chili-garlic sauce, 1 tablespoon fish sauce, ginger, and ½ teaspoon salt in bowl and mix with your hands until thoroughly combined. Divide mixture into 20 portions, about

2 tablespoons each. Roll portions between your wet hands to form meatballs. Transfer meatballs to plate and refrigerate for 15 minutes.

2. Heat oil in 12-inch nonstick skillet over medium-high heat until shimmering. Add meatballs and cook until well browned all over, 5 to 7 minutes. Return meatballs to plate, leaving fat in skillet.

3. Add bell peppers to now-empty skillet; cook until beginning to brown, about 2 minutes. Add rice and cook, stirring frequently, until edges of grains begin to turn translucent, about 1 minute. Stir in water, coconut milk, remaining 1 tablespoon fish sauce, and remaining ½ teaspoon salt and bring to boil. Return meatballs to skillet. Cover, reduce heat to low, and cook for 20 minutes.

4. Without removing lid, remove skillet from heat and let sit, covered, for 10 minutes. Gently stir peas into rice. Sprinkle with peanuts, remaining one-third of scallions, and remaining ¼ cup cilantro. Serve with lime wedges and extra chili-garlic sauce.

Mehshi Bazal

Serves 4 to 6 | **Total Time** 1¾ hours

WHY THIS RECIPE WORKS Stuffed vegetables of all kinds are standards throughout Lebanon, Syria, and Palestine. In this recipe, onion leaves are stuffed with warm-spiced meat and rice. Syrian Jewish cook Sheila Sutton introduced us to this impressive variant particular to the cuisine from the Aleppo region. Whereas stuffed vegetables in the Middle East tend to be cooked in a savory tomato-based sauce, these onion petals are simmered in pomegranate juice, pomegranate molasses, and Aleppo pepper. Sutton says, "The use of cherry and pomegranate is key to the cuisine of Aleppo." This braising medium reduces down to a fruity-sweet-sour sauce that's enriched by the juices of the filling. The sauce lacquers the onions with its ruby-hued shine. In order to easily separate the onion leaves and render them pliable enough for wrapping around the filling, onions are blanched whole (partially cut so the boiling water can reach the interior). Sometimes the rice (medium-grain for its binding quality) is soaked in advance to prevent the raw rice from wicking away all the moisture from the meat, turning it tough. We give the rice a quick dunk in the onion blanching water for 5 minutes, enough to hydrate it and allow the filling to remain tender. Look for large onions that are approximately 12 to 16 ounces each. Serve the onions warm or let rest longer in step 5 and serve at room temperature. We prefer our homemade Baharat (page 243), but you may use store-bought.

One-Pan Turkey Meatballs with Coconut Rice

Substitution: You can use short grain rice in place of medium-grain. Do not use long-grain rice.

- 3 large red onions (about 1 pound each)
- ⅓ cup medium-grain rice, rinsed
- 12 ounces 85 percent lean ground beef
- 1 teaspoon table salt
- ¾ teaspoon baharat
  Pinch cinnamon
- 2 cups pomegranate juice
- 1 tablespoon pomegranate molasses
- ½ teaspoon ground dried Aleppo pepper
- ½ cup pomegranate seeds
- 2 tablespoons chopped fresh parsley

1. Bring 4 quarts water to boil in Dutch oven. Trim ends of onions and arrange on cutting board with 1 cut side down. Starting at top of each onion with tip of knife at core, cut through 1 side. (Onion should remain intact; do not halve onion completely.) Add onions to boiling water and cook, turning occasionally, until onion layers begin to soften and separate, about 15 minutes.

2. Using slotted spoon, transfer onions to cutting board. Once cool enough to touch, gently separate first 7 layers from each onion. Some layers may tear slightly; only 15 layers are needed. Reserve remaining onion cores for another use.

3. Meanwhile, add rice to water left in pot and let sit, off heat, for 5 minutes; drain. Using your hands, gently knead rice, beef, salt, baharat, and cinnamon in bowl until combined. Arrange 1 onion layer on counter with short side facing you. Place 2 tablespoons of rice mixture about ½ inch from bottom and roll up onion to form torpedo shape with tapered ends. Transfer stuffed onion to plate, seam side down. Repeat with 14 more onion layers and remaining rice mixture. (Stuffed onions can be refrigerated for up to 24 hours.)

4. Whisk pomegranate juice and pomegranate molasses together in 12-inch nonstick skillet. Evenly space 12 stuffed onions seam side down around edge of skillet and place three in center. Sprinkle with Aleppo. Bring to vigorous simmer over medium-high heat. Cover, reduce heat to medium-low, and cook for 25 minutes.

5. Using 2 forks, carefully flip onions. Continue to cook, uncovered, until onions are softened and glaze has thickened slightly, 10 to 15 minutes. Off heat, let rest for at least 10 minutes. Gently turn onions to coat with glaze, then transfer to serving platter. Spoon glaze over top and sprinkle with pomegranate seeds and parsley. Serve.

Baharat

Makes 3 tablespoons | **Total Time** 10 minutes

`FAST` `VEGAN`

- 1 tablespoon ground nutmeg
- 1 tablespoon paprika
- 1 teaspoon ground coriander
- 1 teaspoon ground cinnamon
- 1 teaspoon ground cumin

Combine all ingredients in small bowl. (Baharat can be stored in airtight container at room temperature for up to 1 year.)

STUFFING ONION LAYERS

Arrange 1 onion layer on counter with short side facing you. Place 2 tablespoons rice mixture about ½ inch from bottom and roll up onion to form torpedo shape with tapered ends.

Mehshi Bazal

Braised Short Ribs with Wild Mushroom Farrotto

Serves 4 to 6 | **Total Time** 3¾ hours

WHY THIS RECIPE WORKS This delightfully unctuous dinner is made with bone-in short ribs and farrotto, which is similar to risotto but uses hearty farro. Bone-in short ribs are perfect for braising: When cooked slowly, they boast a rich, beefy flavor and a tender, velvety texture. But the marbling that makes them taste so good can result in a greasy final dish. To avoid this, we first roast them for about an hour without anything else in the pot. This way we can render and discard a significant amount of fat. We then build a deeply flavorful braising liquid using cremini and dried porcini mushrooms, aromatics, beef broth, and the porcini's soaking liquid. When the ribs are nearly done, we again defat the cooking liquid and use it to make the farrotto. For a creamy, risotto-like consistency, we crack about half of the farro in a blender to allow the grains to release more of their starch. We remove the short ribs from the pot, stir the farro into the liquid, then put the short ribs back in and cover the pot to ensure that the grains cook evenly. Stirring in some Parmesan, butter, and sherry

vinegar at the end makes for a rich yet bright side for our ribs. To give the dish a fresh finish, we top it with a simple gremolata. We prefer the flavor and texture of whole farro in this recipe. Do not use pearl, quick-cooking, or presteamed farro (check the ingredient list on the package to determine this) for the whole farro.

4 pounds bone-in English-style short ribs, bone 4 to 5 inches long, 1 to 1½ inches of meat on top of bone, trimmed
1 teaspoon table salt
½ teaspoon pepper
¾ ounce dried porcini mushrooms, rinsed
4 cups water, divided
1½ cups whole farro
4 tablespoons unsalted butter, divided
12 ounces cremini mushrooms, trimmed and sliced thin
1 onion, chopped fine
3 garlic cloves, minced, divided
2 teaspoons minced fresh thyme
2 cups beef broth, plus extra as needed
1½ ounces Parmesan cheese, grated (¾ cup)
2 teaspoons sherry vinegar
¼ cup chopped fresh parsley
2 tablespoons minced fresh chives
2 teaspoons grated lemon zest

1. Adjust oven rack to lower-middle position and heat oven to 450 degrees. Pat short ribs dry with paper towels and sprinkle with salt and pepper. Arrange ribs in single layer in Dutch oven. Transfer pot to oven and roast, uncovered, until short ribs are browned, about 1 hour, flipping short ribs halfway through roasting.

2. Microwave porcini mushrooms and 1 cup water in covered bowl until steaming, about 1 minute. Let sit until softened, about 5 minutes. Drain mushrooms in fine-mesh strainer lined with coffee filter, reserving liquid. Chop porcini mushrooms fine. Pulse farro in blender until about half of grains are broken into smaller pieces, about 6 pulses; set aside.

3. Remove pot from oven and reduce oven temperature to 300 degrees. Transfer ribs to plate and discard any fat and juices left in pot. Melt 2 tablespoons butter in now-empty pot over medium heat. Add cremini mushrooms and onion and cook, stirring occasionally, until softened and dry, 8 to 10 minutes. Stir in porcini mushrooms, two-thirds of garlic, and thyme and cook until fragrant, about 30 seconds.

Braised Short Ribs with Wild Mushroom Farrotto

Flank Steak with Farro and Mango Salsa

Flank Steak with Farro and Mango Salsa

Serves 4 | **Total Time** 40 minutes FAST

WHY THIS RECIPE WORKS This easy steak supper combines hearty farro with a fruity fresh mango and red pepper salsa that punches above its weight in the flavor department. Preparing the steak while the farro cooks makes for a quick weeknight meal. To make four equal-size steaks, cut the steak in half lengthwise with the grain, and then cut each piece in half crosswise against the grain. We prefer the flavor and texture of whole farro in this recipe. Do not use pearl, quick-cooking, or presteamed farro (check the ingredient list on the package to determine this) for the whole farro.

2 cups whole farro

1½ teaspoons table salt, divided, plus salt for cooking farro

1 (2-pound) flank steak, trimmed and cut into 4 equal steaks

1 tablespoon ground cumin

1 teaspoon pepper, divided

3 tablespoons extra-virgin olive oil, divided, plus extra for drizzling

1 mango, peeled, pitted, and cut into ¼-inch pieces

1 red bell pepper, stemmed, seeded, and cut into ¼-inch pieces

½ cup finely chopped red onion

½ cup chopped fresh cilantro

2 tablespoons lime juice

1. Bring 2 quarts water to boil in large saucepan. Add farro and 1 tablespoon salt. Return to boil, reduce heat to medium-low, and simmer until farro is tender with slight chew, 15 to 30 minutes. Drain well and set aside.

2. Meanwhile, pat steaks dry with paper towels and sprinkle with cumin, ½ teaspoon pepper, and ¾ teaspoon salt. Heat 2 tablespoons oil in 12-inch nonstick skillet over medium-high heat until just smoking. Cook steaks until well browned and meat registers 120 to 125 degrees (for medium-rare), 5 to 7 minutes per side. Transfer to carving board, tent with aluminum foil, and let rest for 5 minutes.

3. Combine mango, bell pepper, onion, cilantro, lime juice, remaining ¾ teaspoon salt, remaining ½ teaspoon pepper, and remaining 1 tablespoon oil in bowl. Measure out and reserve ½ cup salsa. Toss remaining salsa with farro in bowl. Slice steaks against grain on bias. Serve steaks with farro and reserved salsa, drizzled with extra oil.

4. Stir in reserved porcini soaking liquid, broth, and remaining 3 cups water, scraping up any browned bits, and bring to simmer. Nestle ribs, bone side up, into pot, adding any accumulated juices. Cover, return pot to oven, and cook for 2 hours.

5. Remove pot from oven and transfer ribs to plate. Using wide, shallow spoon, skim excess fat from surface of braising liquid. Stir in farro, then return ribs to pot, along with any accumulated juices. Cover, return pot to oven, and cook until ribs are tender and fork slips easily in and out of meat, 30 to 40 minutes.

6. Remove pot from oven. Transfer ribs to serving platter, brushing any farro back into pot; discard any loose bones. Add Parmesan, vinegar, and remaining 2 tablespoons butter to farro and stir vigorously until mixture becomes creamy, about 2 minutes. Adjust consistency with extra hot broth as needed. Season with salt and pepper to taste.

7. To make gremolata, combine parsley, chives, lemon zest, and remaining garlic in small bowl. Sprinkle individual portions of ribs and farrotto with gremolata before serving.

Plov

Serves 4 | Total Time 2 hours

WHY THIS RECIPE WORKS A fragrant combination of spiced rice, tender meat, and velvety carrots studded with tangy barberries and garnished with soft garlic, Uzbekistan's revered rice dish can be the centerpiece of your table. While the meat and rice traditionally cook together and must finish at the same time, we braise boneless short ribs first and remove the meat to add back when the rice is nearly done. To retain enough braising liquid to ensure perfect rice, we minimize evaporation by using a saucepan rather than a Dutch oven and covering the pot with foil. A grated carrot provides sweet, earthy flavor throughout, while larger carrot chunks become tender but stay intact. Dried barberries give pops of acidity. A head of garlic, simmered with the meat and used to garnish the platter, distinguishes this plov from other Silk Road pilafs. If barberries are unavailable, microwave 2 tablespoons of dried currants and 1 tablespoon of lemon juice in a small bowl, covered, until very steamy, about 1 minute. Add the currants (and any residual lemon juice) to the plov as directed.

- 5 carrots, peeled
- 1 pound boneless beef short ribs, trimmed
- 1½ teaspoons table salt, divided
- 1 tablespoon vegetable oil
- 2 onions, quartered through root end and sliced ¼ inch thick
- 2 tablespoons dried barberries, divided
- 3 garlic cloves, minced, plus 1 head garlic, outer papery skin removed and top ½ inch cut off
- 1 tablespoon ground cumin
- 2 teaspoons ground coriander
- ½ teaspoon pepper
- 1¾ cups water
- 1 cup basmati rice, rinsed
- 2 scallions, sliced thin

1. Adjust oven rack to middle position and heat oven to 350 degrees. Grate largest carrot. Cut remaining 4 carrots into 2 by ½-inch pieces.

2. Pat beef dry with paper towels and sprinkle with ½ teaspoon salt. Heat oil in large saucepan over medium-high heat until shimmering. Add beef and cook until well browned on all sides, 10 to 12 minutes. Transfer beef to bowl.

3. Add onions and remaining 1 teaspoon salt to fat left in saucepan. Cover and cook, stirring occasionally and scraping up any browned bits, until onions are soft, about 5 minutes. Add grated carrot, 1 tablespoon barberries, minced garlic, cumin, coriander, and pepper and cook, stirring constantly,

until garlic and spices are fragrant, 1 to 2 minutes. Spread mixture into even layer. Return beef to saucepan, nestling it into vegetables. Add water and any accumulated beef juices. Place garlic head in center of saucepan. Increase heat to high and bring mixture to vigorous simmer. Remove saucepan from heat; place large sheet of aluminum foil over saucepan, crimp tightly to seal, and cover tightly with lid. Transfer saucepan to oven and cook until meat is fork tender, 1¼ to 1½ hours.

4. Transfer beef and garlic head to cutting board. Stir rice and remaining carrots into cooking liquid (saucepan handle will be hot). Bring to simmer over medium heat. Adjust heat to maintain simmer; replace foil, cover, and cook until liquid level has dropped below rice and rice is half cooked, about 10 minutes. While rice cooks, cut beef into ½-inch cubes. Gently fold beef into rice mixture, making sure to incorporate rice on bottom of saucepan. Replace foil, cover, and continue to cook until rice is tender and moisture is fully absorbed, 10 to 15 minutes. (Check rice every 5 minutes by sliding butter knife to bottom of center of saucepan and gently pushing rice aside; if bottom appears to be drying out, reduce heat slightly.)

5. Pile plov on platter. Sprinkle with scallions and remaining 1 tablespoon barberries. Garnish with garlic head and serve.

Okinawan Taco Rice

Serves 4 | Total Time 35 minutes **FAST**

WHY THIS RECIPE WORKS Matsuzo Gibo created taco rice in 1984 to cater to U.S. Marines stationed in Okinawa, Japan. The delicious, satisfying, and affordable dish has since flourished, becoming hugely popular and an essential addition to Okinawan cuisine. The key to this easy weeknight-friendly recipe is the seasoning for the ground beef. We enhance the typical taco seasoning with umami-rich instant dashi, sweet and complex mirin, and savory soy sauce. Simple steamed short-grain rice provides the perfect foil for the ultraflavorful beef, while creamy Monterey Jack cheese, crisp shredded iceberg lettuce, diced avocado, and tangy salsa take our taco rice to irresistible heights. We developed this recipe with Hondashi instant dashi and McCormick taco seasoning; you can use other brands, but beware that salt levels and flavors may very slightly. You can use our recipe for Homemade Taco Seasoning (page 247) in place of the store-bought packet of seasoning if you prefer. Japanese short-grain rice is commonly sold as sushi rice.

- 2 cups Japanese short-grain white rice
- 2 tablespoons vegetable oil
- 1 onion, chopped fine

Okinawan Taco Rice

Homemade Taco Seasoning

Serves 4 (Makes ¼ cup) | Total Time 10 minutes

FAST VEGAN

  2 tablespoons chili powder
  2 teaspoons cumin
  2 teaspoons cornstarch
  1 teaspoon paprika
  1 teaspoon table salt
  ½ teaspoon granulated garlic
  ½ teaspoon onion powder
  ½ teaspoon dried oregano

Place all ingredients in airtight container and shake to thoroughly combine. (Taco seasoning can be stored at room temperature for up to 1 month.)

NOTES FROM THE TEST KITCHEN

INSTANT DASHI

Dashi is the fundamental stock of Japanese cuisine, made by steeping katsuobushi (aka bonito flakes, or dried, smoked tuna) and kombu (umami-rich dried kelp) in water. It's the base for Japanese dishes like miso soup, ramen, and chawanmushi (a delicate savory custard). Instant dashi is to dashi what powdered bouillon is to chicken stock, convenient to use and store and easy to adjust in concentration. With only a very subtle seafood flavor and a mellow smokiness, instant dashi is exceptionally versatile. Use instant dashi in any recipe that calls for dashi; to add umami to soups, stews, and sauces of all kinds; to enhance the cooking liquid for rice or polenta; to level up your seafood boils or poached fish; or even still in its granulated form in seasoning blends for meat, seafood, and snacks like popcorn.

  1 pound 90 percent lean ground beef
  1 (1-ounce) packet taco seasoning
  1 cup prepared instant dashi
  2 tablespoons ketchup
  2 tablespoons mirin
  2 tablespoons soy sauce
  4 ounces Monterey Jack cheese, shredded (1 cup)
  2 cups shredded iceberg lettuce
  1 avocado, halved, pitted, and cut into ½-inch
    pieces (optional)
  ½ cup jarred tomato salsa
    Lime wedges for serving

1. Place rice in fine-mesh strainer and rinse under running water until water running through rice is almost clear, about 1½ minutes, swishing rice occasionally with your hand. Drain rice well.

2. Combine rice and 2½ cups water in large saucepan and bring to boil over high heat. Cover, reduce heat to low, and cook for 20 minutes. Remove rice from heat; keep covered to keep warm.

3. Heat oil in 12-inch nonstick skillet over medium-high heat until shimmering. Add onion and cook until softened, 3 to 5 minutes. Add beef and cook, using wooden spoon to break meat into pieces, until beef is no longer pink, 3 to 5 minutes. Add taco seasoning and cook until fragrant, about 30 seconds.

4. Stir in dashi, ketchup, mirin, and soy sauce and cook until liquid is thickened, 3 to 5 minutes. Gently fluff rice with fork. Serve beef over rice, topped with Monterey Jack; lettuce; avocado, if using; and salsa (in that order), and with lime wedges.

Steak Burrito Bowls

Serves 4 | **Total Time** 55 minutes

WHY THIS RECIPE WORKS These tangy rice bowls topped with beef make a satisfying dinner in an hour, brightened by the smoky flavor of chipotle chile powder and a tart cherry tomato, cilantro, and scallion salsa. While the rice cooks, there is time to make the salsa and season and cook the steak tips. We prefer the smoky heat of chipotle chile powder in this recipe, but traditional chili powder or ancho chile powder can be substituted. Serve with diced avocado, shredded Monterey Jack cheese, and lime wedges.

2¼ cups water
1½ cups long-grain white rice, rinsed
2 teaspoons table salt, divided
2 tablespoons lime juice, divided
12 ounces cherry tomatoes, quartered
5 scallions, sliced thin
¼ cup minced fresh cilantro
3 tablespoons vegetable oil, divided
½ teaspoon pepper, divided
1 pound sirloin steak tips, trimmed, cut into strips, and sliced thin against grain on bias
2 teaspoons chipotle chile powder

1. Bring water, rice, and 1 teaspoon salt to boil in medium saucepan. Cover; reduce heat to low; and simmer until rice is tender and water is absorbed, about 20 minutes. Fluff rice with fork and fold in 1 tablespoon lime juice; cover to keep warm.

2. Meanwhile, combine tomatoes, scallions, cilantro, 2 teaspoons oil, ¼ teaspoon pepper, ½ teaspoon salt, and remaining 1 tablespoon lime juice in bowl; set aside.

3. Toss beef with 1 teaspoon oil, chile powder, remaining ½ teaspoon salt, and remaining ¼ teaspoon pepper in bowl. Heat 1 tablespoon oil in 12-inch nonstick skillet over high heat until just smoking. Add half of beef, break up any clumps, and cook, without stirring, for 1 minute. Stir beef and continue to cook until browned, about 2 minutes; transfer to bowl. Repeat with remaining 1 tablespoon oil and remaining beef; transfer to bowl.

4. Portion rice into 4 individual serving bowls. Top with beef along with any accumulated juices and tomato mixture. Serve.

Spiced Stuffed Peppers with Yogurt-Tahini Sauce

Serves 4 to 6 | **Total Time** 2 hours

WHY THIS RECIPE WORKS Stuffed peppers are a crowd-pleaser, and the filling of our version is inspired by kibbeh, the Middle Eastern croquette-like dish made from bulgur, beef or lamb, onions, and aromatic spices. Browning beef and shallots with dried mint, sumac, fenugreek, cumin, and mustard seeds develops flavorful bits on the bottom of the pot, creating a savory base for steaming the bulgur. Adding meaty lentils and dried apricots allows us to use less beef; plus, the earthiness of the lentils and sweetness of the apricots round out the flavor. We halve the peppers through the stem for stability, and for deeper flavor, we char (rather than blanch) the peppers under the broiler before stuffing them. Frying shallots for a topping brings out their onion flavor and adds crispy contrast, while a generous sprinkle of dried mint gives the whole dish a vibrant accent. These posh peppers are dressed up further with a drizzle of yogurt-tahini sauce. Look for bell peppers that weigh at least 8 ounces each. If you can't find dried mint, it's better to omit it than to substitute fresh.

½ cup extra-virgin olive oil
6 shallots (3 sliced thin, 3 chopped)
½ cup plain whole-milk yogurt
2 tablespoons tahini
2 tablespoons plus 3 cups water, divided
6 garlic cloves, minced, divided
1 tablespoon lemon juice
4 red bell peppers, halved lengthwise through stem and seeded
1 teaspoon table salt, divided
12 ounces 90 percent lean ground beef
3 tablespoons dried mint, divided
1½ tablespoons ground sumac, plus extra for sprinkling
1 tablespoon ground fenugreek
2 teaspoons ground cumin
2 teaspoons mustard seeds
¾ cup medium-grind bulgur, rinsed
1 (15-ounce) can lentils, rinsed
½ cup dried apricots, chopped

1. Microwave oil and sliced shallots in medium bowl for 5 minutes. Stir and continue to microwave in 2-minute increments until beginning to brown, 2 to 6 minutes. Stir and microwave in 30-second increments until golden brown, 30 seconds to 2 minutes. Using slotted spoon, transfer shallots

Spiced Stuffed Peppers with Yogurt-Tahini Sauce

4. Stir in remaining 3 cups water and bulgur, scraping up any browned bits, and bring to simmer. Reduce heat to low; cover; and simmer gently until bulgur is just tender and no liquid remains, about 10 minutes. Off heat, stir in lentils and apricots, lay clean dish towel underneath lid, and let mixture sit for 10 minutes. Season with salt and pepper to taste.

5. Arrange cooled bell pepper halves cut side up on sheet and divide beef-bulgur mixture evenly among halves, packing mixture and mounding as needed. Bake until warmed through, 20 to 25 minutes. Transfer to serving platter, drizzle with reserved yogurt-tahini sauce, and sprinkle with reserved crispy shallots, remaining 1½ tablespoons mint, and extra sumac. Serve.

Pan-Seared Pork Chops with Dirty Rice

Serves 4 | **Total Time** 1 hour

WHY THIS RECIPE WORKS Wanting an alternative to the typical pork chop dinner, we looked to the South for inspiration and paired flavorful pork with dirty rice—a side dish of cooked rice, cured meats, vegetables, and seasonings. We use a Cajun seasoning mix to add several bold spices at once, and we reinforce it with some garlic and thyme. Since the side of the pork chop that is nestled into the rice during cooking loses its crispness, we save time by browning only one side of the chops and setting them in the pan browned side up. Buy chops of similar thickness so that they cook at the same rate. If you can't find chorizo sausage, use andouille or linguiça. You can make our Cajun Seasoning (page 250) or use store-bought.

2½ cups chicken broth, divided
1 cup long-grain white rice, rinsed
4 (8- to 10-ounce) bone-in pork rib or center-cut chops, ¾ to 1 inch thick, trimmed
1 teaspoon table salt
½ teaspoon pepper
1 tablespoon vegetable oil
4 ounces chorizo sausage, cut into ¼-inch pieces
1 red bell pepper, stemmed, seeded, and chopped fine
1 small onion, chopped fine
6 garlic cloves, minced
1 teaspoon minced fresh thyme or ¼ teaspoon dried
¾ teaspoon Cajun seasoning or chili powder
3 scallions, sliced thin

to paper towel–lined plate and season shallots with salt to taste. Set shallots aside and reserve shallot oil. (Shallots can be stored in airtight container at room temperature for up to 1 month; shallot oil can be refrigerated for up to 1 month.) Whisk yogurt, tahini, 2 tablespoons water, one-third of garlic, and lemon juice together in bowl, then season with salt and pepper to taste; set aside until ready to serve.

2. Adjust oven rack 6 inches from broiler element and heat broiler. Line rimmed baking sheet with aluminum foil and place bell peppers on sheet. Drizzle bell peppers with 2 tablespoons reserved shallot oil and sprinkle with ½ teaspoon salt, then rub all over to coat. Arrange bell peppers skin side up and broil until spotty brown, 9 to 11 minutes. Set aside to cool while making filling.

3. Heat oven to 350 degrees. Cook beef and chopped shallots in large saucepan over medium-high heat, breaking up meat with wooden spoon, until beef is cooked through and shallots are softened and beginning to brown, 8 to 10 minutes. Stir in 1½ tablespoons mint, sumac, fenugreek, cumin, mustard seeds, remaining two-thirds of garlic, and remaining ½ teaspoon salt and cook until fragrant, about 1 minute.

1. Combine 1¼ cups broth and rice in bowl; cover; and microwave until liquid is absorbed, about 10 minutes. Fluff rice with fork.

2. Meanwhile, cut 2 slits about 2 inches apart through fat on edges of each pork chop. Pat chops dry with paper towels and sprinkle with salt and pepper. Heat oil in 12-inch skillet over medium-high heat until just smoking. Cook chops until well browned on first side, about 5 minutes; transfer to plate.

3. Pour off all but 1 tablespoon fat left in skillet. Add chorizo, bell pepper, and onion and cook over medium heat until vegetables are softened, about 5 minutes. Stir in garlic, thyme, and Cajun seasoning and cook until fragrant, about 30 seconds. Stir in remaining 1¼ cups broth and microwaved rice, scraping up any browned bits.

4. Nestle pork chops, browned side up, into pan, adding any accumulated juices. Cover and simmer gently until pork registers 145 degrees, 8 to 10 minutes.

5. Transfer chops to clean plate, brushing any rice that sticks to chops back into skillet, tent with aluminum foil, and let rest for 5 to 10 minutes. Gently fold scallions into rice and season with salt and pepper to taste. Serve.

Kibbeh bil Saineyeh

Cajun Seasoning

Makes about ¾ cup | **Total Time** 10 minutes
`FAST` `VEGAN`

  5 tablespoons paprika
  2 tablespoons garlic powder
  1 tablespoon dried thyme
  1 tablespoon cayenne pepper
  1 tablespoon celery salt
  1 tablespoon table salt
  1 tablespoon pepper

Combine all ingredients in bowl.

Kibbeh bil Saineyeh

Serves 6 to 8 | **Total Time** 1½ hours

WHY THIS RECIPE WORKS Kibbeh bil Saineyeh, a variation on fried kibbeh, is a Lebanese staple cooked throughout the Middle East. In the fried version, sautéed lamb is encompassed within a dough made up of lamb, or sometimes veal, and fine bulgur, and then deep fried. In this less labor-intensive version, the kibbeh dough is layered on the bottom of the pan, topped with fragrant sautéed lamb, covered with more kibbeh dough, and baked. A potluck favorite, it is also perfect on its own for a filling dinner. We serve it with the traditional accompaniments of a tomato-cucumber salad and some plain yogurt to bring a refreshing element to this satiating dish. If you can find it, we recommend using 85 percent or higher lean ground lamb but any ground lamb will do just fine. You can use slivered almonds if you can't find whole blanched almonds.

KIBBEH
5½ tablespoons extra-virgin olive oil, divided
  3 tablespoons walnuts, chopped
  2 tablespoons whole blanched almonds, chopped, plus 15 whole blanched almonds, divided
  2 tablespoons pine nuts
  3 onions, chopped fine, divided
2½ teaspoons ground cinnamon
1¾ teaspoons ground cardamom
  2 teaspoons ground allspice, divided
  3 pounds ground lamb, divided
  2 tablespoons pomegranate molasses
  1 tablespoon ground sumac
  1 tablespoon plus ½ teaspoon table salt, divided

2¼ teaspoons pepper, divided
1 cup fine bulgur, rinsed
2 teaspoons ground cumin
1 teaspoon grated orange zest

CUCUMBER-TOMATO SALAD
3 tomatoes, cored and cut into ¼-inch pieces
2 cucumbers, peeled, seeded, and cut into ¼-inch pieces
½ white onion, chopped fine
½ cup extra-virgin olive oil
⅓ cup fresh chopped fresh mint
¼ cup lemon juice (2 lemons)
½ teaspoon table salt
½ teaspoon pepper

2 cups plain whole-milk yogurt

1. FOR THE KIBBEH Adjust oven rack to middle position and heat oven to 400 degrees. Heat 1 tablespoon oil in 12-inch skillet over medium heat until shimmering. Add walnuts, chopped almonds, and pine nuts and toast until lightly golden, 1 to 2 minutes. Immediately transfer nuts to plate to cool.

2. Wipe skillet clean with paper towels. Heat 2 tablespoons oil in now-empty skillet over medium heat until shimmering. Add 2 onions and cook until softened and just beginning to brown, 5 to 7 minutes. Stir in cinnamon, cardamom, and 1 teaspoon allspice and cook until fragrant, about 30 seconds. Stir in 2 pounds lamb and cook, breaking up meat with wooden spoon, until lamb is no longer pink, about 7 minutes. Using slotted spoon, strain lamb mixture and transfer to large bowl. Stir pomegranate molasses, sumac, 2¼ teaspoons salt, 1¾ teaspoons pepper, and reserved toasted nuts into lamb mixture in bowl; set aside.

3. Brush bottom and sides of broiler-safe 13 by 9-inch baking dish with 1 tablespoon oil. Process remaining 1 pound lamb, bulgur, cumin, orange zest, remaining onion, remaining 1 teaspoon allspice, remaining 1¼ teaspoons salt, and remaining ½ teaspoon pepper in food processor until smooth and well combined, about 30 seconds, scraping down sides of processor bowl halfway through.

4. Working with half of bulgur mixture, break into small (about 1-inch) pieces, scattering them evenly over bottom of prepared dish. With your moistened hands, press bulgur mixture into smooth, even layer, being sure to press into corners of dish and smoothing pieces together to seal. Spread reserved lamb mixture in even layer over top.

5. Using your moistened hands, pinch off small (about 1-inch) piece of remaining bulgur mixture and flatten into thin layer between your palms. Place on top of lamb filling in dish. Repeat with remaining bulgur mixture, pressing and

smoothing pieces together in dish to cover lamb filling completely. (Be sure to press bulgur mixture firmly into thin layer to ensure you have enough to cover dish entirely.)

6. Brush top evenly with remaining 1½ tablespoons oil, then, using sharp knife, score 1½-inch diamond pattern in top layer of kibbeh, being careful not to cut into filling. Split each almond in half at natural breaking point, then place 1 almond half, rounded side up, in center of each diamond.

7. Bake kibbeh until edges are golden brown and have shrunk slightly from sides of pan, 15 to 20 minutes.

8. FOR THE CUCUMBER-TOMATO SALAD While kibbeh bakes, combine all ingredients in bowl. Season with salt and pepper to taste and set aside until ready to serve.

9. Heat broiler element, then broil kibbeh until beginning to brown, about 4 minutes. Let cool for 10 minutes. Serve with yogurt and reserved cucumber tomato salad.

ASSEMBLING KIBBEH BIL SAINEYEH

1. After scattering half of bulgur mixture into prepared dish, press mixture into smooth even layer.

2. After pressing bulgur mixture into flat layer, be sure to smooth any seams to seal.

3. Using your moistened hands, flatten small piece of bulgur mixture into thin layer in your hands.

4. Press and smooth individual bulgur pieces together in dish to cover lamb filling.

Khao Pad Sapparot

Serves 4 to 6 | **Total Time** 1½ hours, plus 20 minutes cooling

WHY THIS RECIPE WORKS In this Thai stir-fry, also called "heavenly rice," rice is stir-fried with pineapple and fresh shrimp. The fruit gives juicy sweetness and Chinese sausage adds meaty flavor. Fish sauce and soy sauce aren't enough to create saltiness and nuance but shrimp paste, a blend of fermented shrimp and salt, gives the dish a slightly funky umami. We bloom curry powder and aromatics in oil before adding the rice, shrimp, egg, and pineapple. Crispy shallots add oniony flavor, cashews give crunch, and cilantro lends freshness. You can swap in ham steak for the Chinese sausage. You will need a 14-inch flat-bottomed wok or a 12-inch nonstick skillet for this recipe. If using a wok, make sure that it is well seasoned so that the rice doesn't stick.

Substitution: You can use 6 cups day-old cooked rice in place of making the rice in this recipe; skip steps 1 and 2 and bring the leftover rice to room temperature before using.

- 2 tablespoons plus ½ cup vegetable oil, divided
- 2 cups jasmine rice, rinsed
- 2⅔ cups water
- 1 tablespoon fish sauce
- 1 tablespoon shrimp paste
- 1 tablespoon soy sauce
- 2 teaspoons sugar
- ¼ teaspoon table salt
- 3 shallots, sliced thin
- 4 ounces Chinese sausage, cut into ½-inch pieces
- 1 pound extra-large shrimp (21 to 25 per pound), peeled, deveined, tails removed, and cut crosswise into thirds
- 2 large eggs
- 4 garlic cloves, minced
- 2 teaspoons curry powder
- 1½ teaspoons grated fresh ginger
- 2 cups ½-inch pineapple pieces
- 3 tablespoons chopped fresh cilantro
- ¼ cup roasted cashews, chopped coarse

1. Heat 2 tablespoons vegetable oil in large saucepan over medium heat until shimmering. Add rice and stir to coat grains with oil, about 30 seconds. Add water, increase heat to high, and bring to boil. Reduce heat to low, cover, and simmer until all liquid is absorbed, about 18 minutes.

2. Off heat, remove lid and place dish towel folded in half over saucepan; replace lid. Let sit until rice is just tender, about 8 minutes. Spread cooked rice onto rimmed baking

Khao Pad Sapparot

sheet and let cool on wire rack for 10 minutes. Transfer sheet to refrigerator and let rice chill for 20 minutes.

3. Meanwhile, whisk fish sauce, shrimp paste, soy sauce, sugar, and salt in small bowl until sugar has dissolved; set aside.

4. Add remaining ½ cup oil and shallots to 14-inch flat-bottomed wok or 12-inch nonstick skillet and cook over medium heat, stirring constantly, until shallots are golden and crispy, 5 to 8 minutes. Using slotted spoon, transfer shallots to paper towel–lined plate and season with salt to taste. Pour off and reserve oil. Wipe pan clean with paper towels.

5. Heat 1 tablespoon reserved oil in now-empty pan over medium heat until shimmering. Add sausage and cook, tossing slowly but constantly, until spotty brown, 2 to 4 minutes. Add shrimp and increase heat to high. Cook, tossing slowly but constantly, until shrimp are just opaque, about 2 minutes; transfer to medium bowl.

6. Heat 1 tablespoon reserved oil in now-empty pan over high heat until shimmering. Add eggs and scramble quickly using rubber spatula. Continue to cook, scraping slowly but constantly along bottom and sides of pan, until eggs just form cohesive mass, 15 to 30 seconds (eggs will not be completely dry); transfer to bowl with shrimp and sausage.

7. Break up any large clumps of rice with your fingers. Add 2 tablespoons reserved oil, garlic, curry powder, and ginger to now-empty pan and cook over medium heat, mashing ingredients into pan, until fragrant, about 30 seconds. Add rice, fish sauce mixture, shrimp-egg mixture, and pineapple and cook, tossing constantly, until mixture is evenly coated, about 3 minutes. Increase heat to medium-high and cook, tossing occasionally, until mixture is heated through, about 4 minutes. Off heat, stir in cilantro. Sprinkle with fried shallots and cashews. Serve.

Pork Fried Rice

Serves 4 to 6 | **Total Time** 1½ hours, plus 20 minutes cooling

WHY THIS RECIPE WORKS Fried rice is the perfect solution for leftover rice; the hard, dry clumps relax into tender distinct grains. Here we add meaty country-style pork ribs, eggs, and peas, cooking the elements separately so each comes out right. A mix of soy sauce, oyster sauce, Shaoxing wine, hoisin sauce, and brown sugar yields a dish with balanced salty, sweet flavors. You will need a 14-inch flat-bottomed wok or a 12-inch non-stick skillet for this recipe. If using a wok, make sure that it is well seasoned so that the rice doesn't stick.

> **Substitution:** You can use 6 cups day-old cooked rice in place of making the rice in this recipe; skip steps 1 and 2 and bring the leftover rice to room temperature before using.

- 6 tablespoons vegetable oil, divided
- 2 cups jasmine rice, rinsed
- 2⅔ cups plus 1 tablespoon water, divided
- ¼ teaspoon baking soda
- 8 ounces boneless country-style pork ribs, trimmed and cut into ½-inch pieces
- ¼ teaspoon cornstarch
- 6 scallions, white and green parts separated and sliced thin
- 2 garlic cloves, minced
- 2 tablespoons oyster sauce
- 4 teaspoons soy sauce
- 1 tablespoon Shaoxing wine
- 1 tablespoon hoisin sauce
- 1 tablespoon packed brown sugar
- 1 teaspoon table salt
- ¼ teaspoon pepper
- 2 large eggs
- ¼ cup frozen peas, thawed

Pork Fried Rice

1. Heat 2 tablespoons vegetable oil in large saucepan over medium heat until shimmering. Add rice and stir to coat with oil, about 30 seconds. Add 2⅔ cups water, increase heat to high, and bring to boil. Reduce heat to low; cover; and simmer until all liquid is absorbed, about 18 minutes.

2. Off heat, remove lid and place dish towel folded in half over saucepan; replace lid. Let sit until rice is just tender, about 8 minutes. Spread cooked rice onto rimmed baking sheet and let cool on wire rack for 10 minutes. Transfer sheet to refrigerator and let rice chill for 20 minutes.

3. Meanwhile, combine remaining 1 tablespoon water and baking soda in medium bowl. Add pork and toss to coat; let sit for 5 minutes. Add cornstarch and toss until well combined.

4. Combine scallion whites, 2 tablespoons oil, and garlic in small bowl; set aside. Whisk oyster sauce, soy sauce, Shaoxing wine, hoisin, sugar, salt, and pepper in second small bowl until sugar has dissolved; set aside.

5. Heat 1 tablespoon oil in 12-inch nonstick skillet or 14-inch flat-bottomed wok over medium-high heat until just smoking. Add pork and increase heat to high. Cook, tossing pork slowly but constantly, until no longer pink, 2 to 6 minutes; transfer to clean medium bowl.

Polenta with Sausage and Peppers

Sorghum Käsespätzle with Caramelized Onions and Kielbasa

6. Heat remaining 1 tablespoon oil in now-empty pan over high heat until shimmering. Add eggs and scramble quickly using rubber spatula. Continue to cook, scraping slowly but constantly along bottom and sides of pan, until eggs just form cohesive mass, 15 to 30 seconds (eggs will not be completely dry). Transfer to bowl with pork and break up any large egg curds.

7. Break up any large clumps of rice with your fingers. Add reserved scallion whites mixture to now-empty pan and cook over medium heat, mashing mixture into pan, until fragrant, about 30 seconds. Add rice, peas, reserved oyster sauce mixture, pork-egg mixture, and scallion greens and cook, tossing constantly, until mixture is evenly coated, about 3 minutes. Increase heat to medium-high and cook, tossing occasionally, until mixture is heated through, about 4 minutes. Serve.

Polenta with Sausage and Peppers

Serves 4 | **Total Time** 35 minutes

WHY THIS RECIPE WORKS It's hard to get more classic than sausage, peppers, and onions—one whiff and you're instantly transported to a baseball game or a street fair, tucking into a larger-than-life sub piled high with this killer combo. To re-create this experience with a bit more elegance, we introduce smoky fire-roasted tomatoes into the equation and serve it all over rich and buttery stick-to-your-ribs polenta (instant all the way), which does an excellent job of sopping up the savory sauce.

4½ cups water, divided
1 cup instant polenta
3 tablespoons unsalted butter
1 teaspoon table salt, divided
¾ teaspoon pepper, divided
1½ pounds sweet or hot Italian sausage
1 red bell pepper, stemmed, seeded, and sliced thin
1 small onion, halved and sliced thin
1 (14.5-ounce) can fire-roasted diced tomatoes

1. Bring 4 cups water to boil in large saucepan. Whisk in polenta; reduce heat to medium-low; and cook until thickened, about 3 minutes. Off heat, stir in butter, ¾ teaspoon salt, and ½ teaspoon pepper. Cover to keep warm.

2. Meanwhile, place sausages in 12-inch nonstick skillet and cook over medium heat until browned all over, 6 to 10 minutes. Increase heat to medium-high, add bell pepper and onion, and cook, stirring occasionally, until vegetables are softened, 4 to 6 minutes. Add tomatoes, remaining ½ cup water, remaining ¼ teaspoon salt, and remaining ¼ teaspoon pepper. Simmer until sausages register 160 degrees, 4 to 6 minutes.

3. Top polenta with sausage and pepper mixture. Serve.

Sorghum Käsespätzle with Caramelized Onions and Kielbasa

Serves 6 | **Total Time** 1½ hours, plus 15 minutes resting

WHY THIS RECIPE WORKS A homey cross between egg noodles and dumplings, spätzle is a slightly chewy, light, and buttery noodle dish traditionally served with chicken paprikash and other stews. For this version, we use a combination of all-purpose flour and sorghum flour and add cheese. Sorghum has a mild, earthy flavor and has been called the most wheat-like of the gluten-free flours. Letting the batter rest before making the noodles is a necessary step; it allows the gluten to relax and results in more tender spätzle. We incorporate the hearty flavors of kielbasa, sauerkraut, mustard, and caraway into our comforting dish. The holes in both a potato ricer and a colander are too big to act as a makeshift spätzle press. Instead, we poke holes in a disposable aluminum pan and set the pan directly over the boiling water. You can use a spätzle maker or a food mill with ¼-inch wide holes if you have one.

5 ounces (1 cup) sorghum flour
5 ounces (1 cup) all-purpose flour
1 teaspoon pepper, divided
¾ teaspoon table salt, divided, plus salt for cooking spätzle
¾ cup whole milk
3 large eggs
1 (13 by 9-inch) disposable aluminum pan
4 ounces fontina cheese, shredded (1 cup)
4 ounces Gruyère cheese, shredded (1 cup)
2 tablespoons unsalted butter
1 tablespoon vegetable oil
14 ounces kielbasa sausage, halved lengthwise and sliced crosswise ½-inch thick
1 large onion, halved and sliced thin
1 cup sauerkraut, drained and squeezed dry
2 teaspoons yellow mustard
¼ teaspoon caraway seeds
2 tablespoons chopped fresh dill

1. Whisk sorghum flour, all-purpose flour, ½ teaspoon pepper, and ½ teaspoon salt together in large bowl. Whisk milk and eggs together in second bowl. Slowly whisk milk mixture into flour mixture until smooth. Cover and let rest for 15 to 30 minutes. Meanwhile, use skewer to poke about forty ¼-inch-wide holes in bottom of disposable pan, moving skewer in circular motions to widen holes as needed. Combine fontina and Gruyère in third bowl.

2. Bring 4 quarts water to boil in Dutch oven. Add 1 tablespoon salt to boiling water and set prepared disposable pan on top of Dutch oven. Transfer half of batter to disposable pan. Use spatula to scrape batter across holes, letting batter fall into water and stirring to prevent clumping. Boil until all spätzle float, about 30 seconds. Using spider skimmer or slotted spoon, transfer spätzle to colander set in large bowl to drain. Repeat with remaining batter. Toss drained spätzle with butter and set aside. Drain leftover cooking water in Dutch oven and wipe pot dry with paper towel.

3. Adjust oven rack 6 inches from broiler and heat broiler. Heat 1 tablespoon oil in now-empty Dutch oven over medium heat until just smoking. Add kielbasa and cook, stirring occasionally, until spotty brown, about 5 minutes. Using slotted spoon, transfer kielbasa to bowl with spätzle.

4. Add onion and remaining ¼ teaspoon salt to fat left in pot and cook, stirring frequently, until onion is golden brown, about 15 minutes, adjusting heat and adding water 1 tablespoon at a time if onion or bottom of pot becomes too dark.

5. Off heat, stir in reserved spätzle-kielbasa mixture, ¾ cup cheese mixture, sauerkraut, mustard, caraway seeds, and remaining ½ teaspoon pepper. Sprinkle remaining cheese mixture evenly over top. Broil until bubbling and cheese is browned in spots, about 5 minutes. Let cool for 10 minutes. Sprinkle with dill. Serve.

CREATING AND USING A DISPOSABLE SPÄTZLE MAKER

1. Use sharp knife to poke about 40 (¼-inch-wide) holes in bottom of disposable pan, moving knife in circular motion to widen holes as needed.

2. Pour half of batter into pan and use spatula to press batter through holes and into boiling water. Repeat with remaining batter.

Cod with Cilantro Rice

Serves 4 | Total Time 40 minutes **FAST**

WHY THIS RECIPE WORKS Inspired by arroz verde (green rice), we toss still-warm white rice with a garlic and cilantro vinaigrette so it drinks up all of the sauce's tart, herbal flavors. For this recipe, it's critical to have uniform grains of rice, so we cook it like pasta—dump the rice into a pot of boiling water (no need for finicky ratios) and drain it when it's done. While all that is happening, we sear cod fillets in a piping-hot skillet to achieve a gorgeous crust before gently finishing them in the oven. Once everything is ready, we drizzle some of the reserved cilantro sauce over the top to tie it all together.

- 3 cups fresh cilantro leaves and stems, chopped coarse
- 2 tablespoons red wine vinegar
- 2 garlic cloves, smashed and peeled
- ¾ teaspoon table salt, divided, plus salt for cooking rice
- ½ teaspoon pepper, divided
- ½ cup plus 1 tablespoon extra-virgin olive oil, divided
- 1 cup long-grain white rice
- 4 (6- to 8-ounce) skinless cod, black sea bass, haddock, hake, or pollack fillets, 1 inch thick

1. Adjust oven rack to middle position and heat oven to 425 degrees. Pulse cilantro, vinegar, garlic, ¼ teaspoon salt, and ¼ teaspoon pepper in food processor until finely chopped, about 12 pulses, scraping down sides of bowl as needed. Transfer to bowl, whisk in ½ cup oil, and set aside.

2. Bring 2 quarts water to boil in large saucepan. Stir in rice and 1 teaspoon salt and cook until rice is tender, about 12 minutes. Drain rice well, return to saucepan, and stir in ¼ cup reserved cilantro sauce; season with salt and pepper to taste. Cover and set aside until ready to serve.

3. Meanwhile, pat cod dry with paper towels and sprinkle with remaining ½ teaspoon salt and remaining ¼ teaspoon pepper. Heat remaining 1 tablespoon oil in 12-inch ovensafe nonstick skillet over medium-high heat until just smoking. Lay fillets in skillet and, using spatula, lightly press fillets for 20 to 30 seconds to ensure even contact with skillet. Cook until golden brown on first side, 1 to 2 minutes.

4. Using 2 spatulas, flip fillets, then transfer skillet to oven. Roast until fish flakes apart when gently prodded with paring knife and registers 135 degrees, 7 to 10 minutes. Transfer cod to platter, drizzle with remaining reserved cilantro sauce, and serve with reserved rice.

Black Rice Bowls with Roasted Salmon and Miso Dressing

Serves 4 | Total Time 1 hour

WHY THIS RECIPE WORKS Black rice is an ancient grain with a deliciously roasted, nutty flavor. It pairs wonderfully with meaty salmon, rich avocado, and crisp vegetables. Because it can be easy to overcook, we boil it to ensure that the grains cook evenly. For silky roasted salmon to top the rice, we preheat a baking sheet in a 500-degree oven and then set the heat to 275 and add the fish. The initial blast of heat firms up the exterior and the fish cooks through gently as the oven temperature slowly drops. If using wild salmon, check for doneness earlier and cook it until it registers 120 degrees.

> **Substitution:** You can use brown rice in place of the black but it may need a few extra minutes of cooking.

- 1½ cups black rice
- ½ teaspoon table salt, plus salt for cooking rice
- 4 (6- to 8-ounce) skin-on salmon fillets, 1 to 1½ inches thick
- ¼ teaspoon pepper
- 1 (8 by 7½-inch) sheet nori (optional)
- ¼ cup unseasoned rice vinegar
- ¼ cup mirin
- 1 tablespoon white miso
- 1 teaspoon grated fresh ginger
- ½ teaspoon lime zest plus 2 tablespoons juice
- 4 radishes, trimmed, halved, and sliced thin
- 1 avocado, sliced thin
- 1 English cucumber, halved lengthwise and sliced thin
- 2 scallions, sliced thin

1. Bring 4 quarts water to boil in Dutch oven over medium-high heat. Add rice and 1 teaspoon salt and cook until rice is tender, 20 to 25 minutes. Drain rice and transfer to large bowl; cover to keep warm.

2. Meanwhile, adjust oven rack to lowest position, line rimmed baking sheet with aluminum foil and place on rack, and heat oven to 500 degrees. Pat salmon dry with paper towels and sprinkle with salt and pepper.

3. Once oven reaches 500 degrees, reduce oven temperature to 275 degrees. Remove sheet from oven and carefully place salmon, skin side down, on hot sheet and roast until center is still translucent when checked with tip of paring knife and registers 125 degrees (for medium-rare), 9 to 13 minutes. Slide fish spatula along underside of fillets and transfer to plate, leaving skin behind; discard skin.

4. While salmon roasts, whisk vinegar, mirin, miso, ginger, and lime zest and juice in small bowl until miso is fully incorporated. Season with salt and pepper to taste. Measure out ¼ cup dressing, drizzle over rice, and toss to combine.

5. Divide rice among individual serving bowls and sprinkle with nori, if using. Top with salmon, radishes, avocado, and cucumber. Sprinkle with scallions and drizzle with remaining dressing. Serve.

Nasi Goreng

Serves 4 to 6 | **Total Time** 1¾ hours, plus 20 minutes cooling

WHY THIS RECIPE WORKS Nasi goreng may be Indonesia's best-known dish. It combines cooked rice with pungent chile paste and a sweet soy sauce called kecap (pronounced "ketchup") manis. Heat comes from Thai chiles; swap in two serranos or two jalapeños if needed. For a milder dish, remove all or a portion of the ribs and seeds from the chiles. Serve nasi goreng with sliced cucumbers and tomato wedges, if desired. It's worth seeking out kecap manis. If it's unavailable, substitute a mixture of 2 tablespoons of molasses, 2 tablespoons of packed dark brown sugar, and 2 tablespoons soy sauce. You will need a 14-inch flat-bottomed wok or a 12-inch nonstick skillet with a tight-fitting lid. If using a wok, make sure that it is well seasoned so that the rice does not stick.

> **Substitution:** You can use 6 cups day-old cooked rice in place of making the rice in this recipe; skip steps 1 and 2 and bring the leftover rice to room temperature before using.

- 2 tablespoons plus ½ cup vegetable oil, divided
- 2 cups jasmine rice, rinsed
- 2⅔ cups water
- 7 large shallots, peeled (4 whole, 3 sliced thin)
- 5 Thai chiles, stemmed
- 4 large garlic cloves, peeled
- 3 tablespoons kecap manis
- 2 tablespoons fish sauce
- 1½ teaspoons table salt, divided
- 4 large eggs
- 12 ounces extra-large shrimp (21 to 25 per pound), peeled, deveined, tails removed, and cut crosswise into thirds
- 4 large scallions, sliced thin
  Lime wedges

Cod with Cilantro Rice

Black Rice Bowls with Roasted Salmon and Miso Dressing

Nasi Goreng

Paella on the Grill

1. Heat 2 tablespoons vegetable oil in large saucepan over medium heat until shimmering. Add rice and stir to coat grains with oil, about 30 seconds. Add water, increase heat to high, and bring to boil. Reduce heat to low, cover, and simmer until all liquid is absorbed, about 18 minutes.

2. Off heat, remove lid and place dish towel folded in half over saucepan; replace lid. Let sit until rice is just tender, about 8 minutes. Spread cooked rice onto rimmed baking sheet and let cool on wire rack for 10 minutes. Transfer sheet to refrigerator and let rice chill for 20 minutes.

3. Meanwhile, pulse whole shallots, Thai chiles, and garlic in food processor until coarse paste forms, about 15 pulses, scraping down sides of bowl as needed; transfer to small bowl and set aside. Whisk kecap manis, fish sauce, and 1¼ teaspoons salt together in second small bowl; set aside. Whisk eggs and remaining ¼ teaspoon salt together in separate bowl; set aside.

4. Add remaining ½ cup oil and sliced shallots to 14-inch flat-bottomed wok or 12-inch nonstick skillet and cook over medium heat, stirring constantly, until shallots are golden and crispy, 5 to 8 minutes. Using slotted spoon, transfer shallots to paper towel–lined plate and season with salt to taste. Pour off and reserve oil. Wipe pan clean with paper towels.

5. Heat 1 teaspoon reserved oil in now-empty pan over medium heat until shimmering. Using paper towel, wipe out pan, leaving thin film of oil on bottom and sides. Add half of egg mixture and gently tilt and shake pan until mixture forms even 10-inch round omelet (if using wok, egg will go up sides of pan). Cover and cook until bottom of omelet is spotty brown and top is just set, about 30 seconds. Loosen edges of omelet with rubber spatula and slide onto cutting board. Gently roll omelet into tight log. Cut log crosswise into 1-inch segments (leaving segments rolled). Repeat with 1 teaspoon reserved oil and remaining egg mixture.

6. Break up large clumps of rice with your fingers. Heat 3 tablespoons reserved oil in now-empty pan over medium heat until just shimmering. Add shallot-chile mixture and cook, mashing mixture into pan, until golden, 3 to 5 minutes. Add shrimp and cook, tossing slowly but constantly, until just opaque, about 2 minutes. Add rice and kecap manis mixture and cook, tossing constantly, until mixture is evenly coated, about 3 minutes. Increase heat to medium-high and cook, tossing occasionally, until mixture is heated through, about 4 minutes. Off heat, stir in scallions. Garnish with egg segments and crispy shallots. Serve with lime wedges.

Skillet Paella

Serves 4 to 6 | **Total Time** 1 hour

WHY THIS RECIPE WORKS Spain's famous rice dish is a showstopping one-pot meal. For the ultimate version, see the next recipe. This skillet rendition delivers serious flavor, too, and in about an hour. Here we focus on quick-cooking shrimp, Spanish chorizo, and either clams or mussels. Because the shrimp, rice, sausage, and clams all cook at different rates, we cook them in stages, first sautéing the shrimp, followed by the sausage, and then setting them aside. We use the sausage's fat to cook the aromatics and herbs before toasting the rice, which then soaks up the flavors of clam juice, tomatoes, and saffron. We steam the clams or mussels toward the end, letting them release their briny liquid into the rice. You will need a 12-inch nonstick skillet with a tight-fitting lid.

- 1 pound extra-large shrimp (21 to 25 per pound), peeled and deveined
- ½ teaspoon chili powder
- ¼ teaspoon pepper
- 2 tablespoons vegetable oil, divided
- 8 ounces Spanish chorizo, sliced ½ inch thick
- 1 onion, chopped fine
- ½ teaspoon minced fresh thyme or ¼ teaspoon dried
- 3 garlic cloves, minced
- 1 cup long-grain white rice, rinsed
- 2 (8-ounce) bottles clam juice
- 1 (14.5-ounce) can diced tomatoes, drained
- ¼ teaspoon saffron threads, crumbled
- 1 dozen clams or mussels, scrubbed, mussels debearded
- ½ cup frozen peas
- 2 tablespoons minced fresh parsley
  Lemon wedges

1. Pat shrimp dry with paper towels and sprinkle with chili powder and pepper. Heat 1 tablespoon oil in 12-inch nonstick skillet over medium-high heat until just smoking. Add shrimp and cook until curled and pink on both sides, about 2 minutes. Transfer to bowl and cover with aluminum foil.

2. Add remaining 1 tablespoon oil to skillet and heat until shimmering. Add chorizo and cook until lightly browned, about 3 minutes. Transfer chorizo to bowl with shrimp.

3. Add onion and thyme to fat left in skillet and cook over medium heat until softened, about 5 minutes. Stir in garlic and cook until fragrant, about 30 seconds. Stir in rice and cook until grains are sizzling and lightly toasted, about 1 minute.

4. Stir in clam juice, tomatoes, and saffron, scraping up any browned bits. Bring to boil, then cover, reduce heat to low, and cook until rice is tender and liquid is absorbed, about 15 minutes.

5. Off heat, stir in cooked shrimp and chorizo. Arrange clams over top and sprinkle with peas. Cover and cook over medium heat until shellfish have opened, about 7 minutes, discarding any that don't open.

6. Remove skillet from heat and let sit, covered, for 5 minutes. Sprinkle with parsley. Serve with lemon wedges.

Paella on the Grill

Serves 8 | **Total Time** 1 hour 55 minutes

WHY THIS RECIPE WORKS Though modern paella is cooked on the stove or in the oven, it was originally made on the grill, and many Spanish cooks still make it that way today. The live fire adds subtle smokiness, and an extra-large cooking surface encourages even development of socarrat, the prized caramelized rice crust that forms on the bottom of the pan. In place of a traditional paella pan, we cook ours in a large, sturdy roasting pan that maximizes the amount of socarrat. Building a large (7-quart) fire and fueling it with fresh coals (which ignite during cooking) ensures that the heat output lasts throughout cooking. We also shorten the outdoor cooking time by using roasted red peppers and tomato paste (instead of fresh peppers and tomatoes), making an infused broth with the seasonings, and grilling (rather than searing) the chicken thighs. To ensure that various components finish cooking at the same time, we stagger the addition of the proteins—first, the chicken thighs, followed by the shrimp, clams, and chorizo. We also place the grilled chicken along the pan's perimeter, where it can finish cooking gently, and the sausage and seafood in the center, where they are partially submerged in the liquid so that they cook through; once the liquid has reduced, the steam keeps them warm. This recipe was developed using a light-colored 16 by 13.5-inch tri-ply roasting pan; however, it can be made in any heavy roasting pan that measures at least 14 by 11 inches. If your roasting pan is dark in color, the cooking times will be on the lower end of the ranges given. The recipe can also be made in a 15- to 17-inch paella pan. If littlenecks are unavailable, use 1½ pounds of shrimp in step 1 and season them with ½ teaspoon of salt.

1½ pounds boneless, skinless chicken thighs, trimmed and halved crosswise

1¾ teaspoons table salt, divided

1 teaspoon pepper

12 ounces jumbo shrimp (16 to 20 per pound), peeled and deveined

6 tablespoons extra-virgin olive oil, divided

6 garlic cloves, minced, divided

1¾ teaspoons hot smoked paprika, divided

3 tablespoons tomato paste

4 cups chicken broth

1 (8-ounce) bottle clam juice

⅔ cup dry sherry

Pinch saffron threads (optional)

1 onion, chopped fine

½ cup jarred roasted red peppers, chopped fine

3 cups Arborio rice

1 pound littleneck clams, scrubbed

1 pound Spanish-style chorizo, cut into ½-inch pieces

1 cup frozen peas, thawed

Lemon wedges

1. Place chicken on large plate and sprinkle both sides with 1 teaspoon salt and pepper. Toss shrimp with 1 tablespoon oil, ½ teaspoon garlic, ¼ teaspoon paprika, and ¼ teaspoon salt in bowl. Set aside.

2. Heat 1 tablespoon oil in medium saucepan over medium heat until shimmering. Add remaining garlic and cook, stirring constantly, until garlic sticks to bottom of saucepan and begins to brown, about 1 minute. Add tomato paste and remaining 1½ teaspoons paprika and continue to cook, stirring constantly, until dark brown bits form on bottom of saucepan, about 1 minute. Add broth; clam juice; sherry; and saffron, if using. Increase heat to high and bring to boil. Remove saucepan from heat and set aside.

3A. FOR A CHARCOAL GRILL Open bottom vent completely. Light large chimney starter mounded with charcoal briquettes (7 quarts). When top coals are partially covered with ash, pour evenly over grill. Using tongs, arrange 20 unlit briquettes evenly over coals. Set cooking grate in place, cover, and open lid vent completely. Heat grill until hot, about 5 minutes.

3B. FOR A GAS GRILL Turn all burners to high, cover, and heat grill until hot, about 15 minutes. Leave all burners on high.

4. Clean and oil cooking grate. Place chicken on grill and cook until both sides are lightly browned, 5 to 7 minutes total. Return chicken to plate. Clean cooking grate.

5. Place roasting pan on grill (turning burners to medium-high if using gas) and add remaining ¼ cup oil. When oil begins to shimmer, add onion, red peppers, and remaining ½ teaspoon salt. Cook, stirring frequently, until onion begins to brown, 4 to 7 minutes. Add rice (turning burners to medium if using gas) and stir until grains are well coated with oil.

6. Arrange chicken around perimeter of pan. Pour broth mixture and any accumulated juices from chicken over rice. Smooth rice into even layer, making sure nothing sticks to sides of pan and no rice rests atop chicken. When liquid reaches gentle simmer, place reserved shrimp in center of pan in single layer. Arrange clams in center of pan, evenly distributing with shrimp and pushing hinge sides of clams into rice slightly so they stand up. Sprinkle chorizo evenly over surface of rice. Cook (covered if using gas), moving and rotating pan to maintain gentle simmer across entire surface of pan, until rice is almost cooked through, 12 to 18 minutes. (If using gas, heat can also be adjusted to maintain simmer.)

7. Sprinkle peas evenly over paella, cover grill, and cook until liquid is fully absorbed and rice on bottom of pan sizzles, 5 to 8 minutes. Continue to cook, uncovered, checking bottom of pan frequently with metal spoon, until uniform golden-brown crust forms, 8 to 15 minutes. (Rotate and slide pan around grill as necessary to ensure even crust formation.) Remove pan from grill, cover with aluminum foil, and let stand for 10 minutes. Serve with lemon wedges.

NOTES FROM THE TEST KITCHEN

TREAT SOCARRAT LIKE COOKIES

Socarrat, the layer of browned rice and browned sugars and proteins from the cooking liquid at the bottom of paella, benefits from a brief rest before serving. This allows the starch, which is flexible when the rice is hot, to crystallize and become rigid, so the socarrat crisps and easily releases from the pan. "It's kind of like a perfectly cooked chocolate chip cookie when you first pull it out of the oven," said Jamie Bissonnette, chef and partner at Toro, a tapas bar in Boston and New York. "If you try to pick it up, it's going to be soggy. But if you wait for it to cool off, it has just the right amount of crunch."

Seared Shrimp with Tomato, Avocado, and Lime Quinoa

Serves 4 | **Total Time** 55 minutes

WHY THIS RECIPE WORKS For an easy main-course quinoa and seafood dish, we pair quinoa with seared shrimp and flavorful Southwestern-inspired ingredients such as chipotle chile powder, avocado, and cilantro. Cooking the shrimp in two batches ensures that they will brown, not steam. A quick, fresh tomato sauce pulls together the juicy, smoky shrimp and quinoa. Toasting the quinoa prior to cooking it enhances its nuttiness. We like the convenience of prewashed quinoa; rinsing removes the quinoa's bitter protective coating (called saponin). If you buy unwashed quinoa, rinse it and then spread it out on a clean dish towel to dry for 15 minutes.

Seared Shrimp with Tomato, Avocado, and Lime Quinoa

1½ cups prewashed white quinoa

1¾ cups water

¾ teaspoon table salt, divided

¼ teaspoon grated lime zest plus 2 tablespoons juice, divided, plus lime wedges for serving

½ cup chopped fresh cilantro, divided

1½ pounds extra-large shrimp (21 to 25 per pound), peeled and deveined

½ teaspoon chipotle chile powder

¼ teaspoon pepper

2 tablespoons extra-virgin olive oil, divided plus extra for drizzling

1 pound tomatoes, cored and cut into ½-inch pieces

3 scallions, sliced thin, white and green parts separated

3 garlic cloves, minced

1 avocado, halved, pitted, and cut into ½-inch pieces

1. Toast quinoa in medium saucepan over medium-high heat, stirring frequently, until quinoa is very fragrant and makes continuous popping sound, 5 to 7 minutes. Stir in water and ¼ teaspoon salt and bring to simmer. Cover, reduce heat to low, and simmer until quinoa is tender and liquid is absorbed, 18 to 22 minutes, stirring once halfway through cooking. Remove quinoa from heat and let sit, covered, for 10 minutes. Fluff quinoa with fork, stir in lime zest, 1 tablespoon lime juice, and ¼ cup cilantro; cover to keep warm.

2. Meanwhile, pat shrimp dry with paper towels, then toss with chile powder, pepper, and ¼ teaspoon salt. Heat 1 tablespoon oil in 12-inch nonstick skillet over medium-high heat until just smoking. Add half of shrimp in single layer and cook, without stirring, until spotty brown and edges turn pink on bottom side, about 1 minute. Flip shrimp and continue to cook until all but very center is opaque, about 30 seconds. Transfer shrimp to clean large plate. Repeat with remaining 1 tablespoon oil and remaining shrimp.

3. Return now-empty skillet to medium-high heat. Add tomatoes, scallion whites, garlic, remaining ¼ teaspoon salt, remaining 1 tablespoon lime juice, and remaining ¼ cup cilantro. Cook until tomatoes soften slightly, about 1 minute. Stir in shrimp and cook until shrimp are opaque throughout, about 1 minute. Transfer to platter, sprinkle with scallion greens and top with avocado. Serve with quinoa and lime wedges, drizzling with extra oil to taste.

Shrimp with Warm Barley Salad

Serves 4 | Total Time 35 minutes FAST

WHY THIS RECIPE WORKS When you want something light and healthful but still hearty enough to feel like a meal, try this dish. Nutty, chewy barley pairs wonderfully with shrimp and crunchy-tart apple. Tangy marinated feta and its herby oil are turned into a dressing for the barley to ensure all that goodness gets dispersed throughout the whole salad. We like to use extra-large shrimp (21 to 25 per pound). Some shrimp are treated with salt or additives like sodium tripoly-phosphate (STPP); if using treated shrimp, skip adding salt to the shrimp in step 2.

1½ cups water
1 teaspoon table salt, divided
1 cup quick-cooking barley
1½ pounds shrimp, peeled and deveined
1 teaspoon pepper, divided
2 tablespoons extra-virgin olive oil
¼ cup cider vinegar
4 ounces marinated feta, crumbled (1 cup), plus ¼ cup marinated feta oil
1 apple, cored, halved, and sliced thin

Shrimp with Warm Barley Salad

1. Bring water and ¼ teaspoon salt to boil in medium saucepan over high heat. Add barley, cover, reduce heat to low, and cook until tender and most of water is absorbed, about 10 minutes. Spread over rimmed baking sheet to cool.

2. Meanwhile, pat shrimp dry with paper towels and sprinkle with ¼ teaspoon salt and ¼ teaspoon pepper. Heat oil in 12-inch nonstick skillet over medium-high heat until just smoking. Add shrimp and cook, stirring occasionally, until opaque throughout, 3 to 6 minutes.

3. Whisk vinegar, feta oil, remaining ½ teaspoon salt, and remaining ¾ teaspoon pepper together in large bowl. Add barley, apple, and feta and toss to coat. Season with salt and pepper to taste and top with shrimp. Serve.

Twice-Cooked Barley with Sautéed Squid

Serves 4 | Total Time 2 hours

WHY THIS RECIPE WORKS This barley recipe borrows elements from Spanish, Portuguese, and Moorish cooking. Inspired by Portuguese seafood rice dishes, it incorporates cara-melized barley with tender pieces of squid. Cooking the barley a second time makes it nicely crispy and intensifies its flavor. Designed to be tomato-forward, our recipe includes sherry for its intriguing sweet undertone, plus coriander, cumin, turmeric, and paprika to create a highly flavorful and bright dish. The squid is prepared simply with olives for a briny pop. We recommend using Pedro Ximenez sherry in this recipe for its sweet, ripe, and complex flavor.

BARLEY
3 tablespoons extra-virgin olive oil, divided
2 onions, chopped fine
1 large red bell pepper, stemmed, seeded, and finely chopped
1 serrano chile, stemmed, seeded, and finely chopped
6 garlic cloves, minced
1½ tablespoons tomato paste
1½ teaspoons smoked paprika
1½ teaspoons ground cumin
1½ teaspoons ground coriander
1 teaspoon table salt
¾ teaspoon pepper
¾ teaspoon ground turmeric
5 tablespoons sherry
1½ cups pearl barley, rinsed

4 cups chicken broth

1 (14.5-ounce) can whole peeled tomatoes, drained with ½ cup juice reserved, tomatoes chopped

1 teaspoon grated lemon zest plus 1 teaspoon juice, plus lemon wedges for serving

SAUTÉED SQUID

1 pound squid, bodies sliced crosswise into ½-inch-thick rings, tentacles left whole

¼ cup extra-virgin olive oil, divided

6 garlic cloves, sliced thin

¼ cup pitted green olives, chopped, divided

2 tablespoons chopped fresh parsley

1 tablespoon lemon juice

½ teaspoon table salt

¼ teaspoon pepper

1. FOR THE BARLEY Heat 2 tablespoons oil in medium saucepan over medium heat until shimmering. Add onions and cook until golden brown, about 8 minutes, stirring often. Add bell pepper and serrano and cook until softened, about 3 minutes, stirring occasionally. Stir in garlic, tomato paste, paprika, cumin, coriander, salt, pepper, and turmeric and cook until fragrant, about 1 minute. Stir in sherry, scraping up any browned bits, and cook until evaporated, about 30 seconds.

2. Stir in barley and cook until toasted, about 3 minutes. Stir in broth and tomatoes and reserved juice and bring to boil. Reduce heat to medium-low; cover and simmer until liquid is absorbed and barley is tender, about 40 minutes. Off heat, stir in lemon zest and juice. Cover and let sit for 10 minutes.

3. Heat 1½ teaspoons oil in 12-inch nonstick skillet over medium-high heat until shimmering. Add half of barley and stir until mixture is evenly coated with oil. Spread barley into even layer in skillet and cook until barley begins to crisp and turns spotty brown, 5 to 7 minutes, occasionally stirring barley and returning to even layer. Transfer to platter and cover loosely with aluminum foil to keep warm. Repeat with remaining 1½ teaspoons oil and remaining barley.

4. FOR THE SAUTÉED SQUID Pat squid dry with paper towels; set aside. Wipe now-empty skillet clean with paper towels. Heat 2 tablespoons oil in skillet over medium-high heat until just smoking. Add half of squid and cook without stirring, until squid is beginning to turn opaque and edges are light golden brown, 1 to 2 minutes. Flip squid, add half of garlic and olives and cook until just opaque, 1 to 2 minutes. Transfer squid to bowl and repeat with remaining 2 tablespoons oil, remaining squid, and remaining garlic and olives. Add parsley, lemon juice, salt, and pepper to bowl with squid and toss to combine. Top barley with squid mixture and serve with lemon wedges.

Twice-Cooked Barley with Sautéed Squid

Stuffed Eggplants with Bulgur

Serves 4 | **Total Time** 1¾ hours

WHY THIS RECIPE WORKS Stuffed eggplant is a fantastic dinner option when you crave a satisfying meal that's also appealingly light. The smaller-size Italian eggplants you often see at summer farmers' market are ideal for stuffing, making this dish all the more appealing. There are countless variations on stuffed eggplant, but we found ourselves enamored of a classic Turkish preparation known as imam bayildi. Most recipes for it are similar: Eggplant is cooked in olive oil and then stuffed with onions, garlic, and tomatoes. Using nutty bulgur as a hearty filling base adds enough heft to the dish to make it a satisfying main course. To ensure that the eggplants are rich and creamy, not watery, we roast them prior to stuffing. The slight caramelizing effect of roasting them on a preheated baking sheet adds depth of flavor. We let the roasted eggplants drain briefly on paper towels, which gets rid of excess liquid, before adding the stuffing. Plum tomatoes lend bright flavor and a bit of moisture, and Pecorino Romano and pine nuts provide richness.

Stuffed Eggplants with Bulgur

Garlicky Fried Rice with Bok Choy

4 (10-ounce) Italian eggplants, halved lengthwise
2 tablespoons extra-virgin olive oil, divided
1 teaspoon table salt, divided
¼ teaspoon pepper
½ cup medium-grind bulgur, rinsed
¼ cup water
1 onion, chopped fine
3 garlic cloves, minced
2 teaspoons minced fresh oregano or ½ teaspoon dried
¼ teaspoon ground cinnamon
  Pinch cayenne pepper
1 pound plum tomatoes, cored, seeded, and chopped
2 ounces Pecorino Romano cheese, grated (1 cup), divided
2 tablespoons toasted pine nuts
2 teaspoons red wine vinegar
2 tablespoons minced fresh parsley

1. Adjust oven racks to upper-middle and lowest positions, place parchment paper–lined rimmed baking sheet on lower rack, and heat oven to 400 degrees.

2. Score flesh of each eggplant half in 1-inch diamond pattern, about 1 inch deep. Brush scored sides of eggplant with 1 tablespoon oil and sprinkle with ½ teaspoon salt and pepper. Lay eggplant cut side down on hot sheet and roast until flesh is tender, 40 to 50 minutes. Transfer eggplants cut side down to paper towel–lined baking sheet and let drain.

3. Toss bulgur with water in bowl and let sit until grains are softened and liquid is fully absorbed, 20 to 40 minutes.

4. Heat remaining 1 tablespoon oil in 12-inch skillet over medium heat until shimmering. Add onion and cook until softened, 5 minutes. Stir in garlic, oregano, cinnamon, cayenne, and remaining ½ teaspoon salt, and cook until fragrant, about 30 seconds. Off heat, stir in bulgur, tomatoes, ¾ cup Pecorino, pine nuts, and vinegar and let sit until warmed through, about 1 minute. Season with salt and pepper to taste.

5. Return eggplant cut side up to parchment-lined sheet. Using 2 forks, gently push eggplant flesh to sides to make room for filling. Mound bulgur mixture into eggplant halves and pack lightly with back of spoon. Sprinkle with remaining ¼ cup Pecorino. (Stuffed eggplant can be refrigerated for up to 24 hours. To serve, increase cooking time to 10 to 12 minutes.) Bake on upper rack until cheese is melted, 5 to 10 minutes. Sprinkle with parsley and serve warm or at room temperature.

Garlicky Fried Rice with Bok Choy

Serves 4 to 6 | **Total Time** 1 hour, plus 20 minutes cooling

WHY THIS RECIPE WORKS Garlic does the heavy lifting flavor-wise in this savory, vegetable-packed rice dish, with help from briny, pungent fish sauce (use a vegetarian fish sauce to make this vegetarian, or use soy sauce). But the best part of this dish is the crunchy hits of rice peppered throughout, where the lime juice and fish sauce concentrate into tiny pops of umami. Cooking the rice undisturbed right at the end is key to getting those magical crispy bits, so don't go stir-crazy. You will need a 14-inch flat-bottomed wok or a 12-inch nonstick skillet for this recipe. If using a wok, make sure that it is well seasoned so that the rice does not stick.

> **Substitution:** You can use 4 cups day-old cooked rice in place of making the rice in this recipe; skip step 1 and bring the leftover rice to room temperature before using.

1½ cups short-grain white rice, rinsed
1½ cups water
 1 teaspoon table salt, divided
 3 tablespoons vegetable oil, divided
1½ pounds baby bok choy, halved lengthwise and sliced crosswise ½ inch thick
10 garlic cloves, minced
 2 tablespoons fish sauce or soy sauce
 1 teaspoon grated lime zest plus 1½ tablespoons juice
 ¼ teaspoon pepper

1. Combine rice, water, and ½ teaspoon salt in medium saucepan and bring to boil over high heat. Reduce heat to low, cover, and simmer for 7 minutes. Let sit off heat for 15 minutes. Spread rice onto rimmed baking sheet and let cool on wire rack for 10 minutes. Transfer sheet to refrigerator and let rice chill for 20 minutes.

2. Heat 1 tablespoon oil in 14-inch flat-bottomed wok or 12-inch nonstick skillet over medium-high heat until just smoking. Add bok choy and remaining ½ teaspoon salt and cook until beginning to soften and char in spots, 2 to 4 minutes. Stir in garlic and cook until fragrant, about 30 seconds. Stir in rice, remaining 2 tablespoons oil, fish sauce, lime zest and juice, and pepper.

3. Firmly press rice mixture into compact, even layer. Cover and cook, without stirring, until rice begins to crisp, about 2 minutes. Uncover, reduce heat to medium, and continue to cook until bottom of rice is golden brown, 4 to 6 minutes. Season with salt and pepper to taste, and serve.

Vegetable Bibimbap with Nurungji

Serves 4 to 6 | **Total Time** 1 hour 25 minutes

WHY THIS RECIPE WORKS Bibimbap, an iconic Korean dish with many variations, features rice mixed together with various toppings ("bibim" means "mixed" in Korean; "bap" is the word for cooked rice). In one version, dolsot bibimbap, the dish is assembled and served in a hot stone bowl. The hot stone, which is coated in sesame oil, crisps the bottom of the rice, developing a satisfying crust called nurunji. This crust then gets combined with the softer rice and other components when the dish is mixed together. Our version trades the stone bowls for a Dutch oven. Because the pot retains heat for a long time, it's able to build a substantial crust of rice. To shorten the preparation process a bit, we use three sautéed vegetable toppings instead of the traditional six or more and turn the pickles and sauce into make-ahead options. You can save extra time by substituting store-bought kimchi for the pickles. For a true bibimbap experience, bring the whole pot to the table before stirring the vegetables into the rice in step 7.

RICE
2½ cups short-grain white rice
2½ cups water
 ¾ teaspoon table salt

VEGETABLES
 ¼ cup water
 3 scallions, minced
 3 tablespoons soy sauce
 3 garlic cloves, minced
 1 tablespoon sugar
 1 tablespoon vegetable oil, divided
 3 carrots, peeled and shredded (2 cups)
 8 ounces shiitake mushrooms, stemmed and sliced thin
10 ounces curly-leaf spinach, stemmed and chopped coarse

BIBIMBAP
 2 tablespoons plus 2 teaspoons vegetable oil, divided
 1 tablespoon toasted sesame oil
 4 large eggs
 1 recipe Sweet and Tangy Chili Sauce (page 266)
 1 recipe Quick-Pickled Cucumber and Bean Sprouts (page 267)

1. **FOR THE RICE** Bring rice, water, and salt to boil in medium saucepan over high heat. Cover, reduce heat to low, and cook for 7 minutes. Remove saucepan from heat and let sit, covered, until rice is tender, about 15 minutes.

2. **FOR THE VEGETABLES** While rice cooks, whisk water, scallions, soy sauce, garlic, and sugar in small bowl until sugar has dissolved. Heat 1 teaspoon oil in Dutch oven over high heat until shimmering. Add carrots and stir until coated. Add ⅓ cup scallion mixture and cook, stirring frequently, until carrots are slightly softened and moisture has evaporated, 1 to 2 minutes. Using slotted spoon, transfer carrots to small bowl.

3. Heat 1 teaspoon oil in now-empty pot until shimmering. Add mushrooms and stir until coated with oil. Add ⅓ cup scallion mixture and cook, stirring frequently, until mushrooms are tender and moisture has evaporated, 3 to 4 minutes. Using slotted spoon, transfer mushrooms to second small bowl.

4. Heat remaining 1 teaspoon oil in now-empty pot until shimmering. Add spinach and remaining ⅓ cup scallion mixture and stir to coat spinach. Cook, stirring frequently, until spinach is completely wilted but still bright green, 1 to 2 minutes. Using slotted spoon, transfer spinach to third small bowl. Discard any remaining liquid and wipe pot clean with paper towels.

5. **FOR THE BIBIMBAP** Heat 2 tablespoons vegetable oil and sesame oil in now-empty pot over high heat until shimmering. Carefully add rice and gently press into even layer. Cook, without stirring, until rice begins to form crust on bottom of pot, about 2 minutes. Using slotted spoon, transfer carrots, mushrooms, and spinach to pot and arrange in piles that cover surface of rice. Reduce heat to low.

6. While crust forms, heat remaining 2 teaspoons vegetable oil in 10-inch nonstick skillet over low heat for 5 minutes. Crack eggs into small bowl. Pour eggs into skillet; cover and cook (about 2 minutes for runny yolks, 2½ minutes for soft but set yolks, and 3 minutes for firmly set yolks). Slide eggs onto vegetables in pot.

7. Drizzle 2 tablespoons chili sauce over eggs. Without disturbing crust, use wooden spoon to stir rice, vegetables, and eggs until combined. Just before serving, scrape large pieces of crust from bottom of pot and stir into rice. Serve in individual bowls, passing pickles and remaining sauce separately.

Vegetable Bibimbap with Nurungji

Sweet and Tangy Chili Sauce

Makes about ¾ cup | **Total Time** 5 minutes FAST

A spicy-tart-sweet Korean chili sauce, gochujang is a standard accompaniment to mixed rice dishes such as bibimbap, but it is equally delicious drizzled on steamed, stir-fried, grilled, or roasted vegetables and proteins or used as a seasoning for soups and stews.

- ¼ cup gochujang paste
- 2 tablespoons toasted sesame oil
- 2 tablespoons unseasoned rice vinegar
- 2 tablespoons honey
- 1½ tablespoons water
- 2 garlic cloves, minced

Whisk all ingredients together in bowl. (Sauce can be refrigerated for up to 4 days; let come to room temperature before serving.)

Quick-Pickled Cucumber and Bean Sprouts

Makes about 2 cups | **Total Time** 10 minutes plus 1 hour pickling VEGAN

Serve these sweet and tangy pickles as a snack or with stir-fries and rice and noodle dishes. Draining the vegetables after 1 hour keeps them crisper.

- 1 cup unseasoned rice vinegar
- 2 tablespoons sugar
- 1½ teaspoons table salt
- 4 ounces (2 cups) bean sprouts
- 1 cucumber, peeled, quartered lengthwise, seeded, and sliced thin on bias

Whisk vinegar, sugar, and salt in medium bowl until sugar and salt have dissolved. Add bean sprouts and cucumber and toss to combine. Gently press on vegetables to submerge. Cover and let sit at room temperature for 1 hour; drain. Serve. (Drained vegetables can be refrigerated for up to 1 day.)

Skillet Rice and Beans with Corn and Fresh Tomatoes

Serves 6 | **Total Time** 1 hour VEGAN

WHY THIS RECIPE WORKS Rice and beans are a familiar combination the world over. This summery recipe produces a delicious weeknight meal with plump beans, soft rice, and fresh-tasting vegetables. We begin by sautéing onions and corn. Garlic, cumin, and cayenne contribute their potent flavors. Toasting the rice briefly before stirring in broth and black beans ensures that it soaks up all of the flavors and becomes fat and tender. We finish by sprinkling tomatoes, scallions, cilantro, and lime juice over the dish before serving. A few variations supply more recipes for this traditional pairing. We prefer the flavor of fresh corn; however, 1½ cups frozen corn, thawed and patted dry, can be substituted.

- 2 tablespoons extra-virgin olive oil, divided
- 12 ounces grape tomatoes, quartered
- 5 scallions, sliced thin
- ¼ cup minced fresh cilantro
- 1 tablespoon lime juice
- 1 onion, chopped fine

- 2 ears corn, kernels cut from cobs
- 4 garlic cloves, minced
- 1 teaspoon ground cumin
  Pinch cayenne pepper
- 1 cup long-grain white rice, rinsed
- 3 cups vegetable broth
- 2 (15-ounce) cans black beans, rinsed

1. Combine 1 tablespoon oil, tomatoes, scallions, cilantro, and lime juice in bowl and season with salt and pepper to taste; set aside for serving.

2. Heat remaining 1 tablespoon oil in 12-inch nonstick skillet over medium-high heat until shimmering. Add onion and cook until softened and lightly browned, 5 to 7 minutes. Stir in corn and cook until lightly browned, about 4 minutes.

3. Stir in garlic, cumin, and cayenne and cook until fragrant, about 30 seconds. Stir in rice and coat with spices, about 1 minute. Stir in broth and beans and bring to simmer. Cover and simmer gently, stirring occasionally, until rice is tender and liquid is absorbed, about 20 minutes.

4. Season with salt and pepper to taste, sprinkle tomato mixture over top, and serve.

VARIATIONS
Skillet Rice and Chickpeas with Coconut Milk VEGAN
Substitute 2 finely chopped yellow bell peppers for corn, 1½ teaspoons garam masala for cumin, and canned chickpeas for black beans. Substitute 1 cup coconut milk for 1 cup broth.

Spanish-Style Skillet Rice and Chickpeas VEGAN
Substitute 2 finely chopped red bell peppers for corn, pinch crumbled saffron threads for cumin, and canned chickpeas for black beans.

Mujaddara

Serves 4 to 6 | **Total Time** 1 hour 25 minutes

WHY THIS RECIPE WORKS This classic Levantine dish is a spectacular example of how a few humble ingredients can add up to a dish that's satisfying and complex. Traditional versions consist of tender basmati rice and lentils seasoned with warm spices and minced garlic and topped with deeply savory fried onions. To give the onions the best crispy texture, we microwave them to remove some of their liquid, then fry them in oil to a deep golden brown. To ensure that the rice and lentils are done at the same time, we parcook the lentils and then set them aside while we prepare the rice. We soak the rice in hot water to ensure that it turns out fluffy, not sticky, and then toast it along with the spices in some of the flavorful frying oil from the onions. Finished with a bracing garlicky yogurt sauce, this pilaf is comfort food at its best. You can use store-bought crispy onions and extra-virgin olive oil in place of the Crispy Onions if you prefer.

YOGURT SAUCE

- 1 cup plain whole-milk yogurt
- 2 tablespoons lemon juice
- ½ teaspoon minced garlic
- ½ teaspoon table salt

RICE AND LENTILS

- 8¾ ounces (1¼ cups) green or brown lentils, picked over and rinsed
- 1 teaspoon table salt, plus salt for cooking lentils
- 1¼ cups basmati rice
- 1 recipe Crispy Onions, plus 3 tablespoons reserved oil (page 270)
- 3 garlic cloves, minced
- 1 teaspoon ground coriander
- 1 teaspoon ground cumin
- ½ teaspoon ground cinnamon
- ½ teaspoon ground allspice
- ¼ teaspoon pepper
- ⅛ teaspoon cayenne pepper
- 1 teaspoon sugar
- 3 tablespoons minced fresh cilantro

1. FOR THE YOGURT SAUCE Whisk all ingredients together in bowl and refrigerate until ready to serve.

2. FOR THE RICE AND LENTILS Bring lentils, 4 cups water, and 1 teaspoon salt to boil in medium saucepan over high heat. Reduce heat to low and cook until lentils are just tender, 15 to 17 minutes. Drain and set aside.

3. Meanwhile, place rice in medium bowl, cover with hot tap water by 2 inches, and let sit for 15 minutes. Using your hands, gently swish grains to release excess starch. Carefully pour off water, leaving rice in bowl. Repeat adding and pouring off cold water 4 or 5 times, until water runs almost clear. Drain rice in fine-mesh strainer.

4. Cook reserved onion oil, garlic, coriander, cumin, cinnamon, allspice, pepper, and cayenne in Dutch oven over medium heat until fragrant, about 2 minutes. Add rice and cook, stirring occasionally, until grain edges begin to turn translucent, about 3 minutes. Stir in 2¼ cups water, sugar, and salt and bring to boil. Stir in reserved lentils, reduce heat

Mujaddara

to low, cover, and simmer gently until all liquid is absorbed, about 12 minutes.

5. Off heat, lay clean dish towel underneath lid and let sit, covered, for 10 minutes. Fluff rice and lentils with fork and stir in cilantro and half of onions. Transfer to serving platter and top with remaining onions. Serve with yogurt sauce.

Koshari

Serves 4 to 6 | **Total Time** 2 hours VEGAN

WHY THIS RECIPE WORKS Considered the national dish of Egypt, koshari evolved as a way to use up leftovers and became a popular street food. The hearty dish usually features lentils, rice, pasta, and chickpeas smothered in a spiced tomato sauce and topped with crispy fried onions. Although the dish takes some time to put together, each element is fairly simple. We cook the lentils and the pasta in boiling water and drain them, then set them aside while we prepare the rice and sauce. Soaking the rice in hot water before cooking eliminates excess starch so it doesn't clump. Using the same spices—coriander, cumin, cinnamon, nutmeg, and cayenne—in the sauce and the rice creates a layered flavor profile. Adding the chickpeas directly to the sauce to simmer infuses them with flavor. The finishing touch: a generous amount of ultrasavory, crunchy fried onions. You can use store-bought crispy onions and extra-virgin olive oil in place of the Crispy Onions if you prefer.

- 1 cup elbow macaroni
- 1 teaspoon table salt, divided, plus salt for cooking pasta and lentils
- 1 cup dried green or brown lentils, picked over and rinsed
- 1 recipe Crispy Onions, plus ¼ cup reserved oil, divided (page 270)
- 4 garlic cloves, minced, divided
- 1½ teaspoons ground coriander, divided
- 1½ teaspoons ground cumin, divided
- ¾ teaspoon ground cinnamon, divided
- ¼ teaspoon ground nutmeg, divided
- ¼ teaspoon cayenne pepper, divided
- 1 (28-ounce) can tomato sauce
- 1 (15-ounce) can chickpeas, rinsed
- 1 cup basmati rice
- 1 tablespoon red wine vinegar
- 3 tablespoons minced fresh parsley

Koshari

1. Bring 2 quarts water to boil in Dutch oven. Add pasta and 1½ teaspoons salt and cook, stirring often, until al dente. Drain pasta, rinse with water, then drain again. Transfer to bowl and set aside.

2. Meanwhile, bring lentils, 4 cups water, and 1 teaspoon salt to boil in medium saucepan over high heat. Reduce heat to low and cook until lentils are just tender, 15 to 17 minutes. Drain and set aside.

3. Cook 1 tablespoon reserved onion oil, 1 teaspoon garlic, ½ teaspoon coriander, ½ teaspoon cumin, ¼ teaspoon cinnamon, ⅛ teaspoon nutmeg, ⅛ teaspoon cayenne, and ½ teaspoon salt in now-empty saucepan over medium heat until fragrant, about 1 minute. Stir in tomato sauce and chickpeas, bring to simmer, and cook until slightly thickened, about 10 minutes. Cover and keep warm.

4. While sauce cooks, place rice in medium bowl, cover with hot tap water by 2 inches, and let sit for 15 minutes. Using your hands, gently swish grains to release excess starch. Carefully pour off water, leaving rice in bowl. Repeat adding and pouring off cold water 4 or 5 times, until water runs almost clear. Drain rice in fine-mesh strainer.

5. Cook remaining 3 tablespoons reserved onion oil, remaining garlic, remaining 1 teaspoon coriander, remaining 1 teaspoon cumin, remaining ½ teaspoon cinnamon, remaining ⅛ teaspoon nutmeg, and remaining ⅛ teaspoon cayenne in now-empty pot over medium heat until fragrant, about 2 minutes. Add rice and cook, stirring occasionally, until grain edges begin to turn translucent, about 3 minutes. Stir in 2 cups water and remaining ½ teaspoon salt and bring to boil. Stir in reserved lentils; reduce heat to low; cover; and simmer gently until all liquid is absorbed, about 12 minutes.

6. Off heat, sprinkle pasta over rice mixture. Cover, laying clean dish towel underneath lid, and let sit for 10 minutes.

7. Return sauce to simmer over medium heat. Stir in vinegar and season with salt and pepper to taste. Fluff rice and lentils with fork and stir in parsley and half of onions. Transfer to serving platter and top with half of sauce and remaining onions. Serve, passing remaining sauce separately.

Wild Mushroom Ragout with Farro

Serves 4 | Total Time 45 minutes FAST VEGAN

WHY THIS RECIPE WORKS Whole-grain farro is popular in Italy and we love it for its slightly sweet, nutty flavor and chewy texture. We decided to give this dish a simple Italian profile and pair it with a mushroom ragout. Chunks of portobellos and other mushrooms add texture while dried porcini add flavor and depth. For the best flavor, we prefer to use a combination of white, shiitake, and oyster mushrooms; however, you can choose just one or two varieties if you like. The woody stems of shiitakes are unpleasant to eat so be sure to remove them. Drizzle individual portions with good balsamic vinegar before serving if desired. We prefer the flavor and texture of whole farro in this recipe. Do not use pearl, quick-cooking, or presteamed farro (check the ingredient list on the package to determine this) for the whole farro.

3½ cups vegetable broth
1½ cups whole farro, rinsed
1 pound portobello mushroom caps, halved and sliced ½ inch wide
18 ounces assorted mushrooms, trimmed and halved if small or quartered if large
2 tablespoons extra-virgin olive oil
1 onion, chopped fine
½ ounce dried porcini mushrooms, rinsed and minced
3 garlic cloves, minced
1 teaspoon minced fresh thyme or ¼ teaspoon dried
¼ cup dry Madeira
1 (14.5-ounce) can diced tomatoes, drained and chopped
2 tablespoons minced fresh parsley

1. Combine broth and farro in large saucepan and bring to simmer over medium heat. Cook until farro is tender and creamy, 20 to 25 minutes. Season with salt and pepper to taste; cover and keep warm.

2. Meanwhile, microwave portobello and assorted mushrooms in covered bowl until tender, 6 to 8 minutes. Drain, reserving mushroom juices.

3. Heat oil in Dutch oven over medium-high heat until shimmering. Add onion and porcini and cook until softened and lightly browned, 5 to 7 minutes. Stir in drained mushrooms and cook, stirring often, until mushrooms are dry and lightly browned, about 5 minutes.

4. Stir in garlic and thyme and cook until fragrant, about 30 seconds. Stir in Madeira and reserved mushroom juices, scraping up any browned bits. Stir in tomatoes and simmer gently until sauce is slightly thickened, about 8 minutes. Off heat, stir in parsley and season with salt and pepper to taste. Portion farro into individual serving bowls and top with mushroom mixture. Serve.

Crispy Onions

Makes 1½ cups | Total Time 35 minutes
FAST VEGAN

It is crucial to thoroughly dry the microwaved onions after rinsing. Be sure to reserve enough oil to use in Mujaddara or Koshari. Any remaining oil may be stored in an airtight container and refrigerated for up to four weeks; it tastes great in salad dressings, sautéed vegetables, eggs, and pasta sauces.

2 pounds onions, halved and sliced crosswise into ¼-inch-thick pieces
2 teaspoons table salt
1½ cups vegetable oil

1. Toss onions and salt together in large bowl. Microwave for 5 minutes. Rinse thoroughly, transfer to paper towel–lined baking sheet, and dry well.
2. Heat onions and oil in Dutch oven over high heat, stirring frequently, until onions are golden brown, 25 to 30 minutes. Drain onions in colander set in large bowl. Transfer onions to paper towel–lined baking sheet to drain; reserve oil.

Creamy Polenta with Radicchio Agrodolce

Creamy Polenta with Radicchio Agrodolce

Serves 4 | **Total Time** 1 hour

WHY THIS RECIPE WORKS Cheesy polenta is often topped with a meat or mushroom ragu but here we counter the creamy grain with pleasingly bitter radicchio and celery in an agrodolce sauce, a sweet and sour reduction of vinegar and sugar with an eye-catching luster. A pinch of baking soda added to the polenta cuts the cooking in half and eliminates the need for constant stirring. While the polenta cooks, we sauté the celery and shallots until they're softened, add fresh thyme for slightly peppery notes, and reduce red wine vinegar and sugar in the same pan. The vinegar and sugar thicken into the signature agrodolce glaze. Grapes provide pops of appropriately wine-y sweetness. Charring the radicchio slightly in a skillet counterbalances the sweetness from the grapes with smoky bitterness, and adds heft. Richness, sweetness, sourness, and bitterness join forces for a vegetarian main to remember. Or serve this as a sensational side dish for meat. You can use parsley if your celery doesn't come with leaves.

5 cups water
½ teaspoon table salt, divided
  Pinch baking soda
1 cup coarse-ground cornmeal
¼ cup extra-virgin olive oil, divided, plus extra for drizzling
1 ounce Parmesan cheese, grated (1 cup), plus extra for serving
3 celery ribs, cut into ½-inch pieces, plus ½ cup celery leaves
2 shallots, sliced thin
1 teaspoon minced fresh thyme or ¼ teaspoon dried
1 cup red wine vinegar
3 tablespoons sugar
3 ounces seedless red grapes, halved (½ cup)
1 head radicchio (10 ounces), halved, cored, and cut into ½-inch pieces
¼ cup whole almonds, toasted and chopped coarse

1. Bring water to boil in large saucepan over medium-high heat. Stir in ¼ teaspoon salt and baking soda. Slowly add cornmeal in steady stream, stirring constantly. Bring mixture to boil, stirring constantly, about 1 minute. Reduce heat to lowest possible setting, cover, and cook for 5 minutes.

2. Whisk cornmeal to smooth out any lumps, making sure to scrape down sides and bottom of saucepan. Cover and continue to cook, without stirring, until cornmeal is tender but slightly al dente, about 25 minutes. (Polenta should be loose and barely hold its shape but will continue to thicken as it cools.) Off heat, stir in 2 tablespoons oil and Parmesan and season with salt and pepper to taste. Cover and keep warm.

3. Meanwhile, heat 1 tablespoon oil in 12-inch nonstick skillet over medium heat until shimmering. Add celery ribs, shallots, and remaining ¼ teaspoon salt and cook, stirring occasionally, until softened and lightly browned, 7 to 9 minutes. Stir in thyme and cook until fragrant, about 30 seconds. Stir in vinegar and sugar; bring to simmer; and cook until liquid is thickened to syrupy glaze, about 10 minutes. Transfer to large bowl and stir in grapes. Cover with aluminum foil to keep warm.

4. Heat remaining 1 tablespoon oil in now-empty skillet over medium-high heat until shimmering. Add radicchio and cook until browned, about 5 minutes. Transfer to bowl with celery mixture and toss to combine. Serve polenta with radicchio mixture, sprinkling with almonds, extra Parmesan, and celery leaves and drizzling with extra oil.

Savory Oatmeal with Peas, Pecorino, and Pepper

THE BEST CORNMEAL FOR POLENTA

Here's what to look for when shopping for polenta. In the supermarket, cornmeal can be labeled anything from yellow grits to corn semolina. Forget the names. When shopping for the right product to make polenta, there are three things to consider: "instant" or "quick-cooking" versus the traditional style, degerminated versus whole-grain meal, and grind size. Instant and quick-cooking cornmeals are parcooked and comparatively bland. Though we loved the full-corn flavor of whole-grain cornmeal, it remains slightly gritty no matter how long you cook it. We prefer degerminated cornmeal, in which the hard hull and germ are removed from each kernel (check the back label or ingredient list to see if your cornmeal is degerminated; if it's not explicitly labeled as such, you can assume it's whole-grain).

As for grind, we found coarser grains brought the most desirable and pillowy texture to our polenta. However, grind coarseness can vary dramatically from brand to brand since there are no standards to ensure consistency: One manufacturer's "coarse" may be another's "fine." Here's how to identify the optimal coarsely ground texture.

TOO FINE

The superfine grains of quick-cooking cornmeal speed the cooking process but lack corn flavor.

STILL TOO FINE

Regular cornmeal (such as Quaker) has a similarly sand-like texture that also cooks up gluey.

JUST RIGHT

A coarser cut, about the size of couscous, retains a soft but hearty texture after cooking.

Savory Oatmeal with Peas, Pecorino, and Pepper

Serves 4 | **Total Time** 35 minutes, plus 2 hours soaking

WHY THIS RECIPE WORKS Oatmeal needn't always be sweet; it can have plenty of savory appeal. Most oatmeal fans agree that the steel-cut version of the grain offers the best flavor and texture, but many balk at the 40-minute cooking time. In this recipe, we decrease the cooking time to only 10 minutes by stirring steel-cut oats into boiling water the night before. This enables the grains to hydrate and soften overnight. In the morning, we add more water and a bit of lemon juice and simmer the mixture for 4 to 6 minutes, until thick and creamy. Stirring in generous amounts of Pecorino and pepper gives these oats a deeply savory flavor, lemon juice augments the cheese's tang, and a topping of peas provides visual appeal and pops of grassy sweetness. A final sprinkle of Pecorino and pepper and a drizzle of olive oil seals the deal—this isn't your typical bowl of breakfast oats. The oatmeal thickens as it cools; thin it with boiling water for a looser consistency. For a heartier meal, top each serving with a fried or soft-cooked egg.

4 cups water, divided
1 cup steel-cut oats
¼ teaspoon table salt
2 teaspoons lemon juice
4 ounces Pecorino Romano cheese, grated fine (2 cups), plus extra for serving
1½ teaspoons pepper
1 cup frozen peas
4 teaspoons extra-virgin olive oil

1. Bring 3 cups water to boil in large saucepan over high heat. Off heat, stir in oats and salt. Cover saucepan and let stand for at least 2 hours or up to 10 hours.

2. Stir remaining 1 cup water and lemon juice into oats and bring to boil over medium-high heat. Reduce heat to medium and cook, stirring occasionally, until oats are softened but still retain some chew and mixture thickens and resembles warm pudding, 4 to 6 minutes. Off heat, whisk in Pecorino and pepper until fully incorporated. Let sit for 5 minutes.

3. While oatmeal rests, microwave peas until warm, 1 to 2 minutes. Stir oatmeal and season with salt and pepper to taste. Divide evenly among 4 bowls. Top each portion with ¼ cup peas. Drizzle each portion with 1 teaspoon oil; sprinkle with additional Pecorino and pepper, if desired; and serve.

Soba Noodles with Roasted Eggplant

Soba Noodles with Roasted Eggplant

Serves 4 | Total Time 45 minutes `FAST`

WHY THIS RECIPE WORKS With its creamy texture and mild flavor, eggplant is a perfect foil to nutty, pleasantly chewy buckwheat soba noodles. Roasting is an easy, hands-off way to cook the eggplant. For the sauce, we start with soy sauce for savory richness. Oyster sauce (regular or vegetarian), toasted sesame oil, and some sugar provide a nice balance of savory and sweet flavors, while a little sake contributes a clean, acidic note that bolsters the sauce. Finally cilantro and sesame seeds add freshness. You may substitute dry vermouth for the sake.

3 pounds eggplant, cut into 1-inch pieces
¼ cup vegetable oil
⅓ cup sugar
3 tablespoons oyster sauce or vegetarian oyster sauce
3 tablespoons toasted sesame oil
5 teaspoons sake
1 tablespoon soy sauce
Pinch red pepper flakes (optional)
12 ounces dried soba noodles
¾ cup fresh cilantro leaves
2 teaspoons sesame seeds, toasted

1. Adjust oven racks to upper middle and lower-middle position and heat oven to 450 degrees. Line 2 rimmed baking sheets with aluminum foil and spray with vegetable oil spray. Toss eggplant with vegetable oil and spread over prepared baking sheets. Roast until well browned and tender, 25 to 30 minutes, stirring and switching sheets halfway through.

2. Combine sugar; oyster sauce; sesame oil; 2 tablespoons water; sake; soy sauce; and pepper flakes, if using, in small saucepan. Cook over medium heat, stirring often, until sugar has dissolved, about 1 minute; cover and set aside.

3. Meanwhile, bring 4 quarts water to boil in large pot. Add noodles and cook, stirring often, until tender. Reserve ½ cup cooking water, then drain noodles and return them to pot. Add reserved sauce and roasted eggplant and toss to combine. Add reserved cooking water as needed to adjust consistency. Serve, sprinkling individual portions with cilantro and sesame seeds.

Teff-Stuffed Acorn Squash with Lime Crema and Roasted Pepitas

Serves 4 | **Total Time** 1 hour

WHY THIS RECIPE WORKS Teff is a gluten-free whole grain indigenous to Ethiopia and Eritrea. It has a mildly nutty, earthy flavor; is packed with nutrients; and ranges in color from dark brown to red to white. For this dish we chose brown teff, which is the most readily available in supermarkets. In Ethiopia, the tiny grains of teff are typically ground into flour to make the flatbread known as injera. Embracing teff as a whole grain, we cook it pilaf-style and make it the base for a savory stuffing to spoon into roasted acorn squash. To showcase teff's versatility, we put a Southwestern spin on our stuffing using the warm and bright flavors of chopped green chiles, chili powder, cumin, coriander, and oregano. After spooning the stuffing into the squash, we top it off with lime crema and toasted pepitas to bring freshness and crunch.

LIME CREMA

½ cup sour cream
2 teaspoons grated lime zest plus 3 tablespoons juice (2 limes)
½ teaspoon table salt

TEFF-STUFFED ACORN SQUASH

1 tablespoon vegetable oil
1 tablespoon chipotle chile powder
1 teaspoon table salt, divided
½ teaspoon ground cumin
½ teaspoon ground coriander
½ teaspoon pepper
¼ teaspoon dried oregano
2 acorn squashes (1½ pounds each), quartered pole to pole and seeded
2 cups vegetable broth
1 cup teff
2 (4-ounce) cans chopped green chiles, drained
½ cup minced fresh cilantro
¼ cup roasted pepitas

1. FOR THE LIME CREMA Whisk all ingredients together in bowl; set aside until ready to serve.

2. FOR THE TEFF-STUFFED ACORN SQUASH Adjust oven rack to middle positions and heat oven to 400 degrees. Line rimmed baking sheet with aluminum foil. Combine oil, chipotle chile powder, ¾ teaspoon salt, cumin, coriander, pepper, and oregano in bowl. Brush flesh side of squash evenly with spice mixture. Place wedges cut side down on prepared sheet and roast until browned on first side, about 20 minutes.

3. Flip wedges so second cut side is in contact with sheet and roast until second side is browned and tip of paring knife slips easily into flesh, about 15 minutes.

4. Meanwhile, bring broth to boil in medium saucepan. Stir in teff and remaining ¼ teaspoon salt, reduce heat to medium-low, cover, and simmer until broth is absorbed, 15 to 20 minutes. Remove from heat and let sit, covered, for 10 minutes. Fluff grains with fork and set aside.

5. Using spoon, scoop flesh from each squash wedge, leaving about ¼-inch thickness of flesh in each shell. Chop squash flesh into rough ½-inch pieces and transfer to large bowl. Gently fold reserved teff, green chiles, and cilantro into squash in bowl, then gently mound teff-squash mixture evenly in squash shells. Drizzle reserved lime crema over top and sprinkle with pepitas. Serve.

Curried Fonio with Roasted Vegetables and Hibiscus Vinaigrette

Serves 4 | **Total Time** 1 hour VEGAN

WHY THIS RECIPE WORKS Tiny but mighty, fonio is a perfect grain for pilaf: This gluten-free and nutrient-rich West African relative of millet not only cooks up quickly, but is also light and fluffy and absorbs flavors well. To create a punchy and flavorful foundation for a fonio pilaf meal, we use curry powder along with fresh garlic and ginger. Sweet butternut squash, red onion, and grassy okra roast at the same time in the oven, but on separate baking sheets so that we can steam the okra first before it gets crispy and brown. We add extra crunch and richness by stirring in chopped roasted cashews to finish, and then we drizzle everything with a sweet-tart vinaigrette made with dried hibiscus flowers. The bright fuchsia flowers—from a plant related to okra and native to Africa—add a unique cranberry-like flavor and color that pulls this striking plate together.

- 1 pound butternut squash, peeled, seeded, and cut into ¾-inch pieces
- 1 red onion, cut through root end into 1-inch wedges
- 2 tablespoons plus 2 teaspoons extra-virgin olive oil, divided
- 1¼ teaspoons table salt, divided
- ¼ teaspoon pepper, divided
- 12 ounces okra, trimmed and halved lengthwise
- 2 garlic cloves, minced
- 1½ teaspoons curry powder
- 1 teaspoon grated fresh ginger
- 2 cups water
- 1 cup fonio
- ⅓ cup roasted cashews, chopped
- ½ cup Hibiscus Vinaigrette
- ¼ cup chopped fresh parsley

1. Adjust oven racks to upper-middle and lower-middle positions and heat oven to 425 degrees. Line 2 rimmed baking sheets with aluminum foil.

2. Toss squash and onion with 1 tablespoon oil, ½ teaspoon salt, and ⅛ teaspoon pepper in bowl, then arrange in even layer on rimmed baking sheet. Toss okra with 2 teaspoons oil, ¼ teaspoon salt, and remaining ⅛ teaspoon pepper in now-empty bowl, then arrange cut side down on second rimmed baking sheet. Cover sheet with okra tightly with foil.

3. Place sheet with squash and onions on lower rack and sheet with okra on upper rack. Roast for 15 minutes, then remove foil from sheet with okra. Continue to roast vegetables until squash and onions are tender and browned, and cut sides of okra are well browned, 7 to 12 minutes.

4. Meanwhile, heat remaining 1 tablespoon oil in medium saucepan over medium heat until shimmering. Add garlic, curry powder, and ginger and cook until fragrant, about 30 seconds. Stir in water, fonio, and remaining ½ teaspoon salt, and bring to simmer. Cover, reduce heat to low, and simmer until liquid is absorbed, about 3 minutes. Off heat, let fonio sit, covered, for 10 minutes, then gently fluff with fork, breaking up any large clumps. Stir in cashews.

5. Divide fonio among individual serving bowls. Top with roasted vegetables and drizzle with vinaigrette. Sprinkle with parsley and serve.

Hibiscus Vinaigrette

Makes 1 cup | **Total Time** 20 minutes

`FAST` `VEGAN`

For an accurate measurement of boiling water, bring a kettle of water to a boil and then measure out the desired amount.

- ½ ounce (½ cup) whole dried hibiscus flowers
- ½ cup boiling water
- ½ cup extra-virgin olive oil
- 2 tablespoons red wine vinegar
- 2 tablespoons sugar
- 1 teaspoon table salt
- 1 teaspoon Dijon mustard
- ½ teaspoon pepper
- 1 tablespoon minced shallot

Combine hibiscus flowers and boiling water in blender jar; let sit for 10 minutes. Add oil, vinegar, sugar, salt, mustard, and pepper and process until only small pieces of flowers remain, about 1 minute. Transfer to small bowl and stir in shallot. (Vinaigrette can be refrigerated for up to 5 days.)

Curried Fonio with Roasted Vegetables and Hibiscus Vinaigrette

Cauliflower Biryani

Serves 4 to 6 | **Total Time** 1 hour `VEGAN`

WHY THIS RECIPE WORKS Biryani places fragrant long-grain basmati center stage, enriching it with saffron and a variety of fresh herbs and pungent spices. Traditional recipes take a long time to develop deep flavor by steeping whole spices and cooking each component on its own before marrying them. We deconstruct this dish to make it easier and faster, while staying true to its warmth and home-style appeal. We pair our rice with sweet, earthy roasted cauliflower, cut the cauliflower into small florets to speed up roasting, and toss it with warm spices to give it deep flavor. While it roasts, we sauté an onion until golden, then cook a jalapeño, garlic, and more spices until fragrant. We add the rice to this flavorful mixture and simmer it until tender. Once the rice finishes cooking, we let the residual heat plump the currants and bloom the saffron while the rice rests. Last, we stir in lots of bright mint and cilantro and our roasted cauliflower. Biryani is traditionally served with a cooling yogurt sauce.

> **Substitution:** You can use long-grain white, jasmine, or Texmati rice in place of the basmati.

- 1 head cauliflower (2 pounds), cored and cut into ½-inch florets
- ¼ cup extra-virgin olive oil, divided
- 1 teaspoon table salt, divided
- ¼ teaspoon pepper
- ¼ teaspoon ground cardamom, divided
- ¼ teaspoon ground cumin, divided
- 1 onion, sliced thin
- 4 garlic cloves, minced
- 1 jalapeño chile, stemmed, seeded, and minced
- ⅛ teaspoon ground cinnamon
- ⅛ teaspoon ground ginger
- 1½ cups basmati rice, rinsed
- 2¼ cups water
- ¼ cup dried currants or raisins
- ½ teaspoon saffron threads, lightly crumbled
- 2 tablespoons chopped fresh cilantro
- 2 tablespoons chopped fresh mint
- 1 recipe Herb-Yogurt Sauce (page 176); optional

1. Adjust oven rack to middle position and heat oven to 425 degrees. Toss cauliflower, 2 tablespoons oil, ½ teaspoon salt, pepper, ⅛ teaspoon cardamom, and ⅛ teaspoon cumin together in bowl. Spread cauliflower onto rimmed baking sheet and roast until tender, 15 to 20 minutes.

2. Meanwhile, heat remaining 2 tablespoons oil in large saucepan over medium-high heat until shimmering. Add onion and cook, stirring often, until soft and dark brown around edges, 10 to 12 minutes.

3. Stir in garlic, jalapeño, cinnamon, ginger, remaining ⅛ teaspoon cardamom, and remaining ⅛ teaspoon cumin and cook until fragrant, about 1 minute. Stir in rice and cook until well coated, about 1 minute. Add water and remaining ½ teaspoon salt and bring to simmer. Reduce heat to low; cover; and simmer until all liquid is absorbed, 16 to 18 minutes.

4. Remove pot from heat and sprinkle currants and saffron over rice. Cover, laying clean folded dish towel underneath lid, and let sit for 10 minutes. Fold in cilantro, mint, and roasted cauliflower. Season with salt and pepper to taste and serve with yogurt sauce, if desired.

Barley Risotto with Roasted Butternut Squash

Serves 8 | **Total Time** 2 hours

WHY THIS RECIPE WORKS In this hearty cold-weather main course, sweet roasted butternut squash is paired with nutty, chewy barley, sage, and Parmesan. With the bran removed, the texture of the cooked grain is pleasantly springy. Also, the pearl barley's starchy interior is exposed, which creates a supple, velvety sauce when simmered. Barley requires more liquid and more time to cook than the usual Arborio rice, but we have found that barley takes well to a modified version of our risotto method. We start traditionally by sautéing aromatics, toasting the grain, and simmering the mixture with wine. We then buck the tradition of adding hot liquid in small intervals and pour in 3 cups of it at once, allowing the barley to simmer and only giving it the occasional stir. The simmering action agitates the barley enough that it releases its starch, making constant stirring unnecessary. Once the barley has absorbed the broth, we add 2 more cups of liquid and continue to simmer. After the grains absorb that liquid, we gradually add more, stirring constantly, until the barley is cooked through. We add half of our squash to the simmering barley to break down and thicken and then stir in the remaining squash pieces right before serving.

1½ cups pearl barley

2 pounds butternut squash, peeled, seeded, and cut into ½-inch pieces (6 cups)

1 tablespoon extra-virgin olive oil

¼ teaspoon table salt

⅛ teaspoon pepper

4 cups chicken or vegetable broth

1 onion, chopped fine

2 garlic cloves, minced

1 cup dry white wine

1½ ounces Parmesan cheese, grated (¾ cup)

1 tablespoon unsalted butter

1 teaspoon minced fresh sage

⅛ teaspoon ground nutmeg

1. Adjust oven rack to upper-middle position and heat oven to 450 degrees. Rinse barley in fine-mesh strainer under cold running water until water runs clear. Drain briefly. Spread grains on rimmed baking sheet lined with clean dish towel. Let dry for 15 minutes.

2. Line second rimmed baking sheet with parchment paper. Toss squash with 2 teaspoons oil, salt, and pepper in bowl to coat. Spread squash over prepared sheet. Roast until tender and golden brown, about 30 minutes; set aside.

3. Meanwhile, bring broth and 4 cups water to simmer in medium saucepan. Reduce heat to lowest possible setting and cover to keep warm.

4. Cook remaining 1 teaspoon oil and onion, covered, in large saucepan over medium-low heat, stirring occasionally, until onion is softened, 8 to 10 minutes. Stir in garlic and cook until fragrant, about 30 seconds. Stir in barley and increase heat to medium. Cook, stirring often, until lightly toasted and aromatic, about 4 minutes. Stir in wine and continue to cook, stirring often, until wine has been completely absorbed, about 2 minutes.

5. Stir in 3 cups warm broth mixture and half of roasted squash. Simmer, stirring occasionally, until liquid is absorbed and bottom of pan is dry, 22 to 25 minutes. Stir in 2 cups warm broth mixture and continue to simmer, stirring occasionally, until liquid is absorbed and bottom of pan is dry, 15 to 18 minutes. Continue to cook, stirring often and adding remaining broth, ½ cup at a time, as needed to keep pan bottom from becoming dry (about every 4 minutes). Continue to add broth until barley is cooked through and still somewhat firm in center, 15 to 20 minutes.

6. Off heat, stir in Parmesan, butter, sage, nutmeg, and remaining squash. Season with salt and pepper to taste, and serve.

Cauliflower Biryani

Barley Risotto with Roasted Butternut Squash

Bean Sides

● FAST (45 minutes or less)   ● VEGAN

Photo: Edamame Salad with Pecorino and Mint

Caesar Green Bean Salad

Southwestern Black Bean Salad

Caesar Green Bean Salad

Serves 4 to 6 | **Total Time** 45 minutes, plus 30 minutes cooling

WHY THIS RECIPE WORKS This inventive approach to Caesar salad turns to green beans instead of leafy greens for the salad base. To keep the flavors bold and prevent the green beans from becoming waterlogged, we blanch them in boiling salted water but then, instead of shocking them in ice water, we transfer them to a towel-lined baking sheet to cool down. To make a Caesar dressing that clings well to the beans, we combine lemon juice, Worcestershire sauce, garlic, anchovies, and extra-virgin olive oil and emulsify the dressing with Dijon mustard. To add texture to the salad and keep with some tradition, we toss crispy croutons into the dressed beans.

DRESSING AND GREEN BEANS

1½ tablespoons lemon juice
 1 tablespoon Worcestershire sauce
 1 tablespoon Dijon mustard
 3 garlic cloves, minced
 3 anchovy fillets, rinsed and minced to paste
 ½ teaspoon pepper
 ¼ teaspoon table salt, plus salt for blanching beans
 3 tablespoons extra-virgin olive oil
1½ pounds green beans, trimmed
 2 ounces Parmesan or Pecorino Romano cheese, shaved with vegetable peeler, divided

CROUTONS

 3 ounces baguette, cut into ½-inch pieces
 2 tablespoons extra-virgin olive oil
 ¼ teaspoon pepper

   1. FOR THE DRESSING AND GREEN BEANS Whisk lemon juice, Worcestershire, mustard, garlic, anchovies, pepper, and salt together in bowl. Whisking constantly, slowly drizzle in oil until emulsified; set aside. (Dressing can be refrigerated for up to 24 hours; whisk to recombine before using.)

   2. Line rimmed baking sheet with clean dish towel. Bring 4 quarts water to boil in large pot. Add green beans and 1½ teaspoons salt. Return to boil and cook until tender, 5 to 7 minutes. Drain green beans in colander and spread in even layer on prepared sheet; let cool completely, about 30 minutes.

   3. FOR THE CROUTONS Meanwhile, toss baguette with oil and pepper, then transfer to 12-inch nonstick skillet (reserve bowl). Cook over medium-high heat, stirring occasionally, until golden brown and crispy 5 to 7 minutes. Return croutons to reserved bowl.

4. Transfer dressing, green beans, and half of Parmesan to bowl with croutons and toss to combine. Season with salt and pepper to taste. Sprinkle with remaining Parmesan. Serve.

DRAINING GREEN BEANS

For bold flavors and to prevent green beans from getting waterlogged, simply drain them and spread them onto a dish towel–lined baking sheet to cool, instead of shocking them in ice water to stop them cooking.

Southwestern Black Bean Salad

Serves 6 to 8 | **Total Time** 25 minutes FAST

WHY THIS RECIPE WORKS Scallions, creamy avocados, tomatoes, and corn contribute mellow aromatic zing, richness, juicy freshness, and welcome sweetness to this colorful bean salad. Sautéing the corn (both fresh and frozen work well) until it's toasty and just starting to brown adds a pleasant nuttiness to the kernels. To give the salad tantalizing brightness, we turn the typical dressing ratio of 1 part acid to 3 parts oil nearly upside down, using more lime juice than olive oil. Honey balances the citrus kick, and chipotle chile in adobo contributes smoky heat. You will need three to four ears to yield 2 cups of fresh kernels. If using frozen corn, be sure to thaw and drain it.

⅓ cup lime juice (3 limes)

¼ cup extra-virgin olive oil, divided

4 scallions, sliced thin

1 tablespoon minced canned chipotle chile in adobo sauce

1 teaspoon honey

½ teaspoon table salt

½ teaspoon pepper

2 cups fresh or frozen corn

2 (15-ounce) cans black beans, rinsed

2 avocados, halved, pitted, and cut into ½-inch pieces

2 tomatoes, cored and chopped

¼ cup minced fresh cilantro

Whisk lime juice, 2 tablespoons oil, scallions, chipotle, honey, salt, and pepper together in large bowl. Heat remaining 2 tablespoons oil in 12-inch nonstick skillet over medium-high heat until shimmering. Add corn and cook until spotty brown, about 5 minutes; transfer to bowl with dressing. Add beans, avocados, tomatoes, and cilantro and toss to combine. Season with salt and pepper to taste. Serve.

Classic Three-Bean Salad

Serves 8 to 10 | **Total Time** 30 minutes, plus 12¾ hours chilling and resting VEGAN

WHY THIS RECIPE WORKS Recipes for this familiar picnic standby—canned green, yellow, and kidney beans tossed in a sweet, vinegary dressing—have changed little since the salad's heyday in the 1950s. To create an updated, fresher-tasting version, we stick with the convenient canned kidney beans but opt for fresh green and yellow beans for a more vibrant flavor and better texture than canned. For the dressing, we rely on vegetable oil for mild richness and red wine vinegar for tang. Heating the oil and vinegar with sugar, garlic, salt, and pepper intensifies the vinaigrette's flavor and sweetness. For the best results, do not skip refrigerating the salad, which is key for allowing the flavors to meld.

8 ounces green beans, trimmed and cut into 1-inch lengths

8 ounces yellow wax beans, trimmed and cut into 1-inch lengths

1 teaspoon table salt, plus salt for blanching beans

1 cup red wine vinegar

¾ cup sugar

½ cup vegetable oil

2 garlic cloves, minced
  Pinch pepper

1 (15-ounce) can red kidney beans, rinsed

½ red onion, sliced thin

¼ cup minced fresh parsley

1. Bring 3 quarts water to boil in large saucepan over high heat. Fill large bowl halfway with ice and water. Add green beans, yellow beans, and 1 tablespoon salt to boiling water and cook until beans are crisp-tender, about 5 minutes. Drain beans and plunge immediately into ice water to stop cooking; let sit until chilled, about 2 minutes. Drain well.

2. Heat vinegar, sugar, oil, garlic, pepper, and salt in small saucepan over medium heat, stirring frequently, until sugar has dissolved, about 5 minutes. Transfer to large bowl and let cool completely, about 15 minutes.

3. Toss green and yellow beans, kidney beans, and onion with cooled vinegar mixture. Refrigerate for at least 12 hours or up to 2 days to let flavors meld.

4. Let salad sit at room temperature for 30 minutes. Stir in parsley and season with salt and pepper to taste. Serve.

Sautéed Fava Beans, Asparagus, and Leek

Serves 6 | **Total Time** 45 minutes FAST VEGAN

WHY THIS RECIPE WORKS Quickly sautéing buttery fava beans with asparagus, leek, and fresh herbs makes for a vibrant, ultraspringy side dish. We blanch and shell the favas and then add them at the end of cooking to preserve their vibrant color and creamy bite. This recipe works best with fresh fava beans; look for them at farmers' markets or supermarkets and choose bright-green, unblemished pods. We like fresh parsley here, but mint, tarragon, or cilantro will also work. Serve alongside grilled meats or seafood.

Substitution: You can use 12 ounces (2 ½ cups) frozen shelled fava beans, thawed, in place of the fresh favas. Be sure to remove the sheaths. Skip step 1 if using frozen favas.

- 2½ pounds fava beans, shelled (2½ cups)
- 2 tablespoons extra-virgin olive oil
- 1 leek, white and light green parts only, sliced thin, and washed thoroughly (1½ cups)
- 1 pound asparagus, trimmed and cut on bias into 1-inch lengths
- ½ teaspoon table salt
- ⅛ teaspoon pepper
- 1 teaspoon grated lemon zest, plus lemon wedges for serving
- 1 tablespoon chopped fresh parsley

1. Bring 1 quart water to boil in medium saucepan. Fill large bowl halfway with ice and water. Nestle fine-mesh strainer into ice bath. Add beans to boiling water and cook for 4 minutes. Using spider skimmer or slotted spoon, transfer beans to strainer set in ice water and let cool, about 2 minutes. Transfer fava beans

Edamame Salad with Pecorino and Mint

Succotash Salad with Butter Beans and Basil

to double layer of paper towels and dry well. Using paring knife, make small cut along edge of each bean through waxy sheath, then gently squeeze sheath to release bean; discard sheath.

2. Heat oil in 12-inch nonstick skillet over medium heat until shimmering. Add leek and cook, stirring frequently until softened, about 4 minutes. Add asparagus, salt, and pepper and stir well. Continue to cook, stirring occasionally, until asparagus is crisp-tender, 3 to 6 minutes. Stir in beans and cook just until beans are warmed through, about 2 minutes. Remove from heat and stir in lemon zest. Season with salt to taste, and transfer to serving bowl. Top with parsley. Serve with lemon wedges.

NOTES FROM THE TEST KITCHEN

FAVAS FOR PEOPLE AND THE PLANET
Fava beans are packed with protein, fiber, and a slew of vitamins and minerals. And the fava plant, an exceptionally robust crop that has thrived worldwide for more than 10,000 years, is also something of an agricultural superstar. Whereas almost all other vegetable crops deplete nitrogen from the soil, legumes such as favas fertilize it by drawing nitrogen from the atmosphere and funneling it into the ground. Their dual-purpose potential is what compelled Hossein Zakeri and Kyle Brasier, plant scientists at California State University, Chico, to study and promote fava beans as a vegetable. Despite being a staple in other parts of the world, they said, favas aren't popular in the United States because pulse crops can't compete with the revenue generated by high-value, soil-depleting harvests like lettuce, strawberries, and almonds. Highlighting favas' nutritional and agricultural benefits, they hope, will turn consumers on to them.

Edamame Salad with Pecorino and Mint

Serves 4 | **Total Time** 40 minutes **FAST**

WHY THIS RECIPE WORKS Inspired by Italian fava bean salads, this salad pairs frozen shelled edamame with a garlicky lemon dressing, pungent Pecorino Romano cheese, and refreshing fresh mint and parsley. We blanch the edamame in heavily salted water for 5 minutes to ensure that they're seasoned all the way through and softened just a bit, allowing the dressing to cling to their exteriors. Frozen shelled edamame come in a

wide range of package sizes. If you can find only a 10-ounce package, there's no need to buy a second package to make up the extra 2 ounces; just make the recipe with 10 ounces of edamame. You needn't thaw the edamame before boiling.

- 3 tablespoons extra-virgin olive oil
- 1 small shallot, minced
- 1 tablespoon lemon juice
- 1 garlic clove, minced
- ½ teaspoon table salt, plus salt for blanching edamame
- ½ teaspoon pepper
- 12 ounces (2 cups) frozen shelled edamame
- 1½ ounces Pecorino Romano cheese, shredded (½ cup)
- ⅓ cup coarsely chopped fresh mint
- ¼ cup coarsely chopped fresh parsley

1. Combine oil, shallot, lemon juice, garlic, salt, and pepper in bowl; set aside.

2. Bring 2 quarts water to boil in large saucepan over high heat. Fill large bowl halfway with ice and water. Line large plate with double layer of paper towels.

3. Add edamame and 1 tablespoon salt to boiling water and cook for 5 minutes (water may not return to boil; this is OK). Drain edamame in colander. Nestle colander into ice bath, submerging edamame. Let sit until edamame are chilled, 3 to 5 minutes.

4. Lift colander from ice bath, allowing excess water to drain, and transfer edamame to prepared plate. Pat dry with additional paper towels.

5. Transfer edamame to bowl with dressing and toss to coat. Add Pecorino, mint, and parsley and toss to combine. Season with salt and pepper to taste. Serve.

Succotash Salad with Butter Beans and Basil

Serves 4 to 6 | **Total Time** 25 minutes, plus 30 minutes resting **VEGAN**

WHY THIS RECIPE WORKS When seasonal summer produce is at its best, it should be allowed to shine, as it does here in this fresh, bright succotash. Here we combine sweet corn (browned to add a hint of caramelized complexity) with mild, creamy butter beans, zucchini, and juicy cherry tomatoes and then douse the mixture in an ultrarefreshing white wine vinaigrette. To keep the flavors clean and unmuddied we avoid using cream or butter for the corn. We stir in fresh basil, which brings a licorice-like flavor, and scallions, which contribute a light savoriness and a pop of green. Do not substitute frozen or canned corn in this recipe.

⅓ cup extra-virgin olive oil, divided
¼ cup white wine vinegar
2 teaspoons table salt, divided
1 teaspoon pepper
1 (15-ounce) can butter beans, rinsed
8 ounces cherry tomatoes, halved
1 zucchini, cut into ½-inch pieces
4 scallions, sliced thin
4 ears corn, kernels cut from cobs (3 cups)
1 garlic clove, minced
2 tablespoons chopped fresh basil

1. Whisk ¼ cup oil, vinegar, 1½ teaspoons salt, and pepper together in large bowl. Add butter beans, tomatoes, zucchini, and scallions and toss to combine.

2. Heat remaining oil in 12-inch nonstick skillet over medium-high heat until shimmering. Add corn and remaining ½ teaspoon salt and cook, stirring occasionally, until softened and just beginning to brown, 5 to 7 minutes. Add garlic and cook until fragrant, about 30 seconds.

3. Transfer corn mixture to bowl with butter bean mixture and toss to combine. Let sit for at least 30 minutes to allow flavors to meld. (Salad can be covered with plastic wrap and refrigerated for up to 2 days.)

4. Stir in basil and season with salt and pepper to taste. Serve.

Gan Bian Si Ji Dou

Serves 4 | **Total Time** 40 minutes `FAST`

WHY THIS RECIPE WORKS Sichuan green beans are irresistible: spicy, aromatic, and tingly all at the same time. In Chinese restaurants, the beans are usually deep-fried, which produces their wrinkled appearance, slightly chewy texture, and intense flavor. To make this dish at home, we broil the beans until the skins start to char and shrivel; this results in a nice chewy texture and deep flavor without frying. Shaoxing wine, Sichuan chiles, and Sichuan peppercorns lend their characteristic flavors, and ground pork adds meaty richness. At the end, we toss the beans into a wok along with yacai (pickled mustard greens) and a drizzle of sesame oil. Yacai is sometimes labeled suimiyacai; for more information, see page 133. We do not recommend substituting other varieties of pickled mustard. Serve with rice. As a main course, this dish will serve two.

1½ pounds green beans, trimmed
2½ tablespoons vegetable oil, divided
½ teaspoon table salt
1 tablespoon Shaoxing wine
1½ teaspoons soy sauce
1 teaspoon sugar
2–4 dried small Sichuan chiles, stemmed, halved lengthwise, and seeded
½ teaspoon Sichuan peppercorns
1 tablespoon minced garlic
1 tablespoon grated fresh ginger
3 ounces ground pork
2 tablespoons yacai
1 teaspoon toasted sesame oil

1. Adjust oven rack 8 inches from broiler element and heat broiler. Combine beans and 1 tablespoon vegetable oil in bowl and toss to coat. Spread on rimmed baking sheet (do not wash bowl). Broil beans until softened and charred in places, 10 to 15 minutes, flipping beans halfway through broiling. Return beans to bowl, add salt, and toss to distribute evenly. Cover with plate. Stir Shaoxing wine, soy sauce, and sugar in small bowl until sugar is dissolved and set aside.

2. Combine remaining 1½ tablespoons vegetable oil, chiles, and peppercorns in 14-inch flat-bottomed wok and cook over medium-low heat until fragrant, about 1 minute. Add garlic and ginger and cook, stirring constantly, until fragrant, about 1 minute. Add pork and mash and smear into wok until pork and garlic mixture are evenly combined. Increase heat to medium-high and continue to cook, chopping meat into ¼-inch chunks with edge of spatula until cooked through, about 2 minutes.

3. Add beans and yacai and toss to combine. Add Shaoxing wine mixture and cook, stirring constantly, until no liquid remains in wok, 1 to 2 minutes. Drizzle with sesame oil and serve.

NOTES FROM THE TEST KITCHEN

THE SECRET TO TENDER CHARRED BEANS
The key to charred, dense, concentrated green beans? Dehydration. In place of deep frying, we use a hybrid broiling-steaming method. The broiling condenses the beans and creates spotty charring. Letting the beans gently steam in their residual heat in a covered bowl ensures that they become fully tender.

White Beans with Tomatoes and Capers

Serves 4 to 6 | **Total Time** 1½ hours, plus 8 hours brining VEGAN

WHY THIS RECIPE WORKS White beans are the showpiece of this simple yet flavor-packed side, so starting with dried beans is well worth the extra time and effort. Their superbly creamy texture and flavor are more satisfying than anything you'll get from a can. After cooking the beans, we toast thinly sliced garlic to bring out its sweetness. Cooking the tomatoes until they're just softened adds a savory sauciness to the dish. We finish with a drizzle of rich, fruity, peppery olive oil.

> **Substitution:** You can use two (15-ounce) cans rinsed cannellini beans in place of the dried; skip steps 1 and 2.

1½ tablespoons table salt for brining
1 pound dried cannellini beans, picked over and rinsed
¼ teaspoon table salt, plus salt for cooking beans
6 tablespoons extra-virgin olive oil, divided
3 garlic cloves, sliced thin
5 ounces grape tomatoes, halved
1 tablespoon capers, rinsed
½ teaspoon dried oregano
½ teaspoon red pepper flakes

1. Dissolve 1½ tablespoons salt in 2 quarts cold water in large container. Add beans and soak at room temperature for at least 8 hours or up to 24 hours. Drain and rinse well. (If you're pressed for time, see page 13 for information on quick brining your beans.)

2. Bring soaked beans and 7 cups water to simmer in large saucepan. Simmer, partially covered, over medium-low heat until beans are tender, 30 to 40 minutes. Remove from heat; stir in 1½ teaspoons salt; cover; and let sit until completely tender, about 15 minutes. Drain beans.

3. Combine ¼ cup oil and garlic in 12-inch nonstick skillet and cook over medium heat until garlic begins to brown lightly at edges, about 3 minutes. Add beans, tomatoes, capers, oregano, pepper flakes, and salt and cook until tomatoes just begin to soften, about 5 minutes, stirring occasionally.

4. Transfer bean mixture to shallow dish and drizzle with remaining 2 tablespoons oil. Serve.

Gan Bian
Si Ji Dou

White Beans
with Tomatoes
and Capers

Garlicky White Beans with Sage

Garlicky White Beans with Sage

Serves 4 to 6 | **Total Time** 1½ hours, plus 8 hours brining VEGAN

WHY THIS RECIPE WORKS This utterly simple preparation showcases creamy cannellini beans combined with ingredients that thrive in their company: garlic, sage, and olive oil. We start by toasting garlic in oil to bring out its sweetness. Fresh sage leaves infuse the dish with herbal complexity; do not substitute dried. We prefer using cooked-from-dried cannellini beans for their extra-creamy texture. Finishing with a drizzle of olive oil adds richness.

> **Substitution:** You can use two 15-ounce cans rinsed cannellini beans in place of the dried; skip steps 1 and 2.

1½ tablespoons table salt for brining
1 pound dried cannellini beans, picked over and rinsed
¼ teaspoon table salt, plus salt for cooking beans
6 tablespoons extra-virgin olive oil, divided
3 garlic cloves, sliced thin
6 fresh sage leaves
¼ teaspoon red pepper flakes

1. Dissolve 1½ tablespoons salt in 2 quarts cold water in large container. Add beans and soak at room temperature for at least 8 hours or up to 24 hours. Drain and rinse well. (If you're pressed for time, see page 13 for information on quick brining your beans.)

2. Bring soaked beans and 7 cups water to simmer in large saucepan. Simmer, partially covered, over medium-low heat until beans are tender, 30 to 40 minutes. Remove from heat; stir in 1½ teaspoons salt; cover; and let sit until completely tender, about 15 minutes. Drain beans.

3. Combine ¼ cup oil and garlic in 12-inch nonstick skillet and cook over medium heat until garlic begins to brown lightly at edges, about 3 minutes. Add sage and pepper flakes and cook until fragrant, about 30 seconds. Add 3½ cups beans (reserve remainder for another use) and salt and cook until just heated through, about 2 minutes. Transfer to shallow serving dish and drizzle with remaining 2 tablespoons oil. Serve.

Stewed Chickpeas and Spinach with Dill and Lemon

Stewed Chickpeas and Spinach with Dill and Lemon

Serves 4 to 6 | **Total Time** 20 minutes `FAST` `VEGAN`

WHY THIS RECIPE WORKS For this Greek-inspired side dish, we wanted chickpeas tossed with a tangle of wilted spinach in a vibrant lemon-and-dill-flavored broth. We start by heating sliced garlic and red pepper flakes in olive oil to infuse the oil with spicy flavor. Canned chickpeas keep the dish weeknight-friendly. Instead of curly-leaf spinach, which requires stemming and chopping, we opt for prep-free baby spinach. A little broth provides a savory backbone that ties the dish together. To add luscious body and a subtle creaminess to the broth, we add the starchy liquid from a can of chickpeas along with the beans. Before serving, we spritz the dish with lemon and stir in a hefty quarter-cup of fresh dill.

  2 tablespoons extra-virgin olive oil, plus extra
    for drizzling
  3 garlic cloves, sliced thin
  ¼ teaspoon red pepper flakes
  2 (15-ounce) cans chickpeas (1 can drained and
    rinsed, 1 can left undrained)
 10 ounces (10 cups) baby spinach
  ½ cup vegetable or chicken broth
  ¼ teaspoon table salt
  ¼ cup chopped fresh dill
  1 tablespoon lemon juice

Cook oil, garlic, and pepper flakes in Dutch oven over medium heat until garlic is golden brown, 3 to 5 minutes. Stir in 1 can drained chickpeas, 1 can chickpeas and their liquid, spinach, broth, and salt. Increase heat to medium-high and cook, stirring occasionally, until spinach is wilted and liquid is slightly thickened, about 5 minutes. Off heat, stir in dill and lemon juice. Season with salt and pepper to taste. Drizzle with extra oil and serve.

Braised Green Beans

Serves 4 to 6 | **Total Time** 1¼ hours `VEGAN`

WHY THIS RECIPE WORKS Slow braising is an underappreciated cooking method for green beans but it turns them into something silky-smooth and altogether different from the bright-green crisp-tender spears that result from quicker

cooking methods. This Mediterranean-inspired version calls for sautéing the aromatics on the stovetop in a Dutch oven before adding the green beans and tomatoes. Transferring the pot to the oven allows for gentle, hands-off simmering until the sauce is thickened and the beans become infused with the flavors of tomato and garlic. The best part is the velvety texture of the beans: The slow cooking renders them so meltingly tender that they're almost creamy.

  5 tablespoons extra-virgin olive oil, divided
  1 onion, chopped fine
  4 garlic cloves, minced
    Pinch cayenne pepper
1½ cups water
  ½ teaspoon baking soda
1½ pounds green beans, trimmed and cut into
    2- to 3-inch lengths
  1 (14.5-ounce) can diced tomatoes, drained with
    juice reserved, chopped coarse
  1 tablespoon tomato paste
  1 teaspoon table salt
  ¼ teaspoon pepper
  ¼ cup chopped fresh parsley
    Red wine vinegar

1. Adjust oven rack to lower-middle position and heat oven to 275 degrees. Heat 3 tablespoons oil in Dutch oven over medium heat until shimmering. Add onion and cook until softened, about 5 minutes. Stir in garlic and cayenne and cook until fragrant, about 30 seconds. Add water, baking soda, and green beans and bring to simmer. Reduce heat to medium-low and cook, stirring occasionally, for 10 minutes. Stir in tomatoes and their juice, tomato paste, salt, and pepper.

2. Cover pot, transfer to oven, and cook until sauce is slightly thickened and green beans can be easily cut with side of fork, 40 to 50 minutes. Stir in parsley and season with vinegar to taste. Drizzle with remaining 2 tablespoons oil and serve warm or at room temperature.

VARIATION
Braised Green Beans with Mint and Feta
Add ¾ teaspoon ground allspice with garlic and cayenne. Substitute 2 tablespoons chopped fresh mint for parsley. Omit 2 tablespoons oil in step 2. Sprinkle green beans with ½ cup crumbled feta cheese before serving.

Southern-Style Baby Lima Beans

Serves 4 to 6 | **Total Time** 1¼ hours

WHY THIS RECIPE WORKS Lima beans are worth getting excited about: The frozen baby variety we call for here are sweet, petite, and tender yet still substantial. The beauty of this recipe is in its simplicity: Frozen baby lima beans are cooked low and slow, seasoned with a few strips of bacon and wedges of onion in the pot. The resulting beans and their smoky, thick, peppery broth are complex and deeply comforting. Stirring frequently as the beans cook emulsifies the bacon fat into the broth, giving it a silky texture. Do not thaw the baby lima beans before cooking.

- 4 slices bacon, cut into ½-inch pieces
- 4 cups chicken broth
- 1½ pounds frozen baby lima beans
- 1¼ cups water
- 1 onion, halved
- 1 teaspoon pepper
- ¾ teaspoon table salt

Cook bacon in large saucepan over medium heat until lightly browned and fat is rendered, 7 to 10 minutes. Add broth, beans, water, onion, pepper, and salt and bring to boil. Reduce heat to medium-low and simmer, stirring occasionally, until beans just begin to break down and liquid is thickened, about 1 hour (liquid will continue to thicken as it sits). Discard onion. Season with salt and pepper to taste. Serve.

NOTES FROM THE TEST KITCHEN

ARE BABY LIMA BEANS AND BUTTER BEANS THE SAME THING?
Yes and no. In the culinary world, many cooks use the terms "lima beans" and "butter beans" interchangeably, but other cooks know "butter beans" as the larger white beans that are typically sold dried or canned and "baby lima beans" as the smaller, greener beans that are typically sold frozen or canned.

Baby Lima Beans

Butter Beans

Ful Medames

Ful Medames

Serves 4 to 6 | **Total Time** 30 minutes FAST VEGAN

WHY THIS RECIPE WORKS Fava beans are hugely popular in Egypt, so it's no surprise that ful medames, a rustic mash of favas flavored with cumin and garlic and topped with a host of fresh ingredients, is one of the nation's most beloved breakfast dishes. It also makes regular appearances as a dip with pita and as a side at lunch or dinner. Traditionally it's made by cooking dried fava beans in a pear-shaped pot for hours until the beans are soft enough to be mashed, but here we save time and the need for specialty cookware by opting for canned beans. After cooking the beans with tahini, garlic, and cumin and mashing them, we stir in some lemon juice and add toppings. Chopped tomato, raw onion, and hard-cooked eggs are customary, along with some parsley and a drizzle of rich olive oil.

1 tablespoon extra-virgin olive oil, plus extra for serving

4 garlic cloves, minced

1 teaspoon ground cumin

2 (15-ounce) cans fava beans

3 tablespoons tahini

2 tablespoons lemon juice, plus lemon wedges for serving

1 teaspoon pepper

1 tomato, cored and cut into ½-inch pieces

1 small onion, chopped fine

2 tablespoons minced fresh parsley

2 Easy-Peel Hard-Cooked Eggs, chopped (optional)

1. Cook oil, garlic, and cumin in medium saucepan over medium heat until fragrant, about 2 minutes. Stir in beans and their liquid and tahini. Bring to simmer and cook until liquid thickens slightly, 8 to 10 minutes.

2. Off heat, mash beans to coarse consistency using potato masher. Stir in lemon juice and pepper. Season with salt and pepper to taste. Transfer to serving dish; top with tomato, onion, parsley, and eggs, if using; and drizzle with extra oil. Serve with lemon wedges.

Easy-Peel Hard-Cooked Eggs

Makes 2 to 6 eggs | **Total Time** 40 minutes
FAST

With this cooking method, the shells practically fly off. Use large eggs that have no cracks and are cold from the refrigerator.

2–6 large eggs

1. Bring 1 inch water to rolling boil in medium saucepan over high heat. Place eggs in steamer basket. Transfer basket to saucepan. Cover, reduce heat to medium-low, and cook eggs for 13 minutes.

2. When eggs are almost finished cooking, combine 2 cups ice cubes and 2 cups cold water in medium bowl. Using tongs or spoon, transfer eggs to ice bath; let sit for 15 minutes. Peel before serving. (Eggs can be refrigerated in their shells in airtight container for up to 5 days.)

French Lentils

Serves 4 to 6 | **Total Time** 1¼ hours VEGAN

WHY THIS RECIPE WORKS For a side dish that highlights smaller French lentils, we use lentilles du Puy, which are grown under strict French and European Union origin laws and are often referred to as "the caviar of lentils." We begin by slowly cooking a mirepoix of carrots, onions, and celery to bring out their sweet flavors. Garlic and thyme add earthy and herbal flavors that complement the lentils, and cooking them in broth makes the dish more rich and complex than using just water. We cook the lentils until completely tender and finish the dish with a splash of olive oil, along with some parsley and lemon juice.

Substitution: We like lentilles du Puy for this recipe; however, you can use any dried lentils, except red or yellow.

2 tablespoons extra-virgin olive oil, divided

2 carrots, peeled and chopped fine

1 onion, chopped fine

1 celery rib, chopped fine

¼ teaspoon table salt

2 garlic cloves, minced

1 teaspoon minced fresh thyme or ¼ teaspoon dried

1¾ cups vegetable or chicken broth

1 cup lentilles du Puy, picked over and rinsed

2 tablespoons minced fresh parsley

2 teaspoons lemon juice

1. Combine 1 tablespoon oil, carrots, onion, celery, and salt in large saucepan. Cover and cook over medium-low heat, stirring occasionally, until vegetables are softened, 8 to 10 minutes. Stir in garlic and thyme and cook until fragrant, about 30 seconds.

2. Stir in broth and lentils and bring to simmer. Reduce heat to low; cover; and simmer gently, stirring occasionally, until lentils are mostly tender but still slightly crunchy, about 35 minutes.

3. Uncover and continue to cook, stirring occasionally, until lentils are completely tender, about 8 minutes. Stir in parsley, lemon juice, and remaining 1 tablespoon oil. Season with salt and pepper to taste. Serve.

Lentilles du Puy with Spinach and Crème Fraîche

Lentilles du Puy with Spinach and Crème Fraîche

Serves 4 to 6 | **Total Time** 1 hour

WHY THIS RECIPE WORKS This lentil side dish is made with lentilles du Puy, which are French green lentils. To flavor the lentils, we use a mirepoix of aromatic onion, carrot, and celery. We sweat the vegetables in olive oil before cooking the lentils in chicken broth for depth of flavor. When cooked properly and with the right amount of liquid, the lentils hold their shape but have a creamy texture. We fold in spinach for a bit of greenery and Dijon for a mustard kick. A dollop of crème fraîche makes for a luxurious finish. By the end of step 2, the lentils should have absorbed most, but not all, of the chicken broth. If the bottom of the saucepan looks dry and the lentils are still somewhat firm, add hot water and continue to cook until the lentils are tender. If you can't find crème fraîche, sour cream works well.

Substitution: You can use other French green lentils in place of the lentilles du Puy. Do not substitute other types of green lentils or black, brown, or red lentils; the cooking times of the other lentil varieties can vary greatly.

1 tablespoon extra-virgin olive oil
½ cup finely chopped onion
¼ cup finely chopped carrot
¼ cup finely chopped celery
½ teaspoon table salt
2 cups vegetable or chicken broth
1 cup dried lentilles du Puy, picked over and rinsed
2 ounces (2 cups) baby spinach
2 tablespoons Dijon mustard
¼ cup crème fraiche

1. Heat oil in large saucepan over medium heat until shimmering. Add onion, carrot, celery, and salt and cook until vegetables are tender, about 5 minutes. Stir in broth and lentils and bring to simmer. Reduce heat to medium-low; cover; and cook, stirring occasionally, until lentils are tender but still hold their shape, about 30 minutes. (Add hot water, ¼ cup at a time, if saucepan becomes dry before lentils are cooked through.)

2. Gently fold in spinach and mustard. Let sit off heat for 5 minutes. Transfer to serving bowl and dollop with crème fraîche. Serve.

New England Baked Beans

New England Baked Beans

Serves 4 to 6 | **Total Time** 4 hours, plus 8 hours brining

WHY THIS RECIPE WORKS Traditionally, New England baked beans were cooked in crocks in dying ovens or ember-filled holes in the ground, where the beans could slowly turn tender overnight. To re-create this gentle cooking environment, we cook the beans in a Dutch oven placed inside a low oven, which surrounds the beans with even, ambient heat. Brining the beans overnight helps jump-start hydration and softens their skins so they cook up tender, with few blowouts. Uncovering the pot for the last hour of cooking ensures that the liquid reduces sufficiently to coat the beans in a thick sauce. Molasses, brown sugar, dry mustard, bay leaf, onion, and salt pork, plus one nontraditional ingredient (soy sauce), give the beans rich flavor.

- 1½ tablespoons table salt for brining
- 1 pound (2½ cups) dried navy beans, picked over and rinsed
- 6 ounces salt pork, rinsed, cut into 3 pieces
- 1 onion, halved
- ½ cup molasses
- 2 tablespoons packed dark brown sugar
- 1 tablespoon soy sauce
- 2 teaspoons dry mustard
- ½ teaspoon pepper
- 1 bay leaf
- ¼ teaspoon table salt

1. Dissolve 1½ tablespoons salt in 2 quarts cold water in large container. Add beans and soak at room temperature for at least 8 hours or up to 24 hours. Drain and rinse well. (If you're pressed for time, see page 13 for information on quick brining your beans.)

2. Adjust oven rack to lower-middle position and heat oven to 300 degrees. Combine soaked beans, 4 cups water, salt pork, onion, molasses, sugar, soy sauce, mustard, pepper, bay leaf, and salt in Dutch oven. (Liquid should cover beans by about ½ inch. Add more water if necessary.) Bring to boil over high heat. Cover pot, transfer to oven, and cook until beans are softened and bean skins curl up and split when you blow on them, about 2 hours. (After 1 hour, stir beans and check amount of liquid. Liquid should just cover beans. Add water if necessary.)

3. Remove lid and continue to cook until beans are fully tender, browned, and slightly crusty on top, about 1 hour. (Liquid will reduce slightly below top layer of beans.)

4. Remove pot from oven, cover, and let stand for 5 minutes. Using wooden spoon or rubber spatula, scrape any browned bits from sides of pot and stir into beans. Discard onion and bay leaf. (Salt pork can be eaten, if desired.) Let beans sit, uncovered, until liquid has thickened slightly and clings to beans, 10 to 15 minutes, stirring once halfway through. Season with salt and pepper to taste, and serve.

NOTES FROM THE TEST KITCHEN

WHAT IS SALT PORK?
Don't confuse salt pork with bacon. Although both come from the belly of the pig and are salt-cured, bacon is heavily smoked and is typically leaner and meatier. Salt pork is unsmoked and used primarily as a flavoring agent (traditionally in dishes like baked beans) and is rarely actually consumed. We recommend buying blocks of salt pork (precut slices can dry out) and portioning it as needed. Look for salt pork that has at least a few streaks of meat throughout. Salt pork can be refrigerated for up to one month.

Drunken Beans

Serves 6 to 8 | **Total Time** 2½ hours, plus 8 hours brining

WHY THIS RECIPE WORKS Soupy beans are a staple at Mexican tables; the cooking liquid thickens slightly from the beans' starches and the dish is as satisfying as any rich stew. One such iteration, known as drunken beans, calls for cooking pinto beans in beer or tequila, which lends subtle, complex flavor to the pot. To make sure the alcohol doesn't make our beans boozy or bitter, we add tequila at the beginning of cooking (evaporating it to mellow its flavor) and beer (lager) partway through (so that its malty notes are present in the finished dish). Brining the beans ensures that they stay tender, creamy, and intact. Sautéing onion, garlic, and poblano chiles in rendered bacon fat creates a flavorful base. Simmering the beans vigorously to finish causes them to release starches that give the cooking liquid a pleasant body. For more spice, add the ribs and seeds from the poblano chiles.

Drunken Beans

2. Adjust oven rack to lower-middle position and heat oven to 300 degrees. Pick leaves from 20 cilantro sprigs (reserve stems), chop fine, and refrigerate until needed. Using kitchen twine, tie remaining 10 cilantro sprigs and reserved stems into bundle.

3. Cook bacon in Dutch oven over medium heat, stirring occasionally, until crispy, 5 to 8 minutes. Using slotted spoon, transfer bacon to paper towel–lined plate and set aside. Add onion, poblanos, and garlic to fat left in pot and cook, stirring frequently, until vegetables are softened, 6 to 7 minutes. Off heat, add tequila and cook until evaporated, 3 to 4 minutes. Return to high heat; stir in soaked beans, 3½ cups water, bay leaves, salt, and cilantro bundle; and bring to boil. Cover, transfer to oven, and cook until beans are just soft, 45 minutes to 1 hour.

4. Remove pot from oven. Discard bay leaves and cilantro bundle. Stir in lager and tomato paste and bring to simmer over medium-low heat. Simmer vigorously, stirring frequently, until liquid is thick and beans are fully tender, about 30 minutes. Season with salt to taste. Serve, passing lime wedges, Cotija, chopped cilantro, and reserved bacon separately.

Cajun Red Beans

Serves 6 to 8 | **Total Time** 3 to 3½ hours

WHY THIS RECIPE WORKS This Cajun classic is a highly flavorful stewed kidney bean dish most often served over a bed of white rice. The best versions balance the sweetness of the beans with a smoky, spicy flavor built on a base of vegetables and herbs. Because the broth benefits from a longer simmering time, we start with unbrined dried kidney beans (canned beans would break apart and turn mushy long before the broth is fully seasoned). We flavor the broth with the trinity of Cajun cooking: onion, bell pepper, and celery. Softening the vegetables in rendered bacon fat lends the cooking liquid a deep, meaty flavor. Cayenne and hot sauce add heat without overwhelming the dish. After cooking the beans covered in the oven until tender, we remove the lid, stir in andouille sausage, and continue to bake uncovered until the liquid thickens. Andouille is the traditional sausage for this dish, but we also had good results with kielbasa.

1½ tablespoons table salt for brining
1 pound (2½ cups) dried pinto beans, picked over and rinsed
30 sprigs fresh cilantro (1 bunch), divided
4 slices bacon, cut into ¼-inch pieces
1 onion, chopped fine
2 poblano chiles, stemmed, seeded, and chopped fine
3 garlic cloves, minced
½ cup tequila
2 bay leaves
1 teaspoon table salt
1 cup Mexican lager
¼ cup tomato paste
2 limes, quartered
2 ounces Cotija cheese, crumbled (½ cup)

1. Dissolve 1½ tablespoons salt in 2 quarts cold water in large container. Add beans and soak at room temperature for at least 8 hours or up to 24 hours. Drain and rinse well. (If you're pressed for time, see page 13 for information on quick brining your beans.)

4 slices bacon, chopped fine
1 onion, chopped fine
1 red bell pepper, stemmed, seeded, and chopped fine
1 celery rib, chopped fine
1 teaspoon table salt
4 garlic cloves, minced

- 1 teaspoon dried oregano
- 1 teaspoon dried thyme
- 6 cups water
- 1 pound (2½ cups) dried small red kidney beans, picked over and rinsed
- 4 bay leaves
- 1 teaspoon pepper
- ½ teaspoon cayenne pepper
- ½ teaspoon hot sauce, plus extra to taste
- 8 ounces andouille or kielbasa sausage, quartered and sliced ½ inch thick

1. Adjust oven rack to lower-middle position and heat oven to 300 degrees. Cook bacon in Dutch oven over medium heat until crispy, about 8 minutes. Stir in onion, bell pepper, celery, and salt and cook until vegetables are softened, about 8 minutes.

2. Stir in garlic, oregano, and thyme and cook until fragrant, about 30 seconds. Stir in water, scraping up any browned bits. Stir in beans, bay leaves, pepper, cayenne, and hot sauce. Increase heat to medium-high and bring to boil.

3. Cover pot and transfer to oven. Bake until beans are tender, 1½ to 2 hours, stirring every 30 minutes.

4. Remove lid and stir in andouille. Continue to bake, uncovered, until liquid has thickened, about 30 minutes. Discard bay leaves and let beans sit for 10 minutes. Season with salt, pepper, and hot sauce to taste. Serve.

Cranberry Beans with Warm Spices

Serves 6 to 8 | **Total Time** 2 to 2½ hours, plus 8 hours brining `VEGAN`

WHY THIS RECIPE WORKS Cranberry beans have a creamy texture similar to that of pinto and cannellini beans and a delicate flavor that we like to highlight with a gently spiced flavor profile. Starting with dried beans (cranberry beans are rarely canned), we sauté aromatic vegetables along with tomato paste for depth of flavor; just a touch of cinnamon imparts a subtle yet distinct warmth. White wine offers acidity, and broth gives the dish a hearty backbone. Letting the beans cook through in the Dutch oven in a moderate oven ensures even texture without the need for constant monitoring. Lemon juice and fresh mint complete this comforting side dish, nicely balancing the warm, rich flavors of the beans.

Substitution: You can use dried pinto beans in place of the cranberry beans.

- 1½ tablespoons table salt for brining
- 1 pound (2½ cups) dried cranberry beans, picked over and rinsed
- ¼ cup extra-virgin olive oil
- 1 onion, chopped fine
- 2 carrots, peeled and chopped fine
- 4 garlic cloves, sliced thin
- 1 tablespoon tomato paste
- ½ teaspoon ground cinnamon
- ¼ teaspoon pepper
- ½ cup dry white wine
- 4 cups vegetable or chicken broth
- 2 tablespoons lemon juice, plus extra for seasoning
- 2 tablespoons minced fresh mint

1. Dissolve 1½ tablespoons salt in 2 quarts cold water in large container. Add beans and soak at room temperature for at least 8 hours or up to 24 hours. Drain and rinse well. (If you're pressed for time, see page 13 for information on quick brining your beans.)

Cranberry Beans with Warm Spices

2. Adjust oven rack to lower-middle position and heat oven to 300 degrees. Heat oil in Dutch oven over medium heat until shimmering. Add onion and carrots and cook until softened, about 5 minutes. Stir in garlic, tomato paste, cinnamon, and pepper and cook until fragrant, about 1 minute. Stir in wine, scraping up any browned bits. Stir in soaked beans, broth, and ½ cup water and bring to boil. Cover, transfer pot to oven, and cook, stirring occasionally, until beans are tender, 1½ to 2 hours.

3. Remove pot from oven. Stir in lemon juice and mint and season with salt, pepper, and extra lemon juice to taste. Adjust consistency with extra hot water as needed. Serve.

Green Bean Casserole

Serves 10 to 12 | **Total Time** 3½ hours

WHY THIS RECIPE WORKS Green bean casserole is a holiday staple, but one that could stand a bit of a refresh. To modernize the dish, we add a crunchier topping and make a homemade mushroom sauce. To save some time, we jump-start the beans in the microwave, which shortens the casserole's baking time. For the sauce, we skip canned soup and instead brown mushrooms to deepen their flavor before stirring in broth, cream, and flour. For an extra-crunchy topping, we add bread crumbs to the standard fried onions. We also hold back on adding the topping until the casserole is mostly cooked through, sprinkling it on top just a few minutes before removing the casserole from the oven. This gives the topping just enough time to toast and turn golden brown without soaking up too much sauce and sogging out.

TOPPING

- 2 slices hearty white sandwich bread, torn into pieces
- 2 tablespoons unsalted butter, melted
- ¼ teaspoon table salt
- 2 cups canned fried onions

CASSEROLE

- 3 tablespoons unsalted butter
- 10 ounces white mushrooms, trimmed and sliced thin
- 1 teaspoon table salt
- ½ teaspoon pepper
- 6 garlic cloves, minced
- ½ teaspoon dried thyme
- ¼ cup all-purpose flour
- 1½ cups vegetable or chicken broth

Green Bean Casserole

- 1½ cups heavy cream
- ½ cup dry white wine or dry vermouth
- 2 pounds green beans, trimmed and cut into 1-inch pieces
- ¼ cup cornstarch

1. FOR THE TOPPING Pulse bread, melted butter, and salt in food processor to coarse crumbs, about 6 pulses. Combine bread crumbs and fried onions in bowl. Set aside.

2. FOR THE CASSEROLE Adjust oven rack to middle position and heat oven to 400 degrees. Melt butter in 12-inch skillet over medium heat. Add mushrooms, salt, and pepper and cook until mushrooms release their liquid, about 5 minutes. Increase heat to medium-high and cook until liquid has evaporated, about 5 minutes. Add garlic and thyme and cook until fragrant, about 30 seconds. Stir in flour and cook until golden, about 1 minute. Slowly whisk in broth, cream, and wine and bring to boil. Reduce heat to medium and simmer, stirring occasionally, until sauce is thickened, about 10 minutes.

3. Toss green beans with cornstarch in large bowl and transfer to 13 by 9-inch baking dish. Pour warm mushroom mixture evenly over green beans.

4. Cover with aluminum foil and bake until sauce is bubbling and green beans are tender, 40 to 50 minutes, stirring green beans halfway through baking. Remove foil and spread topping over green beans. Bake until golden brown, about 8 minutes. Serve.

TRIMMING GREEN BEANS

To trim green beans quickly, line up several beans so stem ends are even. Trim off stems with 1 slice; cut beans as directed in recipe.

Refried Beans

Serves 4 to 6 | **Total Time** 40 minutes **FAST**

WHY THIS RECIPE WORKS For deeply flavored, rich, and creamy refried beans in a hurry, canned beans are just fine. For authentic flavor, we sauté salt pork and use its fat to cook the aromatics and beans. Processing some beans with broth creates the ideal creamy texture; we then pulse the rest for some chunky bites. Onion, garlic, two types of chiles, and cumin give the dish complexity; cilantro and lime juice give it a bright finish. For more spice, add the ribs and seeds from the jalapeño and/or poblano chile.

- ½ cup chicken broth
- 2 (15-ounce) cans pinto beans, rinsed, divided
- 1 tablespoon vegetable oil
- 3 ounces salt pork, rind removed, chopped fine
- 1 small onion, chopped fine
- 1 jalapeño chile, stemmed, seeded, and minced
- 1 poblano chile, stemmed, seeded, and minced
- ¼ teaspoon table salt
- 3 small garlic cloves, minced
- ½ teaspoon ground cumin
- 1 tablespoon minced fresh cilantro
- 2 teaspoons lime juice (optional)

1. Process broth and all but 1 cup beans in food processor until smooth, about 15 seconds, scraping down sides of bowl as needed. Add remaining beans and pulse until slightly chunky, about 10 pulses.

2. Heat oil in 12-inch nonstick skillet over medium heat until shimmering. Add salt pork and cook, stirring occasionally, until fat has been rendered and pork is well browned, about 10 to 15 minutes. Using slotted spoon, discard pork, leaving fat behind in skillet.

3. Add onion, jalapeño, poblano, and salt to fat left in skillet and cook over medium-high heat, stirring occasionally, until softened and beginning to brown, about 5 minutes. Stir in garlic and cumin and cook until fragrant, about 30 seconds. Stir in processed beans, reduce heat to medium, and cook, stirring often, until beans are thick and creamy, about 5 minutes. Stir in cilantro and lime juice, if using, and season with salt and pepper to taste. Serve.

VARIATION

Vegetarian Refried Beans **FAST** **VEGAN**
Substitute 1 cup water for ½ cup broth; add all of water to food processor in step 1. Omit salt pork and add vegetables to skillet when oil is shimmering. Add 2 tablespoons tomato paste, ½ teaspoon dried oregano, and ½ teaspoon chipotle chile powder to skillet with garlic and cumin. Adjust consistency with extra hot water as needed before serving.

Refried Beans

Grain Sides

● FAST (45 minutes or less)   ● VEGAN
Photo: Garlic Fried Rice

Stovetop Steamed Long- or Medium-Grain White Rice

Serves 4 to 6 | **Total Time** 35 minutes `FAST` `VEGAN`

WHY THIS RECIPE WORKS Don't have a rice cooker? You can still make great steamed rice to accompany stir-fries and other dishes. Rinsing the rice washes away excess starch that would otherwise absorb the cooking water and cause the grains to clump. When the rinse water runs clear, you're good to go. Do not stir the rice as it cooks.

> 3 cups water
> 2 cups long- or medium-grain white rice, rinsed

Bring water and rice to boil in large saucepan over medium-high heat. Cook, uncovered, until water level drops below surface of rice and small holes form, about 5 minutes. Reduce heat to low; cover; and cook until rice is tender and water is fully absorbed, about 15 minutes. Serve.

VARIATIONS

Stovetop Steamed Short-Grain White Rice
`FAST` `VEGAN`

Reduce water to 2¼ cups and substitute 2 cups short-grain white rice, rinsed, for long- or medium-grain rice. Bring water and rice to boil in large saucepan over medium-high heat. Reduce heat to low; cover; and cook until rice is tender and water is fully absorbed, about 20 minutes. Remove from heat and let sit for 15 minutes to finish cooking. Serve.

Microwave-Steamed Rice `FAST` `VEGAN`

You can microwave rice with consistent results. This method works with long-, medium-, and short-grain rice. Use the same ratio of water to rice as in the stovetop method.

Combine water and rice in large bowl, cover, and microwave on full power for 5 minutes. Continue to microwave on 50 percent power for 15 minutes. Carefully remove bowl from microwave and let sit covered for 5 minutes to finish cooking. Serve.

Hands-Off Baked White Rice

Hands-Off Baked White Rice

Serves 4 | **Total Time** 45 minutes `FAST` `VEGAN`

WHY THIS RECIPE WORKS Wanting an easy and hands-off version of everyday rice, we found our answer by using the oven. After a few tests, we uncovered two tricks that ensure perfect rice every time: First, be sure to rinse the rice before combining it with the water for cooking, or the excess starch clinging to the rice will make everything taste gluey. Second, to speed up cooking, start with boiling water. For an accurate measurement of boiling water, bring a full kettle of water to a boil and then measure out the desired amount.

> 2¾ cups boiling water
> 1⅓ cups long-grain white rice, rinsed
> 1 tablespoon extra-virgin olive oil
> ½ teaspoon table salt

1. Adjust oven rack to middle position and heat oven to 450 degrees. Combine boiling water, rice, oil, and salt in 8-inch square baking dish. Cover dish tightly with double layer of aluminum foil. Bake rice until tender and water has been fully absorbed, about 20 minutes.

2. Remove dish from oven; uncover; and fluff rice with fork, scraping up any rice that has stuck to bottom. Re-cover dish with foil and let sit for 10 minutes. Serve.

VARIATIONS
Hands-Off Baked Saffron Rice `FAST` `VEGAN`
Stir pinch saffron threads into boiling water before adding to baking dish.

Hands-Off Baked Coconut Rice `FAST` `VEGAN`
Substitute 2 cups water, ¾ cup coconut milk, and ⅛ teaspoon ground cardamom for boiling water; microwave in covered bowl until hot, about 2 minutes. When fluffing cooked rice, stir in 1 tablespoon minced fresh cilantro.

Hands-Off Baked Curried Rice `FAST` `VEGAN`
Stir 1 teaspoon curry powder into boiling water before adding to baking dish. When fluffing cooked rice, stir in ¼ cup raisins.

Basmati Rice Pilaf

Serves 4 to 6 | **Total Time** 55 minutes `VEGAN`

WHY THIS RECIPE WORKS The pilaf method for cooking long-grain white rice relies on using less water and an even, gentle heat to produce distinct grains. Many rice pilaf recipes call for soaking the rice overnight, but we found that simply rinsing the rice before cooking removes excess starch and ensures fluffy, rather than clumpy, grains. For an easy flavor boost, we sauté an onion in the saucepan before adding the rice. Toasting the rice for a few minutes in the pan deepens its flavor. A little less liquid than the traditional ratio of 1 cup of rice to 2 cups of water delivers better results. We place a dish towel under the lid while the rice finishes steaming off the heat; it absorbs excess moisture in the pan and guarantees fluffy, light, and tender rice.

> **Substitution:** You can use conventional long-grain white, jasmine, or Texmati rice in place of the basmati.

1 tablespoon extra-virgin olive oil
1 small onion, chopped fine
¼ teaspoon table salt
1½ cups basmati rice, rinsed
2¼ cups water

1. Heat oil in large saucepan over medium heat until shimmering. Add onion and salt and cook until softened, about 5 minutes. Add rice and cook, stirring constantly, until grains become chalky and opaque, 1 to 3 minutes.

2. Stir in water and bring to boil. Reduce heat to low; cover; and simmer gently until rice is tender and water has been fully absorbed, 16 to 18 minutes.

3. Off heat, lay clean dish towel underneath lid and let sit, covered, for 10 minutes. Fluff rice with fork and serve.

VARIATIONS
Basmati Rice Pilaf with Whole Spices
Omit oil and onion and increase salt to 1 teaspoon. Melt 3 tablespoons unsalted butter in medium saucepan over medium heat. Add 1 teaspoon cumin seeds; 3 green cardamom pods, lightly crushed; and 3 whole cloves and cook, stirring constantly, until fragrant, about 1 minute. Add rice and cook, stirring constantly, until fragrant, about 1 minute. Add 1 cinnamon stick, 1 bay leaf, and salt when stirring in water. Before fluffing cooked rice, discard cardamom, cloves, cinnamon stick, and bay leaf.

Herbed Basmati Rice Pilaf `VEGAN`
Add 2 minced garlic cloves and 1 teaspoon minced fresh thyme to pot with rice. When fluffing cooked rice, stir in ¼ cup minced fresh parsley and 2 tablespoons minced fresh chives.

Basmati Rice Pilaf with Peas, Scallions, and Lemon `VEGAN`
Add 2 minced garlic cloves, 1 teaspoon grated lemon zest, and ⅛ teaspoon red pepper flakes to pot with rice. Before covering rice with dish towel, sprinkle ½ cup thawed frozen peas over top. When fluffing cooked rice, stir in 2 thinly sliced scallions and 1 tablespoon lemon juice.

Basmati Rice Pilaf with Currants and Toasted Almonds `VEGAN`
Add 2 minced garlic cloves, ½ teaspoon ground turmeric, and ¼ teaspoon ground cinnamon to pot with rice. Before covering rice with dish towel, sprinkle ¼ cup currants over top. When fluffing cooked rice, stir in ¼ cup toasted sliced almonds.

Arroz con Tocino

Arroz con Tocino

Serves 4 to 6 | **Total Time** 50 minutes

WHY THIS RECIPE WORKS This garlicky Puerto Rican rice dish studded with bits of salty pork is not only intensely satisfying on its own but also makes the perfect accompaniment to our Habichuelas Guisadas con Calabaza (page 195). Our recipe, developed by Von Diaz, begins with removing the rind of the salt pork to eliminate the chewy bits and then rinsing the pork to tame the saltiness and funk. Cooking the pork over moderate heat keeps it from browning too quickly, allowing ample time for the plentiful fat to fully render. Toasting the rice briefly in the hot liquid fat helps it cook up fluffier. Finally, resting the rice after steaming ensures that each grain is fully cooked and tender throughout. Salt pork can vary in saltiness and funk, so rinse it well and pat it dry with a clean towel before dicing, and adjust the salt to taste. If you can't find salt pork, you can substitute diced thick-cut bacon. We developed this recipe with sushi rice but any short-grain rice will work. Do not rinse the rice before cooking, as it will retain moisture and become mushy.

5½ ounces salt pork, rind removed, rinsed, patted dry, and chopped into ½-inch pieces (about 1 cup)
 1 teaspoon extra-virgin olive oil
 1 large garlic clove, minced
 2 cups short-grain white rice
 3 cups water

1. Cook salt pork and oil in large saucepan over medium heat, stirring often, until pork is browned and fat has been rendered, 7 to 10 minutes. Add garlic and cook until fragrant, about 30 seconds. Add rice and cook, stirring frequently, until edges of grains are translucent, about 2 minutes.

2. Stir in water and bring to boil over high heat. Reduce heat to medium-low and simmer, uncovered, until liquid falls below surface of rice and rice is dotted with small bubbling holes, 7 to 10 minutes.

3. Reduce heat to low, cover, and cook for 17 minutes. Off heat, let rice rest, covered, for at least 10 minutes. Check to ensure that rice is fully cooked; if rice is slightly underdone, let sit, covered, until fully tender, 5 to 10 minutes longer. Fluff rice with fork and season with kosher salt to taste. Serve.

Hot Rice

Hot Rice

Serves 6 | **Total Time** 1 hour

WHY THIS RECIPE WORKS An Ohio favorite, hot rice features buttery rice cooked in a tomato-rich sauce spiced with hot red peppers. To ensure that our dish has the perfect balance of bold tomato flavor and controlled heat, we use canned crushed tomatoes (which are less watery than diced tomatoes) and add several kinds of pepper: paprika for color and depth, red pepper flakes for punch, and sautéed red bell peppers for sweetness. To prevent the rice from turning gummy as it cooks, we rinse it well to wash away its excess starch before adding it to the cooking liquid. Cooking the rice directly in the tomato-pepper mixture, bolstered with savory broth, allows the rice to soak up all the flavors of the cooking liquid like a sponge. Stirring in a few tablespoons of butter at the end gives the rice a luxurious and creamy texture, and finishing with chopped cherry peppers packs a last bit of spicy punch. One 28-ounce can of crushed tomatoes will contain more than enough for this recipe.

- 6 tablespoons unsalted butter, divided
- 2 red bell peppers, stemmed, seeded, and chopped fine
- 1 onion, chopped fine
- 1¼ teaspoons table salt, divided
- 1 tablespoon sugar
- 1 tablespoon paprika
- 1½ teaspoons red pepper flakes
- 4 cups vegetable or chicken broth
- 1½ cups canned crushed tomatoes
- 1½ cups long-grain white rice, rinsed
- 2 tablespoons jarred hot cherry peppers, stemmed, seeded, and chopped fine

1. Melt 3 tablespoons butter in large saucepan over medium heat. Add bell peppers, onion, and ½ teaspoon salt and cook until softened, 6 to 8 minutes.

2. Stir in sugar, paprika, and pepper flakes and cook until fragrant, about 30 seconds. Add broth, tomatoes, rice, and remaining ¾ teaspoon salt and bring to boil. Cover, reduce heat to low, and simmer, stirring occasionally, until rice is tender and liquid is mostly absorbed, 13 to 15 minutes.

3. Off heat, lay clean dish towel underneath lid and let sit for 10 minutes. Stir in cherry peppers and remaining 3 tablespoons butter until combined. Serve.

Com Do

Serves 4 to 6 | **Total Time** 45 minutes **FAST**

WHY THIS RECIPE WORKS Vietnamese food expert Andrea Nguyen calls com do (red rice) a diaspora dish, made popular by its presence on restaurant menus outside Vietnam. Red rice may have originated with a traditional dish that got its color from gac fruit (*Momordica cochinchinensis*), a relative of bitter melon. The diaspora version is often reddened with the help of easily found tomato paste, which we use for both color and depth of flavor. The dish is usually made by stir-frying precooked rice, but for a weeknight version we make the rice from scratch, holding back on the water to re-create the slightly drier texture of fried rice. A splash of soy sauce provides additional depth of flavor while butter gives richness and complexity. Do not use basmati rice in this recipe.

> **Substitution:** You can use conventional long-grain white rice in place of the jasmine.

- 2 tablespoons unsalted butter
- 1½ cups jasmine rice, rinsed
- 4 garlic cloves, minced
- 3 tablespoons tomato paste
- 1¾ cups water
- 2 teaspoons soy sauce
- ½ teaspoon table salt

1. Melt butter in large saucepan over medium-high heat. Add rice and cook, stirring constantly, until grains become chalky and opaque, 1 to 3 minutes. Add garlic and cook, stirring constantly, until fragrant, about 30 seconds. Add tomato paste and cook, stirring constantly, until tomato paste is evenly distributed, about 1 minute.

2. Add water, soy sauce, and salt and bring to boil. Reduce heat to low; cover; and simmer gently until rice is tender and liquid has been fully absorbed, about 20 minutes. Off heat, lay clean dish towel underneath lid and let sit for 10 minutes. Fluff rice with fork and stir to combine. Serve.

Garlic Fried Rice

Serves 4 to 6 | **Total Time** 1 hour, plus 20 minutes
chilling VEGAN

WHY THIS RECIPE WORKS A popular way to use day-old
rice in the Philippines is to make sinangag, a garlicky fried-rice
breakfast dish. Sinangag is usually served with omelets, fried
eggs, cured meats, or corned beef. But if you don't feel like
garlic or rice for breakfast, you can serve sinangag at other
meals to accompany a meaty stir-fry or curry. The key to maximum flavor in the rice is to make the most of the garlic. Some
recipes call for garlic chips, but we find that they overcook
easily, becoming acrid and bitter. Mincing our garlic instead
allows its flavor to permeate the entire dish. Toasting the
minced garlic in oil over medium heat while stirring frequently
ensures that it just cooks to a pale golden brown. We then stir
the rice, salt, and floral white pepper into the garlic and heat it
through. You will need a 12-inch nonstick skillet or a 14-inch
flat-bottomed wok for this recipe. If using a wok, make sure
that it is well seasoned so that the rice does not stick.

> **Substitution:** You can use 6 cups leftover cooked rice in
> place of making the rice in this recipe; skip steps 1 and 2
> and bring leftover rice to room temperature before using.

6 tablespoons vegetable oil, divided
2 cups jasmine rice, rinsed
2⅔ cups water
1 teaspoon table salt
¼ teaspoon white pepper
6 garlic cloves, minced

1. Heat 2 tablespoons oil in large saucepan over medium
heat until shimmering. Add rice and stir to coat grains with
oil, about 30 seconds. Add water, increase heat to high, and
bring to boil. Reduce heat to low, cover, and simmer until all
liquid is absorbed, about 18 minutes.

2. Off heat, remove lid and place dish towel folded in half
over saucepan; replace lid. Let sit until rice is just tender,
about 8 minutes. Spread cooked rice onto rimmed baking
sheet and let cool on wire rack for 10 minutes. Transfer sheet
to refrigerator and let rice chill for 20 minutes.

3. Break up any large clumps of rice with your fingers and
sprinkle with salt and white pepper. Combine remaining
¼ cup oil and garlic in 12-inch nonstick skillet or 14-inch
flat-bottomed wok over medium heat, stirring frequently, until
garlic is crisped and light golden brown, 3 to 5 minutes. Add
rice and cook, tossing constantly, until mixture is thoroughly
combined and heated through, about 3 minutes. Serve.

Arroz Rojo

Serves 6 to 8 | **Total Time** 1¼ hours VEGAN

WHY THIS RECIPE WORKS In northern Mexico, rice is
cooked with broth and tomato to make arroz rojo, a dish of
distinct, tender, mildly spicy red-hued grains. Since it's the
aromatic cooking liquid that infuses the rice with flavor
through and through, we start with broth for savory backbone
and enhance the broth with a mixture of pureed onion and the
obligatory tomatoes. Three minced jalapeños (with some of
the ribs and seeds removed to help moderate their heat), some
garlic, and a tablespoon of tomato paste give our rice spice,
depth, and a deeper red color. Use an ovensafe pot about
12 inches in diameter with a tight-fitting lid so that the rice
cooks evenly and in the time indicated. For more spice, add
the ribs and seeds from the jalapeño chiles.

2 tomatoes, cored and quartered
1 onion, root end trimmed, quartered
3 jalapeño chiles, stemmed, divided
⅓ cup vegetable oil
2 cups long-grain white rice, rinsed
4 garlic cloves, minced
2 cups vegetable or chicken broth
1 tablespoon tomato paste
1½ teaspoons table salt
½ cup minced fresh cilantro
Lime wedges

1. Adjust oven rack to middle position and heat oven to
350 degrees. Process tomatoes and onion in food processor
until smooth, about 15 seconds. Transfer mixture to liquid
measuring cup and spoon off excess until mixture measures
2 cups. Remove ribs and seeds from 2 jalapeños and discard;
mince flesh and set aside. Mince remaining 1 jalapeño,
including ribs and seeds; set aside.

2. Heat oil in Dutch oven over medium-high heat for 1 to
2 minutes. Drop 3 or 4 grains rice in oil; if grains sizzle, oil is
ready. Add rice and cook, stirring often, until rice is light
golden and translucent, 6 to 8 minutes.

3. Reduce heat to medium. Stir in garlic and reserved seeded
jalapeños and cook, stirring constantly, until fragrant, about
1½ minutes. Stir in broth, tomato paste, salt, and tomato-onion
mixture. Increase heat to medium-high and bring to boil.

4. Cover pot; transfer to oven; and cook until liquid is
absorbed and rice is tender, 30 to 35 minutes, stirring well
after 15 minutes. Fold in cilantro and reserved jalapeño with
seeds to taste. Serve with lime wedges.

Arroz Rojo

Almost Hands-Free Risotto with Parmesan

Serves 4 to 6 | **Total Time** 1 hour

WHY THIS RECIPE WORKS Classic risotto can demand half an hour of stovetop tedium for the creamiest results. However, this rich, satisfying risotto requires 5 minutes of stirring, tops. First, we swap out the usual saucepan for a Dutch oven, which has a thick, heavy bottom, deep sides, and a tight-fitting lid—perfect for trapping and distributing heat evenly. Traditional recipes dictate adding the broth in small increments after the wine has been absorbed and stirring constantly after each addition, but we add most of the broth at once and then cover the pan, allowing the rice to simmer until almost all the broth has been absorbed and stirring just twice. After adding the second and final addition of hot broth, we stir the pot constantly for 3 minutes and then turn off the heat. Without sitting over a direct flame, the sauce turns out perfectly creamy and the rice is thickened, velvety, and just barely chewy. To finish, we simply stir in butter and a squeeze of lemon juice.

5 cups vegetable or chicken broth
1½ cups water
4 tablespoons unsalted butter, divided
1 large onion, chopped fine
¾ teaspoon table salt
1 garlic clove, minced
2 cups Arborio rice
1 cup dry white wine or dry vermouth
2 ounces Parmesan cheese, grated (1 cup)
1 teaspoon lemon juice

1. Bring broth and water to boil in large saucepan over high heat. Cover and reduce heat to medium-low to maintain bare simmer.

2. Melt 2 tablespoons butter in Dutch oven over medium heat. Add onion and salt and cook until softened, about 5 minutes. Stir in garlic and cook until fragrant, about 30 seconds. Add rice and cook, stirring often, until grain edges begin to turn translucent, about 3 minutes.

3. Add wine and cook, stirring constantly, until fully absorbed, 2 to 3 minutes. Stir in 5 cups hot broth mixture. Reduce heat to medium-low; cover; and simmer until almost all liquid has been absorbed and rice is just al dente, 18 to 19 minutes, stirring twice during cooking.

4. Add ¾ cup hot broth mixture and stir gently and constantly until risotto becomes creamy, about 3 minutes. Stir in Parmesan. Remove pot from heat, cover, and let sit for 5 minutes. Stir in lemon juice and remaining 2 tablespoons butter. Season with salt and pepper to taste. Before serving, stir in remaining broth mixture as needed to loosen texture of risotto.

VARIATIONS

Almost Hands-Free Risotto with Herbs
Stir in 2 tablespoons minced fresh parsley and 2 tablespoons minced fresh chives before serving.

Almost Hands-Free Risotto with Porcini
Add ¼ ounce rinsed and minced porcini mushrooms to pot with garlic. Substitute soy sauce for lemon juice.

Almost Hands-Free Risotto with Fennel and Saffron
Add 1 finely chopped fennel bulb to pot with onion and cook until softened, about 12 minutes. Add ¼ teaspoon ground coriander and large pinch saffron threads to pot with garlic.

Chelow ba Tahdig

Serves 6 | **Total Time** 1¾ hours

WHY THIS RECIPE WORKS Our version of this showpiece Iranian pilaf marries unusually light and fluffy steamed rice (chelow) with a crisp golden-brown crust known as tahdig. To ensure discrete, evenly cooked grains, we soak the rice in hot water to wash away its excess starch and then boil it briefly. We pack part of the parcooked rice into the bottom of a Dutch oven and then mound the rest on top before adding water, covering the pot, and blasting it with heat. The bottom layer of rice fries while the rest steams. Next, we place the hot pot on a damp dish towel to help the bottom grains contract so the crust releases from the pot more easily. Instead of unmolding the entire portion of rice at once as is traditional, we find it easier to spoon the steamed rice onto a plate before breaking up the crust and scattering the pieces on top. For the best results, use a Dutch oven with a bottom diameter between 8½ and 10 inches. It is important not to overcook the rice during parboiling, as it will continue to cook during steaming. Begin checking the rice at the lower end of the time range.

> **Substitution:** You can use other long-grain rice varieties in place of the basmati.

2 cups basmati rice, rinsed

1 tablespoon table salt for soaking

¼ teaspoon table salt, plus salt for cooking rice

5 tablespoons vegetable oil, divided

¼ cup plain Greek yogurt

1½ teaspoons cumin seeds, divided

2 tablespoons unsalted butter, cut into 8 pieces

¼ cup minced fresh parsley, divided

1. Bring 8 cups water to boil in Dutch oven over high heat. Add rice and 2 tablespoons salt. Boil briskly, stirring frequently, until rice is mostly tender with slight bite in center and grains are floating toward top of pot, 3 to 5 minutes (begin timing from when rice is added to pot).

2. Drain rice in large fine-mesh strainer and rinse with cold water to stop cooking, about 30 seconds. Rinse and dry pot well to remove any residual starch. Brush bottom and 1 inch up sides of pot with 1 tablespoon oil.

3. Whisk yogurt, 1 teaspoon cumin seeds, ¼ teaspoon salt, and remaining ¼ cup oil together in medium bowl. Add 2 cups rice and stir until combined. Spread yogurt-rice mixture evenly over bottom of prepared pot, packing it down well.

4. Stir remaining ½ teaspoon cumin seeds into remaining rice. Mound rice in center of pot on top of yogurt-rice base (it should look like small hill). Poke 8 equally spaced holes through rice mound but not into yogurt-rice base. Place 1 butter cube in each hole. Drizzle ⅓ cup water over rice mound.

5. Wrap pot lid with clean dish towel and cover pot tightly, making sure towel is secure on top of lid and away from heat. Cook over medium-high heat until rice on bottom is crackling and steam is coming from sides of pot, about 10 minutes, rotating pot halfway through for even cooking.

6. Reduce heat to medium-low and continue to cook until rice is tender and fluffy and crust is golden brown around edges, 30 to 35 minutes. Remove covered pot from heat and place on damp dish towel set in rimmed baking sheet; let stand for 5 minutes.

7. Stir 2 tablespoons parsley into rice, making sure not to disturb crust on bottom of pot, and season with salt to taste. Gently spoon rice onto serving platter.

8. Using thin metal spatula, loosen edges of crust from pot, then break crust into large pieces. Transfer pieces to serving platter, arranging evenly around rice. Sprinkle with remaining 2 tablespoons parsley and serve.

Chelow ba Tahdig

Jamaican Rice and Peas

Serves 6 | **Total Time** 1¾ hours, plus 8 hours soaking

WHY THIS RECIPE WORKS Rice and peas—fluffy white rice and creamy red kidney beans enriched with coconut milk and seasoned with scallions, garlic, a Scotch bonnet chile, thyme, and pimento (allspice)—is so foundational in Jamaican cooking that it has been called the nation's "coat of arms." Our version begins with giving dried red kidney beans a long soak. We then simmer the beans until they're tender, using just enough chicken broth and coconut milk to leave the right amount of liquid to cook the rice. Placing a sheet of aluminum foil under the saucepan lid creates a tight seal, guarding against excess evaporation. Once the saucepan is covered in step 4, do not uncover it until after the 10-minute rest.

- 1 cup dried red kidney beans, picked over and rinsed
- 3 cups chicken broth
- 1 (14-ounce) can coconut milk
- 10 sprigs fresh thyme
- 2 scallions, sliced thin
- 4 garlic cloves, chopped coarse
- 1 Scotch bonnet chile
- 2 teaspoons table salt
- ½ teaspoon pepper
- ¼ teaspoon whole allspice berries
- 2 cups long-grain white rice, rinsed
- 2 tablespoons unsalted butter

1. Combine 2 quarts cold water and beans in bowl and soak at room temperature for at least 8 hours or up to 24 hours. Drain and rinse well. (If you're pressed for time, see page 13 for information on quick brining your beans.)

2. Combine soaked beans, broth, coconut milk, thyme sprigs, scallions, garlic, Scotch bonnet, salt, pepper, and allspice berries in large saucepan. Bring to boil over high heat. Cover; reduce heat to medium-low; and simmer until beans are tender, 45 minutes to 1 hour.

3. Drain bean mixture in fine-mesh strainer set over 8-cup liquid measuring cup or large bowl. Discard thyme sprigs and Scotch bonnet. Return bean mixture to saucepan along with 3½ cups bean cooking liquid (add water to equal 3½ cups if needed; reserve any excess for another use or discard).

4. Stir rice and butter into bean mixture. Bring to boil over high heat. Once boiling, stir and place large sheet of aluminum foil over saucepan and cover tightly with lid. Reduce heat to low and cook for 20 minutes. Remove from heat and let rest, covered, for 10 minutes. Transfer rice and bean mixture to shallow serving bowl. Fluff rice with fork and serve.

Jamaican Rice and Peas

Brown Rice Pilaf with Dates and Pistachios

Serves 6 | **Total Time** 1½ hours `VEGAN`

WHY THIS RECIPE WORKS When enriched with just a few judiciously chosen add-ins, simple brown rice pilaf transforms into something memorable. We sauté a base of onions in a Dutch oven; stir in broth, rice, and a bay leaf; and then cover the pot and pop it into the oven to cook in the oven's even heat for about an hour. When the rice is tender, we remove it from the oven, sprinkle sweet chopped dates over the top, cover the pot again, and let it stand for 10 minutes, just enough time for the dates to plump up. After a quick fluff with a fork to incorporate a sprinkling of earthy pistachios and cooling mint, our light, wholesome pilaf is good to go.

Substitution: You can use medium-grain or short-grain brown rice in place of the long-grain.

Brown Rice Pilaf with Dates and Pistachios

VARIATION
Brown Rice Pilaf with Peas, Feta, and Mint

Increase salt to 1 teaspoon. Substitute 1 cup thawed frozen peas for dates. Substitute ½ teaspoon grated lemon zest for pistachios. Sprinkle with ½ cup crumbled feta before serving.

Easy Baked Brown Rice

Serves 4 to 6 | **Total Time** 1 hour 45 minutes   VEGAN

WHY THIS RECIPE WORKS Brown rice should be ultimately satisfying, with a nutty, gutsy flavor and more textural personality—slightly sticky and just a bit chewy—than white rice. Moving the recipe to the oven ensures more even cooking, guards against scorching, and produces light and fluffy grains every time. As with our Hands-Off Baked White Rice (page 298), we rinse the rice before cooking to help the grains stay separate. But for this recipe, we use a slightly higher ratio of liquid to rice. Swapping part of the cooking water for vegetable broth adds savory notes, as does including some finely chopped sautéed onion.

Substitution: You can use short-grain brown rice in place of the long-grain.

1	tablespoon extra-virgin olive oil
1	small onion, chopped fine
¼	teaspoon table salt
2¼	cups water
1	cup vegetable or chicken broth
1½	cups long-grain brown rice, rinsed

1. Adjust oven rack to middle position and heat oven to 375 degrees. Heat oil in Dutch oven over medium heat until shimmering. Add onion and salt and cook until softened and lightly browned, 5 to 7 minutes.

2. Add water and broth, cover, and bring to boil. Off heat, stir in rice. Cover; transfer pot to oven; and bake rice until tender and liquid has been fully absorbed, 1 hour 5 minutes to 1 hour 10 minutes.

3. Remove pot from oven. Fluff rice with fork, scraping up any rice that has stuck to bottom. Lay clean dish towel underneath lid and let sit, covered, for 10 minutes. Serve.

1	tablespoon extra-virgin olive oil
1	onion, chopped fine
½	teaspoon table salt
3¼	cups vegetable or chicken broth
1½	cups long-grain brown rice, rinsed
1	bay leaf
1½	ounces pitted dates, chopped (¼ cup)
⅓	cup shelled pistachios, toasted and chopped coarse
¼	cup minced fresh mint

1. Adjust oven rack to middle position and heat oven to 375 degrees. Heat oil in Dutch oven over medium heat until shimmering. Add onion and salt and cook until softened and lightly browned, 5 to 7 minutes.

2. Stir in broth, cover, and bring to boil. Off heat, stir in rice and bay leaf. Cover; transfer pot to oven; and bake until rice is tender and liquid has been fully absorbed, about 1 hour.

3. Remove pot from oven. Sprinkle dates over rice. Lay clean dish towel underneath lid and let sit, covered, for 10 minutes. Discard bay leaf. Fluff rice with fork, stir in pistachios and mint, and season with salt and pepper to taste. Serve.

VARIATION
Easy Baked Brown Rice with Parmesan, Lemon, and Herbs

When fluffing cooked rice, stir in ½ cup grated Parmesan, ¼ cup minced fresh parsley, ¼ cup chopped fresh basil, 1 teaspoon grated lemon zest, and ½ teaspoon lemon juice.

Wild Rice Pilaf with Pecans and Cranberries

Serves 6 to 8 | **Total Time** 1 hour 5 minutes VEGAN

WHY THIS RECIPE WORKS Properly cooked wild rice is tender yet chewy and pleasingly rustic—never crunchy or gluey. Simmering the wild rice in flavorful liquid and then draining off excess is the surest way to produce fluffy wild rice every time. To enhance the rice's earthy nuttiness, we cook it in a combination of vegetable broth and water. We also add some white rice to our pilaf to balance the wild rice's assertive flavor, and we finish our dish with nuts and dried fruit. Do not use quick-cooking or presteamed wild rice (check the ingredient list on the package to determine this) in this recipe.

2½ cups water, divided
1¾ cups vegetable broth
2 bay leaves
8 sprigs fresh thyme, divided into 2 bundles, each tied together with kitchen twine
1 cup wild rice, rinsed
2 tablespoons extra-virgin olive oil
1 onion, chopped fine
1 large carrot, peeled and chopped fine
1 teaspoon table salt
1½ cups long-grain white rice, rinsed
¾ cup dried cranberries
¾ cup pecans, toasted and chopped coarse
2 tablespoons minced fresh parsley

1. Bring ¼ cup water, broth, bay leaves, and 1 bundle thyme to boil in medium saucepan over medium-high heat. Add wild rice and reduce heat to low. Cover and simmer gently until rice is plump and tender and most of liquid has been absorbed, 35 to 45 minutes. Drain rice and discard bay leaves and thyme. Transfer rice to large bowl, cover, and set aside.

Wild Rice Pilaf with Pecans and Cranberries

2. Meanwhile, heat oil in large saucepan over medium-high heat until shimmering. Add onion, carrot, and salt and cook until vegetables are softened, about 5 minutes. Add white rice and cook, stirring constantly, until grains become chalky and opaque, 1 to 3 minutes.

3. Stir in remaining 2¼ cups water and second thyme bundle and bring to boil. Reduce heat to low; cover; and simmer gently until rice is tender and water has been fully absorbed, 16 to 18 minutes. Off heat, lay clean dish towel underneath lid and let sit, covered, for 10 minutes. Discard thyme and fluff rice with fork.

4. Add white rice, cranberries, pecans, and parsley to bowl with wild rice and toss to combine. Season with salt and pepper to taste. Serve.

VARIATION
Wild Rice Pilaf with Scallions, Cilantro, and Almonds VEGAN

Omit dried cranberries. Substitute toasted sliced almonds for pecans and cilantro for parsley. Add 2 thinly sliced scallions and 1 teaspoon lime juice to pilaf before serving.

Wild Rice Stuffing

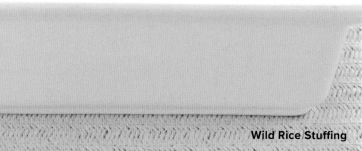

Barley Risotto

Wild Rice Stuffing

Serves 10 to 12 | **Total Time** 2¼ hours

WHY THIS RECIPE WORKS The amount of liquid that wild rice absorbs during cooking varies dramatically depending on the variety. To account for this unpredictability, we boil the rice in extra liquid and then drain the excess (reserving some for later use), so no matter which kind of wild rice is used it will cook perfectly every time. Cream and eggs bind the dressing but on their own are far too rich, so we also add the reserved cooking liquid to lighten the dish and enhance its nutty flavor. Toasted bread crumbs add color and crunch. Covering the casserole while it bakes keeps the surface from getting too crunchy. Do not use quick-cooking or presteamed wild rice (check the ingredient list on the package to determine this) in this recipe.

  2 cups vegetable or chicken broth
  2 cups water
  1 bay leaf
  2 cups wild rice, rinsed
10 slices hearty white sandwich bread, torn into pieces
  8 tablespoons unsalted butter, divided
  2 onions, chopped fine
  3 celery ribs, chopped fine
  4 garlic cloves, minced
1½ teaspoons dried sage
1½ teaspoons dried thyme
1½ cups heavy cream
  2 large eggs
  ¾ teaspoon table salt
  ½ teaspoon pepper

1. Bring broth, water, and bay leaf to boil in large saucepan over medium-high heat. Stir in rice. Return to boil, then reduce heat to low, cover, and simmer until rice is tender, 35 to 45 minutes. Strain rice through fine-mesh strainer, reserving 1½ cups cooking liquid. Discard bay leaf.

2. Adjust oven racks to upper-middle and lower-middle positions and heat oven to 325 degrees. Working in batches, pulse bread in food processor until coarsely ground. Spread crumbs onto 2 rimmed baking sheets and bake until golden, about 20 minutes, stirring occasionally. Let crumbs cool completely.

3. Melt 4 tablespoons butter in 12-inch skillet over medium heat. Add onions and celery and cook until softened and lightly browned, 8 to 10 minutes. Stir in garlic, sage, and thyme and cook until fragrant, about 30 seconds. Off heat, stir in reserved cooking liquid and let cool for 5 minutes.

4. Grease 13 by 9-inch baking dish. Whisk cream, eggs, salt, and pepper together in large bowl. Slowly whisk in warm broth mixture. Stir in rice and bread crumbs. Transfer mixture to prepared dish. (Dressing can be refrigerated for up to 1 day; increase baking time to 1 hour 5 minutes to 1¼ hours.)

5. Melt remaining 4 tablespoons butter in now-empty skillet and drizzle evenly over dressing. Cover dish with aluminum foil and bake on lower rack until set, 45 to 55 minutes. Remove foil and let cool for 15 minutes. Serve.

Oven-Baked Barley

Serves 4 to 6 | **Total Time** 1 hour 35 minutes

WHY THIS RECIPE WORKS With its mild flavor and robust texture, barley makes a great alternative to rice. In fact, our baked white rice recipe (page 298) is the template for this easy barley side dish, with some substantial adjustment in the water-to-grain ratio. Since barley can absorb two to three times its volume in cooking liquid, we use 3½ cups of water to 1½ cups of barley. After an hour-plus stint, covered, in the oven, followed by a 10-minute rest, the grains of barley are separate and fully cooked without being soggy. Be sure to cover the pot when bringing the water to a boil in step 1; any water loss due to evaporation will affect how the barley cooks. Do not use hulled, hull-less, quick-cooking, or presteamed barley (check the ingredient list on the package to determine this) in this recipe.

1½ cups pearl barley, rinsed
3½ cups water
  1 tablespoon unsalted butter
  ½ teaspoon table salt

1. Adjust oven rack to middle position and heat oven to 375 degrees. Spread barley in 8-inch square baking dish. Bring water, butter, and salt to boil in covered medium saucepan over high heat.

2. Pour hot water mixture immediately over barley. Cover baking dish tightly with double layer of aluminum foil. Bake barley until tender and liquid has been fully absorbed, 1 hour 10 minutes to 1 hour 20 minutes.

3. Remove baking dish from oven, uncover, and fluff barley with fork. Re-cover dish with foil and let barley sit for 10 minutes. Serve.

Barley Risotto

Serves 4 to 6 | **Total Time** 1½ hours

WHY THIS RECIPE WORKS Pearl barley makes an excellent alternative risotto. Pearling removes the barley's outer bran so the grain's interior starch can thicken the cooking liquid to a supple, velvety consistency. We use the classic risotto cooking method with one minor change: We add more liquid because barley takes a bit longer to cook than rice. Parmesan and butter enrich the risotto. Do not use hulled, hull-less, quick-cooking, or presteamed barley (check the ingredient list on the package to determine this) in this recipe. The cooking time for pearl barley will vary from product to product, so start checking the barley for doneness after about 25 minutes.

  4 cups vegetable or chicken broth
  4 cups water
  1 tablespoon vegetable oil
  1 onion, chopped fine
  1 carrot, peeled and chopped fine
1½ cups pearl barley, rinsed
  1 cup dry white wine or dry vermouth
  1 teaspoon minced fresh thyme
  2 ounces Parmesan cheese, grated (1 cup), plus extra
    for serving
  1 tablespoon unsalted butter
    Lemon wedges

1. Bring broth and water to boil in large saucepan over high heat. Cover and reduce heat to medium-low to maintain bare simmer.

2. Heat oil in Dutch oven over medium heat until shimmering. Add onion and carrot and cook until softened, 5 to 7 minutes. Add barley and cook, stirring often, until lightly toasted and aromatic, about 4 minutes. Add wine and cook, stirring constantly, until fully absorbed, about 2 minutes.

3. Add thyme and 3 cups warm broth mixture and simmer, stirring occasionally, until liquid is absorbed and bottom of pot is dry, 22 to 25 minutes. Add 2 cups warm broth mixture and continue to simmer, stirring occasionally, until liquid is absorbed and bottom of pot is dry, 15 to 18 minutes.

4. Continue to cook risotto, stirring often and adding warm broth mixture as needed to prevent pot bottom from becoming dry, until barley is cooked through but still somewhat firm in center, 15 to 20 minutes. Off heat, stir in Parmesan and butter. Adjust consistency with remaining warm broth mixture as needed (you may have broth left over). Season with salt and pepper to taste. Serve with lemon wedges, passing extra Parmesan separately.

Barley with Celery and
Miso Dressing

Buckwheat Tabbouleh

Barley with Celery and Miso Dressing

Serves 6 to 8 | **Total Time** 1¼ hours VEGAN

WHY THIS RECIPE WORKS Barley, like many other grains, contains sticky starch that can cause clumping when cooked. To produce a clump-free grain salad featuring barley's pleasant chew and mild nutty flavor, we cook the barley like pasta, boiling it in a large volume of salted water before draining away the excess water—and the excess starch along with it. Once the barley is cooked, we let it cool briefly on a rimmed baking sheet to help it dry thoroughly—further insurance against clumping. We then toss it with an acid-heavy dressing (a 1:1 ratio of oil to acid instead of the typical 3:1 ratio) to give this hearty side a bright lift. Do not use hulled, hull-less, quick-cooking, or presteamed barley (check the ingredient list on the package to determine this) in this recipe. The cooking time for pearl barley will vary from product to product, so start checking the barley for doneness after about 25 minutes.

1½ cups pearl barley, rinsed
    Table salt for cooking barley
  3 tablespoons seasoned rice vinegar
  1 tablespoon white miso paste
  1 tablespoon soy sauce
  1 tablespoon toasted sesame oil
  1 tablespoon vegetable oil
  2 teaspoons grated fresh ginger
  1 garlic clove, minced
  1 teaspoon packed brown sugar
¼–½ teaspoon red pepper flakes
  2 celery ribs, sliced thin on bias
  2 carrots, peeled and grated
  ½ cup minced fresh cilantro

1. Bring 2 quarts water to boil in large saucepan. Add barley and 2 teaspoons salt. Return to boil, then reduce to simmer and cook until tender with slight chew, 25 to 45 minutes. Drain well. Spread barley on rimmed baking sheet and let cool for 15 minutes. (Barley can be refrigerated in airtight container for up to 2 days.)

2. Meanwhile, whisk vinegar, miso, soy sauce, sesame oil, vegetable oil, ginger, garlic, sugar, and pepper flakes together in large bowl. Add barley and toss to coat. Add celery, carrots, and cilantro and stir to combine. Season with salt and pepper to taste. Serve.

Buckwheat Tabbouleh

Serves 4 | **Total Time** 35 minutes, plus 45 minutes cooling and resting VEGAN

WHY THIS RECIPE WORKS Featuring bulgur (a product of the wheat berry), parsley, mint, and chopped tomatoes tossed in a bright lemon vinaigrette, classic Mediterranean tabbouleh has a refreshing flavor profile that makes it a great light side. To give this classic our own spin, we swap the bulgur for another grain: mild, appealingly earthy buckwheat groats. Because buckwheat contains a fair amount of starch, we make sure to cook it pasta-style in plenty of water; the water washes away the excess starch, producing separate, evenly cooked kernels. For the herbs, we add plenty of fresh, peppery parsley; 1½ cups has just enough of a presence to balance well with ½ cup of fresh mint. To ensure undiluted, bright flavor in the final tabbouleh, we salt the tomatoes to rid them of excess moisture before tossing them into the salad.

- ¾ cup buckwheat groats, rinsed
- ½ teaspoon table salt, divided, plus salt for cooking buckwheat
- 3 tomatoes, cored and cut into ½-inch pieces
- 2 tablespoons lemon juice
  Pinch cayenne pepper
- ¼ cup extra-virgin olive oil
- 1½ cups minced fresh parsley
- ½ cup minced fresh mint
- 2 scallions, sliced thin

1. Bring 2 quarts water to boil in large saucepan. Stir in buckwheat and 2 teaspoons salt. Return to boil, then reduce to simmer and cook until tender, 10 to 12 minutes. Drain well. Spread buckwheat on rimmed baking sheet and let cool for 15 minutes. (Buckwheat can be refrigerated in airtight container for up to 2 days.)

2. Meanwhile, toss tomatoes with ¼ teaspoon salt in bowl. Transfer to fine-mesh strainer, set strainer in bowl, and let sit for 30 minutes, tossing occasionally.

3. Whisk lemon juice, cayenne, and remaining ¼ teaspoon salt together in large bowl. Whisking constantly, drizzle in oil.

4. Add drained tomatoes, cooled buckwheat, parsley, mint, and scallions and gently toss to combine. Cover and let sit at room temperature until flavors meld, at least 30 minutes or up to 2 hours. Toss to recombine and season with salt and pepper to taste. Serve.

Bulgur Pilaf

Serves 4 | **Total Time** 50 minutes VEGAN

WHY THIS RECIPE WORKS Bulgur, a form of wheat that's been parboiled and dried so it cooks fast yet retains all the benefits of whole grains, makes a hearty and delicious pilaf-style dish. Onions, garlic, and a dash of soy sauce give the bulgur umami savoriness and a rich mahogany color. After simmering the bulgur until tender, we place a dish towel underneath the lid to absorb moisture and let the bulgur steam gently for 10 minutes, which results in perfectly tender, chewy grains. When shopping, don't confuse bulgur with cracked wheat, which has a much longer cooking time and will not work in this recipe.

- 2 tablespoons extra-virgin olive oil
- 1 onion, chopped fine
- ¼ teaspoon table salt
- 2 garlic cloves, minced
- 1 cup medium-grind bulgur, rinsed
- ¾ cup vegetable or chicken broth
- ¾ cup water
- 1 teaspoon soy sauce
- ¼ cup minced fresh parsley

1. Heat oil in large saucepan over medium heat until shimmering. Add onion and salt and cook until softened, about 5 minutes. Stir in garlic and cook until fragrant, about 30 seconds. Stir in bulgur, broth, water, and soy sauce and bring to simmer. Cover; reduce heat to low; and simmer until bulgur is tender, 16 to 18 minutes.

2. Off heat, lay clean dish towel underneath lid and let sit for 10 minutes. Fluff bulgur with fork, stir in parsley, and season with salt and pepper to taste. Serve.

Basic Farro

Serves 6 | **Total Time** 40 minutes FAST VEGAN

WHY THIS RECIPE WORKS The hulled whole-wheat kernels called farro boast a slightly sweet, wheaty flavor and chewy texture. To make a simple, delicious side dish with this protein- and fiber-rich grain, we start with commonly available pearl farro and toast it in olive oil to bring out its nuttiness. Cooking times can vary among brands of farro, so we use the pasta method, simmering the farro in an abundance of water to produce tender grains without the saucepan going dry. Fresh thyme sprigs and a bay leaf fortify the water (and thus

Basic Farro

1. Combine farro and 1 tablespoon oil in large saucepan. Cook over medium-high heat, stirring frequently, until farro is fragrant and just starting to darken in color, about 6 minutes.

2. Add 2 quarts water, 1 tablespoon salt, thyme sprigs, and bay leaf. Bring to boil over high heat. Reduce heat to medium and simmer until grains are tender with slight chew, 10 to 20 minutes. Drain well. Discard thyme sprigs and bay leaf.

3. Return farro to saucepan. Stir in parsley, if using; garlic; salt; and remaining 1 tablespoon oil. Season with salt and pepper to taste. Serve.

Old-Fashioned Stovetop Grits

Serves 4 | **Total Time** 30 Minutes **FAST**

WHY THIS RECIPE WORKS A staple of the Southern table, grits can be a substantial start to the day or a good addition to the dinner plate. Although the convenience of quick-cooking grits is tempting, we find them a bit too creamy and overprocessed. Old-fashioned grits cook in 10 to 15 minutes, and retain a pleasing, slightly coarse texture. We keep the recipe simple by bringing milk, water, and a pinch of salt to a boil and then slowly pouring the grits into the pot, whisking the entire time to prevent clumping. Finishing the grits over low heat and uncovering them a few times to stir them, ensures that they cook evenly without burning. If you're serving grits for breakfast, they can be drizzled with maple syrup, honey, or molasses. If serving them with dinner, sprinkle with grated Parmesan or shredded cheddar cheese and season with minced fresh herbs. These grits taste best made with whole milk; you can substitute low-fat milk but do not use nonfat milk.

the farro) with extra flavor. We brighten the taste of the grains with fresh parsley, minced garlic, and a drizzle of olive oil. Without parsley, the farro also makes an excellent base for a grain salad.

Substitution: You can also use whole-grain or semi-pearled farro here if you can find it, but note that the cooking time will be on the longer side of the range given. To use whole-grain farro, soak it for at least 8 hours or up to 12 hours and drain it thoroughly before starting with step 1. Do not use quick-cooking farro here.

1½ cups pearl farro
2 tablespoons extra-virgin olive oil, divided
¼ teaspoon table salt, plus salt for cooking farro
2 sprigs fresh thyme
1 bay leaf
2 tablespoons chopped fresh parsley (optional)
1 garlic clove, minced

4 cups whole milk
1 cup water
¼ teaspoon table salt
1 cup old-fashioned grits
2 tablespoons unsalted butter

1. Bring milk, water, and salt to boil in medium saucepan. Pour grits into pot in very slow stream while whisking constantly in circular motion to prevent clumping.

2. Cover and reduce heat to low. Cook, stirring often and vigorously (make sure to scrape corners of pot), until grits are thick and creamy, 10 to 15 minutes. Stir in butter and season with salt and pepper to taste. Serve.

Cheesy Baked Grits

Serves 6 to 8 | **Total Time** 1½ hours

WHY THIS RECIPE WORKS Rich and cheesy grits are a simple but satisfying side dish. In this version, we whisk some of the cheese into the grits, sprinkle the rest on top, and then bake until brown and bubbling on top and creamy in the middle. We begin building flavor by sautéing some chopped onion in butter. Next we bring water—enriched with cream and spiked with a dash of hot sauce—to a boil and whisk in the grits. Once the grits are thickened, we stir in plenty of tangy cheddar cheese along with beaten eggs, which give the dish an airy texture, and then move the grits to the oven to finish.

- 2 tablespoons unsalted butter
- 1 onion, chopped fine
- 1 teaspoon table salt
- 4½ cups water
- 1½ cups heavy cream
- ¾ teaspoon hot sauce
- 1½ cups old-fashioned grits
- 8 ounces extra-sharp cheddar cheese, shredded (2 cups), divided
- 4 large eggs, lightly beaten
- ¼ teaspoon pepper

1. Adjust oven rack to lower-middle position and heat oven to 350 degrees. Grease 13 by 9-inch baking dish. Melt butter in large saucepan over medium heat. Add onion and salt and cook until softened, about 5 minutes. Stir in water, cream, and hot sauce and bring to boil.

2. Add grits to pot in slow, steady stream, whisking constantly in circular motion to prevent clumping. Cover and reduce heat to low. Cook, whisking frequently and vigorously (make sure to scrape corners of pot), until grits are thick and creamy, 10 to 15 minutes.

3. Off heat, whisk in 1 cup cheddar, eggs, and pepper. Pour mixture into prepared baking dish and smooth top with rubber spatula. Sprinkle remaining 1 cup cheddar over top. Bake until top is browned and grits are hot, 35 to 45 minutes. Let casserole cool for 10 minutes. Serve.

VARIATIONS

Cheesy Baked Grits with Sausage and Bell Pepper
Add 1 pound crumbled breakfast sausage and 1 finely chopped red bell pepper to pot with onion; increase cooking time to 8 to 10 minutes.

Cheesy Baked Grits with Pepper Jack Cheese and Bell Pepper
Add 1 finely chopped red bell pepper to pot with onion; increase cooking time to 8 to 10 minutes. Substitute pepper Jack cheese for cheddar.

Creamy Parmesan Polenta

Serves 4 to 6 | **Total Time** 55 minutes

WHY THIS RECIPE WORKS Simple, creamy stovetop polenta makes a perfect bed for toppings ranging from fried eggs to sautéed shrimp and roasted meat to vegetables (see Creamy Polenta with Radicchio Agrodolce, page 271). Adding a pinch of baking soda just as the water comes to a boil is a decidedly nontraditional approach that cuts the cooking time in half. Covering the pot and lowering the heat cooks the polenta gently. If the polenta bubbles or sputters even slightly after the first 10 minutes, the heat is too high. It may help to have a flame tamer (see page 314 for how to make your own). Coarse-ground degerminated cornmeal (with grains the size of couscous) works best here. Avoid instant and quick-cooking products and whole-grain, stone-ground, and regular cornmeal.

Creamy Parmesan Polenta

7½ cups water
1½ teaspoons table salt
    Pinch baking soda
1½ cups coarse-ground cornmeal
 4 ounces Parmesan cheese, grated (2 cups),
    plus extra for serving
 2 tablespoons unsalted butter

1. Bring water to boil in large saucepan over medium-high heat. Stir in salt and baking soda. Slowly add cornmeal in steady stream, stirring constantly. Bring mixture to boil, stirring constantly, about 1 minute. Reduce heat to lowest possible setting, cover, and cook for 5 minutes.

2. Whisk cornmeal to smooth out any lumps that may have formed, making sure to scrape down sides and bottom of saucepan. Cover and continue to cook, without stirring, until cornmeal is tender but slightly al dente, about 25 minutes. (Polenta should be loose and barely hold its shape but will continue to thicken as it cools.)

3. Off heat, stir in Parmesan and butter and season with pepper to taste. Let polenta stand, covered, for 5 minutes. Serve, passing extra Parmesan separately.

TAMING THE FLAME TAMER

A flame tamer keeps polenta, risotto, and sauces from simmering too briskly. To make one, shape a sheet of heavy-duty aluminum foil into a 1-inch-thick ring that fits on your burner, making sure that the ring is of even thickness.

NOTES FROM THE TEST KITCHEN

BUYING CORNMEAL

Shopping for cornmeal can be confusing. Should you get the stuff labeled "cornmeal," "yellow grits," or "corn semolina"? A better approach is to focus on whether the product is "instant" (or "quick-cooking") versus traditional (the former is often bland). We like to use traditional Quaker Yellow Corn Meal.

Fluffy Baked Polenta with Red Sauce

Serves 6 | **Total Time** 3¼ hours, plus 4 hours cooling and chilling

WHY THIS RECIPE WORKS Italians enjoy polenta in many ways—one of which is baking it so that it develops a golden crust and tender, light interior. We complement this type of polenta with a simple red sauce. Cooking the polenta in water lets the corn flavor shine through; stirring in half-and-half at the end brings richness. A healthy dose of nutty Pecorino Romano provides savory backbone. Using a two-step cooking process—first on the stove and then, once the polenta is cooled and cut into blocks, in the oven—brings the desired results. We developed this recipe using Quaker Yellow Corn Meal for its desirable texture and relatively short cooking time. We recommend you use the same product for this recipe. The timing may be different for other types of cornmeal, so be sure to cook the polenta until it is thickened and tender. Whole milk can be substituted for the half-and-half.

POLENTA
 4 tablespoons unsalted butter
 2 tablespoons extra-virgin olive oil
 2 garlic cloves, smashed and peeled
 7 cups water
1½ teaspoons table salt
 ½ teaspoon pepper
1½ cups cornmeal
 3 ounces Pecorino Romano cheese, grated (1½ cups)
 ¼ cup half-and-half

RED SAUCE
 1 (14.5-ounce) can whole peeled tomatoes
 ¼ cup extra-virgin olive oil, divided
 1 onion, peeled and halved through root end
 1 (15-ounce) can tomato sauce
 1 ounce Pecorino Romano cheese, grated (½ cup)
1½ tablespoons sugar
 ¾ teaspoon table salt
 ½ teaspoon garlic powder

1. **FOR THE POLENTA** Lightly grease 8-inch square baking pan. Heat butter and oil in Dutch oven over medium heat until butter is melted. Add garlic and cook until lightly golden, about 4 minutes. Discard garlic.

2. Add water, salt, and pepper to butter mixture. Increase heat to medium-high and bring to boil. Add cornmeal in slow, steady stream, whisking constantly in circular motion to prevent clumping. Reduce heat to medium-low and cook, whisking frequently and vigorously (make sure to scrape corners of pot) until mixture is thick and cornmeal is tender, about 20 minutes.

3. Off heat, whisk in Pecorino and half-and-half. Transfer to prepared pan and let cool completely on wire rack. Once cooled, cover with plastic wrap and refrigerate until completely chilled, at least 3 hours.

4. FOR THE RED SAUCE Process tomatoes and their juice in blender until smooth, about 30 seconds. Heat 1 tablespoon oil in large saucepan over medium heat until shimmering. Add onion cut side down and cook without moving until lightly browned, about 4 minutes. Add pureed tomatoes, tomato sauce, Pecorino, sugar, salt, garlic powder, and remaining 3 tablespoons oil. Bring mixture to boil, reduce heat to medium-low, and simmer until sauce is slightly thickened, about 15 minutes. Remove from heat, discard onion, cover, and keep warm.

5. Adjust oven rack to middle position and heat oven to 375 degrees. Line rimmed baking sheet with parchment paper, then grease parchment. Cut chilled polenta into 6 equal pieces (about 4 by 2 ⅔ inches each). Place on prepared sheet and bake until heated through and beginning to brown on bottom, about 30 minutes. Serve each portion covered with about ½ cup red sauce.

Fluffy Baked Polenta with Red Sauce

Corn Pudding

Serves 6 to 8 | **Total Time** 1 hour

WHY THIS RECIPE WORKS Recipes for this rustic, soufflé-like casserole, a traditional part of many a Thanksgiving spread, often call for boxed corn muffin mix and canned cream corn, but here we opt for a fresher take. We swap out the creamed corn for frozen corn kernels, which have a better texture and more flavor than canned. To ensure a silky base brimming with the flavor of sweet corn, we buzz some of the kernels with cream in a blender. In place of the boxed muffin mix, we simply combine flour, cornmeal, salt, sugar, and a touch of baking soda; for rich flavor and light texture, we add sour cream and melted butter. Baking the mixture for 35 minutes in a 400-degree oven sets the pudding without drying it out. Note that the corn is divided after being microwaved. To double this recipe, bake the pudding in a 13 by 9-inch baking dish and increase the baking time to 45 to 50 minutes. You can use 1 pound of fresh corn kernels (from about four cobs) in place of the frozen corn.

Corn Pudding

1 pound frozen corn
¾ cup heavy cream
½ cup (2½ ounces) all-purpose flour
⅓ cup (1 ⅔ ounces) cornmeal
¼ cup (1¾ ounces) sugar
1¼ teaspoons table salt
¼ teaspoon baking soda
1 cup sour cream
6 tablespoons unsalted butter, melted
1 large egg, lightly beaten

1. Adjust oven rack to upper-middle position and heat oven to 400 degrees. Grease 8-inch square baking dish. Combine corn and ¼ cup water in microwave-safe bowl. Cover and microwave until corn is tender, about 7 minutes. Drain corn.

2. Combine cream and 1½ cups corn in blender and process until coarse puree forms, about 30 seconds. Whisk flour, cornmeal, sugar, salt, and baking soda together in large bowl. Whisk sour cream, melted butter, egg, pureed corn mixture, and remaining corn together in separate bowl. Whisk sour cream mixture into flour mixture until combined. Transfer batter to prepared dish.

3. Bake until edges of pudding are lightly browned and top is slightly puffed, about 35 minutes. Let cool on wire rack for 10 minutes. Serve warm.

Summer Cornbread and Tomato Salad

Summer Cornbread and Tomato Salad

Serves 4 | **Total Time** 1 hour

WHY THIS RECIPE WORKS This summer salad is inspired by panzanella, but instead of Italian bread we swap in sweet cornbread and add fresh corn kernels for juicy pops of flavor. Rather than making cornbread from scratch, we up the convenience factor by opting for prepared cornbread. We then toast it in the oven until golden-brown and crisp on the edges to deepen its flavor and help it stand up to the moisture from the tomatoes and dressing. As for that dressing, mayonnaise, jalapeño, lime juice, and olive oil make for the ideal creamy-tangy-spicy complement to the sweet corn and tomatoes. Thin slices of red onion add crunch and piquant bite. For more spice, add the ribs and seeds from the jalapeño chile.

1 pound prepared cornbread, cut into ¾-inch pieces (about 4 cups)
6 tablespoons extra-virgin olive oil, divided

2 tablespoons mayonnaise
2 tablespoons minced jalapeño chile
2 tablespoons lime juice
1¼ teaspoons table salt
½ teaspoon pepper
1½ pounds mixed tomatoes, cored and cut into ¾-inch pieces
1 small red onion, sliced thin
2 ears corn, kernels cut from cobs
¼ cup fresh basil leaves, torn

1. Adjust oven rack to middle position and heat oven to 400 degrees. Toss cornbread with 2 tablespoons oil on rimmed baking sheet, then spread into even layer. Bake until dry to touch and edges turn golden brown, about 15 minutes, stirring halfway through baking. Let cool for 10 minutes.

2. Whisk mayonnaise, jalapeño, lime juice, salt, pepper, and remaining ¼ cup oil together in large bowl. Add tomatoes, onion, and cornbread and gently toss to coat. Season with salt and pepper to taste. Transfer salad to serving platter and top with corn and basil. Serve.

1. Using a sharp knife, trim and discard stem end. Slice chile in half lengthwise.

2. Use a spoon to scrape out seeds and ribs (reserve if desired). Prepare seeded chile as directed.

Warm Kamut with Carrots and Pomegranate

Serves 4 to 6 | **Total Time** 1¾ hours VEGAN

WHY THIS RECIPE WORKS The rich, nutty flavor and firm texture of the ancient grain Kamut help it stand out even when it is paired with a variety of other assertive ingredients, making it a great candidate for the grain salad treatment. Here we pair it with finely chopped carrots, crunchy green pistachios, cilantro, and purple-red pomegranate seeds for a side dish that's a riot of color and texture. A liberal dash of garam masala and a couple cloves of garlic add their pungent flavors to the mix. After cooking the Kamut using the pasta method and allowing it to cool, we soften the carrots in a skillet, adding garam masala and garlic to bloom them, and then toss in the Kamut to ensure that every bite is seasoned through and through. Soaking the Kamut in water overnight will shorten the cooking time to 35 to 50 minutes. Kamut is also sold as khorasan wheat.

  1 cup Kamut, rinsed and drained
  ¼ teaspoon table salt, plus salt for cooking Kamut
  2 tablespoons vegetable oil
  2 carrots, peeled and cut into ¼-inch pieces
  2 garlic cloves, minced
  ¾ teaspoon garam masala
  ¼ cup shelled pistachios, lightly toasted and chopped coarse, divided
  3 tablespoons chopped fresh cilantro, divided
  1 teaspoon lemon juice
  ¼ cup pomegranate seeds

Warm Kamut with Carrots and Pomegranate

1. Bring 2 quarts water to boil in large saucepan. Stir in Kamut and 2 teaspoons salt. Return to boil, then reduce to simmer and cook until tender, 55 minutes to 1 hour 15 minutes. Drain well. Spread Kamut on rimmed baking sheet and let cool for 15 minutes. (Kamut can be refrigerated in airtight container for up to 2 days.)

2. Heat oil in 12-inch skillet over medium heat until shimmering. Add carrots and salt and cook, stirring frequently, until carrots are softened and lightly browned, 4 to 6 minutes. Add garlic and garam masala and cook, stirring constantly, until fragrant, about 1 minute. Add Kamut and cook until warmed through, 2 to 5 minutes. Off heat, stir in half of pistachios, 2 tablespoons cilantro, and lemon juice. Season with salt and pepper to taste. Transfer to serving bowl and sprinkle with pomegranate seeds, remaining pistachios, and remaining 1 tablespoon cilantro. Serve.

Quinoa Pilaf with Herbs and Lemon

Serves 4 to 6 | **Total Time** 1 hour

WHY THIS RECIPE WORKS Most recipes for quinoa pilaf turn out woefully overcooked because they call for nearly twice as much liquid as they should. We cut the water back to ensure tender grains with a satisfying bite, and give it a stir partway through cooking to ensure that the grains cook evenly. We let the quinoa rest for several minutes before fluffing to help further improve the texture. We also pre-toast the quinoa in the pan before simmering to develop its natural nutty flavor, and finish our pilaf with a judicious amount of boldly flavored ingredients. If you buy unwashed quinoa, rinse it and then spread it out on a clean dish towel to dry for 15 minutes.

1½ cups prewashed white quinoa
  2 tablespoons unsalted butter, cut into 2 pieces
  1 small onion, chopped fine
  ¾ teaspoon table salt
1¾ cups water
  3 tablespoons chopped fresh parsley, cilantro, chives, and/or tarragon
  1 tablespoon lemon juice

1. Toast quinoa in medium saucepan over medium-high heat, stirring frequently, until quinoa is very fragrant and makes continuous popping sound, 5 to 7 minutes. Transfer quinoa to bowl and set aside.

2. Return now-empty saucepan to medium-low heat and melt butter. Add onion and salt and cook until softened and lightly browned, 5 to 7 minutes.

3. Increase heat to medium-high, stir in water and quinoa, and bring to simmer. Cover, reduce heat to low, and simmer until grains are just tender and liquid has been fully absorbed, 18 to 20 minutes, stirring once halfway through cooking. Remove saucepan from heat and let sit, covered, for 10 minutes. Fluff quinoa with fork, stir in herbs and lemon juice, and season with salt and pepper to taste. Serve.

Easy Baked Quinoa with Lemon, Garlic, and Parsley

Serves 4 | **Total Time** 50 minutes VEGAN

WHY THIS RECIPE WORKS There are many ways to prepare quinoa, but this hands-off method delivers perfectly cooked quinoa; plus, it's simple to incorporate flavorful add-ins. Extra-virgin olive oil and minced garlic go right into the baking pan with the quinoa—no sautéing needed. For the cooking liquid, we use vegetable broth spiked with lemon zest; microwaving the mixture until just boiling helps infuse the broth with lemon flavor and also shortens the oven time. Lemon juice and parsley stirred in before serving lend bright notes to this side dish. If you buy unwashed quinoa, rinse it and then spread it out on a clean dish towel to dry for 15 minutes.

1½ cups prewashed white quinoa
  2 tablespoons extra-virgin olive oil
  2 garlic cloves, minced
1½ cups vegetable or chicken broth
  1 teaspoon grated lemon zest plus 1 teaspoon juice
  ¼ teaspoon table salt
  2 tablespoons minced fresh parsley

1. Adjust oven rack to middle position and heat oven to 450 degrees. Combine quinoa, oil, and garlic in 8-inch square baking dish.

2. Microwave broth, lemon zest, and salt in covered bowl until just boiling, about 5 minutes. Pour hot broth over quinoa mixture and cover dish tightly with double layer of aluminum foil. Bake quinoa until tender and liquid has been fully absorbed, about 25 minutes.

3. Remove dish from oven, uncover, and fluff quinoa with fork, scraping up any quinoa that has stuck to bottom. Re-cover dish with foil and let sit for 10 minutes. Fold in lemon juice and parsley and season with salt and pepper to taste. Serve.

VARIATIONS
Easy Baked Quinoa with Scallions and Feta
Substitute 4 thinly sliced scallions for parsley. Fold ½ cup crumbled feta into quinoa before serving.

Easy Baked Quinoa with Tomatoes, Parmesan, and Basil
Omit lemon zest, lemon juice, and parsley. Fold 1 finely chopped tomato, ½ cup grated Parmesan, and 2 tablespoons chopped fresh basil into quinoa before serving.

Easy Baked Quinoa with Curry, Cauliflower, and Cilantro VEGAN

Substitute 2 teaspoons curry powder for lemon zest, and fresh cilantro for parsley. Sprinkle 2 cups small cauliflower florets evenly into dish before baking.

Warm Rye Berries with Apple and Scallions

Serves 4 to 6 | **Total Time** 1½ hours

WHY THIS RECIPE WORKS The earthy, nutty flavor and firm chew of rye berries make them an ideal base for a hearty side dish. Here we pair the whole grain with a tart Granny Smith apple and mild oniony scallions for a warm pilaf-like dish with an irresistible combination of textures and flavors. We find it easiest (and fastest) to cook the rye berries like pasta, simply simmering the kernels in a pot of water until they're tender but still chewy. Soaking the rye berries overnight, while optional, helps shorten the cooking time and prevents the grains from blowing out.

- 1 cup rye berries, rinsed
- ½ teaspoon table salt, plus salt for cooking rye berries
- 2 tablespoons unsalted butter
- 3 scallions, white parts sliced thin, green parts sliced thin on bias
- 1 Granny Smith apple, peeled, cored, and cut into ¼-inch pieces
- ¼ teaspoon pepper
- ¼ teaspoon fennel seeds
- 1 teaspoon sherry vinegar

1. Bring 2 quarts water to boil in large saucepan. Stir in rye berries and 2 teaspoons salt. Return to boil, then reduce to simmer and cook until tender, 50 minutes to 1 hour 10 minutes. Drain well. Spread on rimmed baking sheet and let cool for 15 minutes.

2. Melt butter in 12-inch skillet over medium heat. Add scallion whites, apple, pepper, fennel seeds, and salt and cook, stirring frequently, until apple starts to soften, 2 to 4 minutes. Add rye berries and cook until warmed through, 2 to 5 minutes. Off heat, stir in vinegar and scallion greens. Season with salt and pepper to taste. Serve.

Quinoa Pilaf with Herbs and Lemon

Warm Rye Berries with Apple and Scallions

Under Pressure

● FAST (45 minutes or less)   ● VEGAN
Photo: Pressure-Cooker Braised Tofu with Pumpkin Mole and Apple-Cabbage Slaw

Pressure Cooking 101

Pressure Cooking Beans and Lentils

An electric pressure cooker (aka Instant Pot) makes quick work of cooking dried beans and lentils, cooking them in a fraction of their conventional cooking time. It's a hands-off way to cook dried beans to the perfect tender consistency while infusing them with whatever flavors are added to the cooking liquid, such as hearty herbs, citrus zest, or garlic.

The Instant Pot is the most widely owned electric pressure cooker. We used an Instant Pot to create our bean cooking chart because it is our winning model. Results may vary slightly if using a different model. (See modification instructions below if using a stovetop pressure cooker.) For information on our winning pressure cookers, see page 37.

BRINE THE BEANS
Brining dried beans before cooking is crucial for texture and minimizes busted beans. (It's not necessary for lentils.) Brine 1 pound of beans overnight (or up to 24 hours in advance) in 2 quarts cold water plus 1½ tablespoons table salt. If you are short on time, you can quick brine your beans: Combine water, salt, and beans in the pot, bring to boil using the high sauté function, then turn off the pot and let sit for 1 hour. Drain and rinse beans after brining.

COOKING INSTRUCTIONS

- Combine 1 pound brined beans or 2 cups lentils in pressure cooker with water, 1 tablespoon extra-virgin olive oil (to prevent foaming), and salt. Lock lid into place and close pressure-release valve.

- Select low pressure-cook function and set cooking time according to the chart. (If using stovetop pressure cooker, place cooker on medium heat and start timer once pressure is reached.)

- Turn off pressure cooker or remove from heat once done. Let pressure release naturally for 15 minutes and then quickly release any remaining pressure, or quickly release pressure for brown or green lentils as directed in chart.

- Carefully remove lid, allowing steam to escape away from you. Remove any floating beans or lentils. Drain.

Type of Bean	Water for Cooking	Salt for Cooking	Cook Time (Mins)	Release Type
Black beans	8 cups	½ teaspoon	1*	natural
Black-eyed peas	8 cups	½ teaspoon	1*	natural
Cannellini beans	8 cups	½ teaspoon	4	natural
Chickpeas	8 cups	½ teaspoon	1	natural
Great northern beans	8 cups	½ teaspoon	1	natural
Kidney beans	8 cups	½ teaspoon	3	natural
Navy beans	8 cups	½ teaspoon	1	natural
Pinto beans	8 cups	½ teaspoon	3	natural
Small red beans	8 cups	½ teaspoon	3	natural
Lentilles du Puy	8 cups	½ teaspoon	1*	natural
Brown or green lentils	8 cups	½ teaspoon	3	quick

* As soon as pressure is reached, turn off pressure cooker or remove from heat.

NOTES FROM THE TEST KITCHEN

MODIFYING ELECTRIC PRESSURE COOKER RECIPES FOR THE STOVETOP PRESSURE COOKER
We love the convenience of using a countertop electric pressure cooker and have written all the recipes with it in mind. That said, the recipes can be easily modified to work in a stovetop pressure cooker. Just use these tips.

- Utilize medium heat when softening vegetables or cooking aromatics; medium-high heat is best for browning proteins.
- Bring the cooker to the desired pressure setting over medium-high heat. As soon as the indicator signals that the pot has reached pressure, reduce the heat to medium-low and begin counting the cook time stated in the recipe. Adjust the heat as needed to maintain pressure.
- Remove the cooker from the heat before allowing the pressure to naturally release or quick release.

Pressure Cooking Grains and Rice

The pressure cooker is the best way to cook big batches of grains or rice to have on hand to combine with other recipes or to round out any meal. They store easily and reheat reliably, and it's simple to jazz them up. Try fluffing in some flavored oil, fresh herbs, or any other flavorful ingredients such as toasted nuts or grated cheese.

COOKING INSTRUCTIONS
We also used an Instant Pot when creating this grain cooking chart. Results may vary slightly if using a different model. Follow modification instructions on page 322 if using a stovetop pressure cooker.

PILAF METHOD
Rinse 1½ cups rice or grains, then combine in electric pressure cooker with water amount indicated in chart, 1 tablespoon oil, and ½ teaspoon table salt. Lock lid into place and close pressure-release valve. Select high pressure-cook function and set cook time according to chart. Turn off electric pressure cooker and quick-release pressure. Carefully remove lid, allowing steam to escape away from you. Fluff rice or grains gently with fork. Lay clean dish towel over pot, replace lid, and let sit for 5 minutes. Makes about 4 cups.

BOILING METHOD
Rinse 1½ cups rice or grains, then combine in electric pressure cooker with water amount indicated in chart, 1 tablespoon oil, and 1½ teaspoons table salt. (When cooking wheat berries reduce salt to ½ teaspoon.) Lock lid into place and close pressure release valve. Select high pressure-cook function and set cook time according to chart. Turn off electric pressure cooker and let pressure release naturally for 15 minutes. Quick-release any remaining pressure, then carefully remove lid, allowing steam to escape away from you. Drain cooked rice or grains through fine-mesh strainer. Makes about 4 cups. (To make smaller batch, decrease amount of rice or grains, but keep same amounts of water, oil, and salt.)

Grain/Rice	Cooking Method	Water Amount	Cook Time (Mins)	Release Type
Barley, pearl	boil	8 cups	4	natural
Bulgur, medium-grind	pilaf	2⅓ cups	1	quick
Farro	boil	8 cups	1*	natural
Oat berries (groats)	boil	8 cups	20	natural
Wheat berries	boil	8 cups	30	natural
Quinoa	pilaf	1¾ cups	8	quick
Long-grain white rice	pilaf	2 cups	6	quick
Long-grain brown rice	pilaf	2⅓ cups	22	quick
Wild rice	boil	8 cups	15	natural
Black rice	pilaf	2⅓ cups	18	quick

* Set cook time for 1 minute; as soon as electric pressure cooker reaches pressure, turn it off.

Pressure-Cooker Spiced Chicken Soup
with Squash and Chickpeas

Pressure-Cooker Spiced Chicken Soup with Squash and Chickpeas

Serves 6 to 8 | **Total Time** 1½ hours

WHY THIS RECIPE WORKS We love to make chicken soup in the pressure cooker because it does a great job of creating a substantial broth by extracting body-building gelatin from convenient bone-in, skin-on chicken parts. Then you can shred the meat to add to the soup. This North African take on chicken noodle soup combines chicken with chickpeas and hearty butternut squash, flavored with spices such as coriander, cumin, cardamom, and allspice, that mimic the warmth and subtle heat of bzaar, a Libyan five-spice blend. The chicken turns moist and tender while the squash cooks to silky perfection. Canned chickpeas are a hearty replacement for noodles and only need to be heated through. Chopped cilantro adds a hint of herbal freshness.

- 2 tablespoons extra-virgin olive oil
- 1 onion, chopped
- 1¾ teaspoons table salt
- 2 tablespoons tomato paste
- 4 garlic cloves, minced
- 1 tablespoon ground coriander
- 1½ teaspoons ground cumin
- 1 teaspoon ground cardamom
- ½ teaspoon ground allspice
- ¼ teaspoon cayenne pepper
- 7 cups water, divided
- 3 (12-ounce) bone-in split chicken breasts, trimmed
- 1½ pounds butternut squash, peeled, seeded, and cut into 1½-inch pieces (4 cups)
- 1 (15-ounce) can chickpeas, rinsed
- ½ cup chopped fresh cilantro

Pressure-Cooker Beef Oxtail Soup with White
Beans, Tomatoes, and Aleppo Pepper

1. Using highest sauté or browning function, heat oil in electric pressure cooker until shimmering. Add onion and salt and cook until softened, 3 to 5 minutes. Stir in tomato paste, garlic, coriander, cumin, cardamom, allspice, and cayenne and cook until fragrant, about 30 seconds. Stir in 5 cups water, scraping up any browned bits. Nestle chicken into pot, then arrange squash evenly around chicken.

2. Lock lid in place and close pressure-release valve. Select high pressure-cook function and cook for 20 minutes. Turn off pressure cooker and quick-release pressure. Carefully remove lid, allowing steam to escape away from you.

3. Transfer chicken to cutting board, let cool slightly, then shred into bite-size pieces using 2 forks; discard skin and bones.

4. Using spoon, break squash into bite-size pieces. Stir shredded chicken along with any accumulated juices, chickpeas, and remaining 2 cups water into soup and let sit until heated through, about 2 minutes. Stir in cilantro and season with salt and pepper to taste. Serve.

Pressure-Cooker Beef Oxtail Soup with White Beans, Tomatoes, and Aleppo Pepper

Serves 6 to 8 | **Total Time** 2 hours

WHY THIS RECIPE WORKS White beans offer a creamy, nutty counterpoint to succulent beefy oxtails in the popular Turkish dish etli kuru fasulye, or "white beans with meat." Using canned navy beans means they can be added just to heat through while the oxtails, a great cut for imparting beefy flavor and lustrous body to broth, become moist and tender, thanks to the pressure cooker's ability to draw out their plentiful collagen. We found that browning only half the oxtails is enough to create flavorful fond, so we use this technique to build flavor quickly. Aleppo pepper and spices such as cinnamon and cumin bring out the dish's Mediterranean flavors while preserved lemon gives an intense but subtly sweet citrusy finish. Traditionally the soup is often served with rice pilaf and pickled vegetables. Try to buy oxtails that are approximately 2 inches thick and 2 to 4 inches in diameter. If using frozen oxtails, be sure to thaw them completely before using. If Aleppo pepper is unavailable, substitute ¼ cup paprika and ⅛ teaspoon cayenne pepper. If you can't find preserved lemons, you can substitute grated lemon zest or use our Quick Preserved Lemon (page 240).

4 pounds oxtails, trimmed
1 teaspoon table salt
1 tablespoon extra-virgin olive oil
1 onion, chopped fine
2 carrots, peeled and chopped fine
¼ cup ground dried Aleppo pepper
6 garlic cloves, minced
2 tablespoons tomato paste
¾ teaspoon dried oregano
½ teaspoon ground cinnamon
½ teaspoon ground cumin
6 cups water
1 (28-ounce) can diced tomatoes, drained
1 (15-ounce) can navy beans, rinsed
¼ cup chopped fresh parsley
1 tablespoon sherry vinegar
½ preserved lemon, pulp and white pith removed, rind rinsed and minced (2 tablespoons)

1. Pat oxtails dry with paper towels and sprinkle with salt. Using highest sauté or browning function, heat oil in electric pressure cooker for 5 minutes (or until just smoking). Brown half of oxtails, 4 to 6 minutes per side; transfer to plate. Set aside remaining uncooked oxtails.

2. Add onion and carrots to fat left in pot and cook, using highest sauté or browning function, until softened, 3 to 5 minutes. Stir in Aleppo pepper, garlic, tomato paste, oregano, cinnamon, and cumin and cook until fragrant, about 30 seconds. Stir in water, scraping up any browned bits, then stir in tomatoes. Nestle remaining uncooked oxtails into pot along with browned oxtails and add any accumulated juices.

3. Lock lid in place and close pressure-release valve. Select high pressure-cook function and cook for 45 minutes. Turn off pressure cooker and quick-release pressure. Carefully remove lid, allowing steam to escape away from you.

4. Transfer oxtails to cutting board, let cool slightly, then shred into bite-size pieces using 2 forks; discard bones and excess fat. Strain broth through fine-mesh strainer into large container; return solids to now-empty pot. Using wide, shallow spoon, skim excess fat from surface of liquid; return broth to pot.

5. Stir shredded oxtails and any accumulated juices and beans into pot. Using highest sauté or browning function, cook until soup is heated through, about 5 minutes. Stir in parsley and vinegar and season with salt and pepper to taste. Serve, passing preserved lemon separately.

Pressure-Cooker Pork Pozole Rojo

Serves 4 to 6 | **Total Time** 1 hour, plus 8 hours soaking

WHY THIS RECIPE WORKS This hearty Mexican soup combines the pleasantly chewy taste of hominy, made from dried corn kernels (see page 24), with tender pork and aromatic alliums, and is perfect to make in the pressure cooker. Hominy is an essential ingredient in pozole and we find that dried hominy, which we soak, cooks through properly with the pork. The starches that the hominy releases under pressure give the soup extra body. Country-style pork ribs turn soft and juicy under pressure too and are a leaner, more convenient choice than boneless pork butt. To achieve richness and depth, we first build an intense base by softening onion and blooming ancho chile powder, garlic, and oregano for flavorful fond in the pot. Boneless pork butt can be substituted for the ribs. We like to serve our pozole with shredded cabbage, thinly sliced radishes, diced avocado, cilantro, lime wedges, and a little extra oregano.

> **Substitution:** You can use two 15-ounce cans of hominy, rinsed, in place of the dried hominy; skip step 1.

- 8 ounces (1¼ cups) dried whole white or yellow hominy
- 1 tablespoon extra-virgin olive oil
- 1 onion, chopped fine
- 2 tablespoons ancho chile powder
- 5 garlic cloves, minced
- 1 teaspoon dried oregano
- 4 cups chicken broth
- 1½ pounds boneless country-style pork ribs, trimmed and cut into 1-inch pieces
- 1 teaspoon table salt
- ½ teaspoon pepper
- 2 bay leaves

1. Place hominy and 2 quarts cold water in large container. Let soak at room temperature for at least 8 hours or up to 24 hours. Drain and rinse hominy.

2. Using highest sauté or browning function, heat oil in electric pressure cooker until shimmering. Add onion and cook until softened and lightly browned, 5 to 7 minutes. Add ancho chile powder, garlic, and oregano and cook, stirring frequently, until fragrant, about 30 seconds. Stir in broth, scraping up any browned bits. Stir in hominy, pork, salt, pepper, and bay leaves.

3. Lock lid into place and close pressure-release valve. Select high pressure-cook function and cook for 25 minutes. Turn off pressure cooker and quick-release pressure. Carefully remove lid, allowing steam to escape away from you.

4. Discard bay leaves. Using wide, shallow spoon, skim excess fat from surface of soup. Season with salt and pepper to taste. Serve.

Pressure-Cooker Pork Pozole Rojo

Pressure-Cooker Harira

Serves 6 to 8 | **Total Time** 1 hour

WHY THIS RECIPE WORKS Harira is made in various North African countries; Algerian recipes might contain either lentils or chickpeas and many Moroccan ones use both, paired with lamb or chicken. The energy-giving dish is used to break the fast during the holy month of Ramadan. For our Moroccan version, the electric pressure cooker ensures the lamb and lentils finish cooking at the same rate under pressure. Then we shred the cooked lamb and stir it back into the pot with canned chickpeas. We flavor the proteins with harissa for smoky, spicy heat and fresh tomatoes bring sweetness and acidity. Serve with yogurt, if desired. We prefer our homemade Harissa (page 116), but you may use store-bought.

> **Substitution:** We like lentilles du Puy for this recipe; however, you can use any dried lentils, except red or yellow.

Pressure-Cooker Harira

until fragrant, about 30 seconds. Slowly whisk in broth, scraping up any browned bits and smoothing out any lumps. Stir in lentils, then nestle lamb into pressure cooker and add any accumulated juices.

3. Lock lid in place and close pressure-release valve. Select high pressure-cook function and cook for 10 minutes. Turn off pressure cooker and quick-release pressure. Carefully remove lid, allowing steam to escape away from you.

4. Transfer lamb to cutting board, let cool slightly, then shred into bite-size pieces using 2 forks; discard excess fat and bones. Stir lamb and chickpeas into soup and let sit until heated through, about 3 minutes. Season with salt and pepper to taste. Top individual portions with tomatoes and sprinkle with cilantro. Serve, passing extra harissa separately.

Pressure-Cooker 15-Bean Soup with Sausage

Serves 4 to 6 | **Total Time** 1 hour, plus 8 hours brining

WHY THIS RECIPE WORKS Dry bean soup mixes promise flavorful soup and offer an assortment of beans in one package like chickpea, kidney, lima, and green and yellow split lentils. But the mix can disappoint because different beans cook at different rates, so some get blown out and disintegrate while others stay hard. We brine beans overnight to help prevent blowouts and ensure even cooking; the pressure cooker tenderizes the beans quickly and the smaller ones break down and help to thicken the soup. Instead of using the mix's flavor packet, we build fresh flavor with sausage, vegetables, and herbs. Adding Swiss chard and tomato after pressure is released ensures that they cook briefly and gently.

1 pound lamb shoulder chops (blade or round bone),
  1 to 1½ inches thick, trimmed and halved
¾ teaspoon table salt, divided
⅛ teaspoon pepper
1 tablespoon extra-virgin olive oil
1 onion, chopped fine
¼ cup harissa, plus extra for serving
1 tablespoon all-purpose flour
8 cups chicken broth
1 cup lentilles du Puy, picked over and rinsed
1 (15-ounce) can chickpeas, rinsed
2 tomatoes, cored and cut into ¼-inch pieces
½ cup chopped fresh cilantro

1. Pat lamb dry with paper towels and sprinkle with ¼ teaspoon salt and pepper. Using highest sauté or browning function, heat oil in electric pressure cooker for 5 minutes (or until just smoking). Place lamb in pot and cook until well browned on first side, about 4 minutes; transfer to plate.

2. Add onion and remaining ½ teaspoon salt to fat left in pot and cook, using highest sauté or browning function, until softened, 3 to 5 minutes. Stir in harissa and flour and cook

3 tablespoons table salt for brining
10 ounces (1½ cups) 15-bean soup mix, flavor packet
  discarded, beans picked over and rinsed
2 tablespoons vegetable oil, divided
12 ounces hot or sweet Italian sausage
1 onion, chopped fine
1 carrot, peeled and chopped fine
4 garlic cloves, minced
1 teaspoon minced fresh thyme or ¼ teaspoon dried
4 cups chicken broth
2 bay leaves
8 ounces Swiss chard, stemmed and chopped
1 large tomato, cored and chopped
  Grated Parmesan cheese

1. Dissolve 1½ tablespoons salt in 2 quarts cold water in large container. Add beans and soak at room temperature for at least 8 or up to 24 hours. Drain and rinse well. (If you're pressed for time, see page 322 for information on quick brining your beans.)

2. Using highest sauté or browning function, heat 1 tablespoon oil in electric pressure cooker for 5 minutes (or until just smoking). Brown sausage on all sides, about 2 minutes; transfer to plate.

3. Using highest sauté or browning function, heat remaining 1 tablespoon oil in now-empty pot until shimmering. Add onion and carrot and cook until onion is softened, 3 to 5 minutes. Stir in garlic and thyme and cook until fragrant, about 30 seconds. Stir in soaked beans, broth, and bay leaves, scraping up any browned bits. Add sausage and any accumulated juices to pot.

4. Lock lid in place and close pressure-release valve. Select high pressure-cook function and cook for 25 minutes. Turn off pressure cooker and quick-release pressure. Carefully remove lid, allowing steam to escape away from you.

5. Discard bay leaves. Transfer sausage to cutting board and slice ½ inch thick. Using highest sauté or browning function, bring soup to simmer, stir in chard and tomato, and cook until chard is tender, about 5 minutes. Stir in sliced sausage and season with salt and pepper to taste. Serve, passing Parmesan cheese separately.

Pressure-Cooker Lentil and Chorizo Soup

Pressure-Cooker Lentil and Chorizo Soup

Serves 6 to 8 | **Total Time** 1 hour

WHY THIS RECIPE WORKS Lentils are inexpensive and nutritious and they are eaten all over the world. One iteration popular in Spain is sopa de lentejas con chorizo, an earthy soup of lentils and smoked paprika–scented chorizo sausage. This filling soup is served with varying degrees of brothiness; our version features whole lentils suspended in a creamy, but not too thick, broth. The pressure cooker makes our work easy; we cook the vegetables whole with the lentils under pressure, puree them in the food processor, and then return them to the soup to achieve a velvety broth. A garnish of almonds highlights the soup's Spanish roots. If Spanish-style chorizo is not available, Portuguese linguiça or Polish kielbasa can be substituted.

> **Substitution:** We like lentilles du Puy for this recipe; however, you can use any dried lentils, except red or yellow.

1 tablespoon extra-virgin olive oil, plus extra for drizzling
8 ounces Spanish-style chorizo sausage, quartered lengthwise and sliced thin
4 garlic cloves, minced
1½ teaspoons smoked paprika
5 cups water
1 pound (2¼ cups) lentilles du Puy, picked over and rinsed
4 cups chicken broth
1 tablespoon sherry or red wine vinegar, plus extra for seasoning
2 bay leaves
1 teaspoon table salt
1 large onion, peeled
2 carrots, peeled and halved crosswise
½ cup slivered almonds, toasted
½ cup minced fresh parsley

1. Using highest sauté or browning function, heat oil in electric pressure cooker until shimmering. Add chorizo and cook until lightly browned, 3 to 5 minutes. Stir in garlic and

paprika and cook until fragrant, about 30 seconds. Stir in water, scraping up any browned bits, then stir in lentils, broth, vinegar, bay leaves, and salt. Nestle onion and carrots into pot.

2. Lock lid in place and close pressure-release valve. Select high pressure-cook function and cook for 14 minutes. Turn off pressure cooker and quick-release pressure. Carefully remove lid, allowing steam to escape away from you.

3. Discard bay leaves. Using slotted spoon, transfer onion and carrots to food processor and process until smooth, about 1 minute, scraping down sides of bowl as needed. Stir vegetable mixture into lentils and season with salt, pepper, and extra vinegar to taste. Drizzle individual portions with extra oil, and sprinkle with almonds and parsley before serving.

Pressure-Cooker Hearty Minestrone

Serves 6 | **Total Time** 1½ hours, plus 8 hours brining

WHY THIS RECIPE WORKS Traditionally, beans and the liquid used to cook them—essentially a starchy bean broth—are often used to make minestrone, providing protein and thickening the soup with their starch. We soak beans overnight, then pressure-cook them so they are soft and tender. We sauté vegetables to build flavor, then marry them with the soaked beans, vegetable broth, water, and V8 juice rather than canned tomatoes to give the soup a consistent tomato flavor. Adding a Parmesan rind before pressure-cooking brings richness. Zucchini only cooks for the last 5 minutes so the pieces stay firm, and stirring in basil before serving gives a fresh finish.

1½ tablespoons table salt for brining
 8 ounces (1¼ cups) dried cannellini beans, picked over and rinsed
 ¼ cup extra-virgin olive oil, divided, plus extra for serving
 3 carrots, peeled and cut into ½-inch pieces
 3 celery ribs, chopped
 4 cups chopped green cabbage
 2 garlic cloves, minced
 ¼ teaspoon red pepper flakes
 4 cups vegetable or chicken broth
1½ cups V8 juice
 1 Parmesan cheese rind (optional), plus grated Parmesan for serving
1½ teaspoons table salt
 2 zucchini, cut into ½-inch pieces
 ½ cup chopped fresh basil

Pressure-Cooker Hearty Minestrone

1. Dissolve 1½ tablespoons salt in 2 quarts cold water in large container. Add beans and soak at room temperature for at least 8 hours or up to 24 hours. Drain and rinse well. (If you're pressed for time, see page 322 for information on quick brining your beans.)

2. Using highest sauté or browning function, heat 2 tablespoons oil in electric pressure cooker until shimmering. Add carrots and celery and cook until softened, 5 to 7 minutes. Stir in cabbage, garlic, and pepper flakes and cook until cabbage starts to wilt, about 2 minutes. Stir in soaked beans; 4 cups water; broth; V8 juice; Parmesan rind, if using; and salt.

3. Lock lid into place and close pressure-release valve. Select high pressure-cook function and cook for 30 minutes. Turn off pressure cooker and quick-release pressure. Carefully remove lid, allowing steam to escape away from you.

4. Discard Parmesan rind. Stir in zucchini and cook, using highest sauté or browning function, until tender, about 5 minutes. Stir in basil and remaining 2 tablespoons oil and season with salt and pepper to taste. Serve, passing extra oil and grated Parmesan separately.

Pressure-Cooker Acquacotta

Pressure-Cooker Acquacotta

Serves 6 to 8 | **Total Time** 1½ hours, plus 8 hours brining

WHY THIS RECIPE WORKS The name of this traditional Italian vegetable soup, acquacotta, means "cooked water." Ours features a satiny egg yolk–thickened chicken broth in which creamy cannellinis, tender fennel, and bitter escarole are suspended. Brined, cooked cannellini beans have a beautifully soft texture and the electric pressure cooker is a great way to cook them evenly. To keep the escarole fresh and crunchy, we add it after releasing the pressure. Before adding the egg yolks, we whisk them together with some reserved cooking liquid to avoid curdling; we then stir the mixture into the hot broth, along with parsley and oregano. If escarole is unavailable, you can substitute 8 ounces of kale. Ladling the acquacotta over toasted bread makes an even heartier meal. We prefer Pecorino Romano's salty flavor, but Parmesan can be substituted, if desired.

3 tablespoons table salt for brining

1 pound (2½ cups) dried cannellini beans, picked over and rinsed

1 large onion, chopped coarse

2 celery ribs, chopped coarse

4 garlic cloves, peeled

1 (28-ounce) can whole peeled tomatoes

2 tablespoons extra-virgin olive oil, plus extra for drizzling

1 fennel bulb, stalks discarded, bulb halved, cored, and cut into ½-inch pieces

½ teaspoon table salt

⅛ teaspoon red pepper flakes

8 cups vegetable or chicken broth

1 small head escarole, trimmed and cut into ½-inch pieces (8 cups)

2 large egg yolks

½ cup chopped fresh parsley

1 tablespoon minced fresh oregano

Grated Pecorino Romano cheese

Lemon wedges

1. Dissolve 1½ tablespoons salt in 2 quarts cold water in large container. Add beans and soak at room temperature for at least 8 hours or up to 24 hours. Drain and rinse well. (If you're pressed for time, see page 322 for information on quick brining your beans.)

2. Pulse onion, celery, and garlic in food processor until very finely chopped, 15 to 20 pulses, scraping down sides of bowl as needed; set aside. Add tomatoes and their juice to now-empty processor and pulse until tomatoes are finely chopped, 10 to 12 pulses; set aside.

3. Using highest sauté or browning function, heat oil in electric pressure cooker until shimmering. Add onion mixture, fennel, salt, and pepper flakes and cook until fennel begins to soften, 7 to 9 minutes. Stir in soaked beans, broth, and tomatoes.

4. Lock lid in place and close pressure-release valve. Select high pressure-cook function and cook for 1 minute. Turn off pressure cooker and let pressure release naturally for 15 minutes. Quick-release any remaining pressure, then carefully remove lid, allowing steam to escape away from you.

5. Measure out and reserve 1 cup hot broth. Stir escarole into pressure cooker, 1 handful at a time, and let cook in residual heat until escarole is wilted, about 5 minutes.

6. Gently whisk egg yolks together in small bowl. Whisking constantly, slowly add reserved broth to eggs until combined. Stir yolk mixture, parsley, and oregano into soup. Season with salt and pepper to taste. Top individual portions with Pecorino and drizzle with extra oil. Serve with lemon wedges.

Pressure-Cooker Gigante Bean Soup with Celery and Olives

Serves 6 to 8 | **Total Time** 1 hour, plus 8 hours brining

`VEGAN`

WHY THIS RECIPE WORKS Gigante beans—large white runner beans—are popular in Greece and Spain. Our Greek bean soup features these meaty beans which hold their shape well after cooking. The mellow, vegetal broth comes alive when servings are topped generously with finely chopped tender and slightly sweet celery leaves, kalamata olives, and fragrant fresh marjoram. The floral mixture perfumes the soup and complements the pillowy-soft beans. We soak the gigante beans overnight in salted water, which softens their skins and makes them less prone to bursting. If celery leaves are not available, substitute ¼ cup minced celery plus ¼ cup minced fresh parsley.

Substitution: You can use cannellini beans in place of gigante beans; reduce the time under pressure to 1 minute in step 3.

- 3 tablespoons table salt for brining
- 1 pound (2½ cups) dried gigante beans, picked over and rinsed
- 2 tablespoons extra-virgin olive oil, plus extra for drizzling
- 5 celery ribs, cut into ½-inch pieces, plus ½ cup leaves, minced
- 1 onion, chopped
- ½ teaspoon table salt
- 4 garlic cloves, minced
- 4 cups vegetable or chicken broth
- 2 bay leaves
- ½ cup pitted kalamata olives, chopped
- 2 tablespoons minced fresh marjoram or oregano
  Lemon wedges

Pressure-Cooker Gigante Bean Soup with Celery and Olives

1. Dissolve 3 tablespoons salt in 4 quarts cold water in large container. Add beans and soak at room temperature for at least 8 hours or up to 24 hours. Drain and rinse well. (If you're pressed for time, see page 322 for information on quick brining your beans.)

2. Using highest sauté or browning function, heat oil in electric pressure cooker until shimmering. Add celery pieces, onion, and salt and cook until onion is softened, 3 to 5 minutes. Stir in garlic and cook until fragrant, about 30 seconds. Stir in soaked beans, broth, 4 cups water, and bay leaves.

3. Lock lid in place and close pressure-release valve. Select high pressure-cook function and cook for 6 minutes. Turn off pressure cooker and let pressure release naturally for 15 minutes. Quick-release any remaining pressure, then carefully remove lid, allowing steam to escape away from you.

4. Combine celery leaves, olives, and marjoram in bowl. Discard bay leaves. Season soup with salt and pepper to taste. Top individual portions with celery-olive mixture and drizzle with extra oil. Serve with lemon wedges.

Pressure-Cooker Rustic French Pork and White Bean Stew

Serves 6 | **Total Time** 1½ hours, plus 8 hours brining

WHY THIS RECIPE WORKS This luscious French-inspired stew with its creamy white beans and chunks of pork, fennel, and carrots, tastes as though it simmered all day. But thanks to the pressure cooker, you can make this cold-weather delight, packed with satisfying beans and meat, in under 2 hours. We ensure that each component cooks through evenly by brining the beans and cutting the pork, carrots and fennel into large 1-inch pieces. To keep the cooking time down, we brown only half of the meat, which builds enough flavorful fond on the bottom of the pot to season the stew. We deepen the flavor with sautéed onion, garlic, and herbes de Provence before deglazing the pot with white wine and cooking until all the ingredients are tender. Pork butt roast is often labeled Boston butt in the supermarket.

   1½ tablespoons table salt for brining
    8 ounces (1¼ cups) dried cannellini beans, picked over and rinsed
    3 pounds boneless pork butt roast, trimmed and cut into 1-inch pieces
    1 teaspoon table salt
    ½ teaspoon pepper
    2 tablespoons vegetable oil, divided
    2 onions, chopped
    8 garlic cloves, minced
   1½ teaspoons herbes de Provence
    ⅓ cup all-purpose flour
    1 cup dry white wine
    3 cups chicken broth
    1 pound carrots, peeled and sliced 1 inch thick
    1 fennel bulb, stalks discarded, bulb halved, cored, and cut into 1-inch pieces
    2 bay leaves
    ¼ cup minced fresh parsley
    1 tablespoon lemon juice, plus extra for seasoning

   1. Dissolve 1½ tablespoons salt in 2 quarts water. Add beans and soak at room temperature for 8 to 24 hours. Drain and rinse well. (If you're pressed for time, see page 322 for information on quick brining your beans.)

   2. Pat pork dry with paper towels and sprinkle with salt and pepper. Using highest sauté or browning function, heat 1 tablespoon oil in electric pressure cooker for 5 minutes (or

until just smoking). Brown half of pork on all sides, about 8 minutes; transfer to bowl.

   3. Using highest sauté or browning function, heat remaining 1 tablespoon oil in now-empty pot on until shimmering. Add onions and cook until softened, 3 to 5 minutes. Stir in garlic and herbes de Provence and cook until fragrant, about 30 seconds. Stir in flour and cook for 1 minute. Whisk in wine, scraping up any browned bits and smoothing out any lumps, and cook until slightly reduced, about 1 minute. Stir in soaked beans, broth, carrots, fennel, bay leaves, browned pork with any accumulated juices, and remaining pork.

   4. Lock lid in place and close pressure-release valve. Select high pressure-cook function and cook for 30 minutes. Turn off pressure cooker and quick-release pressure. Carefully remove lid, allowing steam to escape away from you.

   5. Discard bay leaves. Using large spoon, skim excess fat from surface of stew. Stir in parsley and lemon juice and season with salt, pepper, and extra lemon juice to taste. Serve.

Pressure-Cooker Abgoosht

Serves 6 | **Total Time** 2 hours, plus 8 hours brining

WHY THIS RECIPE WORKS Dating back centuries, abgoosht is a rustic Persian stew consisting of lamb simmered with chickpeas and onions as well as potatoes and tomatoes. It is enhanced by spices such as turmeric and cinnamon but the unique flavor of this rich dish comes from limu omani, dried Persian limes. They deliver sweetness, sourness, and muskiness. Once cooked, the solids are mashed into a savory paste, which is served alongside the tart, meaty broth. We speed up the cooking by using a pressure cooker to cook the lamb as well as the chickpeas. The lamb mash is accompanied by a Persian flatbread called sangak (lavash can also be used) and adorned with a number of fresh toppings. Limu omani, also known as black limes, are dried limes that can be found at Middle Eastern markets or online; if you can't find them, substitute 2 tablespoons of fresh lime juice. Sip the broth on its own or stir in pieces of the bread. Use the bread to scoop up the meat paste, and top the paste with herbs, scallions, radishes, and onion before eating.

   1½ tablespoons table salt for brining
    8 ounces (1¼ cups) dried chickpeas, picked over and rinsed
    2 pounds lamb shoulder chops (blade or round bone), ¾ to 1 inch thick, trimmed

1 pound Yukon Gold potatoes, peeled and quartered
2 tomatoes, cored and quartered
1 yellow onion, quartered
2 limu omani
1 tablespoon tomato paste
2 garlic cloves, lightly crushed and peeled
2 teaspoons table salt
1 teaspoon pepper
1 teaspoon ground turmeric
½ cinnamon stick
  Pinch saffron threads
3 cups fresh dill, mint, and/or tarragon leaves
4 scallions, sliced thin
8 radishes, trimmed and sliced thin
1 small red onion, halved and sliced thin
  Sangak or lavash

1. Dissolve 1½ tablespoons salt in 2 quarts cold water in large container. Add chickpeas and soak at room temperature for at least 8 hours or up to 24 hours. Drain and rinse well. (If you're pressed for time, see page 322 for information on quick brining your beans.)

2. Add soaked chickpeas, 7 cups water, lamb, potatoes, tomatoes, yellow onion, limu omani, tomato paste, garlic, salt, pepper, turmeric, and cinnamon stick to electric pressure cooker. Lock lid into place and close pressure-release valve. Select high pressure-cook function and cook for 40 minutes. Turn off pressure cooker and let pressure release naturally for 15 minutes. Quick-release any remaining pressure, then carefully remove lid, allowing steam to escape away from you.

3. Using slotted spoon, transfer large pieces of lamb and vegetables to large bowl. Strain broth through fine-mesh strainer into separate large bowl or container; discard bones, limu omani, and cinnamon stick. Transfer strained solids to bowl with lamb and vegetables.

4. Return broth to pot. Using highest sauté or browning function, bring broth to simmer, then turn off pressure cooker. Stir in saffron and let steep for 5 minutes. Season with salt and pepper to taste.

5. Using potato masher, gently mash lamb mixture until meat is finely shredded and chickpeas and vegetables are mostly smooth. Season with salt and pepper to taste and transfer to shallow serving bowl. Ladle broth into individual serving bowls and serve with lamb mixture, fresh herbs, scallions, radishes, red onion, and sangak.

Pressure-Cooker Rustic French Pork and White Bean Stew

Pressure-Cooker Abgoosht

Pressure-Cooker Calamari, Chorizo, and Chickpea Stew

1½ tablespoons table salt for brining
8 ounces (1¼ cups) dried chickpeas, picked over and rinsed
1 tablespoon extra-virgin olive oil, plus extra for drizzling
2 red bell peppers, stemmed, seeded, and chopped
1 onion, chopped
6 ounces Spanish-style chorizo sausage, sliced ¼ inch thick
4 garlic cloves, minced
2 teaspoons hot smoked paprika
½ cup dry red wine
1 (28-ounce) can diced tomatoes
1 pound squid, bodies sliced crosswise into ¾-inch-thick rings, tentacles halved
1 cup chicken broth
5 ounces (5 cups) baby spinach
1½ teaspoons red wine vinegar

1. Dissolve 1½ tablespoons salt in 2 quarts cold water in large container. Add chickpeas and soak at room temperature for at least 8 hours or up to 24 hours. Drain and rinse well. (If you're pressed for time, see page 322 for information on quick brining your beans.)

2. Using highest sauté or browning function, heat oil in electric pressure cooker until shimmering. Add bell peppers, onion, and chorizo and cook until vegetables are softened and lightly browned, and chorizo is lightly browned, 7 to 9 minutes. Add garlic and paprika and cook, stirring frequently, until fragrant, about 30 seconds.

3. Stir in wine, scraping up any browned bits, and cook until mostly evaporated, about 1 minute. Stir in soaked chickpeas, tomatoes and their juice, squid, and broth. Lock lid into place and close pressure-release valve. Select high pressure-cook function and cook for 20 minutes.

4. Turn off pressure cooker and quick-release pressure. Carefully remove lid, allowing steam to escape away from you. Stir in spinach and let sit until wilted, about 1 minute. Stir in vinegar and season with salt and pepper to taste. Drizzle individual portions with extra oil before serving.

Pressure-Cooker Calamari, Chorizo, and Chickpea Stew

Serves 4 to 6 | **Total Time** 1 hour, plus 8 hours brining

WHY THIS RECIPE WORKS We make a simple classic Catalan stew of chickpeas and spinach into a veritable feast by adding squid. We start by sautéing chorizo to render flavorful fat and soften red peppers and onions. Then we deglaze the pot with red wine and add diced tomatoes to produce a smoky, spicy broth. Finally, in just 20 minutes, the electric pressure cooker cooks the chickpeas and pressure-braises the squid in the aromatic and deeply flavored broth. Using dried chickpeas adds a depth of flavor to the stew. If Spanish-style chorizo is not available, Portuguese linguiça or Polish kielbasa can be substituted. If hot smoked paprika is unavailable, substitute 1¾ teaspoons sweet smoked paprika and ¼ teaspoon cayenne pepper.

Pressure-Cooker Vegetable and Chickpea Stew

Serves 6 to 8 | **Time** 1 hour VEGAN

WHY THIS RECIPE WORKS Our Lebanese-inspired stew stars chickpeas and vegetables flavored with baharat, a bold Middle Eastern spice blend. Using the sauté function, we first brown bell peppers and onion to develop depth, and then add baharat, garlic, and tomato paste before stirring in broth. After cooking the vegetables and broth quickly under pressure, we add delicate zucchini to the stew, simmering it gently to ensure that it stays green and tender and letting the convenient canned chickpeas warm through. A little olive oil drizzled at the end provides richness while chopped mint brings freshness to the warmly spiced dish. We prefer our homemade Baharat (page 243) but you may use store-bought.

- ¼ cup extra-virgin olive oil, plus extra for drizzling
- 2 red bell peppers, stemmed, seeded, and cut into 1-inch pieces
- 1 onion, chopped fine
- ½ teaspoon table salt
- ½ teaspoon pepper
- 1½ tablespoons baharat
- 4 garlic cloves, minced
- 1 tablespoon tomato paste
- 4 cups vegetable or chicken broth
- 1 (28-ounce) can whole peeled tomatoes, drained with juice reserved, chopped
- 1 pound Yukon Gold potatoes, peeled and cut into ½-inch pieces
- 2 zucchini, quartered lengthwise and sliced 1 inch thick
- 1 (15-ounce) can chickpeas, rinsed
- ⅓ cup chopped fresh mint

1. Using highest sauté or browning function, heat oil in electric pressure cooker until shimmering. Add bell peppers, onion, salt, and pepper and cook until vegetables are softened and lightly browned, 5 to 7 minutes. Stir in baharat, garlic, and tomato paste and cook until fragrant, about 1 minute. Stir in broth and tomatoes and reserved juice, scraping up any browned bits, then stir in potatoes.

2. Lock lid in place and close pressure-release valve. Select high pressure-cook function and cook for 9 minutes. Turn off pressure cooker and quick-release pressure. Carefully remove lid, allowing steam to escape away from you.

3. Stir zucchini and chickpeas into stew and cook, using highest sauté or browning function, until zucchini is tender, 10 to 15 minutes. Turn off pressure cooker. Season with salt and pepper to taste. Drizzle individual portions with extra oil, and sprinkle with mint before serving.

Pressure-Cooker Green Gumbo

Serves 6 | **Total Time** 1¼ hours, plus 8 hours brining VEGAN

WHY THIS RECIPE WORKS Green gumbo, originally a Louisiana Lent dish, is set apart from its seafood and meat cousins by its use of greens such as collards and spinach. Although not traditional, we use black-eyed peas and green beans to add flavor, texture, and heartiness. A mix of sturdy and softer greens gives a nice balance of chew and silkiness. We sauté onions, celery, and pepper in the pressure cooker and then stir in the black-eyed peas, collards, and water. As they cook, the starch from the beans and the aromatics in the water create a tasty broth. To complement the earthiness of this vegetarian dish, we amp up the smoky flavor with cayenne and smoked paprika, echoing the taste of gumbos that include smoked meats. A finishing splash of vinegar adds a hit of brightness. Kale can be substituted for collards, and Swiss chard can be substituted for spinach. Serve with your favorite rice (pages 298–299).

- 1½ tablespoons table salt for brining
- 8 ounces (1¼ cups) dried black-eyed peas, picked over and rinsed
- ½ cup vegetable oil
- ½ cup all-purpose flour
- 1 large onion, chopped fine
- 2 celery ribs, chopped fine
- 1 green bell pepper, stemmed, seeded, and chopped fine
- 1 tablespoon minced fresh thyme or 1 teaspoon dried
- 2 teaspoons table salt
- 2 teaspoons smoked paprika
- ¼–½ teaspoon cayenne pepper
- 12 ounces collard greens, stemmed and chopped
- 1½ cups frozen cut okra
- 12 ounces curly-leaf spinach, stemmed and chopped
- 6 ounces green beans, trimmed and cut into 1-inch lengths
- 1 tablespoon cider vinegar, plus extra for seasoning
- 2 scallions, sliced thin

1. Dissolve 1½ tablespoons salt in 2 quarts cold water in large container. Add black-eyed peas and soak at room temperature for at least 8 hours or up to 24 hours. Drain and rinse well. (If you're pressed for time, see page 322 for information on quick brining your beans.)

2. Using highest sauté or browning function, heat oil in electric pressure cooker until shimmering. Add flour and cook, stirring constantly, until mixture is color of milk chocolate, 5 to 10 minutes. Stir in onion, celery, and bell pepper. Cook, stirring frequently, until vegetables have softened, 5 to 8 minutes. Add thyme, salt, paprika, and cayenne and cook, stirring frequently, until fragrant, about 30 seconds.

3. Stir in 5 cups water, scraping up any browned bits and smoothing out any lumps, then stir in soaked black-eyed peas. Arrange collards on top of bean mixture. Lock lid into place and close pressure-release valve. Select high pressure-cook function and cook for 8 minutes.

4. Turn off pressure cooker and quick-release pressure. Carefully remove lid, allowing steam to escape away from you. Stir in okra and bring to simmer using highest sauté or browning function. Stir in spinach, 1 handful at a time, and green beans and cook until vegetables are tender, 5 to 7 minutes. Stir in vinegar and season with salt, pepper, and extra vinegar to taste. Sprinkle individual portions with scallions before serving.

Pressure-Cooker Vegetable Tagine with Chickpeas and Artichokes

Serves 4 to 6 | **Total Time** 1 hour, plus 8 hours brining

VEGAN

WHY THIS RECIPE WORKS Traditional North African tagines—fragrant, spiced stews of braised meats, vegetables, beans, and dried fruits—are long-simmered affairs with myriad ingredients. Here we use the pressure cooker to make a satisfying meatless tagine fast enough for a weeknight without sacrificing flavor. Since delicate vegetables can easily overcook in the pressure cooker, we stir in our artichoke hearts (which we brown first to remove their raw flavor) after the brined chickpeas are cooked. Chopped kalamata olives round out the Mediterranean profile, fresh cilantro lends brightness, and a finishing drizzle of olive oil adds richness to each bowl. Serve with couscous or your favorite rice (pages 298–299).

1½ tablespoons table salt for brining
8 ounces (1¼ cups) dried chickpeas, picked over and rinsed
2 tablespoons extra-virgin olive oil, divided, plus extra for serving
1 onion, halved and sliced thin
4 (2-inch) strips lemon zest
6 garlic cloves, minced
1 tablespoon paprika
½ teaspoon ground cumin
¼ teaspoon ground cinnamon
⅛ teaspoon cayenne pepper
2 tablespoons all-purpose flour
3 cups vegetable broth
1 pound carrots, peeled and sliced ½ inch thick
1 (14.5-ounce) can diced tomatoes
9 ounces frozen artichoke hearts, thawed and patted dry
½ cup pitted kalamata olives, halved
½ cup minced fresh cilantro

1. Dissolve 1½ tablespoons salt in 2 quarts water. Add chickpeas and soak at room temperature for at least 8 hours or up to 24 hours. Drain and rinse well. (If you're pressed for time, see page 322 for information on quick brining your beans.)

2. Using highest sauté or browning function, heat 1 tablespoon oil in electric pressure cooker until shimmering. Add onion and cook until softened, 3 to 5 minutes. Stir in lemon zest, garlic, paprika, cumin, cinnamon, and cayenne and cook until fragrant, about 30 seconds. Stir in flour and cook for 1 minute. Whisk in broth, scraping up any browned bits and smoothing out any lumps. Stir in carrots, tomatoes and their juice, and chickpeas.

3. Lock lid in place and close pressure-release valve. Select high pressure-cook function and cook for 25 minutes. Turn off pressure cooker and quick-release pressure. Carefully remove lid, allowing steam to escape away from you.

4. Heat remaining 1 tablespoon oil in 12-inch skillet over medium heat until shimmering. Add artichokes and cook until golden brown, 5 to 7 minutes. Discard lemon zest from stew. Stir in olives, cilantro, and artichokes and season with salt and pepper to taste. Drizzle individual portions with extra oil before serving.

Pressure-Cooker Easy Weeknight Chili

Serves 4 to 6 | **Total Time** 45 minutes `FAST`

WHY THIS RECIPE WORKS Making a ground beef chili with bold, long-simmered flavor in a pressure cooker is easy because the meat quickly picks up the flavor of the spices while cooking under pressure. A combination of chili powder, cumin, and garlic is all it takes to get the job done. In this dish, beans are an important player, adding heft and chew. We use crushed tomatoes plus chicken broth for a base with the proper consistency. Browning the beef to develop flavor is standard in most ground beef chilis, but we found that browned meat overcooks and becomes gritty in the pressure cooker. To avoid this, we cook the meat until it just loses its pink color. Given the 10-minute cooking time, dried beans aren't an option, so we turn to canned kidney beans. Serve with your favorite chili garnishes.

- 2 tablespoons vegetable oil
- 1 onion, chopped fine
- 2 tablespoons chili powder
- 4 garlic cloves, minced
- 2 teaspoons ground cumin
- ½ teaspoon table salt
- 1 pound 85 percent lean ground beef
- 1 (28-ounce) can crushed tomatoes
- 1 cup chicken broth, plus extra as needed
- 2 (15-ounce) cans kidney beans, rinsed

1. Using highest sauté or browning function, heat oil in electric pressure cooker until shimmering. Add onion and cook until softened, 3 to 5 minutes. Stir in chili powder, garlic cumin, and salt and cook until fragrant, about 1 minute. Add beef and cook, breaking up meat with wooden spoon, until no longer pink, about 4 minutes. Stir in tomatoes, broth, and beans, scraping up any browned bits.

2. Lock lid in place and close pressure-release valve. Select high pressure-cook function and cook for 10 minutes. Turn off pressure cooker and quick-release pressure. Carefully remove lid, allowing steam to escape away from you.

3. Adjust chili consistency with extra hot broth as needed. Season with salt and pepper to taste. Serve.

Pressure-Cooker Vegetable Tagine with Chickpeas and Artichokes

Pressure-Cooker Easy Weeknight Chili

Pressure-Cooker Bean and Sweet Potato Chili

9 garlic cloves, minced
3 tablespoons chili powder
2 tablespoons ground cumin
1–3 teaspoons minced canned chipotle chile in adobo sauce
2½ cups vegetable or chicken broth
2½ cups water
1 (28-ounce) can crushed tomatoes
1 pound white mushrooms, trimmed and quartered
2 bay leaves
2 red bell peppers, stemmed, seeded, and cut into ½-inch pieces
½ cup minced fresh cilantro

1. Using highest sauté or browning function, heat oil in electric pressure cooker until shimmering. Add onion and cook until softened, 5 minutes. Stir in garlic, chili powder, cumin, and chipotle and cook until fragrant, about 30 seconds. Stir in rinsed beans, broth, water, tomatoes, mushrooms, and bay leaves, scraping up any browned bits.

2. Lock lid in place and close pressure-release valve. Select high pressure-cook function and cook for 45 minutes. Turn off pressure cooker and quick-release pressure. Carefully remove lid, allowing steam to escape away from you.

3. Discard bay leaves. Stir in bell peppers. Using highest sauté or browning function, bring chili to simmer and cook until peppers are tender, 10 to 15 minutes. Stir in cilantro and season with salt and pepper to taste. Serve.

Pressure-Cooker Vegetarian Black Bean Chili

Serves 4 to 6 | **Total Time** 1½ hours VEGAN

WHY THIS RECIPE WORKS Vegetarian black bean chili is tricky to make since you can't build flavor with the smoky ham hock or bacon that you typically find in nonvegetarian versions. So we brown a good number of aromatics and spices instead and make sure to use flavorful dried beans rather than canned, letting their creamy texture and meatiness take center stage. The pressure cooker cuts the beans' traditional cooking time in half. Soaking dried beans helps prevent them from bursting, but here we just rinse them since broken beans work to thicken the chili. Serve with your favorite chili garnishes.

1 pound (2½ cups) dried black beans, picked over and rinsed
3 tablespoons vegetable oil
1 onion, chopped

Pressure-Cooker Bean and Sweet Potato Chili

Serves 6 to 8 | **Total Time** 1¼ hours, plus 8 hours brining VEGAN

WHY THIS RECIPE WORKS We make this vegetarian chili with a variety of dried beans paired with hearty chunks of earthy sweet potato. To bring classically spiced chili flavor to the dish, we bloom ancho chile powder, coriander, cumin, oregano, and garlic powder in the pot with chopped onion. Adding one can of crushed tomatoes makes the perfect base because it breaks down into a stewy consistency while maintaining some individual tomato pieces. This dish is so filling and warming that you won't miss the meat. Serve with your favorite chili garnishes.

Substitution: We like a combination of beans but a single variety will also work well.

- 3 tablespoons table salt for brining
- 1 pound (2½ cups) black, navy, pinto, and/or small red beans, rinsed
- 2 tablespoons ancho chile powder
- 1 tablespoon ground coriander
- 2 teaspoons ground cumin
- 2 teaspoons dried oregano
- 1 teaspoon garlic powder
- 1½ teaspoons table salt
- ¼ cup extra-virgin olive oil
- 1 onion, chopped fine
- 1 (28-ounce) can crushed tomatoes
- 2 pounds sweet potatoes, peeled and cut into 1-inch pieces
- ¼ teaspoon baking soda
- ½ cup chopped fresh cilantro, divided
- Lime wedges

1. Dissolve 3 tablespoons salt in 4 quarts cold water in large container. Add beans and soak at room temperature for at least 8 hours or up to 24 hours. Drain and rinse well. (If you're pressed for time, see page 322 for information on quick brining your beans.)

2. Combine chile powder, coriander, cumin, oregano, garlic powder, and salt in bowl. Using highest sauté or browning function, heat oil in electric pressure cooker until shimmering. Add onion and cook until softened, 3 to 5 minutes. Add spice mixture and cook, stirring frequently, until fragrant, about 30 seconds. Stir in tomatoes and 3 cups water, scraping up any browned bits, then stir in soaked beans, potatoes, and baking soda.

3. Lock lid into place and close pressure-release valve. Select high pressure-cook function and cook for 30 minutes. Turn off pressure cooker and quick-release pressure. Carefully remove lid, allowing steam to escape away from you.

4. Adjust consistency with extra hot water as needed. Stir in ¼ cup cilantro and season with salt and pepper to taste. Sprinkle individual portions with remaining ¼ cup cilantro and serve with lime wedges.

Pressure-Cooker Texas-Style Chili con Carne

Pressure-Cooker Texas-Style Chili con Carne

Serves 6 to 8 | **Total Time** 1¼ hours, plus 8 hours brining

WHY THIS RECIPE WORKS Texans are famous for their style of chili featuring chunks of beef in a chile-infused sauce. Our beef cut of choice—boneless short ribs—turns tender in less than 30 minutes in the pressure cooker. Kidney beans cook quickly in the pressured heat and brining the beans first seasons them from the inside out and helps them hold their shape throughout cooking. To thicken our base of chicken broth and crushed tomatoes, we experimented with ingredients like flour and cornstarch, finally settling on corn tortillas. Processing the tortillas in the food processor before adding them to the pot ensures that they melt into the chili, thickening it and giving it a subtle corn flavor. Traditional recipes call for dried chiles, but we find that the pressure cooker does a great job of intensifying the flavor of basic pantry chili powder.

1½ tablespoons table salt for brining

8 ounces (1¼ cups) dried kidney beans, picked over and rinsed

6 (6-inch) corn tortillas, chopped coarse

5 pounds boneless beef short ribs, trimmed and cut into 1-inch pieces

1½ teaspoons table salt

¾ teaspoon pepper

3 tablespoons vegetable oil, divided

1 onion, chopped

3 tablespoons chili powder

2 tablespoons ground cumin

5 garlic cloves, minced

4 teaspoons minced canned chipotle chile in adobo sauce

3 cups chicken broth, plus extra as needed

1 (28-ounce) can crushed tomatoes

2 tablespoons soy sauce

1. Dissolve 1½ tablespoons salt in 2 quarts cold water. Add beans and soak at room temperature for at least 8 hours or up to 24 hours. Drain and rinse well. (If you're pressed for time, see page 322 for information on quick brining your beans.)

2. Process tortilla pieces in food processor to fine crumbs, about 30 seconds; set aside. Pat beef dry with paper towels and sprinkle with salt and pepper. Using highest sauté or browning function, heat 1 tablespoon oil in electric pressure cooker for 5 minutes (or until just smoking). Brown one-quarter of beef on all sides, about 8 minutes; transfer to bowl. Repeat with 1 tablespoon oil and one-quarter of beef.

3. Using highest sauté or browning function, heat remaining 1 tablespoon oil in now-empty pot until shimmering. Add onion and cook until softened, 3 to 5 minutes. Stir in chili powder, cumin, garlic, and chipotle and cook until fragrant, about 30 seconds. Stir in broth, scraping up any browned bits. Stir in soaked beans, tomatoes, soy sauce, browned beef with any accumulated juices, and remaining beef. Sprinkle processed tortillas over top.

4. Lock lid in place and close pressure-release valve. Select high pressure-cook function and cook for 25 minutes. Turn off pressure cooker and quick-release pressure. Carefully remove lid, allowing steam to escape away from you.

5. Adjust chili consistency with extra hot broth as needed. Season with salt and pepper to taste. Serve.

Pressure-Cooker Chicken and Rice with Lemon-Yogurt Sauce

Serves 4 | **Total Time** 1 hour

WHY THIS RECIPE WORKS A steaming bowl of oregano-scented rice studded with sweet peas and briny capers and served alongside juicy chicken breasts, is our idea of a feel-good meal. Bone-in chicken breasts turn moist and tender; browning them before cooking with the rice adds depth to the dish. And the key to avoiding gluey rice? Instead of stirring, which breaks the cooked grains, we simply fluff the rice with a fork to combine it with the peas and capers. A simple make-ahead lemon-flavored yogurt sauce adds brightness to both rice and chicken. If your chicken breasts are larger than 12 ounces, cut them in half crosswise before browning to ensure proper doneness.

LEMON-YOGURT SAUCE

½ cup plain whole-milk yogurt

½ teaspoon grated lemon zest plus 1 tablespoon juice

1 small garlic clove, minced

CHICKEN AND RICE

4 (12-ounce) bone-in split chicken breasts, trimmed

1¼ teaspoon table salt, divided

¼ teaspoon pepper

1 tablespoon extra-virgin olive oil

1 onion, chopped fine

2 celery ribs, sliced ¼ inch thick

4 garlic cloves, minced

2 cups chicken broth

1½ cups long-grain white rice, rinsed

3 bay leaves

¾ cup frozen peas, thawed

4 teaspoons capers, rinsed

2 tablespoons chopped fresh oregano

1. FOR THE LEMON-YOGURT SAUCE Whisk all ingredients together in bowl and season with salt and pepper to taste. Cover and refrigerate for at least 30 minutes to allow flavors to meld. (Sauce can be refrigerated for up to 4 days.)

2. FOR THE CHICKEN AND RICE Pat chicken dry with paper towels and sprinkle with 1 teaspoon salt and pepper. Using highest sauté or browning function, heat oil in electric pressure cooker for 5 minutes (or until just smoking). Place chicken skin side down in pot and cook until well browned on first side, about 5 minutes; transfer to plate.

3. Add onion, celery, and remaining ¼ teaspoon salt to fat left in pot and cook, using highest sauté or browning function, until onion is softened, 3 to 5 minutes. Stir in garlic and cook until fragrant, about 30 seconds. Stir in broth, rice, and bay leaves, scraping up any browned bits. Nestle chicken skin side up into rice and add any accumulated juices. Lock lid in place and close pressure-release valve. Select high pressure-cook function and cook for 4 minutes.

4. Turn off pressure cooker and quick-release pressure. Carefully remove lid, allowing steam to escape away from you. Transfer chicken to cutting board and discard skin, if desired. Tent with aluminum foil and let rest while finishing rice.

5. Discard bay leaves. Add peas and capers and gently fluff rice with fork to combine. Lay clean dish towel over pot, replace lid, and let sit for 5 minutes. Gently fold in oregano. Serve chicken with rice and sauce.

Pressure Cooker Chicken and Warm-Spiced Freekeh

Serves 4 | **Total Time** 45 minutes **FAST**

WHY THIS RECIPE WORKS Smoky, earthy freekeh shines in this satisfying one-pot meal and makes a delicious change from grains like quinoa or bulgur. Cooking the freekeh at the same time as the chicken, in chicken broth instead of water, with warm spices like cinnamon, allspice, and cardamom, makes for a scrumptious dish. If your chicken breasts are larger than 12 ounces, cut them in half crosswise before browning to ensure proper doneness. Do not substitute whole freekeh here, it requires a different cooking method and will not work in this recipe. Serve with Herb-Yogurt Sauce (page 176), if desired.

- 2 tablespoons extra-virgin olive oil, plus extra for drizzling
- 1 onion, chopped fine
- 4 garlic cloves, minced
- ½ teaspoon ground cinnamon
- ¾ teaspoon pepper, divided
- ¼ teaspoon ground allspice
- ⅛ teaspoon ground cardamom
- 2¼ cups chicken broth
- 1½ cups cracked freekeh, rinsed
- 2 (12-ounce) bone-in split chicken breasts, halved crosswise and trimmed
- ½ teaspoon table salt
  Ground dried Aleppo pepper (optional)
  Lemon wedges

Pressure-Cooker Chicken and Rice with Lemon-Yogurt Sauce

Pressure-Cooker Chicken and Warm-Spiced Freekeh

1. Using highest sauté function, heat oil in pressure cooker until shimmering. Add onion and cook until softened, about 5 minutes. Stir in garlic, cinnamon, ½ teaspoon pepper, allspice, and cardamom and cook until fragrant, about 30 seconds. Stir in broth and freekeh. Sprinkle chicken with salt and remaining ¼ teaspoon pepper. Nestle skin side up into freekeh mixture. Lock lid in place and close pressure-release valve. Select high pressure-cook function and cook for 5 minutes.

2. Turn off pressure cooker and quick-release pressure. Carefully remove lid, allowing steam to escape away from you. Transfer chicken to serving dish and discard skin, if desired. Tent with aluminum foil and let rest while finishing freekeh.

3. Gently fluff freekeh with fork. Lay clean dish towel over pot, replace lid, and let sit for 5 minutes. Season with salt and pepper to taste. Transfer freekeh to serving dish with chicken and sprinkle with Aleppo pepper, if using. Drizzle with extra oil and serve with lemon wedges.

Pressure-Cooker Chicken and Barley Risotto with Butternut Squash and Kale

Serves 4 | **Total Time** 1 hour

WHY THIS RECIPE WORKS Pearl barley takes well to being cooked risotto-style; its starchy interior creates a velvety sauce when simmered, while maintaining a pleasant chewiness. The electric pressure cooker's concentrated, moist heat alleviates the need for the constant monitoring that a risotto typically requires. To complement the hearty grain, we use the sauté function to soften onions and butternut squash before adding thyme, wine, and broth to the pot. Bone-in split chicken breasts, which we brown first, conveniently finish cooking atop the risotto. Placing the breasts on top of the barley allows the chicken to render its flavorful juices into the risotto while still keeping the two components distinct. While the chicken breasts rest, we finish the risotto by stirring in baby kale for freshness and whisking in blue cheese for creamy richness. Do not substitute hulled, hull-less, quick-cooking, or presteamed barley (read the ingredient list on the package to determine this) in this recipe. If your chicken breasts are larger than 12 ounces, cut them in half crosswise before browning to ensure proper doneness.

4 (12-ounce) bone-in split chicken breasts, trimmed
½ teaspoon table salt, divided
¼ teaspoon pepper

Pressure-Cooker Chicken and Barley Risotto with Butternut Squash and Kale

1 tablespoon extra-virgin olive oil
4 cups butternut squash, cut into ½-inch pieces
1 onion, chopped fine
¾ cup pearl barley
1 teaspoon minced fresh thyme
½ cup dry white wine
1½ cups chicken broth, plus extra as needed
2 ounces blue cheese, crumbled (½ cup), plus extra for serving
5 ounces (5 cups) baby kale

1. Pat chicken dry with paper towels and sprinkle with ¼ teaspoon salt and pepper. Using highest sauté or browning function, heat oil in electric pressure cooker for 5 minutes (or until just smoking). Place chicken skin side down in pot and cook until well browned on first side, about 5 minutes; transfer to plate.

2. Add squash and onion to fat left in pot and cook, using highest sauté or browning function, until onion is softened, 3 to 5 minutes. Stir in barley and thyme and cook until fragrant, about 1 minute. Stir in wine, scraping up any browned bits, and cook until nearly evaporated, about 1 minute.

3. Stir in broth and remaining ¼ teaspoon salt. Place chicken skin side up on top of squash mixture and add any accumulated juices. Lock lid into place and close pressure-release valve. Select high pressure-cook function and cook for 16 minutes.

4. Turn off pressure cooker and quick-release pressure. Carefully remove lid, allowing steam to escape away from you. Transfer chicken to cutting board and discard skin, if desired. Tent with aluminum foil and let rest while finishing risotto.

5. Add blue cheese to risotto and stir vigorously until risotto becomes creamy. Stir in kale, 1 handful at a time, until wilted, about 1 minute. Season with salt and pepper to taste, and adjust consistency with extra hot broth as needed. Carve chicken from bones and slice ½ inch thick. Transfer risotto to individual serving bowls, top with chicken, and sprinkle with extra blue cheese. Serve.

Pressure-Cooker Chicken with Lentils and Butternut Squash

Serves 4 | **Total Time** 1¼ hours

WHY THIS RECIPE WORKS For a dish inspired by North African flavors, we combine tender chicken with stewed lentils, butternut squash, and warm, floral spices. We bloom the spices and then stir in the lentils, broth, and butternut squash so the spice flavor can infuse into them. We nestle the chicken on top before cooking everything under pressure until the squash softens and melts into the lentils, its sweetness tempering the vegetal legumes. A quick salad of parsley leaves and shallot, with a lemon vinaigrette, adds brightness from the leafy green herbs, and the subtle sharpness from the shallot ties the whole dish together and provides a nice contrast to the braised earthiness of the lentils.

> **Substitution:** We like lentilles du Puy for this recipe; however, you can use any dried lentils, except red or yellow.

    2 large shallots, halved and sliced thin, divided
    5 teaspoons extra-virgin olive oil, divided
    ½ teaspoon grated lemon zest plus 2 teaspoons juice
    1 teaspoon table salt, divided
    8 (5- to 7-ounce) bone-in chicken thighs, trimmed
    ¼ teaspoon pepper
    2 garlic cloves, minced
 1½ teaspoons caraway seeds
    1 teaspoon ground coriander
    1 teaspoon ground cumin

    ½ teaspoon paprika
    ⅛ teaspoon cayenne pepper
    2 cups chicken broth
    1 cup lentilles du Puy, picked over and rinsed
    2 pounds butternut squash, peeled, seeded, and
       cut into 1½-inch pieces (6 cups)
    1 cup fresh parsley or cilantro leaves

1. Combine half of shallots, 1 tablespoon oil, lemon zest and juice, and ¼ teaspoon salt in bowl; set aside. Pat chicken dry with paper towels and sprinkle with pepper and ½ teaspoon salt. Using highest sauté or browning function, heat remaining 2 teaspoons oil in electric pressure cooker for 5 minutes (or until just smoking). Place half of chicken skin side down in pot and cook until well browned on first side, about 5 minutes; transfer to plate. Repeat with remaining chicken; transfer to plate.

2. Add remaining shallot and remaining ¼ teaspoon salt to fat left in pot and cook, using highest sauté or browning function, until shallot is softened, about 2 minutes. Stir in garlic, caraway, coriander, cumin, paprika, and cayenne and cook until fragrant, about 30 seconds. Stir in broth, scraping up any browned bits, then stir in lentils.

Pressure-Cooker Chicken with Lentils and Butternut Squash

3. Nestle chicken skin side up into lentils and add any accumulated juices. Arrange squash on top. Lock lid in place and close pressure-release valve. Select high pressure-cook function and cook for 15 minutes.

4. Turn off pressure cooker and quick-release pressure. Carefully remove lid, allowing steam to escape away from you. Transfer chicken to plate and discard skin, if desired. Season lentil mixture with salt and pepper to taste. Add parsley to shallot mixture and toss to combine. Serve chicken with lentil mixture, topping individual portions with shallot-parsley salad.

Pressure-Cooker Chicken Tagine

Serves 4 | **Total Time** 1 hour

WHY THIS RECIPE WORKS This stew, traditionally cooked in a pot also called a tagine, is a cornerstone of Moroccan cuisine. We find that this balancing act of flavors, heady with spices, salty with olives, and bright with lemon, is well-suited to the electric pressure cooker—the enclosed environment ensures that none of the flavor escapes. For the chicken, we use thighs instead of breasts for deep intensity, and for heft, we add convenient canned chickpeas (some of them mashed into a paste to thicken the tagine) and fresh fennel. Paprika, cumin, and ginger bring depth and a little sweetness, accented by raisins; cayenne adds subtle heat; and brine-cured olives are a salty counterpart to the sweet and complex broth, which aromatic turmeric colors a deep, attractive yellow. Don't core the fennel before cutting it into wedges; the core helps hold the wedges together during cooking.

    2 (15-ounce) cans chickpeas, rinsed, divided
    8 (5- to 7-ounce) bone-in chicken thighs, trimmed
    1 teaspoon table salt
    2 teaspoons extra-virgin olive oil
    5 garlic cloves, minced
 1½ teaspoons paprika
    ½ teaspoon ground turmeric
    ½ teaspoon ground cumin
    ¼ teaspoon ground ginger
    ¼ teaspoon cayenne pepper
    1 fennel bulb, 1 tablespoon fronds minced, stalks discarded, bulb halved and cut lengthwise into ½-inch-thick wedges
    1 cup chicken broth

Pressure-Cooker Chicken Tagine

    3 (2-inch) strips lemon zest, plus lemon wedges for serving
    ½ cup pitted large brine-cured green or black olives, halved
    ⅓ cup raisins
    2 tablespoons chopped fresh parsley

1. Using potato masher, mash ½ cup chickpeas in bowl to paste. Pat chicken dry with paper towels and sprinkle with salt. Using highest sauté or browning function, heat oil in electric pressure cooker for 5 minutes (or until just smoking). Place half of chicken skin side down in pot and cook until well browned on first side, about 5 minutes; transfer to plate. Repeat with remaining chicken; transfer to plate.

2. Turn off pressure cooker. Add garlic, paprika, turmeric, cumin, ginger, and cayenne to fat left in pot and cook, using residual heat, until fragrant, about 1 minute. Stir in fennel wedges, broth, lemon zest, mashed chickpeas, and remaining whole chickpeas. Nestle chicken skinned side up into pot and add any accumulated juices. Spoon some of cooking liquid over top. Lock lid in place and close pressure-release valve. Select high pressure-cook function and cook for 10 minutes.

3. Turn off pressure cooker and quick-release pressure. Carefully remove lid, allowing steam to escape away from you. Discard lemon zest and chicken skin, if desired. Stir in olives, raisins, parsley, and fennel fronds. Season with salt and pepper to taste. Serve with lemon wedges.

Pressure-Cooker Chicken Curry with Chickpeas and Cauliflower

Serves 4 | **Total Time** 1¼ hours

WHY THIS RECIPE WORKS Curries—dishes inspired by Indian flavors—are well suited to cooking under pressure since pressure cookers cook ingredients like proteins and vegetables quickly and amplify the flavor of the spices and seasonings that envelop them. Nutty chickpeas and cauliflower work well for this dish, absorbing the flavors of the sauce and complementing the mild chicken. The chicken's cooking time is too short to allow for cooking dried chickpeas at the same time, so we use canned instead and add them after the chicken is cooked. That way we can monitor their doneness and ensure they don't blow out or become mushy.

    8 (5- to 7-ounce) bone-in chicken thighs, trimmed
    ½ teaspoon table salt
    ¼ teaspoon pepper
    1 tablespoon vegetable oil
    2 onions, chopped fine
    6 garlic cloves, minced
    1 tablespoon curry powder
    2 teaspoons grated fresh ginger
    1 tablespoon tomato paste
    1 teaspoon garam masala
    1 cup chicken broth
    ½ head cauliflower (1 pound), cored and cut into
       1-inch florets
    1 (15-ounce) can chickpeas, rinsed
    ½ cup coconut milk
    ½ cup frozen peas
    ¼ cup minced fresh cilantro

1. Pat chicken dry with paper towels and season with salt and pepper. Heat oil in pressure-cooker pot over medium-high heat until just smoking. Brown half of thighs, skin side down, until golden, about 6 minutes; transfer to plate. Remove and discard skin from browned and unbrowned thighs. Pour off all but 1 tablespoon fat from pot.

2. Add onions to fat left in pot and cook over medium heat until softened, about 5 minutes. Stir in garlic, curry powder, ginger, tomato paste, and garam masala and cook until fragrant, about 1 minute. Stir in broth. Using wooden spoon, scrape up all browned bits stuck on bottom of pot. Nestle chicken with any accumulated juices into pot.

3. Lock lid in place and close pressure-release valve. Select high pressure-cook function and cook for 20 minutes. Turn off pressure cooker and quick-release pressure. Carefully remove lid, allowing steam to escape away from you.

4. Transfer chicken to plate and tent with aluminum foil. Bring sauce to simmer, stir in cauliflower, chickpeas, and coconut milk and cook until cauliflower is tender, about 15 minutes. Stir in peas and cook until heated through, about 2 minutes. Stir in cilantro and season with salt and pepper to taste. Off heat, return chicken to pot and let heat through, about 2 minutes. Serve.

Pressure-Cooker Pork Sausage with White Beans and Mustard Greens

Serves 4 | **Total Time** 1 hour

WHY THIS RECIPE WORKS For our weeknight version of a rich French stew that combines meaty sausage, creamy white beans, and fresh greens, we make things easy by using canned navy beans and keeping the sausages whole. We brown easy-to-find Italian sausages and then pressure-cook them with the beans and peppery mustard greens, adding garlic and thyme for fragrant flavor. For a bright finish, we make lemon-scented bread crumbs to sprinkle over the completed dish along with tangy goat cheese. If mustard greens are unavailable, you can substitute kale.

2 tablespoons extra-virgin olive oil, divided
1 pound hot or sweet Italian sausage (4 sausages)
1 onion, chopped fine
1 tablespoon minced fresh thyme or 1 teaspoon dried
2 garlic cloves, minced
¾ cup chicken broth
¼ cup dry white wine
2 (15-ounce) cans navy beans, rinsed
1 pound mustard greens, stemmed and cut into 2-inch pieces
½ cup panko bread crumbs
2 tablespoons chopped fresh parsley
½ teaspoon grated lemon zest plus 1 teaspoon juice
4 ounces goat cheese, crumbled (1 cup)

1. Using highest sauté or browning function, heat 1 tablespoon oil in electric pressure cooker for 5 minutes (or until just smoking). Brown sausages on all sides, 6 to 8 minutes; transfer to plate.

2. Add onion to fat left in pot and cook, using highest sauté or browning function, until softened, 5 minutes. Stir in thyme and garlic and cook until fragrant, about 30 seconds. Stir in broth and wine, scraping up any browned bits, then stir in beans. Add mustard greens, then place sausages on top. Lock lid in place and close pressure-release valve. Select high pressure-cook function and cook for 2 minutes.

3. Meanwhile, toss panko with remaining 1 tablespoon oil in bowl until evenly coated. Microwave, stirring every 30 seconds, until light golden brown, about 5 minutes. Let cool slightly, then stir in parsley and lemon zest; set aside for serving.

4. Turn off pressure cooker and quick-release pressure. Carefully remove lid, allowing steam to escape away from you. Transfer sausages to plate. Stir lemon juice into bean and mustard greens mixture and season with salt and pepper to taste. Serve sausages with bean and mustard green mixture, sprinkling individual portions with seasoned bread crumbs and goat cheese.

Pressure-Cooker Sopa Seca with Chorizo and Black Beans

Serves 4 | **Total Time** 50 minutes

WHY THIS RECIPE WORKS This vibrant Mexican one-pot pasta, whose name means "dry soup," boasts thin strands of fideos pasta, toasted until golden and then cooked in a tasty broth until it reduces to a thick sauce. The pressure cooker helps us do that quickly. We first make a robust soffrito and then use the intense heat of the sauté function to lightly toast spaghetti before stirring in chipotle chile in adobo sauce, tomato paste, and minced garlic. Next, we stir in a measured amount of chicken broth and a can of black beans for added protein. In just 1 minute under pressure, the pasta is al dente and the liquid nearly absorbed. We give the pasta a quick stir and a brief rest to let it finish cooking gently and the sauce thicken. To complement the deep, earthy, spicy flavors of the spaghetti, we serve an array of traditional garnishes—chopped avocado, crumbled cotija cheese, fresh cilantro, and lime wedges. Be sure to use fresh Mexican chorizo here, not the semicured Spanish or Portuguese versions.

8 ounces spaghetti
1 tablespoon extra-virgin olive oil
1 onion, chopped
1 green bell pepper, stemmed, seeded, and chopped
4 ounces Mexican-style chorizo sausage, casings removed
2 tablespoons minced canned chipotle chile in adobo sauce
2 tablespoons tomato paste
3 garlic cloves, minced
1 cup chicken broth
1 cup water
1 (15-ounce) can black beans, rinsed
10 ounces cherry tomatoes, halved
1 avocado, halved, pitted, and cut into 1-inch pieces
1 ounce cotija cheese, crumbled (¼ cup)
½ cup fresh cilantro leaves
Lime wedges

1. Loosely wrap half of pasta in dish towel, then press bundle against corner of counter to break noodles into 1- to 2-inch lengths; repeat with remaining pasta. Set aside.

2. Using highest sauté or browning function, heat oil in electric pressure cooker until shimmering. Add onion, bell pepper, and chorizo and cook, breaking up meat with wooden spoon, until onion is softened, 3 to 5 minutes.

3. Add spaghetti and cook, using highest sauté or browning function, stirring frequently, until lightly toasted, about 2 minutes. Add chipotle, tomato paste, and garlic and cook, stirring frequently, until fragrant, about 30 seconds. Stir in broth and water, scraping up any browned bits, then stir in beans.

4. Lock lid into place and close pressure-release valve. Select high pressure-cook function and cook for 1 minute. Turn off pressure cooker and quick-release pressure. Carefully remove lid, allowing steam to escape away from you.

5. Stir tomatoes into pasta mixture. Partially cover pot and let sit until pasta is tender and sauce is thickened, 5 to 8 minutes. Season with salt and pepper to taste. Sprinkle individual portions with avocado, cotija, and cilantro. Serve with lime wedges.

Pressure-Cooker Moroccan White Beans with Lamb

Serves 6 to 8 | **Total Time** 1¼ hours, plus 8 hours brining

WHY THIS RECIPE WORKS Loubia is a dish of stewed white beans that is well loved in Morocco. Traditionally, the beans are cooked in a warm-spiced tomatoey base and scooped up with fluffy pita bread, making for a comforting and complete meal. A small amount of meat is used as seasoning, allowing the beans to shine. We use thrifty lamb shoulder chops here for their easy availability and forgiving cook time (other cuts are tough by the time the beans are ready). For this dish, we prefer dried beans to canned for their superior texture; the result is soft, intact beans and melt-in-your-mouth-tender pieces of lamb. Just 1 minute under pressure and then 15 minutes of natural release is perfect for producing beans that are uniformly cooked, as this allows them to cook more gently toward the end.

- 3 tablespoons table salt for brining
- 1 pound (2½ cups) dried great northern beans, picked over and rinsed
- 1 (12-ounce) lamb shoulder chop (blade or round bone), ¾ to 1 inch thick, trimmed and halved
- ½ teaspoon table salt
- 2 tablespoons extra-virgin olive oil, plus extra for serving
- 1 onion, chopped
- 1 red bell pepper, stemmed, seeded, and chopped
- 2 tablespoons tomato paste
- 3 garlic cloves, minced
- 2 teaspoons paprika
- 2 teaspoons ground cumin
- 1½ teaspoons ground ginger
- ¼ teaspoon cayenne pepper
- ½ cup dry white wine
- 2 cups chicken broth
- 2 tablespoons minced fresh parsley

Pressure-Cooker Sopa Seca with Chorizo and Black Beans

Pressure-Cooker Moroccan White Beans with Lamb

1. Dissolve 3 tablespoons salt in 4 quarts cold water in large container. Add beans and soak at room temperature for at least 8 hours or up to 24 hours. Drain and rinse well. (If you're pressed for time, see page 322 for information on quick brining your beans.)

2. Pat lamb dry with paper towels and sprinkle with salt. Using highest sauté or browning function, heat oil in electric pressure cooker for 5 minutes (or until just smoking). Brown lamb, about 5 minutes per side; transfer to plate.

3. Add onion and bell pepper to fat left in pot and cook, using highest sauté or browning function, until softened, about 5 minutes. Stir in tomato paste, garlic, paprika, cumin, ginger, and cayenne and cook until fragrant, about 30 seconds. Stir in wine, scraping up any browned bits, then stir in soaked beans and broth.

4. Nestle lamb into beans and add any accumulated juices. Lock lid in place and close pressure-release valve. Select high pressure-cook function and cook for 1 minute. Turn off pressure cooker and let pressure release naturally for 15 minutes. Quick-release any remaining pressure, then carefully remove lid, allowing steam to escape away from you.

5. Transfer lamb to cutting board, let cool slightly, then shred into bite-size pieces using 2 forks; discard excess fat and bones. Stir lamb and parsley into beans and season with salt and pepper to taste. Drizzle individual portions with extra oil before serving.

Pressure-Cooker Salmon with Wild Rice and Orange Salad

Pressure-Cooker Salmon with Wild Rice and Orange Salad

Serves 4 | **Total Time** 1¼ hours

WHY THIS RECIPE WORKS Despite its name, wild rice is actually an aquatic grass. We love it for its woodsy smokiness, chew, and high nutritional value. The only downside is that it can take nearly an hour to cook. The electric pressure cooker slashes that time, cooking it in just 15 minutes, giving us an opportunity to prepare ingredients for a vibrant, citrusy rice salad studded with juicy oranges and shredded carrots. A generous sprinkling of ground dried Aleppo pepper gives our salmon a uniquely fruity touch of heat that complements the nutty, citrusy flavors in the salad. This recipe works best with farmed salmon; we do not recommend using wild salmon here, as it is much leaner. If the salmon has not reached at least 125 degrees (for medium-rare) after releasing pressure, partially cover the pot and continue to cook using residual heat until it reaches 125 degrees. Do not use quick-cooking or presteamed wild rice in this recipe. If you can't find ground dried Aleppo pepper, you can substitute 1 teaspoon paprika and a pinch cayenne pepper.

　1　cup wild rice, picked over and rinsed
　3　tablespoons extra-virgin olive oil, divided
　½　teaspoon table salt, plus salt for cooking rice
　2　oranges, plus ⅛ teaspoon grated orange zest
　4　(6-ounce) skinless salmon fillets, 1½ inches thick
　1　teaspoon ground dried Aleppo pepper
　1　small shallot, minced
　1　tablespoon red wine vinegar
　2　teaspoons Dijon mustard
　1　teaspoon honey
　2　carrots, peeled and shredded
　¼　cup chopped fresh mint

1. Combine 6 cups water, rice, 1 tablespoon oil, and 1½ teaspoons salt in electric pressure cooker. Lock lid in place and close pressure-release valve. Select high pressure-cook function and cook for 15 minutes. Turn off pressure cooker and let pressure release naturally for 15 minutes. Quick-release any remaining pressure, then carefully remove lid, allowing steam to escape away from you. Drain rice and set aside to cool slightly. Wipe pot clean with paper towels.

2. Add ½ cup water to now-empty pressure cooker. Fold sheet of aluminum foil into 16 by 6-inch sling. Slice 1 orange ¼ inch thick and shingle widthwise in 3 rows across center of sling. Sprinkle flesh side of salmon with Aleppo pepper and ½ teaspoon salt, then arrange skinned side down on top of orange slices. Using sling, lower salmon into pressure cooker; allow narrow edges of sling to rest along sides of insert. Lock lid in place and close pressure-release valve. Select high pressure-cook function and cook for 3 minutes.

3. Meanwhile, cut away peel and pith from remaining 1 orange. Quarter orange, then slice crosswise into ¼-inch pieces. Whisk remaining 2 tablespoons oil, shallot, vinegar, mustard, honey, and orange zest together in large bowl. Add rice, orange pieces, carrots, and mint and gently toss to combine. Season with salt and pepper to taste.

4. Turn off pressure cooker and quick-release pressure. Carefully remove lid, allowing steam to escape away from you. Using sling, transfer salmon to large plate. Gently lift and tilt fillets with spatula to remove orange slices. Serve salmon with salad.

USING A FOIL SLING FOR MORE CONTROL

1. Making a Foil Sling
Fold sheet of aluminum foil into 16 by 6-inch rectangle by folding either in half or thirds, depending on width of foil.

2. Using a Foil Sling for Fish
Arrange fillets in center of sling, on top of citrus slices if called for. Using sling, lower fish into pot; allow narrow edges of sling to rest along sides of insert.

3. Using a Foil Sling for a Soufflé Dish
Place soufflé dish in center of sling. Using sling, lower dish into pot and onto trivet; allow narrow edges of sling to rest along sides of insert.

Pressure-Cooker Salmon with Garlicky Broccoli Rabe and White Beans

Serves 4 | **Total Time** 45 minutes **FAST**

WHY THIS RECIPE WORKS Cannellini beans and broccoli rabe combine with salmon in this flavorful one-pot dish, the pot being the pressure cooker. We start off using the sauté function to make delicate, aromatic garlic chips for a garnish, which adds a crispy, slightly sweet element to the finished dish. Then we switch to high pressure to cook our salmon fillets before removing them and returning to the sauté function to briefly simmer the broccoli rabe and beans to tender perfection in the remaining liquid. A drizzle of olive oil, and dinner is served. This recipe works best with farmed salmon; we do not recommend using wild salmon. If the salmon has not reached at least 125 degrees (for medium-rare) after releasing pressure, partially cover the pot and continue to cook using residual heat until it reaches 125 degrees.

- 2 tablespoons extra-virgin olive oil, plus extra for drizzling
- 4 garlic cloves, sliced thin
- ½ cup chicken or vegetable broth
- ¼ teaspoon red pepper flakes
- 1 lemon, sliced ¼ inch thick, plus lemon wedges for serving
- 4 (6-ounce) skinless salmon fillets, 1½ inches thick
- ½ teaspoon table salt
- ¼ teaspoon pepper
- 1 pound broccoli rabe, trimmed and cut into 1-inch pieces
- 1 (15-ounce) can cannellini beans, rinsed

1. Using highest sauté or browning function, cook oil and garlic in electric pressure cooker until garlic is fragrant and light golden brown, about 3 minutes. Using slotted spoon, transfer garlic to paper towel–lined plate and season with salt to taste; set aside for serving. Turn off pressure cooker, then stir in broth and pepper flakes.

2. Fold sheet of aluminum foil into 16 by 6-inch sling. Arrange lemon slices widthwise in 2 rows across center of sling. Sprinkle flesh side of salmon with salt and pepper, then arrange skinned side down on top of lemon slices. Using sling, lower salmon into pressure cooker; allow narrow edges of sling to rest along sides of insert. Lock lid in place and close pressure-release valve. Select high pressure-cook function and cook for 3 minutes.

3. Turn off pressure cooker and quick-release pressure. Carefully remove lid, allowing steam to escape away from you. Using sling, transfer salmon to large plate. Tent with foil and let rest while preparing broccoli rabe mixture.

4. Stir broccoli rabe and beans into cooking liquid, partially cover, and cook, using highest sauté or browning function, until broccoli rabe is tender, about 5 minutes. Season with salt and pepper to taste. Gently lift and tilt salmon fillets with spatula to remove lemon slices. Serve salmon with broccoli rabe mixture and lemon wedges, sprinkling individual portions with garlic chips and drizzling with extra oil.

Pressure-Cooker Cod with Warm Tabbouleh Salad

Serves 4 | **Total Time** 45 minutes **FAST**

WHY THIS RECIPE WORKS Tabbouleh, a Levantine bulgur salad, tossed with a lemony dressing and fresh herbs, is often served at room temperature. We find it surprisingly elegant served warm (this also cuts down on waiting time) so that's how we serve it, with cod, for a complete dinner. We steam bulgur on its own in a soufflé dish set into the electric pressure cooker on the trivet; this allows us to quickly remove the bulgur when it's done and use the same pot to cook the fish. Meanwhile we stir together our still-warm bulgur with some sweet cherry tomatoes, parsley and mint, and a lemon vinaigrette. When shopping, don't confuse bulgur with cracked wheat, which has a much longer cooking time and will not work in this recipe. Haddock and striped bass are good substitutes for the cod. Thin tail-end fillets can be folded to achieve proper thickness. If the cod has not reached at least 135 degrees after releasing pressure, partially cover the pot and continue to cook using residual heat until it reaches 135 degrees. You will need a 1½-quart round soufflé dish or ceramic dish of similar size for this recipe.

- 1 cup medium-grind bulgur, rinsed
- 1 teaspoon table salt, divided
- 1 lemon, sliced ¼ inch thick, plus 2 tablespoons juice
- 4 (6-ounce) skinless cod fillets, 1½ inches thick
- 3 tablespoons extra-virgin olive oil, divided, plus extra for drizzling
- ¼ teaspoon pepper
- 1 small shallot, minced
- 10 ounces cherry tomatoes, halved
- 1 cup chopped fresh parsley
- ½ cup chopped fresh mint

Pressure-Cooker Cod with Warm Tabbouleh Salad

1. Arrange trivet included with electric pressure cooker in base of insert and add ½ cup water. Fold sheet of aluminum foil into 16 by 6-inch sling, then rest 1½-quart round soufflé dish in center of sling. Combine 1 cup water, bulgur, and ½ teaspoon salt in dish. Using sling, lower soufflé dish into pot and onto trivet; allow narrow edges of sling to rest along sides of insert.

2. Lock lid in place and close pressure-release valve. Select high pressure-cook function and cook for 3 minutes. Turn off pressure cooker and quick-release pressure. Carefully remove lid, allowing steam to escape away from you. Using sling, transfer soufflé dish to wire rack; set aside to cool. Remove trivet; do not discard sling or water in pot.

3. Arrange lemon slices widthwise in 2 rows across center of sling. Brush cod with 1 tablespoon oil and sprinkle with pepper and remaining ½ teaspoon salt. Arrange cod skinned side down in even layer on top of lemon slices. Using sling, lower cod into pressure cooker; allow narrow edges of sling to rest along sides of insert. Lock lid in place and close pressure-release valve. Select high pressure-cook function and cook for 3 minutes.

4. Meanwhile, whisk remaining 2 tablespoons oil, lemon juice, and shallot together in large bowl. Add bulgur, tomatoes, parsley, and mint, and gently toss to combine. Season with salt and pepper to taste.

5. Turn off pressure cooker and quick-release pressure. Carefully remove lid, allowing steam to escape away from you. Using sling, transfer cod to large plate. Gently lift and tilt fillets with spatula to remove lemon slices. Serve cod with salad, drizzling individual portions with extra oil.

Pressure-Cooker Halibut with Carrots, White Beans, and Chermoula

Serves 4 | **Total Time** 45 minutes `FAST`

WHY THIS RECIPE WORKS This dish is full of satisfying contrasts—moist, tender halibut fillets with delicately sweet carrots, white beans, a zesty sauce, and fresh herbs. Because halibut tends to be a more expensive fish, we keep the remaining ingredients pantry friendly. First, we create a base of carrots and canned beans in a splash of broth and use a foil sling for our halibut for easy removal. In less than a minute under pressure, our carrots are cooked to tender perfection, and the beans and broth mingle with the juices from the fish, creating a saucy consistency that coats the halibut. We finish the dish with chermoula, a bright Moroccan sauce, and top it with a fresh herb salad. Swordfish is a good substitute for the halibut. To prevent the halibut from overcooking, be sure to turn off the pressure cooker as soon as it reaches pressure. If the halibut has not reached at least 130 degrees after releasing pressure, partially cover the pot and continue to cook using residual heat until it reaches 130 degrees.

- 1 shallot, sliced thin
- 1 tablespoon extra-virgin olive oil
- 2 teaspoons lemon juice
- 1 pound carrots, peeled
- 1 (15-ounce) can navy beans, rinsed
- ½ cup chicken or vegetable broth
- 4 (6-ounce) skinless halibut fillets, 1½ inches thick
- 3 tablespoons Chermoula, divided
- ¼ teaspoon table salt
- 1 cup fresh parsley or cilantro leaves
- 2 tablespoons sliced almonds, toasted

1. Combine shallot, oil, and lemon juice in medium bowl; set aside. Cut carrots into 2-inch lengths. Leave thin pieces whole, halve medium pieces lengthwise, and quarter thick pieces lengthwise. Combine carrots, beans, and broth in electric pressure cooker.

2. Fold sheet of aluminum foil into 16 by 6-inch sling. Brush halibut with 1 tablespoon chermoula and sprinkle with salt. Arrange halibut skinned side down in center of sling. Using sling, lower halibut into pressure cooker on top of carrot mixture; allow narrow edges of sling to rest along sides of insert.

3. Lock lid in place and close pressure-release valve. Select high pressure-cook function and set cook time for 0 minutes. Once pressure cooker has reached pressure, immediately turn off pot and quick-release pressure. Carefully remove lid, allowing steam to escape away from you.

4. Using sling, transfer halibut to large plate. Tent with foil and let rest while finishing carrot mixture. Stir remaining 2 tablespoons chermoula into carrot mixture and season with salt and pepper to taste. Add parsley and almonds to bowl with shallot mixture and gently toss to combine. Season with salt and pepper to taste. Serve halibut with carrot mixture, topped with parsley salad.

Chermoula

Makes 1½ cups | **Total Time** 10 minutes, plus 30 minutes resting `FAST` `VEGAN`

- 2¼ cups fresh cilantro leaves
- 8 garlic cloves, minced
- 1½ teaspoons ground cumin
- 1¼ teaspoons paprika
- ½ teaspoon cayenne pepper
- ¼ teaspoon table salt
- 6 tablespoons lemon juice (2 lemons)
- ¾ cup extra-virgin olive oil

Pulse cilantro, garlic, cumin, paprika, cayenne, and salt in food processor until cilantro is coarsely chopped, about 10 pulses. Add lemon juice and pulse briefly to combine. Transfer mixture to medium bowl and slowly whisk in oil until incorporated and mixture is emulsified. Cover and let sit at room temperature for at least 30 minutes to allow flavors to meld. (Sauce can be refrigerated for up to 2 days; bring to room temperature before serving.)

Pressure-Cooker Halibut with Lentils, Kale, and Pancetta

Serves 4 | **Total Time** 1 hour

WHY THIS RECIPE WORKS For this beautifully textured meal, we sauté pancetta, onion, carrots, garlic, and thyme and cook lentils in this aromatic base. The electric pressure cooker's even cooking allows lentils to keep their shape and placing kale on top of the lentils helps it wilt but not overcook. So that all components can finish cooking together, we suspend the halibut in a foil sling above the lentils and kale and cook everything for 2 more minutes. Mahi-mahi, red snapper, striped bass, and swordfish are good substitutes for the halibut. If the halibut has not reached at least 130 degrees after releasing the pressure, partially cover the pot and continue to cook using residual heat until it reaches 130 degrees. Serve with lemon wedges.

> **Substitution:** We like lentilles du Puy for this recipe; however, you can use any dried lentils, except red or yellow.

2 tablespoons extra-virgin olive oil, divided, plus extra for drizzling
1 onion, chopped fine
2 carrots, peeled and chopped fine
2 ounces pancetta, chopped fine
2 garlic cloves, minced
½ teaspoon minced fresh thyme or ⅛ teaspoon dried
2 cups water
1 cup lentilles du Puy, picked over and rinsed
½ teaspoon table salt, divided
12 ounces kale, stemmed and chopped
4 (6-ounce) skinless halibut fillets, 1 to 1½ inches thick
¼ teaspoon pepper
½ cup panko bread crumbs
2 tablespoons chopped fresh parsley
½ teaspoon grated lemon zest plus 1 tablespoon juice

1. Using highest sauté or browning function, heat 1 tablespoon oil in electric pressure cooker until shimmering. Add onion, carrots, and pancetta and cook until vegetables are softened and lightly browned, and pancetta is lightly browned, 4 to 6 minutes. Add garlic and thyme and cook, stirring frequently, until fragrant, about 30 seconds. Stir in water, scraping up any browned bits, then stir in lentils and ¼ teaspoon salt. Arrange kale in even layer on top of lentils.

2. Lock lid into place and close pressure-release valve. Select high pressure-cook function and cook for 12 minutes. Turn off pressure cooker and quick-release pressure. Carefully remove lid, allowing steam to escape away from you.

3. Stir lentils and kale gently to combine. Fold sheet of aluminum foil into 16 by 6-inch sling. Arrange halibut skinned side down in center of sling and sprinkle with pepper and remaining ¼ teaspoon salt. Using sling, lower halibut into pot on top of lentil mixture; allow narrow edges of sling to rest along sides of pot.

4. Lock lid into place and close pressure-release valve. Select high pressure-cook function and cook for 2 minutes. Turn off pressure cooker and quick-release pressure. Carefully remove lid, allowing steam to escape away from you. Using sling, transfer halibut to large plate.

5. Meanwhile, toss panko with remaining 1 tablespoon oil in bowl until evenly coated. Microwave, stirring frequently, until light golden brown, 2 to 4 minutes. Let cool slightly, then stir in parsley and lemon zest; set aside for serving.

6. Stir lemon juice into lentil mixture and season with salt and pepper to taste. Serve halibut with lentils, sprinkling individual portions with bread crumb topping and drizzling with extra oil.

Pressure-Cooker Southwestern Shrimp and Oat Berry Bowl

Serves 4 | **Total Time** 1 hour

WHY THIS RECIPE WORKS Oat berries (also known as groats) make a substantial base for a bowl because of their hearty chew and pleasant nuttiness. On the stove, they can take at least 45 minutes to cook, but the high-pressure electric pressure cooker function cuts that in half. Inspired by the Southwestern flavors of fast-casual burrito bowls, we set out to create an elevated at-home version. We first pressure-cook the oat berries. Then we char poblano peppers with garlic and spices to season the cooked oat berries. Finally, we sear shrimp in the same aromatics to double down on flavor. Serve this bowl with an abundance of toppings: corn salsa for zesty sweetness, avocado for rich creaminess, a chipotle-yogurt sauce for smoky coolness, and salty tortilla chips to add a fun crunch. Extra-large shrimp (21 to 25 per pound) also work in this recipe. For more spice, add the ribs and seeds from the poblano chiles.

CHIPOTLE-YOGURT SAUCE

½ cup plain whole-milk yogurt

1½ teaspoons minced canned chipotle chile in adobo sauce

½ teaspoon grated lime zest plus 1 tablespoon juice

1 small garlic clove, minced

SHRIMP AND OAT BERRY BOWL

1½ cups oat berries, rinsed

3 tablespoons extra-virgin olive oil, divided

½ teaspoon table salt, divided, plus salt for cooking oat berries

1 cup frozen corn, thawed

½ cup fresh cilantro leaves

¼ cup finely chopped red onion

1 tablespoon grated lime zest plus 1 tablespoon juice

2 poblano chiles, stemmed, seeded, and sliced thin

4 garlic cloves, minced

¾ teaspoon chili powder

¾ teaspoon ground coriander

1 pound large shrimp (26 to 30 per pound), peeled, deveined, and tails removed

1 avocado, halved, pitted, and cut into ½-inch pieces

1½ ounces corn tortilla chips, broken into 1-inch pieces (½ cup)

1. FOR THE CHIPOTLE-YOGURT SAUCE Whisk all ingredients together in bowl. Cover and refrigerate until flavors meld, at least 30 minutes. Season with salt and pepper to taste. (Sauce can be refrigerated for up to 4 days.)

2. FOR THE SHRIMP AND OAT BERRY BOWL Combine 6 cups water, oat berries, 1 tablespoon oil, and 1½ teaspoons salt in electric pressure cooker. Lock lid into place and close pressure-release valve. Select high pressure-cook function and cook for 20 minutes.

3. Turn off pressure cooker and let pressure release naturally for 15 minutes. Quick-release any remaining pressure, then carefully remove lid, allowing steam to escape away from you. Drain oat berries, transfer to large bowl, and cover to keep warm. Wipe pot clean with paper towels.

4. Meanwhile, stir corn, cilantro, onion, lime juice, and ¼ teaspoon salt together in small bowl; set aside for serving.

5. Using highest sauté or browning function, heat 1 table-spoon oil in now-empty pot until shimmering. Add poblanos and cook until softened and lightly browned, 3 to 5 minutes. Add lime zest, garlic, chili powder, coriander, and remaining ¼ teaspoon salt and cook, stirring frequently, until fragrant, about 30 seconds. Transfer poblano mixture to bowl with oat berries, toss to combine, and season with salt and pepper to taste; set aside.

Pressure-Cooker Halibut with Lentils, Kale, and Pancetta

Pressure-Cooker Southwestern Shrimp and Oat Berry Bowl

Pressure-Cooker Shrimp and White Beans with Butternut Squash and Sage

6. Using highest sauté or browning function, heat remaining 1 tablespoon oil in now-empty pot until just smoking. Add shrimp and cook, tossing constantly, until all but very center is opaque, about 3 minutes.

7. Divide oat berries among individual serving bowls. Top with shrimp, avocado, tortilla chips, and corn salsa. Serve, passing yogurt sauce separately.

Pressure-Cooker Shrimp and White Beans with Butternut Squash and Sage

Serves 4 | **Total Time** 45 minutes FAST

WHY THIS RECIPE WORKS Turning chunks of dense vegetables into tender bites is one of the things a pressure cooker does best. We combine creamy cannellini beans with nutty butternut squash and pair them with shrimp for a complete and comforting meal. Sage pairs well with beans, squash, and shrimp separately, but it becomes magical with all three. As well as adding minced sage to the base, we also use the sauté function to produce fried sage leaves for a crispy garnish. Our favored method for shrimp in the pressure cooker is stirring them in raw at the end of cooking and letting the residual heat cook them through. The indirect heat virtually eliminates the chance of overcooking this delicate protein. Extra-large shrimp (21 to 25 per pound) also work in this recipe.

- 2 tablespoons extra-virgin olive oil, plus extra for drizzling
- 12 fresh sage leaves, plus 1 tablespoon minced fresh sage
- 1 onion, chopped fine
- 4 garlic cloves, minced
- ½ cup dry white wine
- 2 (15-ounce) cans cannellini beans, drained with ½ cup canning liquid reserved, rinsed
- 1½ pounds butternut squash, peeled, seeded, and cut into 1-inch pieces (4 cups)
- ½ teaspoon table salt
- 1 pound large shrimp (26 to 30 per pound), peeled, deveined, and tails removed
- 1 teaspoon grated lemon zest plus 2 teaspoons juice, plus lemon wedges for serving
- 2 tablespoons toasted sliced almonds

Pressure-Cooker Black Beans and Brown Rice

1. Using highest sauté or browning function, cook oil and sage leaves in electric pressure cooker until sage is dark green and crisp, 3 to 5 minutes, flipping leaves halfway through cooking. Using slotted spoon, transfer sage leaves to paper towel–lined plate.

2. Add onion to oil left in pot and cook, using highest sauté or browning function, until softened and lightly browned, about 5 minutes. Add garlic and minced sage and cook, stirring frequently, until fragrant, about 30 seconds. Stir in wine, scraping up any browned bits, and cook until mostly evaporated, about 1 minute. Stir in beans and reserved liquid, squash, and salt.

3. Lock lid into place and close pressure-release valve. Select high pressure-cook function and cook for 3 minutes. Turn off pressure cooker and quick-release pressure. Carefully remove lid, allowing steam to escape away from you.

4. Stir shrimp gently into squash mixture, cover, and let sit until shrimp are opaque throughout, 5 to 8 minutes. Stir in lemon zest and juice and season with salt and pepper to taste. Sprinkle individual portions with almonds and sage leaves and drizzle with extra oil. Serve with lemon wedges.

Pressure-Cooker Black Beans and Brown Rice

Serves 4 to 6 | **Total Time** 1 hour, plus 8 hours brining
`VEGAN`

WHY THIS RECIPE WORKS Beans and rice are classic comfort food the world over. But stovetop recipes can some-times lead to blown-out rice and undercooked beans when the two are cooked together. Here we use the electric pressure cooker to produce fluffy rice and tender beans consistently. We brine our beans, which are the star of this meal, to ensure that they cook through completely. As the beans cook, they impart flavor and color to the brown rice while maintaining structural integrity. For a savory base, we sauté bell peppers, onions, and jalapeños, adding garlic, oregano, cumin, and tomato paste. After adding the broth, we cook the rice and beans together at pressure for 22 minutes and the perfect one-pot dish is ready to eat. We finish this deceptively simple but flavor-packed dish with scallions and a splash of red wine vinegar. For more spice, add the ribs and seeds from the jalapeño chiles.

1½ tablespoons table salt for brining
8 ounces (1¼ cups) dried black beans, picked over and rinsed
1 tablespoon vegetable oil
2 green bell peppers, stemmed, seeded, and chopped fine
1 onion, chopped fine
2 jalapeño chiles, stemmed, seeded, and minced
6 garlic cloves, minced
1 tablespoon tomato paste
2 teaspoons dried oregano
2 teaspoons ground cumin
1¼ teaspoons table salt
2¾ cups vegetable broth
1½ cups long-grain brown rice, rinsed
4 scallions, sliced thin
2 tablespoons red wine vinegar
Lime wedges

1. Dissolve 1½ tablespoons salt in 2 quarts cold water in large container. Add beans and soak at room temperature for at least 8 hours or up to 24 hours. Drain and rinse well. (If you're pressed for time, see page 322 for information on quick brining your beans.)

2. Using highest sauté or browning function, heat oil in electric pressure cooker until shimmering. Add bell peppers, onion, and jalapeños and cook until vegetables are softened and lightly browned, 5 to 7 minutes. Add garlic, tomato paste, oregano, cumin, and salt and cook, stirring frequently, until fragrant, about 30 seconds. Stir in broth, scraping up any browned bits, then stir in soaked beans and rice.

3. Lock lid into place and close pressure-release valve. Select high pressure-cook function and cook for 22 minutes. Turn off pressure cooker and quick-release pressure. Carefully remove lid, allowing steam to escape away from you.

4. Lay clean dish towel over pot, replace lid, and let sit for 5 minutes. Sprinkle scallions and vinegar over rice and beans and fluff gently with fork to combine. Season with salt and pepper to taste. Serve with lime wedges.

Pressure-Cooker Gochujang-Braised Tempeh Lettuce Wraps

Serves 4 | **Total Time** 45 minutes **FAST**

WHY THIS RECIPE WORKS For a vegetarian meal that is fun to eat and easy to make, we turn to lettuce wrapped around sweet, savory tempeh and crisp pickled vegetables. Tempeh, made from fermented soybeans, is high in protein and fiber and has a nutty flavor with a meaty chew, making it the perfect choice for our filling. Cooking in the electric pressure cooker allows the tempeh to soften slightly and soak up the flavorful sauce without drying out. The sauce is sweet and spicy, thanks to gochujang (Korean red pepper paste), honey, soy sauce, sesame oil, ginger, and garlic. Once the tempeh is ready, we remove it from the pot and reduce the sauce further on high. Fresh and crunchy pickled cucumber and bean sprouts offset the spicy tempeh for a refreshing dinner with a kick.

- 1 cup unseasoned rice vinegar
- 2 tablespoons sugar
- 1 cucumber, peeled, quartered lengthwise, seeded, and sliced thin on bias
- 4 ounces (2 cups) bean sprouts
- 4 scallions, sliced thin
- 4 teaspoons toasted sesame oil, divided
- 4 teaspoons grated fresh ginger, divided
- 1 cup water
- 3 tablespoons gochujang paste
- 2 tablespoons honey
- 2 tablespoons soy sauce, plus extra for seasoning
- 4 garlic cloves, minced
- 1 pound tempeh, halved lengthwise and cut crosswise into ½-inch pieces
- 1 tablespoon sesame seeds, toasted
- 2 heads Bibb lettuce (8 ounces each), leaves separated

1. Microwave vinegar and sugar in medium bowl until steaming, 1 to 2 minutes; whisk to dissolve sugar. Add cucumber and bean sprouts to hot brine and let sit, stirring occasionally, for 30 minutes. Drain cucumber mixture and return to now-empty bowl. Stir in scallions, 1 teaspoon oil, and 1 teaspoon ginger; set aside for serving. (Pickled vegetables can be refrigerated for up to 24 hours.)

2. Meanwhile, whisk water, gochujang, honey, soy sauce, garlic, remaining 1 tablespoon oil, and remaining 1 tablespoon ginger together in electric pressure cooker. Arrange tempeh in even layer in pot and spoon sauce over top. Lock lid into place and close pressure-release valve. Select high pressure-cook function and cook for 12 minutes.

3. Turn off pressure cooker and quick-release pressure. Carefully remove lid, allowing steam to escape away from you. Transfer tempeh to serving dish. Using highest sauté or browning function, cook sauce, stirring occasionally, until slightly thickened, 1 to 2 minutes. Season with extra soy sauce to taste. Spoon sauce over tempeh and sprinkle with sesame seeds. Serve in lettuce leaves with pickled vegetables.

Pressure-Cooker Braised Tofu with Pumpkin Mole and Apple-Cabbage Slaw

Serves 4 | **Total Time** 45 minutes **FAST**

WHY THIS RECIPE WORKS We know the electric pressure cooker creates beautifully braised meat dishes, but for a filling vegetarian meal, we wanted to apply the same method to a block of tofu. Tofu is made from pressed soy milk curds and comes in a variety of textures. It makes a perfect blank canvas for flavor. It readily soaks up a sauce's flavorful liquid and becomes tender and creamy. Our sauce, inspired by mole, combines fire-roasted tomatoes, chipotle chiles in adobo, and garlic with golden raisins and cocoa powder. To ensure that the tofu absorbs maximum flavor but still keeps its shape, we cut it into quarters before nestling it into the sauce. After cooking, we remove the tofu from the liquid and whisk in pumpkin puree. Its natural sweetness and mellow squash notes balance the smoky flavors and enhance the luscious, velvety sauce, which we then spoon over the tofu. An easy slaw of cabbage, apple, shallots, and more golden raisins makes for a tart, crunchy sidekick to the creamy tofu. We love serving this braise with brown rice and tortillas for a heartier meal and for sopping up all the delicious sauce.

- ¼ cup cider vinegar
- 1 tablespoon sugar
- ¾ teaspoon table salt, divided
- 2 cups shredded red cabbage
- 1 shallot, sliced thin
- ½ cup golden raisins, divided
- 1 Granny Smith apple, cored and cut into matchsticks
- 1 (14.5-ounce) can fire-roasted diced tomatoes
- 6 garlic cloves, minced
- 1½ tablespoons unsweetened cocoa powder
- 1 tablespoon minced canned chipotle chile in adobo sauce
- 1 teaspoon ground cinnamon
- 2 cups water
- 1 (14-ounce) block firm tofu, quartered
- 1 (15-ounce) can unsweetened pumpkin puree
- 2 ounces cotija cheese, crumbled (½ cup)

1. Microwave vinegar, sugar, and ¼ teaspoon salt in large bowl until steaming, 1 to 2 minutes; whisk to dissolve sugar and salt. Add cabbage, shallot, and ¼ cup raisins to hot brine and let sit, stirring occasionally, for 30 minutes. Drain cabbage mixture and return to now-empty bowl. Stir in apple and set aside for serving. (Slaw can be refrigerated for up to 24 hours.)

2. Meanwhile, process tomatoes and their juice, garlic, cocoa powder, chipotle, cinnamon, remaining ½ teaspoon salt, and remaining ¼ cup raisins in food processor until smooth, 1 to 2 minutes, scraping down sides of bowl as needed. Whisk tomato mixture and water together in electric pressure cooker. Arrange tofu in even layer in pot and spoon some of sauce over top. Lock lid into place and close pressure-release valve. Select high pressure-cook function and cook for 5 minutes.

3. Turn off pressure cooker and quick-release pressure. Carefully remove lid, allowing steam to escape away from you. Transfer tofu to serving dish and tent with aluminum foil. Whisk pumpkin into sauce and cook, using highest sauté or browning function, whisking constantly, until sauce is slightly thickened, 2 to 3 minutes. Season with salt and pepper to taste. Spoon sauce over tofu and sprinkle with cotija. Serve tofu with apple-cabbage slaw.

Pressure-Cooker Gochujang-Braised Tempeh Lettuce Wraps

Pressure-Cooker Braised Tofu with Pumpkin Mole and Apple-Cabbage Slaw

Cook It Slow

*All of the recipes in this chapter will work in a traditional 5- to 7-quart slow cooker

● FAST (45 minutes or less)   ● VEGAN

Photo: Slow-Cooker Lemony Chicken and Rice with Spinach and Feta

Hands-Off Cooking for Beans, Grains, and Rice

Slow cookers really can make your life easier: The food goes in the cooker, you turn it on, and then you go about your business before coming back some time later to a delicious, fully cooked meal. The recipes in this chapter were developed to work in a traditional 5- to 7-quart countertop slow cooker. They will not work using the slow cooker setting on a multicooker.

We slow-cook beans and grains for recipes such as Slow-Cooker Farro Primavera (page 388) and Slow-Cooker Braised Chicken Sausages with White Bean Ragout (page 378). However, a slow cooker also makes sense for simply cooking a batch of beans. Since grains do not need that extended cooking period, except for specific recipes, if you want to simply cook grain to have on hand for other recipes, our test cooks suggest using the stovetop boiling, pilaf, or microwave methods (page 30).

With exacting cooking times and, in most cases, precise amounts of liquid required, bean, grain, and rice dishes can be tricky to cook perfectly in your slow cooker. Here is what we learned:

NO SOAKING NEEDED
When starting with dried beans, we add them right to the slow cooker, no advance soaking or simmering needed. The beans require no prep other than being picked over and rinsed. Dried beans are well suited to low-and-slow cooking, and the gentle simmering heat of the slow cooker helps the beans to cook through evenly.

COOK BEANS ON HIGH
The gentle, steady heat of the slow cooker produces perfectly tender beans and chickpeas after 8 or 9 hours of cooking them on the high setting. But we weren't able to get the same result from cooking on low; even after 16 hours of cooking, we still had crunchy beans. So we cook our baked beans (page 390) and other bean recipes exclusively on high.

USE AN OVAL SLOW COOKER
We found that an oval slow cooker is the perfect vessel in which to cook rice, lentils, wheat berries, and more. The oval shape provides more surface area over which to spread the rice and grains to allow for more even cooking.

TRAP STEAM WITH PARCHMENT
In addition to the right ratio of rice to water, the key to perfectly cooked rice is a parchment shield (see below). Crimping a piece of parchment over the top of the rice creates a vacuum that prevents the grains on top from drying out as the water is absorbed. In addition, condensation builds up on the parchment shield and drips back down onto the rice, creating a superbly even, moist environment. This works beautifully for sides like Slow-Cooker Mushroom Biryani (page 384).

CREATING A PARCHMENT SHIELD

Press 16 by 12-inch sheet of parchment paper firmly onto rice or vegetables, folding down edges as needed.

ADD BOILING WATER
We learned that long-grain white rice, basmati rice, and brown rice all need a head start with boiling water in the slow cooker. We also found that cooking them on high is best, as is using a layer of parchment over the rice to protect the grains on top from drying out as the liquid is absorbed.

A WORD ABOUT INSTANT RICE
In some recipes such as Slow-Cooker Lemony Chicken and Rice with Spinach and Feta (page 375), we found that traditional rice took too long to cook; grains didn't cook through evenly or were blown out and mushy by the time the chicken or beans were done. In those cases, instant white or brown rice (also called minute rice), stirred in toward the end of cooking, holds its shape and absorbs the rich flavors of the cooking liquid and other ingredients.

Five Tips for Making the Best Use of Your Slow Cooker

1. BROWN FOOD OUTSIDE OF THE SLOW COOKER

Browning food first adds color and flavor to food that will be slow-cooked. Brown meat, like turkey for Slow-Cooker Turkey Chili (page 365), in a skillet on the stovetop before adding it to the slow cooker with the broth and vegetables. Or broil ingredients like tomatillos, as we do for Slow-Cooker Tomatillo Chili with Pork and Hominy (page 369), to add flavor and texture before slow-cooking them with other ingredients.

2. SEASON SLOW-COOKED FOOD HEAVILY

Slow cooking can mute flavors, so we like to use lots of spices to build big flavor. But it's not just increasing spices that does that trick; you'll also want to increase their potency. For example, we bloom spices in either a skillet or the microwave to increase flavor. You'll also want to use bold, robust spice rubs for things like roasts. Add strong ingredients such as garlic, lemon or lime juice, vinegar, soy or Worcestershire sauce, anchovies, tomato paste, dried mushrooms, and bold spices to slow-cooker recipes, such as Slow-Cooker Beef and Barley Soup (page 365). And don't forget the salt!

3. USE A THICKENING AGENT FOR SLOW-COOKER SAUCES

The covered environment of a slow cooker means that there is little evaporation, so sauces don't naturally concentrate and reduce. To thicken the sauces of slow-cooked dishes, we often use a roux (a paste of fat and flour), pureed beans, grains, or vegetables that are already in the dish; or instant tapioca, as for Slow-Cooker Vegetables and Tofu with Indian Spices (page 383). Sometimes thickening happens naturally, as in our Slow-Cooker French Lentil Stew (page 372). Brown rice breaks down slightly during cooking, thickening the stew.

4. FINISH WITH FLAVOR

Many slow-cooker dishes need a flavor boost before serving, so we turn to fresh finishers such as herbs, citrus juice, or vinegar, stirred in or sprinkled on top at the end of cooking. We even think outside the box and lean on other flavorful ingredients like brown sugar or coconut milk. Top dishes like our Slow-Cooker Tomatillo Chili with Pork and Hominy (page 369) with fresh cilantro and add a squeeze of fresh lime juice to brighten up any flavors that may have dulled during the long cooking time.

5. KNOW YOUR SLOW COOKER

Using a slow cooker isn't an exact science. Discrepancies in heating power can create dramatically different results in different machines. Some models run hot and fast, while others reach their maximum temperatures more slowly. The tightness of the lid seal can also affect how efficiently a slow cooker heats. Always pay attention to the time ranges given in recipes: Are dishes cooked in your machine typically finished at the lower or higher ends of the time ranges given? The answer tells you if you have a relatively "fast" or "slow" model and allows you to compensate accordingly.

Slow-Cooker Chicken Stew with
Sausage and White Beans

Slow-Cooker White
Chicken Chili

Slow-Cooker Chicken Stew with Sausage and White Beans

Serves 6 to 8 | **Cooking Time** 4 to 5 hours on low

WHY THIS RECIPE WORKS This hearty stew takes its inspiration from classic Tuscan white bean stew but here we combine white beans with both sausage and meaty chicken thighs. Canned beans make our work easy but we find it worthwhile to get out the skillet to brown the chicken and sausage and sauté the aromatics and fennel first, as this step adds a richer, deeper flavor and color to a slow-cooked stew. Sliced fennel, thyme, and red pepper flakes complement the flavors of the Italian sausage. The spinach may seem like a lot at first, but it wilts down substantially. A sprinkling of grated Parmesan cheese enhances the other flavors in the stew. Serve with crusty bread or Garlic Toasts (page 363).

2 pounds boneless, skinless chicken thighs, trimmed
½ teaspoon table salt
¼ teaspoon pepper
3 tablespoons vegetable oil, divided
1 pound hot or sweet Italian sausage, casings removed
2 onions, chopped fine
1 fennel bulb, stalks discarded, bulb halved, cored, and sliced thin
⅓ cup all-purpose flour
6 garlic cloves, minced
1 tablespoon tomato paste
2 teaspoons minced fresh thyme or ½ teaspoon dried
⅛ teaspoon red pepper flakes
4 cups chicken broth, divided, plus extra as needed
½ cup dry white wine
2 (15-ounce) cans cannellini beans, rinsed
2 bay leaves
6 ounces (6 cups) baby spinach
Grated Parmesan cheese

1. Pat chicken dry with paper towels and sprinkle with salt and pepper. Heat 1 tablespoon oil in 12-inch skillet over medium-high heat until just smoking. Brown half of chicken, about 4 minutes per side; transfer to slow cooker. Repeat with 1 tablespoon oil and remaining chicken; transfer to slow cooker.

2. Heat remaining 1 tablespoon oil in now-empty skillet over medium-high heat until just smoking. Add sausage and cook, breaking up meat into rough 1-inch pieces with wooden spoon, until browned, about 5 minutes. Using slotted spoon, transfer sausage to slow cooker.

3. Pour off all but 1 tablespoon fat from skillet, add onions and fennel, and cook over medium heat until softened and lightly browned, 8 to 10 minutes. Stir in flour, garlic, tomato paste, thyme, and pepper flakes and cook until fragrant, about 1 minute. Slowly whisk in 1 cup broth and wine, scraping up any browned bits and smoothing out any lumps; transfer to slow cooker.

4. Stir remaining 3 cups broth, beans, and bay leaves into slow cooker, cover, and cook until chicken is tender, 4 to 5 hours on low.

5. Transfer chicken to cutting board, let cool slightly, then pull apart into large chunks using 2 forks. Discard bay leaves.

6. Stir chicken into stew, then stir in spinach, 1 handful at a time, and let sit until wilted, about 5 minutes. Adjust consistency with extra hot broth as needed. Season with salt and pepper to taste. Serve with Parmesan.

Garlic Toasts

Makes 8 slices | **Total Time** 10 minutes
`FAST` `VEGAN`

Be sure to use a high-quality crusty bread, such as a baguette; do not use sliced sandwich bread. Serve toasts with Slow-Cooker Chicken Stew with Sausage and White Beans (page 362) and Pressure-Cooker Acquacotta (page 330), or even as an appetizer, with one of our bean dips (pages 50–56).

8 (1-inch-thick) slices rustic bread
1 large garlic clove, peeled
3 tablespoons extra-virgin olive oil

Adjust oven rack 6 inches from broiler element and heat broiler. Spread bread evenly in rimmed baking sheet and broil, flipping as needed, until well toasted on both sides, about 4 minutes. Briefly rub 1 side of each toast with garlic, drizzle with oil, and season with salt and pepper to taste. Serve.

Slow-Cooker White Chicken Chili

Serves 6 to 8 | **Cooking Time** 4 to 5 hours on low

WHY THIS RECIPE WORKS Made with hominy, white chicken chili is a fresher, lighter cousin of the thick red chili most Americans know. Hominy helps thicken the broth and flavor the dish; cannellini beans add heartiness; and because there are no tomatoes to mask the other flavors, the chiles, herbs, and spices can take center stage. First we blend the hominy with some chicken broth to make a thick starchy liquid to cook the chicken in. Before adding boneless chicken thighs to the slow cooker, we brown them in a skillet to ensure our chili has big chicken flavor. Sautéing the aromatics—including four jalapeño chiles—and spices together in the skillet also adds a richer, deeper taste; plus, deglazing the pan ensures all the browned bits we develop end up in the slow cooker. Unlike red chili, which uses any combo of dried chiles, chili powders, and cayenne pepper, white chicken chili gets its backbone from fresh green chiles, which contribute vibrant flavor and spiciness. For more spice, add the ribs and seeds from the jalapeño chiles.

Substitution: You can use yellow hominy in place of the white.

3 cups chicken broth, divided, plus extra as needed
1 (15-ounce) can white hominy, rinsed
3 pounds boneless, skinless chicken thighs, trimmed
1 teaspoon table salt
½ teaspoon pepper
3 tablespoons vegetable oil, divided
2 onions, chopped fine
4 jalapeño chiles, stemmed, seeded, and minced
6 garlic cloves, minced
4 teaspoons ground cumin
2 teaspoons ground coriander
3 (15-ounce) cans cannellini beans, rinsed
¼ cup minced fresh cilantro
2 tablespoons minced jarred jalapeños
2 avocados, halved, pitted, and cut into ½-inch pieces

1. Process 2 cups broth and hominy in blender until smooth, about 1 minute; transfer to slow cooker.

2. Pat chicken dry with paper towels and sprinkle with salt and pepper. Heat 1 tablespoon oil in 12-inch skillet over medium-high heat until just smoking. Brown half of chicken, about 4 minutes per side; transfer to slow cooker. Repeat with 1 tablespoon oil and remaining chicken; transfer to slow cooker.

3. Heat remaining 1 tablespoon oil in now-empty skillet over medium heat until shimmering. Add onions and cook until softened and lightly browned, 8 to 10 minutes. Stir in fresh jalapeños, garlic, cumin, and coriander and cook until fragrant, about 30 seconds. Stir in remaining 1 cup broth, scraping up any browned bits; transfer to slow cooker.

4. Stir beans into slow cooker, cover, and cook until chicken is tender, 4 to 5 hours on low.

5. Transfer chicken to cutting board, let cool slightly, then pull apart into large chunks using 2 forks. Stir chicken into chili and let sit until heated through, about 5 minutes. Adjust consistency with extra hot broth as needed. Stir in cilantro and jarred jalapeños and season with salt and pepper to taste. Serve with avocados.

Slow-Cooker Turkey and Rice Soup

Slow-Cooker Turkey and Rice Soup

Serves 6 to 8 | **Cooking Time** 6 to 7 hours on low

WHY THIS RECIPE WORKS Turkey and rice soup is a dish that's perfectly suited to a slow cooker and works well as a tasty weeknight meal. Rice provides rich starch and here we use instant brown rice because traditional rice takes much longer to cook. The hearty flavor of turkey translates easily into a full-flavored soup without requiring any tricks, and turkey thighs (which we prefer for soup) seem to have been designed for the slow cooker's low and steady cooking environment. Made up entirely of dark meat, they are quite big and thick, which means they are nearly impossible to overcook, and they have lots of flavor to spare. As a bonus, they're cheap, too. You can substitute an equal amount of bone-in chicken thighs for the turkey, if desired; reduce the cooking time to 4 to 5 hours. Do not use traditional rice as it takes much longer to cook than instant rice (sometimes labeled minute rice).

- 2 onions, chopped fine
- 4 garlic cloves, minced
- 1 tablespoon vegetable oil
- 1 tablespoon tomato paste
- 2 teaspoons minced fresh thyme or ½ teaspoon dried
- 1¼ teaspoons table salt, divided
- 8 cups chicken broth
- 3 carrots, peeled and sliced ¼ inch thick
- 2 celery ribs, sliced ¼ inch thick
- 2 bay leaves
- 2 pounds bone-in turkey thighs, skin removed, trimmed
- ¼ teaspoon pepper
- 2 cups instant brown rice
- 2 tablespoons minced fresh parsley

1. Microwave onions, garlic, oil, tomato paste, thyme, and ¾ teaspoon salt in bowl, stirring occasionally, until onions are softened, about 5 minutes; transfer to slow cooker. Stir in broth, carrots, celery, and bay leaves. Sprinkle turkey with pepper and remaining ½ teaspoon salt and nestle into slow cooker. Cover and cook until turkey is tender, 6 to 7 hours on low.

2. Transfer turkey to cutting board, let cool slightly, then shred into bite-size pieces using 2 forks; discard bones. Discard bay leaves.

3. Stir rice into soup, cover, and cook on high until tender, 30 to 40 minutes. Stir in turkey and let sit until heated through, about 5 minutes. Stir in parsley and season with salt and pepper to taste. Serve.

Slow-Cooker Turkey Chili

Serves 8 to 10 | **Cooking Time** 4 to 5 hours on low

WHY THIS RECIPE WORKS Turkey chili is a great alternative to classic beef chili, providing a leaner but no less flavorful meal for the dinner table. We add a lot of canned kidney beans to up the protein in the dish without it needing a long time to cook. The rich, red-hued beans also add a pleasant color contrast to the turkey meat. To prevent our ground turkey from drying out, we use a panade—a paste of bread and milk—to provide added moisture. We also found adding broth and a little soy sauce helps reinforce the meatiness of the leaner meat.

- 2 slices hearty white sandwich bread, torn into 1-inch pieces
- ¼ cup soy sauce
- 2 pounds 93 percent lean ground turkey
- 3 tablespoons vegetable oil
- 3 onions, chopped fine
- 1 red bell pepper, stemmed, seeded, and chopped
- ¼ cup chili powder
- ¼ cup tomato paste
- 6 garlic cloves, minced
- 1 tablespoon ground cumin
- ¾ teaspoon dried oregano
- 1¼ cups chicken broth, plus extra as needed
- 2 (15-ounce) cans kidney beans, rinsed
- 1 (28-ounce) can diced tomatoes, drained
- 1 (15-ounce) can tomato sauce
- 1 tablespoon packed brown sugar
- 2 teaspoons minced canned chipotle chile in adobo sauce

1. Mash bread and soy sauce into paste in large bowl using fork. Add ground turkey and knead with your hands until well combined.

2. Heat oil in 12-inch skillet over medium heat until shimmering. Add onions and bell pepper and cook until softened and lightly browned, 8 to 10 minutes. Stir in chili powder, tomato paste, garlic, cumin, and oregano and cook until fragrant, about 1 minute.

3. Add half of turkey mixture and cook, breaking up turkey with wooden spoon, until no longer pink, about 5 minutes. Repeat with remaining turkey mixture. Stir in broth, scraping up any browned bits; transfer to slow cooker.

4. Stir beans, tomatoes, tomato sauce, sugar, and chipotle into slow cooker. Cover and cook until turkey is tender, 4 to 5 hours on low. Break up any remaining large pieces of turkey with spoon. Adjust consistency with extra hot broth as needed. Season with salt and pepper to taste. Serve.

Slow-Cooker Beef and Barley Soup

Slow-Cooker Beef and Barley Soup

Serves 6 to 8 | **Cooking Time** 9 to 10 hours on low or 6 to 7 hours on high

WHY THIS RECIPE WORKS Since pearl barley can absorb two to three times its volume in cooking liquid, we are judicious in the quantity we add to this soup. A modest ¼ cup is all that is needed to lend a pleasing velvety texture without overfilling the slow cooker with swollen grains. We first build a flavorful base in our skillet, sautéing onions, tomato paste, and thyme, and then deglaze the pan with wine to scrape up the flavorful browned bits left behind, which adds deep flavor and allows us to skip the tedious process of browning the meat. We use trimmed beef blade steak, which we shred after it becomes meltingly tender in the slow cooker—no need to cut the meat into pieces to start. Soy sauce adds umami and deep color to the broth. You can substitute an equal amount of beef flat-iron steaks, if desired. Do not use hulled, hull-less, quick-cooking, or presteamed barley (check the ingredient list on the package to determine this) in this recipe.

2 tablespoons vegetable oil

2 onions, chopped fine

¼ cup tomato paste

1 tablespoon minced fresh thyme or 1 teaspoon dried

½ cup dry red wine

1 (28-ounce) can diced tomatoes

4 cups beef broth

2 carrots, peeled and chopped

⅓ cup soy sauce

¼ cup pearl barley, rinsed

2 bay leaves

2 pounds beef blade steaks, ¾ to 1 inch thick, trimmed

½ teaspoon table salt

¼ teaspoon pepper

2 tablespoons minced fresh parsley

1. Heat oil in 12-inch skillet over medium heat until shimmering. Add onions and cook until softened and lightly browned, 8 to 10 minutes. Stir in tomato paste and thyme and cook until fragrant, about 30 seconds. Stir in wine, scraping up any browned bits; transfer to slow cooker.

2. Stir tomatoes and their juice, broth, carrots, soy sauce, barley, and bay leaves into slow cooker. Sprinkle steaks with salt and pepper and nestle into slow cooker. Cover and cook until steaks are tender, 9 to 10 hours on low or 6 to 7 hours on high.

3. Discard bay leaves. Transfer steaks to cutting board, let cool slightly, then shred into bite-size pieces using 2 forks; discard fat and gristle. Stir beef into soup and let sit until heated through, about 5 minutes. Stir in parsley and season with salt and pepper to taste. Serve.

Slow-Cooker Classic Beef Chili

Serves 8 to 10 | **Cooking Time** 6 to 7 hours on low or 4 to 5 hours on high

WHY THIS RECIPE WORKS In this leisurely take on all-American chili, we rely on canned kidney beans for extra heft with minimal effort. Gently simmered ground beef chili is certainly well suited to the slow cooker, but achieving rich taste and tender meat can be a challenge. Most traditional chilis call for browning the beef to develop flavor, but after a long stint in the slow cooker, pre-browned meat can taste overcooked and gritty. Our solution—first mixing the raw beef with a panade of bread and milk (often used in meatballs)—works wonders. We brown this mixture in a flavorful base of onions, chili powder, cumin, oregano, and red pepper flakes before transferring it to the slow cooker. A combination of diced and pureed tomatoes gives our chili the proper consistency, and chipotle chile adds smoky depth. Unconventionally, we also stir in a little soy sauce to boost umami.

2 slices hearty white sandwich bread, torn into 1-inch pieces

¼ cup whole milk

½ teaspoon table salt

½ teaspoon pepper

2 pounds 85 percent lean ground beef

3 tablespoons vegetable oil

3 onions, chopped fine

¼ cup chili powder

¼ cup tomato paste

6 garlic cloves, minced

1 tablespoon ground cumin

¾ teaspoon dried oregano

½ teaspoon red pepper flakes

1 (28-ounce) can tomato puree, divided

1 (28-ounce) can diced tomatoes

2 (15-ounce) cans red kidney beans, rinsed

3 tablespoons soy sauce

1 tablespoon packed brown sugar

2 teaspoons minced canned chipotle chile in adobo sauce

1. Mash bread, milk, salt, and pepper into paste in large bowl using fork. Add ground beef and knead with your hands until well combined.

2. Heat oil in 12-inch skillet over medium heat until shimmering. Add onions and cook until softened and lightly browned, 8 to 10 minutes. Stir in chili powder, tomato paste, garlic, cumin, oregano, and pepper flakes and cook until fragrant, about 1 minute.

3. Add half of beef mixture and cook, breaking up beef with wooden spoon, until no longer pink, about 5 minutes. Repeat with remaining beef mixture. Stir in 1 cup tomato puree, scraping up any browned bits; transfer to slow cooker.

4. Stir remaining tomato puree, diced tomatoes and their juice, beans, soy sauce, sugar, and chipotle into slow cooker. Cover and cook until beef is tender, 6 to 7 hours on low or 4 to 5 hours on high.

5. Using large spoon, skim fat from surface of chili. Break up any remaining large pieces of beef with spoon. Adjust consistency with hot water as needed. Season with salt and pepper to taste. Serve.

Slow-Cooker Tuscan White Bean Soup

2 onions, chopped fine
6 ounces pancetta, chopped fine
8 garlic cloves, minced
1 tablespoon extra-virgin olive oil, plus extra for serving
¼ teaspoon red pepper flakes
4 cups chicken broth
4 cups water
1 pound (2½ cups) dried great northern beans, picked over and rinsed
1 Parmesan cheese rind (optional), plus grated Parmesan for serving
2 bay leaves
1 sprig fresh rosemary

1. Microwave onions, pancetta, garlic, oil, and pepper flakes in bowl, stirring occasionally, until onions are softened, about 5 minutes; transfer to slow cooker. Stir in broth; water; beans; Parmesan rind, if using; and bay leaves. Cover and cook until beans are tender, 9 to 10 hours on high.

2. Nestle rosemary sprig into soup, cover, and cook on high until rosemary is fragrant, about 15 minutes.

3. Discard rosemary sprig; bay leaves; and Parmesan rind, if using. Season with salt and pepper to taste. Serve, passing grated Parmesan and extra oil separately.

Slow-Cooker Tuscan White Bean Soup

Serves 6 to 8 | **Cooking Time** 9 to 10 hours on high

WHY THIS RECIPE WORKS With few ingredients to distract from flaws like mushy beans or a thin broth, Tuscan white bean soup is rarely well prepared in a slow cooker. We create a richly perfumed base for our soup by first microwaving flavorful pancetta along with a lot of onion and garlic. We add dried beans straight to the slow cooker, where the gentle simmering heat helps them cook through evenly. Rosemary is traditional in this soup, but after several hours it gives the broth a bitter, medicinal taste. Instead, we place a sprig of rosemary in the soup to steep for just a few minutes at the end of cooking, which allows us to achieve just the right amount of fresh rosemary flavor. Serve with crusty bread or Garlic Toasts (page 363) to dip into the broth.

> **Substitution:** You can use dried cannellini beans in place of the dried great northern beans.

Slow-Cooker U.S. Senate Navy Bean Soup

Serves 6 to 8 | **Cooking Time** 9 to 10 hours on high

WHY THIS RECIPE WORKS The origins of this mainstay of the U.S. Senate cafeteria may be up for debate, but its list of ingredients is simple and clear: navy beans, ham hocks, onions, and celery. Often the beans are tough or overcooked, the ham flavor is weak, and the broth is thin. So we build layers of flavor by slow cooking the beans and using a combination of ham hock and ham steak for both a nice smoky flavor and lots of meaty bites. To keep the soup's saltiness under control, we rinse the ham hock before cooking and use water rather than chicken stock. We add dried navy beans straight to the slow cooker, where the gentle simmering heat helps them cook through evenly. By the time the ham hock is tender, the beans are perfectly cooked. Carrots make our soup even heartier, and onions and garlic deepen its flavor. A splash of red wine vinegar added just before serving helps to balance the rich, meaty soup with a little acidity. Ham hocks often can be found near the ham and bacon in the supermarket.

- 2 onions, chopped fine
- 2 garlic cloves, minced
- 2 tablespoons vegetable oil
- 2 teaspoons minced fresh thyme or ½ teaspoon dried
- 7 cups water
- 1 pound (2½ cups) dried navy beans, picked over and rinsed
- 1 (12-ounce) smoked ham hock, rinsed
- 8 ounces ham steak, rind removed, quartered
- 3 carrots, peeled and sliced ½ inch thick
- 2 bay leaves
- 1 teaspoon red wine vinegar, plus extra for seasoning

1. Microwave onions, garlic, oil, and thyme in bowl, stirring occasionally, until onions are softened, about 5 minutes; transfer to slow cooker. Stir in water, beans, ham hock, ham steak, carrots, and bay leaves. Cover and cook until beans are tender, 9 to 10 hours on high.

2. Transfer ham hock and ham steak to cutting board, let cool slightly, then shred into bite-size pieces using 2 forks; discard fat, skin, and bones. Discard bay leaves.

3. Stir ham into soup and let sit until heated through, about 5 minutes. Stir in vinegar and season with salt, pepper, and extra vinegar to taste. Serve.

Slow-Cooker Pork and White Bean Stew with Kale

Slow-Cooker Pork and White Bean Stew with Kale

Serves 6 | **Cooking Time** 6 to 7 hours on low or 4 to 5 hours on high

WHY THIS RECIPE WORKS We start with a classic white bean stew and incorporate pork and kale for more heft. Boneless country-style pork ribs require minimal prep work, and thanks to plenty of intramuscular fat, they are moist and fall-apart tender after several hours in the slow cooker. Because dried beans would still be undercooked by the time the pork is done, we use canned white beans here. To give the dish more body, we puree some of the starchy beans with broth before adding them to the slow cooker. To boost the stew's fresh flavor and complement the rich pork and beans, we add whole-grain mustard after the kale is cooked through. Cutting the kale into 1-inch pieces allows the hearty green to become tender in just 20 minutes. Look for country-style pork ribs with lots of fat and dark meat, and stay away from ribs that look overly lean with pale meat, as they will taste very dry after the extended cooking time.

- 3 (15-ounce) cans cannellini beans, rinsed, divided
- 4 cups chicken broth, divided, plus extra as needed
- 2 onions, chopped fine
- 2 tablespoons extra-virgin olive oil, plus extra for serving
- 4 garlic cloves, minced
- 1 tablespoon minced fresh thyme or ¾ teaspoon dried
- ¾ teaspoon table salt, divided
- 1½ pounds boneless country-style pork ribs, trimmed and cut into 1½-inch pieces
- ¼ teaspoon pepper
- 8 ounces kale, stemmed and cut into 1-inch pieces
- 2 tablespoons whole-grain mustard

1. Process one-third of beans and 1 cup broth in blender until smooth, about 30 seconds; transfer to slow cooker.

2. Microwave onions, oil, garlic, thyme, and ¼ teaspoon salt in bowl, stirring occasionally, until onions are softened, about 5 minutes; transfer to slow cooker. Stir in remaining beans and remaining 3 cups broth. Sprinkle pork with pepper and remaining ½ teaspoon salt and stir into slow cooker. Cover and cook until pork is tender, 6 to 7 hours on low or 4 to 5 hours on high.

3. Stir in kale, cover, and cook on high until tender, 20 to 30 minutes. Adjust consistency with extra hot broth as needed. Stir in mustard and season with salt and pepper to taste. Serve, drizzling individual portions with extra oil.

Slow-Cooker Brazilian Black Bean and Pork Stew

Serves 6 to 8 | **Cooking Time** 9 to 10 hours on low or 6 to 7 hours on high

WHY THIS RECIPE WORKS Inspired by feijoada, a classic Brazilian dish loaded with pork and beans, we've created an ultrasatisfying slow-cooker version: creamy black beans in a full-bodied, smoke-and-pork-infused broth, piled high with chorizo and tender, juicy ribs. We skip soaking the beans, instead adding a pinch of baking soda for even cooking. This helps the black beans become tender, not mealy, and gives the stew a more striking color by helping the beans retain their vibrant hue. We discovered that browning the different cuts of meat on the stovetop isn't necessary to achieve full, complex flavor. Adding a ham hock provides enough body and smokiness. Raising the ribs out of the cooking liquid by stacking them on top of the other ingredients keeps them from overcooking and becoming mushy, ensuring a perfect result every time. Serve this hearty dish with rice (see pages 298–299), if desired.

- 5 cups water
- 1 pound (2½ cups) dried black beans, picked over and rinsed
- 4 garlic cloves, peeled and smashed
- 2 bay leaves
- ½ teaspoon table salt
- ¼ teaspoon pepper
- ⅛ teaspoon baking soda
- 1 pound Spanish-style chorizo sausage, halved crosswise
- 1 smoked ham hock
- 1 onion, halved
- 1 (2½- to 3-pound) rack St. Louis–style spareribs, trimmed and cut into 3 pieces
  Orange wedges

1. Combine water, beans, garlic, bay leaves, salt, pepper, and baking soda in slow cooker. Nestle chorizo, ham hock, and onion into bean mixture. Season ribs with salt and pepper. Place ribs on top of bean mixture, taking care to submerge as little of ribs as possible and overlapping as necessary. Cook until beans and ribs are tender, 6 to 7 hours on high or 9 to 10 hours on low.

2. Transfer ribs, ham hock, and chorizo to cutting board and tent with aluminum foil. Discard onion and bay leaves. Transfer 1 cup of beans to bowl and mash with potato masher or fork until smooth; stir mashed beans back into stew in slow cooker.

3. Shred meat from ham hock into bite-size pieces; discard fat and bones. Stir shredded meat into stew. Slice chorizo ½ inch thick. Slice ribs between bones. Transfer meat to platter and serve with stew, passing orange wedges separately.

Slow-Cooker Tomatillo Chili with Pork and Hominy

Serves 8 to 10 | **Cooking Time** 9 to 10 hours on low or 6 to 7 hours on high

WHY THIS RECIPE WORKS In this classic green chili, chunks of pork slowly simmer in a bright sauce made from chiles and tomatillos while hominy both contributes to the dish's heartiness and helps thicken the sauce. The key to achieving the chili's bold flavors in a slow cooker is broiling the tomatillos along with the other aromatics and spices. Once charred, the vegetables and spices take on a rustic, smoky flavor, and we puree them to create a flavorful base. If you can't find fresh tomatillos, you can substitute three 11-ounce cans of tomatillos, drained, rinsed, and patted dry; broil as directed in step 1. Pork butt roast is often labeled Boston butt in the supermarket. For more spice, add the ribs and seeds from the poblano chiles.

Substitution: You can use yellow hominy in place of the white.

- 1½ pounds tomatillos, husks and stems removed, rinsed well, dried, and halved
- 1 onion, cut into 1-inch pieces
- 3 tablespoons vegetable oil
- 4 garlic cloves, minced
- ¾ teaspoon dried oregano
- 1 teaspoon ground cumin
  Pinch ground cloves
  Pinch ground cinnamon
- 2 (15-ounce) cans white hominy, rinsed
- 2½ cups chicken broth, plus extra as needed
- 3 poblano chiles, stemmed, seeded, and chopped fine
- 3 tablespoons instant tapioca
- 2 teaspoons sugar
- 2 bay leaves
- 1 (4-pound) boneless pork butt roast, pulled apart at seams, trimmed, and cut into 1½-inch pieces
- 1¼ teaspoons table salt
- ½ teaspoon pepper
- ¼ cup minced fresh cilantro

1. Position oven rack 6 inches from broiler element and heat broiler. Toss tomatillos and onion with oil, garlic, oregano, cumin, cloves, and cinnamon, then spread onto aluminum foil–lined rimmed baking sheet. Broil vegetables until blackened and beginning to soften, 5 to 10 minutes, rotating sheet halfway through broiling; let cool slightly.

2. Pulse vegetables, along with any accumulated juices, in food processor until almost smooth, about 10 pulses, scraping down sides of bowl as needed; transfer to slow cooker.

3. Stir hominy, broth, poblanos, tapioca, sugar, and bay leaves into slow cooker. Sprinkle pork with salt and pepper and stir into slow cooker. Cover and cook until pork is tender, 9 to 10 hours on low or 6 to 7 hours on high.

4. Discard bay leaves. Adjust consistency with extra hot broth as needed. Stir in cilantro and season with salt and pepper to taste. Serve.

Slow-Cooker White Bean and Tomato Soup

Serves 4 to 6 | **Cooking Time** 6 to 7 hours on low or 4 to 5 hours on high **VEGAN**

WHY THIS RECIPE WORKS This soup fits the bill when you want something wholesome to eat: It's simple, comforting, and nourishing. It relies on a harmonious mix of vegetables for its sweet notes and canned white beans for heartiness. We start the flavorful soup base by sautéing carrot, onion, fennel, and garlic in a skillet until the vegetables are slightly softened and lightly browned, and then add the mixture to the slow cooker. Next, we stir in drained cannellini beans; vegetable (or chicken) broth; canned crushed tomatoes; and a sprinkle of slightly minty, floral dried thyme. We don't rinse the beans, as the starchy liquid clinging to them helps give the soup body. After the vegetables have fully softened and the flavors have mingled in the slow cooker, we puree a measured amount of beans, vegetables, and liquid to create a velvety consistency without the need for flour, ground bread, or heavy cream, keeping this soup gluten- and dairy-free. For a spectacular savory finish, we drizzle the soup with an aromatic kalamata-fennel oil we make by combining olive oil, chopped kalamata olives, ground fennel, and red pepper flakes, microwaving the mixture until fragrant and steeping it before stirring in minced fresh parsley.

Slow-Cooker White Bean and Tomato Soup

SOUP
- ¼ cup extra-virgin olive oil
- 1 cup chopped carrot
- 1 cup chopped onion
- 1 cup chopped fennel bulb
- 3 garlic cloves, minced
- 1¼ teaspoons table salt, divided
- ½ teaspoon pepper
- 3 (15-ounce) cans cannellini beans, drained
- 4 cups vegetable or chicken broth
- 1 (28-ounce) can crushed tomatoes
- ½ teaspoon dried thyme

KALAMATA-FENNEL OIL
- ⅓ cup extra-virgin olive oil
- 3 tablespoons chopped pitted kalamata olives
- 1 teaspoon ground fennel
- ½ teaspoon red pepper flakes
- 1 tablespoon minced fresh parsley

1. FOR THE SOUP Heat oil in 12-inch nonstick skillet over medium heat until shimmering. Add carrot, onion, fennel, garlic, ½ teaspoon salt, and pepper and cook until vegetables begin to soften and brown, 8 to 10 minutes, stirring occasionally. Transfer vegetable mixture to slow cooker.

2. Stir beans, broth, tomatoes, thyme, and remaining ¾ teaspoon salt into slow cooker. Cover and cook until vegetables have softened and flavors have melded, 6 to 7 hours on low or 4 to 5 hours on high.

3. FOR THE KALAMATA-FENNEL OIL Combine oil, olives, fennel, and pepper flakes in small bowl or 1-cup liquid measuring cup and microwave until fragrant, 30 to 60 seconds. Let cool for 5 minutes, then stir in parsley.

4. Transfer 3 cups vegetables and beans (using slotted spoon) and 2 cups liquid (using ladle) to blender. Process until smooth, about 2 minutes. Stir puree into soup in slow cooker. Season with salt and pepper to taste. Serve, drizzling each portion with kalamata-fennel oil.

Slow-Cooker Garden Minestrone

Serves 6 to 8 | **Cooking Time** 9 to 10 hours on high
`VEGAN`

WHY THIS RECIPE WORKS Creating garden-fresh dishes in a slow cooker is a tall order, but we achieve it with this lively minestrone, which incorporates tomato broth, beans for heft, fresh vegetables, and pasta. We microwave the aromatics, then add them to the slow cooker with broth and tomato sauce. Carrots and dried beans—both of which can sustain a long stay in a slow cooker—go in at the same time. Zucchini and chard are added toward the end of cooking, precooked pasta is stirred in last, and basil just before serving. Serve with crusty bread or Garlic Toasts (page 363) to dip into the broth.

Substitution: You can use dried cannellini beans in place of the great northern beans.

1 onion, chopped fine
4 garlic cloves, minced
1 tablespoon plus 1 teaspoon extra-virgin olive oil, divided, plus extra for serving
1½ teaspoons minced fresh oregano or ½ teaspoon dried
⅛ teaspoon red pepper flakes
8 cups vegetable or chicken broth
1 (15-ounce) can tomato sauce

1 cup dried great northern beans, picked over and rinsed
2 carrots, peeled and cut into ½-inch pieces
½ cup small pasta, such as ditalini, tubettini, or elbow macaroni
  Table salt, for cooking pasta
1 zucchini, quartered lengthwise and sliced ¼ inch thick
8 ounces Swiss chard, stemmed and sliced ½ inch thick
½ cup chopped fresh basil
  Grated Parmesan cheese (optional)

1. Microwave onion, garlic, 1 tablespoon oil, oregano, and pepper flakes in bowl, stirring occasionally, until onion is softened, about 5 minutes; transfer to slow cooker. Stir in broth, tomato sauce, beans, and carrots. Cover and cook until beans are tender, 9 to 10 hours on high.

2. Meanwhile, bring 2 quarts water to boil in large saucepan. Add pasta and 1½ teaspoons salt and cook, stirring often, until al dente. Drain pasta, rinse with cold water, then toss with remaining 1 teaspoon oil in bowl; set aside.

3. Stir zucchini and chard into soup, cover, and cook on high until tender, 20 to 30 minutes. Stir in pasta and let sit until heated through, about 5 minutes. Stir in basil and season with salt and pepper to taste. Serve, passing Parmesan, if using, and extra oil separately.

Slow-Cooker Garden Minestrone

Slow-Cooker Black Bean Soup

Serves 6 to 8 | **Cooking Time** 9 to 10 hours on high

WHY THIS RECIPE WORKS To create an easy black bean soup that is robust even after hours in the slow cooker, we add chili powder to our microwaved aromatics, toss in a smoked ham hock (which we later shred), and include chopped celery and carrot. We put dried black beans directly into the slow cooker where the gentle simmering heat helps them cook through evenly. As for texture, we tried thickeners such as flour, but they only muted the overall flavor of the soup. Mashing some of the cooked beans and stirring them back into the finished soup works best, providing excellent body and intensifying flavors and textures. To add a touch of brightness, we stir in minced fresh cilantro. Serve this soup with minced red onion, sour cream, and hot sauce.

- 2 onions, chopped fine
- 6 garlic cloves, minced
- 2 tablespoons vegetable oil
- 2 tablespoons chili powder
- 3 cups chicken broth
- 3 cups water
- 1 pound (2½ cups) dried black beans, picked over and rinsed
- 1 (12-ounce) smoked ham hock, rinsed
- 3 celery ribs, cut into ½-inch pieces
- 2 carrots, peeled and cut into ½-inch pieces
- 2 bay leaves
- 2 tablespoons minced fresh cilantro

1. Microwave onions, garlic, oil, and chili powder in bowl, stirring occasionally, until onions are softened, about 5 minutes; transfer to slow cooker. Stir in broth, water, beans, ham hock, celery, carrots, and bay leaves. Cover and cook until beans are tender, 9 to 10 hours on high.

2. Transfer ham hock to cutting board, let cool slightly, then shred into bite-size pieces using 2 forks; discard fat, skin, and bones. Discard bay leaves.

3. Mash portion of beans with potato masher until soup is thickened to desired consistency. Stir in ham and let sit until heated through, about 5 minutes. Stir in cilantro and season with salt and pepper to taste. Serve.

Slow-Cooker French Lentil Stew

Serves 6 | **Cooking Time** 7 to 8 hours on low or 4 to 5 hours on high

WHY THIS RECIPE WORKS For a warming stew with a deep flavor profile and hearty texture, we turn to lentilles du Puy (French green lentils) and brown rice. The lentils retain some of their texture during cooking without getting too soft in this filling stew, while brown rice adds depth of flavor and also breaks down slightly as it cooks, helping to thicken the dish with its starch. Caramelizing the onions requires getting out a skillet, but the payoff is a richly flavored foundation for the stew. Searching for a hearty green to offer a colorful contrast to the dark lentils, we settled on shredded brussels sprouts, which we add at the end of the cooking time. A little sherry vinegar stirred in just before serving helps to brighten the stew.

Substitution: Short-grain brown rice can be used in place of the long-grain rice. We like lentilles du Puy for this recipe, however you can use any dried lentils, except red or yellow.

- 2 slices bacon, chopped fine
- 3 onions, chopped fine
- ½ teaspoon brown sugar
- ½ teaspoon table salt
- 3 garlic cloves, minced
- 1 tablespoon minced fresh thyme or ¾ teaspoon dried
- 1 tablespoon yellow mustard seeds
- 1½ teaspoons ground coriander
  Pinch cayenne pepper
- 8 cups chicken broth, divided, plus extra as needed
- 4 carrots, peeled, halved lengthwise, and sliced ½ inch thick
- 1 cup lentilles du Puy, picked over and rinsed
- ½ cup long-grain brown rice, rinsed
- 8 ounces brussels sprouts, trimmed, halved, and sliced thin
- 2 tablespoons sherry vinegar

1. Cook bacon in 12-inch skillet over medium heat until crisp, 5 to 7 minutes. Add onions, sugar, and salt, cover, and cook until onions are softened, about 5 minutes. Uncover, reduce heat to medium-low, and continue to cook, stirring often, until onions are caramelized, about 20 minutes. Stir in garlic, thyme, mustard seeds, coriander, and cayenne and cook until fragrant, about 30 seconds. Stir in 1 cup broth, scraping up any browned bits; transfer to slow cooker.

2. Stir remaining 7 cups broth, carrots, lentils, and rice into slow cooker. Cover and cook until lentils are tender, 7 to 8 hours on low or 4 to 5 hours on high.

3. Stir brussels sprouts into stew and let sit until softened, about 5 minutes. Adjust consistency with extra hot broth as needed. Stir in vinegar and season with salt and pepper to taste. Serve.

Slow-Cooker Hearty Vegetarian Chili

Serves 6 to 8 | **Cooking Time** 9 to 10 hours on high
VEGAN

WHY THIS RECIPE WORKS Vegan and vegetarian chilis often rely on a mix of beans and vegetables for heartiness, but neither really adds meaty depth. For a hearty chili that is as rich, savory, and deeply satisfying as any meat chili out there, we start with dried navy beans, which turn tender and creamy with the long simmer. To up the heartiness of the chili and provide textural dimension, we add bulgur. After a quick rinse and a few minutes in the microwave, bulgur needs just 5 to 10 minutes in the slow cooker to fully soften and absorb the rich flavors. We ramp up the intensity and depth of our chili with soy sauce, dried shiitakes, tomato paste, oregano, and cumin. Don't confuse bulgur with cracked wheat, which has a much longer cooking time and will not work in this recipe.

2 onions, chopped fine
3 tablespoons chili powder
¼ cup tomato paste
2 tablespoons vegetable oil
4 teaspoons dried oregano
1 tablespoon ground cumin
1¼ teaspoons table salt, divided
1 pound (2½ cups) dried navy beans, picked over and rinsed
3 tablespoons soy sauce
½ ounce dried shiitake mushrooms, rinsed and minced
⅔ cup medium-grind bulgur, rinsed

1. Microwave onions, chili powder, tomato paste, oil, oregano, cumin, and 1 teaspoon salt in bowl, stirring occasionally, until onions are softened, about 5 minutes; transfer to slow cooker. Stir in beans, 9 cups water, soy sauce, and mushrooms. Cover and cook until beans are tender, 9 to 10 hours on high.

Slow-Cooker Hearty
Vegetarian Chili

2. Microwave bulgur, 2 cups water, and remaining ¼ teaspoon salt in covered bowl until bulgur is softened, about 5 minutes; drain bulgur and stir into chili. Cover and cook on high until bulgur is tender, 5 to 10 minutes. Adjust consistency with extra hot water as needed. Season with salt and pepper to taste. Serve.

Slow-Cooker Black Bean Chili

Serves 6 to 8 | **Cooking Time** 9 to 10 hours on high
VEGAN

WHY THIS RECIPE WORKS Our rich and hearty bean chili is so satisfying and flavorful, no one will miss the meat. Vegetarian versions of black bean chili can be tricky since there are no ham products, like meaty, smoky ham hocks, to build flavor over the long cooking time. To achieve the full flavors we want from black bean chili, we first brown a generous amount of aromatics and spices. A surprise ingredient, mustard seeds, bring an appealing pungency and complexity to the dish. To

Slow-Cooker Black Bean Chili

Slow-Cooker Greek Chicken with Warm Tabbouleh

bulk up the chili, we add red bell peppers, white mushrooms, and canned tomatoes, putting the tomatoes in toward the end because otherwise their acidity prevents the beans from cooking through fully. Minced cilantro and a spritz of fresh lime are essential for welcome brightness.

- 2 tablespoons vegetable oil
- 2 onions, chopped fine
- 2 red bell peppers, stemmed, seeded, and chopped fine
- 2 jalapeño chiles, stemmed, seeded, and minced
- 9 garlic cloves, minced
- 3 tablespoons chili powder
- 4 teaspoons yellow mustard seeds
- 1 tablespoon minced canned chipotle chile in adobo sauce
- 1 tablespoon ground cumin
- 1 tablespoon dried oregano
- 2½ cups vegetable or chicken broth, divided, plus extra as needed
- 2½ cups water
- 1 pound (2½ cups) dried black beans, picked over and rinsed
- 10 ounces white mushrooms, trimmed and halved if small or quartered if large
- 2 bay leaves
- 1 (28-ounce) can whole peeled tomatoes, drained and cut into ½-inch pieces
- 2 tablespoons minced fresh cilantro
  Lime wedges

1. Heat oil in 12-inch skillet over medium heat until shimmering. Add onions and bell peppers and cook until vegetables are softened and lightly browned, 8 to 10 minutes. Stir in jalapeños, garlic, chili powder, mustard seeds, chipotle, cumin, and oregano and cook until fragrant, about 1 minute. Stir in 1 cup broth, scraping up any browned bits; transfer to slow cooker.

2. Stir remaining 1½ cups broth, water, beans, mushrooms, and bay leaves into slow cooker. Cover and cook until beans are tender, 9 to 10 hours on high.

3. Discard bay leaves. Transfer 1 cup cooked beans to bowl and mash with potato masher until mostly smooth. Stir mashed beans and tomatoes into chili and let sit until heated through, about 5 minutes. Adjust consistency with extra hot broth as needed. Stir in cilantro and season with salt and pepper to taste. Serve with lime wedges.

Slow-Cooker Greek Chicken with Warm Tabbouleh

Serves 4 | **Cooking Time** 2 to 3 hours on low

WHY THIS RECIPE WORKS Looking for bright, fresh flavors and heartiness to pair with our Greek-inspired chicken, we thought about adding grain to the dish. However, most grains need to cook for much longer than chicken to become tender enough to eat. Fortunately, our testing revealed that medium-grind bulgur is one of the few hearty grains that can cook through in the slow cooker without breaking down and becoming gummy, so we developed a tabbouleh, which is made with bulgur. We rub the chicken with an aromatic mixture of garlic, oregano, and lemon zest, which seasons both the chicken and the bulgur as it cooks. We drain the bulgur at the end of cooking to remove excess liquid and season it further with olive oil, lemon juice, parsley, and tomatoes to turn the hearty grain into a vibrant salad. Check the chicken's temperature after 2 hours of cooking and continue to monitor until it registers 160 degrees. Don't confuse bulgur with cracked wheat, which has a much longer cooking time and will not work in this recipe.

- 1 cup medium-grind bulgur, rinsed
- 1 cup vegetable or chicken broth
- ¾ teaspoon plus ⅛ teaspoon table salt, divided
- 3 tablespoons extra-virgin olive oil, divided
- 4 teaspoons minced fresh oregano, divided
- 1¼ teaspoons grated lemon zest, divided, plus 3 tablespoons juice
- 1 garlic clove, minced
- ¼ teaspoon pepper
- 4 (12-ounce) bone-in split chicken breasts, skin removed, trimmed
- ½ cup plain Greek yogurt
- ½ cup minced fresh parsley, divided
- 3 tablespoons water
- 8 ounces cherry tomatoes, quartered

1. Lightly coat slow cooker with vegetable oil spray. Combine bulgur, broth, and ¼ teaspoon salt in slow cooker. Microwave 1 tablespoon oil, 1 tablespoon oregano, 1 teaspoon lemon zest, garlic, pepper, and ½ teaspoon salt in bowl until fragrant, about 30 seconds; let cool slightly. Rub chicken with oregano mixture, then arrange, skinned side up, in even layer in prepared slow cooker. Cover and cook until chicken registers 160 degrees, 2 to 3 hours on low.

2. Whisk yogurt, 1 tablespoon parsley, water, remaining ⅛ teaspoon salt, remaining 1 teaspoon oregano, and remaining ¼ teaspoon lemon zest together in bowl. Season with salt and pepper to taste.

3. Transfer chicken to serving dish, brushing any bulgur that sticks to breasts back into slow cooker. Drain bulgur mixture, if necessary, and return to now-empty slow cooker. Add tomatoes, lemon juice, remaining 7 tablespoons parsley, and remaining 2 tablespoons oil and fluff with fork to combine. Season with salt and pepper to taste. Serve chicken with tabbouleh and yogurt sauce.

Slow-Cooker Lemony Chicken and Rice with Spinach and Feta

Serves 4 | **Cooking Time** 4 to 5 hours on low

WHY THIS RECIPE WORKS For a chicken and rice dinner big on flavor but light on prep, we rely on the slow cooker, Mediterranean flavors, and instant rice. We include feta for its briny tang, lemon for brightness, and baby spinach for freshness and color. To start, we microwave aromatics to develop their flavor before adding them to the slow cooker. We then add meaty chicken thighs and cook them until tender. Once the thighs are cooked, we remove them and stir in instant rice, then nestle the chicken on top so it stays warm as the rice cooks. Do not use traditional rice, as it takes much longer to cook than instant rice (sometimes labeled minute rice).

- 1 onion, chopped fine
- 2 tablespoons extra-virgin olive oil
- 3 garlic cloves, minced
- 2 teaspoons minced fresh oregano or ½ teaspoon dried
- 1 teaspoon table salt, divided
- ½ cup chicken broth
- 8 (5- to 7-ounce) bone-in chicken thighs, skin removed, trimmed
- ½ teaspoon pepper
- 1½ cups instant white rice
- 4 ounces (4 cups) baby spinach
- 1 teaspoon grated lemon zest plus 2 tablespoons juice
- 2 ounces feta cheese, crumbled (½ cup)
- 2 tablespoons minced fresh parsley

Slow-Cooker Lemony Chicken and Rice with Spinach and Feta

Slow-Cooker Chicken Thighs with Black-Eyed Pea Ragout

Serves 4 | **Cooking Time** 4 to 5 hours on low

WHY THIS RECIPE WORKS Juicy chicken, tender black-eyed peas, and earthy kale are a great combination for a healthy and comforting supper. The chicken thighs pair beautifully with the rich, slightly spicy canned black-eyed peas, and sturdy kale is a pleasant, slightly bitter counterpoint. Kale is also a perfect match for the slow cooker; after a quick spin in the microwave (along with onion, garlic, and oil) it can be added to the slow cooker simply to soften and cook through. We stir a spoonful of dry mustard into the kale; during cooking, it infuses the chicken with subtle flavor. Pureeing a portion of the peas helps to thicken the juices released from the chicken to make a flavorful ragout. Finishing the peas with hot sauce punches up the dish's heat and acidity.

- 1 pound kale, stemmed and chopped coarse
- 1 onion, chopped fine
- 4 garlic cloves, minced
- 1 tablespoon vegetable oil
- 1 teaspoon dry mustard
- 2 teaspoons minced fresh thyme or ½ teaspoon dried
- ½ cup chicken broth
- 2 (15-ounce) cans black-eyed peas, rinsed, divided
- 8 (5- to 7-ounce) bone-in chicken thighs, skin removed, trimmed
- ¼ teaspoon table salt
- ⅛ teaspoon pepper
- 2 teaspoons hot sauce

1. Microwave onion, oil, garlic, oregano, and ½ teaspoon salt in bowl, stirring occasionally, until onion is softened, about 5 minutes; transfer to slow cooker. Stir in broth. Sprinkle chicken with pepper and remaining ½ teaspoon salt and nestle into slow cooker. Cover and cook until chicken is tender, 4 to 5 hours on low.

2. Transfer chicken to plate. Stir rice into slow cooker. Arrange chicken on top of rice, adding any accumulated juices. Cover and cook on high until rice is tender, 20 to 30 minutes.

3. Transfer chicken to serving platter and tent with aluminum foil. Gently stir spinach into slow cooker, 1 handful at a time, and let sit until wilted, about 5 minutes. Stir in lemon zest and juice, and season with salt and pepper to taste. Transfer rice to dish with chicken and sprinkle with feta and parsley. Serve.

1. Microwave kale, onion, garlic, oil, mustard, and thyme in covered bowl, stirring occasionally, until vegetables are softened, 5 to 7 minutes; transfer to slow cooker.

2. Process broth and one-third of peas in food processor until smooth, about 30 seconds; transfer to slow cooker. Stir in remaining peas. Sprinkle chicken with salt and pepper and nestle into slow cooker. Cover and cook until chicken is tender, 4 to 5 hours on low.

3. Transfer chicken to serving dish. Stir hot sauce into ragout and season with salt and pepper to taste. Serve chicken with ragout.

Slow-Cooker Spice-Rubbed Chicken with Black Bean Salad

Serves 4 | **Cooking Time** 4 to 5 hours on low

WHY THIS RECIPE WORKS We use a Southwestern-inspired spice rub to flavor a whole chicken and pair it with a smoky salad made with canned black beans and frozen corn. Combining the beans with chipotle chile and cooking them with the chicken allows them to absorb some chicken juices and become more flavorful and tender. While the chicken rests, we drain the beans and toss them with bell pepper, corn, sliced scallions, lime juice, and olive oil. Check the chicken's temperature after 4 hours of cooking and continue to monitor until the breast registers 160 degrees and the thighs register 175 degrees.

- 5 teaspoons extra-virgin olive oil, divided
- 1 teaspoon ground cumin
- 1 teaspoon paprika
- 2 teaspoons grated lime zest plus ¼ cup juice (2 limes)
- 1½ teaspoons packed brown sugar
- ¼ teaspoon table salt
- ¼ teaspoon pepper
- 1 (4-pound) whole chicken, giblets discarded
- 1 (15-ounce) can black beans, rinsed
- 1 teaspoon minced canned chipotle chile in adobo sauce
- 1 red bell pepper, stemmed, seeded, and chopped fine
- 1 cup frozen corn, thawed
- 2 scallions, sliced thin

1. Microwave 2 teaspoons oil, cumin, and paprika in bowl until fragrant, about 30 seconds. Let spice mixture cool slightly, then stir in lime zest, sugar, salt, and pepper.

2. Using your fingers, gently loosen skin covering breast and thighs of chicken. Place half of spice mixture under skin, directly on meat in center of each side of breast and on thighs. Gently press skin to distribute spice mixture over meat. Rub entire exterior surface of chicken with remaining spice mixture.

3. Combine beans and chipotle in slow cooker. Place chicken, breast side down, on top of beans. Cover and cook until breast registers 160 degrees and thighs register 175 degrees, 4 to 5 hours on low.

4. Transfer chicken to carving board, tent with aluminum foil, and let rest for 20 minutes.

5. Drain beans and transfer to large bowl. Stir in bell pepper, corn, scallions, lime juice, and remaining 1 tablespoon oil. Season with salt and pepper to taste. Carve chicken, discarding skin if desired. Serve with bean salad.

Slow-Cooker Herbed Chicken with Warm Spring Vegetable Salad

Serves 4 | **Cooking Time** 4 to 5 hours on low

WHY THIS RECIPE WORKS Want a flavorful weeknight dinner that features a juicy whole chicken and crunchy, vibrant spring vegetables such as snap peas? Let your slow cooker do the work for you. A simple aromatic mixture of oil, shallot, garlic, and thyme gives the chicken layers of flavor. We rub the mixture under the skin to give it direct contact with the meat and place the chicken breast side down in the slow cooker to keep the breast meat moist during cooking. We scatter seasoned radish halves around the chicken. While the chicken rests before carving, we stir fresh sugar snap peas into the braised radishes in the slow cooker and cook on high so the snap peas are crisp-tender yet still vibrant. A creamy dill dressing is the perfect flavorful accompaniment to our spring vegetable salad. Check the chicken's temperature after 4 hours of cooking and continue to monitor until the breast registers 160 degrees and the thighs register 175 degrees.

Slow-Cooker Herbed Chicken with Warm Spring Vegetable Salad

¼ cup extra-virgin olive oil, divided
1 shallot, minced
4 garlic cloves, minced, divided
2 teaspoons minced fresh thyme or ½ teaspoon dried
¾ teaspoon plus ⅛ teaspoon table salt, divided
½ teaspoon pepper, divided
1 (4-pound) whole chicken, giblets discarded
1 pound radishes, trimmed and halved
1 pound sugar snap peas, strings removed
¼ cup plain whole-milk yogurt
¼ cup mayonnaise
2 tablespoons minced fresh dill
1 tablespoon red wine vinegar
1 teaspoon sugar
　 Lemon wedges

1. Microwave 3 tablespoons oil, shallot, three-quarters of garlic, thyme, ½ teaspoon salt, and ¼ teaspoon pepper in bowl until fragrant, about 30 seconds; let cool slightly.

2. Using your fingers, gently loosen skin covering breast and thighs of chicken. Place half of oil mixture under skin, directly on meat in center of each side of breast and on thighs. Gently press skin to distribute oil mixture over meat. Rub entire exterior surface of chicken with remaining oil mixture. Place chicken, breast side down, into slow cooker.

3. Toss radishes with remaining 1 tablespoon oil, ¼ teaspoon salt, and remaining ¼ teaspoon pepper in clean bowl, then arrange around chicken. Cover and cook until breast registers 160 degrees and thighs register 175 degrees, 4 to 5 hours on low.

4. Transfer chicken to carving board, tent with aluminum foil, and let rest while finishing vegetables. Stir snap peas into slow cooker, cover, and cook on high until crisp-tender, about 20 minutes.

5. Whisk yogurt, mayonnaise, dill, vinegar, sugar, remaining garlic, and remaining ⅛ teaspoon salt together in large bowl. Using slotted spoon, transfer vegetables to bowl with dressing and toss to coat; discard cooking liquid. Season salad with salt and pepper to taste. Carve chicken, discarding skin if desired. Serve with radish salad and lemon wedges.

Slow-Cooker Braised Chicken Sausages with White Bean Ragout

Serves 4 | **Cooking Time** 3 to 4 hours on low

WHY THIS RECIPE WORKS For this simple and hearty winter braise, sausage, beans, and rosemary are transformed into a rich, warming bean ragout by the gentle simmer of the slow cooker. For the main components of the dish, we use delicately flavored cannellini beans and Italian chicken sausage flavored with spices like fennel and caraway. We combine broth and wine with minced garlic and rosemary for a flavorful cooking liquid that seasons the beans as they cook. Cherry tomatoes add a pop of bright color and fresh flavor. Once the sausage is cooked and the beans are tender, we mash a portion of the beans and tomatoes together to help thicken the ragout. Stirring in some baby spinach right before serving brightens up this comforting dish. Italian turkey sausage can be substituted for the chicken sausage.

2 (15-ounce) cans cannellini beans, rinsed
¼ cup chicken broth
¼ cup dry white wine
2 garlic cloves, minced
1 sprig fresh rosemary
½ teaspoon table salt
½ teaspoon pepper
1½ pounds hot or sweet Italian chicken sausage
8 ounces cherry tomatoes
4 ounces (4 cups) baby spinach
2 tablespoons extra-virgin olive oil

1. Combine beans, broth, wine, garlic, rosemary sprig, salt, and pepper in slow cooker. Nestle sausage into slow cooker and top with tomatoes. Cover and cook until sausage is tender, 3 to 4 hours on low.

2. Transfer sausage to serving dish and tent with aluminum foil. Discard rosemary sprig. Transfer 1 cup bean-tomato mixture to bowl and mash with potato masher until mostly smooth.

3. Stir spinach, 1 handful at a time, and mashed bean mixture into slow cooker and let sit until spinach is wilted, about 5 minutes. Stir in oil and season with salt and pepper to taste. Serve sausages with ragout.

Slow-Cooker Braised Oxtails with White Beans and Tomatoes

Serves 6 to 8 | **Cooking Time** 9 to 10 hours on low or 6 to 7 hours on high

WHY THIS RECIPE WORKS Creamy white beans play a supporting role to succulent, beefy oxtails in this braise, our spin on a Turkish dish, etli kuru fasulye. To ensure rich, meaty flavor, we brown the oxtails in a skillet before sautéing the aromatics. For more aroma, we add a simple yet flavorful combination of eastern Mediterranean ingredients to give the braising liquid its character: sweet diced tomatoes; warm, earthy paprika; red pepper flakes; and pungent oregano. We then deglaze the skillet with broth to ensure a flavorful braising liquid, the key to this humble peasant dish that is surprisingly rich and satisfying. The beans go into the slow cooker with the oxtails to absorb their flavor and become even more tender. After braising, we make sure to remove the fat from the cooking liquid using a fat separator. To finish, we stir in a splash of sherry vinegar and some more fresh oregano to make an aromatic sauce. Try to buy oxtails that are approximately 2 inches thick and 2 to 4 inches in diameter. Oxtails can often be found in the freezer section of the grocery store; if using frozen oxtails, be sure to thaw them completely before using.

- 4 pounds oxtails, trimmed
- 1¾ teaspoon table salt, divided
- ¼ teaspoon pepper
- 2 tablespoons extra-virgin olive oil
- 1 onion, chopped fine
- 1 carrot, peeled and chopped fine
- 6 garlic cloves, minced
- 2 tablespoons tomato paste
- 1 tablespoon minced fresh oregano, divided
- 1 teaspoon paprika
- ½ teaspoon red pepper flakes
- 2 cups chicken broth
- 2 (15-ounce) cans diced tomatoes, drained
- 1 (15-ounce) can navy beans, rinsed
- 1 tablespoon sherry vinegar

Slow-Cooker Braised Chicken Sausages with White Bean Ragout

Slow-Cooker Braised Oxtails with White Beans and Tomatoes

1. Pat oxtails dry with paper towels and sprinkle with ¾ teaspoon salt and pepper. Heat oil in 12-inch skillet over medium-high heat until just smoking. Brown half of oxtails on all sides, 8 to 10 minutes; transfer to plate. Repeat with remaining oxtails; transfer to plate.

2. Add onion, carrot, and remaining 1 teaspoon salt to fat left in skillet and cook over medium heat until vegetables are softened, about 5 minutes. Stir in garlic, tomato paste, 1 teaspoon oregano, paprika, and pepper flakes and cook until fragrant, about 30 seconds. Stir in broth, scraping up any browned bits; transfer to slow cooker.

3. Stir tomatoes and beans into slow cooker. Nestle oxtails into slow cooker, adding any accumulated juices. Cover and cook until oxtails are tender and fork slips easily in and out of meat, 9 to 10 hours on low or 6 to 7 hours on high.

4. Transfer oxtails to serving dish, tent with aluminum foil, and let rest while finishing sauce. Strain cooking liquid into fat separator, reserving solids, and let sit for 5 minutes. Transfer reserved solids and defatted liquid to serving bowl. Stir in vinegar and remaining 2 teaspoons oregano and season with salt and pepper to taste. Spoon 1 cup sauce over oxtails and serve, passing remaining sauce separately.

Slow-Cooker Braised Pork Chops with Campfire Beans

Serves 4 | **Cooking Time** 7 to 8 hours on low or 4 to 5 hours on high

WHY THIS RECIPE WORKS Beans are a classic accompaniment to pork dishes, in many different iterations. This braise complements meaty pork chops with a side of hearty barbecue beans. To create a deeply flavored sauce, we use a small amount of ketchup and molasses for the necessary sweetness and viscosity and then amp up the flavor with onion, chili powder, and liquid smoke. Canned pinto beans turn creamy and tender in the slow cooker as they absorb the smoky flavor of the sauce and help braise the chops. We use blade-cut pork chops, which contain a good amount of fat and connective tissue that help them stay tender and juicy during hours of braising. To really wake up the flavor of the beans before serving, we stir in cider vinegar and Dijon mustard for a hit of piquant freshness.

Substitution: You can use canned navy beans in place of the pinto beans.

Slow-Cooker Braised Pork Chops with Campfire Beans

1 onion, chopped fine
2 garlic cloves, minced
1 teaspoon chili powder
1 tablespoon vegetable oil
2 (15-ounce) cans pinto beans, rinsed
¼ cup ketchup
1 tablespoon molasses
½ teaspoon liquid smoke
4 (8- to 10-ounce) bone-in blade-cut pork chops, ¾ inch thick, trimmed
½ teaspoon table salt
½ teaspoon pepper
1 tablespoon cider vinegar
1 tablespoon Dijon mustard
2 scallions, sliced thin

1. Microwave onion, garlic, chili powder, and oil in bowl, stirring occasionally, until onion is softened, about 5 minutes; transfer to slow cooker. Stir in beans, ketchup, molasses, and liquid smoke.

2. Cut 2 slits about 2 inches apart through fat on edges of each pork chop. Season chops with salt and pepper and nestle into slow cooker. Cover and cook until pork is tender, 7 to 8 hours on low or 4 to 5 hours on high.

3. Transfer chops to serving dish, tent with aluminum foil, and let rest for 5 minutes. Using large spoon, skim fat from surface of sauce. Transfer 1 cup beans to bowl and mash with potato masher until mostly smooth. Stir mashed beans, vinegar, mustard, and scallions into remaining beans, and season with salt and pepper to taste. Serve chops with beans.

Slow-Cooker Pork Loin with Warm Spiced Chickpea Salad

Serves 6 to 8 | **Cooking Time** 2 to 3 hours on low

WHY THIS RECIPE WORKS Inspired by the lively flavors of Moroccan cuisine, we created this satisfying meal featuring moist pork loin and a spice-infused chickpea salad. First we brown the pork in a skillet, and then cook the onion and garlic, and bloom coriander, cumin, and cloves in the same skillet to give them flavor from the pork fond. The pork loin, spices, and onion go into the slow cooker with the chickpeas, infusing them with aroma and flavor as the meat cooks. Once the pork is done, we let it rest for 20 minutes to help the lean meat retain its juices when sliced. Meanwhile we flavor our chickpea salad with dried apricots, roasted red peppers, and shallots to offset its savory spice with a touch of sweetness. A wider, shorter pork loin (about 8 inches long) fits best in the slow cooker. A ⅛-inch-thick layer of fat on top of the roast is ideal. Check the pork's temperature after 2 hours of cooking and continue to monitor it until it registers 140 degrees.

- 1 (3- to 4-pound) boneless center-cut pork loin roast, trimmed and tied at 1-inch intervals
- ½ teaspoon table salt
- ½ teaspoon pepper
- 2 tablespoons extra-virgin olive oil, divided
- 1 onion, chopped fine
- 2 garlic cloves, minced
- 1 teaspoon ground coriander
- ½ teaspoon ground cumin
- ¼ teaspoon ground cloves
- ½ cup chicken broth
- 3 (15-ounce) cans chickpeas, rinsed
- ½ cup dried apricots, chopped
- ½ cup jarred roasted red peppers, rinsed, patted dry, and chopped

Slow-Cooker Pork Loin with Warm Spiced Chickpea Salad

- 1 shallot, sliced thin
- ¼ cup chopped fresh mint
- 1 tablespoon white wine vinegar

1. Pat pork dry with paper towels and season with salt and pepper. Heat 1 tablespoon oil in 12-inch skillet over medium-high heat until just smoking. Brown roast on all sides, 7 to 10 minutes; transfer to plate.

2. Heat remaining 1 tablespoon oil in now-empty skillet over medium heat until shimmering. Add onion and cook until softened and lightly browned, 5 to 7 minutes. Add garlic, coriander, cumin, and cloves and cook until fragrant, about 30 seconds. Stir in broth, scraping up any browned bits; transfer to slow cooker.

3. Stir chickpeas into slow cooker. Nestle roast, fat side up, into slow cooker, adding any accumulated juices. Cover and cook until pork registers 140 degrees, 2 to 3 hours on low.

4. Transfer roast to carving board, tent with aluminum foil, and let rest for 20 minutes.

5. Stir apricots, red peppers, and shallot into chickpea mixture and let sit until heated through, about 5 minutes. Stir in mint and vinegar and season with salt and pepper to taste. Remove twine from roast and slice meat ½ inch thick. Serve with salad.

Slow-Cooker Rustic Pork and White Bean Casserole

Serves 6 to 8 | **Cooking Time** 6 to 7 hours on low or 4 to 5 hours on high

WHY THIS RECIPE WORKS Inspired by classic French cassoulet, we set out to create a casserole we could make in our slow cooker and pack it with beans, vegetables, and smoky pork flavor. For the meat we use easy-prep boneless country-style pork ribs, cutting them into 1½-inch pieces before adding them to the slow cooker. For smoky flavor, bacon is an easy choice, and we microwave it along with the aromatics and vegetables. To bolster the flavor of the casserole, we microwave chopped onions with plenty of garlic, as well as tomato paste for richness and body. To thicken the casserole, we process a can of whole peeled tomatoes and half the beans to a paste before adding them to the slow cooker. The remaining beans are left whole and simmer along with the vegetables and the aromatics. The finishing touch to our rustic dish is crusty toasted croutons made from a small baguette; tossing the croutons with minced fresh oregano and a little olive oil adds a welcome pepperiness.

- 1 (14.5-ounce) can whole peeled tomatoes
- 2 (15-ounce) cans cannellini beans, rinsed, divided
- 2 onions, chopped fine
- 2 slices bacon, chopped fine
- 3 tablespoons tomato paste
- 3 tablespoons minced fresh oregano, divided
- 6 garlic cloves, minced
- 1 teaspoon table salt, divided
- 8 ounces parsnips, peeled and cut into ½-inch pieces
- 4 carrots, peeled and cut into ½-inch pieces
- ¼ cup dry white wine
- 1½ pounds boneless country-style pork ribs, trimmed and cut into 1½-inch pieces
- ¼ teaspoon pepper
- 1 (12-inch) baguette, cut into ½-inch pieces
- 2 tablespoons extra-virgin olive oil, plus extra for drizzling

1. Process tomatoes and their juice and half of beans in blender until smooth, about 30 seconds; transfer to slow cooker.

2. Microwave onions, bacon, tomato paste, 1 tablespoon oregano, garlic, and ½ teaspoon salt in bowl, stirring occasionally, until onions are softened, about 5 minutes; transfer to slow cooker. Stir in remaining beans, parsnips, carrots, and wine. Sprinkle pork with pepper and remaining ½ teaspoon salt and stir into slow cooker. Cover and cook until pork is tender, 6 to 7 hours on low or 4 to 5 hours on high.

3. Adjust oven rack to middle position and heat oven to 450 degrees. Arrange bread in single layer on rimmed baking sheet and bake until browned and crisp, about 10 minutes, stirring halfway through baking. Toss croutons with oil and remaining 2 tablespoons oregano, and season with salt and pepper to taste; set aside for serving.

4. Adjust consistency of filling as needed with hot water. Season with salt and pepper to taste. Top individual portions with croutons and drizzle with extra oil. Serve.

Slow-Cooker Chickpea Tagine

Serves 4 to 6 | **Cooking Time** 8 to 9 hours on high

WHY THIS RECIPE WORKS This Moroccan-style stew gets its heft from chickpeas cooked till tender in the slow cooker, with complex flavor from sweet paprika and garam masala (an Indian blend of warm spices), along with onions, garlic, and orange zest, all of which perfume the sauce. Since many vegetables would be overcooked after hours in a slow cooker, we stir in softened bell peppers and jarred artichokes at the end, cooking them just enough to heat through. Continuing the Mediterranean flavor profile, we add chopped kalamata olives and Greek yogurt to the stew. Golden raisins and honey bring a touch of sweetness, and fresh cilantro brightens up the dish. While we prefer the flavor and texture of jarred whole baby artichokes, you can substitute 12 ounces frozen artichoke hearts, thawed and patted dry, for the jarred.

- 2 onions, chopped fine
- 3 tablespoons extra-virgin olive oil, divided, plus extra for drizzling
- 8 garlic cloves, minced
- 4 teaspoons paprika
- 2 teaspoons garam masala
- 4 cups vegetable or chicken broth, plus extra as needed
- 2 cups water
- 1 pound (2½ cups) dried chickpeas, picked over and rinsed
- 2 (2-inch) strips orange zest
- 2 red bell peppers, stemmed, seeded, and cut into ¼-inch-wide strips
- 2 cups jarred whole baby artichokes packed in water, halved, rinsed, and patted dry
- ½ cup pitted kalamata olives, chopped coarse
- ½ cup golden raisins
- ½ cup plain Greek yogurt
- ½ cup minced fresh cilantro
- 2 tablespoons honey

1. Microwave onions, 2 tablespoons oil, garlic, paprika, and garam masala in bowl, stirring occasionally, until onions are softened, about 5 minutes; transfer to slow cooker. Stir in broth, water, chickpeas, and orange zest. Cover and cook until chickpeas are tender, 8 to 9 hours on high.

2. Microwave bell peppers with remaining 1 tablespoon oil in bowl, stirring occasionally, until tender, about 5 minutes. Discard orange zest. Stir bell peppers, artichokes, olives, and raisins into tagine. Cover and cook on high until heated through, about 10 minutes.

3. Whisk ½ cup hot cooking liquid and yogurt together in bowl (to temper), then stir mixture back into slow cooker. Stir in cilantro and honey. Adjust consistency with extra hot broth as needed. Season with salt and pepper to taste. Serve, drizzling individual portions with extra oil.

Slow-Cooker Vegetables and Tofu with Indian Spices

Serves 4 to 6 | **Cooking Time** 4 to 5 hours on low or 3 to 4 hours on high `VEGAN`

WHY THIS RECIPE WORKS Sauced dishes are especially well suited to the slow cooker because when ingredients have the opportunity to cook for hours, their flavors meld and the result is a bold-tasting dish with complexity. Our version of an Indian sauced vegetable dish does exactly that, using traditional aromatics like onion, garlic, and ginger, and garam masala, a north Indian spice blend, to create layers of aroma and flavor. We use some nontraditional ingredients too: tofu for protein and curry powder to bump up the flavor quotient of the dish. Blooming the aromatics in the microwave helps intensify their flavors. For more savory depth, we include tomato paste. Cubed red potatoes contribute heartiness; precut frozen green beans add bulk and need zero prep. To turn the cooking liquid into an unctuous sauce, we add tapioca, which thickens it and makes it velvety. Then we stir in coconut milk, which is often used in south Indian sauced dishes to create a rich finish. Heating it in the microwave and adding it toward the end of cooking prevents the coconut milk from cooling down our dish and preserves its flavor. Finally, minced cilantro offers a touch of color and freshness. Serve with Spiced Basmati Rice Pilaf (page 299), if desired.

Slow-Cooker
Vegetables and Tofu
with Indian Spices

Substitution: You can use firm tofu in place of extra-firm. Do not use softer varieties such as silken tofu.

- 1 onion, chopped fine
- 3 garlic cloves, minced
- 1 tablespoon vegetable oil
- 1 tablespoon grated fresh ginger
- 1 tablespoon tomato paste
- 1 tablespoon curry powder
- ½ teaspoon garam masala
- ½ teaspoon table salt
- 4 cups vegetable or chicken broth, plus extra as needed
- 1 pound red potatoes, unpeeled, cut into ½-inch pieces
- 14 ounces extra-firm tofu, cut into ½-inch pieces
- 1 tablespoon instant tapioca
- 1 (13.5-ounce) can coconut milk
- 2 cups frozen cut green beans, thawed
- ¼ cup minced fresh cilantro

1. Microwave onion, garlic, oil, ginger, tomato paste, curry powder, garam masala, and salt in bowl, stirring occasionally, until onion is softened, about 5 minutes; transfer to slow cooker. Stir in broth, potatoes, tofu, and tapioca. Cover and cook until potatoes are tender, 4 to 5 hours on low or 3 to 4 hours on high.

2. Microwave coconut milk in bowl, whisking occasionally, until hot, about 3 minutes. Stir coconut milk and green beans into sauce and let sit until heated through, about 5 minutes. Adjust consistency with extra hot broth as needed. Stir in cilantro and season with salt and pepper to taste. Serve.

Slow-Cooker Thai Braised Butternut Squash with Tofu

Serves 4 to 6 | **Cooking Time** 3 to 4 hours on low or 2 to 3 hours on high `VEGAN`

WHY THIS RECIPE WORKS For this easy-to-make main dish, we braise tofu and chunks of butternut squash in a highly aromatic liquid base, making sure this braising medium is loaded with flavor since tofu tends to absorb liquid as it cooks. We use a trio of aromatics (onion, ginger, and garlic), along with Thai red curry paste, and bloom it all in the microwave to meld the flavors. At the end of the cooking time, we take this dish to the next level by adding coconut milk, lime juice, and cilantro.

Substitution: You can use firm tofu in place of extra-firm. Do not use softer varieties such as silken tofu.

- 1 onion, chopped fine
- 3 tablespoons Thai red curry paste
- 2 tablespoons grated fresh ginger, divided
- 4 garlic cloves, minced
- 4 teaspoons vegetable oil, divided
- 2 pounds butternut squash, peeled, seeded, and cut into 1-inch pieces (6 cups)
- 14 ounces extra-firm tofu, cut into ¾-inch pieces
- 1 cup vegetable or chicken broth, plus extra as needed
- 2 teaspoons instant tapioca
- 1 red bell pepper, stemmed, seeded, and cut into ¼-inch-wide strips
- 1 cup canned coconut milk
- 1 tablespoon lime juice, plus extra for seasoning
- ⅓ cup fresh cilantro leaves
- ¼ cup chopped dry-roasted peanuts

1. Microwave onion, curry paste, 1 tablespoon ginger, garlic, and 1 tablespoon oil in bowl, stirring occasionally, until onion is softened, about 5 minutes; transfer to slow cooker. Stir in squash, tofu, broth, and tapioca. Cover and cook until squash is tender, 3 to 4 hours on low or 2 to 3 hours on high.

2. Microwave bell pepper with remaining 1 teaspoon oil in bowl, stirring occasionally, until tender, about 5 minutes. Stir bell pepper, coconut milk, lime juice, and remaining 1 tablespoon ginger into slow cooker. Cover and cook on high until heated through, about 10 minutes.

3. Adjust sauce consistency with extra hot broth as needed. Season with salt, pepper, and extra lime juice to taste. Sprinkle individual portions with cilantro and peanuts before serving.

Slow-Cooker Mushroom Biryani

Serves 4 to 6 | **Cooking Time** 2 to 3 hours on high

WHY THIS RECIPE WORKS The best biryani recipes put fragrant long-grain basmati center stage, enriching it with fresh herbs and pungent spices. However, most recipes develop deep flavor through the time-consuming steps of steeping whole spices and cooking each part of the dish separately before marrying them, as we do for our Chicken Biryani (page 234). For a simple, streamlined, and hands-free version of the dish that still delivers the big, bold flavors we expect from a biryani, we turn to the slow cooker. We like the nutty flavor and fragrant aroma of basmati rice in this dish and we bloom a mixture of aromatics and spices with oil in the microwave to enhance their flavors. We combine the bloomed spice blend, rice, and hot vegetable broth in our slow cooker before topping the rice with hearty, earthy mushrooms. Layering the mushrooms on top of the rice mixture ensures that the rice cooks evenly. Basmati rice cooks best on high, and placing a piece of parchment paper over the mixture prevents the grains on top from drying out as the water is absorbed and promotes even steaming (see more on page 360). Once the rice is cooked, we add spinach, fresh herbs, and raisins before gently fluffing the rice. Biryani is traditionally served with a cooling raita or yogurt sauce. Ideally you should make the sauce before starting the biryani to allow the flavors to meld.

Substitution: You can use long-grain white rice in place of the basmati.

SAUCE

- ¾ cup plain yogurt
- 2 tablespoons chopped fresh cilantro
- 2 tablespoons chopped fresh mint
- 1 garlic clove, minced

BIRYANI

- 1 onion, chopped fine
- 3 tablespoons extra-virgin olive oil
- 4 garlic cloves, minced
- 2 teaspoons garam masala
- 1 teaspoon table salt
- ½ teaspoon turmeric
- ⅛ teaspoon cayenne pepper
- 1½ cups vegetable or chicken broth
- 1½ cups basmati rice, rinsed
- 1 pound cremini mushrooms, trimmed and sliced thin
- 6 ounces (6 cups) baby spinach, chopped coarse
- ¼ cup raisins
- 2 tablespoons chopped fresh cilantro
- 2 tablespoons chopped fresh mint
- ⅓ cup sliced almonds, toasted

1. FOR THE SAUCE Combine all ingredients in bowl and season with salt and pepper to taste. Refrigerate until ready to serve.

2. FOR THE BIRYANI Lightly coat slow cooker with vegetable oil spray. Microwave onion, oil, garlic, garam masala, salt, turmeric, and cayenne in bowl, stirring occasionally, until onion is softened, about 5 minutes; transfer to prepared slow cooker.

3. Microwave broth in bowl until steaming, about 5 minutes. Stir broth and rice into slow cooker. Spread mushrooms evenly on top of rice mixture. Gently press 16 by 12-inch sheet of parchment paper onto surface of mushrooms, folding down edges as needed. Cover and cook until rice is tender and all broth is absorbed, 2 to 3 hours on high.

4. Discard parchment. Sprinkle spinach and raisins on top of rice, cover, and let sit until spinach is wilted, about 5 minutes. Add cilantro and mint, and fluff rice with fork until combined. Season with salt and pepper to taste. Sprinkle with almonds and serve, passing sauce separately.

Slow-Cooker Mushroom Biryani

Slow-Cooker Turkish Eggplant Casserole

Serves 4 to 6 | **Cooking Time** 3 to 4 hours on low or 2 to 3 hours on high

WHY THIS RECIPE WORKS Earthy and versatile, eggplant goes well with beloved Turkish spices; namely, paprika, cumin, cayenne pepper, and cinnamon. We pair this spiced eggplant with bulgur, a popular grain of the region that cooks perfectly in the steamy environment of the slow cooker. We rub the eggplant with a spice mixture and broil it before adding it to the slow cooker, thereby cooking off extra moisture and keeping the slices firm. An herb-yogurt sauce adds a welcome richness and tang to this spiced dish. You will need an oval slow cooker for this recipe. Don't confuse bulgur with cracked wheat, which has a much longer cooking time and will not work in this recipe.

Slow-Cooker Turkish Eggplant Casserole

Slow-Cooker Red Beans and Rice with Okra and Tomatoes

SAUCE
- 1 cup plain yogurt
- ¼ cup chopped fresh parsley
- 2 tablespoons chopped fresh mint
- 1 garlic clove, minced

BULGUR
- 2 teaspoons paprika
- 1½ teaspoons ground cumin
- 1½ teaspoons table salt, divided
- ⅛ teaspoon cayenne pepper
- ⅛ teaspoon ground cinnamon
- 1½ pounds eggplant, sliced into ½-inch-thick rounds
- ¼ cup extra-virgin olive oil, divided
- 1 onion, chopped fine
- 4 garlic cloves, minced
- 1 tablespoon tomato paste
- 1 cup medium-grind bulgur, rinsed
- 1 cup vegetable or chicken broth
- 4 tomatoes, cored and sliced ½ inch thick

1. FOR THE SAUCE Combine all ingredients in bowl and season with salt and pepper to taste. Refrigerate until ready to serve.

2. FOR THE BULGUR Adjust oven rack 6 inches from broiler element and heat broiler. Combine paprika, cumin, ¾ teaspoon salt, cayenne, and cinnamon in bowl. Arrange eggplant in single layer on aluminum foil–lined rimmed baking sheet, brush both sides with 3 tablespoons oil, and sprinkle with spice mixture. Broil eggplant until softened and beginning to brown, 10 to 12 minutes, flipping eggplant halfway through broiling.

3. Lightly coat slow cooker with vegetable oil spray. Microwave onion, garlic, tomato paste, remaining ¾ teaspoon salt, and remaining 1 tablespoon oil in bowl, stirring occasionally, until onion is softened, about 5 minutes; transfer to prepared slow cooker. Stir in bulgur and broth. Shingle alternating slices of eggplant and tomato into 3 tightly fitting rows on top of bulgur mixture. Cover and cook until eggplant and bulgur are tender and all broth is absorbed, 3 to 4 hours on low or 2 to 3 hours on high. Serve, passing sauce separately.

Slow-Cooker Rustic Braised Lentils with Eggplant

Serves 4 to 6 | **Cooking Time** 3 to 4 hours on low or 2 to 3 hours on high

WHY THIS RECIPE WORKS For a hearty vegetarian main, we pair lentilles du Puy with eggplant to create a braised dish bursting with flavor. We broil the eggplant with our aromatics to deepen its taste and ensure that the eggplant cooks evenly and doesn't turn mushy in the slow cooker. We add cherry tomatoes because they break down and create a fresh tomato sauce to envelop the eggplant and lentils. We found it important to put the lentils and broth in the bottom of the slow cooker so that the lentils cook thoroughly and evenly. We then layer the broiled eggplant and fresh tomatoes on the lentils, stirring it all together after it is cooked.

> **Substitution:** We like lentilles du Puy for this recipe, however you can use any dried lentils, except red or yellow.

- 2 pounds eggplant, cut into 1-inch pieces
- 1 onion, chopped fine
- 3 tablespoons extra-virgin olive oil, divided
- 1 tablespoon tomato paste
- 2 garlic cloves, minced
- 2 teaspoons minced fresh thyme or ½ teaspoon dried
- ½ teaspoon table salt
- 2 cups vegetable or chicken broth
- 1 cup lentilles du Puy, picked over and rinsed
- 2 tablespoons red wine vinegar, divided
- 10 ounces cherry tomatoes, halved
- 2 ounces feta cheese, crumbled (½ cup)
- ¼ cup minced fresh parsley

1. Adjust oven rack 6 inches from broiler element and heat broiler. Line rimmed baking sheet with aluminum foil. Toss eggplant and onion with 1 tablespoon oil, tomato paste, garlic, thyme, and salt in bowl. Spread eggplant mixture evenly over prepared baking sheet. Broil until eggplant is softened and beginning to brown, 10 to 12 minutes, rotating sheet halfway through broiling.

2. Combine broth, lentils, and 1 tablespoon vinegar in slow cooker. Spread eggplant mixture and tomatoes evenly on top of lentils. Cover and cook until lentils are tender, 3 to 4 hours on low or 2 to 3 hours on high. Stir in remaining 2 tablespoons oil and remaining 1 tablespoon vinegar. Season with salt and pepper to taste. Sprinkle with feta and parsley and serve.

Slow-Cooker Red Beans and Rice with Okra and Tomatoes

Serves 4 to 6 | **Cooking Time** 8 to 9 hours on high
`VEGAN`

WHY THIS RECIPE WORKS Rather than monitor the stovetop for an hour or two so we could enjoy this Cajun classic, we moved it to the slow cooker, where the moist environment and gentle heat could turn our red beans tender and creamy without a lot of effort. Though the beans cook through perfectly with no advance prep (meaning you can skip the soaking step called for in many recipes), the rice can be a bit of a challenge. Because raw rice would become blown out and mushy by the time the beans are done, we instead stir instant rice in toward the end of cooking. It holds its shape and absorbs the rich flavors of the beans and broth. Using Cajun seasoning means we don't need to include a plethora of spices. Frozen okra, added at the end with some fresh tomatoes, reinforces the Cajun identity of our dish. Serve with hot sauce. Do not use traditional rice as it takes much longer to cook than instant rice (sometimes labeled minute rice).

- 2 tablespoons Cajun seasoning
- 2 tablespoons extra-virgin olive oil
- 3 garlic cloves, minced
- 4 cups vegetable or chicken broth
- 8 ounces (1¼ cups) dried small red beans, picked over and rinsed
- 1 green bell pepper, stemmed, seeded, and cut into ½-inch pieces
- 1½ cups instant white rice
- 2 cups frozen cut okra, thawed
- 2 tomatoes, cored and cut into ½-inch pieces
- 4 scallions, sliced thin

1. Microwave Cajun seasoning, oil, and garlic in bowl until fragrant, about 1 minute; transfer to slow cooker. Stir in broth, beans, and bell pepper. Cover and cook until beans are tender, 8 to 9 hours on high.

2. Stir in rice, cover, and cook on high until rice is tender, 20 to 30 minutes. Stir in okra and let sit until heated through, about 5 minutes. Stir in tomatoes and scallions, and season with salt and pepper to taste. Serve.

Slow-Cooker Farro Primavera

Serves 4 | **Cooking Time** 3 to 4 hours on low or 2 to 3 hours on high

WHY THIS RECIPE WORKS For an interesting take on pasta primavera, we swap out pasta for whole-grain farro and replace cream with nutty Parmesan. Since most of the vegetables for this dish, except the leek, go into the slow cooker at the end to ensure bright colors and fresh flavors, the point of using a slow cooker is the hands-off approach to perfectly cooked farro. To mellow the potent allium flavor of the leek, we give it a head start in the microwave. Once the farro is tender, we stir in some additional broth to help steam the asparagus in the last few minutes of cooking. Peas round out the spring vegetables for our primavera, and a generous portion of Parmesan cheese turns our dish creamy and rich-tasting.

Substitution: You can use pearl farro in place of the whole farro, but the texture may be softer. Do not use quick-cooking or presteamed farro (check the ingredient list on the package to determine this).

- 1 leek, white and light green parts only, halved lengthwise, sliced thin, and washed thoroughly
- 1 tablespoon extra-virgin olive oil
- 2 garlic cloves, minced
- 1 teaspoon minced fresh thyme or ¼ teaspoon dried
- ¼ teaspoon table salt
- 2½ cups vegetable or chicken broth, divided, plus extra as needed
- 1 cup whole farro
- 2 ounces Parmesan cheese, grated (1 cup), plus extra for serving
- 1 pound thin asparagus, trimmed and cut into 1-inch lengths
- 1 cup frozen peas, thawed

1. Lightly coat slow cooker with vegetable oil spray. Microwave leek, oil, garlic, thyme, and salt in bowl, stirring occasionally, until leek is softened, about 5 minutes; transfer to prepared slow cooker.

2. Microwave 2 cups broth in bowl until steaming, about 5 minutes. Stir broth and farro into slow cooker; cover; and cook until farro is tender, 3 to 4 hours on low or 2 to 3 hours on high.

3. Microwave remaining ½ cup broth in bowl until steaming, about 5 minutes. Stir broth and Parmesan into farro until mixture is creamy but still somewhat thin. Stir in asparagus, cover, and cook on high until tender, about 20 minutes. Stir in peas and let sit until heated through, about 5 minutes. Adjust farro consistency with extra hot broth as needed. Season with salt and pepper to taste. Serve, passing extra Parmesan separately.

Slow-Cooker Creamy Farro with Mushrooms and Thyme

Serves 4 to 6 | **Cooking Time** 3 to 4 hours on low or 2 to 3 hours on high

WHY THIS RECIPE WORKS Farro's nutty, mild flavor will happily lend itself to almost any culinary direction, but as it's a popular ingredient in Tuscan cuisine, we decided to give this dish a simple and fresh Italian profile. We start by softening our aromatics—shallots, garlic, and thyme—in the microwave with porcini mushrooms. Cremini mushrooms lend the dish meatiness, and sherry is a natural complement to add complexity. Once the farro is tender, we stir in just enough Parmesan to create a luxurious, creamy texture without overwhelming our well-balanced dish. Finishing with a couple tablespoons of fresh parsley adds brightness and freshness to balance the hearty, savory flavors. Do not use quick-cooking or presteamed farro (check the ingredient list on the package to determine this) instead of the whole farro.

- 2 shallots, minced
- ½ ounce dried porcini mushrooms, rinsed and minced
- 2 tablespoons extra-virgin olive oil, divided
- 3 garlic cloves, minced
- 2 teaspoons minced fresh thyme or ½ teaspoon dried
- ½ teaspoon table salt
- ½ teaspoon pepper
- 2½ cups vegetable or chicken broth, divided, plus extra as needed
- ¼ cup dry sherry
- 8 ounces cremini mushrooms, trimmed and sliced thin
- 1 cup whole farro
- 1 ounce Parmesan cheese, grated (½ cup)
- 2 tablespoons chopped fresh parsley

Slow-Cooker Creamy Farro with Mushrooms and Thyme

1. Lightly coat slow cooker with vegetable oil spray. Microwave shallots, porcini mushrooms, 1 tablespoon oil, garlic, thyme, salt, and pepper in bowl, stirring occasionally, until shallots are softened, about 5 minutes; transfer to prepared slow cooker.

2. Microwave 2 cups broth and sherry in bowl until steaming, about 5 minutes. Stir broth mixture, cremini mushrooms, and farro into slow cooker. Cover and cook until farro is tender, 3 to 4 hours on low or 2 to 3 hours on high.

3. Microwave remaining ½ cup broth in bowl until steaming, about 2 minutes. Stir broth and Parmesan into farro until mixture is creamy. Adjust consistency with extra hot broth as needed. Stir in parsley and remaining 1 tablespoon oil. Season with salt and pepper to taste. Serve.

Slow-Cooker Wheat Berries with Carrots and Orange

Serves 6 to 8 | **Cooking Time** 4 to 5 hours on low or 3 to 4 hours on high

WHY THIS RECIPE WORKS Orange and tarragon are a classic pairing, and it's easy to understand why: Pieces of sweet-tart orange boost and brighten tarragon's grassy licorice notes, creating a remarkably vibrant flavor. This combination shines against a backdrop of mildly nutty wheat berries, especially after we add shredded carrots for crunch and orange zest for a deeper citrus flavor. A simple red wine vinaigrette finishes off this fresh, crowd-pleasing salad with a sophisticated mix of flavors. We found that cooking our wheat berries in a large amount of water, much as we would cook pasta, works best and produces the most evenly cooked results.

Substitution: You can use quick-cooking or presteamed wheat berries (check the ingredient list on the package to determine this) but you will need to decrease the cooking time in step 1. The wheat berries will retain a chewy texture once fully cooked.

- 1½ cups wheat berries
- 1 bay leaf
- 1 teaspoon table salt, divided
- 1 orange plus ⅛ teaspoon grated orange zest
- 1 shallot, minced
- 3 tablespoons red wine vinegar
- 2 tablespoons extra-virgin olive oil
- 1½ tablespoons Dijon mustard
- 1½ teaspoons honey
- 1 garlic clove, minced
- 3 carrots, peeled and shredded
- 1 tablespoon chopped fresh tarragon

1. Combine 5 cups water, wheat berries, bay leaf, and ½ teaspoon salt in slow cooker. Cover and cook until wheat berries are tender, 4 to 5 hours on low or 3 to 4 hours on high.

2. Drain wheat berries, transfer to large serving bowl, and let cool slightly. Cut away peel and pith from orange. Quarter orange, then slice crosswise into ¼-inch-thick pieces.

3. Whisk shallot, vinegar, oil, mustard, honey, garlic, remaining ½ teaspoon salt, and orange zest together in separate bowl. Add orange and any accumulated juices, vinaigrette, carrots, and tarragon to wheat berries, and toss to combine. Season with salt and pepper to taste. Serve.

Slow-Cooker Boston Baked Beans

Serves 6 | **Cooking Time** 8 to 9 hours on high

WHY THIS RECIPE WORKS Boston baked beans are both sweet and savory and make a robust side dish in summer and winter alike. Made from the simplest ingredients, these beans are unified and refined during a long simmer on the stovetop or in the oven but we found a way to get that depth of flavor in the slow cooker. For tender beans in a thick, smoky, slightly sweet sauce, we start by microwaving onion, salt pork, and salt, then slow cook them with navy beans, molasses, and bay leaves. Mild molasses and brown sugar give us the sweetness we want from baked beans, dry mustard and cider vinegar add welcome notes of spice and tanginess, and soy sauce brings smoky umami.

 1 onion, chopped fine
 6 ounces salt pork, rind removed,
   cut into ½-inch pieces
 ½ teaspoon table salt
 6 cups water, plus extra as needed
 1 pound dried navy beans (2½ cups),
   picked over and rinsed
 5 tablespoons molasses, divided
 ¼ cup packed dark brown sugar, divided
 2 bay leaves
 4 teaspoons cider vinegar
 1 tablespoon soy sauce
 2 teaspoons dry mustard

1. Microwave onion, salt pork, and salt in bowl, stirring occasionally, until onion is softened, about 5 minutes; transfer to slow cooker. Stir in water, beans, 2 tablespoons molasses, 2 tablespoons sugar, and bay leaves. Cover and cook until beans are tender, 8 to 9 hours on high.

2. Discard bay leaves. Drain beans, reserving ¾ cup cooking liquid. Return beans to now-empty slow cooker. Stir in reserved cooking liquid, vinegar, soy sauce, mustard, remaining 3 tablespoons molasses, and remaining 2 tablespoons sugar. Cover and cook on high until beans are thickened slightly, about 10 minutes. Season with salt and pepper to taste. Serve.

Slow-Cooker Barbecue Baked Beans

Serves 6 | **Cooking Time** 8 to 9 hours on high

WHY THIS RECIPE WORKS Traditional baked beans rely on a long, slow cooking time in a low oven and require careful adjustment of the cooking liquid in order to get perfectly cooked beans with just the right amount of syrupy, but not cloyingly sweet, sauce. The gentle, steady heat of the slow cooker is the perfect fit for this dish: Cooking on the high setting yields tender, silky beans in 8 to 9 hours. Since cooking on low produces crunchy, inconsistent beans, we cook the beans exclusively on high for this barbecue version of classic baked beans that makes the perfect side for any meal. A surprising ingredient, brewed coffee, enhances the smokiness of the barbecue sauce and adds deep pleasing color to the beans.

 1 onion, chopped fine
 6 slices bacon, chopped
 4 garlic cloves, minced
 1 tablespoon vegetable oil
 ½ teaspoon table salt
5½ cups water, plus extra as needed
 1 pound dried navy beans (2½ cups),
   picked over and rinsed
 ½ cup barbecue sauce, divided
 ½ cup brewed coffee
 2 bay leaves
 1 tablespoon cider vinegar
 2 teaspoons dry mustard
   Hot sauce

1. Microwave onion, bacon, garlic, oil, and salt in bowl, stirring occasionally, until onion is softened, about 5 minutes; transfer to slow cooker. Stir in water, beans, ¼ cup barbecue sauce, coffee, and bay leaves. Cover and cook until beans are tender, 8 to 9 hours on high.

2. Discard bay leaves. Drain beans, reserving ¾ cup cooking liquid. Return beans to now-empty slow cooker. Stir in reserved cooking liquid, vinegar, mustard, and remaining ¼ cup barbecue sauce. Cover and cook on high until beans are thickened slightly, about 10 minutes. Season with salt, pepper, and hot sauce to taste. Serve.

Slow-Cooker Braised Chickpeas

Serves 6 | **Cooking Time** 8 to 9 hours on high
VEGAN

WHY THIS RECIPE WORKS Chickpeas have a great buttery texture and they easily soak up the flavors of other ingredients they're cooked with, making them ideal for cooking in a flavor-packed broth during a long stint in the slow cooker. We infuse the broth with distinctive sweet smoked paprika and a sliced red onion for flavor and texture. Once our chickpeas are perfectly tender and creamy, we drain away all but a cup of the cooking liquid, using what we reserve to create a simple, smoky sauce. Mashing a portion of the beans enhances the creamy consistency of the dish, and citrusy cilantro adds brightness for a simple colorful finish.

- 1 red onion, halved and sliced thin
- 1 tablespoon extra-virgin olive oil
- 1 tablespoon smoked paprika
- 1 teaspoon table salt
- 3 cups vegetable or chicken broth, plus extra as needed
- 3 cups water
- 1 pound (2½ cups) dried chickpeas, picked over and rinsed
- ¼ cup minced fresh cilantro

1. Microwave onion, oil, paprika, and salt in bowl, stirring occasionally, until onion is softened, about 5 minutes; transfer to slow cooker. Stir in broth, water, and chickpeas. Cover and cook until chickpeas are tender, 8 to 9 hours on high.

2. Drain chickpeas, reserving 1 cup cooking liquid. Return one-third of chickpeas and reserved cooking liquid to now-empty slow cooker and mash with potato masher until smooth. Stir in remaining chickpeas and cilantro. Season with salt and pepper to taste. Serve.

Slow-Cooker Barbecue Baked Beans

Slow-Cooker Braised Chickpeas

Nutritional Information for Our Recipes

To calculate the nutritional values of our recipes per serving, we used The Food Processor SQL by ESHA research. When using this program, we entered all the ingredients, using weights wherever possible. We also used our preferred brands in these analyses. Any ingredient listed as "optional" was excluded from the analyses. If there is a range in the serving size, we used the highest number of servings to calculate nutritional values. We did not include additional salt or pepper for food that's seasoned to taste.

	CALORIES	TOTAL FAT (G)	SAT FAT (G)	CHOL (MG)	SODIUM (MG)	TOTAL CARB (G)	DIETARY FIBER (G)	TOTAL SUGAR (G)	ADDED SUGAR (G)	PROTEIN (G)
SNACKS AND APPETIZERS										
Lupini Beans with Garlic, Lemon, and Parsley	180	13	2	0	180	8	2	0	0	12
with Shallot, Urfa, and Cumin	190	13	2	0	180	8	3	0	0	12
Boiled Peanuts	320	28	4	0	590	9	5	3	0	15
Sichuan Snack Peanuts	300	25	4	0	350	11	4	3	1	11
Barbecue-Spiced Roasted Chickpeas	160	9	1	0	310	15	5	1	1	5
Smoked Paprika–Spiced Roasted Chickpeas	150	9	1	0	310	13	5	0	0	5
Coriander-Turmeric Roasted Chickpeas	150	9	1	0	310	14	5	0	0	5
Cumin-Spiced Crispy Lentils	70	1	0	0	290	10	2	1	0	5
Buttered Popcorn	60	5	2	5	40	5	1	0	0	1
Parmesan-Pepper	80	6	2	5	115	5	1	0	0	2
Garlic and Herb	70	5	1	5	40	5	1	0	0	1
Hot and Sweet	70	5	1	5	45	7	1	2	2	1
Cajun-Spiced	70	5	1	5	50	5	1	0	0	1
Popped Wheat Berries	60	0	0	0	50	11	2	0	0	2
Popped Spelt	60	2	0	0	50	11	1	1	0	2
Popped Kamut	60	0	0	0	50	11	1	1	0	2
Chickpea Fries	120	8	1	0	230	9	2	2	0	4
Lemon and Herb Dipping Sauce	190	21	3	10	230	1	0	0	0	0
Calabrian Chile Dipping Sauce	190	21	3	10	200	0	0	0	0	0
Honey and Spice Dipping Sauce	200	21	3	10	180	2	0	2	2	0
Chickpea Crackers	80	3	0	0	85	9	2	2	0	4
Turmeric–Black Pepper Chickpea Crackers	60	3	0	0	80	7	1	1	0	3
Herbes de Provence Chickpea Crackers	60	3	0	0	80	7	1	1	0	3
Farinata	90	6	1	0	230	7	1	1	0	3
Grilled Polenta Wedges with Grilled Scallions and Gorgonzola	170	11	5	15	340	14	1	2	2	4
with Grilled Oranges and Ricotta	150	9	3	10	160	15	2	4	2	3

	CALORIES	TOTAL FAT (G)	SAT FAT (G)	CHOL (MG)	SODIUM (MG)	TOTAL CARB (G)	DIETARY FIBER (G)	TOTAL SUGAR (G)	ADDED SUGAR (G)	PROTEIN (G)
Bean and Beef Taquitos	330	19	3	55	510	27	3	5	5	14
Black-Eyed Pea Fritters with Garlic and Herb Sauce	270	22	3	10	550	14	4	2	0	5
Simple Hummus	140	10	2	0	270	9	3	0	0	4
Big-Batch Simple Hummus	140	10	2	0	270	9	3	0	0	4
Ultracreamy Hummus	160	11	2	0	500	13	4	0	0	6
with Spiced Walnut Topping	350	30	4	0	580	17	5	1	0	7
Sweet Potato Hummus	100	5	1	0	260	11	2	1	0	3
Tepary Bean Dip with Herb and Olive Salad	140	9	1	0	110	12	6	0	0	5
Lemon-Garlic Orca Bean Dip	130	4	1	0	770	20	10	2	0	6
Quick Lemon-Garlic White Bean Dip	100	4	0	0	1030	15	4	1	0	5
Navy Bean and Artichoke Dip	80	1	1	0	490	14	3	1	0	5
Pink Bean and Lima Bean Dip with Parsley	90	2	1	0	310	15	3	1	0	5
Black Bean Dip	100	2	0	0	380	14	4	0	0	5
Greek Layer Dip	390	30	10	20	630	19	5	4	4	14
Toasted Corn and Black Bean Salsa	60	3	0	0	150	7	2	1	0	2
Roasted Tomato Salsa with Black Beans	40	0	0	0	300	8	2	2	0	2
Texas Caviar	190	8	1	0	800	23	6	4	2	7
Cheesy Nachos with Refried Beans	780	48	25	110	125	53	3	2	0	36
TOASTS, PATTIES, TACOS, AND MORE										
Avocado and Black Bean Toast	250	13	2	0	690	26	8	3	0	8
Quick Sweet-and-Spicy Pickled Red Onions	20	0	0	0	55	5	0	5	4	0
Green Fava Bean Toast	590	26	4	0	980	63	17	21	3	23
British-Style Beans on Toast	570	13	3	185	1630	77	14	12	7	28
Molletes	280	21	14	65	520	13	1	3	0	12
Curried Chickpea Salad Sandwiches	490	18	2	5	890	68	5	16	0	11
Herbed Quinoa Cakes with Whipped Feta	560	29	10	130	1260	53	5	14	0	21
Miso Brown Rice Burgers	620	38	5	105	1500	51	3	5	0	10
Sriracha Mayo	70	7	1	5	95	1	0	0	0	0
Fonio, Sweet Potato, and Scallion Cakes	250	12	2	45	620	33	3	4	0	4
Buffalo Blue Cheese Chickpea Patties with Creamy Herb Sauce	420	26	6	85	1100	34	7	3	0	13
Black Bean Burgers	366	11	2	62	528	51	11	3	0	16
Scarlet Runner Mole Burgers	290	11	2	65	1530	34	9	5	0	13
Onigiri	200	7	0.5	0	560	30	3	3	0	7
Quinoa Lettuce Wraps with Feta and Olives	560	29	10	130	1260	53	5	14	0	21
Tomato and Corn Tostadas with Baked Eggs	370	23	8	365	600	22	1	4	0	19
Tempeh Tacos	300	12	2	0	650	38	6	5	1	13
Red Lentil Tacos	280	7	1	0	840	44	6	5	1	11
Black Bean and Sweet Potato Tacos	600	18	2	0	1150	102	9	33	17	12

	CALORIES	TOTAL FAT (G)	SAT FAT (G)	CHOL (MG)	SODIUM (MG)	TOTAL CARB (G)	DIETARY FIBER (G)	TOTAL SUGAR (G)	ADDED SUGAR (G)	PROTEIN (G)
Black Bean, Sweet Potato, and Poblano Tacos	580	21	5	0	1660	83	9	14	0	17
Avocado Crema	20	2	0	0	0	1	1	0	0	0
Breakfast Tacos with Pinto Beans and Cotija Cheese	385	23	6	379	540	23	6	1	0	22
Kale and Black Bean Breakfast Burritos	390	13	3	250	770	50	9	3	0	19
Breakfast Burritos with Poblano, Beans, Corn, and Crispy Potatoes	701	45	11	401	674	47	6	4	0	28
Falafel	500	30	4	0	1020	57	1	2	0	16
Tahini-Yogurt Sauce	70	6	1	0	220	3	0	0	0	2
Ta'ameya with Tahini-Yogurt Sauce	490	31	8	55	330	38	6	9	0	18
Pink Pickled Turnips	5	0	0	0	42	1	1	1	1	0
Spiced Chickpea Gyros with Tahini Yogurt	500	20	7	10	1570	62	8	4	0	23
Shawarma-Spiced Tofu Wraps	510	24	3	0	800	53	2	17	10	23
Sumac Onions	35	3	0	0	100	3	0	1	0	0
Black Bean and Cheese Arepas	267	12	4	13	565	33	2	0	0	7
Pupusas with Beans and Cheese	471	18	8	37	757	59	8	2	0	21
Quick Salsa	20	0	0	0	330	5	0	2	0	1
Curtido	70	0	0	0	950	15	4	9	2	2
Tomatillo Chicken Huaraches	810	28	9	115	1080	90	13	6	0	52
Tacu Tacu with Salsa Criolla	640	28	6	190	1540	76	15	4	0	23
Poblano and Corn Hand Pies	650	35	7	65	980	67	3	2	0	18
New Mexican Bean-and-Cheese Turnovers with Green Chile	1131	83	17	49	1097	76	10	10	0	24
Cauliflower Chickpea Flatbread with Romesco	170	13	3	30	400	7	2	2	0	9
Greek Pita Pizzas with Hummus	563	39	15	67	1006	36	7	4	0	21
Galettes Complètes	420	29	15	320	900	12	1	3	0	28
Rye Crepes with Smoked Salmon, Crème Fraîche, and Pickled Shallots	580	36	20	220	1020	41	5	16	0	24
SOUPS										
Miso Soup with Wakame and Tofu	60	3	0	5	770	7	2	1	0	9
5-Ingredient Black Bean Soup	270	4	2	5	1430	52	0	4	0	18
Chickpea and Garlic Soup	230	7	2	5	950	31	10	1	0	12
White Bean and Sun-Dried Tomato Soup	260	6	3	10	1070	36	10	4	0	17
Lentil and Chorizo Soup	510	23	8	50	1480	44	17	4	0	33
Creamy White Bean Soup with Chorizo Oil and Garlicky Bread Crumbs	380	26	7	20	760	24	5	2	0	12
with Herb Oil and Crispy Capers	320	22	5	10	720	22	5	2	0	9
with Extra-Virgin Olive Oil and Quick Pickled Celery	220	11	2	0	640	23	5	3	1	9
with Lemony Yogurt and Crispy Leeks	290	16	6	15	590	26	5	3	0	11
Creamy Chickpea, Broccoli Rabe, and Garlic Soup	260	15	2	0	810	25	8	1	0	10
Gingery Coconut Carrot Soup with Tofu Croutons	510	43	22	0	520	19	4	6	0	17

	CALORIES	TOTAL FAT (G)	SAT FAT (G)	CHOL (MG)	SODIUM (MG)	TOTAL CARB (G)	DIETARY FIBER (G)	TOTAL SUGAR (G)	ADDED SUGAR (G)	PROTEIN (G)
Tanabour	280	17	11	60	510	25	4	3	0	8
Avgolemono	90	3	1	95	1030	10	0	1	0	4
Kimchi and Tofu Soup	130	6	0	0	1260	10	1	2	0	8
Spring Vegetable Soup with Charred Croutons	390	25	4	0	1970	36	6	8	0	8
Tepary Bean Soup	280	15	2	0	600	29	7	3	0	9
Wild Rice and Mushroom Soup	260	12	7	30	890	29	2	4	0	7
Mushroom and Wheat Berry Soup	310	8	1	0	710	44	7	6	0	11
Minestra di Farro	180	5	1	10	800	29	4	5	0	7
Butternut Squash and White Bean Soup with Sage Pesto	520	27	4	5	1210	55	14	9	0	19
Soupe au Pistou	270	13	3	5	620	28	7	4	0	11
Hearty 15-Bean and Vegetable Soup	220	4	0	0	380	35	7	5	0	12
Garlicky Wild Rice Soup with Artichokes	420	12	2	5	1220	59	7	7	0	20
Acquacotta	510	21	4	40	790	63	7	6	0	17
Ribollita	320	7	2	10	1220	49	18	3	0	16
Lablabi	420	19	3	0	610	49	14	9	0	15
Harissa	110	11	2	0	150	2	1	0	0	1
Coconut Black Bean Soup with Plantains	570	25	13	0	680	73	3	17	0	18
Hot and Sour Soup	130	5	1	30	1030	15	1	10	0	8
Chili Oil	45	5	1	0	85	1	0	0	0	0
Split Pea and Ham Soup	350	10	4	40	960	39	15	6	0	26
Hearty Spanish-Style Lentil and Chorizo Soup with Kale	710	43	14	75	1460	46	12	4	0	36
Chorba Frik	270	13	3	40	850	25	7	3	0	13
Coconut Chicken Soup with Red Rice	370	23	12	80	680	19	1	1	0	23
Gingery Chicken and Rice Soup with Shiitakes	190	6	1	65	960	17	2	2	0	16
Chicken Orzo Soup with Kale and Chickpeas	230	6	1	30	550	26	1	3	0	18
Chicken Barley Soup	230	6	3	55	640	25	5	3	0	18
Italian Wedding Soup with Kale and Farro	310	6	2	25	780	37	6	6	0	27
Madzoon ov Kofte	410	22	13	90	1290	34	4	4	0	19
Beef and Oat Berry Soup	290	12	4	60	900	22	5	3	0	23
STEWS										
Chicken and Rye Dumplings	400	14	5	175	1350	36	3	5	0	40
West African Peanut Stew	420	27	5	70	780	17	5	7	0	29
Italian-Style Lamb Stew with Roman Beans, Green Beans, and Tomatoes	420	17	4	100	980	24	7	5	0	40
Mapo Tofu	400	28	4	25	950	11	2	3	0	19
One-Pot Brazilian Black Bean and Pork Stew	880	42	14	275	1210	30	0	4	0	87
French Pork and White Bean Stew	580	31	10	95	1550	47	16	8	0	32
Posole	430	18	4	110	1550	28	5	6	0	36

	CALORIES	TOTAL FAT (G)	SAT FAT (G)	CHOL (MG)	SODIUM (MG)	TOTAL CARB (G)	DIETARY FIBER (G)	TOTAL SUGAR (G)	ADDED SUGAR (G)	PROTEIN (G)
Hearty Tuscan Bean Stew with Sausage and Cabbage	440	10	3	15	1150	64	22	6	0	23
Congee with Stir-Fried Ground Pork	190	9	3	25	580	19	0	1	0	8
Microwave-Fried Shallots	30	2	0	0	2	2	0	1	0	0
Jamaican Stew Peas with Spinners	560	25	15	70	890	46	10	3	0	36
Beans Marbella	480	11	3	15	1540	78	17	24	7	22
Pasta e Fagioli	450	11	4	15	1000	65	22	8	0	22
Garlicky Shrimp, Tomato, and White Bean Stew	260	10	2	95	660	24	6	8	4	17
Guanimes con Bacalao	550	30	3	50	1460	48	3	6	0	25
Chickpea Bouillabaisse	740	33	5	30	1680	85	11	9	2	20
Chana Masala	210	10	1	0	740	24	7	2	0	8
Bean Bourguignon	330	11	2	0	890	39	10	10	0	14
Palak Dal	400	13	7	30	910	49	13	2	0	23
Adasi	380	12	6	25	570	53	13	4	1	18
Classic Ground Beef Chili	400	21	7	75	1300	26	8	6	0	28
Five-Alarm Chili	380	18	5	50	1070	34	8	11	0	23
Ultimate Beef Chili	530	19	6	135	940	36	11	6	1	50
White Chicken Chili	360	15	4	85	760	20	6	5	0	35
Classic Turkey Chili	310	7	3	45	1110	30	10	11	0	36
Pumpkin Turkey Chili	290	8	2	30	700	30	10	6	0	27
Ultimate Vegetarian Chili	460	13	1	0	700	68	21	11	0	19
Four-Chile Vegetarian Chili	390	11	2	0	1990	59	14	7	0	15
MEAL SALADS										
Marinated Tofu and Vegetable Salad	350	22	3	0	320	17	2	9	3	22
Kale Salad with Crispy Tofu and Miso-Ginger Dressing	690	53	8	0	730	44	12	8	0	20
Edamame and Shrimp Salad	430	25	3	145	910	21	2	10	4	33
Crispy Lentil and Herb Salad	350	31	9	10	320	12	1	7	0	6
Lentil Salad with Oranges, Celery, and Feta	260	14	3	5	350	26	6	6	3	8
Fattoush with Chickpeas	310	20	3	0	340	27	5	4	0	7
Hearty Green Salad with Chickpeas, Pickled Cauliflower, and Seared Halloumi	610	44	16	45	2120	47	9	23	6	26
Warm Broccoli, Chickpea, and Avocado Salad	640	44	6	0	1730	51	20	4	0	18
Roasted Vegetable and Black Chickpea Salad	320	16	5	10	220	44	4	12	0	13
White Bean and Tuna Salad	170	10	2	10	380	12	4	2	0	10
Pinto Bean, Ancho, and Beef Salad with Pickled Poblanos	470	18	8	55	1000	49	12	14	11	28
Chilled Soba Noodles with Spring Vegetables	220	6	1	0	540	37	1	5	0	8
Barley Salad with Celery and Miso Dressing	190	5	1	0	350	35	7	4	1	4

	CALORIES	TOTAL FAT (G)	SAT FAT (G)	CHOL (MG)	SODIUM (MG)	TOTAL CARB (G)	DIETARY FIBER (G)	TOTAL SUGAR (G)	ADDED SUGAR (G)	PROTEIN (G)
Bulgur Salad with Curry Roasted Sweet Potatoes and Chickpeas	560	32	7	15	920	59	12	11	0	15
Bulgur Salad with Spinach, Chickpeas, and Apples	620	30	4	0	650	78	17	15	4	16
Farro Salad with Roasted Eggplant	340	16	2	0	370	46	7	8	0	7
Antipasto Farro Salad with Arugula	360	23	6	25	930	27	5	1	0	12
Millet Salad with Corn and Queso Fresco	230	9	2	0	330	31	3	4	2	5
Quinoa, Black Bean, and Mango Salad with Lime Dressing	420	22	3	0	810	45	7	3	0	10
Quinoa Taco Salad	440	22	4	5	830	47	14	4	0	14
Spelt Salad with Pickled Fennel, Pea Greens, and Mint	210	9	2	5	260	30	4	8	4	6
Oat Berry, Chickpea, and Arugula Salad	280	12	3	10	410	33	6	4	1	10
Wheat Berry Salad with Radicchio, Dried Cherries, and Pecans	200	11	2	5	190	22	4	3	0	5
Black Rice and Sea Bean Salad	320	16	2	0	210	43	5	5	1	5
Harvest Salad	320	16	5	15	510	36	6	14	0	7
Savory Seed Brittle	80	5	1	0	135	6	1	2	2	3
Turmeric Rice and Chicken Salad with Herbs	380	13	3	50	490	45	2	4	0	21
Perfect Poached Chicken	200	5	1	0	125	220	0	0	0	38
Herb-Yogurt Sauce	20	1	1	5	15	2	0	2	0	1
Nam Khao	350	15	3	5	470	46	1	5	3	8
Sprouted Grain Salad	360	18	3	0	490	48	12	12	5	7
Pomegranate Molasses Vinaigrette	60	5	1	0	50	4	0	3	1	0
Hearty Green Salad with Spicy Peanut Chicken	620	29	5	85	1870	48	10	17	5	44
BEAN DINNERS										
Apricot-Glazed Chicken with Chickpeas, Chorizo, and Spinach	882	46	13	197	1339	44	9	15	0	72
Skillet-Roasted Chicken with Garlicky Spinach and Beans	968	59	15	246	1269	49	11	1	0	59
Tunisian Tajine with White Beans	500	29	9	500	840	15	3	2	0	45
Ras el Hanout	20	1	0	0	220	4	2	2	2	1
Mustard-Roasted Chicken with Warm Green Bean and Potato Salad	830	51	12	230	1180	32	5	4	0	57
Braised Chicken and Lentils	846	46	12	241	1711	49	8	9	0	59
Sirloin Steak Tips with Charro Beans	959	44	14	180	1556	70	18	4	0	70
Teriyaki Stir-Fried Beef with Green Beans and Shiitakes	305	15	4	58	947	21	4	12	6	23
Jamaican Oxtail	811	52	21	187	1249	26	4	10		58
Tamale Pie	310	16	5	50	670	23	3	3	0	19
Gochujang Meatballs with Edamame and Sugar Snap Peas	400	22	6	115	870	23	4	9	6	25

	CALORIES	TOTAL FAT (G)	SAT FAT (G)	CHOL (MG)	SODIUM (MG)	TOTAL CARB (G)	DIETARY FIBER (G)	TOTAL SUGAR (G)	ADDED SUGAR (G)	PROTEIN (G)
Hoppin' John	639	40	11	70	1381	46	2	3	0	23
'Nduja with Beans and Greens	420	17	5	215	1190	38	12	6	0	33
Pork Chops with Garlicky Beans and Greens	785	40	12	163	1467	40	10	6	0	67
Bitter Melon with Tofu and Pork	450	36	12	40	780	8	2	1	0	16
Shichimi Togarashi	5	0	0	0	0	1	0	0	0	0
Italian Sausage with Lentils and Kale	477	19	6	54	1157	38	12	6	0	43
Red Beans and Rice with Andouille	520	15	4	35	1470	75	1	4	0	22
Habichuelas Guisadas con Calabaza	345	10	2	16	997	48	11	6	0	20
Sazón	91	2	0	0	65	18	5	1	0	5
Sofrito	18	0	0	0	2	4	1	2	0	1
Whole-Wheat Spaghetti with Greens, Beans, and Pancetta	550	18	6	35	1130	72	15	6	0	27
Braised Lamb Shoulder Chops with Fava Beans	600	20	7	110	1080	48	16	23	0	55
One-Pot Lamb Meatballs with Eggplant and Chickpeas	537	28	9	86	1085	54	13	24	0	24
Spicy Lamb with Lentils and Yogurt	660	35	16	90	840	49	6	8	0	37
Shrimp with Long Beans and Garlic Sauce	320	16	2	180	1890	19	5	7	1	23
Pan-Seared Scallops with Sugar Snap Pea Slaw	320	19	2	46	800	14	2	4	0	23
Roasted Trout with White Bean and Tomato Salad	700	41	6	115	870	30	9	6	0	51
Saumon aux Lentilles	615	30	6	94	1044	38	7	4	0	48
Grilled Swordfish with Eggplant, Tomato, and Chickpea Salad	310	20	3	50	560	15	5	6	0	18
Fava Bean Pesto Pasta	497	21	3	6	306	63	6	5	0	16
Cauliflower and Bean Paella	519	14	2	6	802	78	9	9	0	19
White Bean and Mushroom Gratin	427	19	3	0	757	50	10	6	0	15
White Bean Gratin with Rosemary and Parmesan	260	11	3	10	850	26	7	4	0	14
Cheesy Bean and Tomato Bake	358	13	4	18	719	45	10	7	0	18
White Beans with Caramelized Onions, Fennel, and Gruyère	470	15	7	40	1580	54	10	9	1	27
Burst Cherry Tomato Puttanesca with Roman Beans	280	12	2	0	990	35	11	4	0	10
Loaded Sweet Potatoes	310	12	6	30	540	40	8	7	0	13
Cuban-Style Black Beans and Rice	307	22	7	18	597	22	5	3	0	8
Gigantes Plaki	390	10	2	0	620	60	16	14	0	18
Espinacas con Garbanzos	430	25	4	0	1010	36	11	2	0	15
Stuffed Peppers with Chickpeas, Goat Cheese, and Herbs	539	31	9	21	964	48	10	12	0	20
Vegetable Tagine with Chickpeas and Olives	460	21	2	0	1820	62	13	16	0	11
Garam Masala	20	1	0	0	0	5	3	0	0	1
Fregula with Chickpeas, Tomatoes, and Fennel	557	14	2	0	1094	92	15	14	0	19
Maftoul with Carrots and Chickpeas	410	9	1	0	930	70	7	6	0	13

	CALORIES	TOTAL FAT (G)	SAT FAT (G)	CHOL (MG)	SODIUM (MG)	TOTAL CARB (G)	DIETARY FIBER (G)	TOTAL SUGAR (G)	ADDED SUGAR (G)	PROTEIN (G)
Big-Batch Meatless Meat Sauce with Chickpeas and Mushrooms	180	11	2	0	690	16	2	6	0	4
Thai Red Curry with Lentils and Tofu	191	14	7	0	842	9	3	4	0	11
Herb Vegetable and Lentil Bake with Feta	460	28	7	25	850	41	11	13	0	14
Red Lentil Kibbeh	450	19	3	5	760	60	13	6	0	16
Enfrijoladas	300	11	4	15	740	40	5	2	0	11
Pinto Bean, Swiss Chard, and Monterey Jack Enchiladas	490	28	5	15	1270	57	10	12	1	12
Spicy Basil Noodles with Crispy Tofu, Snap Peas, and Bell Pepper	470	16	1	0	1200	71	2	13	9	12
Stir-Fried Tofu and Bok Choy	300	14	2	0	610	28	3	8	0	14
Panko-Crusted Tofu with Cabbage Salad	410	23	3	95	800	37	1	9	0	16
Glazed Caribbean Tofu with Rice and Pigeon Peas	750	24	3	0	1250	102	4	33	0	29
Braised Tofu with Winter Squash and Coconut Milk	490	36	20	0	30	34	7	9	0	15
GRAIN DINNERS										
Lemon-Oregano Chicken with Farro	705	31	7	162	900	51	9	7	0	58
Pomegranate-Glazed Chicken with Farro Salad	830	34	8	145	810	76	2	17	0	58
Pan-Seared Chicken with Warm Bulgur Pilaf	580	24	7	190	1010	31	5	3	0	60
Roast Chicken with Bulgur, Peas, and Mint	823	50	15	239	1326	28	5	3	0	63
Chicken and Rice with Coconut-Ginger Sauce	943	47	16	233	1386	80	2	17	0	46
One-Pan Chicken and Spinach Rice	665	36	10	169	910	49	2	3	0	35
Homemade Greek Seasoning	18	0	0	0	21	5	2	0	0	1
Khao Man Gai	749	33	9	145	2183	67	3	7	0	44
Chicken Biryani	470	15	8	110	1360	59	2	12	0	24
Chicken Fried Rice with Sausage and Dried Shrimp	460	19	2.5	115	1210	51	1	1	0	21
Arroz con Pollo	842	48	11	177	1004	63	2	4	0	37
Chicken Katsu with Tonkatsu Sauce, Cabbage Salad, and Rice	680	25	3	175	700	66	1	6	0	43
Roast Chicken with Quinoa, Swiss Chard, and Lime	830	52	15	239	1403	24	4	1	0	63
Sheet-Pan Italian Chicken Sausages with Broccoli and Barley	650	35	8	135	1550	46	10	1	0	41
Chicken and Spiced Freekeh with Cilantro and Preserved Lemon	569	24	5	91	582	51	8	4	0	40
Quick Preserved Lemon	5	0	0	0	190	2	1	1	0	0
Lemony Chicken Meatballs with Quinoa and Carrots	720	40	6	100	1080	59	9	9	0	32
One-Pan Turkey Meatballs with Coconut Rice	617	30	11	125	1000	54	4	5	0	33
Mehshi Bazal	310	9	4	40	430	44	4	23	0	14
Baharat	15	1	0	0	0	3	2	0	0	1
Braised Short Ribs with Wild Mushroom Farrotto	732	28	14	224	1634	42	7	6	0	83

	CALORIES	TOTAL FAT (G)	SAT FAT (G)	CHOL (MG)	SODIUM (MG)	TOTAL CARB (G)	DIETARY FIBER (G)	TOTAL SUGAR (G)	ADDED SUGAR (G)	PROTEIN (G)
Flank Steak with Farro and Mango Salsa	835	32	10	154	1092	79	12	20	0	62
Plov	570	26	10	83	1002	59	5	9	0	26
Okinawan Taco Rice	889	36	12	103	1549	95	6	6	0	41
Homemade Taco Seasoning	25	1	0	0	117	5	2	0	0	1
Steak Burrito Bowls	510	17	3	50	1390	62	2	4	0	27
Spiced Stuffed Peppers with Yogurt-Tahini Sauce	520	29	6	40	510	46	10	16	0	21
Pan-Seared Pork Chops with Dirty Rice	715	33	10	157	1268	48	2	2	0	54
Cajun Seasoning	35	1	0	0	1750	7	3	1	0	2
Kibbeh bil Saineyeh	840	62	21	130	1330	37	7	10	0	38
Khao Pad Sapparot	550	25	3	145	770	63	2	8	1	22
Pork Fried Rice	450	18	3	90	960	55	1	4	2	17
Polenta with Sausage and Peppers	500	23	11	75	1720	43	6	4	0	32
Sorghum Käsespätzle with Caramelized Onions and Kielbasa	34	16	0	210	1390	40	3	3	0	30
Cod with Cilantro Rice	620	36	5	75	680	37	0	0	0	35
Black Rice Bowls with Roasted Salmon and Miso Dressing	720	33	6	95	590	64	9	7	0	43
Nasi Goreng	530	22	3	180	1240	65	1	12	9	18
Quick Skillet Paella-Style Rice	400	18	5	105	1110	33	1	3	0	27
Paella on the Grill	897	38	11	204	1792	76	4	5	0	56
Seared Shrimp with Tomato, Avocado, and Lime Quinoa	530	20	3	215	1420	53	10	5	0	35
Shrimp with Warm Barley Salad	560	23	11	190	760	58	2	2	0	24
Twice-Cooked Barley with Sautéed Squid	730	30	4	265	1920	83	17	10	0	29
Stuffed Eggplants with Bulgur	310	15	4	15	680	39	12	14	0	11
Garlicky Fried Rice with Bok Choy	190	3	0	0	500	35	2	2	0	5
Vegetable Bibimbap with Nurungji	560	17	2	125	1290	90	5	16	2	18
Quick-Pickled Cucumber and Bean Sprouts	5	0	0	0	20	1	0	1	1	1
Sweet and Tangy Chili Sauce	45	3	0	0	115	6	0	4	3	0
Skillet Rice and Beans with Corn and Fresh Tomatoes	270	6	1	0	730	48	1	4	0	10
Skillet Rice and Chickpeas with Coconut Milk	300	10	3	0	500	46	7	4	0	8
Spanish-Style Skillet Rice and Chickpeas	260	6	1	0	630	46	6	6	0	8
Mujaddara	460	14	3	5	810	70	9	9	1	14
Crispy Onions	90	5	1	0	100	13	2	6	0	1
Koshari	450	8	1	0	1080	81	12	10	0	17
Wild Mushroom Ragout with Farro	540	15	5	15	760	66	11	19	0	16
Creamy Polenta with Radicchio Agrodolce	370	25	6	20	860	20	2	15	0	15
Savory Oatmeal with Peas, Pecorino, and Pepper	398	24	12	69	992	21	4	3	0	26
Soba Noodles with Roasted Eggplant	770	27	4	0	630	123	9	51	35	14

	CALORIES	TOTAL FAT (G)	SAT FAT (G)	CHOL (MG)	SODIUM (MG)	TOTAL CARB (G)	DIETARY FIBER (G)	TOTAL SUGAR (G)	ADDED SUGAR (G)	PROTEIN (G)
Teff-Stuffed Acorn Squash with Lime Crema and Roasted Pepitas	436	13	2	0	1210	73	12	10	0	13
Curried Fonio with Roasted Vegetables and Hibiscus Vinaigrette	540	30	5	0	1050	67	7	8	3	7
Hibiscus Vinaigrette	140	14	2	0	310	3	0	3	3	0
Cauliflower Biryani	339	11	2	5	831	50	5	9	0	8
Barley Risotto with Roasted Butternut Squash	269	6	2	7	1029	46	9	4	0	10
BEAN SIDES										
Caesar Green Bean Salad	223	15	3	8	376	17	4	5	0	8
Southwestern Black Bean Salad	281	15	2	0	570	33	12	3	0	9
Classic Three-Bean Salad	234	11	1	0	343	29	4	18	11	5
Sautéed Fava Beans, Asparagus, and Leek	103	5	1	0	210	13	5	6	0	6
Edamame Salad with Pecorino and Mint	272	19	5	27	321	12	6	3	0	15
Succotash Salad with Butter Beans and Basil	263	14	2	0	554	30	6	7	0	8
Gan Bian Si Ji Dou	300	22	5	15	650	13	4	6	2	6
White Beans with Tomatoes and Capers	377	14	2	0	268	47	12	2	0	18
Garlicky White Beans with Sage	375	14	2	0	211	46	12	2	0	18
Stewed Chickpeas and Spinach with Dill and Lemon	257	9	1	1	505	35	10	6	0	12
Braised Green Beans	160	12	2	0	532	14	5	7	0	3
Braised Green Beans with Mint and Feta	154	10	3	11	646	14	5	7	0	5
Southern-Style Baby Lima Beans	276	11	3	18	659	31	6	5	0	15
Ful Medames	205	8	1	62	678	23	7	1	0	12
Easy-Peel Hard-Cooked Eggs	70	5	2	185	70	0	0	0	0	6
French Lentils	260	6	1	0	230	41	11	4	0	14
Lentilles du Puy with Spinach and Crème Fraîche	170	10	2	7	732	14	1	6	0	7
New England Baked Beans	580	24	8	24	924	74	12	29	24	19
Drunken Beans	474	12	5	23	560	58	14	5	0	22
Cajun Red Beans	280	7	3	20	630	38	9	3	0	20
Cranberry Beans with Warm Spices	120	2	0	4	389	17	5	4	0	7
Green Bean Casserole	130	7	4	5	300	14	3	5	0	3
Refried Beans	250	15	5	10	750	23	6	2	0	8
Vegetarian Refried Beans	150	4	0	0	350	24	7	2	0	7
GRAIN SIDES										
Steamed Long- or Medium-Grain White Rice	210	0	0	0	0	48	0	0	0	5
Steamed Short-Grain White Rice	210	2	0	0	0	47	1	0	0	7
Microwave-Steamed Rice	230	0	0	0	5	53	1	0	0	4
Hands-Off Baked White Rice	240	4	0	0	300	48	0	0	0	5
Hands-Off Baked Saffron Rice	240	4	0	0	300	48	0	0	0	5
Hands-Off Baked Coconut Rice	330	13	9	0	300	49	0	0	0	6

	CALORIES	TOTAL FAT (G)	SAT FAT (G)	CHOL (MG)	SODIUM (MG)	TOTAL CARB (G)	DIETARY FIBER (G)	TOTAL SUGAR (G)	ADDED SUGAR (G)	PROTEIN (G)
Hands-Off Baked Curried Rice	280	4	0	0	300	56	0	7	0	6
Basmati Rice Pilaf	180	3	0	0	100	34	0	1	0	3
Basmati Rice Pilaf with Whole Spices	223	6	4	15	333	38	1	0	0	3
Herbed Basmati Rice Pilaf	180	3	0	0	100	35	0	1	0	3
Basmati Rice Pilaf with Peas, Scallions, and Lemon	190	3	0	0	100	37	1	1	0	4
Basmati Rice Pilaf with Currants and Toasted Almonds	200	3	0	0	100	41	1	5	0	4
Arroz con Tocino	436	22	8	22	703	52	0	0	0	6
Hot Rice	388	14	8	35	817	56	3	10	0	9
Com Do	233	3	0	0	584	45	3	4	0	6
Garlic Fried Rice	340	14	1	0	390	49	0	0	0	6
Arroz Rojo	111	10	1	0	334	6	1	2	0	2
Almost Hands-Free Risotto with Parmesan	491	16	9	37	1056	62	3	3	0	18
Almost Hands-Free Risotto with Herbs	707	28	13	110	1372	63	3	3	0	42
Almost Hands-Free Risotto with Porcini	413	11	2	0	1134	68	5	4	0	9
Almost Hands-Free Risotto with Fennel and Saffron	410	12	6	25	960	59	4	6	0	13
Chelow ba Tahdig	368	16	4	12	236	50	1	1	0	5
Jamaican Rice and Peas	557	20	16	14	707	79	6	3	0	16
Brown Rice Pilaf with Dates and Pistachios	269	7	1	0	498	48	4	8	0	6
with Peas, Feta, and Mint	260	7	3	10	820	41	3	3	0	7
Easy Baked Brown Rice	200	4	1	0	200	37	2	1	0	4
with Parmesan, Lemon, and Herbs	240	7	2	5	370	37	2	1	0	8
Wild Rice Pilaf with Pecans and Cranberries	360	12	4	10	430	58	4	13	0	6
with Scallions, Cilantro, and Almonds	300	9	3	10	430	46	3	2	0	7
Wild Rice Stuffing	361	21	12	92	317	36	3	4	0	9
Oven-Baked Barley	200	3	1	5	200	39	8	0	0	5
Barley Risotto	310	8	3	10	680	45	9	2	0	9
Barley with Celery and Miso Dressing	181	4	0	0	212	33	7	2	0	4
Buckwheat Tabbouleh	260	15	2	0	424	30	6	3	0	6
Bulgur Pilaf	210	8	2	0	510	31	5	2	0	6
Basic Farro	482	15	6	0	286	82	8	19	0	12
Old-Fashioned Stovetop Grits	350	14	8	40	250	44	1	12	0	12
Cheesy Baked Grits	450	32	19	180	530	27	1	2	0	14
Cheesy Baked Grits with Sausage and Bell Pepper	630	49	24	200	770	28	1	3	0	20
Cheesy Baked Grits with Pepper Jack Cheese and Bell Pepper	460	32	19	180	530	28	1	3	0	14
Creamy Parmesan Polenta	210	10	5	25	940	20	2	0	0	10
Fluffy Baked Polenta with Red Sauce	567	35	15	70	1297	45	4	10	0	19
Corn Pudding	346	24	14	92	339	31	2	9	0	5

GRAIN SIDES *Continued*	CALORIES	TOTAL FAT (G)	SAT FAT (G)	CHOL (MG)	SODIUM (MG)	TOTAL CARB (G)	DIETARY FIBER (G)	TOTAL SUGAR (G)	ADDED SUGAR (G)	PROTEIN (G)
Summer Cornbread and Tomato Salad	613	35	6	48	891	67	3	8	0	11
Warm Kamut with Carrots and Pomegranate	191	8	1	0	165	27	5	5	0	6
Quinoa Pilaf with Herbs and Lemon	196	6	3	10	298	29	3	1	0	6
Easy Baked Quinoa with Lemon, Garlic, and Parsley	310	11	2	0	430	43	5	2	0	9
with Scallions and Feta	360	15	4	15	600	45	5	3	0	12
with Tomatoes, Parmesan, and Basil	370	15	4	10	680	44	5	3	0	15
with Curry, Cauliflower, and Cilantro	344	12	2	3	475	48	6	2	0	12
Warm Rye Berries with Apple and Scallions	66	4	2	10	143	8	2	5	0	0
UNDER PRESSURE										
Pressure-Cooker Spiced Chicken Soup with Squash and Chickpeas	210	7	1	60	690	16	4	3	0	22
Pressure-Cooker Beef Oxtail Soup with White Beans, Tomatoes, and Aleppo Pepper	590	28	10	200	1480	17	4	4	0	64
Pressure-Cooker Pork Pozole Rojo	400	17	3	85	920	35	1	2	0	27
Pressure-Cooker Harira	200	6	1	20	1270	20	4	4	0	15
Pressure-Cooker 15-Bean Soup with Sausage	320	10	3	15	1030	37	2	7	0	20
Pressure-Cooker Lentil and Chorizo Soup	370	17	5	25	950	30	7	5	0	21
Pressure-Cooker Hearty Minestrone	280	11	2	0	1420	35	17	8	0	11
Pressure-Cooker Acquacotta	300	6	1	45	1110	48	25	7	0	15
Pressure-Cooker Gigante Bean Soup with Celery and Olives	120	5	1	0	600	15	4	2	0	5
Pressure-Cooker Rustic French Pork and White Bean Stew	720	37	12	140	1470	44	17	8	0	48
Pressure-Cooker Abgoosht	310	7	2	65	980	46	3	5	0	29
Pressure-Cooker Calamari, Chorizo, and Chickpea Stew	440	17	5	200	910	40	9	10	0	29
Pressure-Cooker Vegetable and Chickpea Stew	190	8	2	0	790	27	4	7	0	5
Pressure-Cooker Green Gumbo	390	19	3	0	900	43	10	6	0	14
Pressure-Cooker Vegetable Tagine with Chickpeas and Artichokes	290	8	1	0	660	44	11	11	0	11
Pressure-Cooker Easy Weeknight Chili	340	17	5	50	900	26	7	9	0	22
Pressure-Cooker Vegetarian Black Bean Chili	420	9	2	0	670	67	16	12	0	21
Pressure-Cooker Bean and Sweet Potato Chili	370	8	1	0	840	62	6	13	0	15
Pressure-Cooker Texas-Style Chili con Carne	610	30	10	115	1380	38	8	6	0	48
Pressure-Cooker Chicken and Rice with Lemon-Yogurt Sauce	800	30	8	180	1280	63	2	5	0	65
Pressure-Cooker Chicken and Warm-Spiced Freekeh	850	40	9	175	990	54	12	2	0	68
Pressure-Cooker Chicken and Barley Risotto with Butternut Squash and Kale	800	34	11	185	870	51	10	5	0	67
Pressure-Cooker Chicken with Lentils and Butternut Squash	750	41	10	200	1050	48	9	8	0	47
Pressure-Cooker Chicken Tagine	410	13	3	135	1490	37	10	12	0	37

	CALORIES	TOTAL FAT (G)	SAT FAT (G)	CHOL (MG)	SODIUM (MG)	TOTAL CARB (G)	DIETARY FIBER (G)	TOTAL SUGAR (G)	ADDED SUGAR (G)	PROTEIN (G)
Pressure-Cooker Chicken Curry with Chickpeas and Cauliflower	330	11	3	135	800	24	7	6	1	35
Pressure-Cooker Pork Sausage with White Beans and Mustard Greens	820	47	17	85	1600	54	11	6	2	44
Pressure-Cooker Sopa Seca with Chorizo and Black Beans	520	22	6	30	840	65	10	7	0	19
Pressure-Cooker Moroccan White Beans with Lamb	340	11	4	20	410	40	13	3	0	19
Pressure-Cooker Salmon with Wild Rice and Orange Salad	700	34	7	95	480	55	6	11	1	43
Pressure-Cooker Salmon with Garlicky Broccoli Rabe and White Beans	510	30	6	95	690	17	6	2	0	43
Pressure-Cooker Cod with Warm Tabbouleh Salad	380	12	2	75	690	33	6	3	0	36
Pressure-Cooker Halibut with Carrots, White Beans, and Chermoula	390	13	2	85	670	28	8	6	0	39
Chermoula	80	7	1	0	0	3	1	0	0	1
Pressure-Cooker Halibut with Lentils, Kale, and Pancetta	480	14	3	95	740	38	8	6	0	48
Pressure-Cooker Southwestern Shrimp and Oat Berry Bowl	660	28	5	145	510	72	13	6	0	31
Pressure-Cooker Shrimp and White Beans with Butternut Squash and Sage	270	7	1	80	600	34	8	5	0	18
Pressure-Cooker Black Beans and Brown Rice	360	5	1	0	600	66	9	4	0	13
Pressure-Cooker Gochujang-Braised Tempeh Lettuce Wraps	390	19	5	0	510	32	3	15	11	29
Pressure-Cooker Braised Tofu with Pumpkin Mole and Apple-Cabbage Slaw	320	8	3	15	850	48	8	31	3	15
COOK IT SLOW										
Slow-Cooker Chicken Stew with Sausage and White Beans	460	13	4	127	1141	39	7	5	0	44
Garlic Toasts	150	6	1	0	240	19	0	1	0	3
Slow-Cooker White Chicken Chili	410	20	3	135	960	19	7	3	0	39
Slow-Cooker Turkey and Rice Soup	469	14	4	88	1100	52	4	7	0	33
Slow-Cooker Turkey Chili	339	13	3	63	1074	31	9	10	0	27
Slow-Cooker Beef and Barley Soup	342	18	5	70	987	17	5	6	0	26
Slow-Cooker Classic Beef Chili	441	20	6	62	950	40	10	13	0	28
Slow-Cooker Tuscan White Bean Soup	373	13	4	20	834	44	10	5	0	21
Slow-Cooker U.S. Senate Navy Bean Soup	371	11	2	43	1101	41	10	5	0	29
Slow-Cooker Pork and White Bean Stew with Kale	420	19	5	75	1200	30	9	5	0	31
Slow-Cooker Brazilian Black Bean and Pork Stew	997	65	22	209	1318	40	10	2	0	63
Slow-Cooker Tomatillo Chili with Pork and Hominy	429	24	7	87	1004	25	4	7	0	28
Slow-Cooker White Bean and Tomato Soup	560	24	4	5	1026	67	15	12	0	23
Slow-Cooker Garden Minestrone	200	3	1	0	970	32	7	2	0	12

	CALORIES	TOTAL FAT (G)	SAT FAT (G)	CHOL (MG)	SODIUM (MG)	TOTAL CARB (G)	DIETARY FIBER (G)	TOTAL SUGAR (G)	ADDED SUGAR (G)	PROTEIN (G)
Slow-Cooker Black Bean Soup	357	10	2	26	811	46	11	5	0	24
Slow-Cooker French Lentil Stew	300	5	1	0	580	51	12	6	0	16
Slow-Cooker Hearty Vegetarian Chili	300	5	1	0	580	51	13		0	16
Slow-Cooker Black Bean Chili	290	5	1	0	430	48	3	12	0	15
Slow-Cooker Greek Chicken with Warm Tabbouleh	470	14	3	150	750	32	5	3	0	54
Slow-Cooker Lemony Chicken and Rice with Spinach and Feta	926	50	14	247	1234	67	2	3	0	49
Slow-Cooker Chicken Thighs with Black-Eyed Pea Ragout	715	45	11	234	1720	29	9	9	0	50
Slow-Cooker Spice-Rubbed Chicken with Black Bean Salad	867	53	14	231	1497	31	10	4	0	66
Slow-Cooker Herbed Chicken with Warm Spring Vegetable Salad	950	70	17	230	870	17	5	9	0	61
Slow-Cooker Braised Chicken Sausages with White Bean Ragout	1188	37	8	164	1368	139	35	7	0	36
Slow-Cooker Braised Oxtails with White Beans and Tomatoes	702	46	17	151	1124	22	6	5	0	49
Slow-Cooker Braised Pork Chops with Campfire Beans	520	16	5	115	760	39	8	9	4	52
Slow-Cooker Pork Loin with Warm Spiced Chickpea Salad	350	13	3	95	660	20	3	14	0	37
Slow-Cooker Rustic Pork and White Bean Casserole	693	24	5	90	1171	78	14	11	0	42
Slow-Cooker Chickpea Tagine	508	14	2	3	1181	80	16	26	0	21
Slow-Cooker Vegetables and Tofu with Indian Spices	280	15	9	0	750	26	4	5	0	9
Slow-Cooker Thai Braised Butternut Squash with Tofu	282	18	8	1	812	27	5	6	0	10
Slow-Cooker Mushroom Biryani	320	11	2	5	440	47	2	10	0	8
Slow-Cooker Turkish Eggplant Casserole	260	13	3	5	640	33	8	9	0	7
Slow-Cooker Rustic Braised Lentils with Eggplant	269	10	3	11	834	35	9	9	0	12
Slow-Cooker Red Beans and Rice with Okra and Tomatoes	290	5	1	0	640	48	7	3	0	11
Slow-Cooker Farro Primavera	373	13	4	13	1318	52	11	11	0	17
Slow-Cooker Creamy Farro with Mushrooms and Thyme	263	10	3	11	497	33	5	6	0	13
Slow-Cooker Wheat Berries with Carrots and Orange	166	4	1	0	215	31	5	4	0	4
Slow-Cooker Boston Baked Beans	570	24	8	25	1200	70	12	26	21	19
Slow-Cooker Barbecue Baked Beans	494	16	4	19	945	66	14	13	0	24
Slow-Cooker Braised Chickpeas	359	8	1	4	766	54	10	11	0	19

Conversions and Equivalents

The recipes in this book were developed using standard U.S. measures following U.S. government guidelines. The charts below offer equivalents for U.S. and metric measures. All conversions are approximate and have been rounded up or down to the nearest whole number.

EXAMPLE

1 teaspoon = 4.9292 milliliters, rounded up to 5 milliliters
1 ounce = 28.3495 grams, rounded down to 28 grams

Volume Conversions

U.S.	Metric
1 teaspoon	5 milliliters
2 teaspoons	10 milliliters
1 tablespoon	15 milliliters
2 tablespoons	30 milliliters
¼ cup	59 milliliters
⅓ cup	79 milliliters
½ cup	118 milliliters
¾ cup	177 milliliters
1 cup	237 milliliters
1¼ cups	296 milliliters
1½ cups	355 milliliters
2 cups (1 pint)	473 milliliters
2½ cups	591 milliliters
3 cups	710 milliliters
4 cups (1 quart)	0.946 liter
1.06 quarts	1 liter
4 quarts (1 gallon)	3.8 liters

Weight Conversions

Ounces	Grams
½	14
¾	21
1	28
1½	43
2	57
2½	71
3	85
3½	99
4	113
4½	128
5	142
6	170
7	198
8	227
9	255
10	283
12	340
16 (1 pound)	454

Conversions for Common Baking Ingredients

Because measuring by weight is far more accurate than measuring by volume, and thus more likely to produce reliable results, in our recipes we provide ounce measures in addition to cup measures for many ingredients. Refer to the chart below to convert these measures into grams.

Ingredient	Ounces	Grams
Flour		
1 cup all-purpose flour*	5	142
1 cup cake flour	4	113
1 cup whole-wheat flour	5½	156
Sugar		
1 cup granulated (white) sugar	7	198
1 cup packed brown sugar (light or dark)	7	198
1 cup confectioners' sugar	4	113
Butter		
4 tablespoons (½ stick or ¼ cup)	2	57
8 tablespoons (1 stick or ½ cup)	4	113
16 tablespoons (2 sticks or 1 cup)	8	227

* U.S. all-purpose flour, the most frequently used flour in this book, does not contain leaveners, as some European flours do. These leavened flours are called self-rising or self-raising. If you are using self-rising flour, take this into consideration before adding leaveners to a recipe.

† In the United States, butter is sold both salted and unsalted. We recommend unsalted butter. If you are using salted butter, take this into consideration before adding salt to a recipe.

Oven Temperature

Fahrenheit	Celsius	Gas Mark
225	105	¼
250	120	½
275	135	1
300	150	2
325	165	3
350	180	4
375	190	5
400	200	6
425	220	7
450	230	8
475	245	9

Converting Temperatures from an Instant-Read Thermometer

We include doneness temperatures in many of the recipes in this book. We recommend an instant-read thermometer for the job. Refer to the table above to convert Fahrenheit degrees to Celsius. Or, for temperatures not represented in the chart, use this simple formula:

Subtract 32 degrees from the Fahrenheit reading, then divide the result by 1.8 to find the Celsius reading.

To convert 160°F to Celsius:
160°F − 32 = 128°
128° ÷ 1.8 = 71.11°C, rounded down to 71°C

Classic
Three-Bean
Salad

Index

Note: Page references in *italics* indicate photographs.

C

K

L

S